T0336735

Information Security in Diverse Computing Environments

Anne Kayem
Department of Computer Science, University of Cape Town, South Africa

Christoph Meinel
Hasso-Plattner-Institute for IT Systems Engineering, University of Potsdam, Potsdam, Germany

A volume in the Advances in Information Security, Privacy, and Ethics (AISPE) Book Series

Information Science
REFERENCE
An Imprint of IGI Global

Managing Director:	Lindsay Johnston
Production Editor:	Jennifer Yoder
Development Editor:	Erin O'Dea
Acquisitions Editor:	Kayla Wolfe
Typesetter:	Thomas Creedon
Cover Design:	Jason Mull

Published in the United States of America by
Information Science Reference (an imprint of IGI Global)
701 E. Chocolate Avenue
Hershey PA, USA 17033
Tel: 717-533-8845
Fax: 717-533-8661
E-mail: cust@igi-global.com
Web site: http://www.igi-global.com

Library of Congress Cataloging-in-Publication Data

Information security in diverse computing environments / Anne Kayem and Christoph Meinel, editors.
    pages cm
 Includes bibliographical references and index.
 Summary: "This book provides the latest empirical research and theoretical frameworks in the area of information security, presenting research on developing sufficient security measures for new environments by discussing challenges faced by researchers as well as unconventional solutions to these problems"-- Provided by publisher.
    ISBN 978-1-4666-6158-5 (hardcover) -- ISBN 978-1-4666-6159-2 (ebook) -- ISBN 978-1-4666-6161-5 (print & perpetual access) 1. Computer security. 2. Data protection. 3. Information technology--Security measures. I. Kayem, Anne, 1975- II. Meinel, Christoph, 1954-
 QA76.9.A25.I54154 2014
 005.8--dc23
                                    2014013850

This book is published in the IGI Global book series Advances in Information Security, Privacy, and Ethics (AISPE) (ISSN: 1948-9730; eISSN: 1948-9749)

British Cataloguing in Publication Data
A Cataloguing in Publication record for this book is available from the British Library.

For electronic access to this publication, please contact: eresources@igi-global.com.

Advances in Information Security, Privacy, and Ethics (AISPE) Book Series

ISSN: 1948-9730
EISSN: 1948-9749

MISSION

As digital technologies become more pervasive in everyday life and the Internet is utilized in ever increasing ways by both private and public entities, concern over digital threats becomes more prevalent.

The **Advances in Information Security, Privacy, & Ethics (AISPE) Book Series** provides cutting-edge research on the protection and misuse of information and technology across various industries and settings. Comprised of scholarly research on topics such as identity management, cryptography, system security, authentication, and data protection, this book series is ideal for reference by IT professionals, academicians, and upper-level students.

COVERAGE

- Privacy Issues of Social Networking
- Tracking Cookies
- IT Risk
- Telecommunications Regulations
- Security Information Management
- Information Security Standards
- Cyberethics
- Cookies
- Security Classifications
- Device Fingerprinting

IGI Global is currently accepting manuscripts for publication within this series. To submit a proposal for a volume in this series, please contact our Acquisition Editors at Acquisitions@igi-global.com or visit: http://www.igi-global.com/publish/.

Titles in this Series

For a list of additional titles in this series, please visit: www.igi-global.com

Network Topology in Command and Control Organization, Operation, and Evolution
T. J. Grant (R-BAR, The Netherlands) R. H. P. Janssen (Netherlands Defence Academy, The Netherlands) and H.
Monsuur (Netherlands Defence Academy, The Netherlands)
Information Science Reference • copyright 2014 • 320pp • H/C (ISBN: 9781466660588) • US $215.00 (our price)

Cases on Research and Knowledge Discovery Homeland Security Centers of Excellence
Cecelia Wright Brown (University of Baltimore, USA) Kevin A. Peters (Morgan State University, USA) and Kofi
Adofo Nyarko (Morgan State University, USA)
Information Science Reference • copyright 2014 • 357pp • H/C (ISBN: 9781466659469) • US $215.00 (our price)

Analyzing Security, Trust, and Crime in the Digital World
Hamid R. Nemati (The University of North Carolina at Greensboro, USA)
Information Science Reference • copyright 2014 • 281pp • H/C (ISBN: 9781466648562) • US $195.00 (our price)

Research Developments in Biometrics and Video Processing Techniques
Rajeev Srivastava (Indian Institute of Technology (BHU), India) S.K. Singh (Indian Institute of Technology (BHU),
India) and K.K. Shukla (Indian Institute of Technology (BHU), India)
Information Science Reference • copyright 2014 • 279pp • H/C (ISBN: 9781466648685) • US $195.00 (our price)

Advances in Secure Computing, Internet Services, and Applications
B.K. Tripathy (VIT University, India) and D. P. Acharjya (VIT University, India)
Information Science Reference • copyright 2014 • 405pp • H/C (ISBN: 9781466649408) • US $195.00 (our price)

Trust Management in Mobile Environments Autonomic and Usable Models
Zheng Yan (Xidian University, China and Aalto University, Finland)
Information Science Reference • copyright 2014 • 288pp • H/C (ISBN: 9781466647657) • US $195.00 (our price)

Network Security Technologies Design and Applications
Abdelmalek Amine (Tahar Moulay University, Algeria) Otmane Ait Mohamed (Concordia University, USA) and
Boualem Benatallah (University of New South Wales, Australia)
Information Science Reference • copyright 2014 • 330pp • H/C (ISBN: 9781466647893) • US $195.00 (our price)

Security, Privacy, Trust, and Resource Management in Mobile and Wireless Communications
Danda B. Rawat (Georgia Southern University, USA) Bhed B. Bista (Iwate Prefectural University, Japan) and
Gongjun Yan (University of Southern Indiana, USA)
Information Science Reference • copyright 2014 • 577pp • H/C (ISBN: 9781466646919) • US $195.00 (our price)

www.igi-global.com

701 E. Chocolate Ave., Hershey, PA 17033
Order online at www.igi-global.com or call 717-533-8845 x100
To place a standing order for titles released in this series, contact: cust@igi-global.com
Mon-Fri 8:00 am - 5:00 pm (est) or fax 24 hours a day 717-533-8661

To the scientists who work tirelessly to transform our dreams for a better world into reality and whose research results in solutions make the lives of the poorer population of the world easier...

Table of Contents

Section 1
Privacy, Anonymity, and Trust Management

Section 4
Cloud Security

Detailed Table of Contents

Section 1
Privacy, Anonymity, and Trust Management

Chapter 1
Anne V. D. M. Kayem, University of Cape Town, South Africa
Richard Ssembatya, University of Cape Town, South Africa
Mark-John Burke, University of Cape Town, South Africa

Information security is generally discussed in terms of preventing adversarial access to applications and to the data these applications handle. The authors note, however, that increasingly, creating information security solutions that are based on the difficulty of discovering the solution is no longer a truly viable approach. Some of the reasons for this include the increasing availability of faster processing power, high-performance computing systems, and big data availability. On the opposite end, issues such as frequent power outages in resource-constrained environments make applying standard security schemes challenging. In this chapter, the authors discuss examples that highlight the challenges of applying conventional security solutions to constrained resource environments. They postulate that effective security solutions for these environments require rather unconventional approaches to security-solution design. Such solutions would need to take into consideration environmental and behavioral factors in addition to drawing inspiration in certain cases from natural or biological processes.

Chapter 2

Security is an interesting area, one in which we may well be guilty of misunderstanding the very people we are working for whilst trying to protect them. It is often said that people (users) are a weak link in the security chain. This may be true, but there are nuances. In this chapter, the authors discuss some of the work they have done and are doing to help users understand their information and device security and make informed, guided, and responsible decisions. This includes Device Comfort, Annoying Technologies, and Ten Commandments for designers and implementers of security and trust systems. This work is exploratory and unfinished (it should in fact never be finished), and this chapter presents a step along the way to better security users.

Chapter 3

Streaming data emerges from different electronic sources and needs to be processed in real time with minimal delay. Data streams can generate hidden and useful knowledge patterns when mined and analyzed. In spite of these benefits, the issue of privacy needs to be addressed before streaming data is released for mining and analysis purposes. In order to address data privacy concerns, several techniques have emerged. K-anonymity has received considerable attention over other privacy preserving techniques because of its simplicity and efficiency in protecting data. Yet, k-anonymity cannot be directly applied on continuous data (data streams) because of its transient nature. In this chapter, the authors discuss the challenges faced by k-anonymity algorithms in enforcing privacy on data streams and review existing privacy techniques for handling data streams.

Chapter 4

With the widespread use of online systems, there is an increasing focus on maintaining the privacy of individuals and information about them. This is often referred to as a need for privacy protection. The author briefly examines definitions of privacy in this context, roughly delineating between keeping facts private and statistical privacy that deals with what can be inferred from data sets. Many of the mechanisms used to implement what is commonly thought of as access control are the same ones used to protect privacy. This chapter explores when this is not the case and, in general, the interplay between privacy and access control on the one hand and, on the other hand, the separation of these models from mechanisms for their implementation.

Chapter 5

Conditional Access (CA) is typically used by pay-television operators to restrict access to content to authorized subscribers. While several commercial CA solutions exist for structured broadcasting, Internet-based television, and video-on-demand services, these solutions are mostly proprietary. Use of proprietary solutions incurs royalty payments and increased cost of components for Set-Top-Box manufacturers. In many developing countries Set-Top-Boxes for the migration to Digital Television will be subsidized by government. An efficient, flexible, and open conditional system that does not incur royalties or require specialised security hardware would be beneficial for these countries. In this chapter, the authors explore conditional access solutions that draw on the area of cryptographic key management and distribution for IPTV environments. They wrap up with propositions on how an open Cryptographic Access Control (CAC) system can be implemented practically by pay-television operators who have to handle a large number of subscriptions.

Section 2
Cyber-Defense Challenges

Chapter 6

This chapter explores the challenges facing those involved in cyber defense at a national, organizational, and individual level. As the global economy grows more dependent on the Internet and connected infrastructure, the risk and impact of attack grows. A long-standing response to attacks of various kinds conducted on the Internet has been to filter traffic but not to respond. In some cases, reactive action is taken, but even where attribution is possible, prosecution is rare. In recent months, several countries have stated their policy of military response where they feel that their national infrastructure is threatened. The risk to organizations, civilian populations, and individuals is discussed in the case of such militant response or retaliation. The chapter further considers aspects such as reputation, neutrality, and the concept of Internet "kill switches."

Chapter 7

Security and privacy have become important issues when dealing with Internet Protocol version 6 (IPv6) networks. On one hand, anonymity, which is related to privacy, makes it hard for current security systems to differentiate between legitimate users and illegitimate users, especially when the users need to be authenticated by those systems whose services they require. On the other hand, a lack of privacy exposes legitimate users to abuse, which can result from the information gained from privacy-related attacks. The current problems inherent within IPv6-enabled networks are due, in part, to the fact that there is no standard available telling companies about the current deficiencies that exist within IPv6 networks. The purpose of this chapter is to show a balance between the use of privacy and security, and to describe a framework that can offer the minimum standard requirement needed for providing security and privacy to IPv6 networks.

Chapter 8

Abdulrahman Al-Mutairi, University of London, UK
Stephen D. Wolthusen, University of London, UK & Gjøvik University College, Norway

Whilst the security and integrity of exterior gateway protocols such as the Border Gateway Protocol (BGP) and, to a lesser extent, interior gateway protocols, including the Multi-Protocol Label Switching (MPLS), have been investigated previously, more limited attention has been paid to the problem of availability and timeliness that is crucial for service levels needed in critical infrastructure areas such as financial services and electric power (smart grid) networks. The authors describe a method for modeling adversaries for the analysis of attacks on quality of service characteristics underpinning such real-time networks as well as a model of policies employed by MPLS routers based on simplified networks and give an analysis of attack vectors based on assumed adversaries derived from the introduced method.

Chapter 9

Maurice Dawson, University of Missouri – St. Louis, USA
Marwan Omar, Nawroz University, Iraq
Jonathan Abramson, Colorado Technical University, USA
Dustin Bessette, National Graduate School of Quality Management, USA

Hyperconnectivity is a growing trend that is driving cyber security experts to develop new security architectures for multiple platforms such as mobile devices, laptops, and even wearable displays. The futures of national and international security rely on complex countermeasures to ensure that a proper security posture is maintained during this state of hyperconnectivity. To protect these systems from exploitation of vulnerabilities it is essential to understand current and future threats to include the laws that drive their need to be secured. Examined within this chapter are the potential security-related threats with the use of social media, mobile devices, virtual worlds, augmented reality, and mixed reality. Further reviewed are some examples of the complex attacks that could interrupt human-robot interaction, children-computer interaction, mobile computing, social networks, and human-centered issues in security design.

Section 3
Forensics, Malware Detection, and Analysis

Chapter 10

P. Vinod, SCMS School of Engineering and Technology, India
P. R. Rakesh, SCMS School of Engineering and Technology, India
G. Alphy, SCMS School of Engineering and Technology, India

The threats imposed by metamorphic malware (capable of generating new variants) can easily bypass a detector that uses pattern-matching techniques. Hence, the necessity is to develop a sophisticated signature or non-signature-based scanners that not only detect zero day malware but also actively train themselves to adapt to new malware threats. The authors propose a statistical malware scanner that is effective in discriminating metamorphic malware samples from a large collection of benign executables.

Previous research articles pertaining to metamorphic malware demonstrated that Next Generation Virus Kit (NGVCK) exhibited enough code distortion in every new generation to defeat signature-based scanners. It is reported that the NGVCK-generated samples are 10% similar in code structure. In the authors' proposed methodology, frequencies of opcodes of files are analyzed. The opcodes features are transformed to new feature spaces represented by similarity measures (37 similarity measure). Thus, the aim is also to develop a non-signature-based scanner trained with small feature length to classify unseen malware and benign executables.

Chapter 11

The ever-increasing use of mobile devices for communication and entertainment has made these devices an increasingly attractive target for malicious attacks. Thus, mobile device security has emerged as an important research area. Although malicious exploits for mobile phones have been steadily developing over the last decade, the emergence of smart-phone technology is proving to be a turning point in development of such malicious exploits. With the increase in sophistication of smartphones and their use for day-today activities, mobile threats (e.g., viruses, spyware, and malware) has also increased. This trend can be attributed to the fact that phone users want to communicate, and viruses want to be communicated. This chapter presents a state-of-the-art review of the developments in this important field of mobile malware.

Chapter 12

Science provides the basis for truth claims in forensics. Very little research has been done to explore the scientific basis of digital forensics. The work that has been done vary widely in what they propose; in most cases it is unclear how the philosophical remarks about such forensic science apply to digital forensics practice, or that the practical suggestions are a sufficient basis to claim that practice based on them is scientific. This chapter provides an initial exploration of the potential of decision problems from the field of algorithmics to form this scientific basis. There is no doubt that decision problems operate in the scientific domain and decision problems look similar to hypotheses to be of immediate practical use. The chapter suggests that, if decision problems are used in this manner, it is clear that current digital forensics have only scratched the surface of what is possible. Probabilistic complexity classes, for example, offer interesting possibilities for performing complex tests in relatively short times, with known error rates. Using decision problems as a demarcation criterion makes it possible to distinguish between digital forensic science (or simply digital forensics) and digital forensic craft, which should be called digital investigative technique or some other suitable term that does not imply that its use leads to scientific truths.

Chapter 13

Siddharth Singh, University of Allahabad, India
Tanveer J. Siddiqui, University of Allahabad, India

Recent advancement of multimedia technology has posed serious challenges to copyright protection, ownership, and integrity of digital data. This has made information security techniques a vital issue. Cryptography, Steganography, and Watermarking are three major techniques for securing information and ensuring copyright ownership. This chapter presents an overview of transform domain techniques for image steganography. The authors discuss the characteristics and applications of image steganography and briefly review Discrete Cosine and Wavelet transform-based image steganography techniques. They also discuss the various metrics that have been used to assess the performance of steganography techniques and shed light on the future of steganography.

Section 4
Cloud Security

Chapter 14

Anne V. D. M. Kayem, University of Cape Town, South Africa
Rotondwa Ratshidaho, University of Cape Town, South Africa
Molulaqhooa L. Maoyi, University of Cape Town, South Africa
Sanele Macanda, University of Cape Town, South Africa

Supported by the Web 3.0 platform that enables dynamic content sharing, social networking applications are a ubiquitous information exchange platform. Content sharing raises the question of privacy with concerns typically centered on vulnerabilities resulting in identity theft. Identifying privacy vulnerabilities is a challenging problem because mitigations are implemented at the end of the software development life cycle, sometimes resulting in severe vulnerabilities. The authors present a prototype experimental social networking platform (HACKMI2) as a case study for a comparative analysis of three popular industry threat-modeling approaches. They focus on identified vulnerabilities, risk impact, and mitigation strategies. The results indicate that software and/or asset-centric approaches provide only a high-level analysis of a system's architecture and are not as effective as attacker-centric models in identifying high-risk security vulnerabilities in a system. Furthermore, attacker-centric models are effective in providing security administrators useful suggestions for addressing security vulnerabilities.

Chapter 15

Maxim Schnjakin, Potsdam University, Germany
Christoph Meinel, Potsdam University, Germany

Cloud Computing as a service-on-demand architecture has grown in importance over the previous few years. One driver of its growth is the ever-increasing amount of data that is supposed to outpace the growth of storage capacity. The usage of cloud technology enables organizations to manage their data with low operational expenses. However, the benefits of cloud computing come along with challenges and open issues such as security, reliability, and the risk to become dependent on a provider for its service. In general, a switch of a storage provider is associated with high costs of adapting new APIs and additional charges for inbound and outbound bandwidth and requests. In this chapter, the authors present a system that improves availability, confidentiality, and reliability of data stored in the cloud. To achieve this objective, the authors encrypt users' data and make use of the RAID-technology principle to manage data distribution across cloud storage providers. Further, they discuss the security functionality and present a proof-of-concept experiment for the application to evaluate the performance and cost effectiveness of the approach. The authors deploy the application using eight commercial cloud storage repositories in different countries. The approach allows users to avoid vendor lock-in and reduces significantly the cost of switching providers. They also observe that the implementation improved the perceived availability and, in most cases, the overall performance when compared with individual cloud providers. Moreover, the authors estimate the monetary costs to be competitive to the cost of using a single cloud provider.

Chapter 16

Jan H. P. Eloff, SAP Innovation Center Pretoria, South Africa & Department Computer
    Science, University of Pretoria, South Africa
Mariki M. Eloff, University of South Africa, South Africa
Madeleine A. Bihina Bella, SAP Innovation Center Pretoria, South Africa
Donovan Isherwood, University of Johannesburg, South Africa
Moses T. Dlamini, University of Pretoria, South Africa
Ernest Ketcha Ngassam, University of South Africa, South Africa

The increasing demand for online and real-time interaction with IT infrastructures by end users is facilitated by the proliferation of user-centric devices such as laptops, iPods, iPads, and smartphones. This trend is furthermore propounded by the plethora of apps downloadable to end user devices mostly within mobile-cum-cloud environments. It is clear that there are many evidences of innovation with regard to end user devices and apps. Unfortunately, little, if any, information security innovation took place over the past number of years with regard to the consumption of security services by end users. This creates the need for innovative security solutions that are human-centric and flexible. This chapter presents a framework for consuming loosely coupled (but interoperable) cloud-based security services by a variety of end users in an efficient and flexible manner using their mobile devices.

Foreword

Bruce Schneier (n.d.), the well-known security specialist, said: "Complexity is the worst enemy of security." Every year, novel products, technologies ideas, companies, and research are introduced, yet weakening levels of security in complex information systems are more and more evident. Ranging from mobile to the cloud, the increase in information system complexity creates serious information security challenges.

In the face of rapidly evolving technologies, information security is receiving increasingly more attention, mainly due to hardware and software innovations that have emerged in recent years. Powerful processors not only make time-intensive computations occur much faster but also have facilitated provoking more security violations. Attacks on computing systems have shifted from being simple attacks perpetrated by socially maladjusted teenagers to a concerted criminal activity. Moreover, the general population is provided with a broad range of powerful computing capabilities, much more than most people need, giving them many avenues through which they can cause damage to themselves.

Therefore, it makes sense to explore alternative or unconventional approaches to addressing problems of security by including the support of user and provider requirements in certain cases, and in others, finding ways around problems that emerge due to resource constraints such as limited bandwidth, power outages, and limited computational or processing power. Furthermore, the advent of platforms and/or environments like cloud computing and service-oriented architectures raise even more intricacies in the security measures that are needed to handle platforms with varying performance requirements and processing capabilities.

This book, written by internationally recognized experts, takes a noteworthy stride towards providing unconventional solutions to the security challenges posed by rapid software and hardware innovations. All chapters were subjected to a peer-review process. The first section of the book considers trust management, privacy and access control, and anonymity to support users to securely make use of innovative computing capabilities.

The second section of the book deals with security challenges resulting from the increasing degree of networking among the individual elements of current infrastructures. Section three of the book looks at techniques to identify criminal activities in computing systems, other types of attack monitoring, as well a copyright protections. The final section of the book describes approaches to secure innovative cloud-based solutions by considering social networking and personalization of security services.

This book should be read by both advanced practitioners and researchers working on innovative security challenges. From a researcher's point of view, the book chapters provide a solid foundation to understand the scope of work in this field. The book can also provide practitioners with a working knowledge on these challenges and their solutions, as security administrators need to understand the types of challenges that they may face and their solutions. The techniques and methods discussed in the book provide insight into how security challenges of rapidly changing technologies can be approached in the best possible way.

Marijke Coetzee
University of Johannesburg, South Africa

Marijke Coetzee *is a Professor and the Sub-Head: Research and Advancement in the Academy for Computer Science and Software Engineering at the University of Johannesburg, South Africa. The main focus of her research is on Information Security and Trust Management. She is a rated NRF researcher and has co-authored more than 40 papers published in peer-reviewed local and international conference proceedings and journals. She acts as reviewer for various national and international conferences, is the external moderator of a number of post-graduate subjects at other tertiary institutions, and a co-chair of the ISSA (Information Security for South Africa) conference. She is a member of the ACM, IEEE, and SAICSIT.*

REFERENCES

Schneier, B. (n.d.). *Software complexity and security*. Retrieved from https://www.schneier.com/crypto-gram-0003.html

Preface

The competent programmer is fully aware of the strictly limited size of his own skull; therefore he approaches the programming task in full humility, and among other things he avoids clever tricks like the plague.

Edsger Wybe Dijkstra (1972)

The emergence of social networks, cloud computing, and more recently, big data management on the Web in addition to data mining and statistical data analysis tools have made privacy violations easier to provoke and consequently a serious threat to society. Individuals now release more personal information from which complex deductions can be made about their behavioral patterns and often in ways that are unpredictable or unknown to the users. This problem of uncontrolled information release is further compounded by the fact that different nations and societies have differing notions on what privacy is.

This book emerges from the need to create a niche and impress upon business as well as government leaders the importance of information security in relation to handling constrained resource settings. Why is this important to business and government? Goodman and Harris (2010) provide a number of compelling reasons in support of their claim that there is a growing tsunami of information insecurity triggered by increased Internet connectivity in the developing world. Amongst their top reasons are that increased information insecurity can be provoked by:

1. Increased prevalence of malware due to a lack of security regulations.
2. Security vulnerabilities from the use of cheaper or older systems.
3. Exposure of sensitive information to adversaries due to limited knowledgeability of information technology use.
4. Increased affordability of mobile and Internet technologies in Africa and the developing world in general will lead to increased information insecurity if adequate countermeasures are not implemented.

Some reasons for addressing these issues include the fact that:

- Providing good information security in diverse computing environments will reduce (or at least not increase) the vulnerabilities of newer and more expensive systems in the developed world to vulnerabilities generated from interacting with weaker systems in the developing world. A direct consequence of this would be increased global online commerce in a trusted framework.
- Good information practices will reduce the prevalence of malware and issues like information theft and privacy violations that come with malware attacks.

So then why do we need to reason about how to build information security models and mechanisms to handle information insecurity scenarios such as the ones that typically emerge in the context of the developing world? Perhaps we should begin with a definition of what we mean by resource-constrained environments and what they mean in the developing world context. Resource constrained environments can be described as a context in which information technology applications are unable to operate optimally because of a lack of computational power and/or the technological support required to ensure that the computing systems operate optimally. For instance, frequent power outages can make it impossible to implement and run algorithms that are computationally intensive, and likewise, bandwidth limitations might make activities such as downloading large volumes of cloud storage data impossible. In the security scenario, the implication of implementing standard solutions in resource-constrained environments can mean that we are unable to provide firm guarantees of data or system protection. For example, a biometric system designed to operate optimally in a highly fault-tolerant system where power outages are a very rare occurrence might give some rather unpredictable results if the power outages were increased in frequency to once every two hours instead of once every two years!

As is the case in most computing environments, tools for enhancing performance and security in resource-constrained scenarios can help counter the argument that Internet communications from the developing world are likely to create a situation of information insecurity. Furthermore, instead of ignoring these communications on the basis that they do not account for a big enough proportion of global communications to be worth factoring into system design, we can find ways to rethink current security designs in order to circumvent violations. By rethinking our philosophies of security design and implementation, we can find effective ways of evaluating the changes that need to be made in current systems in order to enforce security and privacy globally in a successful manner.

CHALLENGES AND OPPORTUNITIES

In the coming years, the need for privacy protection in resource-constrained environments that are typical of the developing world will only increase because of the growing prevalence of Internet connectivity due to reduced costs of technology. Previously, the rapid growth of the Internet and increases in processing power resulted in more consumer personal information in possession of business organizations. This paradigm continues to hold even in relatively unreliable networks and in secure scenarios where access to security solutions are overlooked either due to ignorance or in order to avoid the cost of security software. The Internet continues to expand, however, and communications are not bounded geographically. As a consequence, relatively secure networks are receiving and sharing information with devices and/or systems on relatively insecure networks. Some of the challenges and opportunities that lie ahead for ensuring effective privacy and security on the Internet as device affordability increases in the developing world include:

- Business organizations need to be aware of the need for investing in privacy and security and the consequences of not doing so.
- Privacy legislation needs to be reviewed globally against changing technology and accessibility.
- Penalties for privacy and security breaches should be strong enough to deter adversarial behavior and ensure adherence to policy compliance.
- Accounting and auditing procedures need to be specified to handle different cultural contexts in the global scenario.

ORGANIZATION OF THIS BOOK

In this book, we present 17 chapters aimed at emphasizing our philosophy of intricate security problems in diverse computing environments. For coherency, we have ordered the chapters in terms of similarity of topic. The topics we tackle range from security issues pertaining to the network layer and how these affect quality of service to the human-centric issues that often get ignored in the design, evaluation, and analysis of security mechanisms.

Section 1: Trust Management, Privacy, and Anonymity

In Chapter 1, A. Kayem, R. Ssembatya, and M. J. Burke present the idea of designing security solutions for intricate computing environments. The focus is on the challenges involved in achieving this in environments that do not adhere to more conventional security scenarios. Some problems and avenues for future research work are highlighted and discussed to pave the way for the discussion in Chapter 2 on trust management and, more specifically, the rules that need to be taken into account when making room for human factors in enforcing trust effectively.

In Chapter 2, S. Marsh, N. Dwyer, A. Basu, T. Storer, K. Renaud, K. El-Khatib, B. Esfandiari, S. Noël, and M. V. Bicakci present the ten commandments of designing security applications that users can trust and use.

Chapter 3 follows with a discussion on data stream anonymity. A. Sakpere and A. Kayem present various anonymity-preserving algorithms, discussing the drawbacks of applying these algorithms to ensure data stream anonymity. Ensuring data-stream anonymity is particularly useful in the developing world context, where access to specialized data-mining expertise or resources is generally minimal and in certain cases non-existent. It makes sense, therefore, to extend current data-stream-anonymity-preserving algorithms that are geared for static data to cope with streaming data.

S. Osborn provides an insightful discussion in Chapter 4 on the often-debated issues of privacy and access control. The pros and cons of each approach to security enforcement are analyzed, and notions that overlap between the two concepts are discussed in relation to how they can sometimes be confused.

In Chapter 5, G. Harding and A. Kayem extend the discussion of access control and privacy to the domain of Pay-TV and more specifically methods of guaranteeing secure access to TV bouquets. The authors discuss existing IPTV conditional access schemes and propose an efficient conditional access framework for enabling flexible TV channel bouquet formation and distribution. This is particularly useful in the context of the developing world where low incomes and job instability imply that the buying power of users might be more dynamic than that of users in the developed world.

Section 2: Network Security

In Chapter 6, our discussion on the challenges of enforcing security in resource-constrained environments continues with B. Irwin's presentation of the current and future challenges in cyber-defense. The big questions here are, When is it all right for a state to treat cyber attacks as an act of warfare? and, more importantly, What implications does this have for developing world countries, particularly in Africa, where technological and intellectual expertise is scarce?

H. Rafiee and C. Meinel extend this discussion with the proposition of the idea of a necessary standard for IPv6 networks in Chapter 7, in order to design a framework that allows for the enforcement of minimum security and privacy requirements in IPv6 networks. The authors highlight the fact that ensuring security and privacy in IPv6 networks is challenging in part due to the fact that standards for indicating to companies and organizations what the current deficiencies are within IPv6 networks are non-existent. Furthermore, there is no methodology that clearly outlines how possible security and/or privacy issues can be detected or mitigated in current IPv6 security protocols, how to detect possible problems within current IPv6 security protocols, or how to offer solutions for resolving these issues. In this case, we note that transitioning from IPv4 to IPv6 has highlighted issues of security and privacy that go beyond simply extending existing solutions to meet the new computing environment conditions.

In Chapter 8, A. Al-Mutairi and S. Wolthusen visit the issue of availability and timeliness in Interior Gateway Protocols such as Multi-Protocol Label Switching in critical infrastructure areas and propose a method of adversary modeling for analyzing network attacks that target quality-of-service parameters. Adversary modeling, particularly if automated, is particularly useful for cases in which specialized knowledge is unavailable or difficult to obtain.

Finally, to wrap up this section, in Chapter 9, M. Dawson, M. Omar, J. Abramson, and D. Bessette consider the human factors that create challenges in designing security architectures to cope with the tsunami of information technology. In particular, they focus on and highlight the human-centered issues that need to be addressed in designing security and/or privacy-preserving mechanisms.

Section 3: Forensics, Malware Detection, and Analysis

Data anonymity raises the issue of fraudulent distortions of information and so it is befitting to continue in Chapters 10 and 11 with discussions on malware. In Chapter 10, P. Vinod, P.R. Rakesh, and G. Alphy, propose a malware analysis system. The proposed system relies on a statistical scanner that discriminates between metamorphic malware samples from a large collection of benign executables. Experimental results indicate that the proposed statistical generator effectively identifies metamorphic and benign malware instances.

N. Goel, B. Raman, and I. Gupta, continue the malware discussion in Chapter 11 with a special focus on the rather neglected area of mobile malware. The authors present a state-of-the-art review of various developments in the field of mobile malware.

In Chapter 12, M. Oliver presents a philosophical perspective on the emergence of the area of forensics in information security. Forensics is oftentimes a useful tool for identifying "silent" malware behaviours and mitigating the impact that these malware attacks can have on system security.

S. Singh and T. Siddiqui wrap up this section in Chapter 13 by introducing the notions and major issues involved in implementing steganographic schemes in scenarios involving big multimedia data generation and analysis. Steganography is an art of hidden communication in which a secret message is communicated by hiding it in a cover file, so that the very existence of the secret message is not detectable. In contrast, standard approaches based on cryptography, steganographic-like watermarking techniques, facilitate enforcing copyright ownership by using notions of imperceptibility. Steganographic techniques are particularly useful for enforcing copyright legislature in developing world scenarios where law enforcement authorities sometimes lack the expertise required to enforce international copyright laws. Steganographic schemes, by nature of their imperceptibility and robustness against signal processing operations present a viable approach to copyright enforcement. The authors discuss the applications of steganography, particularly in the field of information security.

Section 4: Cloud Security

In Chapter 14, threat-modeling tools are compared in terms of efficacy in detecting vulnerabilities in social networking scenarios. The authors, R. Ratshidaho, M. Maoyi, S. Macanda, and A. Kayem, present a comparative analysis, highlighting the pros and cons of these tools in detecting threats in a prototype social networking environment.

Social networking applications like cloud computing have become popular because of the flexible opportunities for information sharing that these environments provide. Like social networks, cloud computing environments present new security challenges that need to be addressed in order to encourage users to trust these systems. As we have mentioned before, the security challenges that emerge in the usage of these applications can be more difficult to address when the constraints of the environments are unpredictable and/or different from the standard case.

M. Schnjakin and C. Meinel consider these sorts of issues and how information security can be innovated in proposing methods of implementing personalization of security services in mobile cloud infrastructures in Chapter 15.

J. Eloff, M. Eloff, M. Bihina-Bella, D. Isherwood, M. Dlamini, and E. Ngassam present a follow-up proposal on an approach to guaranteeing security and availability in public clouds by guaranteeing confidentiality with encryption and using RAID technology to ensure availability across platforms in Chapter 16. Their approach has the advantage of preventing vector lock-in and also a reduced cost in switching service providers.

Finally, we wrap-up in Chapter 17 with concluding remarks on enforcing information security in resource-constrained environments and discuss potential directions for future work.

Anne V. D. M. Kayem
University of Cape Town, South Africa

Christoph Meinel
University of Potsdam, Germany

REFERENCES

Dijkstra, E. W. (1972). *The humble programmer.* Paper presented at the ACM Turing lecture. Retrieved from https://www.cs.utexas.edu/~EWD/transcriptions/EWD03xx/EWD340.html

Goodman, S., & Harris, A. (2010). The coming African tsunami of information insecurity. *Communications of the ACM, 53*(12), 24–27.

Acknowledgment

First and most importantly, we would like thank all the authors for their excellent contributions to this book. Your work has brought to life our dream, conceptualizing this topic and packaging in a manner that is accessible to a wide audience.

Second, our heartfelt gratitude goes to all the reviewers who provided insightful and constructive feedback on the contributed chapters. Thank you for making the time in what must be a very busy schedule.

Finally, but not the least, a special note of thanks to Mr. Brett Synder who was brave enough to start the process of creating this manuscript with us, and to Ms. Erin O'Dea for continuing the process with us. Your guidance and answers to our questions made everything much easier.

Anne V. D. M. Kayem
University of Cape Town, South Africa

Christoph Meinel
University of Potsdam, Germany
February 11, 2014

Section 1
Privacy, Anonymity, and Trust Management

Chapter 1
Diversity in Security Environments:
The Why and the Wherefore

Anne V. D. M. Kayem
University of Cape Town, South Africa

Richard Ssembatya
University of Cape Town, South Africa

Mark-John Burke
University of Cape Town, South Africa

ABSTRACT

Information security is generally discussed in terms of preventing adversarial access to applications and to the data these applications handle. The authors note, however, that increasingly, creating information security solutions that are based on the difficulty of discovering the solution is no longer a truly viable approach. Some of the reasons for this include the increasing availability of faster processing power, high-performance computing systems, and big data availability. On the opposite end, issues such as frequent power outages in resource-constrained environments make applying standard security schemes challenging. In this chapter, the authors discuss examples that highlight the challenges of applying conventional security solutions to constrained resource environments. They postulate that effective security solutions for these environments require rather unconventional approaches to security-solution design. Such solutions would need to take into consideration environmental and behavioral factors in addition to drawing inspiration in certain cases from natural or biological processes.

INTRODUCTION

The notion of resource constrained environments is tightly coupled with the growing field of information and communication technologies for development. Resource constrained environments however, are not a peculiarity of developing nations only but more generally of geographic locations where access to technological infrastructure is limited. For instance, in remote areas access to water, transportation, and electricity is sometimes hindered by factors that include cost of connection, low population density, and the infrastructural cost. In these cases, it is often not feasible cost-wise

DOI: 10.4018/978-1-4666-6158-5.ch001

to set up the required infrastructure to make the service available to the population. Therefore, we define resource constrained environments to be areas in which convention methods of technology distribution are hindered by environmental and cost factors. Consequently, providing or implementing technological solutions in these environments requires that one step back and re-evaluate the options in order to find effective methods of addressing the challenges that emerge in the affected areas.

In this chapter and book in general, we focus specifically on the problems of implementing security solutions in resource constrained environments. Factors such as bandwidth limitations, power outages, limited access to information technology, make implementing security solutions in conventional ways challenging. For instance, the popularity of smart phones in emerging economies has resulted in an increased access to social networking media. However, oftentimes the laws on privacy in these countries are quite different from what they are in the United States where the application was designed and implemented. When information gets leaked or exposed to unauthorized parties it is difficult if not impossible to prosecute the malicious user. The problem is further compounded by the fact that the lack of proper security regulations or legislature is creating a growing danger of what has been termed the "tsunami of information insecurity"(Goodman and Harris, 2010).

As Goodman et al. (Goodman and Harris, 2010) point out, cellphones are more affordable and accessible than regular computers are in most African countries. There several reasons for this, but two of the most cited ones include portability and usage simplicity. Frequent power outages make the idea of a small, low-power intensive device that can guarantee communication anytime and anywhere, attractive. Likewise, the usage simplicity of cellphones has addressed an

issue that regular computers have struggled with for decades, that is ensuring that the device is simple enough to use irrespective of the education or tech savvy-ness of the user. Cellphones however are rapidly evolving and some of the current smartphones, though considerably more expensive than the first generation of cellphones, can by themselves operate as though they were mini-computers.

Using cellphones to access the Internet has also become a common practice in recent years and with this the host of privacy and security problems that emerge naturally in this environment. Lack of proper knowledge of or inability to pay for expensive security enforcing applications, is creating a growing situation of information insecurity for the users of these devices.

In this chapter we consider two cases of information insecurity scenarios that are created by factors such as constraints in resource availability, and social media access on mobile devices, due to their popularity in Africa. The rest of the chapter is structured as follows, in Section 2, we discuss factors such as power outages and bandwidth limitations in resource constrained environments. We evaluate the impact of these factors on information security and highlight some potential solutions for addressing these issues. In Section 3, we consider the issues such as the following:

1. Social media use on mobile phones amongst teenagers, and how privacy breaches can be exploited for bullying, and harassment.
2. Personal healthcare data management on mobile devices and the challenges of adopting standard electronic healthcare management systems in developing countries.
3. Enforcing privacy preservation on crime data via anonymity algorithms.

We offer concluding comments and discuss avenues for future work in Section 4.

RESOURCE CONSTRAINED ENVIRONMENTS

In this section we look at the impact that power outages and low bandwidth on standard security implementations. Increasing demands for power in the world in general has resulted in a series of large scale power outages. Furthermore, deregulation and increasing interconnections among grids have left a complex topographical landscape of organizations and technology that transcends traditional national borders (Sveen, Hernantes, Gonzalez, and Rich, 2010). In Africa in general the impact of this has been consistently applying the concept of load shedding whereby people in rural areas can be left without power for extended periods of time. Battery powered devices like mobile ones are attractive because they do not rely on being continuously connected to a power source in other to remain operational (Yamada and Matsumura, 2012).

If we were to consider how this affects security enforcement, one could imagine the case of remote access to healthcare records. In this case access to the backend server is critical in an emergency-management scenario in order to ensure a "correct" diagnosis. Power outages however, put the dependability of these systems in jeopardy and so in recent years there has been a strong drive to make health records accessible on personal mobile devices such as cellphones. Making healthcare records available to users in this way raises questions that are centered around privacy and security of the data. For instance, how do we design access control schemes that enforce data security in ways that adhere to the security policies of both the data owner (patient) and the hospital (healthcare provider)? What happens if the device is stolen or if a patient's password is stolen? When storage limitations preclude storing all of the data on the mobile device, how does one handle "off-loading" extra data to a third-party storage provider? Finally, when the data is trans-ferred to a third-party storage provider, how does one guarantee that the data is stored securely?

Securing data in resource constrained environments such as the one we have just described, require more than designing an efficient security and/or privacy-preserving algorithm or scheme. Use case scenarios need to be taken into account as is the usual case, but we need to go one step further to support these schemes with data management algorithms that can adapt to and cope with changing conditions in a dynamic manner. For example, if we were to revisit the medical healthcare case that we discussed in the preceding paragraph, we might imagine having auto-destruct algorithms to deal with stolen phone cases or dynamic data transfer to handle situations of data "offloading" from the mobile device to the storage server.

SOCIAL MEDIA USE ON MOBILE PHONES

Social media use on mobile phones is also another popular communication method. Applications like FaceBook (FaceBook, 2014), WhatsApp (WhatsApp, 2014), Instagram (Instagram, 2014), and Twitter (Twitter, 2014) are widely used to share messages and photographs. Unfortunately, in many cases the users of these applications are not always aware of the privacy-preserving measures that they need to be taking.

There are many potential problems with social networks especially for the teenagers using them in African countries where there is a strong sense of community. Social networking involves using web services to share information with others. A user creates a profile that may include a personal webpage and a blog. Social networking sites allow users to connect with friends, and communicate using chat applications. A large proportion of African teenagers have access to a social network, usually via a mobile phone. Most teens use these sites to stay in touch with their friends but increasingly, teens also use these sites to make new friends, flirt, and/or organize social events. Along with these benefits come some risks. Social networks are typical open to all and can be used by other teens to perpetrate cyber bullying and harassment. Cyber bullying or harassment can take several forms such as: publicizing private messages, posting threatening messages, posting embarrassing photos, and spreading rumors.

Designing effective security schemes in this situation requires working on discovering behavioral patterns amongst teens in Africa, that are different from that observed in other teens elsewhere and that lead to privacy violations. Furthermore, we need to discover methods of encouraging teens to adopt safe social networking practices to avoid cyber victimization. This requires in addition to the standard requirements that one would take into account in designing a security scheme for this scenario, a study of the cultural and behavioral practices and find ways of amending or designing security schemes that are effective.

E-HEALTH APPLICATIONS AND MOBILE SECURITY

Electronic healthcare management systems provide a flexible platform for facilitating access to healthcare information from the user's perspective (Petri et al., 2012). In recent years, we have seen a plethora of these systems, each aimed at enabling cost-effective accessibility to information. Typical examples include, Dossia that was sponsored by Walmart (Dossia, 2014) and MyHealtheVet (MyHealtheVet, 2014).

While a lot of these systems have enjoyed reasonable success in the developed world, adoption in developing countries has been challenging because of the inherent limitations in the technological infrastructure. We studied a couple of electronic healthcare management systems in terms of the security and usability of these systems and noted that their reliance on online access control mechanisms is the key hindrance to successful adoption in developing countries.

Therefore, sole reliance on systems that require remote or Internet based access is limiting particularly in resource constrained scenarios where access to the server can be disrupted by factors such as power outages and bandwidth limitations that make satisfying quality of service agreements challenging (Ssembatya et al., 2013).

Daglish and Archer (Daglish and Archer, 2009) have argued that one of the ways of providing efficient healthcare is to grant patients increased control with respect to their healthcare data. The idea is that in cases where the records at the hospital are unreachable, having a localized and current version of he patient's data can be useful in making a "correct" diagnosis and treatment (Weber-Jahnke and Obry, 2012). The schemes that we studied are heavily provider centric and are not designed to facilitate localized offline access, particular from the patient's end. A further constraint of relying online accessibility to the data is that when disruptions occur during connections to the server, as can happen in resource constrained environments, access control decisions need to be re-validated which is a time-consuming process (Chen et al., 2012b).

One of the approaches we have proposed for addressing this problem is to enable patients to store copies of their most current healthcare data on a mobile device. The reason for this proposition is that mobile devices are a lightweight and cost-effective storage device that are relatively cheap to acquire in developing countries (Chen et al., 2012a). Evidently, in allowing localized medical data storage, an adequate access control mechanism is needed in order to ensure that data manipulation and access adheres to the security policies of the healthcare provider.

CRIME REPORTING AND THE ISSUE OF ANONYMITY ON THE WEB

Various campaigns in developing countries indicate that there is a need for a convenient and anonymous crime reporting framework that is suited to the context of the developing world. Typical reporting channels that go beyond conventional approaches include mobile centric approaches. However, users have expressed the concern that mobile devices do not provide the same guarantees of anonymity that other reporting channels do. As a result, while several campaigns have been launched to encourage mobile crime reporting, usage popularity has been rather slow with the result that serious crime often goes unreported.

One of the methods of addressing this concern is to design a framework that the reporting of crimes anonymously through a secure platform. The framework comprises of two components namely, a reporting module that is facilitated by unstructured supplementary service data (USSD) on a mobile phone and an anonymization module that is supported by a k-anonymization algorithm (Burke and Kayem, 2013). The advantage of using USSD is that it is available to anyone with a mobile phone and reports can not be traced to the participant. Anonymization has the advantage of guaranteeing user privacy in the management of the reported data. Additionally, the anonymized data can be made available to third party data mining service providers for analysis without raising privacy concerns.

In this case as in the previous two, we note that special and sometimes different scenarios arise in resource constrained environments and that these scenarios require rethinking security solution approaches. In some cases, this requires some slight changes or modifications to existing schemes, while in others such as the social networking cases the impact of cultural beliefs on behavioral inclinations might require completely rethinking security design approaches.

CONCLUSION

In the preceding sections we outlined some of the reasons behind the challenges of implementing standard security solutions in resource constrained environments that are characteristic of rural areas. We noted that for reasons pertaining to cost, and limitations of resources in many cases users prefer to have full control over their data. Our aim therefore, was to argue that by taking into account the constraints of the environment, we can re-engineer security solutions to cope the changes that emerge in these environments.

Specifically, we considered the problems that arise in healthcare data and social media-access scenarios drawing attention to the fact that the environmental and behavioral factors

that impact on security enforcement are beyond the scope of the current quasi-standard schemes. As well the increasing complexity of the data access scenarios implies by default that effective security would be impossible even with most efficient algorithms if we were to ignore the behavioral factors involved.

The advantage of this approach is that users can access information is a secure manner by dynamically adjusting the data management scenario to cope with perceived environmental changes. Additionally, the security administrator of the system now only has to preset required parameters and let the system run, without having to manually handle every change.

In a nutshell, if "security and privacy-preservation" is defined as the ability of a system to inspire confidence in its users by guaranteeing data protection, then we can postulate that augmenting security schemes to integrate parameters that facilitate coping with the environment is a good way to go. Can we guarantee that these theories will work well in practice?

An implementation and experimentation aimed at testing and validating the hypothesis will probably give a more accurate view. One might ask what is to stop a legitimate user from being coerced into attempting to circumvent security schemes that are stand-alone? The assumption is that the SA would specify what actions a user can perform legitimately and implement these policies so that they are incorporated automatically into the security scheme. The assumption that diverse computing environments require alternative solution approaches. Are there other approaches that may be more effective? Is there a good way to define adequate monitoring thresholds to decide on when to dynamically switch protection modes to cope with changing scenarios?

REFERENCES

Burke, M. J., & Kayem, A. V. D. M. (2014). K-Anonymity for Privacy Preserving Crime Data Publishing in Resource Constrained Environments. In *Proceedings for the 8th International Symposium on Security and Multinodality in Pervasive Environments*. (In Press).

Chen, T., & Zhong, S. (2012). Emergency Access Authorization for Personally Controlled Online Health Care Data. *J. Med. Syst., 36*(1), 291-300. DOI=10.1007/s10916-010-9475-2

Chen, T.-S., Liu, C.-H., Chen, T.-L., Chen, C. S., Bau, J.-B., & Lin, T. C. (2012, December). Secure Dynamic Access Control Scheme of PHR in Cloud Computing. *Journal of Medical Systems, 36*(6), 4005–4020. doi:10.1007/s10916-012-9873-8 PMID:22926919

Daglish, D., & Archer, N. (2009). Electronic Personal Health Record Systems: A Brief Review of Privacy, Security, and Architectural Issues. In *Proceedings of the IEE 2009 World Congress on Privacy, Security, and Trust and the Management of e-Business*, (pp. 110-120). IEE.

Dossia. (2014). *Dossia*. Retrieved from http://www.dossia.org

FaceBook. (2014). *FaceBook*. Retrieved from https://www.facebook.com

Goodman, S., & Harris, A. (2010, December). The Coming African Tsunami of Information Insecurity. *Communications of the ACM, 53*(12), 24–27. doi:10.1145/1859204.1859215

Instagram. (2014). *Instagram*. Retrieved from http://instagram.com

MyHealtheVet. (2014). *MyHealtheVet*. Retrieved from https://www.myhealth.va.gov/index.html

Ssembatya, R., Kayem, A., & Marsden, G. (2013). On the challenge of adopting standard EHR systems in developing countries. In *Proceedings of the 3rd ACM Symposium on Computing for Development* (ACM DEV '13). ACM. DOI=10.1145/2442882.2442911

Sveen, F. O., Hernantes, J., Gonzalez, J. J., & Rich, E. (2010). Towards understanding recurring large scale power outages: An endogenous view of inter-organizational effects. In *Proceedings of the 5th international conference on Critical Information Infrastructures Security* (CRITIS'10). Springer-Verlag.

Twitter. (2014). *Twitter*. Retrieved from https://twitter.com

Vuorimaa, P., Harmo, P., Hämäläinen, M., Itälä, T., & Miettinen, R. (2012). Active life home: a portal-based home care platform. In *Proceedings of the 5th International Conference on PErvasive Technologies Related to Assistive Environments* (PETRA '12). ACM. DOI=10.1145/2413097.2413133

Weber-Jahnke, J.H., & Obry, C. (2012). Protecting privacy during peer-to-peer exchange of medical documents. *Information Systems Frontiers, 14*(1), 87-104. DOI=10.1007/s10796-011-9304-2

WhatsApp. 2014. *WhatsApp*. Retrieved from https://www.whatsapp.com

Yamada, T., & Matsumura, T. (2012). Battery-Aware IT Control Method for Effective Battery Use During Power Outage. In *Proceedings of the 2012 IEEE International Conference on Green Computing and Communications* (GREENCOM '12). IEEE Computer Society.

ADDITIONAL READING

Chen, R.-S., & Liu, I.-F. (2013, April). Research on the effectiveness of information technology in reducing the Rural-Urban Knowledge Divide. *Computers & Education*, *63*, 437–445. doi:10.1016/j.compedu.2013.01.002

Hongladarom, S. (2004, February). Making Information Transparent as a Means to Close the Global Digital Divide. *Minds and Machines*, *14*(1), 85–99. doi:10.1023/B:MIND.0000005137.58950.c9

Miller, F. P., Vandome, A. F., & McBrewster, J. (2009). *Global Digital Divide: Internet, Developing Country, Information and Communication Technologies for Development, Global Internet Usage, Inveneo, One Laptop ... on the Information Society, Rural Internet*. Alpha Press.

Sveen, F. O., Hernantes, J., Gonzalez, J. J., & Rich, E. (2010). Towards understanding recurring large scale power outages: an endogenous view of inter-organizational effects. In *Proceedings of the 5th international conference on Critical Information Infrastructures Security* (CRITIS'10), Christos Xenakis and Stephen Wolthusen (Eds.). Springer-Verlag, Berlin, Heidelberg, 43-54.

Yu, L. (2011, December). The divided views of the information and digital divides: A call for integrative theories of information inequality. *Journal of Information Science*, *37*(6), 660–679. doi:10.1177/0165551511426246

KEY TERMS AND DEFINITIONS

Bandwidth: This is a measurement of the bit rate of available or consumed data communication resources expressed in bits per second or multiples of it (bit/s, kbit/s, Mbit/s, Gbit/s, etc.).

Green Computing: This is the study and practice of environmentally sustainable computing. This includes designing, and using computer systems and subsystems, efficiently little or no impact to the environment.

Mobile Devices: Battery-powered devices characterized by being lightweight and highly portable.

Privacy: Laws or rules aimed at protecting users' personal information.

Resource-Constrained Environments: These are environments that are characterized by a lack of computing resources and/or other resources required to run a computing system efficiently. A key drawback of implementing security solutions in these environments is their vulnerability to adversarial access.

Security: A scheme that adheres to the notions of Confidentiality, Availability, and Integrity.

Social Media: Applications for group communication and information sharing.

Chapter 2

Foreground Trust as a Security Paradigm:
Turning Users into Strong Links

Stephen Marsh
University of Ontario, Canada

Karen Renaud
University of Glasgow, UK

Natasha Dwyer
Victoria University, Australia

Khalil El-Khatib
University of Ontario, Canada

Anirban Basu
KDDI R&D Laboratories, Japan

Babak Esfandiari
Carleton University, Canada

Tim Storer
University of Glasgow, UK

Sylvie Noël
University of Trento, Italy

Mehmet Vefa Bicakci
Carleton University, Canada

ABSTRACT

Security is an interesting area, one in which we may well be guilty of misunderstanding the very people we are working for whilst trying to protect them. It is often said that people (users) are a weak link in the security chain. This may be true, but there are nuances. In this chapter, the authors discuss some of the work they have done and are doing to help users understand their information and device security and make informed, guided, and responsible decisions. This includes Device Comfort, Annoying Technologies, and Ten Commandments for designers and implementers of security and trust systems. This work is exploratory and unfinished (it should in fact never be finished), and this chapter presents a step along the way to better security users.

INTRODUCTION

Security involves difficult decisions. They are difficult because security is a process, one in which there are continuous updates, alterations, considerations and adjustments to settings, requirements, and a myriad of different profiles and patterns. Security is also a relationship between the person actually using the system we are trying to make secure, and the things they have no control over or understanding of, like the system itself (see for example Flink, 2002).

DOI: 10.4018/978-1-4666-6158-5.ch002

Often, we hear that users are the weakest link in the security chain. A simple web search will reinforce that view. For example: "You can implement rock solid network security; enforce strong, complex passwords; and install the best anti-malware tools available. Most security experts agree, however, that there is no security in the world that can guard against human error." (Techhive, 2012). Of course, there are studies that address this, particularly where passwords are concerned, such Notoatmodjo and Thomborson (2009), Yan et al. (2004) and Adams and Sasse (1999). There are also approaches from HCI that directly counter that view (Sasse et al, 2001). As well, there is a nascent understanding of the different aspects of users that affect IS (cf. Frangopoulos et al, 2013). In general however, it is accepted wisdom that educating users in their own defence is needed.

Today, the decisions we must make about security of many kinds occupy an important place. Whilst security has always been paramount, the difference now is the tools we use. Computers, either on desktop, laptop, or in our pockets, help us to do things more quickly. They can also help put us into difficult situations more quickly. Information – private, heretofore shared only with a chosen few, can be exposed to the many. Protecting information, devices, and people, is the task of information security.

We conjecture that, if a system is not compromised already it most certainly can be. Attacks are more sophisticated, targeted and widespread. We pour more and more intellectual capital into defences against the adversaries. But to what end? Systems now not compromised can be, and many are, with or without our knowledge whilst their own complexity increases. This ultimately results in more frustration at the very least on the part of the users we are trying to defend, and we arrive at a challenging confusion: the system is broken.

Enhanced security mechanisms such as more complex login procedures or systems that put more demands on users do not ultimately help the user engage with the security process – at the least they encourage the user to rebel (Norman, 2010). As an aside, this also appears to be the case for the very developers we depend on (Bodden et al, 2013). In our work we aim to provide systems that leverage human social norms, in particular, in our work, trust and comfort, and their darker siblings distrust and discomfort. These are tools that have been used by humans for millennia in situations of risk. The paradigm that most interests us in this instance is what Dwyer (2011) calls Foreground Trust. Foreground Trust is a toolset to allow devices to present information to users in order to allow them to make their own trust (and hence security)-focused decisions. Our most recent work in this area has been concerned with integrating comfort and trust reasoning techniques into mobile devices, which we call Device Comfort, and which is examined below.

Security experts understand of course, the power of crowdsourced security – not least, there is an understanding that engaging people in the process of personal security in public places ('If you see something, say something') has potential not only to increase security but also to increase *awareness* of security.

We are beginning the journey of designing and creating systems, models, and interfaces for, whilst thinking of, the Turing Complete User (Lialina, 2012) – the user who employs devices and applications to do many different things, sometimes all at once; the user who understands that there are different ways to do the same thing, and that individual applications for different tasks may or may not be the way in which they want to accomplish their tasks. Given their inherent understanding of 'how they do things,' these users deserve to be brought into the security relationship. Moreover, since, we believe, everyone can be engaged in processes that concern them, we aim to make real users into real Strong Links in the process – understanding, engaged, and responsive.

This chapter explores some of the work we have been doing with the ultimate goal of being able to engage users in the process of security, by bringing to the foreground the trust decisions that users will need to make in order to become part of the process, to understand the process and their part in it, and to ensure that they understand why and how they fit. Ironically, much of the work doesn't involve users in the early stages, but puts in place the things we need to bring them in. This chapter represents a step along the way. One in which we are producing interfaces, rules and methodologies that we conjecture may help in the security and trust process. The next steps, as the chapter discusses below, more readily involve the users we are trying to bring into the fold.

This chapter discusses the Device Comfort paradigm as a security tool for both information and personal security from a high level perspective. As well, we will discuss a set of 'commandments' for trust and comfort; commandments that we feel can benefit any security technology where humans are a concern (and this is, of course, all of them).

The chapter is organized as follows: in the next section we introduce our view of trust as the enabling paradigm for greater understanding. Following that, we describe the work we are doing in the areas of Device Comfort, Foreground Trust, Trust Models and Annoying Interfaces. We then discuss the Ten Commandments for trust (and security) models that we believe can help us move along the path of understanding for people. We conclude with future work.

TRUST? HOW DO WE DO THIS?

Our work has built on the Computational Trust (Marsh, 1994; Marsh & Dibben, 2005) paradigm, and investigated the concept of Foreground Trust as a tool in the ongoing security process. Foreground Trust was first introduced in Dwyer (2011) as a means of facilitating online interactions. The basic premise is this: everyone has his or her own different way of viewing trust: predispositions, evidence, subjective notions, and so forth. This premise runs counter to the view

of trust as a rational decision that dominated the research area for a long time. The rational choice position assumes that a person forms trust and security decisions based on the principle of what benefits that person the most, in other words, from a position of self-interest (see Ostrom, 1998 for an overview). So there is a 'correct' trust and security response in every context that can be calculated. Following these assumptions, the appropriate role of technology is to 'disappear' on those occasions where we might otherwise be directly faced with trust and security issues. For example, there should be no need to prompt the user for a password to access a system if it can readily identify the user through other means. This can go beyond the usual biometrics (fingerprint, face recognition) and rely on indications such as the presence of other familiar devices (social zones, as in Marsh et al, 2011) keystroke patterns (cf. Crawford, 2013) or even the angle the user tilts the device when using it. Trust, according to this view, is something that can be managed in the background, and automatically handled by the system. Rogers (2006) draws a comparison between how mainstream technology has been designed to serve people and the lifestyle of the landed aristocracy in England, whose every need is attended to with as little thought or action on the part of the individual aristocrat. But as Greenfield (cited in Shute, 2009) points out 'we don't do "smart" very well yet'. Although computing technology has been around for a considerable amount of time, technology automation has not been achieved (Langheinrich, 2003), and this is an indication that technology that seeks to fully automate a user's experience may be working in the wrong direction.

Recent research challenges the dominance of rational thought and argues that trust is complex and is a combination of 'rational', 'emotional' and 'intuitive' thinking: for instance, driven by 'exploitation-aversion' rather than 'risk-aversion' (Bohnet & Zeckhauser, 2004). Many motivations drive trust-based decisions including the valuing of justice (Chiu et al., 2009) and reciprocity (Cox, 2004). Relying solely on 'rationalism' will always 'explain trust away or explain everything but trust' (James, 2002; Möllering, 2005, p. 7). In this chapter, we believe that trust is at the very least a combination of 'rational' thinking and what is known as 'feeling' or intuition (Möllering, 2001). Although it may be argued that it is impossible to separate these different ways of thinking, it is clear that trust draws on an assemblage of sensibilities. Rather than a rationalist understanding, we adopt a situated and contextualized understanding that embraces the differences between people's priorities. There is nothing new here. In the 1980s and 1990s, the focus on context began to influence technology development. In Lucy Suchman's groundbreaking text, *Plans and Situated Actions* (1987) she argues that technological development that ignores context results in unsuccessful technology

It's pointless at this level then to tell people that they may trust 'this much' or 'because 100 others do' – but it is entirely correct to tell them that '100 others do', that the history we have seen is this, that the other information we know about this person is that, that the risks and consequences we can see are the following, and so on, and *let them make their own trusting decisions*. This last is key: people have a lot to offer when at trust and security, and we are simply helping them see the path. We argue that technology should be designed to work with the capabilities of humans, not to replace human thinking, and thus should combine the strengths of humans and technology. Computers can only measure outcomes and do not process the subtleties of intention (Nooteboom, 2002). For instance, if we trusted someone with our money, but that person was robbed of our money, then although a failure has occurred, this is not necessarily a breach of trust. Jensen (2010) argues that when considering trust, responses are not binary (yes or no) decisions or easily resolvable; that a lot of interactions happen in the 'grey area', the space where it is not immediately clear what to do and may not have been encountered

before. People have a sophisticated ability to make sense and cohesion out of ambiguity and complexity in a context while technology excels at the processing, storing and searching of data (Sokoler & Svensson, 2007). Technology design should therefore aim to combine the two powers of people and technology.

To enable individuals to make their own trusting decisions, we suggest that designers present the trust evidence that is relevant to an individual. This is not a straightforward task as trust is an idiosyncratic outlook, although we do share some principles of trust, we all have our own take on trust. The trust evidence falls into three general categories according to Cofta (2006); continuity, competence and motivation. In short, continuity evidence is connected with time and is a reflection of how long someone has been a member of communities relevant to the trust interaction. Competence evidence indicates whether someone has the skills to deliver on a trust interaction. Motivation evidence is an insight into whether those in a trust interaction have encapsulated interest. So a designer of a digital environment could make an educated guess of what an individual might wish to include in these above categories and present this information to the individual user.

We extend this to the world of computational devices (ubiquitous computing, mobile computing, etc.) and develop it via the Device Comfort paradigm (cf Marsh et al, 2011), itself predicated on the Biometric Daemon (Briggs and Olivier, 2008). Here, individual devices have their own views of trust: in the environment, in the user, in the information they receive and process, and so on. These views are arrived at through internal trust models that take evidence just as a person would, and arrive at their own *subjective* trust levels. The key here is that no single device needs to be able to know the trust model of any other (just as with humans).

The final link in this Foreground Trust chain is that devices can help humans understand better what the security implications of different behaviours, or information flows, or tools and techniques are. They don't do this by telling people. In the Device Comfort model, they do it by helping them understand the following:

- The Device's own level of comfort (or constructed trust) in a given situation, action, location, etc.
- The reasons for this – evidence that the person needs to form *their own* trusting decisions;
- The risks, consequences, policies in place, and *the reasons for them.*

Ultimately, we hope to help the user better understand (improve, implement…) their own security posture as a result of being able to understand and appreciate that of the environment around them (physical and cyber). And then, when users are involved, we hope that they will acknowledge themselves as the strong links they in fact are when empowered instead of removed from the problem – a part of the security process, not apart from it.

As a side note, our approach matches the expectations the public have regarding technology. In general, technology is becoming increasingly configurable by and accessible to users. Arguably, models of security that aim to exclude the user from the process are working on out of date assumptions about the role of consumers. Gradually, technology has developed that has allowed users more and more of an integral role in the shaping of digital environments. The boundaries between developer, designer, and user have become blurred. For instance, in the last five years we have seen the rise of 'do it yourself' (DIY) technology media. As an example, users with little training have accessed media-making technology, such as cameras, and uploaded the results to be distributed widely over the Internet and thus broadcast their perspective globally. Users have become, in the words of Toffler (1980), 'prosumers': a blend of customer, consumer and producer. Why would issues such as security and trust be handled or

regarded differently to how one voices one's opinion? Users now expect technology to meet their own needs and preferences.

In the following sections, we describe work we have done in Device Comfort and Annoying Technologies as examples of Foreground Trust in practice, before we present our Ten Commandments for Trust and Security to design for the engaged user.

PRACTICALITIES

On the journey toward formal and intuitive understanding, we are working on several different tools to enhance *understanding* and *engagement*, which we briefly document here. Most of them come under the umbrella of Computational Trust, but through extension into actual interfaces and devices.

Device Comfort

Device Comfort actualizes Foreground Trust by allowing devices (systems) to reason with and about computational trust (cf. Marsh, 1994) and to communicate this reasoning (the 'feelings') to the user in a human-oriented, understandable and accessible manner.

Device Comfort also allows the device itself to make trust-based decisions, comfort-based decisions, and policy-based decisions *independent* of the user. These decisions adjust security posture, allow or disallow actions or background activity, information sharing, and so on. We have written extensively about Device Comfort elsewhere (Marsh & Briggs, 2010, Marsh, 2010, Marsh et al, 2011) and so only provide an overview of the concept here.

Originally aimed at mobile devices, powerful machines with the 'same old' users, in our research Device Comfort is now being applied across devices in critical infrastructures and smart cities, augmented infrastructure awareness, and less mobile devices with user focused applications.

The premise of Device Comfort is to Advise, Encourage, and Warn about (as for a constitutional monarch) and if necessary Proscribe, actions for the users of the device. Of course, as the Ten Commandments below make explicit, this is what all security methodologies and tools should be doing.

Device Comfort uses the sensing capabilities of the application and/or device. This includes not only what a device can sense for itself, but also what it might be told by the devices around it, or by its users or owners for example. The more information a device has, the more we can integrate into comfort. At its simplest, Device Comfort is a measure based on reasoning about the following:

The user's identity (we have views about how to achieve this recognition, but continuous authentication, for instance as explored by Crawford (2013) and Bicakci, (2013) shows great promise given that we are already using the capabilities of devices. Thus, even if not the reasoning application or system, mobile personal devices can have input to the comfort decision.

- Enhanced trust reasoning about the user, and the ongoing *relationship* with respect to trust that the device has in the user (and/ or owner).
- The current task (for instance, making a call, sending text, sending pictures, email, etc).
- The current location (which virtually all mobile devices can determine with some accuracy).
- A comfort policy-base (provided by the owner of the device, as well as the owners of any information the device stores or can access, basically presented to the device, and thus the user, on access).
- An extended exposition of Device Comfort, including formalization, is given in Marsh et al (2011).

In much of our development (see for example Marsh et al (2011) and Bicakci, (2013)) we have focused on mobile devices (smartphones) and developed a tuple space information architecture to feed the comfort engine, which then communicates with the user through a reasonably non-intrusive interface as much as possible. We have very carefully considered how the mechanism becomes human-oriented through the interface (consider Annoying Technologies, below) whilst engaging and encouraging the trust relationship. We aim, through the interface to give the user second thoughts, encourage anticipatory regret if possible, and learn from what the device can tell them about the situations they find themselves in – and in this way, to learn about security for themselves and their information.

As we discuss in Storer at al (2013), there are several benefits to such a relationship-based approach:

- It is more flexible and adaptive to user needs than explicit authentication (which may be either too intrusive or not secure enough *in context*);
- It allows for multiple *personas* for a user. Where 'Bring Your Own Device' becomes more prevalent, for instance, adding the user's context into the device's reasoning and sensing capabilities allows more security for different information at different times.

In addition, as the device becomes accustomed to its user's normal patterns of behaviour, it can adjust its own behavior accordingly. Actions that enhance the device's sense of comfort are permitted transparently. Conversely, actions that make the device 'feel' uncomfortable in particular contexts are resisted, although rarely actively prevented. Indeed, rather than prevent, we take the view that engaging the user – sometimes playfully and sometimes in rather more annoying a fashion, has merit.

Annoying Technologies

The Comfort device should actively prompt the user, in order to help them better to engage with the security. Bear in mind that this process is not only about the information the user may be working with, but the device itself, the context, and the user (in other words – security may be about the physical as well as the 'cyber').

Annoying Technology employs designs that extend conventional user interface components with the goal of expressing the device's sense of comfort integrated with the completion of a user's task. User interface design research has largely been concerned with investigating the interaction methods that support a user to complete their desired tasks in an intuitive and convenient manner (Poppe, 2007). Here, we present designs that actively obstruct the user if necessary, in order to express the device's discomfort in a specific context, for a specific action, in the hope of giving the user enough time to have 'second thoughts.' The designs are intended to convey the device's discomfort as a warning concerning the proposed action. However, the obstruction will not normally prevent the user from completing the action if they insist on doing so. In fact, we wish to be annoying in the same sense that a conscience, or a best friend, might be annoying when we are about to do something 'wrong' – in other words we actively leverage the foreground trust 'relationship' between user and device that the device comfort methodology aims to build.

The following figures (from Storer et al (2013)) illustrate some examples of obstructive user interfaces. In these examples, consider that the user has begun an action that the device perceives as undesirable. Each figure shows a different, annoying, dialogue box for a user to confirm the prospective action that has been configured by the device to make the response from the user harder, but not impossible.

In Figure 2, we see two different views. In the first, the device is 'comfortable' (in the sense of Device Comfort described above) with the actions of the user, thus the user is required to simply 'swish and flick' (to borrow a phrase from the wizarding world) to confirm their actions. However, if the device is in an 'uncomfortable' state – perhaps as a result of prior actions, perhaps because of its location, or other applications running – the user is required to do far more in the way of movement to confirm the action they have initiated.

Figure 3 is an extension, of sorts, of the dexterity requirement. Here, the user is forced to click on the 'OK' button, to confirm the action, several times, whilst the button itself moves to a different place every time it is clicked.

In each case, the dialogue can be configured to be more or less obstructive, depending on the device's comfort level, the action itself, and other

Figure 1. Temporal annoyance

Figure 2. Dexterity

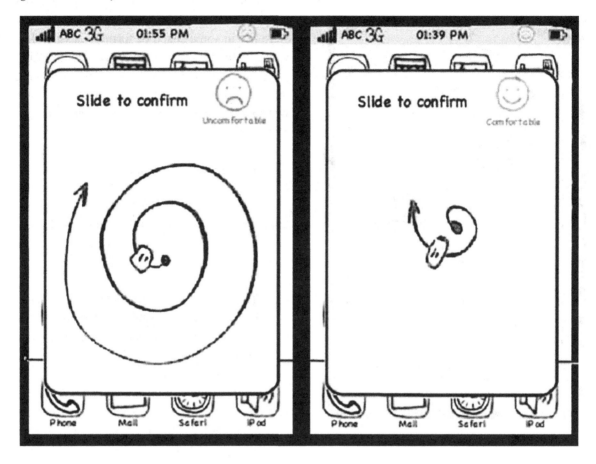

device comfort-related measures. As well, this annoyance can be mitigated or perhaps reversed to make the action more intuitive if the device is in a state of comfort, for instance when the action is being undertaken in a predefined location, or if the action is regularly undertaken in specific places or times, for instance.

We are building several other examples of these 'annoyance' techniques – see Storer et al (2013) for more details. However, the points here should be made clear. Firstly, the device does not in face *forbid* the action – it merely makes it harder to do, and the more 'uncomfortable' it is – indeed, the more strict its security posture – the more the user has to do to achieve the action. Secondly, the device *requires attention* – the action required bears some form of cognitive or physical burden. Finally, as can be seen in Murayama et al (2012) and Oikawa & Murayama (2008), there is a need for accommodation of differences, to allow different users to respond or register discomfort differently.

But why would we do this to our poor users? Simply, in order to have them *think* more about what they are doing, and in thinking, achieve engagement, not with the device, but with the security process. It is our hope (which will be investigated in future work) that this 'getting in the face of' the user achieves far more than the more traditional dialog box that people quite happily click through to achieve the task they want to achieve (often with less than desirable results in the longer term). In the continuing relationship that foreground trust enables and device comfort actualizes, annoyance is a valuable tool, not to be overused, in engaging the user in the security process.

Figure 3. Movement

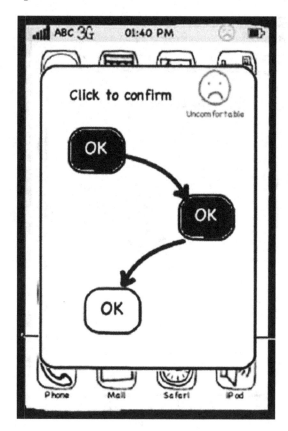

TEN COMMANDMENTS FOR REAL PEOPLE

Of course, the process and the tools are of little use when the models and predictions are opaque to the user. In Marsh, Basu & Dwyer (2012) we presented a discussion of the complexity of trust models that are, as all should be, human-focused. This was further extended in Marsh, Basu and Dwyer (2012a) (because everyone needs ten commandments) with the addition of the final two in the list. The spirit of Foreground Trust and these commandments is further exhibited in Basu et al (2014a, 2014b), where helping the user to understand preferences and privacy is key.

To re-emphasize the arguments there and above: too much complexity is not helpful. Whilst these commandments are likely not particularly unique, they did not at the time exist for the Trust

Management world within which they were first proposed. We would be heartily surprised if they were not in some shape or form discussed elsewhere in the usable security world, but bringing them into trust and security, and acknowledging the interconnectedness of the two, is always worthwhile. The commandments, and a discussion, follow.

1. The model is for people.

   The work we do, in all of the fields computers touch, is for people, and will at some point touch people, either directly or indirectly. They must be considered in the models we deploy.

2. The model should be understandable, not just by mathematics professors, but also by the people who are expected to use and make decisions with or from it.

   Too often, the consensus seems to have been that complexity in our models and our security is a good thing. We do not agree. Of course, the underlying models may well be extensively mathematical – although consider that, given recent revelations, even complex mathematics isn't necessarily the protection it was once thought to be. Now consider further that, fragile as it is, trust, the way people use it, has survived to this day as an excellent tool for judging risk, *whilst acknowledging its frailty*. Indeed, in the absence of any trustworthy (sic) security, it may well become all we have left.

3. Allow for monitoring and intervention. Humans weigh trust and risk in ways that cannot be fully predicted. A human needs to be able to make the judgment, especially when the model is in doubt.

   Models have edges, and the world has nuances that those edges may not take into account. A little human input and understanding at the edges, prompted by the system when it reaches an edge, may make the different between good and bad decisions.

4. The Model Should Not Fail Silently, but Should Prompt for and Expect Input on 'Failure' or Uncertainty

Following from the third commandment, if the model or system fails, it should say so. It's not enough, and it is not satisfactory, for a trust or security system to silently allow transgressions because it doesn't know how to handle them. An encryption system with a back door that allows snooping *is not* doing the job we *trust* it to do, and it should say so.

5. The Model Should Allow for a Deep Level of Configuration. Trust and Security Models Should not Assume What is `Best' for the User. Only the User Can Make That Call

If we wish our users to be engaged, we must engage them. Mobile devices are extremely configurable, and are configured by their users, even if only at a superficial level. Foreground Trust, Device Comfort and Annoying Technologies aim to bring an engagement with the user so that the user can see for themselves how their actions and configurations count.

6. The Model Should Allow for Querying: A User May Want to Know More about a System or a Context

Understanding breeds acceptance. Asking for clarification shows a need to understand. Answering queries breeds understanding (and engagement).

7. The Model Should Cater for Different Time Priorities

In some cases, a trust/security decision does need to be made quickly. But in other cases, a speedy response is not necessary. Indeed, considering events like flash crashes, it's possible to conjecture that a little caution, more haste less speed, in our models is not a bad thing. Consider the first commandment.

8. The Model Should Allow for Incompleteness

Many models aim to provide a definitive answer. Human life is rarely like that. A more appropriate approach is to keep the case open, allowing for new developments, users to change their minds, and for situations to be re-visited.

9. Beware Your Context

Trust (and security) is an ongoing relationship that changes over time. Do not assume that the context in which the user is situated today will be identical tomorrow.

10. Acknowledge Fragility

It is important to acknowledge risk up front (which is what all trust, including Foreground Trust, does). Security often says "this is secure, you may trust it", whilst trust, more honestly, says "you may trust this, *this much* – and if you do, *these risks exist*" – with that honesty comes the ability to put in place controls for the risk that security effectively hides from us.

Quite simply, the Ten Commandments for trust and security aim to bring users into the mix, to engage them actively in the decisions our systems make. We are quite prepared and happy to accept the view that they may be intuitive or obvious, and would ask – if they are obvious, why are our systems and models so very dedicated to decreasing user understanding and reducing user engagement in the process? Such a course of action can only work for so long before those users try to break the process, ironically with actions that we perceive make the users the weakest link, and so the cycle continues.

Let us, for the sake of argument, consider the sending of a sensitive work-related email in an insecure context and apply the Ten Commandments if possible. Consider:

1. The email might be urgent enough that it needs to be sent even if there is risk of snooping. It should be possible for the system to disappear and allow the sending.
2. The system should explain why it is allowing, while still warning the user of the risks: "This email seems urgent, just know that in this environment people might be able to snoop in!"
3. "You are sending this email via a wireless network, are you confident that nobody who shouldn't read your email isn't going to?"
4. "This is foreign territory for me, I'm not able to determine if it is safe to send this email without anyone potentially snooping in".
5. Follow up to 4: "maybe to make sure nobody can snoop in you should encrypt this email (or increase the encryption strength) this one time."
6. Provides the reasoning/explanation/justification as to why it is worried about spying: "text analysis points to important/urgent message", "use of wireless network", "unfamiliar wireless router", and follows up with why it is still ok letting it be sent: "risk/reward analysis," "confident keystrokes, so you seem to know what you're doing today," and so forth.
7. Goes back to the first commandment.
8. "If you keep using me for other tasks I could try to get more certainty about how risky it is to send this email from here."

9 and 10 need no further clarification in the case of this example.

As can be seen, applying the commandments to specific examples and working through them provides valuable input not only to design decisions but also to the quality of interaction between comfort-enabled device and user.

There are many next steps. Whilst some work has been done with 'real' people, much more is needed. The next section examines the future, whilst keeping an eye on what has been achieved thus far.

MOVING FORWARD INTO THE FUTURE, WITH AN EYE ON MCLUHAN'S REAR VIEW MIRROR

In this chapter, we have proposed a set of guidelines, tools and techniques to actively engage users in their security-focused decision making through trust. However, we have not as yet done nearly enough work with the users themselves (Dwyer, (2011), Basu et al (2014a, 2014b) notwithstanding). Much of the future for this work lies in examining how users perceive the technologies we have developed, and their effectiveness. As we have noted above and has been discussed elsewhere, users are quite adept at bypassing (or ignoring) security warnings or pop up windows. We will be actively investigating the same phenomenon with Annoying Technologies both within and outside of the context of a relationship between device and user. Does the relationship make a difference? If it does, does a relationship help with the more prosaic warnings currently used? How much, and in what contexts?

As well, at the level of the user, we are concerned with what type of trust and security issues people are most interested in, and why? Insights into this question can help designers tailor interfaces that meet the expectations of users and work with their interests and aptitudes. Exploration of this question will tell us what elements of an interface users might want to configure or personalize and what aspects might be left in 'default' mode. This leads to another question for further development, how should information about trust and security be best presented to users? Information visualisation research can be applied to this specific area, the representation of trust and security data. Visual images are never ideologically neutral; there is always support of one type of worldview over another (Thaler & Sunstein, 2008). Which one does a user wish to engage with and how does the designer of a system help a user negotiate the choice? Some research has found that visual messages inspiring fear and apprehension simply don't work (Kraak et al, 2012) but often this seems to be the default choice for the design of information about trust and security. Government communiqués about identity theft come to mind. Surely there are better ways? In addition, we will explore other ways of presenting users with trust and comfort information beyond the visual, including sound and tactile feedback..

A third future research question is how can the area of trust and security research learn from the areas of technology that currently empower users and communities? The use of technology in the music domain is a good example. Digital technology has allowed musicians to re-claim creative freedom and circumvent the marketing and distribution structures established by corporations (Oliver and Green, 2009).

We are at a stage where the technologies we have been creating and designing can now be actively deployed and observed. If engaging users in security is the goal, the next steps will aim to do just that.

REFERENCES

Adams, A., & Sasse, A. (1999). Users are not the enemy. *Communications of the ACM, 42*(12), 40–46. doi:10.1145/322796.322806

Basu, A., Corena, J., Kiyomoto, K., Marsh, S., Vaidya, J., & Guo, G. (2014b). Privacy preserving trusted social feedback. In *Proceedings of the ACM Symposium on Applied Computing (SAC) TRECK track*. New York: ACM Press.

Basu, A., Corena, J., Kiyomoto, S., Vaidya, J., Marsh, S., & Miyake, Y. (2014a). PrefRank: Fair aggregation of subjective user preferences. In *Proceedings of the ACM Symposium on Applied Computing (SAC) RS track*. New York: ACM Press.

Bicakci, V. (2013). *Anomaly Detection for Mobile Device Comfort*. (Masters of Applied Science Thesis). Carleton University.

Bodden, E., Hermann, B., Lerch, J., & Mezini, M. (2013). *Reducing human factors in software security architectures. In Proceedings Fraunhofer Future Security Conference 2013*. Germany: Fraunhofer Verlag.

Bohnet, I., & Zeckhauser, R. (2004). Trust, risk and betrayal. *Journal of Economic Behavior & Organization, 55*(40), 467–484. doi:10.1016/j.jebo.2003.11.004

Briggs, P., & Olivier, P. (2008). Biometric daemons: Authentication via electronic pets. In *Proceedings CHI 2008* (pp. 2423–2432). New York: ACM Press.

Chang, H., & Schroeter, K. (2010). Creating safe and trusted social networks with biometric user authentication, ethics and policy of biometrics. In *Proceedings 3rd International Conference on Ethics and Policy of Biometrics and International Data Sharing*. Retrieved on March 29, 2013 from http://www.comp.polyu.edu.hk/conference/iceb/

Chatfield, C., Carmichael, D., Hexel, R., Kay, J., & Kummerfeld, B. (2005). Personalisation in intelligent environments: Managing the information flow. In *Proceedings OZCHI '05: 17th Australian conference on Computer-Human Interaction*. Canberra: Computer-Human Interaction Special Interest Group (CHISIG) of Australia.

Chiu, C., Huang, H., & Yen, C. (2010). Antecedents of trust in online auctions. *Electronic Commerce Research and Applications, 9*(2), 148–159. doi:10.1016/j.elerap.2009.04.003

Cofta, P. (2006), Distrust. In *Proceedings of Eight International Conference on Electronic Commerce* (pp. 250-258). New York: ACM Press.

Cox, J. (2004). How to identify trust and reciprocity. *Games and Economic Behavior, 46*(2), 260–281. doi:10.1016/S0899-8256(03)00119-2

Crawford, H. (2013). *A Framework For Continuous, Transparent Authentication On Mobile Devices*. (PhD Thesis). University of Glasgow, Glasgow, UK.

Dwyer, N. (2011). *Traces of digital trust: an interactive design perspective*. (PhD thesis). Victoria University, Victoria, Australia.

Flink, C. W. (2002). Weakest Link in Information System Security. In *Proceedings of Workshop for Application of Engineering Principles to System Security Design*. Retrieved on October 3rd, 2013 from http://www.acsac.org/waepssd/papers/01-flink.pdf

Frangopoulos, E. D., Eloff, M. M., & Venter, L. M. (2013). Psychosocial risks: Can their effects on the security of information systems really be ignored? *Information Management & Computer Security, 21*(1), 53–65. doi:10.1108/09685221311314428

Jensen, C. (2010). The role of trust in computer security. In *Proceedings of the 4th IFIP WG 11.11 International Conference on Trust Management*. Morioka, Japan: Springer.

Kaminski, P., Agrawal, P., Kienle, H., & Müller, H. (2005). <username>, I need you! initiative and interaction in autonomic systems. In *Proceedings of the 2005 workshop on Design and evolution of autonomic application software*. Retrieved on 25th April, 2013 from http://www.deas2005.cs.uvic.ca/

Kraak, V. I., Story, M., & Wartella, E. A. (2012). Government and school progress to promote a healthful diet to American children and adolescents: A comprehensive review of the available evidence. *American Journal of Preventive Medicine, 42*(3), 250–262. doi:10.1016/j.amepre.2011.10.025 PMID:22341162

Langheinrich, M. (2003). When trust does not compute: The role of trust in ubiquitous computing. In *Proceedings of Privacy Workshops of Ubicomp'03*. Retrieved on 16 May 2006 from http://www.ubicomp.org/ubicomp2003/program.html?show=workshops

Lecture Series, Krete. (n.d.). Retrieved 17 Jan 2011 from http://www.forth.gr/onassis/lectures/2010-06-28/presentations_10/Identity_management_and_privacy.pdf

Lialina, O. (2012). *The Turing Complete User*. Retrieved on 30th November, 2013 from http://contemporary-home-computing.org/turing-complete-user/

Marsh, S. (1994). *Formalising Trust as a Computational Concept*. (PhD Thesis). University of Stirling, Stirling, UK.

Marsh, S. (2010). Comfort Zones: Location Dependent Trust and Regret Management for Mobile Devices. In Proceedings LocationTrust 2010: workshop on location as context for trust at IFIPTM 2010. Springer.

Marsh, S., Basu, A., & Dwyer, N. (2012). Rendering unto Cæsar the things that are Cæsar's: Complex trust models and human understanding. In *Trust Management VI, Proceedings of IFIPTM 2012* (AICT) (vol. 374, pp. 191-200). New York: Springer.

Marsh, S., Basu, A., & Dwyer, N. (2012a). Security Enhancement With Foreground Trust, Comfort, And Ten Commandments For Real People. In Proceedings INTRICATE-SEC 2012. Academic Press.

Marsh, S., & Briggs, P. (2010). Defining and Investigating Device Comfort. In *Proceedings of the 4th IFIP WG 11.11 International Conference on Trust Management*. Morioka, Japan: Springer.

Marsh, S., Briggs, P., El-Khatib, K., Esfandiari, B., & Stewart, J. (2011). Defining and Investigating Device Comfort. *Information and Media Technologies*, 6(3), 914–935.

Marsh, S., & Dibben, M. (2005). Trust, Untrust, Distrust and Mistrust – An Exploration of the Dark(er) Side. In P. Herrmanm, V. Issarny, & S. Shiu (Eds.), Trust Management (LNCS) (vol. 3477, pp. 17–33). Berlin: Springer. doi:doi:10.1007/11429760_2 doi:10.1007/11429760_2

Marsh, S., Wang, Y., Noël, S., Robart, L., & Stewart, J. (2013). Device Comfort for mobile health information accessibility. In *Proceedings Privacy, Security and Trust (PST), eleventh annual conference*. IEEE.

Möllering, G. (2001). The nature of trust: from Georg Simmel to a theory of expectation, interpretation and suspension. *Sociology*, 35(2), 403–420. doi:10.1177/S0038038501000190

Möllering, G. (2005b). *Understanding trust from the perspective of sociological neoinstitutionalism: The interplay of institutions and agency.* MPIfG Discussion Paper 05/13, Max Planck Institute for the Study of Societies, Cologne. Retrieved 11 February 2009 from http://edoc.mpg.de/270955

Möllering, G. (2006a). Trust, institutions, agency: Towards a neoinstitutional theory of trust. In R. Bachmann, & A. Zaheer (Eds.), *Handbook of trust research*. Cheltenham, UK: Edward Elgar. doi:10.4337/9781847202819.00029

Murayama, Y. F., Saito, Y., & Nishioka, D. (2012). Usability issues in security. In *Proceedings Security Protocols XX - 20th International Workshop, Revised Selected Papers* (LNCS) (vol. 7622, pp. 161–171). Cambridge, UK: Springer Verlag.

Nooteboom, B. (2002). *Trust: forms, foundations, functions, failures and figures*. Cheltenham, UK: Edward Elgar. doi:10.4337/9781781950883

Norman, D. (2010). When security gets in the way. *Interactions (New York, N.Y.)*, 16(6).

Notoatmodjo, G., & Thomborson, C. (2009). Passwords and Perceptions. In *Proceedings of the 7th Australasian Conference on Information Security*. Academic Press.

Oikawa, Y. F. H., & Murayama, Y. (2008). Towards an interface causing discomfort for security: A user survey on the factors of discomfort. In *Proceedings Second International Conference on Secure System Integration and Reliability Improvement* (pp. 173–174). Yokohama, Japan: IEEE Press.

Oliver, P., & Green, G. (2009). Adopting new technologies: Self-sufficiency and the DIY artist. In *Proceedings UK Academy for Information Systems Conference 2009*. Retrieved 17 July 2010 from http://aisel.aisnet.org/ukais2009/38

Ostrom, E. (1998). Behavioral approach to the rational choice theory of collective action. *The American Political Science Review*, 92(1), 1–22. doi:10.2307/2585925

Poppe, R., Rienks, R., & van Dijk, B. (2007). Evaluating the future of HCI: Challenges for the evaluation of emerging applications. In Artifical Intelligence for Human Computing, (pp. 234-250). Berline: Springer.

Preneel, B. (2010). *Identity management and privacy*. Onassis Foundation Science.

Rogers, Y. (2006). Moving on from Weiser's vision of calm computing: Engaging UbiComp experiences. In *Proceedings of International Conference of Ubiquitous Computing*. Retrieved 9 July 2009 from http://dx.doi.org/ doi:10.1007/11853565_24

Sasse, M. A., Brostoff, S., & Weirich, D. (2001). Transforming the 'Weakest Link' — A Human/Computer Interaction Approach to Usable and Effective Security. *BT Technology Journal, 3*(19), 122–131. doi:10.1023/A:1011902718709

Shute, T. (2009). Towards a newer urbanism: Talking cities, networks, and publics with Adam Greenfield. *Ugotrade*. Retrieved 3 March, 2012 from http://www.ugotrade.com/2009/02/27/towards-a-newer-urbanism-talking-citiesnetworks-and-publics-with-adam-greenfield/

Sokoler, T., & Svensson, M. (2007). Embracing ambiguity in the design of nonstigmatising digital technology for social interaction among senior citizens. *Behaviour & Information Technology, 26*(4), 343–352. doi:10.1080/01449290601173549

Storer, T., Marsh, S., Noël, S., Esfandiari, B., & El-Khatib, K. (2013). Encouraging second thoughts: Obstructive user interfaces for raising security awareness. In *Proceedings PST 2013: Privacy Security and Trust, Eleventh Annual Conference*. IEEE.

Suchman, L. (1987). *Plans and situated actions: The problem of human-machine communication*. New York: Cambridge University Press.

Techhive. (2012). *Users are still the weakest link. David Jeffers, editorial*. Retrieved June 30, 2002 from http://www.techhive.com/article/260453/users_are_still_the_weakest_link.html

Thaler, R., & Sunstein, C. (2008). *Nudge: Improving decisions about health, wealth, and happiness*. New Haven, CT: Yale University Press.

Toffler, A. (1980). *The third wave*. Bantam Books.

Yan, J., Blackwell, A., Anderson, R., & Grant, A. (2004). Password Memorability and Security: Empirical Results. *IEEE Security & Privacy*, 25–31.

KEY TERMS AND DEFINITIONS

Comfort: A feeling of happiness and security.

Computational Trust: Formalisations, models, and implementations of human (interpersona) trust norms to artificial reasoning systems.

Device Comfort: Formalisation of of human sense of comfort within user-facing mobile devices.

Information Security: The practice of attempting to protect individual's information stored in computational devices, usually using tools such as encryption.

User Engagement: The practice of building (on) relationships between people and technology, usually via user interface design or interaction design.

APPENDIX

Additional Readings

1. For up to date research results around trust and its siblings, we recommend the following conferenceproceedings, published yearly:
    a. IFIPTM Trust Management, published by Springer AICT. See www.ifiptm.org for more information.
    b. PST (Privacy Security and Trust) conferences, co-sponsored by IEEE.
    c. IEEE International Conference on Trust, Security and Privacy in Computing and Communications (IEEE TrustCom)
2. The topic of usable security, upon which this chapter touches, is best reviewed by following the excellent SOUPS - Symposium on Usable Privacy and Security - see http://cups.cs.cmu.edu/soups/
3. Device Comfort is also, as the article mentions, a side look at Ubiquitous Computing, in a way. Here, the Ubicomp conference proceedings are great resources.
4. Heather Crawford's PhD thesis from the University of Glasgow in 2013 discusses how mobile devices can authenticate users transparently, touching on several of our ten commandments: "A framework for continuous, transparent authentication on mobile devices" (http://theses.gla.ac.uk/4046/)

Chapter 3
A State-of-the-Art Review of Data Stream Anonymization Schemes

Aderonke B. Sakpere
University of Cape Town, South Africa

Anne V. D. M. Kayem
University of Cape Town, South Africa

ABSTRACT

Streaming data emerges from different electronic sources and needs to be processed in real time with minimal delay. Data streams can generate hidden and useful knowledge patterns when mined and analyzed. In spite of these benefits, the issue of privacy needs to be addressed before streaming data is released for mining and analysis purposes. In order to address data privacy concerns, several techniques have emerged. K-anonymity has received considerable attention over other privacy preserving techniques because of its simplicity and efficiency in protecting data. Yet, k-anonymity cannot be directly applied on continuous data (data streams) because of its transient nature. In this chapter, the authors discuss the challenges faced by k-anonymity algorithms in enforcing privacy on data streams and review existing privacy techniques for handling data streams.

INTRODUCTION

The need for data protection, especially when needed for analysis, research and data mining purposes has led to the development of several privacy enforcing schemes. Considerable attention has been given to static data protection (Issa, 2009; Iyengar, 2002; Samarati, 2001; Sweeney, 2001, 2002a, 2002b). Static data are non-real time and so the constraints for processing and/or analysis are not time sensitive. Conversely, there is a lot

of data that evolves with time and space, typically referred to as data streams with many real world applications (Guo & Zhang, 2013).

Data streams are real-time and continuous data flows that are ordered implicitly by arrival time or explicitly by timestamps (Golab & Özsu, 2003). The order in which streaming data arrives cannot be pre-determined (Golab & Özsu, 2003). Streaming data emerges from various electronic sources (such as mobile phones or computers) and is expected to be processed online in real-time with minimum

DOI: 10.4018/978-1-4666-6158-5.ch003

delay (Zakerzadeh & Osborn, 2013). In Figure 1, we illustrate that streaming data emerge from a source and essentially has a target destination. Examples of applications that use data streaming include web applications, financial applications and security applications (Zakerzadeh & Osborn, 2013). Data streams can also be a form of temporal data (Wang, Xu, Wong, & Fu, 2010). Temporal data is time-critical because the snapshot available at each timestamp must be made available for necessary action (Wang et al., 2010).

Analyzing data streams in real time helps to reveal hidden knowledge and patterns that might need immediate intervention (such intervention could be to detect anomalies in data streams). For example, in many developing nations like South Africa, about 3.3 million crimes occur yearly, this implies that on the average, thousands of crimes occur daily. Suppose the Crime Report Data Stream (CRDS) has the schema: CRDS (Victim-Name, VictimSex, VictimAge, VictimAddress, CrimeSuffered, SuspectDescription). Analyzing and studying such reported crime in real-time is useful in helping to trap the criminals or suspects in a relatively short period. Furthermore, predictions of future crime or disaster occurrences can be identified. According to Qiu, Li, & Wu (2007), many companies usually outsource the mining of their data to a third party due to lack of in-house expertise. An implication of this is that many law

enforcement agencies particularly in developing countries may lack in-house expertise to mine and/or analyze crime reports/data in real time. In order to release the data to a third party, there is a need to ensure proper data anonymization in order to prevent the persons and/or systems analyzing the anonymized data, from identifying the subjects. Accumulating streaming data over long periods can result in delayed predictions and/or reactions thereby subsequently resulting in a late intervention after analysis.

In order to preserve privacy in data streams, a naive approach is to exclude explicit identifiers such as names and/or identification numbers. However, sensitive details about a subject are deducible through linking attacks. Examples of a subject's sensitive information include crime suffered and medical condition. A linking attack occurs if the combination of non-explicit identifiers (such as date of birth, address and sex) can be used to identify individuals when joined to an external or publicly available table (Li, Ooi, & Wang, 2008; Wang, Li, Ai, & Li, 2007; Zakerzadeh & Osborn, 2013). Non-explicit identifiers used for linking attacks are "Quasi-Identifiers".

We present a simple example of how a linking attack can occur in Figure 2 by joining publicly available data, Table 1, with a supposedly anonymous streaming data in Figure 2, whose explicit identifier, Name, has been removed. Table 1 is a

Figure 1. Illustration of data streams

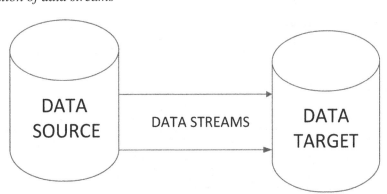

portion of a publicly available table and it contains all individuals at a particular address. Table 1 has the attribute "name" as its explicit identifier. Figure 2 shows that the data in the stream has its explicit identifier removed in order to disguise the identity of the individual to whom the data refers. However, when a join operation was performed on both the publicly available data, Table 1, and the supposedly anonymous streaming data in Figure 2, using the common attributes (date of birth and sex), the supposedly anonymous data in the stream, with details "female, 14/05/1964, rape" as values of the attributes 'sex', 'date of birth' and 'reported crime' respectively was re-identified to be an individual, Ronke living in 6 Alma Road, Rosebank and thus, revealing her sensitive information as a rape victim. This indicates that simply removing explicit identifiers does not guarantee data anonymity and privacy. According to Sweeney (Sweeney, 2002b), as cited in (Sweeney, 2000), 87% of the population in the United States were uniquely identified by the combination of gender, zip code and date of birth using the data of 1990 census. Hence, there is a need for better approach to anonymize data.

BACKGROUND: ANONYMIZATION TECHNIQUES

There are two classifications for anonymization techniques namely perturbative and non-perturbative methodsGkoulalas-Divanis & Loukides, 2013). Figure 3 illustrates this classification.

Perturbative Method

The perturbative method produces untruthful data (Gkoulalas-Divanis & Loukides, 2013; Bayardo & Agrawal, 2005; Jiang & Clifton, 2006; Wang et al, 2007). For instance, the outcome of using the perturbative method may imply that the age of a 30-year-old crime victim becomes 60-year-old in order to preserve privacy. Examples of data anonymization techniques that fall under perturbative include swapping and the additive noise amongst others.

Swapping

Swapping enforces privacy by exchanging the values associated with an attribute in two records/tuples (Dalenius & Reiss, 1982; Sweeney, 2001).

Figure 2. Illustration of linking attack

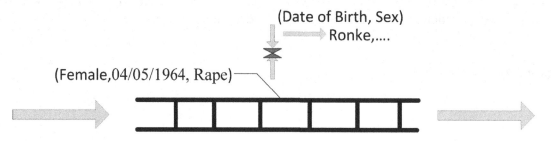

Table 1. Publicly available table

Name	Date of Birth	Sex	Address
Ronke	04/05/1964	Female	6 Alma Road, Rosebank
Wilson	16/09/1986	Female	10 Alma Road, Rosebank
Ayokunle	17/06/1973	Male	10 Dikens Road, Salt River
Lydia	18/05/1975	Male	10 Railway Station Road, Salt River

Figure 3. Classification of anonymisation techniques

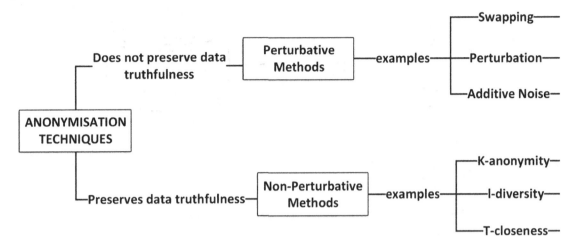

It could be as simple as randomly choosing two records and swapping the values of one of their attributes (Taylor, Reiter, Duncan, Lambert, & Singer, 2003). For instance using swapping, the age of a 70-year-old burglary victim can become that of a 20-year-old rape victim in order to preserve privacy. From Figure 4 below, the age of 20 year old Rape victim, Alice, is been swapped for that of 70-year old burglary victim, Bob, in order to in order to preserve privacy on the attribute "age". The use of such data for crime analysis and mining with reference to age is likely to provide a wrong intervention because the age of a rape victim will be understood to be 70 years old and thus leading to wrong intervention for women that are 70 years old.

Additive Noise/Randomization Method

This involves adding noise randomly by increasing or decreasing attribute values of individual records. This increase or decrease could be sufficiently large such that original values of individual records (i.e. the record's value before anonymization) cannot be re-identified (Aggarwal & Philip, 2008).

We provide an illustration of how the randomization process works by considering a table of n records denoted by $R = \{r_1, r_2, ..., r_n\}$, where r_i

denotes individual record on the table and a noise component derived independently from the probability distribution Pr (Y) denoted by $Y = \{y_1, y_2, ..., y_n\}$. To achieve randomization, we add to each record,, $r_i \in R$,, a noise component, $y_i \in Y$. Thus the anonymized or perturbed records are denoted by by $r_1 + y_1$, $r_2 + y_2$, ..., $r_n + y_n$ (Aggarwal & Philip, 2008).

Non-Perturbative Methods

This method preserves data truthfulness (Gkoulalas-Divanis & Loukides, 2013; Jiang & Clifton, 2006; W. Wang et al., 2007) because of its use of generalization and suppression. Examples of non-perturbative methods include k-anonymity, ℓ -diversity, t-closeness.

K-Anonymity

A first step for k-anonymity to occur is to identify all attributes in the dataset that that could be linked with external dataset (Sweeney, 2002b); such attributes are referred to as 'Quasi-Identifier' (QI). K-anonymity ensures that each entity's quasi-values in the released table corresponds to at least (k-1) other individuals whose information

Figure 4. Illustration of swapping technique

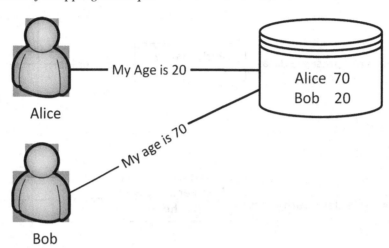

also appears in the release, where k is a pre-assigned integer variable and k>1 (Samarati, 2001; Sweeney, 2001, 2002b). As an illustration of how k-anonymity works, assume an attacker attempts to identify a man, Walex, in the released table based on his birthdate, gender and zipcode, which the attacker knows, k-anonymity ensures there are other (k-1) individuals in the release table with the same birthdate, gender and zipcode. As a result, K-anonymity is effective for counteracting linking attacks. In general, it reduces the probability of linking attacks to at least $\frac{1}{k}$.

K-anonymity is achieved using generalization and suppression (Samarati, 2001; Sweeney, 2002a). Generalization involves "replacing (or recoding) a value with a less specific but semantically consistent value" (Sweeney, 2002a). For instance, a specific year of birth '1984' can be generalized to '198*', representing the year of birth in the interval '1980–1989'. Suppression involves withholding a value completely (Sweeney, 2002a). To illustrate suppression, a given specific year of birth, 1984, can be replaced with '****' to denote a null or a withheld value. Table 2 shows dataset that needs to undergo anonymization. Table 3 is an anonymized version of table 2 using k-anonymity, where k = 2 and QI = (Year of Birth, Sex, Ad-

dress). From table 3, each sequence of values in the QI has at least two occurrences. In particular, record1 [QI] = record3 [QI] and record2 [QI] = record4 [QI]. The probability of a linking attack occurrence on a k-anonymized table is at least 1/k. Therefore, for the anonymized records in table 3, the probability of linking attack is at least ½. This probability seems high, however, if the value of k is increased to 4, the probability will be at least ¼. Thus, the higher the value of k, the lower the probability of linking attacks.

Figure 5 represents the different possible levels of generalization for the attribute "Year of Birth (1984-1986)". The figure also shows that at the lowest level of a generalization tree, the least information loss occurs while the highest information loss occurs at the highest level (total suppression). An implication of this is that generalization can ultimately lead to suppression, which occurs at the highest level of a generalization tree.

Formal Definition of the K-Anonymity Concept

- **Quasi-Identifier (QI):** Assume a set of private data (PD) has attributes, $A_1, A_2 ...,$ A_n, then PD = $\{A_1, A_2,...,A_n\}$. QI is a subset $\{A_{i,...,} A_j\}\{A_{1,...} A_n\}$ whose value can

Table 2. Crime report data streams

Name	Year of Birth	Sex	Address	Reported Crime
Ronke	1989	Female	6 Alma Road, Rosebank	Rape
Ayokunle Ola	1973	Male	10 Dikens Road, Salt River	Car Hijacking
Wilson	1986	Female	10 Alma Road, Rosebank	Rape
Lydia Otoks	1975	Male	24 Dikens Road, Salt River	Burglary

Table 3. Anonymised crime report data streams of table 2

Name	Year of Birth	Sex	Address	Reported Crime
****	198*	Female	Alma Road, Rosebank	Rape
****	197*	Male	Dikens Road, Salt River	Car Hijacking
****	198*	Female	10 Alma Road, Rosebank	Rape
****	197*	Male	Dikens Road, Salt River	Burglary

be used to identify an individual through linking/joining with a publicly released data. From table 2, Year of Birth, Sex and Address are examples of QI.

- **K-Anonymity:** A dataset, PD, satisfies k-anonymity *if and only if* each sequence of values in PD (QI) appears at least k times, where k > 1. (Note: QI $\subseteq$ {$A_{1...}A_n$}).

K-Anonymity Classifications

K-anonymity can be generally classified into two main groups namely Hierarchy-Based Generalization and Hierarchy-Free Generalization (Zakerzadeh & Osborn, 2013). The next sub-sections explain each of the classes in detail.

Hierarchy-Based Generalization

A domain is an acceptable value each attribute of a table can draw from (Silberschatz, Korth, & Sudarshan, 1997). In hierarchy-based generalization, the domain of each attribute is usually stated by means of a hierarchy called Domain Generalization Hierarchy (DGH) (Iyengar, 2002; Sweeney, 2002b). The acceptable values of each attribute are usually constructed from its DGH

(Zakerzadeh & Osborn, 2013). Figure 6 depicts the DGH of the attribute 'Enrolled_Degree'. From the figure, the attribute 'Enrolled_Degree' can have its generalized value drawn from any of the three different levels in the hierarchy namely DGH_0, DGH_1 and DGH_2. Value Generalization Hierarchy (VGH) of an attribute emerges from its DGH. Figure 7 shows the VGH of the attribute 'Enrolled_Degree' which emerges from its DGH in Figure 6. Figure 7 shows how and which of the values in a particular level maps up to values in a higher level of the VGH.

The hierarchy-based generalization expects the data analyst or programmer to specify explicitly the DGH and VGH of each attribute before the generalization or anonymization process begins (Zakerzadeh & Osborn, 2013). Examples of algorithms that make use of Hierarchy-Based Generalization are in (Iyengar, 2002; Samarati, 2001; Sweeney, 2002b).

Hierarchy-Free Generalization

This approach uses clustering and partitioning to produce a generalized/anonymized data/result. To illustrate the concept of clustering, suppose there are x objects that need to undergo partition into

Figure 5. Generalization hierarchies

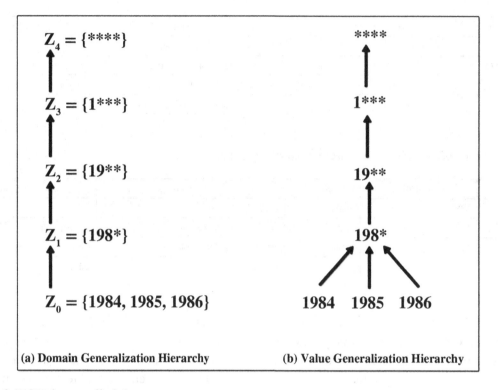

(a) Domain Generalization Hierarchy   (b) Value Generalization Hierarchy

Figure 6. DGH for enrolled degree

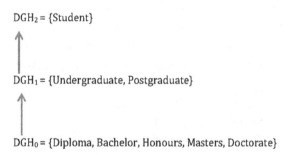

y groups of similar object. Clustering approach divides these objects into y partitions (clusters) and ensures that objects in each partition (cluster) are more similar to each other than to objects in other partitions (Aggarwal, Han, Wang, & Yu, 2003). For more reading on clustering, please refer to (Aggarwal et al., 2003).

To illustrate the concept of clustering in k-anonymization, suppose we have a dataset that contains 20 records where QI = (Age, Gender) and k = 5. The use of clustering approach in order to achieve k-anonymity ensures the following occur:

- The total number of records in a cluster is at least 5.
- All records in a cluster have the same generalized value for age and gender attributes.

Hierarchy-Free Generalization does not require a user-defined generalization tree or hierarchy like Hierarchy-Based Generalization. It automatically does the generalization using clustering approach. Examples of algorithms that make use of Hierarchy-Free Generalization are in (Kabir, Wang, & Bertino, 2011; Tassa & Gudes, 2012).

Why K-Anonymity is Preferred?

K-anonymity is preferred over the perturbative method because it does not compromise the integrity (truthfulness) of data (Bayardo & Agrawal, 2005; Sweeney, 2002b). As a result, the anonymized data produced by the k-anonymity algorithm is reliable and useful for statistical analysis, research and data mining purposes. Secondly,

Figure 7. VGH for enrolled degree

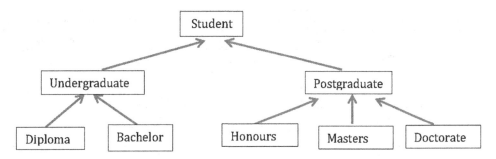

k-anonymity algorithm produces anonymous data that meets the recommendation of census agencies (Jiang & Clifton, 2006). Census agencies, which deals regularly with private data, have discovered that as long as data are aggregated over a group of people, its release does not violate privacy (Jiang & Clifton, 2006).

L-Diversity

K-anonymity can effectively prevent identity disclosure but it is insufficient to prevent attribute disclosure. Li, Li, & Venkatasubramanian (2007) and Machanavajjhala, Kifer, & Johannes (2007) observed the following weaknesses about k-anonymity.

1. K-anonymity does not protect against attacks based on background knowledge. This attack happens as a result of prior knowledge of additional external information that is available to the attacker (Ciriani, Foresti, & Samarati, 2007). In order to illustrate this, we assume Mike and Gabriel are friends. Mike used an anonymous crime reporting system to provide information on a recent murder committed by Gabriel. Sequel to this, Gabriel was arrested and imprisoned. Based on an anonymous public release in order to appreciate citizens who reported crime in the past few months, Gabriel came across the anonymous table (table 4.1). His careful examinations of the table, allowed him conclude that his own murder case was one of records 2, 7, 8, 9. A further analysis made him to rule out records 7, 8, and 9 as his aunty whose postal code is in the generalized group 78** is 70 years old which is not in the age bracket of 31 – 40 leaving him with only record 2. A careful analysis of the anonymous crime reporter in record 2 made him conclude that it must have been Mike who reported him. He came to this conclusion because Mike is the only one he knows who lives in an area with the postal code, 7701 which is in the generalized group 77** and of course he knows that Mike's age is 27 which falls in the generalized age group of 0 – 30.

2. K-anonymity can create groups that leak information due to a lack of diversity in the attribute that stores sensitive information. An attribute is sensitive if it contains private information whose value must be unknown for any individual in the dataset (e.g. crime suffered by a person, medical condition suffered by an individual). A sensitive attribute lacks diversity if an equivalence class is homogenous i.e. has the same value for its sensitive attribute. An equivalence class is a set of k-anonymous records that have the same values for its quasi-identifiers. Table 4.2 below has three Equivalence Classes namely {77**, 0 - 30}, {79**, 40 - 60} and {78**, 31 - 40}. The equivalence classes {79**, 40 - 60} and {78**, 31 - 40} are homogenous with respect to the values of their sensitive attributes.

Table 4. Crime report table

Explicit Attribute	Quasi-Identifier		Sensitive Attribute
Name	Postal Code	Age	Reported Crime
Ronke	7700	20	Bulgary
Ayokunle Ola	7701	27	Murder
Wilson	7802	31	Murder
Lydia Otoks	7903	48	Rape
Walex Olu	7902	50	Rape
Jossy Temmy	7706	21	Bulgary
Sammy Okposi	7890	35	Murder
Anne Chuks	7900	60	Rape
Edwin James	7804	38	Murder

In order to address the deficiencies of the k-anonymity scheme, the concept of ℓ-diversity was introduced to support k-anonymity. ℓ-diversity ensures that each equivalence class has at least ℓ well represented values in the sensitive attributes where $\ell \geq 2$ (Li et al., 2007; Machanavajjhala et al., 2007). In a simplest explanation, the term "well represented" means that ℓ-diversity ensures there are at least ℓ-distinct values for the sensitive attribute in each equivalence class (Li et al., 2007). In order to counter probabilistic inference attacks that may result from the use of distinct ℓ-diversity, two stronger notions namely entropy ℓ-diversity and recursive (c, ℓ)-diversity were introduced. Probabilistic inference attack occur when a sensitive attribute has one value appearing more frequently than other values in an equivalence class; making it possible for an attacker to conclude that an entity in that class is very likely to have the more frequent value. For more reading on entropy ℓ-diversity and recursive (c, ℓ)-diversity, please refer to Machanavajjhala et al. (2007).

T-Closeness

ℓ-diversity requires that the distribution of a sensitive attribute values in an equivalence class be at least ℓ well represented. As a result, the homogeneity and adversarial background knowledge attacks faced by k-anonymity could be minimal. However, Li et al. (2007) discusses some limitations of ℓ-diversity as follows:

1. It could be difficult and unnecessary to achieve especially when the possible values of a sensitive attribute are widely apart. Assume that the original data has a single sensitive attribute named criminal degree, which can take only two possible values: major and minor. In addition, there are 1000 records with 99% of them being major offences and 1% being minor. These two values have very wide sensitivity degrees. In a situation like this, it is difficult to ensure ℓ-diversity effectively.

2. Is insufficient to prevent attribute disclosure from similarity attack. A similarity attack occurs if an attacker can learn important information in an equivalence class when their sensitive attributes are distinct but similar semantically.

3. Is insufficient to prevent attribute disclosure from skewness attack.

In order to overcome these limitations, t-Closeness ensures that the distribution of values of a sensitive attribute(s) in an equivalence class is

Table 5. A 3-anonymous crime report table

Equivalence Class	Explicit Attribute	Quasi-Identifier		Sensitive Attribute
	Name	Postal Code	Age	Reported Crime
1	****	77**	0-30	Bulgary
	****	77**	0-30	Murder
	****	77**	0-30	Bulgary
2	****	79**	40-60	Rape
	****	79**	40-60	Rape
	****	79**	40-60	Rape
3	****	78**	31-40	Murder
	****	78**	31-40	Murder
	****	78**	31-40	Murder

the same as that of the entire table. Assuming the crime type distribution in a table is 35%, 40% and 25% for rape, murder and theft are respectively; t-Closeness will ensure similar ratio holds for each of the equivalence class.

Information Loss Metrics

Data anonymization usually leads to information loss. The degree of information loss of an anonymized data determines its utility and quality. In general, a low information loss infers a good utilization of an anonymized data. Information loss metrics measures how much an anonymized data differs from its initial or original form (Issa, 2009). Common information loss metrics include the following:

- **Precision Metric (Prec):** This takes the height of generalization hierarchy into consideration. For a given cell of an anonymized table, prec is calculated by finding the ratio of the cell's generalization level to the total possible generalization levels (Sweeney, 2002a).
- **Discernibility Metric (DM):** It penalizes each tuple based on the number of tuples that are indistinguishable from it (Bayardo & Agrawal, 2005).

- **Classification Metric (CM):** It counts those tuples which have their class labels different from the majorities (Guo & Zhang, 2013; Iyengar, 2002). CM calculates information loss for data transformation based on the fact that the intended usage of the anonymized data is for predictive modeling (Iyengar, 2002).
- **Generalized Loss Metrics (GLM):** It considers the size of a cluster and the entire data distribution (Iyengar, 2002). This metrics calculate information loss based on the fact that the intended usage of data is not known at the time of release (Iyengar, 2002).

The GLM is suitable for data streams because it takes both the size of equivalence classes (clusters) and data distribution into account (Cao, Carminati, Ferrari, Member, & Tan, 2011). Information loss in streaming data should be calculated incrementally and the final information loss is the sum of partial information loss.

$$\text{GLM (for categorical column)} = M_p - 1 / M - 1$$

From equation 1 above, Mp is number of leaf nodes in the subtree at node P and M is the total number of leaf nodes in T. From Figure 7 and using Equation 1, the GLM is ($\frac{2-1}{5-1} = \frac{1}{4}$) when the specific value of a Bachelor student is generalised to 'Undergraduate'. This is obtained by using the number of nodes in the undergraduate subtree, which is 2, and the total number of leaf nodes in the tree, which is 5.

GLM (for numerical column) = $(U_i - L_i) / (U - L)$

From equation 2 above, L_i and U_i are lower and upper endpoint of an interval in which a specific cell value is generalised to. L and U are the lower and upper bound value of the column.

To illustrate equation 2, suppose year of birth is a numerical attribute with domain range [1900 - 2000]. If this year of birth is generalized into any of the following category: [1900 - 1920], [1921 - 1940], [1941 - 1960], [1961 - 1980] and [1981 - 2000]. A value, 1985, which is generalized into [1981 – 2000], has its information loss as:

$$\frac{Ui - Li}{U - L} = \frac{2000 - 1981}{2000 - 1900} = \frac{19}{100} = 0.19$$

The information loss of an anonymized tuple, r, with s attributes is calculated by averaging the information loss of all its attributes (Zakerzadeh & Osborn, 2013). Equation 3 below represents this mathematically.

$$infoloss\left(r\right) = \frac{1}{s}\sum_{i=1}^{s}infoloss\left(i\right) \qquad (3)$$

DATA STREAM ANONYMIZATION

In the last decade, k-anonymity and other complementary privacy preserving techniques have emerged to encourage users and data holders to share and release information without fear of data disclosure. Such complementary algorithms include ℓ -diversity (Machanavajjhala et al., 2007), t-closeness (Li et al., 2007). However, all of these

techniques were conceptualized for static data and cannot be directly applied to continuous/flowing data (data streams) (Cao & Carminati, 2011; Guo & Zhang, 2013; W. Wang et al., 2007; Zakerzadeh & Osborn, 2013; Zhang & Yang, 2010). The reasons are as follows:

- Data streams have a temporal dimension i.e. there is a maximum delay acceptable between inflowing data and its corresponding anonymized output. In some applications, the anonymized output triggers other actions. Hence, the receiving application should have strong guarantees on the maximum delay of its input data (Cao & Carminati, 2011).

- These techniques assume a record is for an individual i.e. an individual cannot appear twice in a data set. In streaming data, this is not realistic (Cao & Carminati, 2011).

- The technique assumes data is static, but data streams are continuous and transient in nature (Wang et al., 2007). As a result, the main memory is typically too small compared to the size of data stream.

- Random access to data stream is not possible. (Wang et al., 2007)

Differences between Data Streams Anonymization and Static Data Anonymization

Table 6 summarizes the differences between static data anonymization and data stream anonymization as identified by Guo and Zhang (2013).

Principles of Data Stream Anonymization

In order to apply k-anonymity to data streams, current propositions in the literature incorporate a buffer/sliding window and delay constraints (Cao & Carminati, 2011; Guo and Zhang 2013; Zhang & Yang, 2010; Zakerzadeh & Osborn, 2013). The

Table 6. Tabular differences between static data anonymization and data stream anonymization

Static Data Anonymization	Data Streams Anonymization
It does not require real-time process.	It requires a real time process.
The fastest approach for obtaining an approximate solution is in polynomial time.	Processing time should not be more than O (|S|) which is linear to data stream size.
In order to achieve generalization with the least information loss, it requires multiple scans.	Multiple scans of data are not possible because data flows at high speed and only one scan is possible.

buffer holds the portion of the streaming data in order for the anonymisation process to occur. Delay constraints could be time or count-based. Time-based delay constraint specifies the time-duration for which a record can stay in the buffer while count-based specifies the maximum number of records the buffer can store. Figure 8 illustrates adaptability of k-anonymity to data streams.

Guo and Zhang (2013) came up with fundamental principles (as illustrated in Figure 8) on which anonymisation schemes for data streams should be designed:

- Scanning of data should occur only once and the time complexity for data stream anonymization should not be more than (O\|S\|) which is linear to the data stream size, S. Just like clustering of data stream, anonymization of data stream can be divided into the online and offline. The online division scans the records in the stream once and stores them in a buffer. The offline division fetches the records from the buffer and carries out the anonymisation process. Thresholds such as delay constraint are set on the buffer. Delay constraint and other thresholds are explained in the next point.

- Threshold should be set for the following parameters: size of buffer, waiting time of a tuple (delay constraint), k-anonymized cluster and reusable k-anonymized cluster set . Each of these parameters is explained as follows: The size of buffer depicts the total number of tuples under consideration for anonymization at an instant of time.

Delay constraint specifies how long a tuple can stay in the buffer, which could be count-based and/or time-based. k-anony-mized cluster is a cluster that has satisfied k-anonymization requirements on data streams. Re-usable k-anonymized cluster set is a collection of k-anonymized clusters that have successfully satisfied k-anonymity and have also output some anonymised tuples; as a result, they are kept for re-use if their information loss is lower than a certain threshold, δ. Any subsequent record(s) whose Quasi-values fall into any of the cluster in the reusable k-anonymized cluster set can be output immediately without going through k-anonymization because the cluster has already gone through the process of k-anonymization.

By keeping a k-anonymized cluster for re-use, we mean keeping the structure and not its content (records). Suppose a cluster (20 – 30, Male) is a k-anonymized cluster that satisfies the condition(s) necessary for a cluster to be saved for future use; such condition include low information loss. The structure i.e. (20 – 30, Male) will be saved for future use by subsequent records that fit into it. An advantage of this is a low information loss in the overall system. Therefore, assuming a record with a specific value of (25, Male) arrives in the data streams later on, this data might not need to undergo k-anonymization because there is a cluster (i.e. 20 – 30, Male) in the re-usable k-anonymized cluster set this record can fit in to.

Figure 8. A diagrammatic sketch of how k-anonymity can be applied to data streams

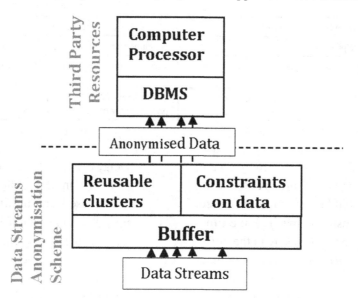

- The space occupied by the data streams anonymization scheme should be constrained. There should not be an infinite growth of space occupation. In a data-stream anonymization scheme, most of the space stores the newly arrived tuples and the k-anonymized clusters. As a result, the maximal number of elements in the buffer should be constrained; this is achievable by using the delay constraint. Likewise, the maximal number of reusable clusters should also be constrained and the existence time of a reusable cluster can be used to achieve that.
- Re-usable k-anonymized cluster set should be encouraged and its reusable strategy employed should be as simple as possible.

Review of Work on Data Stream Anonymization

Data stream anonymization can occur using either the perturbative or the non-perturbative methods. The perturbative method uses technique such as random noise while the non-perturbative uses k-anonymity and/or ℓ-p diversity.

Data Stream Anonymization Using Perturbative Method

To the best of our knowledge, only one documented work achieves data anonymization using the perturbative method. The next paragraph explains this work.

The work of Li, Sun, Papadimitriou, Mihaila, & Stanoi (2007) achieved privacy on streaming data using the random noise technique of the perturbative method. Their work achieves data stream anonymization by modifying the values of incoming data through the addition of noise. $E \in \mathbb{R}^{T \times N}$ denotes the random noise where N is the number of streams and T is the current time-stamp. The input consists of N data streams, denoted as $A_1, \ldots, A_N$. Each E_t^i is the noise added to the ith stream at time t. Hence, the anonymized (perturbed) stream is $A^* = A + E$.

A major weakness of this work is that the anonymized data becomes too difficult to analyze as a result of too much artificial noise (Guo & Zhang, 2013). Also, it can only handle numeric data (Guo & Zhang, 2013).

Data Stream Anonymization Using Non-Perturbative Method

This is achievable through k-anonymity and/or ℓ-diversity using Hierarchy-Based Generalization or Hierarchy-Free Generalization.

Hierarchy-Based Generalization of Data Stream Anonymization

Data stream anonymization under this category is based on tree structures (Guo & Zhang, 2013). Examples are SKY: Stream K-anonYmity (Li et al., 2008), SWAF: Sliding Window Anonymization Framework (Wang et al., 2007), KIDS: K-anonymIzation Data Stream (Zhang & Yang, 2010) and Zhou et al (2009).

SKY (Stream K-AnonYmity)

SKY is the first reported work that considers the use of non-perturbative method (k-anonymity) for data streams anonymization (Li et al., 2008).

Description

SKY takes as input, parameters such as Data Stream, specialization tree, k (value to be used for k-anonymity) and delay constraint. Data Stream represents the set of inflowing data that needs to undergo anonymization. Each quasi-identifier attribute, q_i $(i = 1, \ldots, n)$ has a predefined DGH_i. The specialization tree is a directed tree, where each node is a vector: $v_1, \ldots, v_n$; the value of each is drawn from DGH_i.

When SKY reads a record from the stream, it searches the specialization tree to find the most specific node that generalizes the new record. SKY's specialization tree nodes are either 'candidate' or 'work'. Candidate nodes are those that are yet to satisfy k-anonymity. Work nodes are those that have satisfied k-anonymity and kept for future re-use. When a new tuple, tp, arrives, SKY searches the specialization tree to locate the best node to place tp. If SKY places tp in a working node, tp will be output immediately. If otherwise (i.e. in a candidate node), it may not be output until the node has satisfied k-anonymity and/or delay constraint.

Drawbacks

There are no criteria for choosing re-usable (working) nodes; it keeps and re-uses all nodes that have satisfied k-anonymity irrespective of its degree of information loss. A consequence of this is that SKY can lead to high information loss because a node that resulted in high information loss can be saved for re-use.

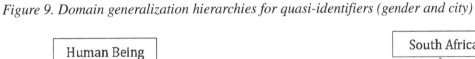

Figure 9. Domain generalization hierarchies for quasi-identifiers (gender and city)

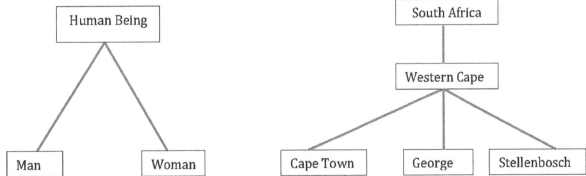

The time and space complexity of this algorithm is O ($|S|^2$log$|S|$) and O ($|S|$) respectively which is unacceptable for data stream anonymization (Guo & Zhang, 2013). One main reason for this could be that there is no constraint defined on working and candidate nodes.

Its use of a specialization tree for anonymizing numerical values makes the process of finding a suitable hierarchy difficult (Zakerzadeh & Osborn, 2013).

Susceptibility to re-identification attack if the hierarchy used for generalization is discovered (Zakerzadeh & Osborn, 2013).

Strengths

SKY's strategy of keeping any node that has satisfied k-anonymity for future use could lead to reduction in loss of information.

SKY use not more than three seconds to complete anonymization of no more than 151, 246 tuples.

SWAF (Sliding Window Anonymization Framework)

SWAF incorporated sliding window on data streams. Sliding window contains the most recent part of the stream. As new tuples arrives in the stream, SWAF replaces the oldest ones in the sliding window. Wang et al. (2007) illustrated data stream as a sequence, $S = \{s_1 p_1 \ldots s_n p_n\}$, in an incremental order; each s_i is a tuple with sequence number p_i, $p_i < p_j$ denotes that p_i arrived before p_j. Each s_i comprises of m vectors, which represents attributes values.

Figure 10. SWAF framework

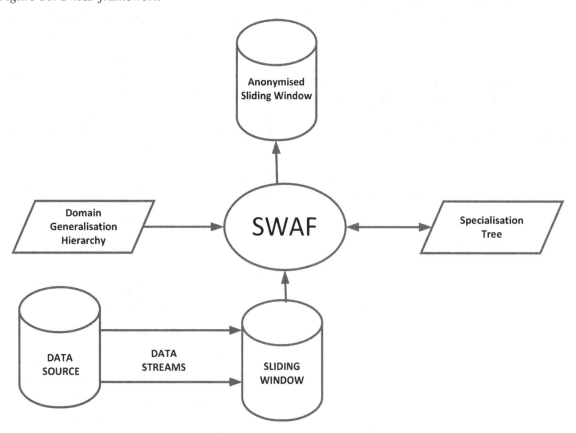

Description

As illustrated in Figure 10, SWAF makes use of a specialization tree that consists of generalized nodes. In the initial stage, the sliding window behaves as a static data set, and SWAF runs an algorithm on the window in order to generate a specialization tree. As the sliding window is being update, SWAF uses another algorithm to adjust continuously the specialization tree. SWAF obtains a k-anonymity for the data in the sliding window from the specialization tree.

The specialization tree shown in Figure 11 below is a derivative of the DGH in Figure 9. The children of a node in a specialization tree must be such that the combination of the children will return into the parent node without any form of overlapping and redundancy. The numbers (0, 1, 2) represent the attributes id used for the generalization. The id 0 stands for no attribute, 1 stands for the first attribute (sex) and 2 stands for the second attribute (city). The children of a node must split it on the same attribute. The children of the root node ({Human Being, Western Cape}) split the root node using the attribute 'city'. These children are {Human Being, Cape Town} and {Human Being, George}. In a similar manner, the first child {Human Being, Cape Town} was further split into {Man, Cape Town} and {Woman, Cape Town} using the attribute, 'gender'.

Drawbacks

Its time complexity will rise to O ($|S| \delta^2$) if the tree degenerates. Its use of a specialization tree for anonymizing numerical values makes the process of finding a suitable hierarchy difficult (Zakerzadeh & Osborn, 2013). Susceptibility to re-identification attack if the hierarchy used for generalization is discovered (Zakerzadeh & Osborn, 2013).

It has no restriction on the maximum number of records that can form a k-anonymized node. For instance, if k is set to 50, there is a possibility that a node can overshoot that limit and have about 70 records in the node.

Strength

Its time and space complexity of $O(|S| \delta \log \delta)$ and $O(|\delta|)$ respectively is better than some existing data stream anonymization algorithm based on clustering (Guo & Zhang, 2013).

Kids (K-Anonymization Data Stream Base on a Sliding Window)

KIDS is similar to SWAF. It also makes use of a sliding window. One of the major contributions of KIDS is the incorporation of distribution density (Zhang & Yang, 2010).

Figure 11. Specialization tree for Figure 9

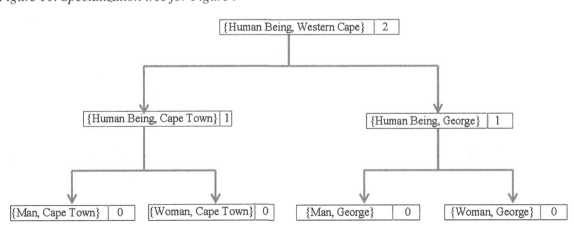

Description

KIDS consists of two parts: construction and update (adjustment) of specialization tree.

- **Tree Construction:** At this point, which is the initial stage, data in the sliding window is static. The root is the most general value of all Quasi-Identifiers. For example, all tuples of a sliding window may be generalized to root node: Human Being, South Africa (i.e. Human Being is the most general form of the attribute gender and South Africa is the most general form of the at-

tribute city; where gender and city are QI). The construction of other nodes emerges from the root. An illustration of this is in Figures 12 and 13.

- **Adjustment of the Tree:** When a new tuple arrives in the sliding window, it is generalized into the most specific node, of the specialization tree. Then the tree updates in one of the following situations:
    - If the node can be further specialized as a result of the new tuple and child node is not violated. Then the node splits.

Figure 12. Modified domain generalization hierarchies for Figure 9(B)

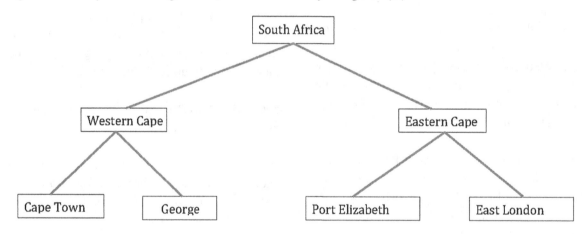

Figure 13. Modified specialization tree of Figure 11

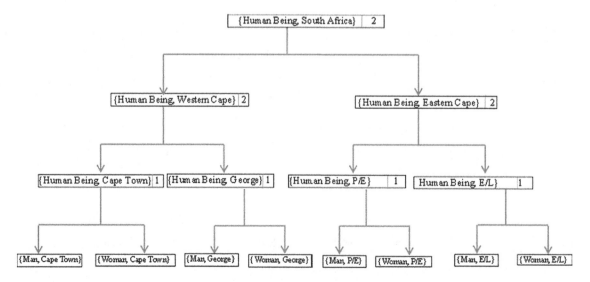

○ If the node contains k-1 frozen tuples, then the tuples will be released as a result of the new tuple. A frozen node contains tuples less than k or has its information loss more than a certain threshold.

● **Distribution Density:** Distribution density parameter helps to predict future data that will arrive in the stream. A node with a high distribution density prediction is set aside for future re-use. This helps to reduce information loss.

Drawbacks

The time and space complexity is too high for data streams (Guo & Zhang, 2013). Its use of a specialization tree for anonymizing numerical values makes the process of finding a suitable hierarchy difficult (Zakerzadeh & Osborn, 2013). Susceptibility to re-identification attack if the hierarchy used for generalization is discovered (Zakerzadeh & Osborn, 2013).

Strength

Its incorporation of distribution density parameter helps to reduce information loss because any node with high prediction of future occurrence is preserved for future use.

Continuous Privacy Preserving Publishing of Data Streams

A major idea behind this work is that the timeliness of data publishing was considered as a factor of preference rather than a hard deadline (Zhou et al., 2009). In view of this, delay factor, which is a parameter, was incorporated into the calculation of information loss for this work.

Description

Zhou et al. (2009) achieved anonymization of data streams by generalizing tuples and grouping them into equivalence classes. Their anonymization algorithms consist of the following three steps:

● An algorithm which is randomized because it decides if tuples in an equivalence class should be published based on its information loss without considering distribution of data in the stream.

● The distribution of data in the stream is taking into consideration in decision making.

● In a bid to further reduce information loss, existing data in the stream are examined for possibility of publishing with future data.

The major weakness of this work is that the time and space complexity is too high for data streams (Guo & Zhang, 2013; Zakerzadeh & Osborn, 2013).

Hierarchy-Free Generalization of Data Stream Anonymization

Data streams anonymization algorithms/schemes under this category make use of clustering to achieve privacy (k-anonymization) in data streams. These data streams anonymization schemes do not use trees to achieve anonymization. An implication of this is that DGH and VGH are not required as inputs. Examples are CASTLE: Continuously Anonymizing STreaming data via adaptive cLustEring (Cao & Carminati, 2011), B-CASTLE (Wang, Lu, Zhao, & Yang, 2010), FAANST: Fast Anonymizing Algorithm for Numerical STreaming data (Zakerzadeh & Osborn, 2013), FADS: Fast clustering-based k-Anonymization approach for Data Streams (Guo & Zhang, 2013).

CASTLE (Continously Anonymising STreaming Data Via Adaptive CLustEring)

CASTLE is the first data stream anonymization algorithm to achieve anonymization using both k-anonymity and ℓ-diversity (Cao & Carminati, 2011). It takes three parameters as inputs, which are k, δ and β. K is the value for k-anonymity which determines the minimum number of tuples that can be in a cluster, δ is a threshold that specifies the maximum publishing delay deadline and β is the maximum number of clusters that can be formed (Wang et al, 2010). CASTLE maintains two sets of clusters namely k-Anonymized Clusters and non-k_s-Anonymized Clusters. The k-Anonymized Clusters are clusters kept for future re-use because its tuples have satisfied k-anonymity and have been output. The non-k_s-Anonymized Clusters are those whose tuples are yet to expire and have not been output.

Description

At the initial stage, there are no clusters in memory. The first record CASTLE receives forms a cluster. For subsequent arriving records, CASTLE determines the best cluster to place them amongst the exiting clusters. On the other hand, it could be that no existing cluster can accommodate the new record. In such instance, one of the existing clusters undergoes enlargement e.g. a cluster [20-25, Cape Town] as values of attribute age and city can be expanded to [20-30, Western Cape] to accommodate a newly arrived tuple, tp(28, Stellenbosch). In Figure 14, we illustrate that anonymization process is triggered in CASTLE as soon as a new record emerges from a data source and enters into the buffer or sliding window. CASTLE achieves this by searching for the best cluster to place such a new record. In cases where there is/are no existing cluster (s) that can accommodate such a new record, CASTLE either merge some existing clusters or forms a new cluster in order to accommodate the new record.

Figure 14. Diagrammatic illustration of castle

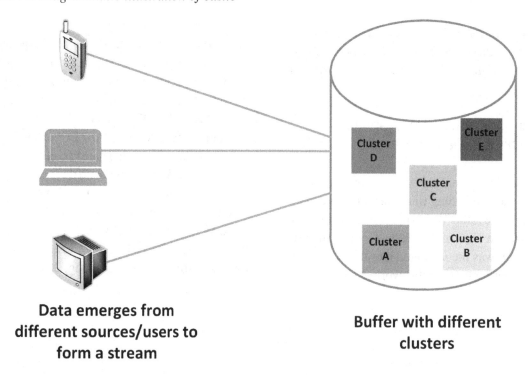

Data emerges from different sources/users to form a stream

Buffer with different clusters

Enlargement of a cluster indicates a greater loss of information because its QI interval will be enlarged. To minimize loss of information, CASTLE chooses the cluster that calls for the smallest enlargement. However, CASTLE ensures information loss is less than a predefined threshold because of cluster enlargement. If the enlargement of a cluster will warrant its information loss to exceed the threshold, the new record forms a new cluster.

CASTLE satisfies delay constraints by checking for an expiring record whenever a new tuple arrives. CASTLE outputs/publishes its anonymized data in two ways. Firstly, a cluster of size equal to or greater than k is output if it contains any expiring record(s). Secondly, if a cluster with its size less than k contains an expiring record, CASTLE checks for other cluster(s) that requires the least enlargement for merging to occur, this ensures that all records in the resultant cluster can be k or greater than k. Afterwards, the records in the resultant cluster can be output. If the information loss of a cluster whose tuples have already been output meets a certain threshold, this cluster will be stored for subsequent re-use. Such clusters are k-anonymized clusters.

CASTLE enforces ℓ-diversity by ensuring that all records belonging to the same QI group have at least ℓ distinct values for the sensitive attribute. CASTLE considered only a single sensitive attribute for ℓ-diversity.

Drawbacks

Tassa & Gudes (2012) noted that data anonymization using local recoding leads to the lowest information loss. CASTLE uses global recoding. A better approach will be to consider local recoding. Local recoding is a cell-level generalization of each tuple (Issa, 2009). To illustrate local recoding, assume a specific year of birth "1984" appears in several records, it may be left unchanged in some, or generalized to 198*, or totally suppressed in other records.

Whenever a record in a cluster with size lower than k has expired, CASTLE attempts to look for neighbouring clusters to merge. Instead of merging the clusters, a better approach might just be to remove only the expiring record and retain the other un-expiring records.

CASTLE does not restrict the size of a cluster. An implication of this is that the size of a cluster could far exceed k. It also does not have a specification for the possible number of initial and final clusters.

CASTLE verifies whether every tuple fits into all available clusters in order to select the one with the least information loss. This verification time increase with |S| making its time complexity to be O ($|S^2|$) which is too high (Guo & Zhang, 2013).

CASTLE checks for an expiring tuple on the arrival of a new one. A better approach could be the activation of an automatic alert whenever a tuple is due/expired rather than waiting for a new tuple to arrive before checking.

Strengths

CASTLE can achieve low information loss because it re-uses a cluster that has satisfied k-anonymity and a certain re-use constraint. CASTLE improves data quality of anonymised tuples by managing outliers. Outliers are tuples that are far away from other tuples.

B-CASTLE (B- Continuously Anonymizing Streaming Data via Adaptive Clustering)

B-CASTLE (Wang et al, 2010) was initiated as a result of the following weaknesses of CASTLE. Firstly, CASTLE does not restrict the maximum number of tuples that a cluster can have. This may make some clusters to have more tuples than the others and this may lead to high information loss. Secondly, CASTLE's merge operation re-clusters all tuples without consideration of the data streams distribution. This operation goes further to split any cluster with more than 2k tuples. This result in higher information loss and increase in the time complexity spent in the process of splitting.

Description

B-CASTLE provides solution to the weaknesses of CASTLE above as follows:

- To solve the first weakness, B-CASTLE introduced a threshold, α, to the cluster size. This ensures that no cluster has more than α tuples.
- B-CASTLE solves the second weakness by merging a cluster with size less than k (if it contains an expiring/expired tuple) with its nearest cluster. This process is performed recursively until the resultant cluster has more than k tuples.

Drawbacks

B-CASTLE does not restrict the size growth of its reusable cluster set. As a result, its time and space complexity is the same as that of CASTLE (Guo & Zhang, 2013).

Strengths

It solves the weaknesses of the splitting operation of CASTLE by setting a threshold on the size of a cluster. As a result, there is no need to break huge clusters into small ones, as it is the case in CASTLE.

Delay-Sensitive Approaches for Anonymizing Numerical Streaming Data (Reviewed-FAANST)

Zakerzadeh & Osborn (2013) came up with a delay-sensitive FAANST as a result of the deficiency of their previous algorithm: FAANST (Zakerzadeh & Osborn, 2011). A brief description of their previous algorithm (FAANST) comes up below before a discussion on its improvement.

DESCRIPTION: REVIEW OF FAANST

FAANST operates in two phases. A round simply connotes what happens when the processing window (buffer) has reached its limit (i.e. maximum size).

Phase 1

This is the first time the algorithm runs. When the number of tuples in the buffer has reached it maximum size, FAANST partitions tuples into different cluster(s) using k-means clustering algorithm. Any cluster whose size is at least k will have its records output irrespective of their information loss. Only cluster whose information loss is not more than a certain threshold is set aside for future re-use while those whose information loss exceeds the threshold are not set-aside for future use. The algorithm waits again to have its memory filled up.

In Figure 15, we illustrate that FAANST & Reviewed-FAANST start anonymization process as soon as the buffer is full unlike in CASTLE where anonymization process is triggered by the entry of a new record into the buffer.

Phase 2

This occurs when at least one round has executed i.e. from the second round to the end. When the window gets to its limit, tuples falling into one of the accepted clusters (i.e. those clusters set aside for future use) is output while other tuples are partitioned into k' using k-means clustering algorithm.

Drawbacks of FAANST

Some tuples may stay in the system for long and expire before they are output. It does not take the time each tuples stay in the system into consideration. For instance, if two tuples were output by the

Figure 15. Diagrammatic illustration of reviewed-FAANST

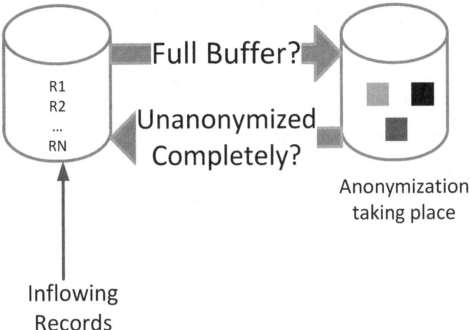

same cluster but with different delay, assume one with 10 seconds delay and the other 60 seconds, FAANST will not differentiate between these two.

Proposed Solution to Solve the Weaknesses

To solve these weaknesses, delay sensitive approach (Zakerzadeh & Osborn, 2013) introduces:

- Proactive and passive deadline monitoring system, in order to ensure a tuple does not exceed its stipulated deadline.
- Cost metric which takes into consideration the time each tuple stays in the system.
    1. **Passive Deadline Monitoring Solution:** It saves the arrival time of each tuples. At the end of each round, it checks each tuple that is yet to be output to ensure it has not exceeded its due time. Those that have exceeded the deadline are suppressed and output.

2. **Proactive Deadline Monitoring Solution:** This solution has an extra attribute for storing the time of last visit for each tuple. The initial time of every tuple is its arrival time. A simple heuristic (calculated by current time – TimeOfLastVisit) determines if a tuple can still stay in the system and not expire before the next round. If the heuristic solution predicts that a tuple will expire in the next round, then such a tuple will be output in the present anonymization round. Otherwise, it retains such tuple for the next round of anonymization.

Drawbacks of Delay-Sensitive FAANST (Reviewed-FAANST)

According to Tassa & Gudes (2012), local recoding leads to lower information loss. This work used global recoding which has a greater information loss than local recoding.

Tuples in a cluster that satisfies k-anonymity are output irrespective of their information loss. There might be a need to study and see how those clusters that have very high information loss can undergo improvement such that privacy and delay constraint is satisfied.

Does not incorporate new privacy techniques such as ℓ-diversity, t-closeness, and - differential privacy. Passive solution leads to more execution time as a result of checking to see if a tuple has exceeded its deadline.

Strength

It has a faster running speed than one of its predecessor, CASTLE because its cluster size is limited to O (k) by the clustering algorithm. As a result, it does not make use of merge and split operations as it is in CASTLE.

Fast Clustering-Based K-Anonymization Approach for Data Streams (FADS)

FADS (Guo & Zhang, 2013) take four parameters as input in order to achieve data stream anonymization. The parameters are Data Stream (S), the k-anonymity requirement (k), the delay constraint (which should be greater than k) and the reuse constraint (T_{kc}). T_{kc} imposes a constraint on the re-usable clusters. set_{kc} is a set that contains all the reusable clusters.

Description

FADS process is as follows: It reads a tuple, tp, from S and stores it into buffer, $Set_{tp,}$ during each round. Range of numeric attribute updates as new tuple arrives. If some tuple, tp, is ripe for release, FADS refreshes the re-usable cluster set by removing k-anonymized cluster that has existed for more than T_{kc}. Afterwards, it calls on a procedure to publish tp. Finally, when no more tuple arrives in S, FADS call a procedure to publish the remaining tuples in Set_{tp}.

If the number of tuples in a buffer is less than k, it is impossible for anonymization to take place. In such an instance, expiring tuple(s) is/are suppressed or output with a re-usable cluster.

ℓ-Diversity and FADS

To conform to ℓ-diversity, the sensitive attributes of tuples in a cluster should have at least ℓ well-represented values. In order words, the probability of associating a tuple with a sensitive value is at most $1 / \ell$. ℓ is the total number of values for a sensitive attribute.

In a cluster, the number of tuples with the same sensitive value should not be greater than $|C| / \ell$, C is the cluster containing the tuples. Since the size of cluster should not be less than k, the initial threshold for the number of tuples with a corresponding sensitive value can be set to k / ℓ.

If t is chosen to be published with a reusable k-anonymized cluster in set_{kc}, it should be checked if the insertion of t will make sensitive values to correspond to more than $|C| / \ell$.

Drawbacks of FADS

The idea of using suppression when tuples ready for publication is less than k can incur a greater loss of information. ℓ-diversity can only handle a single sensitive attribute. The scheme does not incorporate t-closeness.

The clustering approach adopted in FADS may release a newly arrived tuple early before its time limit just because it is one of the k-1 nearest neighbour of a tuple due for release. This may lead to an extra information loss particularly if it is possible that the tuple could have been released in future with a cluster that has lower information loss.

Strength of FADS

It has a low time and space complexity of O (|S|) and O (|QID|) respectively.

CONCLUSION

This chapter has discussed extensively on data stream anonymity and future research directions. We first presented an overview of techniques of achieving data anonymity that can ensure data protection and privacy whilst minimizing information loss. From our discussion, we can surmise that k-anonymity algorithms are well suited to enforcing data stream anonymity. We also reviewed the literature on existing data anonymity algorithms, highlighting their pros and cons with respect to handling data stream anonymization.

REFERENCES

Aggarwal, C., Han, J., Wang, J., & Yu, P. (2003). A framework for clustering evolving data streams. In *Proceedings of the 29th international conference on Very large data bases* (vol. 29, pp. 81-92). VLDB Endowment.

Aggarwal, C., & Philip, S. (2008). *A general survey of privacy-preserving data mining models and algorithms*. Springer. doi:10.1007/978-0-387-70992-5_2

Bayardo, R., & Agrawal, R. (2005). Data privacy through optimal k-anonymization. In *Proceedings. 21st International Conference on* (pp. 217-228). IEEE.

Cao, J., Carminati, B., Ferrari, E., Member, S., & Tan, K. (2011). Castle: Continuously anonymizing data streams. *IEEE Transactions on Dependable and Secure Computing, 8*(3), 337–352.

Ciriani, V., Foresti, S., & Samarati, P. (2007). Microdata Protection. In Secure Data Management in Decentralized Systems (pp. 291-321). Springer.

Dalenius, T., & Reiss, S. (1982). Data-swapping: A technique for disclosure control. *Journal of Statistical Planning and Inference*. doi:10.1016/0378-3758(82)90058-1

Golab, L., & Özsu, M. (2003). Issues in data stream management. *SIGMOD Record, 32*(2), 5–14. doi:10.1145/776985.776986

Guo, K., & Zhang, Q. (2013). Fast clustering-based anonymization approaches with time constraints for data streams. *Knowledge-Based Systems*. doi:10.1016/j.knosys.2013.03.007

Issa, R. (2009). *Satisfying K-anonymity: New Algorithm and Emirical Evaluation*. (Masters Thesis). Carleton University.

Iyengar, V. (2002). Transforming data to satisfy privacy constraints. In *Proceedings of the eighth ACM SIGKDD international conference on Knowledge discovery and data mining*, (pp. 279–288). ACM.

Jiang, W., & Clifton, C. (2006). A secure distributed framework for achieving k-anonymity. *The VLDB Journal, 15*(4), 316–333. doi:10.1007/s00778-006-0008-z

Kabir, M., Wang, H., & Bertino, E. (2011). Efficient systematic clustering method for k-anonymization. *Acta Informatica*, 51–66. doi:10.1007/s00236-010-0131-6

Li, F., Sun, J., Papadimitriou, S., Mihaila, G. a., & Stanoi, I. (2007). Hiding in the Crowd: Privacy Preservation on Evolving Streams through Correlation Tracking. In *Proceedings of 2007 IEEE 23rd International Conference on Data Engineering*, (pp. 686–695). IEEE. doi: doi:10.1109/ICDE.2007.367914

Li, J., Ooi, B., & Wang, W. (2008). Anonymizing streaming data for privacy protection. In *Proceedings of Data Engineering*, (pp. 1367-1369). IEEE.

Li, N., Li, T., & Venkatasubramanian, S. (2007). t-Closeness: Privacy beyond k-anonymity and l-diversity. *International Conference on Data Engineering (ICDE)*, (3), 106–115.

Machanavajjhala, A., Kifer, D., & Johannes, G. (2007). l-diversity: Privacy beyond k-anonymity. *ACM Transactions on Knowledge Discovery from Data, 1*(1), 3.

Qiu, L., Li, Y., & Wu, X. (2007). Protecting business intelligence and customer privacy while outsourcing data mining tasks. *Knowledge and Information Systems, 17*(1), 99–120. doi:10.1007/s10115-007-0113-3

Samarati, P. (2001). Protecting respondents identities in microdata release. *IEEE Transactions on Knowledge and Data Engineering*, 1–29.

Silberschatz, A., Korth, H. F., & Sudarshan, S. (1997). Database Concepts. McGraw-Hill.

Sweeney, L. (2001). *Computational disclosure control: A Primer on Data Privacy Protection.* (Doctoral Dissertation). MIT, Cambridge, MA.

Sweeney, L. (2002a). Achieving k-anonymity privacy protection using generalization and suppression. *International Journal of Uncertainty, Fuzziness and Knowledge-Based Systems, 10*(5), 1–18. doi:10.1142/S021848850200165X

Sweeney, L. (2002b). k-anonymity: A model for protecting privacy. *International Journal of Uncertainty, Fuzziness and Knowledge-Based Systems, 10*(5), 1–14. doi:10.1142/S0218488502001648

Tassa, T., & Gudes, E. (2012). Secure Distributed Computation of Anonymized Views. *ACM Transactions on Database Systems, 37*(2). doi:10.1145/2188349.2188353

Taylor, P., Reiter, J. P., Duncan, G., Lambert, D., & Singer, E. (2003). Estimating Risks of Identification Disclosure in Microdata. *Journal of the American Statistical Association*, 37–41. doi:10.1198/016214505000000619

Wang, K., Xu, Y., Wong, R. W., & Fu, A. C. (2010). Anonymizing temporal data. In *Proceedings of Data Mining (ICDM)*, (pp. 1109–1114). ICDM. doi: doi:10.1109/ICDM.2010.96

Wang, P., Lu, J., Zhao, L., & Yang, J. (2010). B-CASTLE: An Efficient Publishing Algorithm for K-Anonymizing Data Streams. In *Proceedings of Intelligent Systems (GCIS), 2010 Second WRI Global Congress on* (Vol. 2, pp. 132-136). IEEE. doi: doi:10.1109/GCIS.2010.196

Wang, W., Li, J., Ai, C., & Li, Y. (2007). Privacy protection on sliding window of data streams. In *Proceedings of Collaborative Computing: Networking, Applications and Worksharing,* (pp. 213-221). IEEE.

Zakerzadeh, H., & Osborn, S. (2011). FAANST: fast anonymizing algorithm for numerical streaming data. In *Data Privacy Management and Autonomous Spontaneous Security* (pp. 36–50). Springer. doi:10.1007/978-3-642-19348-4_4

Zakerzadeh, H., & Osborn, S. (2013). Delay-sensitive approaches for anonymizing numerical streaming data. *International Journal of Information Security*. doi:10.1007/s10207-013-0196-7

Zhang, J., & Yang, J. (2010). KIDS: K-anonymization data stream base on sliding window. In *Proceedings of Future Computer and Communication (ICFCC),* (pp. 311–316). IEEE.

Zhou, B., Han, Y., Pei, J., Jiang, B., Tao, Y., & Jia, Y. (2009). Continuous privacy preserving publishing of data streams. In *Proceedings of the 12th International Conference on Extending Database Technology: Advances in Database Technology* (pp. 648-659). ACM.

ADDITIONAL READING

Aggarwal, C., Han, J., Wang, J., & Yu, P. (2003). A framework for clustering evolving data streams. In *In Proceedings of the 29th international conference on Very large data bases-Volume 29 (pp. 81-92). VLDB Endowment.*

Aggarwal, C., & Philip, S. (2008). *A general survey of privacy-preserving data mining models and algorithms* (pp. 11–52). Springer, US. doi:10.1007/978-0-387-70992-5_2

Cao, J., Carminati, B., Ferrari, E., Member, S., & Tan, K. (2011). Castle: Continuously anonymizing data streams. *Dependable and Secure Computing, IEEE Transactions on, 8(3), 337-352., 8(3),* 337–352.

Ciriani, V., Foresti, S., & Samarati, P. (2007). Microdata Protection. In Secure Data Management in Decentralized Systems (pp. 291-321). Springer US.

Golab, L., & Özsu, M. (2003). Issues in data stream management. *SIGMOD Record, 32(2),* 5–14. doi:10.1145/776985.776986

Guo, K., & Zhang, Q. (2013). Fast clustering-based anonymization approaches with time constraints for data streams. *Knowledge-Based Systems.* doi:10.1016/j.knosys.2013.03.007

Li, F., Sun, J., Papadimitriou, S., Mihaila, G. a., & Stanoi, I. (2007). Hiding in the Crowd: Privacy Preservation on Evolving Streams through Correlation Tracking. *2007 IEEE 23rd International Conference on Data Engineering,* 686–695. doi: doi:10.1109/ICDE.2007.367914

Li, J., Ooi, B., & Wang, W. (2008). Anonymizing streaming data for privacy protection. *In Data Engineering, 2008. ICDE 2008. IEEE 24th International Conference on (pp. 1367-1369). IEEE.,* 1367–1369.

Li, N., Li, T., & Venkatasubramanian, S. (2007). t-closeness: Privacy beyond k-anonymity and l-diversity. *International Conference on Data Engineering (ICDE), (3),* 106–115.

Machanavajjhala, A., Kifer, D., & Johannes, G. (2007). l-diversity: Privacy beyond k-anonymity. *ACM Transactions on Knowledge Discovery from Data (TKDD), 1(1), 3.ACM Transactions on Knowledge Discovery from Data (TKDD), 1(1), 3., 1.*

Sweeney, L. (2001). *Computational disclosure control. A Primer on Data Privacy Protection.* Doctoral Dissertation, MIT.

Sweeney, L. (2002a). Achieving k-anonymity privacy protection using generalization and suppression. *International Journal of Uncertainty. Fuzziness and Knowledge-Based Systems, 10(5),* 1–18. doi:10.1142/S021848850200165X

Sweeney, L. (2002b). k-anonymity: A model for protecting privacy. *International Journal of Uncertainty. Fuzziness and Knowledge-Based Systems, 10(5),* 1–14. doi:10.1142/S0218488502001648

Wang, K., Xu, Y., Wong, R. W., & Fu, A. C. (2010). Anonymizing temporal data. *In Data Mining (ICDM), 2010 IEEE 10th International Conference on,* 1109–1114. doi: doi:10.1109/ICDM.2010.96

Wang, P., Lu, J., Zhao, L., & Yang, J. (2010). B-CASTLE: An Efficient Publishing Algorithm for K-Anonymizing Data Streams. *In Intelligent Systems (GCIS), 2010 Second WRI Global Congress on (Vol. 2, pp. 132-136). IEEE.* doi: doi:10.1109/GCIS.2010.196

Wang, W., Li, J., Ai, C., & Li, Y. (2007). Privacy protection on sliding window of data streams. *In Collaborative Computing: Networking, Applications and Worksharing, 2007. CollaborateCom 2007. International Conference on (pp. 213-221). IEEE.*

Zakerzadeh, H., & Osborn, S. (2011). FAANST: fast anonymizing algorithm for numerical streaming data. In *Data Privacy Management and Autonomous Spontaneous Security* (pp. 36–50). Springer Berlin Heidelberg. doi:10.1007/978-3-642-19348-4_4

Zakerzadeh, H., & Osborn, S. (2013). Delay-sensitive approaches for anonymizing numerical streaming data. *International Journal of Information Security.* doi:10.1007/s10207-013-0196-7

Zhang, J., & Yang, J. (2010). KIDS: K-anonymization data stream base on sliding window. *In Future Computer and Communication (ICFCC), 2010 2nd International Conference on, 2*(IEEE), 311–316.

Zhou, B., Han, Y., Pei, J., Jiang, B., Tao, Y., & Jia, Y. (2009). Continuous privacy preserving publishing of data streams. *In Proceedings of the 12th International Conference on Extending Database Technology: Advances in Database Technology (pp. 648-659). ACM.*

KEY TERMS AND DEFINITIONS

Anonymization: We define anonymization or the process of ensuring privacy through data anonymity as a method of completely hiding the identity of an individual. Anonymization can also be referred to as de-identification. Anonymization makes it impossible to learn to whom a particular record refers to.

Data Streams: Describe data objects that are transient in nature. One can also view data streams as being time-dependent or time critical and hence are implicitly tagged with a real-time processing requirement.

Explicit Attributes: These are attributes in the data set that uniquely identify an individual. They are usually removed before release of data. Examples include Name, Student Number, Telephone Number, Account Number.

K-Anonymity: This is a privacy-preserving technique that ensures that each individual's record corresponds to at least (k-1) other individuals with respect to their QI.

ℓ-Diversity: This is a privacy-preserving technique that ensures all records that have same quasi-values have diverse values for their sensitive attributes.

Quasi-Identifier (QI): These identifiers are usually formed from a combination of attributes whose values when taken together can potentially identify an individual. Example of such combination of attributes includes Birth Date, Sex, and Address.

Sensitive Attributes: These attributes contain private information whose value must not be discovered for any individual in the dataset. These are always released directly because they are required for analysis and research purposes but their other corresponding attributes (i.e. explicit and QI) must have been properly anonymized. Examples include Type of Crime, salary, medical condition.

Chapter 4
Is It Privacy or Is It Access Control?

Sylvia L. Osborn
The University of Western Ontario, Canada

ABSTRACT

With the widespread use of online systems, there is an increasing focus on maintaining the privacy of individuals and information about them. This is often referred to as a need for privacy protection. The author briefly examines definitions of privacy in this context, roughly delineating between keeping facts private and statistical privacy that deals with what can be inferred from data sets. Many of the mechanisms used to implement what is commonly thought of as access control are the same ones used to protect privacy. This chapter explores when this is not the case and, in general, the interplay between privacy and access control on the one hand and, on the other hand, the separation of these models from mechanisms for their implementation.

INTRODUCTION

The right to privacy is enshrined in international and national covenants and charters on human rights. Concern for the privacy of on-line data began with the introduction of computing systems. By 1980 the OECD published its guidelines dealing with the privacy of information and transborder flow of information, OECD (1980). In the database community, the Hippocratic database paper, by Agrawal, et al. (2002), is considered the seminal paper in introducing privacy concerns to the database community. Meanwhile, access control has always been a part of computer systems.

We begin by examining definitions and dimensions of privacy preservation, continue with an introduction to Sandhu's OM-AM framework, consider the available mechanisms for implementing

access-related models, and then comment on how all these ideas t together. We also briefly discuss the user. Our hope is that if there are gaps in the effective protection of information, this analysis might help to show where the gaps are.

PRIVACY VS. ACCESS CONTROL IN COMPUTER SYSTEMS

In this section, we review some definitions of access control and privacy, in order to crystalize their similarities and differences. Because the discussion of access control is shorter, we proceed with it first, followed by some definitions of privacy, and finally highlight their similarities and differences.

DOI: 10.4018/978-1-4666-6158-5.ch004

Access Control

Access control deals with controlling who has what kind of access to various resources. The resources can be physical (that is a computer system) or strictly deal with data. The data can describe documents, inventory, shipping requisitions for a large company, allocation of university courses to classrooms, the destination of an aircraft carrier, etc. In other words, although a lot of data concerns individuals, there is also a lot of other data dealing with other things. There are three well-known access control models. In the first, Discretionary Access Control (DAC), data is owned by the individual computer user (e.g. personal files in Unix); in Mandatory Access Control (MAC), control is centralized and it is assumed that the enterprise owns (and labels) all the data. The third is Role-based Access Control (RBAC), where permissions are grouped into roles and roles are assigned as a unit to users. RBAC has been shown to be able to simulate both MAC and DAC, Osborn, Sandhu, & Munawer, (2000).

The basic components of an RBAC system are users (U) or subjects, permissions (P) which are pairs (o, a) where "o" represents an object to be protected and "a", an access mode on this object. Roles (R) consist of a set of permissions, represented by a permission-role assignment (PRA). Users' membership in roles is represented by a user-role assignment (URA). Roles can be arranged in a hierarchy such that a senior role inherits the permissions of its junior(s), and members of a senior role are also members of its juniors.

Privacy

Privacy, on the other hand, typically infers that the data in question relates to human beings, or possibly to corporations. It is related to the right to privacy which is enshrined in international and national covenants and charters on human rights. The Merriam-Webster dictionary defines privacy as "freedom from unauthorized intrusion" (Web, 2014). The classic version of the Hippocratic oath contains the following[1]:

What I may see or hear in the course of the treatment or even outside of the treatment in regard to the life of men, which on no account one must spread abroad, I will keep to myself, holding such things shameful to be spoken about.

A definition given in a previous ISSA paper by Renaud, & Galvez-Cruz, (2010) is:

Privacy is the faculty and right that a person has to dene, preserve and control the boundaries that limit the extent to which the rest of society can interact with or intrude upon. At the same time, he or she retains full control over information generated by, and related to, him or her.

Here we begin to see one of the issues: when a data provider gives their information to, say, a company with whom they do business, they no longer have direct control over the data. The question of ownership, if that is a term we want to use, becomes clouded.

An interesting examination of the dimensions concerning privacy from a technical point of view has been given by Barker et al. (2009). They discuss four orthogonal aspects of data privacy, three of which are shown in Figure 1.

Following Purpose along the x-axis, privacy protection decreases (purpose becomes more general) as one moves further from the origin. The first point refers to data given to a service for a Single use. Next comes Reuse Same, which allows multiple uses of the provided data for the original purpose. The third point, Reuse Selected, represents multiple uses of the data by the data collector for related purposes, e.g. in a medical situation, the information is provided to the health care professional for medical reasons, and some of it is released to the insurer. The Reuse Any

Figure 1. Data privacy taxonomy from Barker et al. (2009)

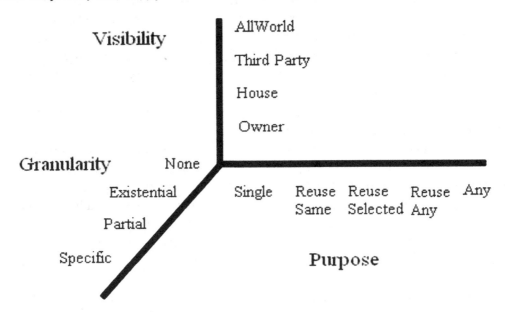

point allows the data to be used in the future for unforeseen purposes, such as for example, medical research. Finally the Any point allows any reuse of the data, and should probably not be encouraged.

The y-axis in Figure 1 deals with visibility, i.e. who can see the data. The first non-origin point is labeled Owner. In general this would refer to the data provider whose information is being discussed. It might also refer to data stored in somecloud service to which the cloud-providing company has no access { only the person storing data there has access. The next point is House, where the entity storing the data, which might be a company with whom the data provider is doing business, or a company like Google who might use some of the data to provide more/better service, may assume ownership and treat the data in some way not immediately obvious to the data provider. Third Party refers to data users who are authorized by the house to see the data, usually under some agreement with the house concerning the nature of the use of the data. The final point, All World, refers to data which is publicly exposed for anyone with access. An example would be information posted on a publicly available web page.

The z-axis shows different granularities with which information can be released. Moving out from the origin, just the Existence of something may be revealed; the next point, Partial would be the release of a range, like $100,000 - 150,000 for salary; and the least privacy occurs with the release of a Specific piece of information in its raw form.

The 4th dimension given in Barker, et al. (2009) is Retention. To comply with various rules and legislation, data may have an expiry date.

The granularity axis in the previous discussion leads us to another aspect of privacy. Discrete facts or raw data can be revealed, as would be the case for the specific point in the taxonomy. Or to turn it around, access to the individual attribute values of a person can be protected as an example of privacy protection.

Often the databases which contain these facts are also to be used for statistical queries. Mechanisms for hiding individuals' information for these statistical applications include k-anonymity from Sweeney (2002) and differential privacy, McSherry (2010). Informally, k-anonymity means that in data over which statistical queries are run, each individual is indistinguishable from k - 1 others, even if the released data is combined with publicly available information. Differential privacy describes a statistical database release in which the absence or presence of a single element will not affect the output of a query in a significant way.

An enhancement of treatment of data with a purpose for access has been described in Byun & Li (2008). They introduce the idea of a purpose tree, where a more general purpose (e.g., marketing) appears as an ancestor of a more specific purpose (e.g., telemarketing). They also distinguish between intended purpose and access purpose: the requester of access to private data must provide an access purpose, and the provider of the private data gives an intended purpose for which they are willing to allow access. E.g. a data provider can allow their address to be used for the shipping purpose but not for marketing. Propagation in the purpose tree takes place, so that an access request with a specific purpose is allowed if the data provider has indicated a more general (an ancestor in the purpose tree) intended purpose.

In Al-Harbi & Osborn (2011), we investigated the integration of such purposes with RBAC. We showed that purpose becomes an additional component of some permissions. It does not need to be present for all data access, e.g. for inventory it would not be necessary but it would for access to the customer's address. In RBAC, such permissions are inherited by senior roles, so that it somewhat muddies the model. Role activation needs to be accompanied by an access purpose, and has to filter out permissions if their intended purpose does not comply with the access purpose for a given role activation.

Similarities and Differences

From the preceding discussion it should be clear that access control in its traditional form is not adequate to protect privacy. At least two similarities are:

1. Facts (attribute values) are to be made available (read) or not to other users.
2. (Similarity with DAC) the decisions about what is visible to whom are made by individuals, not by some security administrator.

The differences include the following:

1. When privacy is of concern, the resource being protected is data concerning an individual or an enterprise.
2. There may be an additional issue of the purpose for the access which can be part of the privacy discussion.
3. Privacy becomes an obligation when the data provider (the person, let's say, who is being described by the data) is no longer the sole owner of the information, but has given the data to another organization whose obligation it now is to protect their privacy.
4. Something not yet discussed: There are other issues dealing with data which the data provider might never have owned (or at least was not aware they owned), i.e. are not strictly related to data explicitly given by the data provider, such as tracking clicks on a web page, using the GPS on a mobile device to track location, and using face recognition software for tagging photos.

THE OM-AM MODEL

In a 2000 paper, Ravi Sandhu introduced the OM-AM model (Sandhu, 2000). We will briefly outline this framework, and then discuss mechanisms which have been used and are available for implementing privacy protection and access control.

The Model

Software engineering practice tells us that to implement a system, we should start with more abstract requirements and move towards implementation. The OM-AM model highlights this distinction as it applies to access control systems. The Objective and Model (the OM) describe what the requirements are, and the Architecture and Mechanism (the AM) give the how for application of the requirements.

In the previous section, we have studied the OM part for privacy concerns. The objective for privacy preservation can be briefly summarized as information hiding/sharing in a very discretionary fashion. The addition of purpose for use of individual attribute values complicates the model.

We will now look very briefly at the AM - the architectures and the mechanisms.

Architecture and Mechanisms

It is possible to look at a separate architecture/mechanism for each component of a model, as Sandhu did in Sandhu, (2000). However, this discussion will be more general.

For Access Control in a centralized computer system, the architecture commonly used is that of a security kernel or reference monitor. The reference monitor interrupts and validates each access request. It may check an access matrix, or access control list to verify that the user can perform the requested operation. In a distributed environment, this checking can be performed by a service if a service-oriented architecture is being used.

One very general solution is the architecture and details of the XACML framework, in particular the data ow architecture given in OASIS (2005); this framework provides a set of standards (involving PDP, PEP, etc.) for implementing a broad range of policies whose details are expressed in XACML. The architecture is an example of a way of representing the reference monitor, accompanied by a set of standards. Here the access control model is expressed as a set of policies encoded in XACML. Examples of XACML policies for MAC, DAC and RBAC can be found.

To enforce privacy requirements, simple obligations by a "house", which stores private facts, to keep these facts secret can be expressed in XACML. This XACML framework is, thus, one example of an Architecture/ Mechanism which can be used to enforce both access control and privacy requirements.

A wide range of cryptographic protocols are available, which are extensively discussed in Kayem, Akl, & Martin, (2010). The encryption/decryption is performed to validate the access, so the architecture is still a reference monitor, but the mechanism is encryption. We see from Kayem, Akl, & Martin, (2010) that cryptographic mechanisms can be used to protect hierarchical arrangements of rights, so it is a valid mechanism to enforce an RBAC model, for example.

For Privacy of facts, the mechanisms seem to be the same as those used for standard access control. One exception is when an access purpose must be matched with an intended purpose, for which mechanisms need to be enhanced.

For statistical privacy, special techniques are required. Statistical databases typically contain large amounts of data against which only summary queries are allowed. The objectives are expressed in complex definitions of k-anonymity or differential privacy, and the architecture for implementing these objectives is usually a specialized database system.

THE USER

To add another dimension to this discussion, we need to look at users. In the database textbooks, it is common to distinguish between "casual" or even "naive" users, and the database administrator who is supposed to understand all the details and implications of a complex data model. It clearly requires an expert to express access control requirements directly in XACML. Slightly less expertise is required for someone to design roles for an RBAC system, and have them automatically translated into XACML. Neither of these users would be a naive user, as they would require technical knowledge to write raw XACML, and at least thorough knowledge of the application environment to design an RBAC system. Statistical databases are not used by what could be called "casual" users; they are used by statisticians or researchers. Many repositories of facts concerning individuals are used and managed by these casual users. In a social network, it is a naive user who is specifying "privacy" settings (one could argue that what the user is doing is specifying access control to the data which they initially own). Any model provided to such a user needs to be one which allows them to understand the implications of what they are doing.

DISCUSSION

As far as the Objective and Mechanism are concerned, we have highlighted some differences between maintaining privacy and enforcing access control. In both, there are scenarios where controlling reading of facts is the issue, and the same mechanisms can be used to achieve both objectives. Some models are only suitable for expert users. Others can be used by casual users. One could say that we have many adequate mechanisms, and if systems are not achieving their objectives, it might be that the objectives and models are not well understood by the user, or that the mechanisms are not being employed.

ACKNOWLEDGMENT

The financial support of the Natural Sciences and Engineering Research Council of Canada is gratefully acknowledged.

REFERENCES

Agrawal, R., Kiernan, J., Srikant, R., & Xu, Y. (2002). Hippocratic databases. In *Proceedings of 28th International Conference on Very Large Data Bases*, (pp. 143-154). Morgan Kaufmann.

Al-Harbi, A. L., & Osborn, S. L. (2011). *Mixing privacy with role-based access control*. Paper presented at the Fourth International C* Conference on Computer Science & Software Engineering. Montreal, Canada.

Barker, K., Askari, M., Banerjee, M., Ghazinour, K., Mackas, B., & Majedi, M. et al. (2009). A data privacy taxonomy. *Lecture Notes in Computer Science*, 5588, 42–54.

Byun, J.-W., & Li, N. (2008). Purpose based access control for privacy protection in relational database systems. *The VLDB Journal*, *17*(4), 603–619. doi:10.1007/s00778-006-0023-0

Kayem, A. V. D. M., Akl, S. G., & Martin, P. (2010). Adaptive Cryptographic Access Control. Springer.

McSherry, F. (2010). Privacy integrated queries: an extensible platform for privacy- Preserving data analysis. *Communications of the ACM*, *53*(9), 89–97. doi:10.1145/1810891.1810916

OASIS. (2005). *eXtensible Access Control Markup Language (XACML) version 2.0*. Retrieved from http://docs.oasis-open.org/xacml/2.0/access_control-xacml-2.0-core-spec-os.pdf

OECD. (1980). *Guidelines on the protection of privacy and transborder ows of personal data*. Retrieved from http://www.oecd.org/ http://www.oecd.org/document/18/0,3746, en_2649_34223_1815186_1_1_1_1,00.html

Osborn, S., Sandhu, R., & Munawer, Q. (2000). Conguring role-based access control to enforce mandatory and discretionary access control policies. *ACM Transactions on Information and System Security*, *3*(2), 1–23. doi:10.1145/354876.354878

Renaud, K., & Galvez-Cruz, D. (2010). Privacy: Aspects, dentitions and a multi-faceted privacy preservation approach. In *Proceedings of Information Security South Africa Conference 2010*. ISSA.

Sandhu, R. S. (2000). Engineering authority and trust in cyberspace: The om-am and rbac way. In *Proceedings of ACM Workshop on Role-Based Access Control*, (pp. 111-119). ACM.

Sweeney, L. (2002). k-anonymity: A model for protecting privacy. *International Journal of Uncertainty, Fuzziness and Knowledge-Based Systems*, *10*(5), 557–570. doi:10.1142/S0218488502001648

Web. (2014). *Merriam Webster On-line dictionary*. Retrieved from www.merriam-webster.com

ADDITIONAL READING

Wang, W., Li, J., Ai, C., & Li, Y. (2007). Privacy protection on sliding window of data streams. *In Collaborative Computing: Networking, Applications and Worksharing, 2007. CollaborateCom 2007. International Conference on (pp. 213-221). IEEE*

Yee, G. O. M. (2012). *Privacy Protection Measures and Technologies in Business Organizations: Aspects and Standards* (I. G. I. Global, Ed.).

Zakerzadeh, H., & Osborn, S. (2011). FAANST: fast anonymizing algorithm for numerical streaming data. In *Data Privacy Management and Autonomous Spontaneous Security* (pp. 36–50). Springer Berlin Heidelberg. doi:10.1007/978-3-642-19348-4_4

Zakerzadeh, H., & Osborn, S. (2013). Delay-sensitive approaches for anonymizing numerical streaming data. *International Journal of Information Security*. doi:10.1007/s10207-013-0196-7

Zhang, J., & Yang, J. (2010). KIDS: K-anonymization data stream base on sliding window. *In Future Computer and Communication (ICFCC), 2010 2nd International Conference on, 2*(IEEE), 311–316.

Zhou, B., Han, Y., Pei, J., Jiang, B., Tao, Y., & Jia, Y. (2009). Continuous privacy preserving publishing of data streams. *In Proceedings of the 12th International Conference on Extending Database Technology: Advances in Database Technology (pp. 648-659). ACM.*

KEY TERMS AND DEFINITIONS

Access Control: This refers to security features that control who can access resources in a computing system.

Authentication: This is the process of determining whether a user is, in fact, who he/she is declared to be. In private and public computer networks (including the Internet), authentication is commonly done through the use of passwords.

Authorisation: This is s the function of specifying access rights to resources, which is related to information security and computer security in general and to access control in particular.

Information Security: This is the practice of defending information from unauthorized access, use, disclosure, disruption, modification, perusal, inspection, recording or destruction. Usually this is achieved by verifying three properties namely, confidentiality, integrity, and availability.

Privacy: This is the ability an individual or group has to seclude information about themselves and have this information be expressed selectively.

Role-Based Access Control: This is a method of regulating access to computer or network resources based on the roles of individual users within an enterprise. In this context, access is the ability of an individual user to perform a specific task, such as view, create, or modify a file.

Trust Management: This is an abstract system that processes symbolic representations of social trust, usually to aid automated decision-making process. Such representations, e.g. in a form of cryptographic credentials, can link the abstract system of trust management with results of trust assessment. Trust management is popular in implementing information security, specifically access control policies.

ENDNOTES

[1] From www.medterms.com

Chapter 5
Design of an IPTV Conditional Access System Supporting Multiple–Services

Gregory L. Harding
University of Cape Town, South Africa

Anne V. D. M. Kayem
University of Cape Town, South Africa

ABSTRACT

Conditional Access (CA) is typically used by pay-television operators to restrict access to content to authorized subscribers. While several commercial CA solutions exist for structured broadcasting, Internet-based television, and video-on-demand services, these solutions are mostly proprietary. Use of proprietary solutions incurs royalty payments and increased cost of components for Set-Top-Box manufacturers. In many developing countries Set-Top-Boxes for the migration to Digital Television will be subsidized by government. An efficient, flexible, and open conditional system that does not incur royalties or require specialised security hardware would be beneficial for these countries. In this chapter, the authors explore conditional access solutions that draw on the area of cryptographic key management and distribution for IPTV environments. They wrap up with propositions on how an open Cryptographic Access Control (CAC) system can be implemented practically by pay-television operators who have to handle a large number of subscriptions.

INTRODUCTION

In the television industry, Conditional Access (CA) is the application of cryptography for controlling access to content. The term is most commonly used in reference to the traditional scheduled programming that is distributed over digital broadcast mediums such as satellite, terrestrial, and cable.

Pay-television (or premium television) content, which consists primarily of high quality video and audio streams, is by its nature a high-bandwidth

application. Traditional television broadcast networks have limited bandwidth and typically it is infeasible to encrypt the data stream with a different key for each valid subscriber. In recent years, increasing availability of fast home broadband connections has allowed the advent of streaming Internet Video-on-demand (VOD) services which do establish individual network connections (unicast) to clients. This type of application is reportedly responsible for a large percentage of global bandwidth usage, placing a strain on dis-

DOI: 10.4018/978-1-4666-6158-5.ch005

tribution networks. Unicast distribution of "live television" (including scheduled programming) to a large number of receivers is extremely inefficient. Multicast facilitates efficient distribution of this type of content over IP networks.

Pay-TV operators are heavily reliant on conditional access systems to support their business model. CA systems are also used for free-to-view (FTV) television broadcasts (distinct from free-to-air (FTA) in which broadcast content is not encrypted at all). Encryption of FTV content can be for reasons such as restricting access to content by physical region. National borders, for example in order to prevent viewers in nearby countries from accessing content that is ultimately paid for by tax-payers.

Within a country, regional boundaries might also be defined on the basis of broadcast licenses and advertising. The South African Broadcasting Corporation (SABC) for instance, plans to switch to digital terrestrial television (DTT). The benefits of digital television include greater efficiency in usage of the radio spectrum, and better picture quality. The SABC, as is the case for similar broadcasting agencies in the developing world, could use a CA system to control access to pay-television to within national or community boundaries, and/or for ensuring that only valid license holders are able to access TV. This is important in creating a trusted environment where valid subscribers get reliable access to their subscription content.

Motivation and Objectives

This chapter was inspired in part by the need of a South African set-top-box (STB) manufacturer for an open, royalty-free conditional access mechanism for IPTV that is based on tested academic research in cryptographic key management. The objective of this research therefore is to study existing research in key management systems and design and implement end-to-end framework that is both theoretically robust and practically implementable.

Existing commercial CA systems are closed, and proprietary. To the best of our knowledge, while there is much research in the area of group key management, there is little available research that specifically addresses the design of a complete conditional access system for IPTV.

Further, conditional access systems might rely on "security by obscurity". That is, the strength of their security is dependent on an attacker not having knowledge of the workings of the system. Kerckhoff's principle should be applied: an attacker having knowledge of the algorithms used should not compromise the security of the system.

CA systems used in some IPTV deployments are based on DRM mechanisms, use a simple key distribution centre (SKDC) approach, or encapsulate broadcast CA systems in IP packets. There is arguably room for improvement in terms of security and efficiency.

Contributions

We consider the problems that are encountered when attempting to deliver pay-TV content to a large group of authorized subscribers in a developing world setting. A survey and assessment is made of techniques in key management and distribution, reliable key delivery, and secure storage.

The core achievement of this research is the design of a framework as a solution to these problems that can be used as the basis for a conditional access system. The framework uses an efficient key-tree based method for sharing a group key and associated updates with a large group of subscribers. This attempts to minimize overhead related to key management. Practical considerations for pay-TV subscriber management mean that the subscriber database is generally separate from the key server's data structures. Therefore it is not required that the data in the key trees be sorted. This allows a technique for growing full key trees that reduces the amount of data to be sent for a key update, which we believe to be novel in this application.

A hierarchical key structure for grouping subscribers according to the services they have selected is used to allow flexible viewing selections that are cryptographically enforced. This structure also allows service groupings known as bouquets to share a common bouquet access key (BAK) for encrypting control words of the constituent services. Furthermore, this multiple service architecture allows for different services and bouquets to be managed with specialized key trees that suited to the business model for that particular service or group of services. The conditions for storing keys securely without the need for a smartcard as a tamper-resistant storage device are discussed.

Outline

This section provides a brief outline of the remainder of this chapter. Section 2 covers general background information on television distribution, and digital pay television in particular as well as an overview of networking, cryptography, and secure communications. In Section 3 a detailed assessment of cryptographic key management and access control techniques is undertaken with consideration for the specific requirements of a conditional access system for IPTV. Section 4 outlines the design and implementation of the conditional access framework. Some results and a performance evaluation are presented in Section 5. We conclude in Section 6, with a summary and a discussion of avenues for future work.

BACKGROUND

Television Distribution

Television is an integral part of the fabric of modern society. It has been widely available for the better part of a century, and has become established as a primary medium for the distribution of news and entertainment. It provides a means for organisa- tions such as governments and corporations to reach large audiences efficiently and effectively. The role television has played in forming public opinion since the mid-twentieth century cannot be understated. It is a technology that has truly made the world a smaller place.

Historically, television has been broadcast to viewers either by means of terrestrial radio transmissions and cable networks. The advent of telecommunications satellites in the 1960s and 70s saw the introduction of "direct-to-home" satellite television broadcasts.

Internet Protocol Television

Internet Protocol Television (IPTV) refers to the delivery of television content over an IP network. It is distinct from video content provided by Internet services such as Youtube (although the security principles described in this thesis could apply to such services). Montpetit et al. (2010) provide a comprehensive overview of the technologies involved.

Multicast Networking

An IP network is packet-switched. Messages are broken up into packets and routed from a source to a destination either directly on a local network segment, or via intermediate routers. Unicast refers to a packet being sent to a single destina- tion. Broadcast involves simultaneous delivery to all destinations on a local network segment. Multicast involves simultaneous delivery of the packets to a particular set of destinations who have registered an interest in receiving them by joining a particular multicast group.

The important factor is that broadcast, and particularly multicast, are features implemented by the network infrastructure. The source host transmits a single packet that is delivered to multiple destinations by the network switching and routing equipment. This significantly reduces the load on the source host and the network that would be caused by the successive or simultaneous establishment of multiple unicast connections.

Broadcast is a feature implemented in IPv4 but not available in IPv6, and is primarily restricted to local networks and associated technologies. It makes use of a specific broadcast address to which packets sent will be received by all hosts on a particular network segment. It is not routed because it causes tremendous load on receiving hosts and the network, even if they are not interested in receiving the packets.

We distinguish with television broadcasting by satellite or terrestrial radio signals. Conceptually this delivery of information to all receivers is the same. However it is a highly efficient and scalable use of radio technologies to distribute from a single transmitting source to multiple receivers, all of which are interested in receiving the signal (assuming they are powered-on and tuned to the correct frequency). An IP network has broader, more general applications. Typically it is not dedicated to television delivery and the assumption cannot be made that all hosts want to receive all packets. IP multicast facilitates efficient use of the network infrastructure. Clients indicate the groups they are interested by communicating with their nearest router using the Internet Group Management Protocol (IGMP) on IPv4 networks and Multicast Listener Discovery (MLD) on IPv6 networks. This router in turn communicates with other routers, and so they build up routing tables that ensure only relevant traffic passes through them. Groups are identified by specific IP addresses. In IPv4 the range of addresses from 224.0.0.0 to 239.255.255.255 is allocated to multicast. IPv6 uses the ff00::/8 address block.

Data is usually sent to a multicast group using UDP datagrams. TCP is not applicable to multicast traffic as it only supports two-way, one-to-one connections. The Real-time Transport Protocol (RTP) is commonly used, encapsulated in UDP datagrams, for delivering streaming media content. It defines various profiles for different types of content. RTP Control Protocol (RTCP) is complementary protocol primarily used by receiving clients to communicate statistics back to the server that it can use to tune its output (such as quality-of-service and rate limiting parameters). Secure RTP (SRTP) is a particular profile defined by RTP for encryption, integrity verification, and message authentication. It uses AES with a counter stream cipher mode of operation.

Return Path

While many modern cable television deployments do provide two-way communications, satellite and terrestrial distribution networks are pure broadcast environments. They do not provide any in-band mechanism for return communication from the viewer to the operator (head-end).

A return-path (or return-channel) is a communications channel that the receiver may use to transmit data to the head-end. The lack of a return path places certain limitations on the type of services that can be offered on these networks (For example, video-on-demand). The routing strategies and return path features offered by the various television transmission methods are summarised in Table 1.

This research primarily considers the situation where a permanent return-path is available. This could be IPTV, two-way cable TV, or a satellite or terrestrial broadcast system augmented with a separate return channel (for example, a satellite set-top-box with an IP connection, or a satellite-IP hybrid). Such a hybrid system could be useful for

Table 1. Comparison of television transmission methods

	Broadcast	Unicast	Multicast	Return Channel
Satellite	✓			X
Terrestrial	✓			X
Cable	✓			✓ (some)
IPTV		✓	✓	✓

countries such as South Africa, where broadband Internet access is currently limited in terms of bandwidth and data usage caps.

PAY TELEVISION

Subscription

The pay television or premium television industry operates a predominantly subscription based business model. They are funded partly or fully by paying subscribers, as opposed to advertising revenue, or public-funding. This allows a broader selection of channel content types to cater to viewers' interests.

Pay-Per-View

Pay-per-view (PPV) is a service which might be offered by pay television operators to existing subscribers or once-off to customers who have the necessary equipment to receive the transmission. All viewers would tune-in at a scheduled time to receive the broadcast. PPV can be viewed as a short-term subscription.

Video-on-Demand

Video-on-demand (VOD) is a service which allows viewers to individually choose content from a selection and watch it at their leisure. This is achieved in different ways, depending on the transmission mechanism being used. In a pure broadcast environment, Push-Video-on-Demand (PVOD) requires a subscriber to have a device with a local storage capability (usually a digital video record (DVR) with a hard disk). A selection of content is background downloaded from a dedicated broadcast channel and saved to the disk. Once some content is available on the disk, the subscriber is able to view it at their convenience.

CONTENT PROTECTION

In order to enforce their business model, pay TV operators need some way of restricting access to their content to only paid-up subscribers. In early cable TV systems, access could be restricted by using signal filters at the cable taps for each subscribers' premises to remove certain channels from their signal. This method was not scalable and as the number of channels and subscribers increased, alternatives had to be found. Methods of distorting or scrambling the signal with interference signals were used. With the advent of digital television, encryption and associated key management schemes have done much towards solving the problem.

Challenges

In many forms of secure communications all parties share at least some interest in maintaining that security. Content protection is primarily aimed at protecting the interests of service operators and copyright holders. Thus there is little incentive for customers to take steps to maintain security, and when these steps are enforced on legitimate customers they are seen as an unwelcome hindrance (particularly in the case of DRM applied to media such as music and books i.e. outside the confines of a controlled distribution network).

It is both pragmatic and prudent for operators and vendors of such security systems to work on the assumption that the system can never be completely secure. Given enough time and resources, any system can be broken.

The goal therefore is to ensure that the cost of breaking the system is more expensive than using it legitimately would be. It should be more costly and/or onerous for potential customers to attempt avoiding having to pay for a subscription than to simply pay. Particularly, it should not be possible for illegitimate efforts to piggyback on the legitimate network. For example, a criminal organization that attempts a pirate redistribution of the service for commercial gain should not be able to make use of the operator's distribution network. This is a problem with over-the-air transmissions via terrestrial and satellite where cloning smartcards or sharing decryption keys obtained from legitimate subscriptions are often the only steps necessary to set up an illegal commercial operation.

If some part of the content distribution network is vulnerable, the strength of other areas is irrelevant. The primary weakness in any such system is at the point where, by necessity, it must be decrypted in order for customers to view it. This is addressed by employing an end-to-end chain of trust. The data is transmitted securely by the CA schemes discussed in this thesis. The receiving device (STB) then sends it to a television via an encrypted signal using the HDCP (High-bandwidth Digital Content Protection) protocol, where the source device cryptographically authenticates the destination device before sending the data. The destination (television) displays the content. In theory the only way to extract the content would be to record a lower quality version via analogue device outputs. The high quality digital data is encrypted from its source at the operator all the way to the TV.

Digital Rights Management

Digital rights management (DRM) and conditional access aim to achieve similar goals: namely the protection of content that is ultimately distributed to untrusted users.

DRM is a widely applicable term that refers to any mechanism for restricting the use of content or hardware. Broadly, DRM associates content with a set of usage rights and protects both the content and the rights, usually by cryptographic means. It attempts to associate a unique copy of some content with a specific authorised user. Each authorised user would receive their own copy of the content.

This is done in such a way a user should only be able to access his/her own copy of the content, and then only in the manner deemed acceptable by the provider of the content. For DRM to be effective, only trusted hardware or software should be able to decrypt and interpret the rights, and provide a user with access to the content only if the rights and additional authorisation information permit doing so. Azad, Ahmed, & Alam, (2010) provides an overview of research in DRM.

DRM attempts to restrict the use of content that is distributed or distributable outside the confines of a controlled system (i.e. an untrusted distribution channel). Conditional access benefits by being part of a more tightly controllable system. It is distinct from DRM in that it attempts to protect a single copy of content that is shared by all users.

A chain of trust must be maintained from the content source to the eventual destination (a television, for example) for any content protection to be complete. However both DRM and CA systems suffer from an inevitability: ultimately the content must be provided to the user in some accessible, unencrypted form. At that point all the protections used earlier in the chain become irrelevant and an attacker no longer has to break strong encryption: he/she simply has to workaround any obstacles or hindrances to copying or recording the content.

DIGITAL VIDEO BROADCASTING

The Digital Video Broadcasting (DVB) Project defines a comprehensive set of open standards that are widely used in Europe, Australia, Africa and other parts of the world for the broadcast of digital television. They specify most aspects of digital television to allow interoperability and compatibility between networks and equipment. For example, the DVB-S standard (1997) specifies modulation, encoding and transmission characteristics, and data formats and protocols for satellite television.

The newer DVB-IPTV (2009) includes specifications for the use of protocols such as RTSP and RTP, and multicast networking. The standards also define the DVB Conditional Access framework (DVB-CA) (2005) that allows operators to use various commercial conditional access solutions. Major vendors of such solutions include Irdeto (2011), NDS (2011) and Nagravision (2011). These systems are typically closed, and proprietary, with almost no information publicly available on the exact mechanisms that are used to achieve the required objectives. In DVB-CA video is scrambled with a control word (CW) which is used as a seed to a pseudorandom number generator. Either the common scrambling algorithm (DVB-CSA (2011)) or optionally some variant of it is used, as decided by the vendor of the particular conditional access system. The subscribers' receiving equipment needs a compatible descrambler. The CW is common for all subscribers of the system and is changed often (every few seconds) to minimize the impact of key discovery. The effective key size is 48-bits.

This small key, which is potentially vulnerable to brute force attacks, is needed to allow real-time descrambling on relatively constrained embedded systems. Newer versions of DVB-CSA, which take faster hardware into account, provide stronger AES-based encryption.

The DVB-CA standard species the existence of Entitlement Control Messages (ECMs), which contain CW updates, and Entitlement Management Messages (EMMs) which contain other instructions and key updates for the CA system. These messages are opaque, and usually encrypted, with their format and content specific to the particular conditional access system in use. They are decrypted and processed by the CA system, which must ensure that it provides a control word to the descrambler in a timely fashion.

Any mechanism that fits into this specification can be used to securely deliver the CWs. In the most simplistic system, the CA system might store a static, globally shared master key in smartcards (which are tamper resistant). This key would use symmetric encryption to decrypt the control words. Obviously the impact of this single key being compromised is severe.

More complex systems will encrypt the CW with an intermediate key-encryption-key (KEK). The intermediate KEK is usually stored on authorised smartcards and periodically updated using a message encrypted with a smartcard's public key. One such message would need to be delivered per smartcard in circulation. The performance and bandwidth requirements scale linearly $O(n)$ with this approach, sometimes referred to as Simple Key Distribution Centre. Even more advanced systems employ hierarchies of keys that allow securely delivering these keys in a more efficient manner.

It should be noted that the use of a control word allows flexibility in the system: it can be updated very frequently without incurring further rekey operations; it facilitates the "modular" interchange of CA systems; and in fact it allows multiple CA systems to be used simultaneously, SimulCrypt, with an ECM for each system containing the same control word.

SECURE TWO-PARTY COMMUNICATIONS

Attacks and Vulnerabilities

Before attempting to secure a system, it is necessary to have an understanding of the types of threats and attacks that the system could possibly be subjected to. In normal communications, a message is passed from a sender to a receiver. It may pass through multiple intermediaries (network routers) along the way. Attacks by a third party on this data flow can be classified as either active or passive. In a passive attack, the message arrives at the receiver unmodified from the form that it left the sender. In an active attack the message received is altered or not received at all. Interception is a passive attack on confidentiality. Modification is an active attack on integrity. Interruption is an active attack on availability. Fabrication is an active attack on authenticity. Figure 1 illustrates these four forms of attacks.

Security Objectives and Services

Information security has certain objectives that need to be met dependent on the requirements of the particular application. These desirable properties known as security services are implemented by various underlying mechanisms and protocols.

CRYPTOGRAPHY

Provision of the aforementioned security services is primarily accomplished by performing certain transformations to the data before sending, and again once it has been received. These transformations make use of cryptography: data is encrypted with a secret key to provide confidentiality, for example. Only parties who hold the appropriate secret key for decryption will be able to understand the message.

Symmetric Cryptography

With symmetric cryptography, the same secret key is used to decrypt the data as was used to encrypt it. Block ciphers such as DES (Data Encryption Standard) and AES (Advanced Encryption Standard) are examples of symmetric cryptography. The primary issue with symmetric cryptography is finding a way to securely distribute the secret key to all concerned parties. If the secret key is intercepted, the encryption is worthless.

Figure 1. Possible forms of attack on a message sent from Alice to Bob. Eve is the attacker.

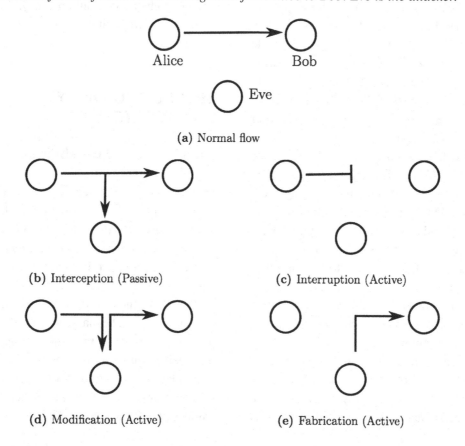

Various methods of secure key distribution exist. A key might be pre-shared between a group of users (for example, by physically entering the same password into multiple computers, or loaded onto a STB during production in the factory). The Diffie-Helman key establishment protocol allows two parties to securely negotiate a key over an insecure channel.

Asymmetric Cryptography

Asymmetric cryptography (also known as public/private key cryptography) uses a separate key for the encryption and decryption steps. Encryption is typically performed with a public key which can be widely distributed without concern for security. Only the holder of the private key is able to decrypt the message. RSA (1978) is a widely used example of an asymmetric cryptographic algorithm.

Asymmetric cryptography is significantly slower than symmetric and is only suitable for encrypting small amounts of data. Often communications protocols might start with asymmetric cryptography to share a symmetric "session key" which is then used for the remainder of the communications. An initial exchange of public keys allows the parties to encrypt messages that can only be read by the other.

Trusted Third Party to Establish Authentication

Unless two parties have communicated in some way and shared some secret information known only to each of them, it is usually necessary to make use of a trusted third-party for authentication (that is, for one or both of the parties to verify that the other is who it claims to be).

This service is normally provided by a certification authority. Such an authority will cryptographically sign a certificate containing the public key of a party whose identity they can verify in some way. That certificate can then be used in future exchanges with unknown entities, who are able to verify it using the public key of the certification authority.

PROPOSED CA FRAMEWORK

Primarily, a conditional access system needs to ensure that only legitimate users are able to access content, and that they are only able to access the content they are authorised to receive. That is, it must protect content from outsiders who have no subscription, and it must protect against subscribers being able to illegitimately elevate their access privileges.

Any transmission medium has maximum available bandwidth. For example, we might assume that a single high-definition (HD) television service requires an average 12 Mbit/s for a suitable quality video stream. An associated 6-channel surround sound audio stream ("5.1") might have a bit rate of 320 kbit/s. A satellite television transponder with a maximum effective bandwidth of 64 Mbit/s would therefore be able to transmit a maximum of 5 such HD television services. Other transmission mediums such as cable or IP networks have higher available bandwidth. However it is not unlimited. A CA system should attempt to minimise the data transfer overhead that it imposes.

The system should be designed with the view that it will be compromised, and steps should be taken to minimise the impact of any such compromise. An ideal conditional access system should be sufficiently general and broadly applicable to different business models. For example, a system that is dependent on batched key updates to keep bandwidth usage acceptable imposes restrictions on the flexibility of subscription periods that can be offered to subscribers. A system that requires services to be grouped in a particular way imposes restrictions on the content selection choices available to a subscriber.

A conditional access system must reasonably support an operator with tens to hundreds of channels, and millions of subscribers. The system needs to scale well in these ranges. The core is to securely share appropriate keys amongst the authorised subscribers so that they are able to decrypt the content. The mechanism by which the keys are shared needs to be secure against collusion between users, and it must provide forward and backward secrecy.

SECURE BROADCASTING

In the pay-television scenario, a single source (the head-end server) needs to transmit a large amount of data simultaneously to a large number of receivers (the subscribers). The data transmission is continuous, which is known as streaming, and consists of video and audio streams, and other supporting information such as an electronic program guide (EPG). It is measured in terms of bandwidth requirements (transfer rate), rather than total data size.

In a typical over-the-air (OTA) broadcast network (such as satellite and terrestrial television), it is necessary to encrypt this data because it is otherwise impossible to control access to it. Anyone who can acquire or fabricate the necessary reception equipment could intercept the transmission. On a cable or IP network, although the subscriber's connection and access is controllable by the network operator, encryption is also highly desirable to protect against interception attacks. Such attacks are very possible over large public networks such as the Internet or by means of illegal taps into private cable networks which are difficult to detect due to the networks' size.

It should be clear that attempting to secure this data transmission using the previously discussed mechanisms for two-party communications would require a separate encrypted video stream for each individual subscriber. So while that would meet the security requirements for controlling subscriber access, it is an extremely inefficient use of limited and costly bandwidth.

HIERARCHY OF KEYS

The solution is to encrypt the video or data stream only once and then transmit it to all subscribers. It is necessary to securely share the key used to encrypt the video stream with all subscribers. The data encryption key can itself be encrypted with a private "key-encryption-key" (KEK). If a key is associated with each subscriber, and known only to that subscriber and the server, then the data encryption key can be securely transmitted to all subscribers. This is a 2-level key hierarchy. The data encryption key that is shared amongst the entire group of subscribers is called a group key (GK). This key hierarchy is illustrated in Figure 2.

DVB Key Hierarchy

In the DVB-CA system, the actual key used to encrypt the streamed data is known as a Control Word (CW) (see "Digital Video Broadcasting"). While the group key could be used as the CW directly (provided it meets the standard format for DVB descrambler equipment), it makes more sense to introduce a third level in the key hierarchy. The control word is encrypted with the group key. For the purpose of this chapter, it is assumed that the actual data to be encrypted by a conditional access system is a continuous series of control words.

Group Rekeying

The group key needs to be changed every time a new subscriber is added (to prevent them being able to decrypt any transmissions made prior to their joining) or an old subscriber is removed (to prevent them being able to decrypt any future transmissions). This is referred to as rekeying.

Figure 2. Illustration of a two-level key structure

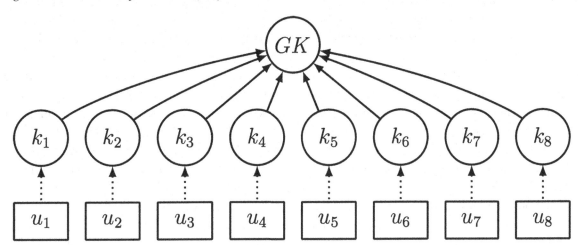

In a network with a large number of users, and frequent join and remove operations taking place, the overhead in terms of bandwidth and server load for these key distributions can be significant if the simple protocol described above is used.

For example, assume a network has 10 million users and the size of a rekey message is 68 bytes (256-bit AES key and initialization vector, 32-bit key identifier). Then for every join or leave operation the server needs to perform 10 million encryption operations, and needs to transmit approximately 650 MB of incompressible data. If the data is broadcast or multicast, then every client needs to receive all the data to find the one key message applicable to them. If the data is unicast then the load on a client is negligible, however the server needs to make 10 million outgoing connections: which places high demands on a system that can multicast all other data (video and audio).

Stateful and Stateless

Zhu and Jajodia (2010) classify methods for group rekey operations as either stateful or stateless. This state refers to the information a client needs to hold in order to receive and interpret a new key update message.

In a stateful system, a client needs to hold keys that have been previously distributed in order for it to be able to decrypt new keys. As an example, consider the situation in which each new group key is encrypted by the previous group key.

In a stateless system, a client does not need to hold previous keys and can immediately interpret any new key update message. A trivial example is one in which each client shares the same symmetric key. That key never changes and is used to encrypt and decrypt group key update messages.

A stateful system requires a reliable key distribution mechanism so that clients receive all key updates. It is therefore best suited to applications that are able to maintain semi-permanent network connections, for example. Stateless systems are useful for applications in which no such connection is available. For example, distribution of encrypted content on DVDs.

Logical Key Hierarchy (LKH)

To reduce load on the server and the network infrastructure, the users can be divided into two subgroups, each with an intermediate key-encryption-key. This intermediate key can be used to encrypt the group key, and itself be encrypted with the users' private encryption keys. When a group rekey operation takes place, only half of the users need to receive a new intermediate key that is those belonging to the subgroup to which the new member is added (or from which an existing member is removed, respectively). They also receive a new group key encrypted with their new intermediate key. The other half of the users only need to receive the new group key encrypted with their existing intermediate key. Thus the required bandwidth and number of encryption operations is nearly halved.

This approach can be extended by halving each group again and adding a new layer of intermediate keys. In that case approximately only a quarter of the original bandwidth and encryption operations is required. If this process is repeated until each subgroup has only two users, the number of keys involved in a rekey operation is exactly the number between the affected user and the group key. This tree structure is known as Logical Key Hierarchy (LKH) (Wallner et al., 1999). If the tree is full and balanced, the complexity of a rekey operation is O(logN). In fact it is not necessary that the tree structure be binary as described above. Wong (2000) found the optimal degree to be 4.

Assume that Figure 3 represents some initial state of an LKH tree containing 8 members, U_1 - U_8. Each member holds a key Ki known only to that member and the key server. GK is the group key shared by all members. K_{123} is known only to the members of the subtree containing users U_1, U_2 and U_3. Likewise, the key K_{456} is known to U_4, U_5 and U_6, and K_{78} to U_7 and U_8.

Given this tree structure, the following procedures are followed to update keys when a new member joins or an existing member has its access revoked.

Join Operation

To add a new member, U_9, the key server locates an intermediate node in the tree that is not full and attaches a new child node there containing K_9. See Figure 4. K_{78} is this joining point. The key there and the group key GK need to be updated.

The key server generates new random keys K_{789} and GK′ to replace them respectively. These new keys then need to be securely delivered to U_9 and to the existing members that need them.

Wong (2000) distinguishes between three mechanisms for distributing these keys to users. These differ in how to determine the grouping of new keys and which existing keys to use to encrypt the update messages. The selection of existing keys used to encrypt new keys needs to be done in such a way as to avoid revealing new keys to users who should not hold them. With user-oriented rekeying, the server creates a message containing exactly the keys needed by a particular user and encrypts it with a key held by that user (and other users with the same requirements).

With key-oriented rekeying, each new key is encrypted separately, perhaps multiple times with different existing keys. Figure 5 shows the key messages that would be sent to perform the same group rekeying as above with the key-oriented strategy.

In practice, implementing user or key oriented rekeying involves establishing multiple unicast connections or having multiple multicast subgroups. Group-oriented rekeying is the most straightforward to implement and results in the fewest rekey messages.

Group-oriented rekeying creates a single message containing all new keys encrypted as necessary. Members U_7 and U_8 need K_{789}. All the users need GK′. Since exactly U_7 and U_8 hold the previous key K_{78} and U_9 does not, it can be used to encrypt K_{789}. Likewise all existing members hold GK which can be used to encrypt GK′. These update messages are shown in Figure 6.

Leave Operation

In Figure 7, member U_5 is removed. Key K_{456} needs to be replaced with a new key K_{46} and GK′ is replaced with GK″. However since U_5 holds both of these existing keys, they cannot be used to encrypt their replacements. GK″ is therefore encrypted separately with K_{123} and K_{789}. K_{46} is en-

Figure 3. Logical key hierarchy

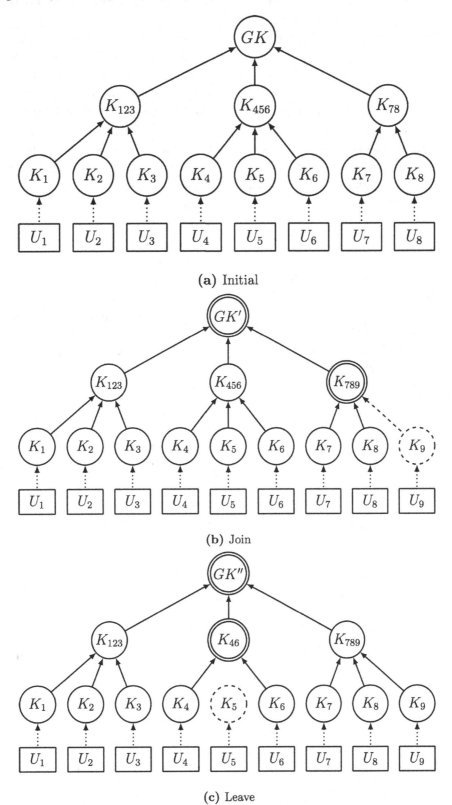

(a) Initial

(b) Join

(c) Leave

crypted with K_4 and K_6. Finally, GK'' is encrypted with the new K_{46} which members U_4 and U_6 will obtain after decrypting the previous message.

LKH+

Perlman (1997) suggests an improvement to LKH which he calls "LKH+". In the case of a join operation, existing members apply a one-way hash function to the updated keys. This saves significantly on the bandwidth required to transmit the actual keys.

Figure 4. User-oriented rekeying strategy when member U9 joins

$$s \to U_9 : \langle K_{789}, GK' \rangle_{K_9}$$
$$s \to U_7, U_8 : \langle K_{789}, GK' \rangle_{K_{78}}$$
$$s \to U_1, \cdots, U_6 : \langle GK' \rangle_{GK}$$

Figure 5. Key-oriented rekeying strategy when member U_9 joins

$$s \to U_9 : \langle GK' \rangle_{K_9}$$
$$s \to U_9 : \langle K_{789} \rangle_{K_9}$$
$$s \to U_7, U_8 : \langle K_{789} \rangle_{K_{78}}$$
$$s \to U_1, \cdots, U_8 : \langle GK' \rangle_{GK}$$

ONE-WAY FUNCTION TREES (OFT)

McGrew & Sherman (1998) propose a technique based on one-way functions applied bottom-up in a key tree. The key server maintains a binary tree. Associated with each node i of the tree are two keys: the node key and the blinded key. By blinded key, we imply that such a key cannot be used to derive the node key due to the fact that we use a one-way function to generate the node key.

Each leaf node is associated with a group member and the node key K_i of a leaf node is known only to that member and the key server. The node key of an interior node is derived from the blinded keys of its left and right children by combining the keys using a mixing function such as bitwise exclusive-or (XOR).

Each member knows only its own node key and the blinded keys of the sibling nodes on the path from its leaf node to the root. It can use these to derive the node keys on its path to the root. The node key of the root node is the group key. See Figure 8 for an example.

Join Operation

When a new member joins the group, an existing leaf node is split into two. The existing member is placed as the left child and the new member becomes the right child. For example in Figure 9

Figure 6. Group-oriented rekeying strategy when member U_9 joins

$$s \to U_1, U_2, \cdots, U_8 : \langle GK' \rangle_{GK}, \langle K_{789} \rangle_{K_{78}} \qquad \text{(multicast)}$$
$$s \to U_9 : \langle K_{789}, GK' \rangle_{K_9} \qquad \text{(unicast)}$$

Figure 7. Group-oriented rekeying strategy for member U5 leave

$$s \to U_1, U_2, \cdots, U_9 : \langle GK'' \rangle_{K_{123}}, \langle GK'' \rangle_{K_{789}}, \langle K_{46} \rangle_{K_4}, \langle K_{46} \rangle_{K_6}, \langle GK'' \rangle_{K_{46}}$$

Figure 8. One-Way Function Tree: In this example, member U3 holds node key K3 and the corresponding blinded keys

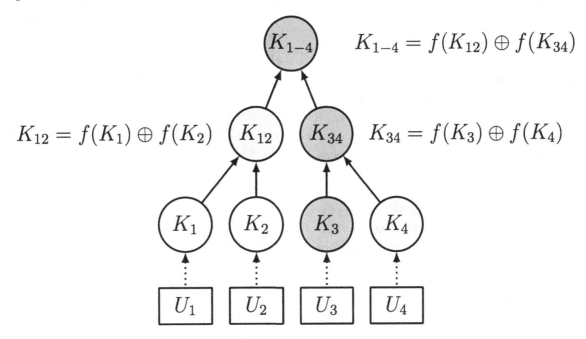

member U_5 has joined the group originally shown in Figure 8. Some existing leaf node is chosen, in this case the one that was associated with U_3. U_3 now becomes the left child and receives a new key K'_3. Likewise the right child for the new member becomes a new key, K_5. Then the original K_3 is replaced with

$$K_{35} = f\left(K'_3\right) \oplus f\left(K_5\right), K_{34} \text{ with } K_{345} = f\left(K_{35}\right) \oplus f\left(K_4\right), \text{and} K_{1-4} \text{ with } K_{1-5} = f\left(K_{12}\right) \oplus f\left(K_{345}\right)$$

In general, if the key K_x for node x is updated, its blinded key needs to be distributed to the members in the subtree rooted at its sibling node s. These members already hold the node key Ks which can be used for encryption. Therefore $Kb_{35} = f(K_{35})$ will be encrypted with K_4 and $Kb_{345} = f(K_{345})$ with K_{12}. K'_3 can be encrypted with K_3 as only the security of its blinded key is compromised for further use. It is assumed that K_5 and other blinded keys required by U_5 are transmitted

as part of some separate secure communication. The updated keys would be distributed as follows (Ks_5 is some key known only to the server and member **U_5**).

$$s \rightarrow U_5 : K_5, Kb'_3, Kb_4 Kb_{12Ks5} \left(\text{Unicast}\right)$$
$$s \rightarrow U_1,...,U_4 : K'_{3K3}, Kb_{35K4}, Kb_{345K12}$$

Leave Operation

When a member leaves, the update process is similar. It is necessary to differentiate between two cases. In the first case, the sibling of the leaf node associated with the removed node is also a leaf node. In this case, the member associated with the sibling is reassigned to the parent node and given a new key. For example, Figure 9b shows U_1 being removed from the group shown in Figure 9a. The nodes K_1 and K_2 are removed, and U_2 is reassigned to its original parent node, and given a new key K'_2. The key update message is multicast as follows:

$$s \rightarrow U_2, \ldots, U_5 : K'_{2K2}, Kb'_{2K345}$$

In the second case, the sibling is an intermediate node --- the root of a subtree. The parent node is then replaced by the sibling and one of the leaf nodes in the subtree need to be changed so the node key (and therefore the blinded key that was known to the removed member) is updated. Figure 9c illustrates this by removing U_4

Assume members U_2, U_5 and U_6 have been revoked (shown as filled nodes). The remaining members can be represented by the subsets of nodes from the group. K'_3 is the leaf node in the sibling subtree that is arbitrarily selected to be changed (in order to change the blinded key of K_{35} that was know to U_4).

Subset-Difference Rekeying (SDR)

Subset-Difference Rekeying is a stateless protocol for group rekeying proposed by Naor et al. (2001). It works on the basis of users possessing information about other users in such a way that when a user is removed, the remaining users can recalculate the group key without the removed user being able to.

The key server maintains a binary tree, and as with the other techniques, the leaf nodes represent subscribers. Consider the two subtrees rooted at the internal nodes, or vertices, V_x and V_y, where V_y is a descendant node of V_x. S_x and S_y are sets of users (leaf nodes) in each of these subtrees respectively and $S_y \subset S_x$. Then S_{xy} is the subset of users contained in S_x but not S_y, that is $S_{xy} = S_x \setminus S_y$. A key is associated with each subset such that if a subset describes a selection of members, less the revoked members, it can be used to encrypt the new group key for distribution to valid members. In the example shown in Figure 10, assume members U_2, U_5 and U_6 have been revoked (shown as filled nodes). The remaining members can be

represented by the subsets $Sab = \{U_9, \cdots, U_{16}\}$, $Sde = \{U_7, U_8\}$ and $Scf = \{U_1, U_3, U_4\}$.

The challenge is to partition the valid members into a minimal number of subsets and encrypt the group key with each associated key. Clearly a member will be included in many possible subsets and it is necessary to determine a way to minimize the number of keys that the member must store.

This method hinges on it perpetually retaining information about removed members. That is, the nodes associated with revoked users must remain in the tree. Thus over time as the number of revoked users grows, so will the number of subsets, and the number of separate encryptions of the group key that must take place. The server memory usage also increases with time.

MARKS

Multicast Key Management using Arbitrarily Revealed Key Sequences (MARKS) Briscoe, (1999) takes a different approach. A binary tree is used, but the nodes are not associated with group members. Instead membership duration is divided into fixed time periods. The key server maintains a binary hash tree where the key associated with each node is derived from the key in its parent node by application of a one-way hash function. Two distinct functions are used to derive the left and right child keys respectively. Leaf-nodes represent the group key to be used for some fixed time period. Once the time period has passed, the next successive leaf node's key is used. Figure 11 shows a key hierarchy for 8 time periods (T1 to T8). Members have knowledge of f and g and by providing a member with the keys of intermediate nodes it can derive the larger set of keys associated with its time period.

Figure 9. OFT: Member join and leave operations. In (a) U_5 joins. Then U1 is removed in (b) and finally U_4 removed in (c). Nodes marked with double circles have changed. Their respective blinded keys need to be distributed to the subtrees rooted at their siblings.

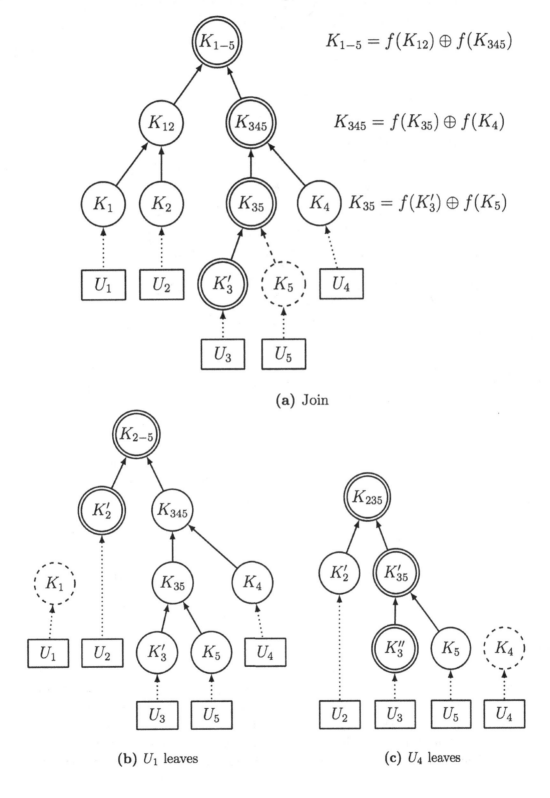

$$K_{1-5} = f(K_{12}) \oplus f(K_{345})$$

$$K_{345} = f(K_{35}) \oplus f(K_4)$$

$$K_{35} = f(K_3') \oplus f(K_5)$$

(a) Join

(b) U_1 leaves   **(c)** U_4 leaves

Figure 10. Subset-difference rekeying. Part of a tree containing 16 group members.

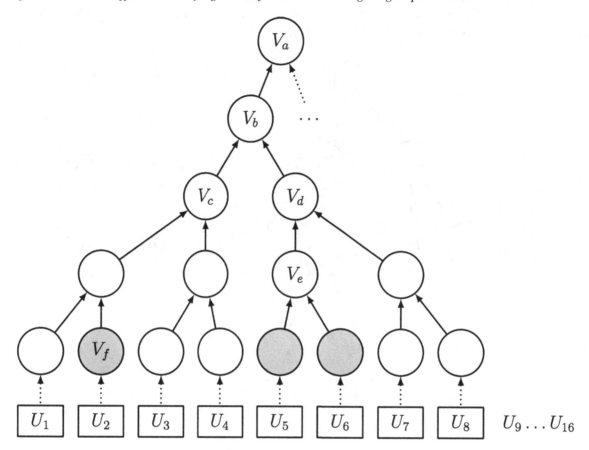

F-PPC Key Refreshment Scheme

Sun et al. (2008) propose the Flexible Pay-per-Channel (F-PPC) model which incorporates both a group rekey operation and a method for more efficiently handling the problem of multiple services ("channels").

They claim superior performance for their binary-tree based group rekey operation over other methods. Their method relies on each subscriber not possessing some secret associated with itself that is possessed by every other subscriber. While similar to SDR, this method does not have the benefit of statelessness. To varying extents all the other rekeying methods we have discussed depend on subscribers having access to only a very limited subset of information that is possessed by others (in the form of intermediate tree nodes).

However in F-PPC the secret associated with a subscriber has permanence. Once created, there is no method to update it for the duration of the subscription. Also, knowledge of the secret is held by all other subscribers. This makes the system particularly vulnerable to collusion between any two or more subscribers in a way that would be difficult to stop without regenerating the entire tree.

Basic Attack on FPPC Rekey Operation

Say an attacker purchases two independent subscriptions, A and B for the purposes of this example, with full access to all services. If the attacker can somehow retrieve from B the secret associated with A, he can then unsubscribe both A and B and still be able to obtain the new group

Figure 11. MARKS: the children nodes at each level are derived from their parent node by applying one-way functions

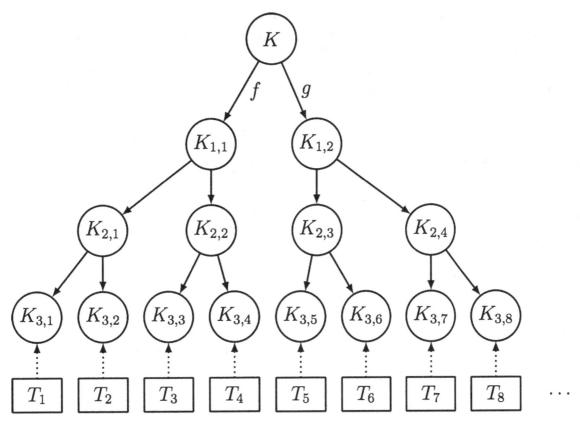

key that is generated after removal of A from the system, and can continue to do so in perpetuity as he now has complete information about the system. Even if this is discovered by the operator, there is no way to stop the authorised access to content without regenerating the entire FPPC tree. Even so, it would not be burdensome for the attacker to repeat the process.

The security of this technique therefore hinges entirely on the security of subscriber local storage (ie. the smartcard or other encrypted storage). Furthermore, the technique is stateful and therefore provides minimal benefit over LKH and OFT. The single point of failure and the scale of potential compromise makes this method unsuitable for our purposes.

MULTIPLE SERVICE ARCHITECTURE

Thus far we have only considered the case of a single group key being shared amongst the subscribers. Typically, pay-TV operators provide multiple content services ("channels") and offer a selection of subscription choices to their customers. Whilst a single key could be used to encrypt all services, this would only differentiate between subscribers and non subscribers. Thus any valid subscriber would technically be able to decrypt the content streams for every service. Any finer grained subscription choices would have to be simulated by the set-top-box/client software (for example, by blacking out channels which are not in the subscriber's entitlements).

Clearly this is not a cryptographically-secure approach, and is essentially "security-by-obscurity". The question arises of how to implement finer grained access controls that strictly restrict a subscriber to his/her subscription choice. The technical limitations of any such technique should be carefully considered so as not to impose undue restrictions on the business model and service offerings of the operator.

Flexible Pay-Per-Channel

The multiple service architecture suggested by F-PPC allows a subscriber to make a completely arbitrary selection of services. Subscribers are placed into groups along with other subscribers which the same selection of services. A subscriber is in exactly one such subscription group. Associated with each subscription group G_x is a Group Authorisation Key (GAK), GK_x. Associated with each service Si is a group, the members of whom have access to a Service Authorisation Key (SAK), SK_i. The subscription groups themselves are members of the service authorisation groups. Therefore a member of a particular subscription group uses his GAK to decrypt the SAK for each service his subscription group is authorised for. The group rekey mechanism used for distributing these GAKs and SAKs is separate from this hierarchy structure for associating groups.

Allowing completely arbitrary selections of services is a feature demanded by customers of pay-TV operators, (Vermeulen, 2012). Aside from business model considerations, technical reasons limit the ease with which such a feature can be implemented. With completely arbitrary selection of services, for each service a subscriber either does or not does subscribe to it. Therefore the number of possible combinations of m services is 2m. For example, if 3 services are available $2^3 = 8$ groupings of subscribers are possible. See Table 2 for an example of possible subscription selections of 3 services, by 6 users. Their particular choices have resulted in 4 groupings.

However with realistic numbers of services, the number of possible groupings rapidly becomes unrealistic for implementation purposes. For example, 100 services would allow a maximum of 2^{100} possible groupings. With F-PPC, the numbers of groupings is bounded by the number of subscribers, n. Practically n $<<$ 2^m -1, and in the worst case, each subscriber has a unique service selection. Therefore the number of groupings is given by max(2^m, n). Nevertheless, an implementation of this mechanism without additional restrictions in place can easily become impractical.

RELIABLE KEY DELIVERY

Multicast and broadcast packet delivery is inherently unreliable. On an IP network, these routing schemes depend on UDP datagrams. UDP provides no guarantees that a datagram will be received at its destination, and if it is received, there is no guarantee of correctness or that multiple packets are received in the order they were sent. The possibility of a multicast packet not being correctly received by all interested participants needs to be considered. If a member misses a key update,

Table 2. Example subscriptions for users {U_1;... ; U_6}. Users are grouped into exactly one of {G_w;...;G_z} along with other users who have matching subscriptions.

	U_1	U_2	U_3	U_4	U_5	U_6
S_1	●	●	●			
S_2		●		●	●	●
S_3	●	●	●	●		●
	G_X	G_Y	G_X	G_W	G_Z	G_W

especially with a stateful rekeying algorithm, he will not be able to decrypt the transmission or further key updates.

In a DVB network with no return-path, certain data that needs to readily available is repeatedly transmitted in a loop, sometimes know as a carousel. In an IP network, a client who has missed out on some keys can fallback to a unicast request for those keys. Obviously it is necessary to minimize the number of such requests, otherwise the performance of the system can degrade to that where all keys are supplied individually to subscribers with unicast, which is a situation these mechanisms are trying to avoid.

DVB Satellite, Cable, and Terrestrial networks make use of two levels of error correction. Firstly, 16 bytes of optional Reed-Solomon error correction information can be added to the 188 byte MPEG transport stream (TS) packets, resulting in a packet size of 204 bytes. Secondly, internal to the DVB transmitter a convolutional code is used with various code rates (commonly 1/2, 3/4, 5/6, 7/8). This is commonly termed "FEC" (Forward Error Correction) in STB configuration menus.

Various solutions have been proposed to the problem of reliable multicast networking. Examples are Pragmatic General Multicast (PGM) (Speakman et al., 2001) and Scalable Reliable Multicast (SRM) (1997). These protocols either replace UDP or implement an additional layer above UDP, but they are complex (Zhu, & Jajodia, 2010), and often require extensive support from network equipment.

Application level solutions to the problem specifically consider the problem of reliable key distribution. These are primarily Weighted Key Assignment with Batched Key Retransmission (WKA-BKR) (Setia, Zhu, & Jajodia, 2002), and Proactive FEC-based Key Delivery (Yang et al., 2001) which uses Reed-Solomon erasure correction codes. Zhu et al. have proposed a hybrid method, WFEC-BKR in an extension to SDR that incorporates "self-healing" (Zhu, Setia, & Jajodia, 2003).

WKA-BKR improves significantly on the bandwidth usage of the multi-send approach wherein each key update message would be sent multiple times. A weight is assigned to each key based on the number of users that hold the key. Keys held by more users are weighted higher and are retransmitted more times than keys with lower weights.

BATCHED UPDATES

Depending on the application, it is not always necessary to immediately perform a group rekey on a member joining or leaving. This is especially the case with pay-TV. If, for example, the content is offered on a subscription basis it is only necessary to perform a group rekey operation at the end of the subscription period (say, at month end). In that case, multiple members might be revoked at the same time and depending on the rekeying strategy being used some benefit can be gained in combining the operations.

Apart from reasons of subscription periods, and depending on the business requirements of a particular operator, the revocation of a member can be delayed until some other batch rekey frequency. The member might then be able to access content for slightly longer than their subscription period but this might not have any negative impact on the security of the system or finances of the operator. Batched key updates of this sort are addressed by Setia et al. (2000) and Yang et al. (2001).

PROPOSED KEY MANAGEMENT FRAMEWORK

Overview

We designed a conditional access framework based on an implementation of the key management and distribution scheme and assessed its viability via experimentation on a prototype implementation.

Figure 12. F-PPC Approach to supporting multiple services. Each user is a member of exactly one user group G_j according to his subscription preferences and receives a Group Authentication Key, GK_j. The user group is in turn a member of one or more subscription groups S_1; ; S_3. Members of subscription group S_k will have Service Authentication Key S_k for each service their group is authorised for.

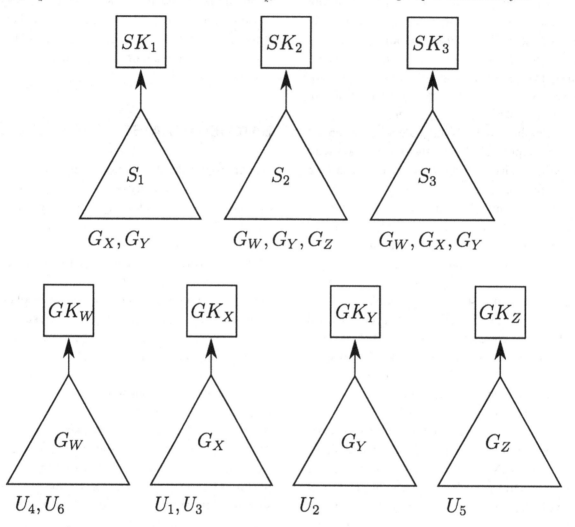

The conditional access system design for this implementation consists of the LKH+ scheme that incorporates a one-way hash function for reducing the size of join messages and a unique "grow" operation that reduces the number of messages that need to be sent for certain types of joins, combined with an adaptation of the multiple service architecture used in F-PPC that allows groupings of channels to share a single key. The solution also attempts to exploit the properties of multicast packet routing for greater efficiency and

increased security. Finally, consideration is given to secure storage of keys at the receiving end to prevent unauthorised disclosure.

Key Hierarchy

This implementation uses the 4-level key hierarchy shown in Figure 13. A user key (UK) is shared between a subscriber and the server and known only to these two parties. The mechanism by which such a key can be shared can vary.

Figure 13. Key hierarchy

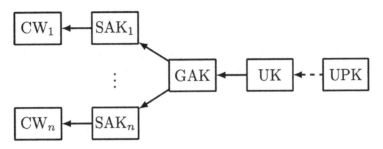

For example, it can be a pre-shared key inserted into a set-top-box's non-volatile memory at the time of manufacture. For this implementation, each set-top-box is provided with a public/private key pair at the time of manufacture. The public key certificate is signed by an appropriate certification authority (this certification authority would be internal to the manufacturer, operator, or conditional access vendor). A negotiation protocol is specified whereby a symmetric key is provided by the server to the subscriber. The symmetric key would typically remain unchanged for the duration of the subscription but the use of the public/private key pair allows for the option to update it if necessary.

The user key can decrypt a Group Authentication Key (GAK), a group key shared amongst users with the same viewing preferences (ie. matching subscription selections). The GAK then decrypts a bouquet authentication key (BAK). In order to maintain compatibility with DVB descrambling equipment and the DVB-CA framework, the actual data stream that is encrypted by our system is the sequence of control words (CWs) used to scramble the video. These control words are updated frequently (as often as every few seconds). The BAK is used to decrypt the control words of each service associated with it. The encrypted CW is transmitted along with the encrypted video content in ECMs. It can be updated as often as the operator likes, without needing the more expensive group rekey operations to be performed so frequently. Further, the distribution of these CWs

is stateless --- if any particular CW is missed by a receiver, it will be able to start decrypting as soon as it receives the next CW (typically within a few seconds), thus resulting in minimal disruption.

Group Key Refreshment

The implementation makes use of the LKH+ algorithm, which in practice is found to perform better than OFT, Briscoe, (1999). This is due to OFT using a binary tree (degree of 2), whereas LKH is not restricted in this way. Wong (2000) found that the optimal degree for a LKH tree is 4, which reduces the height of the tree significantly and therefore the number of key update operations that need to be performed for any join or leave operation.

The literature gives little consideration to the specifics of building and maintaining the structure of a LKH tree. The $O(\log_d n)$ performance of a LKH tree assumes the tree is balanced, however the algorithm does not guarantee this. Haroon (2004) proposes a mechanism for balancing a binary LKH tree based on AVL rotations, however this does not extend to LKH trees of variable degree.

Splitting Leaf Nodes

Once all leaf nodes in a LKH tree of a particular height are full, some mechanism is required for "growing" the tree to insert further members. One approach is to split an existing leaf node by moving it down one level and inserting a new intermediate node as its parent. See Figure 14 for an example. The key update message would be transmitted as follows:

The number of keys to be updated by this method for inserting a new member into an already full tree by this method is $O(\log_d n)$, assuming the tree is balanced initially.

Subtree Insertion Approach

The method used in this implementation, which we believe is novel in this application, is to generate a new root node and insert the existing tree as its first child as a subtree. All existing members thus only have to receive a single key update as follows:

$$s \rightarrow U_4 : GK', K_{456 K_4} \left(\text{unicast} \right)$$

$$s \rightarrow U_1, \dots, : U_3 : GK'_{GK}$$

This approach offers $O(1)$ performance in terms of multicast key updates and keys to be processed by users and maintains a balanced tree structure.

The height of the tree is maintained by inserting h intermediate nodes. The height of the new tree is thus h + 1 as expected and capacity is d-times larger than it was prior to the grow operation. Note that the implementation only allocates memory for the nodes as it is required. Thus in Figure 15 memory for only 7 key nodes is allocated.

Nodes associated with members who have left are marked as unused. On subsequent joins, these unused nodes will be re-purposed before another grow operation takes place. For the pay-TV application, the assumption is made that over time the client base will always grow, and the tree is designed to perform efficiently under this condition.

Service Grouping

In order to support multiple services, subscribers are separated into groups using a method similar to F-PPC. The problem with the technique is discussed in Section 3.4.2. Completely flexible service selection can in the worst case degrade to the situation where each subscriber has a unique

Figure 14. One approach to inserting a new member, U_4, into a full LKH tree

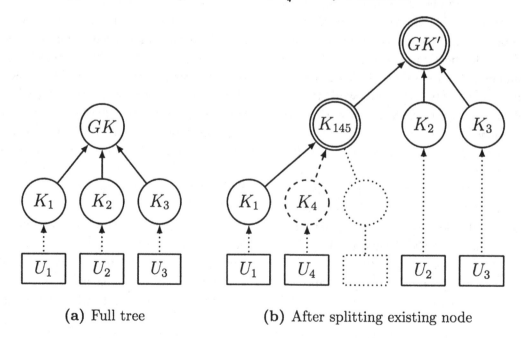

(a) Full tree   (b) After splitting existing node

Figure 15. Subtree insertion approach. Inserting a new member, U_4, into a full LKH tree.

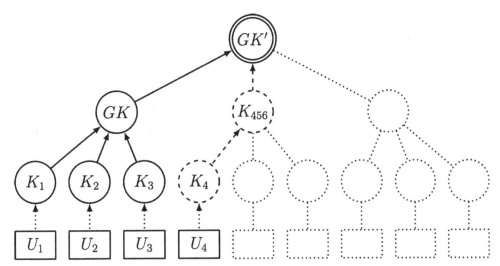

selection. The performance of a key update will be O(n) in that any change in membership will result in at least n update messages being transmitted.

We expand the notion of Service Authorisation Keys to include Bouquet Authorisation Keys (BAKs). Bouquets are operator-defined groupings of services defined by DVB, usually used for convenience in package selection.

A bouquet will be treated as an atomic unit of subscription that contains one or more services. All services in the bouquet can be encrypted with the same key, with no loss of security. The impact of a single BAK compromise is greater than that of a SAK compromise in that it will potentially decrypt multiple services. However it is equivalent to the compromise of a GAK and no more or less likely.

Each LKH+ group is assigned to a separate multicast group. Depending on subscriber distribution characteristics and network infrastructure, this can reduce network load. Primarily, however, it ensures that clients do not receive key updates related to groups they are not interested in.

Simulating Flexible Service Selection

As an aside, I provide a suggestion for simulating flexible service selection. This suggestion is compatible with the proposed multiple service

architecture. Proceed by defining a number of service groupings based on popularity. For example, the most popular services will be in more groupings while the least popular services will be in fewer groupings. These groupings could be refined over time based on subscription history, and will potentially be quite numerous. When a new subscriber joins with a selection of services S, find a grouping G such that S G. The objective is to minimise the size of set G\S so that the subscriber has minimal access to services for which he is not paying. Receiver software could be used to enforce the subscription by disallowing these services.

Example

Refering to Table 2 and Figure 12, if we assume that the keys $\{S_1; ...; S_3\}$ are service bouquets and the SK_i keys are used as BAKs. Suppose a new subscriber U_7 joins with subscription $\{S_1; S_3\}$. He is therefore allocated to group GX. The key trees involved are shown in Figure 16. The LKH+ join algorithm is followed and so an updated GKX will be multicast to users. It is also necessary to update the group keys for each of the bouquets for which GX is a member, thus SK_1 and SK_3 will be updated. The leaf node keys associated with

GX in each of those trees will be updated, and any intermediate keys on the path to the root. Key updates will be delivered as follows:

Note the distinction between member and subscriber/user. The system architecture uses multiple trees to support multiple services. A member of a tree may be either a subscriber or a group of subscribers.

Multi-Device Subscriptions

Modern households often have multiple potential viewing devices: televisions in more than one room, and mobile devices such as tablets and smart-phones, for example. An operator may wish to enable a single subscription to access content on these various devices, possibly for an additional fee per device. This should still maintain the security properties of the system. It must be possible to revoke access for individual devices.

We propose a further extension to the F-PPC service grouping model to allow this, by introducing another level in the key hierarchy for multiple device subscriptions. This extension is illustrated in Figure 17. Devices associated with a particular subscription are grouped together and share a Subscription Authorisation Key (SAK). Each device has an associated Device Key (DK). The SAK is used to decrypt the User Key. Additional considerations need to be implemented to ensure that devices on a single subscription are being used within the subscriber's household (or other authorised location). Various approaches to this are possible. For example, devices might need to be able to communicate with each other on a local network. Alternatively, the

Figure 16. Multiple service architecture: example of user U_7 joining with subscription $\{S_1; S_3\}$. Keys in nodes marked with a double circle are updated.

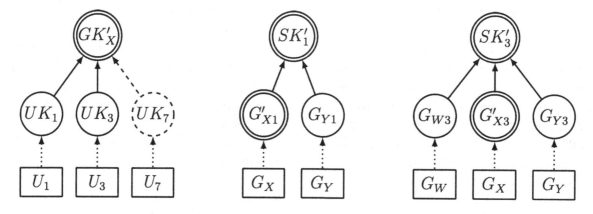

Figure 17. Extended key hierarchy to support multi-device subscriptions

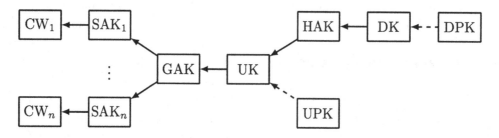

ISP could verify the devices are connecting from the same network endpoint. The expansion of this idea and a possible cryptographic solution to ensuring devices are in the same household is relegated to future work.

INITIAL KEY ESTABLISHMENT

It is assumed that the client and server share a symmetric encryption key, the User Private Key (UPK). The means of sharing this key are dependant on the particular application and operator's requirements. For purpose specific devices such as STBs, the simplest case is that a unique key is installed on the device in the factory. Alternatively, the system-on-a-chip will have a unique key associated with its serial number, both of which are know to the manufacturer and supplied to the operator.

Protocol for Dynamic Key Establishment

Mobile devices such as smart phones and tablets are increasingly popular and prevalent. The trend is towards supplying media to these devices. Such media would be accessible via a third-party ap-

Table 3. Legend: dynamic key establishment protocol

A	Application
K	Trusted Kernel
S	Key Server
K_{AS}	Key to be shared between A and S
K_{UA}, K_{UK}	Public keys of A and K respectively
KR_S	Private key of S
C_A, C_S, C_K	Certificates of A, S, and K, including respective public keys (X.509)
N_A	Nonce generated by A, used to identify this particular interaction
H	Cryptographic hash function

plication installed on the device. It is necessary for the server and the application to share a symmetric key. However the server has no prior knowledge of the device. It needs some way of verifying that the application is trusted before sharing this key. We assume that a trusted kernel (or other secure component of the operating system) is running on the device. The kernel should be able to verify the integrity of applications before executing them, and acts as a trusted intermediary.

The kernel should be able to verify the integrity of applications before executing them, and acts as a trusted intermediary in the following protocol.

$$A \rightarrow A : C_A, C_K, N_A \tag{1}$$

$$S \rightarrow K : \left\langle \left\langle K_{AS}, N_A \right\rangle_{KU_A}, A, C_S \right\rangle_{KU_K}, \\ \left\langle H\left(\left\langle K_{AS}, N_A \right\rangle_{KU_A}, A, C_S \right) \right\rangle_{KR_S} \tag{2}$$

$$K \rightarrow A : \left\langle K_{AS}, N_A \right\rangle_{KU_A} \tag{3}$$

The application needs to take necessary precautions to ensure secure storage of keys provided to it. The trusted kernel should provide encryption services to applications. If the local security of the device is circumvented (commonly referred to as "jailbreaking") so that an untrusted kernel executes, then the security of the protocol fails and an unauthorised application could be supplied with keys. A practical implementation of this protocol would need to take this possibility into account. Further platform-specific steps might need to be taken to disqualify such devices.

KEY SERVER OPERATIONS

The subscribe, change subscription, and unsubscribe operations are assumed to be conducted out-of-band. For example a customer might call the pay-TV operator's call centre and provide personal information, payment details, and a unique device identifier such as a serial number.

Therefore at the time the subscriber is added to the tree, the necessary key updates are made by the server and multicast to the current subscribers. The new subscriber is not necessarily online at that time. When it comes online it must use the rekey request protocol to receive the necessary keys.

Dynamic Subscriptions

In the case of a mobile device, a subscription might be obtained by an "in-app" purchase mechanism (for example Apple iOS in-app purchases). A separate protocol can be defined for communicating the selected services along with payment verification information to the key server. In this case, the protocol would supply the user with necessary keys immediately and then trigger the multicast updates.

Subscribe

The server creates a new subscriber entry and associates it with the leaf node of a particular service group tree. The symmetric key in the associated node is shared with the subscriber, encrypted with the UPK. This is shown in Algorithm 1.

Change Subscription

A subscriber's subscription selection changes. He moved to the new subscriber group. Keys of services that were in the previous subscription are not updated. Suppose the subscriber's existing subscription is given by the set S_E, and his new subscription by S_N. The members of these sets are bouquets which are themselves sets of services.

These bouquets can be divided into 3 groups, shown in Figure 18. $S_E \setminus S_N$ are the bouquets no longer subscribed to: the subscriber needs to be removed from these. $S_N \setminus S_E$ are the new bouquets

Algorithm 1. Add new subscriber

Algorithm 1 Add New Subscriber

1: **procedure** ADDSUBSCRIBER(*subscription, userId, userKey*)

2:     *userGroup* ← MATCHSUBSCRIPTION(*subscription*)

3:     **if** *userGroup* = ∅ **then**   ▷ no matching user group
4:         *userGroup* ← NEWLKHTREE
5:         ADDSUBSCRIPTION(*userGroup, subscription*)
6:         *userGroup*.INSERT(*userId, userKey*)   ▷ *userId* joins *userGroup*
7:         **for all** *service* ∈ *subscription* **do**
8:             *service*.INSERT(*userGroup*) ▷ authorise new group for this bouquet
9:         **end for**
10:     **else**   ▷ found matching user group
11:         *userGroup*.INSERT(*userId, userKey*)
12:         **for all** *service* ∈ *subscription* **do**
13:             *leafNode* ← *service*.FINDLEAFNODE(*userGroup*)
14:             *leafNode*.REKEY
15:         **end for**
16:     **end if**
17: **end procedure**

Figure 18. Difference in subscription sets when changing selection

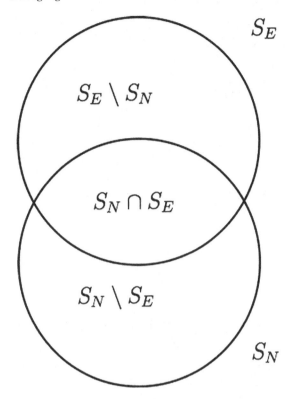

to which the subscriber was previously not subscribed and must be added. $S_E \setminus S_N$ are bouquets which the subscriber has retained. These do not need to be updated.

Unsubscribe

A subscriber is removed entirely. Algorithm 2 shows the operation.

Multicast Rekey Message

The format of key update message as multicast by the key server is shown in Table 4.

It is assumed that the multicast network infrastructure prevents clients from sending information to the multicast group. Therefore it can safely be assumed that messages are from the key server. If this is not the case, a signature needs to

be added to the message for integrity verification. Denial-of-service attacks could distribute bad key update messages intentionally to corrupt the keys stored by clients.

Key Recovery Fallback

The following protocol is defined for client-initiated unicast communication with the key server. This is used when the subscriber initially comes online, and subsequently in the event that it missed some keys and needs to request retransmission. The client establishes a TCP connection to the server and identifies itself. The server responds by sending the updated keys, encrypted with the pre-shared symmetric key UPK.

MULTICAST GROUP SECURITY

Additional protections can be added at the Internet service provider's multicast network level. Specifically, an ISP possesses sufficient information to associate a particular endpoint in the network with a particular subscriber. This information could be used to restrict access to multicast groups based on the subscription associated with that endpoint.

A restriction of this type would mean that an attacker who holds a legitimate subscription but is illegitimately redistributing content would not only have to redistribute decryption keys but also the encrypted content itself. This is because anyone who is not a legitimate subscriber would not be able to join the multicast groups used to distribute the encrypted services, even if they received the keys through some illegitimate means. This would prevent the illegitimate users "piggy-backing" of the legitimate network.

Secure Key Storage

A critical aspect of the security of a cryptographic system is the security of the keys themselves. The discussion thus far has considered mechanisms for

Algorithm 2. Remove subscriber

Algorithm 2 Remove Subscriber

1: **procedure** REMOVESUBSCRIBER($userId$)

2:     $userGroup \leftarrow$ USERGROUPFORID($userId$)
3:     $userGroup$.REMOVE($userId$)

4:     $subscription \leftarrow$ SUBSCRIPTION($userGroup$)
5:     **for all** $service \in subscription$ **do**
6:         $leafNode \leftarrow$ FINDLEAFNODE($userGroup$)
7:         $leafNode$.REKEY
8:     **end for**
9: **end procedure**

Table 4. Rekey message format

Size (Bytes)	Name	Description
1	type	Update type (key data or one-way)
1	count	Number of indivdual key updates in this message
		...
4	updateId	ID of updated key
4	updateVer	Version of updated key
4	decryptId	ID of key used to encrypt payload
4	decryptVer	Version of key used to encrypt payload
16	iv	Initialisation Vector
16	payload	Encrypted Payload:
(16)	updatedKey	Updated Key (AES 128-bit)
		...
4	crc	CRC 32-bit Checksum
54	Total Size	

securely transmitting keys over a network so that only appropriately authorised users will receive them. However once the keys are in the possession of the user, steps need to be taken to prevent their unauthorised disclosure via other channels.

The standard method of protecting keys is in a tamper-resistant device such as a smartcard. The smartcard is able to perform cryptographic operations and often the majority of client-side key handling operations are performed within it. However smartcards incur additional costs and have limitations. Special hardware is required in a set-top-box to interface with them, and this restricts the deployment of a CA system that depends on them to devices with applicable hardware (therefore eliminating devices such as smart-phones and tablets). Royalties are often payable, and smartcards are limited in their processing power and storage capacities potentially restricting the type and frequency of cryptographic operations they can perform.

Therefore in situations were subsidies are involved or otherwise minimizing cost is a factor, or where various types of devices need to be able to receive content, a system secure without the need for a smartcard is necessary. Contemporary STB hardware typically makes use of a secure boot mechanism. Usually some area of the silicon in the device's system-on-a-chip (SoC) and/or its flash memory chips is able to check a cryptographic signature of the software that will be loaded into memory. This ensures that no unauthorised (unsigned) software is able to run on the device. Together with encryption of the applicable areas of non-volatile storage (flash, or hard disk), and encryption of random access memory (RAM encryption is prevalent in STB devices), reasonable assurance can be had that an attacker will not be able to access keys stored on a STB. This assurance is often not sufficient, however. Development of a set-top-box platform might involve multiple parties – the hardware manufacturer (who also develops driver software), user interface software developers, conditional access vendor, pay-TV operator, and increasingly on modern set-top-boxes and media devices, third-party application ("app") developers. This provides multiple avenues for software that will be signed and legitimately running on the device that could potentially gain access to keys via some exploit.

Payne (2007) proposes VAULTS, "a cryptographic access control architecture secure against privileged attackers". He describes a complete access control framework targeted at a multi-user, Unix-like, general purpose operating system. Data stored in this framework is secure even against a user with root access or physical access to the storage medium (such as hard disks). This is distinct from the usual access control scheme that uses active protection enforced by the kernel. Even in a system with full-disk-encryption (FDE), legitimate users might be able to elevate their privileges thus allowing unauthorised access to data belonging to other users.

VAULTS depends on the system having some form of trusted-computing or secure boot module and provides a combination of access control and a cryptographic file system. The secure bootstrap process ensures that the kernel is trusted (the process of assessing/auditing the security of the kernel prior to signing is not considered).

Briefly, each user has a secure repository known as a "vault" (an encrypted area used to store keys, fingerprints (hashes) of system programs, and "tickets" used to access cryptographically protected files. These are decrypted at login and their contents are only accessible by cryptographically verified processes. The secure kernel prevents access to vaults when they are stored in memory. Apart from user vaults, various system vaults and a public-key infrastructure are defined. The kernel acts as an intermediary, decrypting les on behalf of users who hold valid tickets. Users never has direct access to the actual protection keys.

Implementation

A C++ prototype of the conditional access system consisting of client and server components that implement the aforementioned communications protocols and key management scheme was developed. A simulation application provides the server with multiple join and leave requests to collect experimental data.

The simulation bypasses the IP networking interface by directly triggering a large number joins and leaves within the server module. A sample of the total clients added are simulated to monitor their key processing and storage. The component responsible for passing messages to the clients simulates an unreliable multicast network by randomly injects errors into packets, dropping certain packets, and randomly reordering packets before delivering them. The probability of these events occurring is adjustable to simulate the varying reliability of real networks. All key update messages are encrypted with AES in the Cipher-Block-Chaining mode of operation. A randomly generated initialization vector is transmitted along with each encrypted key update message. For simulation purposes, key establishment is achieved by sending a unique symmetric key to each client. This is used for further cryptography operations.

RESULTS AND EVALUATION

Experiments were performed on an Apple Mac-Book Pro with a 2.66 GHz Intel Core i7 processor and 8 GB of RAM. For testing purposes, 50 services and an initial 50,000 subscribers was used. The subscribers are successively joined. Thereafter the simulation increases the subscriber base to 500,000 with varying rates for losing subscribers.

In order to generate experimental data for each test, a number of initial subscribers, **N**, with random subscription choices are successively added to the system. Thereafter, for bandwidth tests, the simulation randomly adds and removes subscribers in a ratio of 9:1 until the subscriber count reaches 2**N**. The simulation uses 50 services divided evenly into 5 bouquets, unless otherwise specified. The subscription choice for a given subscriber is a random selection of between 1 and 5 of the bouquets. A degree of 4 was used for key trees, unless otherwise specified.

Memory Consumption

The graph in Figure 19 shows the memory consumption of the server application as the number of initial subscribers increases to 50,000. Memory consumption is measured using the Mach kernel's task info() utility function. Total resident memory of the process is sampled for 1,000 users added. The graph shows linear memory consumption, O(N) for N subscribers, as is expected. The actual total is approximately 14.5 MB for 50,000 users (degree 4). Projecting this to 10 million subscribers, as an approximation of a large operator, memory usage would be 2.9 GB which is can easily be accommodated in a suitable server's random access memory. Figure 20 shows how total memory consumption is related to degrees of the LKH trees. It is expected that a higher degree has lower memory consumption because fewer intermediate nodes are required.

Figure 19. Server memory consumption for varying numbers of subscribers

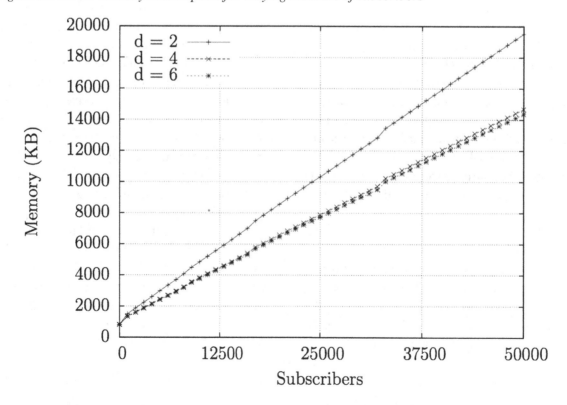

Figure 20. Server memory consumption for varying degrees of the LKH trees

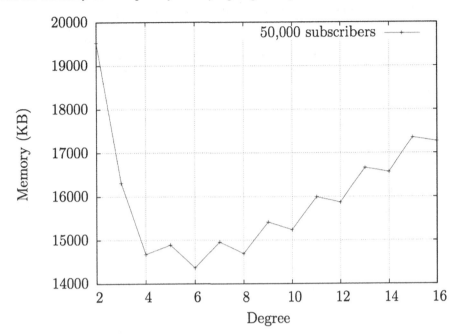

The server process was run for each of the degrees from 2 to 16 and 50,000 subscribers were added. Minimum memory usage was found to be achieved with a degree of 6, which uses 25% less memory than a binary tree. With further increases to the degree, memory usage starts to increase approximately linearly. It is observed that even degrees use less memory than the adjacent odd degrees. This is due to wasted space caused by the memory manager's alignment rules. The implementation makes a large number of dynamic memory allocations. Using a memory pool could reduce or eliminate wasted space.

The total number of nodes N in a single full tree of height h and degree d is given by:

$$N = \frac{1 - d^{h+1}}{1 - d}$$

where the height h for n members is given by:

$$h - \log_d n$$

Figure 21 compares the total number of nodes allocated for 50,000 subscribers to the number that would be needed for a single tree. The graph shows that increasing the degree causes the total number of nodes to tend towards the minimum required which would be 50,000 nodes (no intermediate nodes). The overhead of additional keys to support the multiple service architecture is shown to be approximately constant and minimal. This is because of the system property that restricts a subscriber to exactly one grouping. Dividing **N** subscribers amongst multiple trees uses approximately the same number of nodes as a single tree containing all N subscribers. The overhead comes from the nodes comprising the service trees.

To assess differences in performance between the two approaches to growing a full tree (splitting leaf nodes and subtree insertion) 50,000 members were added to a single tree and the total number of key updates were counted. Subtree insertion results in fewer total key updates than splitting leaf nodes. Additionally, the subtree insertion approach was significantly faster in our implementation (Table 5).

Figure 21. Total nodes to support 50,000 subscribers for varying degrees of the constituent trees. Compared against the number of nodes for a single tree of 50,000 subscribers.

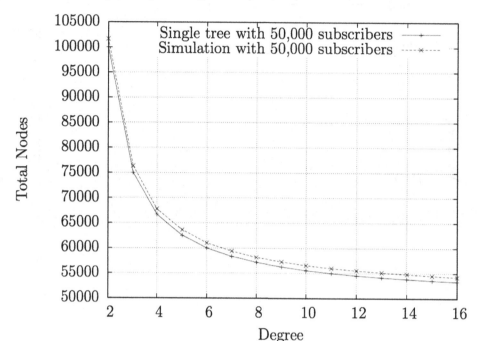

Table 5. Time to insert 50000 users

	Time	
	Total (s)	**Average (msec)**
Subtree Insertion	3.83	0.077
Leaf Node Splitting	25.97	0.519

This improvement is due to the single update message required to replace the group key when the tree grows in the subtree insertion approach. Subtree insertion performs marginally better in this case as shown in Figure 22. This is because new subscribers are inserted into subtrees that are initially empty and so joins after a grow operation affect fewer existing subscribers.

While the subtree insertion operation supports rapidly growing the tree, as presented in this thesis it does not cater for shrinking the tree again in the case of a large number of members being removed. While memory associated with user keys is freed when those users are removed, the structure of intermediate nodes remains.

With the leaf nodes splitting approach, if all siblings of a particular leaf node are removed, the intermediate parent node can be eliminated to shrink the tree (this was not implemented). The tree will become unbalanced, and rebalancing the tree is nontrivial and potentially expensive in terms of key updates. In this implementation, the leaf node to split is chosen from the shortest subtree. Finding the shortest subtree causes the leaf node splitting operation to be time consuming relative to the subtree insertion approach.

Bandwidth usage was calculated by increasing the number of subscribers from 50,000 to 100,000, with randomized adding and removing of subscribers in a 9:1 ratio. This simulates a pay-TV operator that is growing overall, with a 10% rate of turnover.

Total data sent by the server is divided by the total number of add and remove operations. The results are shown in Table 6. The average data required to deliver key updates for add or remove operation using LKH trees is 13.35 KB or 4.8 KB when using LKH+ key-trees.

Figure 22. Weight of subtree insertion compared to splitting leaf nodes. Inserting nodes into a single tree of degree 4.

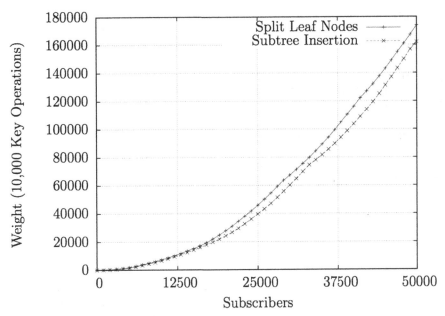

Table 6. Update Size per Add/Remove Operation. Total shown is the bandwidth required to increase subscribers from 50,000 to 100,000.

	Average Update Size (KB)			Total (MB)
	Add	Remove	Combined	
LKH	13.21	14.57	13.35	817.3
LKH+ Joins	3.71		4.81	294.7

These figures can be compared against unicast distribution of a group key to all subscribers, or equivalently, multicasting the group key to all users encrypted with their UPK. A single add or remove operation with 100,000 subscribers would require transmitting 5,272 KB per group key, assuming the same update message size. This could be reduced to 1,367 KB for joins by using a one-way function. The bandwidth savings of using the proposed solution is many orders of magnitude, allowing more frequent updates to be performed.

These size calculations are based on the key update packet format that we defined earlier and exclude the size of UDP and IP packet headers. This represents all outgoing key updates from the server, including initial unicast delivery to subscribers. All keys are transmitted only once, with no batched updates.

The implementation supports an optional batch mode. The effect of batched updates on outgoing server bandwidth and client operations was tested by varying the number of add/remove operations per batch. Figure 23 shows that bandwidth initially reduces significantly as batch size increases, then flattens out for a batch size of about 300. At that point the multicast group updates have reduced to almost zero, and the remaining bandwidth usage is for initial unicast transmission of keys to joining members.

Similarly, the average number of key updates that a client has to process drops significantly with increase in batch size as shown in Figure 24. Note that for any single batch update operation, the number of key updates that a client processes will not be reduced from that of a non-batch operation (and may in fact be slightly greater).

These results show that use of even moderately sized batches result in an appreciable reduction in bandwidth overhead. In a pay-TV environment,

Figure 23. Effect of batches on outgoing server bandwidth. Data transfer required to increase subscribers from 50,000 to 100,000, with 10% turnover.

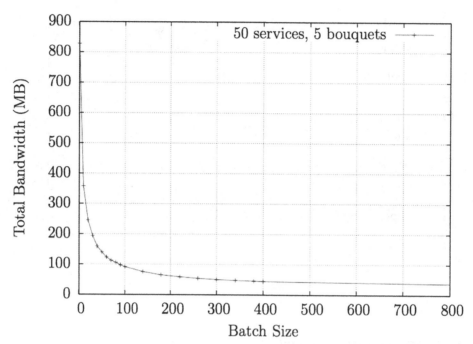

dependant on subscriber turnover rates and subscription periods, batches could be run daily or every few days.

FUTURE RESEARCH DIRECTIONS

Summary

In proposing this area of research, the following questions were posed. How best can existing research in key management techniques be combined to provide a flexible and practical conditional access system for IPTV? The proposed solution and results have shown that it is possible to successfully develop a workable framework that could be used as a basis for a commercial CA system.

The protocols that have been designed and presented do not require a smart card as a secure storage mechanism. All that is required is a system that can verify the integrity of authenticated code and assure that is guaranteed not to disclose keys. Different components (processes) within the system can exchange keys similarly, for example using Diffie-Helman key exchange or a public-key infrastructure using a framework similar to VAULTS.

The system keeps shared keys on hand for each user, and incorporates a key negotiation protocol. It is therefore suitable for encrypted VOD content on a per-user basis using the User Key directly. An extension supporting multiple devices was proposed and expansion on this could be an area for future work.

Directions for Future Work

Software

Additional work on the software would require developing more comprehensive networking code, integration with a proper subscriber management system that possibly incorporates direct sign-up, integrating the server and client with a media streaming framework such as the Live555 libraries (which supports RTP, RTCP, and RTSP),

Figure 24. Effect of batches on average number of keys processed by clients per add/remove operation

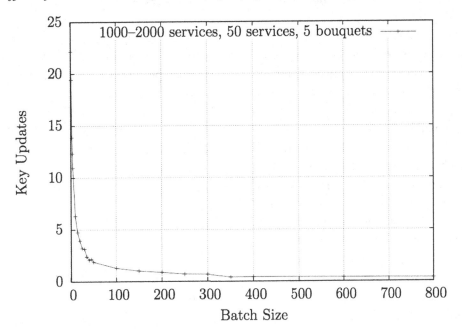

Green Technology

The current global trend is towards energy saving and "green" technology. From both a legislated and ethical standpoint, developing devices such as set-top-boxes that have minimal power consumption is highly desirable. A critical component of this is the standby power consumption of a device. That is, how much power it uses when in standby mode.

In the European Union, for example, legislation states that electrical devices sold after December 2012 should use no more than 0.5 Watts in standby mode (or 1 Watt if they display information such as a clock when in standby). This places restrictions on the operation of a set-top-box. Typically, satellite set-top-boxes in standby only disable their video and audio outputs and otherwise maintain full connections to the satellite network. This is in order to receive software updates, altered programme schedules, and most importantly, group key updates and other entitlement information. If

modification to comply with the DVB-IPTV standard, and general performance and robustness improvements.

such a set-top-box is properly powered-o for any period of time (often only possible by physically unplugging it), once turned on again it often takes quite a while to start descrambling video. This is because of the carousel fallback mechanism that is in place for recovering after missed key updates. In any system with no return-path, the only way to distribute potentially missed keys to clients is to continuously broadcast them.

The design of the conditional access system therefore has direct implications on the power usage and environmental impact of a set-top-box. While these power savings for a single set-top-box might seem insignificant, cumulatively they are very significant. A multiple-tuner, high-definition satellite PVR might use as a much as 100 Watts when operating. If this is reduced to 1 Watt when in standby, a savings of 99 Watts is achieved. Assuming the majority of set-top-boxes are in standby most of the time, in a network with 5 million subscribers a total power reduction of 495MW is possible (almost a third of the total power generation capacity of Koeberg Nuclear Power Station).

Maintaining a STB network connection and other processing functions with less than 1 Watt of power is not feasible with current technology. It should therefore be clear that any stateful conditional access system needs to rely on a fallback mechanism to supply missed key updates to devices that have been o or in standby. The time complexity of the aforementioned carousel mechanism is O(n), for a system with n subscribers. In practice this creates a bad user experience as the waiting period for a system with a realistic subscriber base can be up to an hour (a very poor user experience if this occurs every time the STB is turned on. Overcoming this might require a reduction in the frequency of key updates, potentially resulting in a reduction of the security of the system).

In an IPTV network, a return path is available. A reliable fallback method is therefore for a client to establish a unicast connection to the key server and request the latest group key. However, dependant on the frequency of key updates, this will degrade to the situation where all clients need to establish a fallback connection every time they are powered on. This will negatively impact network bandwidth and place extremely high demand on the server. A stateless conditional access system would avoid many of these problems. Additions or modifications to a technique such as SDR that accounts for the poor performance in the case of removed users would be a good direction for future work. Academic research in this area is on-going.

Network Simulation

More comprehensive network simulation with a system such as NS-3 would be relevant if detailed information about a real topology was available. This would need to include the operator network, ISPs and other intermediate service providers, end users' networks, and so forth. Such a simulation would allow measurements of traffic flow, and more accurate simulation of failures.

CONCLUSION

We have highlighted the primary problem areas in granting conditional access to pay-TV content and have proposed some workable solutions for resource-constrained environments to address the problems that we highlighted. There is much scope for future work in extending the solution, and in fact in the greater problem of end-to-end content security.

REFERENCES

Azad, M., Ahmed, A., & Alam, A. (2010). Digital Rights Management. *International Journal of Computer Science and Network Security*, *10*, 11.

Briscoe, B. (1999). MARKS: Zero side eect multicast key management using arbitrarily revealed key sequences. In *Proc. First International Workshop On Networked Group Communication* (NGC'99). NGC.

Cruickshank, H., Howarth, M., & Iyengar, S. A. (2005). *Comparison between satellite DVB conditional access and secure IP multicast*. Paper presented at the 14th IST Mobile and Wireless Communications Summit. New York, NY.

European Telecommunications Standards Institute. (1997). *Digital Video Broadcasting: Framing structure, channel coding and modulation for 11/12 GHz satellite services*. European Standard EN 300-421. Author.

European Telecommunications Standards Institute. (2009). *Digital Video Broadcasting: Transport of MPEG-2 TS Based DVB Services over IP Based Networks*. ETSI TS 102 034, August 2009. Author.

European Telecommunications Standards Institute. (2011, September). Digital Video Broadcasting: Support for use of the DVB Scrambling Algorithm version 3 within digital broadcasting systems. *ETSI TS*, *100*, 289.

Floyd, S., Jacobson, V., Liu, C., McCanne, S., & Zhang, L. (1997, December). A reliable multicast framework for light-weight sessions and application level framing. *IEEE/ACM Transactions on Networking, 5*(6), 784–803. doi:10.1109/90.650139

Haroon, J. (2004). *Decentralized key management for large dynamic multicast groups using distributed balanced trees.* (Master's thesis). National University of Computer and Emerging Sciences, Lahore, Pakistan.

Irdeto, B. V. (2011). *Irdeto.* Retrieved from http://www.irdeto.com/

McGrew, D. A., & Sherman, A. T. (1998). Key establishment in large dynamic groups using one-way function trees. *IEEE Transactions on Software Engineering.*

Montpetit, M., Mirlacher, T., & Ketcham, M. (2010). IPTV: An end to end perspective. *The Journal of Communication, 5,* 5.

Nagravision, S. A. (2011). *Nagravision.* Retrieved from http://www.nagravision.com/

Naor, D., Naor, M., & Lotspiech, J. (2001). Revocation and tracing schemes for stateless receivers. In *Advances in Cryptology* (pp. 41–62). Springer-Verlag. doi:10.1007/3-540-44647-8_3

NDS. (2011). *NDS VideoGuard.* Retrieved from http://www.nds.com/

Payne, C. A. (2007). Cryptographic Access Control Architecture Secure Against Privileged Attackers. In *Proceedings of the 2007 ACM workshop on Computer security architecture.* ACM.

Perlman, R. (1997). *"LKH+": Simplication of LKH, an observation from the conference floor.* Academic Press.

Rivest, R. L., Shamir, A., & Adleman, L. (1978, February). A method for obtaining digital signatures and public-key cryptosystems. *Communications of the ACM, 21*(2), 120–126. doi:10.1145/359340.359342

Setia, S., Koussih, S., Jajodia, S., & Harder, E. (2000). *Kronos: A scalable group rekeying approach for secure multicast.* Paper presented at the IEEE Symposium on Security and Privacy. Oakland, CA.

Setia, S., Zhu, S., & Jajodia, S. (2002). A comparative performance analysis of reliable group rekey transport protocols for secure multicast. Performance Evaluation, 21-41.

Speakman, T., Crowcroft, J., Gemmell, J., Farinacci, D., Lin, S., & Leshchiner, D. et al. (2001). *PGM Reliable Transport Protocol Specication. Request for comments 3208.* Internet Engineering Task Force.

Sun, H., Chen, C., & Shieh, C. (2008, October). Flexible-Pay-Per-Channel: A New Model for Content Access Control in Pay-TV Broadcasting Systems. *IEEE Transactions on Multimedia, 10*(6), 1109–1120. doi:10.1109/TMM.2008.2001381

Vermeulen, J. (2012). *Subscriber selected DStv channels demanded, My Broadband Tech News.* Retrieved from http://mybroadband.co.za/news/broadcasting/56271-subscriber-selected-dstv-channels-demanded.html

Wallner, D. M., Harder, E. J., & Agee, R. C. (1999). *Key management for multicast: Issues and architectures.* Request for comments 2627, Internet Engineering Task Force (June 1999).

Wong, C. K. (2000). Secure group communications using key graphs. *IEEE/ACM Transactions on Networking, 8*(1), 16–30. doi:10.1109/90.836475

Yang, Y., Li, X., Zhang, X., & Lam, S. (2001). Reliable group rekeying: design and performance analysis. In Proceedings of ACM SIGCOMM 2001 (pp. 27-38). ACM.

Zhu, S., & Jajodia, S. (2010). Scalable group key management for secure multicast: A taxonomy and new directions. In S. C. H. Huang, D. MacCallum, & D. Du (Eds.), *Network Security* (pp. 57–75). Springer. doi:10.1007/978-0-387-73821-5_3

Zhu, S., Setia, S., & Jajodia, S. (2003). Adding reliable and self-healing key distribution to the subset dierence group rekeying method. In *Proceedings of the 5th COST 264 International Workshop on Networked Group Communications*. Springer-Verlag.

ADDITIONAL READING

Byun, J.-W., & Li, N. (2008). Purpose based access control for privacy protection in relational database systems. *The VLDB Journal*, *17*(4), 603–619. doi:10.1007/s00778-006-0023-0

Kayem, A. V. D. M., Akl, S. G., & Martin, P. (2010). Adaptive Cryptographic Access Control, volume 48 of Advances in Information Security. Springer, 2010.

Meinel, C., & Sack, H. (2014). *Internet-Working: Technological Foundations and Applications*. Berlin, Germany: Springer.

Menezes, A. J., van Oorschot, P. C., & Vanstone, S. A. (1997) Handbook of Applied Cryptography. CRC Press. Taylor & Francis Group. New York, USA.

Osborn, S., Sandhu, R., & Munawer, Q. (2000). Conguring role-based access control to enforce mandatory and discretionary access control policies. *ACM Transactions on Information and System Security*, *3*(2), 1–23. doi:10.1145/354876.354878

Sandhu, R. S. (2000). Engineering authority and trust in cyberspace: the om-am and rbac way. In ACM Workshop on Role-Based Access Control, pages 111-119, 2000.

Yee, G. O. M. (Ed.). (2012). *Privacy, Protection Measures and Technologies in Business Organizations: Aspects and Standards*. USA: IGI Global.

KEY TERMS AND DEFINITIONS

Access Control: Restricts who can join a network or make use of a service. Once a user is authenticated, it grants them access in accordance with their associated authorisations.

Authentication: Is the process of one entity verifying the identity of another checking it is who it claims to be. Authentication might be conducted mutually or in one direction only. It protects against fabrication attacks. For example, the pay-TV operator needs to authenticate subscribers (specifically their receiving device) to associate them with a valid subscription.

Availability: A system must remain available for those for whom it is intended. Denial-of-service and interruption are attacks against availability.

Confidentiality: Ensures that information is only disclosed to authorised recipients. An attacker eavesdropping on a network will not be able to read the information. It is protection against interception attacks. In the context of pay-TV, confidentiality is required to ensure that only authorised subscribers are able to access content.

Integrity: Is the ability to ensure that the data received is unchanged from what was sent. It provides protection against modification attacks as well as corruption of data that might occur in transit.

Non-Repudiation: Is the ability of a system to ensure that a user cannot deny involvement in communications that have been sent or received and acknowledged. In the context of business systems, such a service would be required to prove a customer placed an order, for example.

Section 2
Cyber-Defense Challenges

Chapter 6
Standing Your Ground:
Current and Future Challenges in Cyber Defense

Barry V. W. Irwin
Rhodes University, South Africa

ABSTRACT

This chapter explores the challenges facing those involved in cyber defense at a national, organizational, and individual level. As the global economy grows more dependent on the Internet and connected infrastructure, the risk and impact of attack grows. A long-standing response to attacks of various kinds conducted on the Internet has been to filter traffic but not to respond. In some cases, reactive action is taken, but even where attribution is possible, prosecution is rare. In recent months, several countries have stated their policy of military response where they feel that their national infrastructure is threatened. The risk to organizations, civilian populations, and individuals is discussed in the case of such militant response or retaliation. The chapter further considers aspects such as reputation, neutrality, and the concept of Internet "kill switches."

INTRODUCTION

The realization of cyberwarfare, and cyber attacks has increased since the significant events of May 2007, in what has become termed the Estonian Incident. Denial of Service attacks affecting nation states have subsequently occurred on a number of occasions. In recent months the discovery of the Flame malware has raised more questions in terms of the offensive capability of nation states, with this software exhibiting previously unprecedented sophistication. At the opposing end of the spectrum individuals and organizations often bear the brunt of malicious online activity. This chapter considers the challenges that emerging Internet states need to consider as part of their future development and planning. An integral part of this is to consider the approach taken when individuals and organizations detect and need to decide on an appropriate response to such attacks.

Section 2 briefly explores the evolution of Security on the Internet, considering the substantial changes that have taken place. This is followed in Section 3 by a discussion of current challenges faced in cyber defense. The future challenges from the perspective of the author are explored in Section 4.

DOI: 10.4018/978-1-4666-6158-5.ch006

EVOLUTION OF SECURITY

The Internet has transitioned from its largely academic roots, where the principles of openness and data sharing were paramount to a global network, vital to global commerce and communication. Possibly as a factor of the rapid growth, legal systems globally have failed to keep up, and the ease with which actions may be performed on or against system located in areas geographically distant to the instigator, have made the enforcement of traditional laws difficult. The question of legal jurisdiction in such cross border incidents greatly complicates the resolution from a law enforcement perspective. The long standing principle employed by many network administrators has been to protect the border and implement appropriate technologies to manage the communications of what has become an increasingly hostile, exterior network to those hosts within their organization. This thin veil of security, aptly described by Bill Cheswick as a "sort of crunchy shell around a soft, chewy center" (Cheswick, 1990), has probably never been more apt. The initial approach taken with the widespread adoption of firewall systems was to block the known bad (blacklisting), which has transitioned to largely block everything except what we need (whitelisting). In both approaches, the majority of organizations still focus their defensive efforts outwards. The act of blocking itself takes many forms. Considering the case of the traditional IP Firewall, a block is often differentiated between two states: Deny: in which IP datagrams matching the rule are discarded, and Block: in which prior to the discard a protocol relevant error message is sent indicating this has occurred.

In the case of blocking, the RFC specifications for the ICMP protocol provide for fairly specific signaling as to why a packet may have been dropped (IANA, 2008) (which may not have been only due to security reasons). A similar approach is taken when dealing with email, where spam is either discarded (preferably pre-acceptance) or a notification of the message having been quarantined or tagged is sent.

In recent years many organizations have started to consider the implications of focusing defensive resources inwards on their networks. While in many ways this has been primarily driven by technologies such as DLP (Data Loss/Leak Prevention), a secondary driver has been seen to be the mitigation of risk and liability. Considering the scenario of an administrator detecting repeated port scanning activity from a source, the response has usually consisted of a number of distinct phases.

- **Attribution:** The source(s) are identified, initially as an IP address, and then resolved using various methods to a source organization. This organization may be an endpoint, or in the case of consumer Internet access, an Internet service provider.
- **Action:** The identified sources are blocked, usually at the firewall or routing infrastructure at the point where the administrator has control.
- **Complaint:** A notification of the malicious activity is sent to the responsible organization, usually as an email directed to the abuse@ email address, which is required to exist as per RFC 2142 (Crocker, 1997). This is not always successful, as the addresses often do not exist or no response is received. An escalation path is typically followed with the provider of network access to that organization.

In severe cases such as Denial of Service (DoS) attacks an organization may need to liaise with their upstream network provider(s) in order to perform mitigation actions as close to the ingress point of the traffic as possible. In some circumstances, Network Providers may de-announce targeted network address blocks, resulting in all traffic destined for these ranges of addresses being dropped. An alternate approach is selective null-routing of the traffic on specific network devices, which causes it to be dropped. In either of these scenarios, the targeted organization can end up suffering a more substantial outage than was initially caused by an attack.

This raises the question of responsibility. Network Providers usually have clauses dealing with disconnection or dropping of traffic built into their operation agreements and Acceptable Use Policies (AUP) with their clients. When these are considered, what has traditionally been dealt with as a technical network operational issue can a list of sites not complying to the norm is maintained at http://www.rfc-ignorant.org/ now be seen to be a potentially significant element in organizational risk management.

One of the most prevalent forms of abuse complaints is the Cease and Desist type most commonly led by firms acting on behalf of media companies and groups such as the Motion Picture Association of America (MPAA - http://www.mpaa.org/) and Recording Industry Association of America (RIAA - http://www.riaa.com/) against claims copyright violators. This is a request that the recipient cease form a particular action or potentially face legal action. The validity of these claims in areas outside of the jurisdiction of the organizations issuing them has become a hotly debated topic. While much of the legal groundwork and debates has been around piracy and copyright violation, the lessons learned can be well applied to shutting down malicious activity form a cyber defense point of view.

One of the most contentious topics raised within the Information Security community in recent years, is that of strike-back or aggressive self defense of one's assets against an aggressor. Parallels have been dawn between existing law dealing with one right to defend one's own property and person in the physical world, but no definitive legislation has been passed in this area clearly defining the so-called rules of engagement. This has been variously described as going a step

beyond just blocking traffic, but rather attempting to shut down the source of the malicious activity. To a large extent this is still a legal grey-area. Legitimate take downs have been conducted, but these have consumed substantial resources, and been executed under judicial warrants. Should individuals, organizations, and nations have the right, and ability, to defend their networks and systems from attack?

CURRENT CYBER DEFENSE ISSUES

In recent months a number of states the USA (Alexander, 2011), but also notably Russia and China (Manson, 2011), have stated that they will respond with physical force using their military to perceived major threats against their cyber infrastructures. Some thought into this possibility by Waxman (2010), who highlights the point that Military attacks are considered illegal under international law, with exceptions for self-defense or when authorized by the U.N. Security Council. While military action in response to an electronic threat may seem extreme, it provides a useful entry into the discussion of cyber defense and the problems being faced by a range of partied online today.

This section opens with a consideration of the context in which the three primary classes of entity on the internet experience cyber defense. This is followed by a brief discussion around the problem of attribution, incident response, and ongoing defensive measures to support operational needs.

Context

The context in which current cyber defense issues needs to be considered can be broken down into three broad groups. These groups are important to consider both as groupings of increasing vulnerability, but also as groups which can have positive impacts on the overall state of online safety.

Individual

Individual users represent the most significant portion of the Internet user base, by some orders of magnitude, yet have a disproportionally insignificant ability to influence activities and policy. Conversely it is this body that has the most opportunity to influence the realities of the day-to-day running of the Internet. This group of users is also as a whole the most exposed to, and under resourced with regards to skills, knowledge and finance to deal with malicious activity. This population may also be vulnerable to either recruitment or co-option into performing malicious activity, whether motivated by political, socio-economic, or criminal ideals.

Organizational

Organizations range in size from SME operations to multinational organization, with operational capacities exceeding some nation states. At the smaller end of this spectrum, organizations are often unaware that they have been attacked or are party to an attack on others. An example of this is evidenced by the prevalence of phishing activity hosted on the websites of these organizations, which often goes undetected until reported to the hosting provider. Unless staff are highly motivated, incidents are often ignored or go unreported. Larger organizations have the resources, from a legal, technical and financial standpoint to be able to deal with substantial activity, and are often compelled to given the risk of damage to brand and/or reputation in the event of incidents, such as data disclosure, defacements or outages.

These bodies consist of individuals working towards a common goal, but at the same time the organization, particularly at the larger end of the spectrum, is seen as a faceless entity. Employee dissatisfaction or disillusionment, may well account for the significant proportion of incidents reported by organization originating from inside the network. Employees may also neglect their responsibilities for cyber security as it may be seen as the organizations problem.

National

The interests of a nation state are the most significant. A nation state may choose to act when the situation with a particular incident targeting the state as a whole, or significant elements such as critical infrastructure or financial services becomes critical.

This decision may be due to a (perceived) threat to National infrastructure, and could be regarded as valid in terms of self-defense under International Law. This could be Internet infrastructure residing within the national boundaries, or other so-called critical infrastructure such as electrical power, water or general telecommunications.

The resources that a nation state is able to bear are substantial, ranging from seizing administrative control of network ingress points to direct military intervention. Given these resources, consideration must be given as to what an appropriate response to a given threat is.

Attribution

One of the biggest challenges facing cyber security professionals is that of attribution. This is a well established problem, where systems involved in cybercrime, or other malicious activity, are rarely those which can be attributed to the perpetrators of such actions. This is further complicated by situations where IP addresses are shared due to technologies such as network address translation (NAT) or Proxy servers. On the case of the former, it's often near impossible to apportion responsibility to a party behind the NAT gateway.

While many parties involved in Information Security are primarily concerned with the attribution of responsibility. These same parties are often hard pressed to be able to perform the attribution process within their own organization when receiving complaints from other parties. A particular area of concern is wireless networks, where there is a history of malicious activity being performed using either open wireless networks or having intruded on the networks. The same can be said of shared computing resources such as Internet cafes, computer laboratories or consoles at schools or universities. Legislation such as South Africa's Electronic Communications and Transactions Act (Republic of South Africa, 2002), and similar legislation elsewhere, places a burden of record keeping on organizations for attribution. Recent media attention has focused on the anti-piracy legislation enacted in France and the United Kingdom, where Internet Service Providers have been tasked to attribute claims of copyright infringement to their users, and act against repeat offenders.

A larger problem exists with the rise of the use of networks of compromised systems in order to execute nefarious activities online, as explored by Clarke and Landau (2010). The question of where the attribution should lie in the event of an individual's system being part of a botnet denial of service attack needs to be considered. Should the individual be held responsible (when the software is almost certainly installed on their system unbeknownst to them)? Alternately, should the parties running the botnet be held liable? What about the party who rented the botnet in order to execute the attack? Current legal frameworks have extreme difficulty when dealing with issues such as this.

Blind altering of traffic, or any kind of aggressive or intrusive response to these kinds of hosts is likely to do more harm than good, in terms of reputational damage to the organization perpetuating it, and to the often innocent and unaware targets (McMahan, 1994). Consider the extreme of where an actor makes use of a botnet either of its own creation or obtained via rental of compromised systems to attack another party.

Attribution efforts are likely to lead to the endpoints, who may be guilty of nothing more than practicing poor digital hygiene. It may be near on impossible to locate the operators or executors of the attack.

Response

In an ideal world perpetrators of malicious acts would be brought to book. Given the complications of attribution many organizations cease their response at the point where services have been restored and the threat mitigated. Follow-up and further investigation is usually only warranted in cases where substantial financial loss or other damage has occurred. One of the areas where a positive response has been seen is in the areas of combating phishing and spamming operations. When dealing with these, the majority of providers acting fairly swiftly in the take-down of these operations.

Pursuing further actions in response to an incidents, particularly those taking place cross-border, requires both substantial motivation, the involvement of law enforcement, and financial resources. The high profile cases involving the shutdown of the Maraposa (Thompson, 2010) and DNSchanger (Federal Bureau of Investigation, 2011) botnets are examples of where this has been successful.

Operational Defense

Organisms as, part of their ongoing biological process, process stimuli and produce a response. Considering malicious activity as a stimulus the idea that needs to be discussed is what an appropriate response to this stimulus is? The first point to consider with regard to cyber defense is as to whether the stimulus is recognized, with much malicious activity going undetected for extended periods of time. The chances of this occurring in a timely manner increase with the relative 'size' of the target, but other factors also influence this. Once recognized, the choice as to whether to respond needs to be made. Assuming a response is decided on there are a number of options which can be followed. The gamut of options runs form ignoring the incident as nuisance traffic, to actively altering, to engaging with law enforcement and pursuing legal avenues at the other.

From an operational perspective the primary concern is to return the organization to normality. In practical terms, in the case of malicious traffic coming over the network, this means blocking incoming network traffic, thereby mitigating the threat. This can be done at either their own boundary, or in conjunction with upstream providers.

From this point complaints and notification of the activity can be passed top parties identified by the attribution process. Remedial action is generally likely to occur other than in cases involving phishing and spamming, which have a raise awareness level, and are generally recognized to be criminal activities. The general understanding of a port-scan or brute for attempt against a service is less clear cut.

FUTURE CHALLENGES

Considering the issues discussed above, five distinct areas deemed to pose particular challenges in terms of ongoing and future cyber defense. These are discussed below.

Aggression

The first of these areas to consider is what constitutes aggression. Being able to quantify the degree of the attack is key in being able to then respond with appropriate force (being one of the tenets of most common understandings of the concept of self-defense in the physical world) (Hoisington, 2009). Two of the most common activities observed by hosts on the Internet are generic portscanning and bruteforcing of common services - particularly the Secure Shell protocol (SSH). While the former can be seen as the physical equivalent of checking if a door is unlocked, the latter is an active attempt to achieve an intrusion on a system. While portscanning is largely an annoyance it could be potentially part of a more sophisticated attack. The counterargument to this is that a sophisticated targeted attack is likely to be more subtle, and hence less likely to be detected. Common responses to the brute-forcing issue (also increasingly common with VoIP services) is to alter the source host after a specified number of connections. The matter that needs to be considered is how should one respond to threats on a larger scale. Waxman (2010) discusses the concept of both for and its appropriateness in the context of the United Nations Charter.

Reputation

The reputation of parties transacting on the Internet is especially important. In the event of organizations or net-blocks persisting with malicious behavior. They could become subject to altering or blackhole routing by other parties online. If the problem is severe enough upstream providers may need to resort in termination of their uplink.

While this approach may be appropriate for end users or organizations on the 'edge' of the network, a number of problems become apparent when one considers the impact that such accounts could have if applied higher up the connectivity chain. The potential exists for organizations and individuals to be significantly impacted should an ISP servicing them consistently fail to respond to malicious traffic exiting their network. This has already been seen in the realm of anti-spam solutions where large blocks of IP address space have been tagged as spam sources and hence had e-mail emanating from them tagged as spam, or rejected. Countries seen as havens for criminal activity could face sanction from network providers, and other states, particularly those with the capability to provide network transit. In the past, large portions of Korean and Nigerian address space have been ltered by US and European providers, due to spam and scam emails emanating from these countries. African nations are particularly at risk given the recent inux of Internet connectivity, and the relatively low skill levels and awareness around cyber security.

Kill-Switches

Following from the discussion above, consideration needs to be given to the issue of does one county have the right to kill traffic to other countries, particularly when providing transit for links from submarine cables to landlocked neighbors. An example of a situation where this could have been considered was during the cyber attacks on Georgia, related to the geostrategic conflict involving South Ossetia in 2008 (Hollis, 2011). Much of this traffic was routed though terrestrial breoptic links running though Turkey. The net result was that Turkish internet users were negatively affected. Related to this is the concept of proverbial kill-switches, which have been proposed by a number of governments with the intention of being able to isolate the countries network in the event of a major threat. The practicalities of implementing such a system aside, the number of parties potentially affected should such a system be realized. When one considers highly connected countries such as the Netherlands, United Kingdom, and USA and the impact on the global network should they theoretically sever their communication paths, the negative impact and collateral damage against innocent parties both internal and (possibly unwittingly) using these Internet Exchange points for transit would be significant.

Neutrality and Mutual Aid

The concepts of a neutral state and military mutual-aid need to be reassessed as the world becomes increasingly connected. Consider the case of a country who has declared its neutrality in a dispute between two others. Traffic for one of the disaffected parties transits though the neutral state.

How would interfering with the traffic in transit be interpreted. Related to this is the concept of traditional military mutual aid agreements, such as the NATO bloc. How will these treaties be bought to bear in the future should member states be threatened not by physical hostilities, but rather against their telecommunications networks and other critical infrastructure? This issues were raised within NATO following the Estonian incidents of 2007, and revisited in the aftermath of the Attacks on Georgia (Tikk et al., 2008).

International Co-Operation

As legal systems mature, and law enforcement skills are developed we are likely to see increased collaboration in dealing with malicious activity. This has to some extent been seen with takedown operations against spam operations and botnet control nodes; although these have been largely driven by the private sector, with Microsoft in particular having taken a leading role.

CONCLUSION

This chapter has presented a number of challenges faced by information security practitioners. These areas are not clear cut and will require substantial discussion and debate in the near future. The debate around the impact of these identified areas will need to be considered at all levels. Each of the identified challenges will impact differently for the varying classes of consumers.

The evolution of the global network is likely to consider and become even more pervasive, and critical to our social and economic lives, as individuals, organizations and nations. Part of this evolution needs to be in terms of ensuring its ongoing integrity, from technical, economic, and legal perspectives. Probably the single most important challenge facing all stakeholders within cyber defense is that of raising the general awareness at grassroots level. If individuals take responsibility for the security of endpoint systems, a reduction in rates of compromise will follow, along with a drop in the malicious activity emanating from such systems.. The action doesn't need to be complex, but rather ensuring good practice. Vendors such as Microsoft, Adobe, Google and Mozilla have made great strides in increasing the ease with which software updates are obtained. Much as a motor vehicle requires checking of the wear of tires and functioning of lights and indicators in order to be considered roadworthy, possibly the same should apply to endpoint systems?

REFERENCES

Alexander, D. (2011). *U.S. reserves right to meet cyber attack with force.* Academic Press.

Brenner, S. W., & Clarke, L. L. (2010, October). Civilians in cyberwarfare: Conscripts. *Vanderbilt Journal of Transnational Law, 43*(4), 10111076.

Cheswick, B. (1990). The design of a secure internet gateway. In *Proc. Summer USENIX Conference.* USENIX.

Clark, D. D., & Landau, S. (2010). The problem isn't attribution: It's multi-stage attacks. In *Proceedings of the Re-Architecting the Internet Workshop.* ACM.

Crocker, D. (1997). *Mailbox Names for Common Services, Roles and Functions.* RFC 2142 (Proposed Standard), May 1997.

Federal Bureau of Investigation. (2011). *International cyber ring that infected millions of computers dismantled.* Author.

Hoisington, M. (2009). Cyberwarfare and the use of force giving rise to the right of self-defense. *Boston College International and Comparative Law Review, 32*(1), 439.

Hollis, D. (2011, January). Cyberwar case study: Georgia 2008. *Small Wars Journal.*

Internet Assigned Numbers Authority (IANA). (2008). *ICMP type numbers.*

Manson, G. P. (2011). Cyberwar: The united states and china prepare for the next generation of conict. *Comparative Strategy, 30*(2), 121–133. doi:10.1080/01495933.2011.561730

McMahan, J. (1994, January). Self-defense and the problem of the innocent attacker. *Ethics, 104*(2), 252290. doi:10.1086/293600

Republic of South Africa. (2002) *Electronic communications and transactions act.* Author.

Thompson, M. (2010). *Mariposa botnet analysis* (Technical report). Defence Intelligence.

Tikk, E., Kaska, K., Rnnimeri, K., Kert, M., TalihŠrm, A-M., & Liis Vihul. (2008). *Cyber attacks against Georgia: Legal lessons identied.* Academic Press.

Waxman, M.C. (2010). Cyber-Attacks and the Use of Force: Back to the Future of Article 2(4). *Yale Journal of international Law, 36*(2).

ADDITIONAL READING

Andrew, D., & Chi, H. (2013). An empirical study of botnets on university networks using low-interaction honeypots. In *Proceedings of the 51st ACM Southeast Conference* (ACMSE '13). ACM, New York, NY, USA, Article 44, 2 pages. DOI=10.1145/2498328.2500094 http://doi.acm.org/10.1145/2498328.2500094

Duong, D., Pearman, J., & Bladon, C. (2013). The nexus cognitive agent-based model: coevolution for valid computational social modeling. In *Proceeding of the fifteenth annual conference companion on Genetic and evolutionary computation conference companion* (GECCO '13 Companion), Christian Blum (Ed.). ACM, New York, NY, USA, 1431-1436. DOI=doi:10.1145/2464576.2482723 http://doi.acm.org/10.1145/2464576.2482723

Qian, Y., Tipper, D., Krishnamurthy, P., & Joshi, J. (2007). *Information Assurance: Dependability and Security in Networked Systems*. San Francisco, CA, USA: Morgan Kaufmann Publishers Inc.

Venegas-Andraca, S.E. (2012). Quantum walks: a comprehensive review. *Quantum Information Processing* 11, 5 (October 2012), 1015-1106. DOI=10.1007/s11128-012-0432-5 http://dx.doi.org/10.1007/s11128-012-0432-5

KEY TERMS AND DEFINITIONS

Attribution: Idea of describing perceived threat activities with respect to observations of system behavior.

Cyber Attack: Malicious activity, perpetrated by code or user behavior aimed at gaining unauthorized access to information and/or destroying the integrity of existing information.

Cyber Defense: Means acting in anticipation to oppose an attack against computers and networks.

Cyber Law: Government regulations aimed at ensuring fair use and practices of information sharing on the Internet.

Internet Security: Branch of computer security related to the behavior of malicious code on the Internet.

Military Cyber Policies: Internet policies implemented by the military in order to safeguard state security.

Proactive Cyber Defense: Will most often require additional security from internet service providers.

ENDNOTES

[1] Such as the numerous attacks during the Arab Spring unrest in Early 2011

[2] This would include groups such as the Occupy movement, and those targeting financial institutions as part of the response to the 2008 financial crisis.

[3] Prime examples of this would include the hackivist vigilante groups of Anonymous and LulzSec and their various offshoots.

Chapter 7
Necessary Standard for Providing Privacy and Security in IPv6 Networks

Hosnieh Rafiee
University of Potsdam, Germany

Christoph Meinel
University of Potsdam, Germany

ABSTRACT

Security and privacy have become important issues when dealing with Internet Protocol version 6 (IPv6) networks. On one hand, anonymity, which is related to privacy, makes it hard for current security systems to differentiate between legitimate users and illegitimate users, especially when the users need to be authenticated by those systems whose services they require. On the other hand, a lack of privacy exposes legitimate users to abuse, which can result from the information gained from privacy-related attacks. The current problems inherent within IPv6-enabled networks are due, in part, to the fact that there is no standard available telling companies about the current deficiencies that exist within IPv6 networks. The purpose of this chapter is to show a balance between the use of privacy and security, and to describe a framework that can offer the minimum standard requirement needed for providing security and privacy to IPv6 networks.

INTRODUCTION

IPv6 (Deering & Hinden, 1998) is the successor version of Internet Protocol version 4 (IPv4). These protocols are what makes communication possible across the Internet. Without the use of an IP address, it would not be possible to access the information located on many distributed repositories in many different locations across the world.

When the Internet Engineering Task Force (IETF) first proposed IPv6, the main assumption was to have a highly secure protocol which could support Internet Protocol Security (IPsec) (Kent, & Seo, 2005) natively, thus solving any problems dealing with end-to-end communications. However, this assumption proved to be unsupported. Unfortunately many implementers, and vendors alike, have not supported or have not

DOI: 10.4018/978-1-4666-6158-5.ch007

activated IPsec. One reason for this is because of the complexity that is involved in configuring IPsec and also the key management involved. This protocol thus remains with only the basic protection mechanisms in play so companies and governments are thus unwilling to widely deploy IPv6 or to replace their current IPv6 backbones with one making use of the IPsec protocol.

But the story does not end here. The development of a new address scheme for IPv6, which was necessitated by the IPv4 address space exhaustion, has led to new technology waves in which several volunteer experts and companies have become involved in looking for the flaws in IPv6. They are doing this in order to provide new security protocols to the users' of IPv6-enabled networks so that they can have the same security that exists when using IPv4, or maybe even higher.

The increased use of clouds and other repositories on the internet, in order to service and support many users at the same time, exposes this data to the vulnerabilities exploited by several types of privacy and security attacks. Today, we are living in an information technology world where governments and companies try to collect as much information as possible about their competitors. They do this so that they can overcome any possible threats from other governments or companies. Along with the risk of competitors, there are also individual/groups of attackers who are interested in obtaining the information available in those repositories so that they can misuse this information for their own criminal purposes. This is why, today, cyber attacks (attacks that are accomplished using cyber methods) are one of the main concerns of both societies and governments. Over the past 10 to 15 years multiple cyber attacks have occurred targeting both governmental agencies and private companies. The damage estimates are placed at more than $1 billion. Based on an official report from the United States Homeland Security Agency, in 2011 there were more than 106,000 incidents reported of which 5000 needed an urgent response.

Unfortunately, nobody knows yet, whether or not through the use of all security protocols, if IPv6 nodes will have the security level that is necessary to prevent several types of attacks or whether there are still many uncoverd flaws that might prevent the current services from being available to users or that can leak confidential information. What if there is a system that helps to show the current flaws in IPv6 networks and enables the user to do further tests to discover uncovered flaws in order to find a solution before these vulnerabilities can be used, like a tool in the hand of criminals? The remaining sections of this chapter are organized as follows:

Section 2: Introduce different meanings for privacy, anonymity and security in general and survey the current approaches in use in the application and network layers by explaining their issues and by introducing any available solutions.
Section 3: Explains some of the possible attacks in use across the internet.
Section 4: Surveys the currently available tools
Section 5: Introduces a system which can be used as a basic consultant system
Section 6: Explains the security recommendations for use in IPv6 networks and gives a basic security requirement.
Section 7: Summarizes this chapter.

PRIVACY, SECURITY, ANONYMITY, AND THEIR CONFLICTS

It is not easy to come up with a unique definition of privacy, security and anonymity. This is because some entities (such as users' data that can be an IP address, bank information, a post on social networking website, medical data, etc.) that are considered confidential for one group of people may not be considered confidential for another group of people. In other words, people have different interpretations of what constitutes privacy.

This is why they are easily confused between the meaning of privacy, anonymity and security and they perceive them to be the same while in fact each is an entity unto itself. Privacy is the act of allowing users to choose what entities they want to share with others and what entities they want to keep from others. Security, on the other hand, is the ability to protect these entities and this is usually possible by the use of cryptographic approaches. Of course encryption of the users' information also protects their privacy. But this approach does not allow a user to choose what data he wants to share with others and what data he wants to keep private. Moreover, the gathering of a user's location information via their IP address, for security purposes, might infringe on their privacy. Anonymity is the act of hiding a node's real identity so that its IP address or his other identities will be unseen by the other nodes on the Internet. For example, to remain anonymous, a user can use a Virtual Private Network (VPN) or proxy software, such as Tor, so that his real IP address would remain hidden behind several other groups of trusted computers. In other words, the node would hide its identity by making use of intermediate groups of trusted nodes thus masking its real identity. But hiding the IP address, or the identity of a user, does not necessarily protect the users' information from prying eyes. This means that, if the data is not encrypted, an attacker is capable of obtaining users' information, and then backtracking, using this information to further invade a user's privacy.

In 1995, the European Union (EU) (EU DPD, 1995) attempted to define privacy and come up with the first Data Protection Directive (DPD). This was the first attempt made by governments to officially define privacy so that they could pass laws to protect it. Unfortunately, later, European countries had a different interpretation of this DPD and used their own interpretation as a base for their laws as applied to a user's privacy. So, some countries decided only to concern themselves with location based tracking, while other countries only

worried about some of their users' data while still others looked for absolute privacy so they think that everything should be kept confidential. So again, in 2012, the EU proposed another DPD (EU DPD, 2012) that tried to unify the meaning of privacy. According to this proposal, "privacy consists of personal data that concerns any information relating to an individual, whether it relates to his or her private, professional or public life. It can be anything from a name, a photo, an email address, bank details, posts on social networking websites, medical information, or a computer's IP address".

Another attempt at defining privacy also took place in 2012 when a group of people at the IETF proposed a standard (Cooper et. al., 2013) in which they tried to unify the meaning of privacy and anonymity so that all people, wishing to make implementations while observing privacy, would have a document that they could use as a reference for insight while doing their work.

As explained earlier, privacy is a user's entity so it is not bound to any particular Open Systems Interconnections (OSI) layer but some layers might have a stronger impact on a user's privacy than others. Two examples of these layers are the application layer and the network layer. In the next subsections we will explain what constitutes privacy in these two layers

Privacy in the Application Layer

Most of the user's confidential data, that is used by particular applications or is stored in some databases, reside then in the application layer. This data then might be accessible, over the internet, through the use of the user friendly name of your computer, called the Domain Name Service (DNS) name (Mockapetris, 1987). Since people are willing to use the online storage for easy accessibility to their data from everywhere, attackers are also willing to try to find ways to gain access to this confidential data. The data transferred across the internet can be in plaintext or encrypted. So when the data is not encrypted and the user uses unsafe networks, or when it is easy to obtain a user's computer identity (that can be the DNS name of his computer), then there is a possibility that an attacker will eavesdrop on the network in order to obtain the information that the user is not willing to share with him. There are currently several approaches that can be used in the application layer to make data anonymous. These approaches are more focused on processing data in a way that removes any confidential data from them, thereby making it harder for an attacker to identify the owner of this data. The confidential information is removed from the data through the use of different algorithms. The work of Truta and Vinay (2006) provides an example of privacy protection used to protect medical data. They use k-anonymity algorithms where their algorithm categorizes and sub categorizes data into different classes based on similar properties, or based on the level of damage they might inflict on a user's health, etc. Then they try to group each category through the use of symbols, such as greater or smaller. They also remove any addresses or names from the data that would aid the attacker in identifying the data's owner. From the output of their algorithm you might obtain something like x number of people who have an age greater than 20 and less than 35 in the area of *secret_area, and* are under the category of *secret_letters_for-group-category*. In this case, this information might only be useful for statistical purposes.

The other attempt at providing privacy in the application layer has to do with giving users the ability to choose or hide their data on their public website, such as their profile. Google and Facebook are two big companies that observe user privacy using this approach. This allows users to also share their data with a group of confidential users and not the public.

However useful this might prove to be, there are, unfortunately, some companies, where people store their data, that can be easily hacked or that don't provide the high degree of protection that is necessary to prevent this data from intentionally being exposed to governments or other competing companies. Some companies might even store their confidential data on some public websites

Privacy in the Network Layer

One of the important protocols used in the network layer is the IP. IP addresses form the core of the addressing scheme used across computer networks to identify a user with his computer or to identify different devices. As explained in a prior section, a user might use the DNS name of a computer to access an entity. But this DNS name does not have any meaning without its mapping to an IP address. This means that any DNS name is mapped to one or several IP addresses. The IP address can thus provide an attacker with the means of finding the location of a user and then to track his movements over the internet. By knowing the user's location, he might be able to accomplish other criminal acts. If he knows when the user is at work, he can plan to rob his house when he isn't there. Another example would be to track very important politicians in order to carry out some form of terrorism. However, location tracking is not always done for criminal purposes as it may be done solely for advertising or security purposes. For instance, when you take a trip to an unfamiliar place, it is nice to have Google Maps available to show you where restaurants and shopping centers are located near where you are staying. It does this by storing your home IP address (the IP address of where you usually use to connect to the Google server) and comparing it to the new IP address that you just obtained from the server where you are staying. By doing this, they can also prevent unauthorized access to your account on their server by trying to verify you.

Knowing a user's IP address can lead to obtaining a user's confidential information. Especially if the user always uses the same IP address, or does not encrypt his data, or connects using an unsecure network. So this can allow an attacker to gain access to this user information during its transfer across the network, which could result in harm to a user's privacy. It was for this reason that some research work (Silva, Dias, & Ricardo) was conducted to address the issue of anonymity in the network layer by hiding the user's identity, his IP address. This would give users the ability to anonymously surf the Internet or anonymously access websites. One example might be by encrypting the payload and then submitting it through many different intermediate nodes. The drawback to using this process is that the receiver is known to all communicating nodes and may also be well known to the attacker. Another example would be the use of a VPN, or other single entity controlled solution, i.e., using servers that are owned by entities, such as companies, to provide encryption and protection for the nodes. However, if this single node is compromised, then this will have an effect on the privacy of all nodes that used that node to start their VPN connection. Generally, the approaches just explained will cause delays or will end up being a single point of failure.

There are currently some countries, like Germany, that enforce their Internet Service Providers (ISPs) to change the range of IPv4 addresses in use once per week in order to protect their users' privacy by disallowing an attacker to track their users or to learn of their exact location. This range of IP address can be from a different location of the country.

The Privacy Extension standard RFC (Narten, Draves, & Krishnan, 2007) is the first attempt in IPv6 enabled network to observe privacy by generating a temporary Interface ID (IID). An IID consists of the 64 rightmost bits of the 128 bit IPv6 address. The 64 leftmost bits of an IPv6 address represent the subnet prefix and the user's network. The IPv6 address is in hexadecimal format. For example, if the IPv6 address of a computer is *2020:126:897:abc:ef2:8bc:683:a741* then the subnet prefix is *2020:126:897:abc* and the IID is *ef2:8bc:683:a741*. The Privacy Extension uses two different approaches for the generation of the IID portion of an IPv6 address, which is

not based on a Media Access Control (MAC) address. A MAC address is a 48- bit hexadecimal number used by network adapters to uniquely identify themselves on a Local Area Network (LAN). Narten et al. (2007) assign a short lifetime to these temporary IIDs so they are not valid for long periods of time. Unfortunately this approach does have some drawbacks that afford attackers the ability to track users across networks. The list of these issues is as follows (Rafiee & Meinel, 2013):

- When a node joins a new network with a different subnet prefix, if the option in the router advertisement tells the node to extend the lifetime of its address, and if the maximum lifetime of that address has not been reached, then the node will keep its current IID without generating a new one.

- The node may still respond to requests from other nodes using the IID that was generated based on the MAC address. This can happen because this mechanism prompts the node to generate its public address based on a MAC address. There are different types of subnet prefixes: link-local subnet prefix, i.e.,the value of fe08:: and global subnet prefix, i.e., any subnet prefixes that are obtained from a router or make use of other servers, such as a Dynamic Host Configuration Protocol version 6 (DHCPv6) (Droms et al., 2003). The public addresses are the addresses that make use of a global subnet prefix. These addresses might also be defined on DNS servers or have associated DNS records.

- Another problem can occur when the node cuts its current connections with other nodes because the maximum lifetime for this IID has expired. In general the preferred lifetime is 1 day and the maximum lifetime is one week.

- Nodes may require a stable storage area in which to store both the history and the currently generated IID. This is done to preclude the use of an already used value.

If there is no stable storage area available, and the node does not use a good randomization algorithm, then the node may be unable to make use of a greatly randomized IID.

Stable Privacy Enhanced IID Generation (Gont, 2013) was proposed in order to address some issues that exist with the current IID generation mechanisms in use today. It uses a pseudo random function *F()*, and also some other parameters, as an input to this function thus enabling a node to generate a unique IID, which would be the same for the same subnet prefix, but will change with different subnet prefixes. This approach can significantly decrease the possibility of scanning attacks making it dissimilar to the approach that is based on MAC as it will not have the same IID in different networks. A problem with this approach, though, is that the node generates the same IID for the same subnet prefix and keeps it for as long as the subnet prefix is valid. This means that once the attacker finds the node's IP address, and if the node is fixed in one network, then the attacker will have enough time to try to gather as much confidential information as possible during the time that the subnet prefix is valid. In real life, the subnet prefixes are not frequently changed and they can be valid for several months to years. This is true for all countries except Germany, as was mentioned earlier with regard to IPv4 networks, which I assume will be same for IPv6 networks.

Router Advertisement (RA) based Privacy (Rafiee & Meinel, 2013) is a possible solution to the problem of privacy in the network layer. It tries to address the existing problems with the Privacy Extension and Stable Privacy Enhanced approaches make use of a randomized algorithm which is not based on the MAC address and they also force the node to change its IID whenever it receives a new router advertisement message. Dissimilar to Stable Privacy Enhanced IID, it will keep its IID for a short period of time for each subnet prefix. Therefore, if the user's identity is exposed to an attacker, the attacker probably won't have enough time to track this node or to obtain confidential information.

MECHANISMS USED TO ATTACK IPV6 ENABLED NETWORKS

There are many possibilities for attacks' classifications. Many attacks may make use of similar techniques to attain their goals. This means their way of doing it almost is similar, but their purpose might be different, or they might have a similar purpose as well. For accomplishing these attacks, one might need to misuse a/many intermediate services. The attacks might have an effect on both the privacy and security of the users or may only harm the privacy or security of users. The attack might be easy to detect or hard to detect depending on the nature of this attack. There is currently some work being done to try to detect attacks and then drawing a graph that compares attack patterns to similar attacking scenarios that are available in their database (Roschke, Cheng & Meinel, 2010). Here we try to categorize these attacks based on the impact that the attack has on the entities' privacy and security.

User's Identity Detection

The attacks in this category can be divided into two subcategories: passive and active.

Passive Detection

A passive attack is one where the attacker does not perform any process that involves the sending of a lot of packets to the target network, which could enable the security system, in target networks, to detect his malicious behavior. One of these passive approaches is the reconnaissance of target networks in order to obtain general information about the network and the nodes (any host in this network such a router a computer, etc.) in that network. This is usually the first step that an attacker would execute. Some information that might be obtained through the use of this step is the information about firewalls, subnet prefixes used in this network, and general information about the type of organization/company or the place he wants to attack. If during this phase the attacker is able to obtain any IP addresses or nodes' information, such as the OS being used, servers, routers, etc., then as we explained earlier, finding an IP address of a node might lead to location tracking or leakage of the confidential information. This is because an attacker might be able to eavesdrop (silently listening to the network) all/part of the packets sent/received to/from a victim node in the target network. This might give this attacker the ability to gather any confidential information about the user of this node. Usually this attack is successful if there is no security mechanism in place for protecting a user's data. This is why, this phase of an attack is more concerned with a user's privacy. If the attacker is in the same network as other nodes, then he is able to change his network adapter status to promiscuous mode and eavesdrop on all packets being transferred in this network. This allows him also to obtain the other nodes' IP addresses, especially in an IPv6 network, where by default, Neighbor Discovery Protocol (NDP) (Narten et al., 2007) is active. The use of NDP is proposed for IPv6 networks to ease the IP address configuration process. Nodes in the network use 5 different types of Internet Control Message Protocol version 6 (ICMPv6) for the purpose of configuring their IP address and detecting neighboring nodes in this network.

Active Detection

The attacks in this category are involved with actively initiating processes in order to obtain a user's data. This means that these attacks are also involved with invading a user's privacy. In order to expand the information obtain from the Reconnaissance phase, one might need to scan the target

network. This allows an attacker to obtain the IP addresses of the nodes. This step concerns privacy more than security. In IPv6 networks, because of the large address space (2^{128} unique IP addresses), scanning attacks are not really feasible but the attacker does have the possibility of sending and receiving multicast ICMPv6 echo messages in order to obtain the node's IP addresses. It is also possible to obtain node's IP addresses from DNS servers. One way to do this is by querying the DNS server for different domains. Another way is to obtain a copy of the DNS zone file during a zone transfer from a master to a slave DNS server. A zone is a portion of domain space that is authorized and administered by a primary name server and one or more secondary name servers. A name server can be a master or a slave. Master or primary name servers are the ones from which other name servers can transfer zone files. So attacking DNS servers is a means of obtaining IP addresses. After obtaining IP addresses, the attacker needs to detect the running services on each node in this network. Port scanning is one of the popular ways to detect the services running on each node in this network. This step is concerned more with a user's security than his privacy. This step is performed to enable an attacker to later look for security flaws in target services so that, later, he will be able to compromise the node and access the user's data.

Active Data Collection

Attacks in this category are divided into two subgroups; bugs in implementations or during configurations, and other attacks.

Bugs in Implementations or During Configurations

The standard documents defining Internet procedures, i.e, RFCs, usually explain what to implement but in most cases give the implementers the choice of how to go about implementing. Human errors are a well-known problem in all computer systems. It is impossible for programmers to consider all of the possible conditions that their code must handle, so their code could cause problems during run-time. This is why implementers put so much effort into stress testing their implementations. One stress testing approach is fuzz testing. With this test random and unexpected data are used as inputs to the system being tested to find the conditions under which the system crashes or leaks information. Unfortunately attackers also make use of this approach to attack target protocols and services in IPv6 networks. They send packets containing invalid data, but with the correct checksum. By doing this they can crash the victim's system or force the protocol to leak information. The chance of this attack being successful increases when the protocol or service is not configured correctly. This too can lead to the leakage of information.

Other Attacks

Most attacks in this subgroup are a result of spoofing or the combination of spoofing and Distributed Denial of Service (DDoS) Attacks. Spoofing is the act of modifying data. DoS is the act of denying a node or a group of nodes access to their desired services. These attacks appear in different layers of the OSI model: network, application, etc. They occur using different formats and attack both privacy and security. Nikander, Kempf & Nordmark (2004) explained a list of NDP vulnerabilities. Hogg & Vyncke (2009) explain the attacks used against network layer protocols in IPv6 networks.

One example of these attacks is a smurfing attack where the attacker sends a lot of ICMPv6 messages using a spoofed source IP address, i.e., uses a victims' IP address as a source IP address and then sends it to a broadcast IP address. This results in all nodes in the network responding to that message by sending messages to the victim's node.

The Man in the Middle (MITM) attack is an example of a spoofing attack where the attacker tries to interrupt communications between two nodes. This is accomplished by presenting itself in a way that the two communicating nodes think that they are communicating directly with each other while their communication is actually via the attacker's node. This is a form of information leakage. Another spoofing attack occurs during the authentication process between one node and another node. The authentication is usually based on the source IP address or some other identity number existent in the packets. The attacker can spoof this data and easily impersonate itself as the other node to obtain unauthorized access to data or to make unauthorized modifications. Spoofing attacks might not be possible if the node where to use a security mechanism, but the chance for DDoS attacks actually increases when the node uses a security mechanism to protect its data. This is because the verification process takes more time than when not using a security mechanism and this time factor makes the node to susceptible to DDoS attacks.

AVAILABLE PENETRATION TESTING TOOLS

Currently there are several research groups and individual researchers actively involved in testing IPv6 networks for vulnerabilities in a variety of IPv6 protocol suites. These include addressing mechanisms, extension headers, fragmentations, tunneling or the dual stack networks (using IPv4 and IPv6 at the same time).

Single and Multi Function Tools

This section introduces some tools that are available for use in IPv6 networks. An example of such a tool for this endeavor is The Hacker Choice (THC)[1] Attack Suite, which was created by and is supported by some individual researchers. In spite of being considered one of the most complete tools available on the Internet with which to initiate a large variety of attacks in IPv6 networks, one needs to call each attack separately, one by one, using the required parameters in order to execute these attacks. Another shortcoming of this tool is that no reports are prepared indicating whether or not the attacks were effective on the network and what hosts were vulnerable to what attacks. A third problem is that there is no good documentation for developers to use in writing additional code for their testing purposes. This is due to the fact that each tool might be developed by a different individual developer and so there is no consistency in the code. This means that the code might not be able to be used as a library.

There are other tools available, but they only have a single functionality and they thus can be used only for a specific purpose. For example, nmap (Lyon, 2009), halfscan6, etc. are used for scanning or for locating live nodes in IPv6 networks. SendIP[2], Scorpio[3], isic6[4], etc. are used to generate and manipulate IPv6 packets. Lecigne & Neville-Neil (2006) developed tools to test the IPv6 stack of FreeBSD during Google summer code. Later they extend their code to also evaluate IPv6 stack protocol in other Operating System (OS) such as Windows and Linux[5]. Some other tools are used just for testing a particular service. Web applications are one example of important target services in IPv6 networks. Ottow et al. (2012) explain the modifications required in order to be considered a valid current tool to be used for penetration testing of web applications based on checklists containing the most prevalent security issues. One example of a modification is related to a node scanning mechanism that should consider the IPv6 large address space and modify its scanning mechanism accordingly. Another issue of concern is that none of these tools can be used for scanning a network when DNS Security Extension (DNSSEC) (Arends et al., 2005) and NSEC3 are used. DNSSEC is an extension to the DNS used in the validation of DNS query operations.

It verifies the authenticity and integrity of query results obtained from a signed zone. It introduces new Resource Records (RRs) (DNS servers store data in a specific structure called RR) for the authentication and verification purpose. One of these important RRs is the NSEC/3 (Laurie et al., 2008) which is used for NXDOMAIN responses. A NSEC RR includes the names of the successor and predecessor to a query response for the purpose of preventing replay attacks. All query responses in NSEC3 are the result of a SHA1 hash of the names so that it is not possible for the attacker to obtain the identities of the nodes by querying a DNS server. This is because the identities are not in plain text.

A FLEXIBLE FRAMEWORK

The tools currently available for penetration testing in IPv6 networks lack the ability to generate reports and do not focus on all available protocols used in IPv6 networks. They are also not capable of checking to see whether or not a combination of two or more protocols can be used to generate new attacks. One example relates to the vulnerability of the DNS server. Today, the nature of attacks used against DNS has changed to the point where attackers use this protocol, as a tool, to perform attacks against various other services available in the network. To address this problem we developed a new, flexible framework[6]. This framework not only detects the services in use in a network automatically but also performs attacks. It also generates vulnerability reports which administrators can use in resolving the detected security flaws in their network. This also provides for extensions from three perspectives: service discovery, attacks, and reports. This is a user space with an easy to use framework. It consists of two main components: attack and report/monitoring. They can be installed for use in two different linux-based nodes in IPv6 networks. Each of these components consists of a web interface and a backend library. The flexibility of the framework gives users the ability of dragging and dropping their own scripts or to extend the framework by using other external scripts or codes that are available on the internet via the provided web interface. They can add and save their commands, which contain the required parameters, via this interface so that, later, the backend component can compile the external scripts and codes and save them in a directory and then save the path to the compiled code in its database. The framework will consider and run these scripts and codes during the next user-triggered network service execution. During the execution phase, the commands will pass through to the backend component in order to trigger a standard console command. The web interface is written in PHP.

New Node Discovery Algorithm

Attack components make use of two phases to process any attack: service discovery and execution of attacks. For service discovery, first it employs ICMPv6 multicast echo messages. In the case where it does not receive a response from the nodes in the targeted networks, it then uses a new algorithm, which uses the DNS to obtain infor-mation about the nodes having associated DNS records. To do this it executes the following steps:

1. If a zone transfer request is possible, then ask for the whole copy of the zone file. Otherwise go to step 2.
2. If the DNSSEC is not enabled, report a failure and stop scanning. Otherwise go to step 3.
3. If the DNS server uses NSEC, then start zone walking. Otherwise go to step 4. Zone walking is the process of sending different query requests to the DNS server on which DNSSEC is supported. This is done in order to retrieve the available legitimate DNS names of nodes, which then leads to being able to obtain the node's identities. Because

in DNSSEC, the zone file is signed offline, it always responds to the query with the two closest legitimate names. If DNSSEC uses NSEC, then this response is in plain text. As an example an attacker might ask for an invalid name like "invalid.example.com". The DNS server would respond with two valid names, which are alphabetically close to that name, such as internal.example.com and nat.example.com.

4. If the DNS server uses NSEC3, start zone walking, gather hashed data, execute the dictionary attack offline, and then go to step 5.
5. If any records are left, do brute force attacks and repeat this step until no unknown record is available.

We gathered a list of popular domains and stored them in our database by using Alexa.com. We also tried to use a whole zone transfer request on these found domains. When our database was full of popular records, we ran the above algorithm for about 2 hours (Rafiee et al., 2013) on a com-puter with a 2.60 GHz CPU. We scanned one million domains. Among them, 55160 domains (5.5%) were not secure, which enabled us to obtain a copy of the zone file by using an AXFR query. This helped us to gather 1.43×10^6 RRs which we stored in our mysql database for later use in a dictionary attack against NSEC3. By using this approach, we were able to find the plain text for over 50% of the third level domains (example: www.google.com, www in this combination is the third level domain) in our target network on one public website.

The next phase of the attack component is to trigger all available attacking scripts for selected services for a certain period of time. This time was chosen by the user when this attack script was added to the framework. It also activates the report/monitoring component so that it is ready to monitor the network. The task of the report server is to act as a basic consulting system that advises the user of any security and privacy flaws in his network. When the report/monitoring component receives a wake up message from the attack component, it will retrieve the list of attacks from the database of the attack component, and then starts monitoring the network to find out whether or not the attack was effective. This is done by sending probe messages or silently sniffing the network. For example, to see whether a node set its IP address based on a fake router advertisement message, the monitoring service sniffs the network to obtain the unsolicited neighbor advertisement message. To improve the reports, the user can easily add new scripts to detect the effectiveness of the attacks. For some types of attacks this phase may have problems in generating the report. This is because this framework does not install any external component or activate SNMP on any node in the target network. This does not mean that the ability to use this protocol does not exist. If the user wants to manually enable SNMP on any nodes in his network, then he can configure this framework for the SNMP protocol.

Vulnerability Detection Algorithm

To better find the vulnerabilities that exist in the target network, we need to consider the cases where one service can use, as a means of attack, other services, so as to be able to enhance the system with this algorithm. We also need to use machine learning approaches in order to automate the process for adding new protocols. The steps of the vulnerability Detection algorithm are as follows:

Store the Current Root Vulnerability of Existing Trees

In this step, we need to manually (or use any online databases) feed the system with all the vulnerabilities of known protocols. This is necessary in order to have a consistency of keywords

used for all protocols. For example, if your NDP protocol is vulnerable to IP spoofing and message spoofing, then the keyword can be spoofing. This means that one should then use the same keyword for a spoofing vulnerability in all other protocols. In this step all the dependencies should also be specified. This means there are two variable to be consider as inputs to the system, i.e., L and D, where L is the list of vulnerabilities for a specific protocol, V is all available vulnerabilities for all protocols and D consists of the dependency lists.

$$L = \left\{ \forall l \in V, \exists D \therefore l \rightarrow D \right\} \qquad (1)$$

For example, if l is spoofing (keyword), then D is the array of vulnerabilities that spoofing can lead to, such as cache poisoning, unauthorized access to the system, MITM, etc. These are all dependent on spoofing.

Definition 1: TV where T represents a tree structure. To prove that it is a tree, we assume that T has n members and we define a matrix $M(T)_{n \times n}$ that specifies whether or not there is an edge (dependency) between two vulnerabilities in T. We initially set M(T) to zero. So,

$$\forall t_i \in T, \exists t_j, t_k \in T \text{ where } t_j, t_k \text{ are adjacents of } t_i \therefore M\left[t_j, t_k\right] \neq 0 \qquad (2)$$

Adjacent vertexes are the vertexes that are directly connected to each other with an edge. This means neighboring vulnerabilities are dependent on t_i.

From Definition 1 we can generate a tree structure containing l as a root and many Ds as the leaves of this tree. The leaves might directly or indirectly connect to the l. The tree will be useful later as a report component that gives users more precise information about the vulnerabilities in the system. But for finding out whether or not the vulnerability of a service might be used as a means of attacking other service, then only the root level vulnerabilities play an important role in determining that.

Execute an Attack on Other Services Using the Root Vulnerabilities of a Particular Service

For example, spoofing is the root attack when an attacker spoofs the source IP address in a DNS query message and then uses the victim node's IP address instead of his own IP address. Then he asks for a query that requires a large response. He can also ask for different queries. The DNS server will then respond to those queries. This means that the victim node will then, as a result of this, receive several large packets that were never requested. Thus the victim node will be kept busy processing those packets. This attack is applicable if there is no authentication during the DNS query process involving the DNS server and clients. DoS attacks are thought of as both an attack against privacy and security. It is considered as such because the user is not able to share his chosen information with others due to the fact that the attacker has prevented the running of any service on his node.

Evaluation of the Framework

We evaluated our framework by considering some factors such as the time it takes to uncover what services are in use in the network and what attacks are being perpetrated along with the time needed to generate the report describing said services and attacks. We ran our framework using a testbed of 17 nodes. As we were in the same network as the other nodes, we did not need to use our DNS based scanning algorithm. We could have easily used ICMPv6 echo messages. After we found the list of available nodes, we tried to call one of the external codes which can be used to give us the general information about the available services in the network. Our results showed that it takes

the total of 5.99 seconds to find the list of nodes and to do the port scan for ssh and http.

The duration of time for the attacks is a variable time to be determined by the user and input using the framework's web interface. If the user chose a value of 40 seconds, then the duration of the attack would be 40 seconds. To enhance the framework by using more attacks, we implemented new attacks with which to evaluate the IPv6 protocols. These attacks entailed the use of fuzz mechanisms, evaluating DNS protocols such as multicast DNS (mDNS) (Cheshire, & Krochmal, 2013) and the evaluation of Mobile IPv6. Some instances of the new attacks are as follows:

Attacks Against Multicast DNS (mDNS)

DNS is one of the application layer services that uses an IP address. This is why the existing attack tools for DNS need some modification to support IPv6. mDNS is one of the new operations of DNS used in a local link in the absence of a unicast DNS server. Domain names using the multicast DNS end with *.local*. mDNS is used for finding printers or other shared folders of different OSs, or for checking the uniqueness of names used in local links. When a host joins a network that supports multicast DNS, it tries to set its local hostname, like *mydomain.local*, and then it sends a multicast DNS message to all nodes on that local link to see whether or not the chosen name is unique. We implemented a Man In The Middle (MITM) attack using C++ by extending the packet-manipulation-library[7]. Using a *Sniffer* object, provided by the packet-manipulation-library, the component analyzed all traffic on UDP port 5353. Each host name query (AAAA, i.e. IPv6 RRs) was stored in a map laid out to remember the questioner and the host name in question. Every time a DNS response was received by our framework, the map was checked for a matching answer. If found, the attack was carried out against the original questioner. For example, if nodes A and B want to communicate together, then node B will ask the name of node A using mDNS in order to connect via its name. Node A picks up a name and tries to check the uniqueness of this name by sending a mDNS message. Our MITM components (in our framework) receive this message as well as does Node B. Our component can then spoof that message and claim to own that name. There is no security proposed for mDNS, so it is easy for this to happen. Or our component could wait for node A and B to start their connection. First the MITM component will send out unicast goodbye packets to B indicating that the original host name holder gave up his authority over the name (node A will not hold onto A's name anymore). Then the MITM component sends another spoof unicast mDNS message to node B claiming to be allowed to use name A and continues the communication and then redirects the communication to the real A. In this case it plays a MITM attack. According to the mDNS RFC, the node should not accept unicast messages. However, we discovered that all current mDNS implementations accept unicast messages, which meant that we were able to successfully execute our attacks.

Fuzz Attacks

Fuzz testing is one of the popular testing approaches used by industries. To better test an IPv6 protocol stack, we implemented fuzz attacks. The code is called by our framework, which is then responsible for the creation and sending of fuzzy IPv6 packets as well as monitoring the target machines. Our first approach falls into the category of random input generation. We used scapy to generate our own packets, as it allows for the generation of invalid packets, which is useful for the fuzz approach. Our experimental results show that many packets are being rejected in the early stages because of invalid formats. In some cases the victim node's crashed and we had to reboot the system. In order to improve our results we used grammar based fuzz mechanisms. Grammar based

fuzz mechanisms are more precise. To facilitate the process of grammar based fuzzing we used the Peach Fuzzer framework[8]. On the day that we ran our code, we could not find any malfunction in nodes that accepted our IPv6 plain packets. However, as we did not have access to the IPv6 implementation stack, it was not easy to evaluate the target nodes' completely.

The last step, and the most important step for the framework, is the generation of reports. Based on our experiments, it takes an average of 9.77 seconds to generate a report about one protocol, like the NDP. This report varies from one protocol to another as it is dependent on many factors such as how fast the victim nodes respond to attacks, the duration of the attacks, and whether the report component needs to send a probe message to gather data from the nodes in the network, or whether that just sniffing will suffice.

SECURITY AND PRIVACY RECOMMENDATIONS

Enabling IPv6 might be a nightmare for many governments, companies or places who are still not sure about how to deploy this protocol without interrupting their running services or without the fear of privacy and security attacks. This is why many people felt that there was a need for a deployment guide for this protocol. To address this issue, the National Institute of Standards and Technology (NIST) (Frankel et al., 2010), with the help of many individual experts or companies, gathered a guideline, which supports most of the protocols used in IPv6 networks. However, even though this work is so promising, it unfortunately, despite the attempt to prepare a good document, contains several mistakes in descriptions of protocols and their protective capabilities. This is why, it cannot be considered a reliable source for people who are new to IPv6 and do not have any experience in this area. Usually these guidelines are used by non-experienced people more than experienced ones. One example occurs in the security section and concerns the description of Cryptographically Generated Addresses (CGA) (Aura, 2005).

To address the concerns surrounding IPv6 deployment and to offer a minimum standard, we will cover some of the protocols used in IPv6 networks. Our coverage includes the DNS, Mobile IPv6, and the IPv6 protocol itself, such as IPv6 addressing schemes and the IPv6 dual stack mode.

DNS Security and Privacy Recommendations

The DNS is one of the fundamental protocols used by the internet. It allows for the translation of the user friendly names of nodes in the network to their IP addresses. This protocol only provides protection by use of a basic security mechanism which is authenticated based on the source IP address. DNS is vulnerable to many security flaws such as cache poisoning, spoofing, etc. (Atkins & Austein, 2004). Because the DNS is usually a public node, which must be accessible over the internet, privacy for this protocol does not make sense. But ignorance of security flaws might lead to exposing the identity of nodes in the targeted network, as was through the use of our framework in a prior section. In other word, the lack of security on this node could lead to serious privacy and security issues for other nodes. Some of the things that need to be considered for this protocol are as follows:

- Secure Authentication during zone transfer, DNS update (updating a/ record/s by a client to a DNS server) or resolver authentication (authentication of a DNS resolver during query response with clients or other resolvers). There are two solutions here; using DNSSEC with NSEC3 or using CGA-TSIG (Rafiee, Loewis & Meinel, 2013):

  ◦ Use DNSSEC with NSEC3 to authorize zone transfers. To decrease the chance of a dictionary attack, the use of popular names is not recommended. The protocol also needs to pick up a random signed name as a response to an invalid name that is not available in the DNS server. This will decrease the chance of guessing the third level domains, as the two letters will not be close in alphabetical order.

  ◦ Use CGA-TSIG when Secure Neighbor Discovery (SeND) (Arkko et al., 2005) is available in the network. This decreases the complexity of the use of DNSSEC and will also exhibit the same problem that exists in NSEC3.

Mobile IPv6 (MIPv6)

Mobile IPv6 (MIPv6) (Perkins, Johnson, & Arkko, 2011) was designed to allow users to move from one network to the other network without any interruption in their connections. There are only a few implementations of MIPv6. One of these implementations is UMIP[9], which is not a stable version (Based on our experiments carried on three Computers which support Debian). Like some other protocols that are susceptible to spoofing attacks, MIPv6 is also vulnerable to spoofing attacks. This is the reason why it is not recommended to use this protocol without having IPsec enabled or using some other security mechanism in its stead. The following recommendations made concerning the use of MIPv6:

Use SeND or some other security approach to configure IPv6 for a Mobile Node (MN). MN is a node, such as a laptop, etc. that can move from one place to another. UMIP does not support SeND. UMIP only supports radvd[10], which is a daemon used to send Router Advertisement (RA) messages, which allows nodes, that support NDP, to configure their IP addresses. The other option for configuring the IP address is to use DHCPv6. However, it is not secure either. If an attacker is in a Home Network (the network where the MN first made its connection and started its communication with the other nodes, known as Correspondent Nodes. The Home Agent (HA) in this network maintains the status of the MN) or the Foreign Network (the network to where MN moved and expects to continue his communication with other nodes without interruption. The Foreign Agent (FA) in this network maintains the status of MN) so that he can then use a spoofing attack and play a MITM role. However, the chance of a MITM attack decreases when the node uses IPsec. This is because, by using IPsec, a secure channel is established between the MN and his communicating node.

In general, key management may pose a problem when using IPsec. This is because the administrator might need to manually exchange the keys between MN, HA, FA and/or CNs.

IPv6 Addressing Scheme

As explained earlier, NDP and DHCPv6 are two popular approaches used to configure the IPv6 address of nodes. Unfortunately DHCPv6 does not support any mechanism that would enable nodes to authenticate the DHCP servers or clients. This means it is vulnerable to spoofing attacks. For example, if a malicious node is inside a network, then it can claim to be a DHCP server. Nodes in this network will accept this DHCP server since they cannot distinguish between the legitimate and illegitimate DHCP servers. Some administrators try to limit the access to their DHCP-enabled network by including the MAC address of all legitimate clients on their DHCP access list. However, the attacker can spoof a MAC address of one of legitimate node and then initiate his attacks. NDP has the same problem. A malicious node in the network can claim to be a router and redirect all the traffic to his desired place. These are some recommendations for generating IP addresses:

- It is recommended that SeND be used, including the use of the CGA or a Simple Secure Addressing Scheme (SSAS) (Rafiee & Meinel, 2013) options. SSAS is faster than CGA and provides the node with a good level of security that is even higher than that of CGA.
- For privacy reasons, the IP addresses should only be valid for a short period of time.
- Using DHCPv6 is not recommended since there is no way for authorizing nodes. If this is a local network that no external users can access, the local network might be safe. In this case then, for privacy, DHCPv6 can make use of any random approach for the generation of IIDs.

Dual Stack

Dual stack is the state of concurrently using both IPv6 and IPv4 in parallel. It is the most preferable scenario during the coexistence of both IPv4 and IPv6. This means the nodes can process packets send/receive to/from other nodes with IPv4 or IPv6 contents simultaneously. This is done due to the fact that we are in a migration period from IPv4 to IPv6. This means some networks might support only IPv4 and some both. One problem with dual stack is the fact that we need to configure all services with both IPv4 and IPv6 addresses, but unfortunately IPv4 addresses are nearly exhausted. One solution is to use Network Address Translation (NAT) in IPv4 networks. According to the IETF definition "NATs are used to interconnect a private network consisting of unregistered IP addresses with a global IP network using limited number of registered IP addresses". However, NAT creates a problem for end-to-end communication. Recommendations for the use of the dual stack relate to the consideration of security issues within IPv4 and IPv6 enabled networks. This means that if one wants to have a secure network, and to partially support IPv6, then it needs to ensure that all the security protocols are installed in the target network. This can be done by using one of the tools that penetrate IPv6 networks, and then using the tools that detect IPv4 vulnerabilities. The problem that many people ignore is the case where the network only supports IPv4. They are not aware that, by default, the current OS supports IPv6 and in most cases they are activated automatically during the installation of the OS. One example of these protocols, in IPv6 suites, is NDP. In the Windows OS, this feature, by default, is activated. This is why, in dual stack mode, or in IPv6 mode only, tools for both protocols should be used to penetrate the networks and uncover possible flaws.

CONCLUSION

In this chapter we explained the different meaning given to privacy, security, and anonymity from different points of view. We also covered the problems affecting both security and privacy in the network layer and application layer. We then categorized attacks based on their impact on privacy and security. We evaluated different available IPv6 tools used for penetration testing, we introduced our own flexible framework that can make use of all the external tools and finally we enhanced this framework with new attacks. We evaluated our framework by considering the time required to scan the network, execute attacks, and generate reports. This framework can be used as a basic consulting system, which helps people learn of the flaws in their network and then shows them what to install as a security protocol to safeguard it. Our framework makes use of a new vulnerability algorithm. We also introduced a new scanning algorithm which makes use of DNSSEC and NSEC3. Finally we explain our recommendation for some of the protocols in IPv6 networks to show how one can observe privacy and security in this areana.

REFERENCES

Arends, R., Austein, R., Larson, M., Massey, D., & Rose, S. (2005, March). DNS Security Introduction and Requirements. *RFC*. Retrieved March 2005, from http://www.ietf.org/rfc/rfc4033.txt

Arkko, J., Kempf, J., Zill, B., & Nikander, P. (2005, March). *SEcure Neighbor Discovery (SEND)*. Retrieved from http://tools.ietf.org/html/rfc3971

Atkins, D., & Austein, R. (2004, August). Threat Analysis of the Domain Name System (DNS). *RFC*. Retrieved August 2004, from http://www.ietf.org/rfc/rfc3833.txt

Aura, T. (2005, March). *Cryptographically Generated Addresses (CGA)*. Retrieved from http://www.ietf.org/rfc/rfc3972.txt

Cheshire, S., & Krochmal, M. (2013, February). *Multicast DNS*. Retrieved from http://tools.ietf.org/html/rfc6762

Cooper, A., Tschofenig, H., Aboba, B., Peterson, J., Morris, J., Hansen, M., & Smith, R. (2013, July). *Privacy Considerations for Internet Protocols*. Retrieved from http://tools.ietf.org/html/rfc6973

Deering, S., & Hinden, R. (1998, December). Internet Protocol, Version 6 (IPv6) Specification. *RFC*. Retrieved from http://www.ietf.org/rfc/rfc2460.txt

Droms, R., Bound, J., Volz, B., Lemon, T., Perkins, C., & Carney, M. (2003, July). Dynamic Host Configuration Protocol for IPv6 (DHCPv6). *RFC*. Retrieved July 2003, from http://www.ietf.org/rfc/rfc3315.txt

EU DPD. (1995). *European Union Data Protection Directive: Processing of Personal Data and on the free movement of such data*. Retrieved from http://eur-lex.europa.eu/LexUriServ/LexUriServ.do?uri=CELEX:31995L0046:en:HTML

EU DPD. (2012). *European Union Data Protection Directive*. Retrieved from http://europa.eu/rapid/press-release_IP-12-46_en.htm?locale=en

Frankel, S., Graveman, R., Pearce, J., & Rooks, M. (2010, December). *Guidelines for the Secure Deployment of IPv6*. Retrieved from http://csrc.nist.gov/publications/nistpubs/800-119/sp800-119.pdf

Gont, F. (2013). *A method for Generating Stable Privacy-Enhanced Addresses with IPv6 Stateless Address Autoconfiguration (SLAAC)*. Retrieved from http://tools.ietf.org/html/draft-ietf-6man-stable-privacy-addresses (Work In Progress)

Hogg, S., & Vyncke, E. (2009). *IPv6 Security*. Cisco Press.

Kent, S., & Seo, K. (2005, December). Security Architecture for the Internet Protocol. *RFC*. Retrieved December 2005, from http://www.ietf.org/rfc/rfc4301.txt

Laurie, D., Sisson, G., Arends, R., & Blacka, D. (2008, March). *DNS Security (DNSSEC) Hashed Authenticated Denial of Existence*. Retrieved from http://tools.ietf.org/html/rfc5155

Lecigne, C., & Neville-Neil, G. V. (2006, August). *Walking through FreeBSD IPv6 stack*. Retrieved from http://clem1.be/gimme/ipv6sec.pdf

Lyon, J. F. (2009). *Nmap Network Scanning: The Official Nmap Project Guide to Network Discovery and Security Scanning*. Academic Press.

Mockapetris, P. (1987, November). *Domain Names - Implementation and specification*. Retrieved from http://tools.ietf.org/html/rfc1035

Narten, T., Draves, R., & Krishnan, S. (2007, September). *Privacy Extensions for Stateless Address Autoconfiguration in IPv6*. Retrieved from http://tools.ietf.org/html/rfc4941

Narten, T., Nordmark, E., Simpson, W., & Soliman, H. (2007, September). Neighbor Discovery for IP version 6 (IPv6). *RFC*. Retrieved September 2007, from http://www.ietf.org/rfc/rfc4861.txt

Nikander, R., Kempf, J., & Nordmark, E. (2004, May). *IPv6 Neighbor Discovery (ND) Trust Models and Threats*. Retrieved from http://tools.ietf.org/html/rfc3756

Ottow, C., Vliet, F. V., Boer, P. D., & Pras, A. (2012). The Impact of Ipv6 on Penetration Testing. Springer.

Perkins, C., Johnson, D., & Arkko, J. (2011, July). *Mobility Support in IPv6*. Retrieved from http://tools.ietf.org/html/rfc6275

Rafiee, H., Loewis, M. V., & Meinel, C. (2013). Challenges and Solutions for DNS Security in IPv6. In Architectures and Protocols for Secure Information Technology Infrastructures. Hershey, PA: IGI Global. DOI: doi:10.4018/978-1-4666-4514-1.ch006

Rafiee, H., & Meinel, C. (2013). *Router Advertisement based privacy extension in IPv6 autoconfiguration*. Retrieved from http://tools.ietf.org/html/draft-rafiee-6man-ra-privacy

Rafiee, H., & Meinel, C. (2013). SSAS: A Simple Secure Addressing Scheme for IPv6 AutoConfiguration. In *Proceedings of the 11th IEEE International Conference on Privacy, Security and Trust (PST)*. IEEE.

Rafiee, H., Mueller, C., Niemeier, L., Streek, J., Sterz, C., & Meinel, C. (2013). *A Flexible Framework For Detecting IPv6 Vulnerabilities*. Submitted to ACM Conference.

Roschke, S., Cheng, F., & Meinel, C. (2010). Using Vulnerability Information and Attack Graphs for Intrusion Detection. In *Proceedings of the 6th International Conference on Information Assurance and Security (IEEE)*, (pp. 68 - 73). IEEE. doi: doi:10.1109/ISIAS.2010.5604041

Silva, P. M., Dias, J., & Ricardo, M. (n.d.). *Survey on Privacy Solutions at the Network Layer: Terminology, Fundamentals and Classification.* Retrieved from http://paginas.fe.up.pt/~prodei/dsie11/images/pdfs/s6-4.pdf

Truta, T. M., & Vinay, B. (2006). Privacy Protection: p-Sensitive k-Anonymity Property. In *Proceedings of the 22nd International Conference on Data Engineering workshops*. IEEE.

ENDNOTES

1 http://www.thc.org/thc-ipv6/

2 http://snad.ncsl.nist.gov/ipv6/sendip.html

3 http://www.secdev.org/projects/scapy/

4 http://isic.sourceforge.net/

5 http://clem1.be/ipv6-attacks/

6 http://www.hpi.uni-potsdam.de/meinel/security_tech/ipv6_security/ipv6ssl.html

7 https://code.google.com/p/packet-manipulation-library

8 http://peachfuzzer.com

9 http://www.umip.org/

10 http://www.litech.org/radvd/

Chapter 8
A Security Analysis of MPLS Service Degradation Attacks Based on Restricted Adversary Models

Abdulrahman Al-Mutairi
University of London, UK

Stephen D. Wolthusen
University of London, UK & Gjøvik University College, Norway

ABSTRACT

Whilst the security and integrity of exterior gateway protocols such as the Border Gateway Protocol (BGP) and, to a lesser extent, interior gateway protocols, including the Multi-Protocol Label Switching (MPLS), have been investigated previously, more limited attention has been paid to the problem of availability and timeliness that is crucial for service levels needed in critical infrastructure areas such as financial services and electric power (smart grid) networks. The authors describe a method for modeling adversaries for the analysis of attacks on quality of service characteristics underpinning such real-time networks as well as a model of policies employed by MPLS routers based on simplified networks and give an analysis of attack vectors based on assumed adversaries derived from the introduced method.

INTRODUCTION

Multi-Protocol Label Switching (MPLS) protocol is widely deployed not only as an interior gateway protocol within single organization networks, but also in networks where well-defined Quality of Service (QoS) characteristics are critical including electric power, financial services, and other critical infrastructure networks where demanding

hard real-time requirements are in place. Whilst such networks were historically isolated, the current, so-called Next Generation Network (NGN) infrastructure visualizes such networks on top of internet substrate protocol (Lee and Knight, 2005).

Unlike in the case of the Border Gateway Protocol (BGP) exterior gateway protocol, even the existence of flows may not be visible due to the implementation of different routing techniques

DOI: 10.4018/978-1-4666-6158-5.ch008

such as labels aggregation that is used for efficiency purposes (Rosen, Viswanathan, & Callon, 2001) or due to the confidentiality of traffic flows, also some routing policies must be considered confidential (Subramanian et al., 2005). However, at the same time MPLS networks tend to be better managed and monitored, imposing limitations on what an adversary may be considered capable of. In this work we describe a simplified network model to capture selected timing characteristics and identify the relevant parameters which may be subjected to deliberate attacks that may affect QoS directly or indirectly. To this end we also provide a simplified model of MPLS routing policies that is then forming the base of an analysis of attack vectors that adversaries of different capabilities may deploy to violate the QoS characteristics of given network flows.

Based on the above, we model common adversaries with more limitations that could emerge in MPLS networks. Then, we give an analysis primarily for QoS-related attack classes that adversaries may be able to deploy depending on the level of adversary capabilities ascribed, which itself provides guidance for the security requirements levied on MPLS routers and links interconnecting these routers.

Adversaries may seek to affect QoS parameters of a particular traffic flow and the relevant service level agreements (SLA) rather than launching Denial of Service (DoS) attacks against the entire network. Also, adversaries may seek to exploit knowledge of the attacked network to inform their possible attack targets and strategies as this will give insights into response behavior to disturbances induced by the adversary directly, by non-malicious traffic and incidents on shared network resources, or combinations of these.

The main contributions of this work are therefore the adversary modeling method that could be used to extract more suitable adversary models for specific security analysis for MPLS networks, based on which we perform a threat analysis describing several classes of attacks

which an adversary may launch against policy mechanisms by manipulating the policy engines directly through mis-using the used signaling protocols or by altering the decision elements that policy engines use for routing processes; mainly, label entries in label stack.

RELATED WORK

As our work is motivated by the notion of mapping the QoS requirements which is mainly defined by hard real-time characteristics into the underlying networks for a well defined security analysis, we find that works addressing the availability and functionality of real-time networks are closely related. Indeed, a well designed real-time network that is capable of processing real-time traffic efficiently requires well studied and analyzed techniques to make sure all of the components in such networks act consistently and accordingly.

Yerraballi (Yerraballi and Mukkamalla, 1996) presented a way to analyze real time systems ability to meet the deadlines of tasks; particularly, by addressing the problem of end-to-end schedulability in distributed real-time system. Some of the concerns were discussed in the case that execution time changes (e.g arrival changes) in fixed priority scheduling environment. Alternatively, Thiele (Thiele, Chakraborty, & Naedele, 2000) presented a performance analysis approach using real time calculus which extends the basic concepts of network calculus. Basically, the presented method is aimed to analyze the flow of event streams through a network of computation and communication resources in any event stream environment.

Stoimenov (Stoimenov, Chakraborty, & Thiele, 2010) proposed an interface algebra based on the real time interfaces for verifying buffer overflow/ underflow constraints and the worst-case traversal time (WCTT). Indeed the main contribution was the confirmation of the composability of multiple components while satisfying the buffer and WCTT constraints. In addition, Stoimenov et al. presented a simplified real calculus model for basic components in real time systems. Both of the presented analysis approaches provided by Thiele et al. and Stoimenov et al. show how strict and sensitive is the environment that is used to assure the real-time applications requirements provision.

On the other hand, assuring the security of real-time networks requires a rigorous security analysis of the associated network components and mechanisms. Consequently, some efforts; remarkably, have been paid to analyze the security of multiple protocols, mechanisms and implementations of real-time networks. One of the major signaling protocols used in MPLS networks is label distribution protocol (LDP). An analysis of LDP from the insider attack perspective was reported by Guernsey (Guernsey, Engel, Butts, & Sheno, 2010) demonstrating several exploits that may cause route modification, traffic injection and Denial of Service (DoS); mainly, by BGP update messages poisoning or by injecting malicious traffic directly into Label Switched Paths (LSPs). However, the relatively small number of MPLS nodes that are physically secured limits the likelihood of such attacks. Furthermore, the mentioned attacks were only theoretically highlighted. However, our work aims to demonstrate the mis-use of LDP messages and the subsequent effects on the QoS of the routed traffic.

Grayson (Grayson, Guernsey, Butts, Spainhower, & Shenoi, 2009) provided a further security analysis of BGP/MPLS virtual private networks (VPNs); mainly, for the possibility of integrity threats. Grayson et al. discussed the VPNs integrity by addressing some of the possible attacks on route and traffic injection and paid some attention to DoS attacks, but placed less emphasis on the reconnaissance and QoS degradation resulting in policy-driven attacks that we are considering here. It should be noted that DoS or route injection might not be the main goals of attacks; however, the adversary may seek to affect the QoS of the processed traffic. Missing such security concerns could lead to attacks

that have long-lasting impacts on QoS or traffic direction that may go far beyond transitive faults (Bilski, 2009). Moreover, the problem of routing traffic according to the requirements of QoS is known as the QoS routing problem (Alkahtani, Woodward, & Al-Begain, 2003) which requires integration with a number of additional protocols. For example, finding suitable paths is relatively complicated and employs various mechanisms such as Integrated Services (IntServ) (Clark, Braden, & Shenker, 1994), Differentiated Services (DiffServ) (Blake et al.,1998) and Traffic Engineering (TE) (Awduche and Agogbua, 1999), which could themselves be targeted or attacked by adversaries.

The main alternative for the MPLS control plane to LDP is the extension of existing protocols for signaling; this is realized both in the form of the Resource Reservation Protocol for Traffic Engineering (RSVP-TE) and Multi-protocol Extensions for BGP (MP-BGP). Spainhower (Spainhower, Butts, Guernsey, & Shenoi, 2008) analysed the security properties of RSVP-TE. Spainhower et al. claimed that the trust relationship between Provider Edge (PE) and Customer Edge (CE) nodes could be violated by using a fabricated RSVP-TE message to perform resource reservation inside MPLS domain in case this type of messages is allowed at the PE node which leads to the possibility of launching DoS attack against MPLS by mis-using path messages to exhaust the network resources. Also, a reconnaissance attack was introduced that could allow attacker to gain topology information by revealing the record route object (RRO) in the reservation message. However, most of the mentioned attacks could be mitigated by good configuration practices; particularly, on the MPLS edges.

Although, the research studies listed above have added a remarkable effort to the research of real-time networks security by addressing the security of MPLS and the associated protocols, the possibility of affecting the network parameters was not included within the analyses framework.

In other words, the QoS assurance and stability issues in terms of information security have not been addressed in those studies which could lead to a misguided security analysis, vulnerabilities assessment and risk mitigation.

REAL-TIME NETWORKS

Traffic in networks may belong to a large number of applications that have different characteristics to be considered in traffic routing; mainly, those characteristics are related to availability and timeliness which are dependent on network metrics such as bandwidth, time delay and jitter. In order to meet the real-time deadlines for multiple applications, the underlying networks need to sufficiently manage and offer the required network resources according to the deadlines of each traffic flow in the network. Generally, most of the introduced solutions include Resource Reservation Protocol (RSVP), TE, DiffServ, constraint-based routing and the emerging model MPLS enable the underlying networks firstly to satisfy and assure the bandwidth requirement; then, satisfy the time delay and jitter. We refer the reader to ITU-T Recommendation Y.1540 by Nt'l Telecommuncation Union (2011) for time delay and jitter definitions.

Therefore, an upper bound must be set on bandwidth of each path that real-time traffic traverses where the total bandwidth of a concerned path is seen as the sum up of the bandwidth of each link along that path. Formally, let the total bandwidth of a path *P* be *B*total and the required bandwidth of the real-time flow be *B*, therefore, the upper bound on the required bandwidth is expressed as following:

$$B \leq B_p^{total} \tag{3.1}$$

Apparently, the time delay that a packet experiences in the network could be seen as the sum up of all local time delays of a sequence of nodes on the path that the packet traverses. Therefore,

a bound must be set on the concerned path for time delay. Formally, let the time delay that a packet *i* may experience in network be T_i, the upper bound on time delay of the packet *i* be T_i^{max} and the maximum time delay (the sum up of all the maximum local delays) of a sequence of nodes along the path *p* that the packet traverses be T_p^{max}. Hence, the bound on the time delay that may be experienced by the packet could be expressed as follows:

$$T_i \leq T_i^{max} \leq T_p^{max} \tag{3.2}$$

Similarly, the underlying network must ensure that the hard real-time flow is treated as per the jitter requirement by setting an upper bound J^{max} on jitter *J* as following:

$$J \leq J^{max} \tag{3.3}$$

Jitter J for each packet could be calculated continuously using the difference of packet spacing for the current packet *i* and the previous packet *i-1* according to the following formula:

$$J = J + \left(\left\| \left(Diff_{i-1,i} \right) \right\| - J \right) / 16 \tag{3.4}$$

We refer the reader to Jacobson (Jacobson, Frederick, Casner, & Schulzrinne, 2003) for more details concerning jitter calculations and measurement.

MPLS AND POLICY ROUTING

MPLS is a connection oriented switching mechanism designed for fast routing decision based on indexed label entries instead of longest prefix matching for IP addresses. MPLS provides Traffic Engineering (TE) implicitly (Awduche and Agogbua, 1999) to enable load balancing on available links and perform fast re-routing in case of link failure (Usui, Kitatsuji, & Yokota, 2011). By guaranteeing bandwidth for various traffic flows, Traffic Engineering can satisfy the constraints for QoS requirements such as bandwidth as well as administrative policies. The other main two requirements for QoS are jitter and time delay that require MPLS to add class based classification to different traffic flows in order to serve each class differently. By setting the experimental filed in label headers at the ingress Label Switching Router (LSR), the core LSRs could buffer and schedule the packets accordingly. Both techniques TE and class based treatment are needed to guarantee QoS requirements (e.g. bandwidth, jitter and time delay) (Fineberg, 2003).

MPLS is not used only in network backbone but also is used for QoS provision if combined with differentiated services because it is ideal for traffic engineering. MPLS protocol is working at layer 2.5 in the Open Systems Interconnection (OSI) model, hence, it encapsulates any layer 3 (network layer) protocol over layer 2 (data link). MPLS adds a shim header between layer 2 and 3 headers as shown in figure 1. MPLS shim has the label stack which contains label entries.

In MPLS, packets with the same desired treatment (e.g. same destination) are assigned to a class or what is known as Forward Equivalence Class (FEC) which represents the forwarding treatment for flow (flows) of packets in the MPLS domain.

Those FECs are encoded as a 32-bit label (a short fixed-length identifier). The label header contains four fields: 20-bit label value field, 3-bit experiment field (EXP) for experimental use (e.g QoS and priority), 1-bit bottom of stack (S) which is set to one to indicate the last label in the label stack and zero for other labels and 8-bit time to live (TTL) field (Rosen et al.,2001). The label is then inserted to each packet once at the MPLS edge router and forwarded to the next hop. The network layer header is not analyzed at any of the subsequent hops. Actual forwarding of packets is based on labels rather than IP addresses (He and Botham, 2008).

The MPLS forwarding scheme is done by mapping the incoming label into next hop and outgoing label which replaces the incoming label when the packet is forwarded along a pre- computed label switched path (LSP). To establish LSPs, MPLS uses some signalling protocols such as Label Distribution Protocol (LDP). We refer the reader to Andersson (Andersson, Doolan, Feldman, Fredette, & Thomas, 2007) for details concerning the LDP specifications. However, for establishing LSPs with some specific constraints (e.g. bandwidth), some signalling protocols are used such as Resource Reservation Protocol (RSVP) and Constrained based LDP (CD-LDP). We refer the reader to Awduche et al. (2001) and Jamoussi et al. (2002) for details concerning RSVP and CD-

Figure 1. MPLS packet format

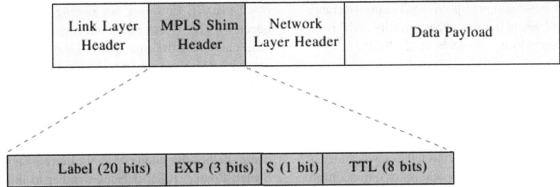

LDP respectively. The goal of using the latter two protocols is to map the available resources to the required services by the traffic flows to enable QoS routing in such environment.

The set-up LSPs are then used to offer end to end QoS for traffic flows using QoS routing algorithm to assure the QoS services for different flows according to network parameters change (e.g. bandwidth, time delay or jitter) and routing/administrative polices. In addition, each flow is treated as required based on hop-by-hop basis. The main contribution by MPLS is the provision of QoS based on flow-by-flow basis rather than packet-by-packet basis. Indeed, MPLS leads to the isolation of high priority flows (e.g. real time-traffic) from the ordinary data flows which have no strict parameters.

Moreover, LSPs in MPLS could be set up with various priorities in order to serve important LSPs better than less important ones. Therefore, the LSPs with higher priority can pre-empt (tear down) the ones with less priority. Before a new LSP is established, if there is a lack of resources, the set-up priority of the new LSP is compared with the holding priority of the other LSPs to determine the ability of the new LSP to pre-empt the already established LSPs. Pre-emption mechanism is included in RSVP-TE protocol to allow an LSP with higher priority to pre-empt other LSPs with lower priority. The pre-empted LSPs are then re-established if possible. Basically, each LSP has a set-up and holding priorities that specify the capability of an LSP to pre-empt the other LSPs and the capability of an LSP to resist such pre-emption respectively. The priority range is 0-7 where 0 is the highest priority and 7 is the lowest priority (Awduche et al., 2001).

A SIMPLIFIED MPLS POLICY MODEL

The act of routing the traffic in MPLS according to the desired QoS is subjected to a wide range of polices (e.g. routing or admission). In addition,

there are different technologies that MPLS has to adopt in order to deliver QoS such as IntServ, DiffServ and TE which would lead to different implementations with different policies in MPLS networks. Therefore, focusing on a simplified policy model that is concerned with the QoS routing/re-routing of traffic in MPLS would lead to a clear security analysis process.

Our simplified policy model describes how the network system is supposed to treat traffic as expected. Mainly, there is a need for a guaranteed QoS by establishing (LSPs) and bind flows to them. We assume such LSPs are already established. However, we need to identify the QoS metrics that are considered in establishing and maintaining such paths as well as re-routing of traffic among them according to network changes. There are four metrics in our simplified MPLS policy model: bandwidth (B), time delay (T), jitter (J) and packet loss (L).

While, bandwidth and time delay metrics are used to establish the constrained LSPs, the time delay, jitter and packet loss metrics are used to monitor the processed flows and adjust the routes according to the constraints on each of them. Therefore, bandwidth to be reserved as well as using the class based treatment based on hop-by-hop for the other two requirements (time delay and jitter). For simplicity we are going to assume that flows are served as per Class Based Queues (CBQ). There are only two different service classes: Real-Time (RT) class and Best-Efforts (BE) class. BF class may borrow bandwidth from RT class whenever it is not used but not the vice versa. It should be noted that BE flows are not sharing the same queue with RT flows. However, flows from the same class share the same queue. There are back-up paths which are set-up to be used in case of failure or sudden changes in network domain shared by all LSPs.

The MPLS policy model could be split into two phases: the admission phase and the routing phase. In the admission phase, the ingress Label Switch Router (LSR) decides whether to initiate a new LSP in response to a request for RT flow by making the constraints computation on the available resources and the request requirements (*B, T*) as shown in figure 2. The paths are calculated to find a set of paths that satisfies the bounds or constraints simultaneously. Firstly, the policy engine finds the set of paths that satisfy the constraint B by removing the paths with residual bandwidth less than requested B using the equation-3.1. Then, selects paths satisfy the constraint T using the equation-3.2. It has to be noted that if no path could be found for a new HRT request LSPs pre-emption is used.

The other phase is the routing phase where the flows are forwarded along their assigned LSPs as shown in Figure 3. Also, where the flows status is monitored and feed-backed to the admission phase as shown in Figure 2. Each traffic flow is forwarded, buffered in queues and scheduled inside MPLS domain through LSRs based on labels. As the packet received at any of the LSRs, it is checked if it has a label, otherwise, it is going to be dropped. Then, the label is processed and if it belongs to the same LSR (self label), that label

is popped (removed) and the packet is processed again as if it is recently received as shown in Figure 3.

Otherwise, the LSP table which is known as Explicit-Routes Information Base is checked to find entries for the processed label. Finally, the packet is label switched into the associated LSP if an entry is exist, otherwise, the packet is simply dropped. Moreover, we assume that the strategy to react to overload bandwidth in each LSP is limited to delay accumulation then packet discarding which could be done by assuming the queue length is limitedly fixed. However, the traffic is monitored for adjustment periodically at every time interval m to keep the three metrics *L, T* and *J* within the assigned bounds.

According to Gurijala and Molina (2004), QoS traffic could be monitored periodically and passively by calculating the concerned metrics averages. Hence, the average time delay for a specific flow could be calculated by dividing the total delays for all received packets (excluding the lost packets) by the total number of the received packets at every time interval *m*. Similarly, the

Figure 2. Admission phase for LSPs requests

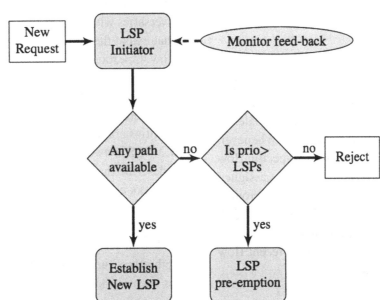

Figure 3. Routing phase for packets

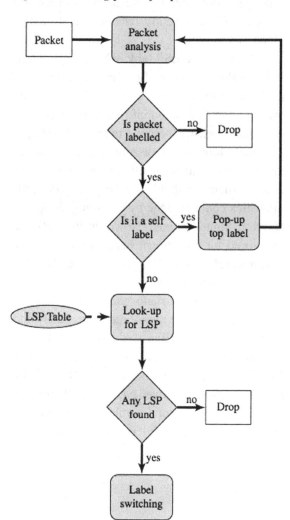

ADVERSARY MODEL FOR MPLS NETWORKS

Describing the adversary forms the cornerstone of any information security analysis. Indeed, no information security analysis of any system could be successfully accomplished without describing what the adversary is capable of. Moreover, measuring the effectiveness of any introduced solution for any information security vulnerability needs clearly defined and variable adversary capabilities which would enable analysts to determine the acceptable levels of risks and the sufficient countermeasures (Olsen, 2005).

Protocol adversary models mainly are prescribed for security analysis of cryptographic systems and mostly assume the worst case scenario. For example, Dolev-Yao adversary model (Dolev and Yao, 1983) assumes that the adversary has unlimited access to the message which increases the adversary strength, while, more variable limitations on adversary in MPLS networks have to be considered. Although, Syverson (Syverson, Tsudik, Reed, & Landwehr, 2001) claimed that the compromised core scenario is sufficient to assess the studied security because the other defined adversaries could perform only subsets of the compromised core scenario actions, analyzing adversaries with less capabilities would reveal to what extent the system is vulnerable in order to allow some room for accepting the risk, especially, in the case where usability is chosen over security as in QoS networks.

Suitable adversary models with variable capabilities are needed to capture different threats in MPLS networks. Therefore, we would like to describe the adversary properties that MPLS networks could face in sections 6.1-5. Then we use the adversary properties in a specified MPLS security analysis to extract different adversary models in section 6.6. Our adversary modeling method is not unique as a similar modeling method has been introduced by Olsen (2005). However,

packet lost rate is calculated for each traffic flow at every time interval *m* as the ratio of the lost packets to the total sent packets. However, jitter is sampled at every time interval *m* as it is updated as per packet basis using the equation-3.3. Whenever, one of the monitored metrics for a specific flow at least exceeds the threshold and the assigned bandwidth was not violated, the flow is re-routed to another path that satisfies the specified QoS requirements; otherwise, a signaling message is sent to the source to block the most recent flow (Chen, Chen, & Chian, 2007).

our modeling method focuses on the MPLS networks properties and aims to help the researchers to model their own adversary models for different security analysis of MPLS networks.

Adversary Goals and Motivations

The adversary goals and motivations are important to direct the security analysis efforts and justify the ability that the adversary could gain in order to affect networks that may carry time sensitive traffic for various military, financial, electric power, health and other critical infrastructure organizations. The main goal for the adversary that MPLS networks may face is to affect the QoS parameters of traffic flows for multiple reasons such as degradation of the services that different traffic flows are supposed to receive or upgrading certain traffic flows services on the starvation of others. However, the adversary may also aim to minimize the ability of network operators to notice that the system is under attack in order to make considerable gains of the launched attacks.

Adversary Knowledge

Information about the attacked networks would assist adversaries to prepare, adopt and launch the applicable attacks for the specified goals. For instance, information about the used protocols or the set-up processes of the connections among network nodes forms the basic knowledge that the adversary would need. We assume that the adversary initially has a complete knowledge of the MPLS networks operational information (e.g how MPLS networks work generally). Moreover, the adversary is assumed to have a detailed description of the signaling protocols used in MPLS networks; particularly, the LDP and RSVP protocols and the way to simulate them (e.g signaling messages fabrication). However, the adversary knowledge about the targeted MPLS network or the associated flows needs to be specified. An adversary with

detailed information about the routing tables in the attacked network, for example, is more capable to launch successful attacks against that network than an adversary with zero knowledge.

The adversary knowledge could be divided into four classes as follows:

Topology Information

Whilst, the topology information in simple networks; mainly, is related to the arrangement of network elements (e.g point to point, bus or star), there is a distinct difference in MPLS networks between the physical or logical topology. The physical topology refers to the physical interconnections among network nodes (e.g physical locations of links on nodes) as well as the links specification details (e.g time delay, bandwidth capacity and link types). However, the logical topology refers to the logical interconnections among nodes in network. For example, some nodes can communicate as if they are physically connected while there is no direct link attached between them; hence, other nodes lay alongside that logical path may not be aware of such connection. It should be noted that the next hop for a packet may not be the actual current hop (downstream hop). The logical topology information in MPLS; mainly, encompasses the information about the next hop and the interface for each packet. Also, the forwarding plane information for each MPLS node may include such information. Whilst, the Forwarding Information Base (FIB) that is used for non-labeled packets routing is used to find the proper interface for forwarding a packet, Label Forwarding Information Base (LFIB) has information about the Next Hop Label Forwarding Entry (NHLFE) that contains the packet next hop. Also, the Explicit Routing Table (ERT) and the VPN routing tables contain entries for the explicit routes (tunnels) and VPN routes respectively that have been established on the MPLS network with the associated labels.

Control Information

The exchanged information (e.g requests, replies and announcements) among network nodes in order to establish connections (e.g label requests) or required services (e.g resource reservation) represents the control information. Indeed, control information encompasses the signaling messages of different protocols. The main LDP signaling messages are label allocation, release, withdraw and request messages as well as the notification messages. On the other hand, the main RSVP-TE signaling messages are the path (request) and reserve (accept) messages. In addition, the control information includes the network mapping tables such as the network layer routing tables, the label bindings and the VPN routing tables that routers receive and forward among each others.

Traffic Information

The information that belongs to traffic flows in the attacked network represents the traffic information class. The traffic knowledge encompasses the type of traffic that passes through the attacked network, the priority of the traffic and the time periods of such information (past, present or updated information). While, past information for traffic describes the details about traffic during previous time periods, the present and updated information for traffic describe the details about traffic in the current period and the current and future period respectively.

Policy Information

The policy information refers to the collection of rules that MPLS network nodes use to accomplish the desired operation according to the required services. The policy information encompasses a wide range of rules that is used in network management. However, the policy information in MPLS could be divided into three classes of policy: label bindings, routing tables and routing policy. Label biddings policy represents the collection of rules

that governs the labels management such as label allocation, distribution and retention. However, routing table policy refers to the desired actions on routing tables. For example, which routing table to be shared with which router or the parameters that are needed to be injected to the routing tables (e.g hop counts) as well as the allowed protocols that are used for such actions.

Routing policy represents the collection of rules that each node in MPLS network use for making decisions on the received packets. For example, a LSR in MPLS may decide to carry some configured actions (e.g drop packet) on specific packets if they are received at a particular link. Routing policy also encompasses the main operations on packets label stack (push, swap and pop). According to Rosen (Rosen, Viswanathan, Callon, 2001), each LSR may push one or more labels onto the label stack, swap (replace) the top label of the label stack by a specified one or pop (remove) the label stack. Indeed the adversary may have access to one or more of the network information classes at the same time. Therefore, the level of knowledge that the adversary may have gained of each information class could be presented on a scale of zero to 10 where zero means that the adversary has no knowledge about that information class and 10 means that the adversary is aware of the information class entirely. It should be noted that a description of the knowledge level that the adversary has must be provided. For example, let us consider an adversary that has gained information of the physical topology of the topology information class and the control information class entirely which includes the signaling messages and label bindings; however, the adversary has no access to the traffic or policy information in the attacked network.

Then, the adversary has a level of knowledge of 5 for the topology information class, a level of knowledge of 10 for the control information class and zero level of knowledge for the traffic and policy information classes respectively as shown in figure 4.

Figure 4. An adversary with a certain level of knowledge of topology, control, traffic and policy information classes

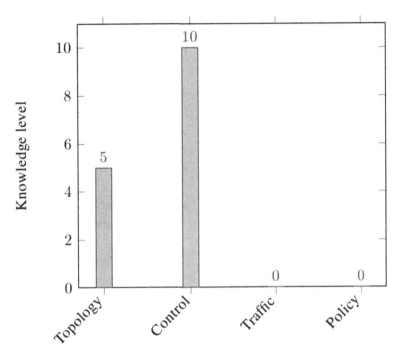

Intervention Type

The intervention type specifies the network elements that the adversary has access to in order to intervene to launch attacks. The adversary may compromise one or more of MPLS network principals and/or may have access to one or more of the links attached to them. Network principals are defined as the set of entities interacting within a system. In our adversary model, the MPLS network principals are restricted to the customer edges (ingress/egress edges of the customer network according to the flow direction), MPLS edges (ingress/egress edges of the customer network according to the flow direction) and MPLS core LSRs (LSRs inside the MPLS domain).

It should be noted that having access to particular links would add more/less power to the adversary as the links that are attached directly to the MPLS edges increase the possibility of affecting the edges themselves as well as the ability

to affect most of the processed traffic especially, on links attached to the egress LSR where packets are sent in network layer format because of the penultimate hop popping mechanism (Rosen, Viswanathan, & Callon, 2001).

Intervention Operation

The operations that the adversary may run on one of the network elements in order to intervene in the system processes for malicious intents are read, intercept or write operations. The intervention operations are defined as following:

- **Read Operation:** The adversary can read (observe) all messages that pass through the compromised entity.
- **Intercept Operation:** The adversary can block, reorder, delay (restrict) and suppress any message of choice that passes through the compromised entity.

- **Write Operation:** The adversary could insert his own messages onto the compromised entity.

Adversary may run one or more of the intervention operations. Hence, the given intervention operations must be specified in the adversary model. It should be noted that compromising one of the network principals (customer edge, MPLS edge or MPLS core LSR) implies the full set of intervention operations (read, intercept or write).

Multi-Intervention

The adversary could be working alone or interacting with other adversaries for more malicious intents. The other adversaries may have different capability limits (e.g intercept operation on one of the core link). The other adversary capabilities must be clarified in order to measure the capabilities of multi-intervention adversaries in the targeted network where the multi-intervention adversaries with lower capabilities could achieve a powerful level of combined capabilities. Also, the information flow between the adversaries and the way they coordinate has to be specified. For example, are the adversaries using a synchronous channel to communicate for the attacks or they are assumed to work separately.

Extracted Adversary Models

After specifying the possible properties of the adversary that could emerge in MPLS networks, we give examples of extracting suitable adversary models in order to use the models for a security analysis of MPLS networks in next section. It should be noted that the following adversary models are mainly for adversaries with limited capabilities because stronger adversary models and scenarios such as the compromised node scenario are not suitable for MPLS security analysis. Indeed, the relatively small number of MPLS nodes that are usually physically secured limits the likelihood of such scenarios. The extracted adversary models are listed below:

LDP-Messages Manipulating Adversary

The adversary has the ability to fabricate and send LDP label withdraw/release messages to the upstream/downstream LSRs in order to remove label entries in LFIB. The LDP-messgaes manipulating adversary has the following properties:

- **Adversary Knowledge:** Topology information about any flow of choice; particularly, the location of the link that the attacked flow traverses. Control information about any flow of choice; particularly, the label that is assigned for that flow to the upstream or downstream LSR.
- **Intervention Type:** Adversary has access to at most one chosen core link.
- **Intervention Operation:** Write.
- **Multi-Intervention:** No (single adversary).

Label Manipulating Adversary

The adversary has the ability to spoof the used labels and has the following properties:

- **Adversary Knowledge:** Topology information about any flow of choice (the link that the flow of concern traverses). Control information about any flow of choice (the label stack assigned for that flow as well as label stack associated with high priority flows to the upstream or downstream LSR).
- **Intervention Type:** Adversary has access to at most one chosen core link.
- **Intervention Operation:** Intercept and Write.
- **Multi-Intervention:** No (single adversary).

LSP Injection Adversary

The adversary has the ability to inject messages (e.g flow) into attacked LSP that passes through the given link by spoofing the associated label stack.

- **Adversary Knowledge:** Topology information about any LSP of choice (the link that the attacked path traverses). Control information about the attacked LSP (the label stack assigned for attacked LSP).
- **Intervention Type:** Adversary has access to at most one chosen core link.
- **Intervention Operation:** Write.
- **Multi-Intervention:** No (single adversary).

Resource Exhaustion Adversary

The adversary has the ability to fabricate and send a RESV message to initiate explicit LSPs over the attacked network.

- **Adversary Knowledge:** Topology information about the attacked LSRs (e.g LSRs addresses). Control information (how the RSVP messages are used to set-up explicit LSPs among the LSRs in the attacked network).
- **Intervention Type:** Adversary has access to at most one core link.
- **Intervention Operation:** Write.
- **Multi-Intervention:** No (single adversary).

Following our method in extracting the required adversary model based on the possible adversary properties introduced in section 6.1-5 would lead to a well guided MPLS network security analysis. Subsequently, the security analysts could calculate the acceptable level of risk as well as the effectiveness of the countermeasures using the security analysis results accurately.

THREAT ANALYSIS

In this section, we show how our extracted adversary models in section 6.6 are used to address different threats in MPLS network using the simplified MPLS policy model in section 5. We used network simulator NS (version 2) to demonstrate some of the presented attacks. NS-2 is a popular and powerful simulation tool that has the ability to simulate MPLS networks. Our simulated network is shown in figure 5. Our simulated network consists of the MPLS domain and the customer domain. The MPLS domain is made up of multiple LSRs (LSR-2, 3, 4, 5, 6, 7, 8, and 9). The LSRs are bounded by two MPLS edges (ingress and egress LSRs) represented by LSR-1 and LSR-10 respectively.

The customer domain is made up of the source and the destination represented by node-0 and node-11 respectively. Each two adjacent nodes are connected by at most one link. Each LSR can implement the QoS scheduling for the traffic flows that traverse the attached links.

For simplicity, we assume that there is only one HRT traffic flow at source rate of *290kbps* which is attached to an LSP takes the shortest path through LSR-1 → LSR-2 → LSR-4 → LSR-6 → LSR-8 → LSR-10 as shown in Figure 5 with a guaranteed bandwidth of *300kbps*. It should be noted that the source rate and the path bandwidth are chosen arbitrarily.

Our analysis results revealed different types of attacks that may cause degradation of Quality of Service or even Denial of Service in some cases. In this section we will introduce the attacks that may lead to full disablement of Quality of Service that HRT flow should receive inside MPLS network with examples. Then, we will present two practical examples with simulations and results of the attacks that may lead to partial degradation of Quality of Service inside MPLS networks. Finally, we will use the simulated attacks results to prove that such attacks may not be detected or observed by network operators.

Quality of Service Treatment Level Disablement

Attacks under this category are concerned with preventing the HRT flow from getting the guaranteed Quality of Service either by manipulation of LSRs policy engines or by manipulation of labels belong to the HRT flow.

First of all, whereas the initiation of LSPs and the binding of specific traffic flows to them are done at the ingress LSR according to our simplified policy model in section 5, any changes to the policies of LSRs or traffic flows inside the MPLS domain may not be reported to or received by

ingress LSR. For example, if a resource release message was sent from one of the LSRs downstream of the ingress LSR (e.g. LSR-2) which serves the pre-computed LSP that the HRT flow traverses then the resources will be released from the downstream LSRs (LSR-4, 6, 8, 10) and the treatment of the underlying traffic flow of the released LSP will be no longer subjected to the desired Quality of Service and such actions may not be reported to the ingress LSR.

The LDP-messages manipulating adversary has the ability to fabricate a label release message to downgrade Quality of Service treatment for the HRT flow on any of the links that the HRT flow

Figure 5. MPLS Simulation Network Topology

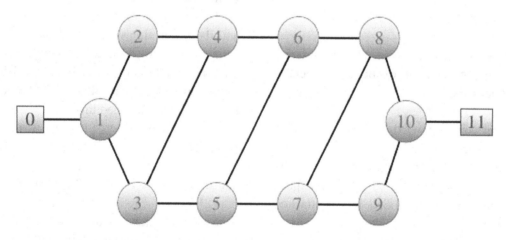

Figure 6. Hard real-time flow path

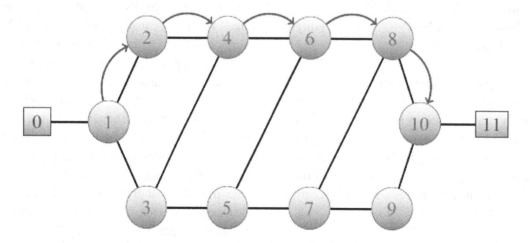

traverses as shown in Figure 6. Subsequently, the label release message will propagate towards the MPLS egress and the label entries will be removed from the affected LSRs which means that any flow belongs to the removed label will not be recognized by the downstream LSRs and hence the HRT flow will be treated as an unrecognized flow; therefore, the downstream LSRs may treat the HRT flow as one of the BE flows or drop the flow packets as suggested by our simplified MPLS policy model as shown in Figure 3.

The second attack under this category takes advantage of the independent processing of flows on LSRs and because the decisions of binding flow to LSPs are based on labels according to our simplified policy model in section 5, the label manipulating adversary that is introduced in section 6.6 could only replace labels stack belongs to the LSP that serves the HRT flow which passes through the compromised link (e.g the link between LSR-2 and LSR-4) to a label of choice that redirect traffic of concern into another LSP that does not comply with required Quality of Service in order to assure its delivery to the egress LSR to conceal the degradation attack. Therefore, the HRT flow is not going to be attached to the assigned LSP in the downstream LSRs and hence the required Quality of Service treatment is no longer applied.

Traffic Fluctuation

This type of attacks is based on the notion of Quality of Service parameters sensitivity to the sudden changes in the networks environment. According to Bilski (2009), the mitigation procedure to re-route the high bandwidth traffic around the affected cables in the Mediterranean Sea which have suffered cuts in 2008 did not consequently affected only the Quality of service of the re-routed connections, but, the Quality of Service of connections from other parts of the world to unacceptable level and such deterioration of Quality of Service may last for months.

The resource exhaustion adversary could initiate a longer and wider LSP with highest priority on the compromised link between LSR-3 and LSR-4 to make sure it crosses almost all of the other LSPs and utilizes most of the network resources. In our network the ideal path for this type of attacks is the path that passes through LSR-3 → LSR-4 → LSR-6 → LSR-5 → LSR-7 → LSR-8 → LSR-10 as shown in Figure 7. Consequently, according to our simplified MPLS policy model in section 5, almost all of the initiated LSPs are going to be torn down and re-established because of the LSPs pre-emption mechanism. The sudden tear down of almost all of the initiated LSPs, the re-establishing and re-routing pro-

Figure 7. Fabricated path

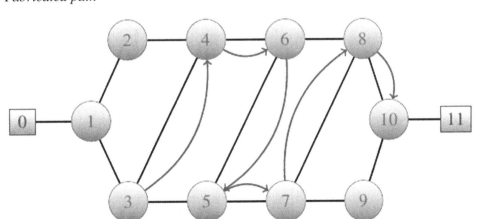

cesses of the traffic flows among them would affect the QoS parameters of the HRT flows inside the MPLS domain. Indeed, it could disable most of the LSPs from being re-established as long as that fabricated LSP keeps occupying the network resources.

Alternatively, the adversary could only initiate a longer LSP that interferes with most of the established LSPs discretely. The main idea here is to create a flapping environment inside the MPLS domain. In order to demonstrate this type of attacks, a fabricated LSP with a guaranteed bandwidth of *200kbps* was initiated over the path that passes through LSR-3 →LSR-4 →LSR-6→ LSR-5 →LSR-7 →LSR-8 →LSR-10 as shown in Figure 7.

Then, a traffic flow at source rate of *200kbps* was attached at the time *5sec* to the fabricated LSP in order to show how a slight flapping situ-

ation could affect the other traffic flows even if they are not sharing the same LSP. Our results show a slight changes in the Quality of Service parameters that belong to HRT traffic flow as the time delay reached *75ms* as shown in figure 8 with no changes to the packet loss value as the bandwidth was not violated, however, the jitter violated the specified bound which is *3ms* and reached *3.4ms* as shown in Figure 9 compared to the jitter in normal operation.

LSP Injection

Deliberately injecting traffic flows into other LSPs does not only affect the integrity of LSPs; but, the QoS of the traffic flows already attached into the injected LSPs could be affected too. The LSP injection adversary introduced in section 6.6 could inject a malicious flow into any LSP that

Figure 8. HRT flow time delay in fluctuating attack compared to normal operation

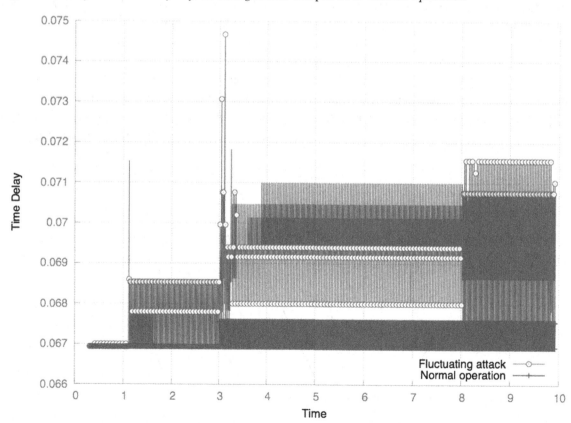

Figure 9. HRT flow jitter in fluctuating attack compared to normal operation

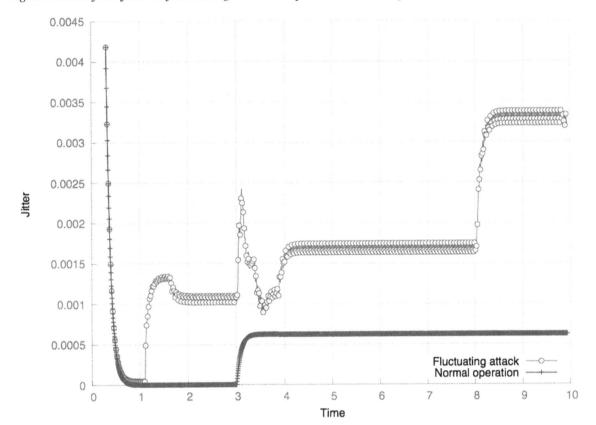

carries HRT traffic flow and passes through the compromised link. More interestingly, this attack could be launched against any HRT traffic flow in the MPLS domain by fabricating the label stack for the targeted LSP that serves the HRT traffic flow of concern and push a label into the label stack belongs to any LSR's label that the HRT traffic flow passes through. The targeted LSR then would pop (remove) the label on top and process the next label on label stack according to the policy engine in figure 3. Subsequently, the malicious flow would be attached to the targeted LSP causing an integrity violation and QoS degradation as our results showed.

We have demonstrated by simulation how the injection of even a low rate traffic flow could hugely affect the QoS of the HRT traffic flow that traverses the attacked LSP. Our LSP injection adversary could inject a traffic flow at source rate

of *10kbps* into the LSP that serves the HRT traffic flow only to fill up the allowed bandwidth for that LSP which is *300kbps* on the compromised link between LSR-2 and LSR-4. Consequently, the time delay and jitter of the HRT traffic flow have increased dramatically to exceed *90ms* and *4ms* compared to *67ms* and *0.6ms* in normal operation as shown in figures 10 and 11 respectively. However, the packet loss value was not changed because the bandwidth was not violated.

Attacks Concealment

Covering attacks and traces is an important strategy for attackers in general. However, the notion of attack concealment is more important for quality of service degradation attacks; mainly, because the attacks are only successful as they are periodically being launched in network domain to degrade the

Figure 10. HRT flow time delay in injection attack compared to normal operation

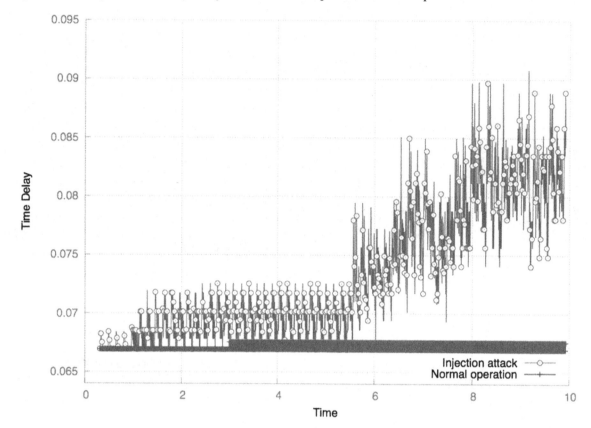

quality of service of the targeted traffic. Also, attacks concealment is useful to make it harder for the network operator to track down the source of attacks such as the compromised link. Because quality of service monitoring in our simplified MPLS policy model introduced in section 5 are mainly based on the analysis of the mean values of time delay and packet loss or the current updated value of jitter, the implementation of our attacks could not be discovered or mitigated if they were periodically launched to affect the HRT traffic flow of concern partially on packet basis.

For illustration, we arbitrarily assume that the metrics samples are taken periodically every *60sec*. Therefore, if both of our simulated attacks only last for *5sec* the sampling results for packet loss rate, average delay time and jitter in the traffic fluctuation attack are: 0%, 68m and0.9ms respectively. Also, the sampling results for packet

loss rate, average delay time and jitter in the LSP injection attack are: 0.3%, 69ms and 1.2ms respectively. Unfortunately, this type of attacks is very difficult to discover as the bounds on the QoS parameters; particularly, the average time delay and jitter bounds has not been violated.

CONCLUSION

The demands for a guaranteed quality of service for diversity of applications and the degree of criticality of those applications (e.g financial services or critical mission communications) increasingly force the Internet Service Providers (ISPs) to adopt, develop and secure their networks accordingly. Securing the underlying networks is the most important step in providing quality of service because any violation to the quality of

Figure 11. HRT flow jitter in injection attack compared to normal operation

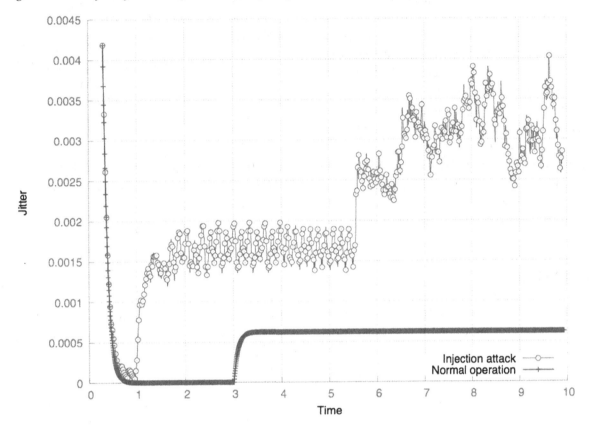

service deadlines or the SLA may not be detected, mitigated or subjected to further assessment in design process as the case with other elements. Therefore, some efforts have been made to study the security of main elements of such networks; mainly, the signaling protocols. For example, the security analysis of signaling protocols such as LDP or BGP and the resource managing protocols such as RSVP. However, analyzing the security of individual protocols solely in addition to the lack of the suitable adversary model may lead to a weak assessment of the vulnerabilities or threats of the analyzed system; especially, in case of certain type of attacks such as those targeting the policy model.

This work provides an analysis of the real-time networks security; mainly, in the context of MPLS core networks based on restricted adversary models. We illustrated the mapping of hard real-time characteristics onto the core networks and differentiation into service classes. Furthermore, a method for deriving a suitable adversary in MPLS network was introduced in order to highlight the ability of limited adversary to take advantages of potential vulnerabilities of MPLS networks. These limitation and restrictions on the adversary are important to direct the security study of real-time systems based on MPLS networks correctly from the common security issues into the availability and stability of the networks operation. Then, restricted adversary models were extracted for further security analysis.

Therefore, some practical attacks have been demonstrated using the network simulator NS (version 2) which is a discrete event simulator targeted at networking research that has the ability to simulate MPLS networks and quality of service mechanisms. Our simulation scenarios showed how different techniques could be applied by an adversary with a limited capability to affect the quality of service of traffic flows of choice. Finally, we explain how such attacks might not be reported to network operators or trigger the monitoring servers. We hope that the introduced method for extracting suitable adversary models help researchers to construct the required adversary model for a well defined security analysis in MPLS networks and the revealed attacks results raise the concerns about quality of service provision in the backbone networks as well as the security of control protocols used at core systems.

REFERENCES

Agrawal, Cruz, Okino, & Rajan. (1999). Performance bonds for flow control protocols. *IEEE/ACM Transactions on Networking, 7*(3), 310–323.

Alkahtani, M. S., Woodward, M. E., & Al-Begain, K. (2003). An overview of quality of service (qos) and qos routing in communication networks. In *Proceedings of 4th PGNET 2003 Symposium*, (pp. 236-242). Liverpool, UK: PGNET.

Andersson, Doolan, Feldman, Fredette, & Thomas. (2007). *LDP specification*. IETF, RFC 5036.

Audsley, N. C., Burns, A., Davis, R. I., Tindell, K. W., & Wellings, A. J. (1995). Fixed priority pre-emptive scheduling: An historical perspective. *Real-Time Systems, 8*(2-3), 173–198. doi:10.1007/BF01094342

Awduche & Agogbua. (1999). *Requirements for traffic engineering over mpls*. IETF, RFC 2702.

Awduche, Berger, Gan, Li, Srinivasan, & Swallow. (2001). *Rsvp-te: Extensions to rsvp for lsp tunnels*. IETF, RFC 3209.

Bilski, T. (2009). Fluctuations and lasting trends of qos on intercontinental links. *Quality of Service in Heterogeneous Networks, 22*, 251–264. doi:10.1007/978-3-642-10625-5_16

Blake, Black, Carlson, Davies, Wang, & Weiss. (1998). *An architecture for differentiated services*. IETF, RFC 2475.

Chen, J. L., Chen, M. C., & Chian, Y. R. (2007). QoS management in heterogeneous home networks. *Computer Networks, 51*(12), 3368–3379. doi:10.1016/j.comnet.2007.01.032

Chen, T. M., Walrand, J., & Messerschmitt, D. G. (1989). Dynamic priority protocols for packet voice. *IEEE Journal on Selected Areas in Communications, 7*, 632–643. doi:10.1109/49.32327

Clark, D., Braden, B., & Shenker, S. (1994). *Integrated service in the internet architecture: an overview*. Program on Internet and Telecoms Convergence.

Cruz, R. L. (1991). A calculus for network delay. Part I. network elements in isolation. *IEEE Transactions on Information Theory, 37*(1), 114–131.

Dolev, D., & Yao, A. C. (1983). On the security of public key protocols. *IEEE Transactions on Information Theory, 29*(2), 198–208.

Fineberg. (2003). *Qos support in mpls networks*. White Paper.

Grayson, D., Guernsey, D., Butts, J., Spainhower, M., & Shenoi, S. (2009). Analysis of security threats to mpls virtual private networks. *International Journal of Critical Infrastructure Protection, 2*(4), 146–153. doi:10.1016/j.ijcip.2009.08.002

Guernsey, D., Engel, A., Butts, J., & Sheno, S. (2010). Security analysis of the mpls label distribution protocol. In *Proceedings of the Fourth Annual IFIP Working Group 11.10 International Conference on Critical Infrastructure Protection*, (vol. 342, pp. 127–139). IFIP.

Gurijala & Molina. (2004). Defining and monitoring qos metrics in the next generation wireless networks. In *Telecommunications Quality of Services: The Business of Success, 2004. QoS 2004* (pp. 7–42). IEE.

He, L., & Botham, P. (2008). Pure mpls technology. In *Proceedings of Availability, Reliability and Security*, (pp. 253–259). ARES.

Jacobson, Frederick, Casner, & Schulzrinne. (2003). *Rtp: A transport protocol for real-time applications*. IETF, RFC 3550.

Jain (1998). *Myths about congestion management in high speed networks*. Arxiv preprint cs/9809088.

Jamoussi, L., Andersson, R., Callon, R., Dantu, L., Wu, P., Doolan, T., … Girish, M. (2002). *Constraint-based lsp setup using ldp*. IETF, RFC 3212.

Lee, S., & Knight, D. (2005). Realization of the next-generation network. IEEE *Communications Magazine*, *43*(10), 34–41. doi:10.1109/MCOM.2005.1522122

Lehoczky, J. P. (1990). Fixed priority scheduling of periodic task sets with arbitrary deadlines. In *Proceedings of Real- Time Systems Symposium*, (pp. 201–209). Academic Press.

Li, A. B., & Liebeherr, J. (2007). A network calculus with effective bandwidth. *IEEE/ACM Transactions on Networking, 15*(6), 1442–1453.

Nt'l Telecommuncation Union (2011). *ITU-T Recommendation Y.1540, Internet protocol aspects Quality of service and network performance-Internet protocol data communication service IP packet transfer and availability performance parameters*. Author.

Olsen, O. (2005). *Adversary modeling*. (Master's thesis). Gjovik University College.

Rosen, A. V., & Callon, R. (2001). *Multiprotocol label switching architecture*. IETF, RFC 3031.

Rosen, Y. R., Tappan, Farinacci, Fedorkow, Li, & Conta. (2001). *MPLS label stack encoding*. IETF, RFC 3032

Spainhower, M., Butts, J., Guernsey, D., & Shenoi, S. (2008). Security analysis of rsvp-te signaling in mpls networks. *International Journal of Critical Infrastructure Protection*, *1*(1), 68–74. doi:10.1016/j.ijcip.2008.08.005

Stoimenov, N., Chakraborty, S., & Thiele, L. (2010). An interface algebra for estimating worstcase traversal times in component networks. Leveraging Applications of Formal Methods, Verification, and Validation, 6415, 198–213.

Subramanian, L., Caesar, M., Ee, C. T., Handley, M., Mao, M., Shenker, S., & Stoica, I. (2005). HLP: a next generation inter-domain routing protocol. *ACM, 35*(4), 13–24.

Syverson, Tsudik, Reed, & Landwehr. (2001). *Towards an analysis of onion routing security*. Academic Press.

Thiele, Chakraborty, & Naedele. (2000). Real-time calculus for scheduling hard real-time systems. In *Proceedings of Circuits and Systems*, (vol. 4, pp. 101–104). IEEE.

Usui, T., Kitatsuji, Y., & Yokota, H. (2011). A study on traffic management cooperating with ims in mpls networks. *Telecommunication Systems*, 1–10.

Wang, Z., & Crowcroft, J. (1996). Quality-of-service routing for supporting multimedia applications. *IEEE Journal on Selected Areas in Communications*, *14*(7), 1228–1234.

Xiao, X., & Ni, L. M. (1999). Internet qos: A big picture. *IEEE Network*, *13*(2), 8–18. doi:10.1109/65.768484

Yerraballi, R., & Mukkamalla, R. (1996). Scalability in real-time systems with end-to-end requirements. *Journal of Systems Architecture, 42*, 409–429. doi:10.1016/S1383-7621(96)00031-8

ADDITIONAL READING

Alouneh, S., & Sa'ed, A. "Fault tolerance and security issues in MPLS networks." *Proceedings of the 10th WSEAS international conference on Applied computer science*. World Scientific and Engineering Academy and Society (WSEAS), 2010.

Armitage, G. (2000). MPLS: the magic behind the myths [multiprotocol label switching]. *Communications Magazine, IEEE, 38*(1), 124–131. doi:10.1109/35.815462

Behringer, Michael H. "Analysis of the Security of BGP/MPLS IP Virtual Private Networks (VPNs)." (2006).

Bilski, T. (2009). *"Disaster's impact on internet performance–case study."Computer Networks* (pp. 210–217). Springer Berlin Heidelberg.

Ghein, L. D. (2006). *MPLS fundamentals*. Cisco Press.

Huang, Weizheng, and Chris G. Guy. "A Study of Constraint-based Routing with MPLS."

Khurana, H. et al. (2010). Smart-grid security issues. *Security & Privacy, IEEE, 8*(1), 81–85. doi:10.1109/MSP.2010.49

Perros, Harry G. *Connection-oriented networks: SONET/SDH, ATM, MPLS and optical networks*. Wiley. com, 2005.

Porwal, M. K., Yadav, A., & Charhate, S. V. "Traffic Analysis of MPLS and Non MPLS Network including MPLS Signaling Protocols and Traffic distribution in OSPF and MPLS." *Emerging Trends in Engineering and Technology, 2008. ICETET'08. First International Conference on*. IEEE, 2008.

Stallings, W. (1998). *High speed networks*. Prentice Hall.

KEY TERMS AND DEFINITIONS

Adversary Modelling: The process of setting the assumptions, explicit and implicit, which have been made with regards to the adversary in any given situation.

DoS Attacks: The prevention of authorized access to resources or the delaying of time-critical operations. (Time-critical may be milliseconds or it may be hours, depending upon the service provided.

MPLS: Multiprotocol Label Switching is a mechanism in high-performance telecommunications networks that directs data from one network node to the next based on short path labels rather than long network addresses, avoiding complex lookups in a routing table. The labels identify virtual links (paths) between distant nodes rather than endpoints. MPLS can encapsulate packets of various network protocols. MPLS supports a range of access technologies, including T1/E1, ATM, Frame Relay, and DSL.

QoS: Quality of Service (QoS) refers to the capability of a network to provide better service to selected network traffic over various technologies.

Real-Time Networks: Any network in which the time at which packet is processed is significant. This is usually because the packets correspond to real-time applications or systems. The end-to-end time spent in processing packets must be sufficiently small for acceptable timeliness.

Threat Analysis: The examination of threat sources against system vulnerabilities to determine the threats for a particular system in a particular operational environment.

Chapter 9
The Future of National and International Security on the Internet

Maurice Dawson
University of Missouri – St. Louis, USA

Jonathan Abramson
Colorado Technical University, USA

Marwan Omar
Nawroz University, Iraq

Dustin Bessette
National Graduate School of Quality Management, USA

ABSTRACT

Hyperconnectivity is a growing trend that is driving cyber security experts to develop new security architectures for multiple platforms such as mobile devices, laptops, and even wearable displays. The futures of national and international security rely on complex countermeasures to ensure that a proper security posture is maintained during this state of hyperconnectivity. To protect these systems from exploitation of vulnerabilities it is essential to understand current and future threats to include the laws that drive their need to be secured. Examined within this chapter are the potential security-related threats with the use of social media, mobile devices, virtual worlds, augmented reality, and mixed reality. Further reviewed are some examples of the complex attacks that could interrupt human-robot interaction, children-computer interaction, mobile computing, social networks, and human-centered issues in security design.

CYBER SECURITY

Cyber terrorism is on the rise and is constantly affecting millions every day. These malicious attacks can affect one single person to entire government entities. These attacks can be done with a few lines of code or large complex programs that have the ability to target specific hardware. The authors investigate the attacks on individuals, corporations, and government infrastructures throughout the world. Provided will be specific examples of what a cyber terrorist attack is and why this method of attack is the preferred method of engagement today. The authors will also identify software applications, which track system weaknesses and vulnerabilities. As the United States (U.S.) government has stated, an act of cyber terrorism is an act of war; it is imperative that we explore this new method of terrorism and how it can be mitigated to an acceptable risk.

DOI: 10.4018/978-1-4666-6158-5.ch009

Information assurance (IA) is defined as the practice of protecting and defending information and information systems by ensuring their availability, integrity, authentication, confidentiality and non repudiation. This definition also encompasses disaster recovery, physical security, cryptography, application security, and business continuity of operations. To survive and be successful, an enterprise must have a disaster recovery strategy and response plan in place to mitigate the effects of natural disasters (e.g., floods, fires, tornadoes, earthquake, etc.), inadvertent actions by trusted insiders, terrorist attacks, vandalism, and criminal activity. In order to lay the groundwork for this review properly, it is essential to detail current processes techniques being utilized by officials within the government to accredit and certify systems to include their IA enabled products (Dawson, Jr., Crespo, & Brewster, 2013).

BACKGROUND

Cyber security has become a matter of national, international, economic, and societal importance that affects multiple nations (Walker, 2012). Since the 1990s users have exploited vulnerabilities to gain access to networks for malicious purposes. In recent years, the number of attacks on United States networks has continued to grow at an exponential rate. This includes malicious embedded code, exploitation of backdoors, and more. These attacks can be initiated from anywhere in the world from behind a computer with a masked Internet Protocol (IP) address. This type of warfare, cyber warfare, changes the landscape of war itself (Beidleman, 2009). This type of warfare removes the need to have a physically capable military and requires the demand for a force that has a strong technical capacity e.g. computer science skills. The U.S. and other countries have come to understand that this is an issue and has developed policies to handle this in an effort to mitigate the threats.

In Estonia and Georgia there were direct attacks on government cyber infrastructure (Beidleman, 2009). The attacks in Estonia rendered the government's infrastructure useless. The government and other associated entities heavily relied upon this e-government infrastructure. These attacks help lead to the development of cyber defense organizations that drive laws and policies within Europe.

LAWS AND POLICIES TO COMBAT TERRORISM

The events of 9/11 not only changed policies with the U.S. but also policies with other countries in how they treat and combat terrorism. The United Nations (U.N.) altered Article 51 of the U.N. charter. This article allows members of the U.N. to take necessary measures to protect themselves against an armed attack to ensure international peace and security.

Israel is a country with some of the most stringent policies towards national and international security. This country requires all citizens to serve in the military to include multiple checkpoints throughout the country. This country has utilized stringent checks in the airport long before 9/11, however, now they have additional measures to ensure the nation's security as they are surrounded by countries that have tried to invade before. Israel has also deployed more Unmanned Air Vehicles (UAVs), and Unmanned Ground Vehicles (UGVs) to patrol the border in the event something occurs.

The United Kingdom (U.K.) has the Prevention of Terrorism Act 2005 and the Counter-Terrorism Act 2008 which was issued by Parliament. The first act was created to detain individuals who were suspected in acts of terrorism. This act was intended to replace the Anti-terrorism, Crime and Security Act 200 I as it was deemed unlawful. These acts seem to mirror the same ones, created in the U.S., to monitor potential terrorists and terrorists. The U.K. also shared their information with the U.S. for coordinating individual that may be of risk.

In the U.S., the methods for national security were enhanced to ensure no threats occur on U.S. soil. These changes include enhanced security in all ports of entry. The signing of the Homeland Security Act of 2002 (HS Act) (Public Law 07-296) created an organization that received funding and lots of resources for monitoring the security posture of this country. Additional changes include enhanced monitoring of citizens and residents within the country to prevent terrorist activities by the mention of key words e.g. bomb, explosive, or Al Qaeda.

The USA Patriot was signed into law by President George W. Bush in 2001 after September 11, 2001 (Bullock, Haddow, Coppola, & Yeletaysi, 2009). This act was created in response to the event of 9111 which provided government agencies increased abilities. These increased abilities provided the government rights to search various communications such as email, telephone records, medical records, and more of those who were thoughts of terrorist acts (Bullock, Haddow, Coppola, & Yeletaysi, 2009). This allowed law enforcement to have the upper hand in being proactive to stopping potential acts against U.S. soil. In the 2011 year, President Obama signed an extension on the USA Patriot Act. This act has received criticism from the public due to the potential to be misused or abused by those in power. This act has allowed government agencies to impede on constitutional rights.

The Protecting Cyberspace as a National Asset Act of 2010 was an act that also amends Title 11 of the Homeland Security Act of 2002. This act enhanced security and resiliency of the cyber and communication infrastructure within the U.S. This act is important as the President declared that any cyber aggressions would be considered an act of war. This is also important as Estonia's entire digital infrastructure was taken down by hackers who supported the former Soviet rule. This type of attack could be damaging to the infrastructure in the U.S.- causing loss of power for days or more which could result in death. In an area, such as the Huntsville Metro, we could have multiple nuclear facility melt downs, loss of ISR capabilities, and communication to the warfighter that we are supporting.

Additional changes from this act include the ability to carry out a research and development program to improve cyber security infrastructure. At the moment all government organizations must comply with the Federal Information Security Management Act (FISMA) of 2002. This act has shown many holes within the U.S. cyber security infrastructure to include those organizations that are leads. This act provides DHS the ability to carry out the duties described in the Protecting Cyberspace as a National Asset Act of 2010.

Stuxnet Worm

During the fall of 2010 many headlines declared that Stuxnet was the game-changer in terms of cyber warfare (Denning, 2012). This malicious worm was complex and designed to target only a specific system. This worm had the ability to detect location, system type, and more. And this worm only attacked the system if it met specific parameters that were designed in the code. Stuxnet tampered directly with software in a programmable logic controller (PLC) that controlled the centrifuges at Natanz. This tampering ultimately caused a disruption in the Iranian nuclear program.

America's Homeland Security Preparing for Cyber Warfare

The Department of Homeland Security (DHS) is concerned with cyber attacks on infrastructure such as supervisory control and data acquisition (SCADA) systems. SCADA systems are the systems that autonomously monitor and adjust switching among other processes within critical infrastructures such as nuclear plants, and power grids. DHS is worried about these systems as they are unmanned frequently and remotely accessed. As they are remotely accessed, this could allow anyone to take control of assets to critical infrastructure remotely. There has been increasing mandates and directives to ensure any system deployed meets stringent requirements. As the Stuxnet worm has become a reality, future attacks could be malicious code directly targeting specific locations of critical infrastructure.

Cyber Security Certification and Accreditation Processes to Secure Systems

The Department of Defense Information Assurance Certification and Accreditation Process (DIACAP) is the process that the Department of Defense (DoD) utilizes to ensure that risk management is applied to Automated Information Systems (AIS) to mitigate IA risks and vulnerabilities (Dawson, Jr., Crespo, & Brewster, 2013). DIACAP is the standard process that all services utilize to ensure that all DoD systems maintain IA posture throughout the systems life cycle. DIACAP

is the replacement of the Department of Defense Information Technology Security Certification and Accreditation Process (DITSCAP). Figure 2 displays the process which includes five key steps. The first step is to initiate and plan the IA C & A process. The second step is to implement and validate the assigned IA controls. The third step is to make the certification determination and accreditation decision. The fourth step is to maintain authorization to operate and conduct reviews. The final step is to decommission the system.

The Common Criteria (CC), an internationally approved set of security standards, provides a clear and reliable evaluation of security capabilities of Information technology (IT) products (CCEVS, 2008). By providing an independent assessment of a product's ability to meet security standards, the CC gives customers more confidence in the security of products and leads to more informed decisions (CCEVS, 2008). Since the requirements for certification are clearly established, vendors can target very specific security needs while

Figure 1. DIACAP stages (Department of Defense, 2007)

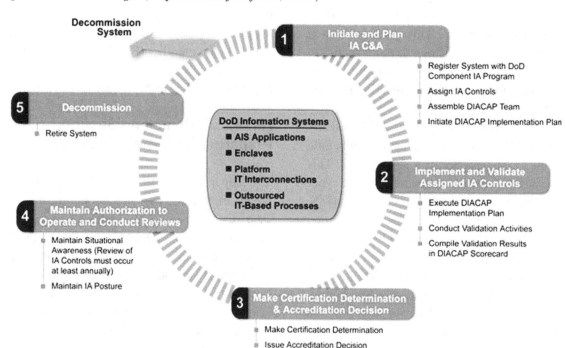

Figure 2. Process for building virtual world representations of real world items

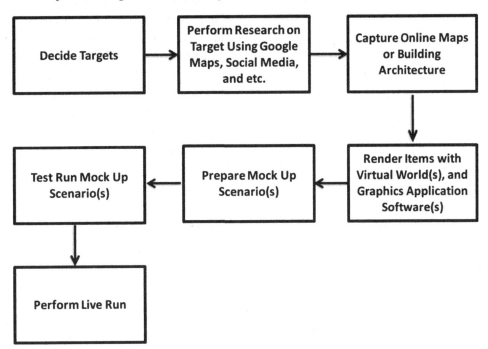

providing users from other countries to purchase IT products with the same level of confidence, since certification is recognized across all complying nations. Evaluating a product with respect to security requires identification of customer's security needs and an assessment of the capabilities of the product. The CC aids customers in both of these processes through two key components: protection profiles and evaluation assurance levels (CCEVS, 2008).

The CC is the process that replaced the Orange Book. The CC has evaluated assurance levels (EAL) 1 through 7. EAL products 1 through 4 may be used and certified in any of the participating countries. However, EAL 5 through 7 must be certified by the countries national security agency, that is the United States' national agency is the National Security Agency and United Kingdom's national agency is the Communication Electronics Security Group (CESG). By all accounts, the NSA'a Orange Book program, in which the NSA forced vendors through prolonged product testing at Fort Meade, MD was a dismal failure. Also, the government's failure to Orange-Book-tested

products, which were often out of date after years of testing, was a blow to the vendors that invested huge sums in the Orange Book Evaluations.

Additionally the National Security Agency (NSA) and DHS sponsors a joint venture known as the National Centers of Academic Excellence in IA Education (CAE/IAE), IA 2-year Education and Training (CAE/2Y) and IA Research (CAE/R) programs. Students that attend institutions with these designations are eligible to apply for scholarships and grants which they repay through government service. These programs were created to address the lack of available talent in IA. Table 1 shows the Committee on National Security Standards (CNSS) that institutions must map to in order to receive the designation as a NSA/IAE.

Since the purpose was to expand the numbers of IA personnel, it is hard to evaluate the program's real success (Bishop & Taylor, 2009). One of the major problems is the lack of resources to all institutions who are NSA/IAE. Even though this program is targeted towards post high school efforts, more reforms are currently taking place in the K-12 educational areas.

Table 1. CNSS training standards

Standard	Year	Description
NSTISSI 4011	1994	Information Systems Security Professionals
CNSS 4012	2004	Senior Systems Manager
CNSS 4013	2004	System Administrators in Information Systems Security
CNSS 4014	2004	Information Systems Security Officers (ISSOs)
NSTISSI 4015	2000	System Certifiers
CNSS 4016	2005	Risk Analysis

Human Computer Interaction

Future national and international threats that will be directly correlated to the Internet will be many as more devices are added to the Internet the problem of security also multiplies. Richard Clarke mentions that there are currently 12 billion devices currently connected to the Internet; this figure is supposed to grow to 50 billion in ten years (Clarke, 2012). Our dependence and interdependence with the internet creates new challenges as the more devices that are put online, the more exposure or vectors we are creating. The number of devices on the Internet is growing exponentially. As more applications for technology and wireless technologies are adopted, we are going to see this grow even further. What comes to mind are the self-driving vehicles that will be coming in a few years. We already have some self-driving cars, but they are not widely adopted yet or available to the public. When this does happen, we are going to see another exponential growth rate and the number of connected devices as each automobile will constitute at least a single IP address if not probably more.

Communication is the on-going and never ending process through which we create our social reality. Never in history has this been truer, as the computing and communication platforms that we have today far exceed anything that has ever been planned or projected. Information technology has radically altered the process in the way people learn and communicate. Weiser notes the most profound technologies are those that disappear. They weave themselves into the fabric of everyday life until they are indistinguishable from it (Weiser, 1991). An example has been the explosive growth of SMS texting, email, and social media. As these technologies are weaved into our lives, so are the dangers.

Research Projects

Many of the research projects that have taken place in mixed reality have been in educational domains and military domains. The focus of mixed reality research and education is to expand the capability of students to learn and interact and retain constructed knowledge and for businesses to maximize the knowledge that they have. Interesting new ways of looking at problems and topical areas enhance the learning experience and enhance capabilities, such as the ability to create a physical environment when it does not exist in the real world. Researchers (Park et al., 2008) studied human behavior in urban environments using human subjects in a virtual environment which demonstrated that virtual reality and mixed reality have the capability to model human behavior and that the products of these research projects are useful and may save time and money. Tn many situations, they provide an environment for simulation and analysis and design that would not be possible in the real world.

Most mixed reality devices, at this point, are running on the internet or another network in order to communicate with one another, connectivity is very important. Since the devices are entering cyberspace, they are going to be exposed to the same sorts of risks that any device connecting to cyberspace will encounter. Researchers (Cheok et al., 2005) state that mixed reality is "the fusion of augmented and virtual realities". Mixed reality is more than virtual and more than augmented reality, by combining the two we are able to create real time learning environments, research experiments, and knowledge based collaboration areas that are enhanced by the application of mixed reality.

Using games for learning and for entertainment is one of the areas for different types of mixed reality applications. Researchers (Pellerin et al., 2009) describe a profile management technique for multiplayer ubiquitous games. Multiplayer ubiquitous games use different types of net aware skills me network aware objects and network objects such as an RFTD tag which allows the participant to interact with the physical environment. Hardware and software to support multiplayer ubiquitous game MUG is dependent on planning out the architecture in this specific example and NFC smartcard is used as well as a reader and a HTTP server the NFC smartcard communicates with NFC reader which in turn communicates with the HTTP server. This is done in order to create a mechanism which as the authors state's guarantees a stronger identification scheme than just a login password and might help Fortson common online game cheats". The previous was an example of an approach that is used to handling player profiles and allows interactions and centralized and decentralized ways. This is very similar to the CCNx 1.0 protocol which is also or which also has a goal of allowing centralized and decentralized interactions are communication.

Virtual Worlds

With the continual rise of virtual world environments, such as OpenSimulator (OpenSim) and Second Life (SL), they have the ability to be used for positive or negative gains in military warfare in the areas of training (Dawson, 2011). OpenSim is an open source multi-user 3D application server designed by taking the advantage and making a reverse-engineering to the published Application Programming Interface functions (APIs) and specific Linden Lab open source parts of the SL code

(Dawson & Al Saeed, 2012). One of the strengths for creating any virtual environment is making it accessible by a variety of users through using various protocols. OpenSim provides a method for virtual world developers to create customized virtual worlds easily extensible through using the technologies that fit with their needs. For example, a terrorist could create a virtual representation of a building by using publicly available drafting plans. This virtual representation would serve as scenario based training for terrorists. Additionally, this would allow for terrorists of different cells or groups to communicate freely. The first step would be for the terrorists to decide their targets. Once targets are decided then they would perform research on the target. This research would be on all related items such as technologies, physical infrastructure, and personnel. In the next steps the individual would capture any online maps or building architectural diagrams that would allow these areas to be rendered with the virtual world. Once the rendering of these areas has been completed a mock up scenario would be prepared. This would allow a test run to occur and later a live run. These steps can be prepared with the use of open source technology at no expense to the terrorist. See the figure below which outlines the processes described.

With the possible scenario presented policing the virtual worlds may become a necessity to maintain national security (Parti, 2010). The U.S. Army is currently implementing a program known as Military Open Simulator Enterprise Strategy (MOSES). MOSES runs on OpenSim and is moving towards a Common Access Card (CAC) enabled environment for secure and encrypted communications (Maxwell & McLennan, 2012). In Figure 3 displayed is an interrogation scenario in MOSES. Additionally the U.S. could follow a model similar to Estonia where kids from the age of seven to nineteen learn how to develop software programs. This would help in deterring threats to include having future developers build security into the software from the beginning.

Figure 3. MOSES incerro_qacion scenario

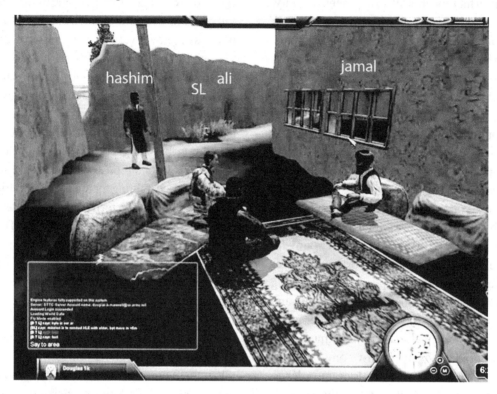

Open-Source Software for Cyber Security

Researchers, as well as scientists, have long advocated for the use of open source software for improving the nation's security posture. Open source software can be used as an effective tool in order to protect government networks and defend them against cyber criminals. Corporation, government agencies, and educational institutions have been seriously considering incorporating open source security into their systems security because of the many advantages offered by open-source software; those advantages are exemplified by lower cost ownership, customizability (the ability of modifying the code to meet security requirement) and reasonable security. In fact, DHS has already established a $10 million program to fund research efforts aimed at finding open-source software that could be used for security purposes and boost existing cyber defenses (Hsu, 2011). What

is encouraging about the future of open source software for security is that the threat landscape is rapidly changing attacks are becoming highly organized as well as sophisticated, and the cost of commercial software security continues to rise; this trend, in turn gives open source software a cutting edge where businesses and governments are enticed to take advantage of the many benefits offered by open source software. Since the US government is looking for ways to cut costs and business organizations are looking at security as a financial burden; it is a matter of time before open-source software becomes mainstream and a competitive security solution.

Back Track Linux

Back track is a Linux-based operating system designed for digital forensics and network penetration testing (Myers, 2012). It is named after the search algorithm, "Backtrack" and is considered an essential security component for all security professionals. Backtrack has become a very popular open source security component for all security professionals and hacker because it contains a set of security tools that can perform virtually any security task ranging from attack simulation and vulnerability assessment to web application security and wireless hacking. Backtrack is mainly a penetration testing tool which is used to assess the security of a network, application or system.

Backtrack Linux is a free open-source software that can be downloaded free from http://www. backtrack linux.org. This security software comes bundled with many other tools that could be installed and run separately from Backtrack; those tools include Nmap, Wireshark, and Metasploit, just to name a few. Backtrack was designed with security in mind, which includes an environment that makes security testing an easy and efficient task for security professionals. It is considered a one-stop-shop and a superior security solution for all security requirements because it offers capabilities that can be used for a variety of security activities such as server exploitation, web application security assessment, and social engineering (BackTrack Linux, 2011).

Tools and Methods for Monitoring Networks

Monitoring traffic across networks is of great interest to systems administrators due to the fact that this traffic has a tremendous impact on the security of networks and provides them with network situational awareness. The ability to monitor and analyze network traffic in real time can help detect and possibly prevent cyber criminals from breaking into information systems networks. Network monitoring software enables us to understand the state of network and determine the potential existence of malicious or abnormal network behavior. Network monitoring tools can prove valuable in preventing unauthorized access by providing insight into the volume of data traffic

that flows over a network, examining and analyzing such data, and ultimately preventing security incidents. Over the years, the open-source security community has developed published open-source tools that are capable of monitoring network traffic and deterring possible attacks. More specifically, open-source software tools are capable of examining most activities within a computer network including malicious activity such as scanning attempts, exploits, network probing, and brute force attacks (Celeda, 2011). Described are some of the most common open-source software tools that are being used for network security monitoring. An example of this is Snort, the open source software developed by Sourcetire and used for intrusion detection and prevention (Snort, 2012). Snort is one of the most widely adopted network monitoring technologies that can be used by network administrators as a defensive technique to report suspicious network traffic activity and alert system administrators about potential cyber-attacks. Snort has gained considerable popularity and attention among other network monitoring tools because it combines the benefits of signature based tools and anomaly detection techniques (Roesch, 1999). Another reason behind Snort popularity and success is that Snort is capable of performing real time traffic analysis and packet logging on IP networks (Tuteja & Shanker, 2012). Furthermore, Snort's strength comes from its intrusion prevention capabilities which is a new feature added to Snort. The intrusion prevention feature allows Snort to take preventive actions, such as dropping or re-directing data packets, against potentially malicious traffic (Salah & Kahtani, 2009).

Nmap ("Network Mapper") is a free open source utility for discovering networks and performing security auditing (Sadasivam, Samudrala, & Yang, 2005). Nmap is a valuable and widely used network scanner that has the ability to scan rapidly and discover hosts and services by sending specially designed packets to the target host analyzes and responds. NMAP is different from other port scanner software applications in that it does not just send packets at some predefined constant rate, instead, nmap takes into account network conditions such as latency fluctuations, network congestion, and the target interference with the scan during the run time. Nmap has some advanced network discovery capabilities that go beyond basic port scanning and host scanning; Nmap can identify the type and version of an operating system, what type of firewalls are being used on the network, and what listening services are rum1ing on the hosts. Nmap runs on major operating system such as Microsoft windows, Linux, and Solaris. NMAP has become one of the most useful network scanning tools that network administrators cannot afford to ignore especially because this tool has proven to be flexible, intuitive interface (the new Zenmap with the graphical user interface), deployable, cross platform and most importantly it is free.

TOOLS AND METHODS FOR NETWORK ATTACKS

Network attacks pose a significant challenge to information systems due to the dramatic impact such attacks have on computer networks. Network attacks could paralyze entire networked systems, disrupt services, and bring down entire networks. In the recent years, network attacks have increased exponentially and have evolved rapidly in complexity to evade traditional network defenses (e.g. intrusion detection systems, amd firewalls). As computer networks grow and evolve to include more applications and services; malicious hackers continue to exploit inevitable vulnerabilities in network based applications. This, in turn, creates a fertile ground for hackers to develop and implement complex attacks and break into critical information assets. Below are a few network attacks illustrating the dangers and consequences of network attacks to include methods to defend against those attacks.

Hackers use a portscan attack, one of the most popular reconnaissance techniques, to break into vulnerable network services and applications. Most of the network services need to use TCP or UPD ports for their connections. Further, a port scan allows hackers to listen via open and available ports by sending a message to each port one at a time and waiting to receive a response. Once the port replies to a message, a hacker would then dig further and attempt to find potential vulnerabilities, flaws, or weaknesses in that port and ultimately launch a port scan attack which can compromise a remote host. The consequences of port scans are numerous and diverse ranging from draining network resources, to congesting network traffic, to actual exploitation of network devices. Cyber criminals utilize a plethora of free, open-source software tools to launch a port scan attack; one of the most popular security tools is Nmap (as explained in the section above). Nmap provides some attractive probing capabilities, such as the ability to determine a host's operating system and to provide a list of potential flaws in a port, all of which could help hackers launch a port scan attack.

Combating a port scan attack requires deploying firewalls at critical locations of a network to filter suspicious or unsolicited traffic. Also, security gateways must be able to raise alerts, and block or shutdown communications from the source of the scan (Check point security, 2004).

A SYN attack which is also known as SYN Flooding targets the TCP/IP stack. It exploits a weakness in the way that most hosts implement the TCP three-way handshake. When Host Y receives the SYN request from X, it maintains the opened connection in a listen queue for at least 75 seconds (Reed, 2003). Many implementations can only keep track of a very limited number of connections. A malicious host can exploit the small size of the listen queue by sending multiple SYN requests to a host thus making the system crash or becoming unavailable to other legitimate connections. The ability of removing a host from the network for at least 75 seconds can be used as a denial-of-service attack, or it can be used as a tool to implement other attacks, like IP Spoofing (Rouiller, 2003). Mitigating this attack requires the implementation of several solutions such as network address translation (NAT), Access control lists (ACL), and routers.

Another attack, which is known as IP address spoofing or IP spoofing, refers to the creation of Internet Protocol (IP) packets with a forged source IP address, called spoofing, with the purpose of hiding the true identity of the packet (sender) or impersonating another host on the network. IP address spoofing is a form of denial of service attacks where attackers attempt to flood the network with overwhelming amounts of traffic without being concerned about receiving responses to attack packets. Implementing packet filters at the router using ingress and egress (blocking illegitimate packets from inside and outside the network) is the best defense against the IP spoofing attack. It's also a good practice to design network protocols in a way that they are not reliant on the IP address source for authentication (Surman, 2002).

Issues with Android Phones and Other Mobile Devices

Smartphones are becoming a more integrated and prevalent part of people's daily lives due to their highly powerful computational capabilities, such as email applications, online banking, online shopping, and bill paying. With this fast adoption of smartphones, imminent security threats arise while communicating sensitive personally identifiable information (PII), such as bank account numbers and credit card numbers used when handling and performing those advanced tasks (Wong, 2005; Brown, 2009).

Traditional attacks (worms, viruses, and Trojan horses) caused privacy violations and disruptions of critical software applications (e.g., deleting lists of contact numbers and personal data). Malware attacks on smartphones were generally "proof of concept" attempts to break through the phone's system and cause damage (Omar & Dawson, 2013).

However, the new generation of smartphone malware attacks has increased in sophistication and is designed to cause severe financial losses (caused by identity theft) and disruption of critical software applications (Bose, 2008). Because smartphones are becoming more diverse in providing general purpose services (i.e., instant messaging and music), the effect of malware could be extended to include draining batteries, incurring additional charges, and bringing down network capabilities and services (Xie, Zhang, Chaugule, Jaeger, & Zhu, 2009).

Smartphones are rapidly becoming enriched with confidential and sensitive personal information, such as bank account information and credit card numbers, because of the functionality and powerful computational capabilities built into those mobile devices. Cyber criminals, in turn, launch attacks especially designed to target smartphones, exploiting vulnerabilities and deficiencies in current defense strategies built into smartphones' operating systems. Bhattacharya (2008) indicated that because of skill and resource constraints, businesses are ill-prepared to combat emerging cyber threats; this claim is true for smartphones as well, given the fact that those mobile devices are even less equipped with necessary protections, such as antivirus and malware protection software. Some services and features, such as Bluetooth and SMS, create attack vectors unique to smartphones and thus expand the attack surface. For example, in December, 2004, A Trojan horse was disguised in a video game and was intended to be a "proof of concept," which signaled the risks associated with smartphones that could potentially compromise the integrity and confidentiality of personal information contained in smartphones (Rash, 2004). Attackers can easily take advantage of those services provided by smartphones and subvert their primary purpose because they can use Bluetooth and SMS services to launch attacks by installing software that can disable virus protection and spread via Bluetooth unbeknownst to smartphone users.

With the development of it to movative features and services for smartphones, security measures deployed are currently not commensurate because those services and features, such as MMS and Bluetooth, are driven by market and user demands, meaning that companies are more inclined to provide more entertainment features than security solutions. In turn, this further increases vulnerabilities and opens doors for hackers to deploy attacks on smartphones. Furthermore, Mulliner & Miller (2009) argue that the operating systems of smartphones allow the installation of third-party software applications, coupled with the increase in processing power as well as the storage capacity. Scenarios like this pose worse security challenges because hackers could exploit those vulnerabilities, which are further compounded by users' lack of security awareness. Smartphone attackers are becoming more adept in designing and launching attacks by applying attack techniques already implemented on desktop and laptop computers; smartphones' enhanced features, such as music players and video games, produce easy-to exploit targets by sending seemingly benign files via music or video game applications to users and luring them into downloading such files. Becher, Freiling, and Leider (2007) indicated that attackers could exploit such vulnerabilities to spread worms autonomously into smartphones. Therefore, hackers usually use a combination of technical expertise along with some social engineering techniques to trap users into accepting and downloading benign applications, which are used later to execute malicious code and affect critical applications running on smartphones.

Android's core components, such as Linux and connectivity media, are vulnerable to attacks through which personal and confidential information is likely to be compromised. Android's threats are further amplified by the fact that users are limited to using their smartphones for basic services and functions, such as email and SMS/MMS. Users lack the programming mind-set to protect their Android smartphones and stay current with the latest security software updates. This gives hackers an edge to target Android smartphones in the hope of gaining unauthorized access to disable core services (email and web browsing); abuse costly services (i.e., sending MMS/SMS and making calls to high-rate numbers); eavesdrop on calls and most importantly compromise sensitive information to be sold for a price. Android's open-source nature further increases security vulnerabilities because attackers can easily exploit this feature to modify the core applications and install malicious software, which could be used to compromise Android-based smartphones and ultimately cause disruption and monetary loss.

Dangers of Social Networks

Virtual communication has become a distinct area of interest for many as it has become second nature and also weaved into our everyday life. People tend to create a social reality that is based on the cmmection to the internet and using tools that assist communication. These tools have danger sides that a vast majority does not see or think about on a daily basis. Currently, there has never been a higher danger in the social networks for the public than there is now. This danger is easily spread to everyone who use this mode of communication based that people unintentionally make themselves vulnerable. With a connection to a vast number of social networks, people are easily consumed by submitting personal information via the Internet. The time is now for the public to understand where they stand in the future of the internet connectivity and what they can do to assist or lessen this danger.

Trend in Social Networks

People of all ages are beginning to learn to use social networks to stay in touch, reconnect, and meet new people and find out about new places. These websites usually allow the user to present a profile of himself through a long list of very detailed information (Conti, Hasani, & Crispo, 2011). A vast majority of businesses are beginning to use these social networks to find new employees, expand and market and product line, and also to advertise their brand. These primary reasons are based on several distinctions that will help companies grow and expand due to the majority of customers who search for products via social networks. Customers are becoming more tech savvy by using mobile devices to gain internet connectivity in various locations. This helps create a realistic and educational feel to understand specific product information that is only based online.

Social networks have become the largest branding and marketing areas for this era. Sites such as Twitter, Facebook, Instagram, Pinterest, and many others have risen in this past decade and have continued to increase with customers based on their usability and features. These sites have risen in popularity in the last few years, typically growing from basic technologies as participation increases and user expectations shape and form the media (Fitzgerald, 2008). Increase use within these sites also dictates an increase in the population in users who are becoming friendlier in the social media aspect.

Online social networking sites have become integrated into the routine of modern-day social interactions and are widely used as a primary source of information for most. Research found that Facebook is deeply integrated in user's daily lives through specific routines and rituals (Debatin, Lovejoy, Horn, & Hughes, 2009). Facebook is a social networking tool that is used in various instances that help people connect to people or businesses connect to people. It is the mere change in security that people and businesses will need the most help. These areas are vital to the metamorphic adaptions of today's society. Change is needed, and with this change, new adaptions for online security are required and mandated in some instances.

Online security can be looked at by a virtual standpoint in the relation of consumers and businesses. Many businesses use social media and online social networks to communicate to one another in a sense that many users are also using the same technology to find new information. Online information security risks, such as identity theft, have increasingly become a major factor inhibiting the potential growth of e commerce (Wang, 2010). A base system of online security is needed to help fulfill many business expectations and also promote or generate business in different geographic locations.

A Geographic Location

In definition, Hochman et al (2012) defines Instagram as a recent fad in mobile photo sharing applications that provide a way to snap photos, tweak their images and share then on various social networks with friends, family, and complete strangers (2012). This type of social media helps create a realistic feel for people to see photos of specific areas where people are located. This also helps create a uniformed timeline scheduled photos that describe a story of one's life. As security is a high need in this type of online social media, it is best used in personal and business use.

Pinterest is also a varying tool of online social media that houses has many users who also use other networking tools. Pinterest allows members to "pin" items or images found on the internet to a pin board, which can then be easily shared through an email link or by following the creator (Dudenhoffer, 2012). This networking tool can also be paired up with other social media tools such as Tnstagram, Twitter, and Facebook. These networking tools also create a justification that helps creates a total profile immersion for people virtually. Security within this profile is currently weak; changes and adaptions can help create a justification for areas of higher influences such as these networks.

The popularity of these sites provides an opportunity to study the characteristics of online social network graphs at large scale (Mislove, Marcon, Gummadi, Drushel, & Bhattacharjee, 2007). A leading cause of the rise of these sites has been with consumers fining it easy to use and navigate to find information on and within these sites. The usability of these sites makes it very easy for customers of all ages to navigate through processes, which require personal information. When people subject themselves into giving information to the virtual world, they also subject themselves in becoming vulnerable for virtual threats.

No matter how easy an internet site can be to submit sensitive information, no site is purely safe and danger free. This is why the connection to internet connectivity is a matter that needs to be handled with high importance. A dire need to have security at its maximum has never been such an item then it is today. From every angle, people are becoming vulnerable to attacks from predators who deem themselves capable of obtaining information. As vital information is spread throughout the system of technology based environments, this information can also be spread throughout the world.

WHO IS CONNECTED AND WHY?

The main focus for the impact of the digital age is the critical mass population of the people in the world. People are beginning to use, read, analyze, and interact virtually younger and more often than ever before. This preliminary change occurs because now people begin to interact with social networks at a younger age. Learning starts to develop at a younger age because many of the cognitive abilities are beginning to be developed and acquired when children are younger, thus giving them the ability to develop an interest in fields they may want to work in as an adult.

Businesses

Businesses begin to look at the advertising site of their work in relation to how it can assist them with sales and goals. Since marketing is such a large portion of business, brands especially need to look and see what advertisements they can use to assist them in reaching their goals. The future of advertisements and marketing is based on the consumer today, and where they look to find information in regards to their purchases. The future of the internet connectivity and adaptation is directly linked through the suitability of use for the internet.

An important factor to look at when it comes to firm development is to look at the dire need for firms to develop their niche successfully. The virtual sector of businesses is extremely dependent on the absolute use of the user and the internet. Businesses tend to adapt to a series of modules that are formulated with their overall mission as a company. Leaning to technology-based marketing is one way to look at the overall spectrum of the businesses.

Companies are moving online media to the core of their programs because of how often consumers use social media for information-gathering purposes (Grainger, 2010). A feature that gives customers a more realistic feel such that they can obtain information in quickly is an online feature. This feature is used in many tactics for marketing and advertising based that many customers are prone to find items that assist them with what they are looking for via online. The connection must also be secure and safe for consumers such that viable personal information is used for online purchases.

Internet connectivity can also create justifications for businesses that have a niche for merchandising to customers, not on location. This avenue also needs an increase in data that are transmitted through various servers and websites. Servers are the basis of information modification; they help provide a space and location for all information to be transmitted within a network. Businesses are taking part of this big shift based that the value of information to be able to be moved with this the-savvy environment is easier than ever. Servers also offer a sense of protection for business material to be saved and updated. Since safety is a big issue due to weather, it is feasible for businesses to purchase servers. Moreover, prices have also decreased with reflection to the safety of a server. Not only does a price reflect an adjustment towards the quality and value of the item at hand, but it is also noted on the overall performance of the machine or equipment.

Institutions are also a main contributor or purchaser of servers and internet connections based that they using online connections more than ever. A main factor that needs to be adjusted with institutions is the feasibility factor of what has been given at hand for the item to be installed, adjusted, and used with the institution. This feasibility also dictates a specific privacy that needs to be labeled at a specific standard for the institution to use. If these privacy areas are not up to a specific level, the institution is not and will not be able to use these items in conjunction with its mission or vision values.

Schools

The future of institutions is founded via the internet and the connectivity that these institutions have with the internet. With this, more schools are using web design formats that are very user friendly, such that more information can be placed virtually. With more information being placed virtually, more students will have access virtually to this sort of information. This also gives the institution the power to place a majority of their application processes; faculty related work, as well as communication online and able to be accessed by any faculty member or student at any time.

The vulnerability of this information being accesses by outside threats is high in regards to how secure the information is. Many institutions place a restriction to the limitation of the access of where it can be obtained. This limits the user capability of accessing information. Limiting this information can lead to problems internally as opposed to externally based that not all users will agree and comply with the polity regulations.

Institutions can create a wall that assists the blockage of information sharing through a semipermeable layer, which is accessed by users and administrators. This barrier helps to control the amount of information sharing that can be displayed accordingly in regards to virtual threats. Creating this wall helps give administrators more control to information that is shared as well as provides a sate avenue for users at the lower level. When a barrio is promoted, it can also create a justification or rule that helps threats stay at bay and never reach core areas of information. The vital elements of this can be displayed in Figure 4.

WHERE DO PEOPLE CONNECT?

A rise in the digital social media arena has a direct impact towards the world, and with this many of the companies are beginning to respond with technological changes. With increasing technological advances. business can operate more smoothly, more effectively, and more efficiently to better facilitate operations and management. More tools are available for businesses that have the desire to take their business and marketing virtually. This has led to the increase of mobile device use since most users of social media use these applications in various locations.

Marketing has become a direct and distinct changing factor in business competition. With this, more businesses have begun to change their style ru1d location of advertisements. It is a clear example that more customers arc beginning to change their overall plans based on how they are able to obtain information on a general basis. With this, it is assumed that many businesses are

Figure 4. Private cloud enterprise data center (Social-Cast VMware, 2012)

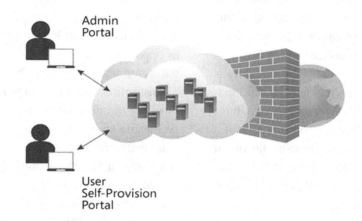

also creating new, avenues and paths for marketing advertisements to be able to reach customers at various distances. This is also why it is very important for a business to have the ability to connect over a large geographic area with ease.

It can be determined that social networks via Internet connectivity are the best ways for businesses to connect to people. Businesses of all stature are beginning to look at the possibility of marketing strategies reaching customers in geographic locations. A large trend for mass adoption for businesses is to connect to customers via mobile devices; this in turn will lead to customers being able to connect to businesses at various levels. This trend increases the use of mobile devices based that a majority of the users are using these devices for a purpose.

One item that can be dictated with the high use of internet connectivity and mobile devices is the ability for outside sources to obtain information via mobile. This path will change the overall spectrum of how customers can purchase goods via online and where they can go to gain security for their purchases. It is then up to the providers of the mobile devices to create secure internet services for the customers' sake depending on how the customer is able to cooperate with technology. Even as the security of the internet service increases for the customer, it also must

increase at the business end. This is to ensure that all employees and persons involved in online transactions are being monitored by a service that can provide safety throughout the purchase and delivery of the product.

INTERNET STALKING

The increase of the social networking trend can be based on the security features of for every user.

Internet stalking can be noted by a threat from an outside source that harms or conflicts harm to a piece of information or person. These threats can international or nation depending on where the organization or user is geographically located. With internet stalking being noted more often in today's society; it is also presumed that people are also becoming more vulnerable to attacks from internet insecurity. Insecure internet can be looked at based on what the user currently is using in terms of connectivity but can always be looked at as a threat to any customer.

When international threats are aimed at consumers, it can be perceived as a threat that is directed to the nation based that it is from outside the country. These circumstances can be legal or illegal based on the source of the threat. Many users see these types of threats as being identified as acts of terror based that many users do not know much information about the types of threats that are visible.

An example is noted from a post on social media that included valuable and private information. Any post can be noted in becoming a threat to outside sources such as a tweet from twitter, a picture from Instagram, or a post on Facebook. Twitter is less than three years old, commands more than 41 million users as of July 2009 and is growing fast (Kwak, 2010).

From this point, an invader or Internet stalker can take into account the vital information and begin to look up where the user lives or where the user is updating his or her status. This can be done by researching with the Internet for items which are displayed virtually and can denote where the user lives. In this example, it is noted that the user Mustaza Mustafa is posting this status with Hongkait. Location information for users is stored in the About section of a user's profile on FaceBook.

Google earth is an application that can help look up locations and geographic areas on maps to help determine where items, businesses, and people are located. With this application, Internet stalking can be made easier by a method of inputing a location for a specific item, person, place or business to locate where it is. Since there is a very low security with this application, this option can be used with most location-based information given specific circumstances.

A phenomenon of cyber-stalking and virtual harassment will be the set of focus for the next generation. It is with this type of harassment that schools and institutions become the most vulnerable based on the population of these locations. Areas of improvement will be creating secure environments for students and faculty based on online communication. These areas will be an avenue for major threats as long as they are unsecure for cyber stalkers to pass through and obtain information.

Figure 5. Post on Facebook, a scoial media application (Mustafa, 2012)

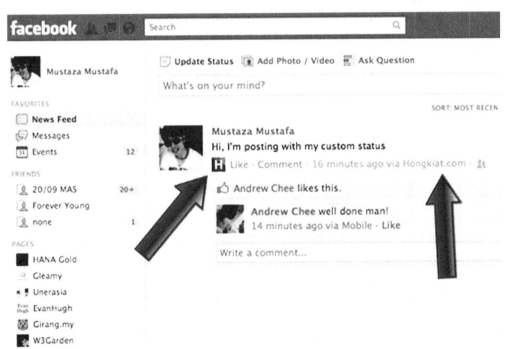

Schools

Institutions, schools, colleges and universities can be noted as main areas for Internet stalking based on the number of users who use the Internet to connect, obtain information, and to communicate. With the increase in interest on the social trend, schools and institutions are adapting to modify more programs to be taught online. This adaption has the ability to help increases the student population for the school as well as increases the amount of adult learners who will use the internet to obtain information. This increase can also upset and hurt the population by leading stalker and other predators into getting involved with or becoming involved with internet stalking. As schools and universities become the highest areas for teens and students, they also become the most vulnerable.

Finn (2004) conducted an exploratory study to show that 339 students at the University of New Hampshire, about 10% to 15% of students reported repeated communication threatened, insulted, or harassed, them (Finn, 2004). This type of negative communication can result in various types of lawsuits, endangerment, or even physical harassment, which can lead into negative effects and/or reputations for institutions. Internal and even external customers can be the main causes of threats to the institution based on what information is current stored and what information is being obtained.

University communication and connectivity systems need to be impeccable in order to ensure secure networks for students and faculty. In terms of financially affordable, these systems need to have various departments that are capable of tracking of where the sources are going towards, coming from, and how they are able to obtain information. This type of security is currently necessary and will be necessary for the future with the increase in students and the usability of online platforms. This type of security also creates a unified system with the university's reputation to promote a positive secure environment.

Internet stalking also increases the risk of vulnerability for the institution in terms of international attacks from outside sources. These attacks or acts of terror can be terminated or at the least lessened by having a secure server internet connection. A secure internet connection needs to be set up with many specific requirements such that all users have access to information and communication within this method. Internet connectivity is increasingly moving off the desktop and into the mobile and wireless environment, particularly for specific demographic groups (Lenhart, Purcell, Smith, & Zickuhr, 2010). As the internet connections become a main target point of importance for institutions, security in these areas will also increase based on the amount of users.

Leading to Intelligence Gathering

The various types of information that social media customers input via the internet can be viewed and retrieved by outside sources. The information gathered leads to a negative activity from international customers. In various instances, personal, financial information can be gathered and used against the user for purposes of threats that can harm or steal the identity of the user.

Intelligence Gathering from Other Countries via Internet Connectivity

With the high trend of social networking scattering the internet's surface, social media are available in every country, thus increasing the use of internet connectivity. This availability of information helps create a mix between businesses and customers in terms of how information is related. Intelligence gathering is one way of using the available information and putting it to good use depending on the source of the receiver. Businesses can use this type of work by targeting special performance enhancing customers who are local and idealistic to the values that the company brings to the table. It is also valuable in terms of online social marketing because it is feasible for businesses to assist with advertising online as compared to physical.

An international point of view that collaborates intelligence gathering can be noted based that internet connectivity is what brings users from various locations together in one normal new setting. This virtual environment setting becomes a normal atmosphere for many users based that most users are not currently satisfied with physical aspects of businesses. Using intelligence gathering from other countries helps institutions and businesses gather a list of potential customers from varying backgrounds that can help modify the existing performance of the business. A modification for a business is looked at by an increased way information is displayed and given to customers. This method should increase sales within the business, such that there is an absolute return on investment for the business.

Institutions can use intelligence gathering to help create new avenues for students to prosper. With this, distance learning and online collaborative learning can be assisted such that these are the main areas that are affected by the online networking. These changes also increase the power and connectivity of the specific institution to the student learner in the sense that they feel connected and secure. These are the most important items in any aspect of online networking in a business or educational field.

Privacy Laws

The U.S., Canada, and European Union (EU) provide a useful launching pad for the examination of cross-border privacy issues. With this, the U.S. has maintained a severe high maintenance cost for its security in the internet connections. This is a main reason why many institutions and businesses have created variances for what is allowed to be passed via the internet. In creating these variances, it also can be noted on how businesses prepare media and advertisements and also the security in these messages.

With Europe's high trade cost and online businesses, there is a high need for privacy to be placed in situations where customers will feel safe. It is this need that the EU uses to assume and vary its security online. Many businesses are accustomed to this type of development processes such that it is now accustomed to the normal activity for online marketing. Even the applications used via the internet connection do not use instances where privacy can be breached. It is with this type of process that businesses become safe from outside attacks.

FUTURE OF INTERNET CONNECTIVITY: SOCIAL NETWORKS

As internet connectivity becomes the more favorable and usable feature in a business industry, many businesses, customers, and people in general will begin to look for more ways to use this type of connection. The basis of a secure internet connection service begins with several items, which dictate how people use the connectivity, what they use it for, and where they use it. Many businesses will also become more conformable with the adaptability of internet usage in terms of security, mobility, and marketing. Overall, social networking is keen to fir development in businesses and keen for connections for people.

EMERGING TECHNOLOGIES AND THE INTERNET

Innovations and Numbers on the Growth of Ubiquitous and Mixed Reality Related Technologies

Google Glass is a wearable computer and a variant of the head mounted display (HMD). What is interesting about this innovation is that it is more than the headset. Google has connected this to the internet in many ways, not the least of which is being connected to the users Google+ account, which enables the user to share photos and videos with others. Using Google+ the user is connected to all their contacts from their Gmail account. Glass provides a way for the user to interact in different ways with the internet, through the rich media environment that is supported by Google. Google glass could be integrated into internet security in many of the same ways in which the traditional mixed reality system that has been described in this chapter.

Google Glass may not have its uses defined, yet many have made prognostications on uses for the augmented reality system. It is quite a visionary type of product with associated services. Many have recently written about potential uses for Google Glass. Some of the best ideas arc very close to some of the existing fields of virtual and augmented reality. The fact that the actual headset is so innovative, small, and connected, is intriguing and opens the door for many types of new applications or revisiting the old applications with the new technologies. Many envision that Google Glass will be used in the operating room to provide real time information to surgeons, as well as, augmenting education on many different levels.

Emerging technologies that are changing things as we speak is the idea of content centric networking. Xerox PARC is currently developing Content Centric Network (CCN), and making the software open source. One of the advantages of this technology is going to be that the data maintains its integrity no matter where it is transmitted; as there are security keys that are incorporated in their peer to peer demonstration of the CCN, which can ride on top of protocols or run natively. Such technology is essentially for mixed reality environments which necessitate a need for sharing information locally and quickly.

An interesting way that we conceived to view ubiquitous wireless technologies and technologies that represent mixed reality is to view the specific technology or group technologies in a feedback control loop. Using such a model we can construct the following control loop using.

At the beginning of the loop is the need for knowledge and learning, which may be in individuals need, and or a formalized educational program. The next step in the feedback loop is the comparer; in this model it will represent grades, 21st-century technology skills, self-fulfillment and self-efficacy. To the right of the compare is the reducer, which consists of pedagogy and technologies that are ubiquitous wireless, and quite possibly on the mixed reality continuum. Lastly is learning and knowledge which again can represent or present informally or formally, as in individuals self-fulfillment, self-efficacy, educational achievement, mastery of a topic. The feedback control loop moves left to right, in the feedback loop itself runs from learning and knowledge back to the need for knowledge and learning. A chart has been created to help visualize the model.

Using this model we make some assumptions, the first is that this is an activity that individuals want to engage in. The second which is illustrated by the comparer, they have a need. The reducer once again is going to representative of the technologies that we arc looking at in this chapter. We arc looking at mobile devices, different types of mixed reality that are used for knowledge creation and collaboration. Therefore we are looking at the technologies in this paper as a reducer in the Ubiquitous Learning Technology Control Loop (ULTCL). While this framework is not predictive in nature, or does not prescribe, it does segment or compartmentalize the topical area which makes it useful for analysis of new and emerging technologies that are found in mixed reality environments.

Dangers

Cyber-attacks happen on all types of organizations and individuals. They can start in many different places, including any device that's connected to the Internet. This becomes highly problematic in our modern society when we have devices such as copy machines that are hooked up to the Internet in order to update themselves report usage, install

Figure 6. Ubiquitous learning technology control loop

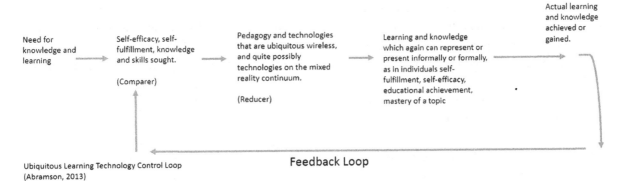

Ubiquitous Learning Technology Control Loop
(Abramson, 2013)

software, etc. Having all these devices connected to the Internet increases our exposure and vulnerability. With so many targets we need to create an orderly way to look for threats. As the threats have increased through the years, we become more vulnerable to these threats. An interesting point about the intrusion detection systems is that they are part hardware and part software. Therefore when we implement one of these solutions we need to make sure that we are up to date with the hardware and software maintenance so that we get the updates that will keep the organization safe.

There are many research papers and projects that have demonstrated the usefulness of virtual and mixed reality environments in many different fields. It is important that the cyber warrior believes that they are in a different environment. Believability has been a requirement for successful implementations of mixed reality and virtual reality. Human computer interaction (HCI) is essential to making the cyber warriors feel that they are immersed in cyberspace. Since cyberspace cannot be seen by the naked eye, we need to gather the data and information that is necessary and make the user be able to see it in a virtual and productive environment. The potential of ubiquitous, mobile and mixed reality technologies to deter Internet threats is enhanced by these characteristics, as we now have the ability to have individuals who are

in geographically separate areas, work together as one to solve new threats and problems. Mixed reality may be able to bridge the gap of recognition of security threats.

Incorporation of mixed reality should only require the changing of the inputs to the user or cyber warrior from game to actual data and information and the integration and implementation of a head mounted device (HMO) and quite possibly new input devices including brain to game interfacing. The process of creating a visual environment in which users can be active participants with real data with the purpose of solving problems and deterring threats, opens the process up to gamification. This permits the analysis of threats and also using the threat log and data for training as well, including one excited in a game based scenario.

Device Innovation

The characteristics of the devices that we use to connect to the internet are becoming smaller and more powerful. Contemporary mobile devices are extremely powerful, students can gather information off the Internet, download files, take pictures, email, and alter portalble document format (.pdf) files of any document that they have downloaded, analyze, synthesize and type up documents, all without any intervention or training from the university. They can also participate in an online discussion, call, email, text, video chat on certain phones and devices, including Apple iPhone and iPod touch. Such areas and technologies are mentioned, as these platforms illustrate what is possible from a technological standpoint, the critical mass of the technology, and show how they have been adopted into organizations and more importantly the individual as many of the changes that we have seen have been driven by the adoption of the individual and used without any intervention of the organization or university. This makes technology

or technological forces great. Thus combined with other forces has helped changed our society, no matter where we live. A ubiquitous device is one that is defined as always connected and allows access to content, anytime and anywhere (Hummel and Hlavacs, 2003). Internet bandwidth has become fast and more importantly wireless and ubiquitous, which has provided for the growth of many types of mobile wireless devices. Figure 7 and 8 displays the cyber warrior enviornments to include associated processes.

Figure 7. Cyber warrior technolgy infrastructure

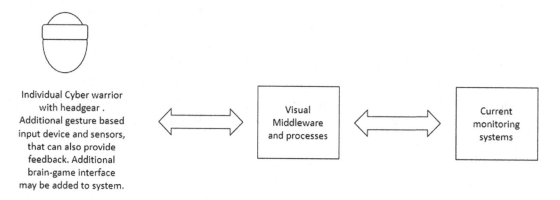

Figure 8. Cyber warrior scanning and interaction processes

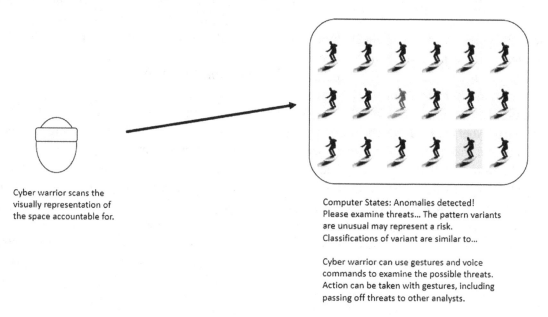

EMERGING AREAS IN HUMAN COMPUTER INTERACTION FOR COUNTERING CYBER ATTACKS

One of these areas is the use of head mounted displays (HMDSs) which may use spatial immersive display technology. By using these types of devices we can create environments which help reduce some of the complexity that is involved with detection of cyber threats. Seeing mixed reality used in this capacity has been seen in popular fiction literature. Ender's Game (1985) is a science fiction novel by Orson Scott Card. In the novel the most talented young are trained using vit1ual reality and augmented reality games. The US military has been using virtual reality for training and development. Specific examples include soldiers shooting and field training with armor, infantry, aviation, artillery, and air defense. One of the first modern implementations of this was at the Defense Advanced Research Projects Agency (DARPA) Simnet facility at Ft. Knox, KY in 199Os. Inside of the facility were multiple types of units that had a representation of the vehicle and tools that they would use on the battlefield. As one of the authors was a participant in this event, computers made a compelling and immersive environment for units to train together and against one another. It is not hard to imagine extending this type of technology in order to create an immersive environment that makes the detection of cyber threats easier to identify from the mass of data and information that may or may not be detected using more conventional means.

Mixed reality will make it easier to find these threats by a reduction of the complexity. Reducing complexity and increasing the understandability of threats will make it easier to work in an environment in which portions can be turned on and off. Current virtual reality and gaming technologies allow for the generation of the monitoring and subsequent training environments described. Of the first elements in a project that would be used to protect and monitor cyber-attacks would be to create a 3-D world in which systems/cyberspace can be modeled. Since many of the cyberspace attacks cyber-attacks target specific cities towns and businesses, we can use the geography as a starting point. From the generalized location we can create a highly granular or defined area of vulnerability and concern. This can be done by using many existing geographical databases such as Google. After this step we can focus on the mechanics of the 3-D world many tools are available for this purpose including dark basic which is a game engine that can house the navigation and parameters of the 3-D world. Therefore most if not all of the hardware and software systems and technology do exist for the creation and implementation of such a system.

Currently there are many open source and commercial versions of software that will permit the player/user to work against an AT or human opponent in order for the development of their ethical hacking skills. Users that immerse themselves in this type of technology are helping develop their skills sets, the future use of virtual and mixed reality to these types of systems will only enhance the understanding and help the user prepare for work as a cyber-warrior. Google code currently has a project emu-os that is a simulation ("Emuos- EmuOS is an open-source hacking game and simulator. - Google Project Hosting," 2012) that pits hacker against hacker, by doing this the user is gaining real-world and real-time experience.

The latest IDC predictions at the time of writing this chapter show that mobile devices are passing out PCs in how users connect to the internet. Software as a service (SaaS) and Platforms as a service (PaaS) are all reporting exponential growth which helps confirm the mobile computing trends that we are seeing. There are many different reports out that describe the most popular mobile devices, a common theme among all of them is the smart phone and tablets ("IDC Predicts 2013", 2012). Therefore we can see that the internet infrastructures are changing to meet the needs of a more mobile device oriented market.

Figure 9. Post university cyber lab

Figure 10. Systems of systems

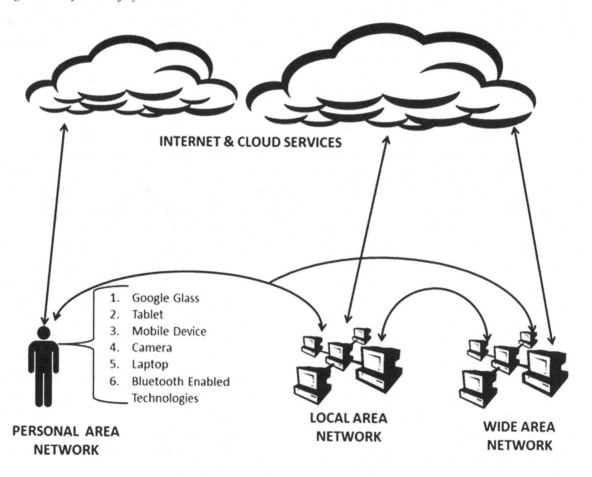

Mobile device security is going to become even more important as more people are going to be using these devices for all sorts of tasks, including those oriented around virtual and mixed reality.

Enhanced Collaboration and Learning with New Technologies

Collaboration is important and is enhanced with virtual and mixed reality systems. Collaboration is an important part of the new learning paradigm and has been proven effective in the supporting collaboration as e-learning tools are readily available on most mobile devices. Collaboration is enhanced by the use of mobile technologies and is a key intention of the knowledge age. Turoff (2000) proposed that collaboration provides a solution to learning outside of the physical classroom. In addition to collaboration, facilitation, and updated educational methodologies are key components to E-learning and M-learning (Hiltz, Benbunan-Fich, Coppola, Rotter, & Turoff, 2000). Collaborative learning is the promotion of learning through social interaction; it is one of the five properties identified by Klopfer et al., (2004), which support the established forms of learning through the use of mobile technologies (Naismith, Lonsdale, Vavoula, & Sharples, 2004). Figure 9 shows the Post University Cyber Lab with network forensics sosfteware running during a live class demonostartion.

Systems of Systems Concepts

When discussing hyperconnectivity it is necessary to discuss systems of systems concepts. Systems of systems is a collection of systems tied together to create a more complex system (Popper, Bankes, Callaway, & DeLaurentis, 2004). An example of this is Figure 10 below which displays a few methods to be connected to the internet and network traffic scenarios. When thinking about the possibilities of hyperconnectivity the personal area network (PAN) is an excellent example as it allows multiple technologies to be interconnected with soil ware applications. The Google Glass has the potential to all global positioning system (GPS), social media, digital terrain overlays, and synchronization with other devices. This increases the complexity of the system as it becomes part of a larger systems which multiples the number of potential vulnerabilities.

CONCLUSION

The futures of national and international security depend on multiple complex countermeasures to ensure that a proper security posture throughout its lifecycle. To effectively protect these systems from exploitation of vulnerabilities, it is a necessity to further comprehend all the current threats and how they exploit the current vulnerabilities. Additionally, one must be able to effectively gauge the future threats and have a strong grasp on the laws that drive their need to be secured such as enhanced privacy laws by the national governments. Examined within this chapter are the potential security related threats with the use of social media, mobile devices, virtual worlds, augmented reality, and mixed reality. Further reviewed were examples of the complex attacks that could interrupt human-robot interaction, children computer interaction, mobile computing, social networks, and more through human centered issues in security design. This book chapter serves as a guide to those who use multiple wired and wireless technologies but fail to realize the dangers of being hyperconnected.

REFERENCES

Armbrust, M., Fox, A., Griftlth, R., Joseph, A. D., Katz, R., Konwinski, A., & Zaharia, M. (201 0). A view of cloud computing. *Communications of the ACM, 53*(4), 50-58.

BackTrack Linux. (2011). *BackTrack Linux.* Retrieved March 22, 2013, from www.backtrack-linux.org

Becher, M., Freiling, F., & Leider, B. (2007). On the effort to create smartphone worms in Windows Mobile. In *Proceedings of the 2007 IEEE Workshop on Information Assurance.* United States Military Academy. Retrieved March 22, 2013, from http://pil.informatik.uni-mannheim.de/filepool/publications/on-the-effort-to-create-smartphone-worms-in-windows-mobile.pdf

Beidleman, S. W. (2009). Defining and Deterring Cyber War. Barracks, PA Army War College. Retrieved March 10, 2013, from http://www.hsdl.org/?abstract&doc=ll8653&coll=limited

Bhattacharya, D. (2008) *Leardership styles and information security in small businesses: An empirical investigation.* (Doctoral dissertation, University of Phoenix). Retrieved March 9, 2013, from www.phoenix.edu/apololibrary

Bishop, M., & Taylor, C. (2009). A Critical Analysis of the Centers of Academic Excellence Program. In *Proceedings of the 13th Colloquium for Information Systems Security Education* (pp. 1-3). Retrieved March 9, 2013, from http://nob.cs.ucdavis.edu/bishop/papers/2009-cisse/

Bose, A. (2008). *Propagation, detection and containment of mobile mal ware.* (Doctoral dissertation, University of Michigan). Retrieved March 11, 2013, from www.phoenix.edu/apololibrary

Brown, B. (2009). *Beyond Downadup: Security expert worries about smart phone, TinyURL threats: Malware writers just waiting for financial incentive to strike, F-Secure exec warns.* Retrieved March 20, 2013, from http://business.highbeam.com/409220/article-1G1-214585913/beyond-downadup-securityexpert-worries-smart-phone

Bullock, J., Haddow, G., Coppola, D., & Yeletaysi, S. (2009). *Introduction to homeland security: Principles of all-hazards response* (3rd ed.). Burlington, MA: Elsevier Inc.

National Security Agency, Common Criteria Evaluation and Validation Scheme (CCEVS). (2008). *Common criteria evaluation and validation scheme -- Organization, management, and concept of operations* (Version 2.0). Retrieved from National Information Assurance Partnership website: http://www.niap-ccevs.org/policy/ccevs/scheme-pub-l.pdf

Celeda, P. (2011). *Network security monitoring and behavior analysis.* Retrieved March 22nd, 2013 from http://www.terena.org/activities/campus-bp/pdf/gn3-na3-t4-cbpd133.pdf

Cheok, A., Fernando, 0., & Liu, W. (2008). The magical world of mixed reality. Innovation: The Magazine of Research and Technology. *National University of Singapore and World Scientific Publishing, 8*(1), 70–73.

Cheok, A. (2009). Mixed Reality Entertainment and Art. *International Journal Of Virtual Reality, 8*(2), 83–90.

Cheok, A., Man Fung, H., Yustina, E., & Shang Ping, L. (2005). Mobile Computing With Personal Area Network and Human Power Generation. *International Journal of Software Engineering and Knowledge Engineering, 15*(2), 169–175. doi:10.1142/S0218194005002348

Clarke, R. & Knake, R. (2010). *Cyber war: The next threat to national security and what to do about it.* New York, NY: Ecco.

Conti, M., Hasani, A., & Crispo, B. (2011). Virtual Private Social Networks. In *Proceedings of the First ACM Conference on Data and Application Security and Privacy.* New York, NY: ACM.

Dawson, M. (2011). Applicability of Web 2.0: Training for Tactical Military Applications. Global TIME, 1, 395-398.

Dawson, M. E. Jr, Crespo, M., & Brewster, S. (2013). DoD cyber technology policies to secure automated information systems. *International Journal of Business Continuity and Risk Management, 4*(1), 1–22. doi:10.1504/IJBCRM.2013.053089

Dawson, M. E., & Saeed, AI, T. (2012). Use of Open Source Software and Virtualization in Academia to Enhance Higher Education Everywhere. *Culling-edge Technologies in Higher Education, 6*, 283–313. doi:10.1108/S2044-9968(2012)000006C013

Debatin, B., Lovejoy, J. P., Horn, A. K., & Hughes, B. N. (2009). Facebook and Online Privacy: Attitudes, Behaviors, and Unintended Consequences. *Journal of Computer-Mediated Communication, 15*(1), 83–108. doi:10.1111/j.1083-6101.2009.01494.x

Denning, D. E. (2012). Stuxnet: What Has Changed? *Future Internet, 4*(3), 672–687. doi:10.3390/fi4030672

Dudenhoffer, C. (2012). Pin lt! Pinterest as a Library Marketing Information Literacy Tool. *College & Research Libraries News, 73*(6), 328–332.

Dyck, J., Pinelle, D., Brown, B., & Gutwin, C. (2003). Learning from Games: HCI Design Innovations in Entertainment Software. In Proceedings of Graphics Interface, (pp. 237-246). Retrieved March 18, 2013, from http:/lhci.usask.ca/publica tions/view.php?id=88

EPOC Features. (2012). Retrieved from http://www.emotiv.com/epoc/features.php

Finn, J. (2004). A Survey of Online Harassment at University Campus. *Journal of Interpersonal Violence, 19*(4), 468–483.

Fitzgerald, D. C. (2008). *Intersections of the Self: Identity in the Boom of Social Media* (Doctoral Dissertation). Available from ProQuest Dissertations and Thesis Full Texts Database: http:!/search.proguest.com/docview/304607151

Fraser, M., Hindmarsh, J., Best, K., Heath, C., Biegel, G., Greenhalgh, C., & Reeves, S. (2006). Remote Collaboration Over Video Data: Towards Real-Time e-Social Science. *Computer Supported Cooperative Work, 15*(4), 257–279. doi:10.1007/s10606-006-9027-y

Google Project Hosting. (2012). *Emu-as- EmuOS Is an Open-source Hacking Game and Simulator*. Retrieved March 11,2013, from http://code.google.com/p/emu-os/

Grainger, J. (2010). *Social Media and the Fortune 500: How the Fortune 500 Uses, Perceives and Measures Social Media as a Marketing Tool* (Doctoral Dissertation). Available from ProQuest Dissertations and Thesis Full Texts Database: https://cdr.lib.unc.edu/indexablecontent?id=uuid:ae530f99-9b8d-43a4-9fa4-9f12c5b00a2l&ds=DATA FILE

Hiltz, S. R., Benbunan-Fich, R., Coppola, N., Rotter, N., & Turoff, M. (2000). Measuring the Importance of Collaborative Learning for the Effectiveness of ALN: A Multi-Measure, Multi-Method Approach. *The Journal of Asynchronous Learning, 4*(2), 103–125.

Hochman, N., & Schwartz, R. (2012). Visualizing Instagram: Tracing Cultural Visual Rhythms, Association for the Advancement of Artificial Intelligence. In *Proceedings of Sixth International AAAI Conference on Weblogs and Social Media*. Retrieved March 18, 2013 from, http://www.aaai.org/ocs/index.php/lCWSM/lCWSM12/paper/viewFile/4782/5091

Hsu, J. (n.d.). *U.S considers open-source software for Cyber security*. Retrieved March 22, 2013, from http://www.teclmewsdaily.com/2644-cybersecurity-open-source.html

Hummel, K. A., & Hlavacs, H. (2003). *Anytime, Anywhere Learning Behaviour Using a Web Based Platform for a University Lecture. In Proceedings of SSGRR 2003*. Aquila.

Kwak, H., Lee, C., Park., H., & Moon, S. (2010). What is Twitter, a Social Network of News Media?. In *Proceedings of the 19111 International Conference on World Wide Web*. Academic Press.

Lenhart, A., Purcell, K., Smith, A., & Zickuhr, K. (2010). *Social Media & Mobiler Internet Use Among Teens and Young Adults*. Pew Research Center. Retrieved March 20, 2013, from http://web.pewinternet.org//media/Files/Reports/2010/PlPSocialMediaandYoungAdultsReportFina!withtoplines.pdf

Lewis, B. K. (2012). *Social Media and Strategic Communications: Attitudes and perceptions Among College Students* (Doctoral Dissertation). Available from ProQuest Dissertations and Thesis Full Texts Database: http://www.prsa.org/Intelligence/PRJournal/Documents/2012LewisNichols.pdf

Lopez, C. (2009). Immersive technology melds Hollywood, warrior training. *Soldiers, 64*(5), 27.

Lotring, A. (2005). Training the millennlal sailor. *U.S. Naval Institute Proceedings, 131*(12), 36–37.

Mac, R. (2013). *No One Is More Excited For Google Glass Than Facebook CEO Mark Zuckerberg*. Retrieved March 28, 2013 from http://www.forbes.com/sites/ryanmac/2013/02/21/no-one-is-moreexcited-for-google-glass-than-facebook-ceo-mark-zuckerberg/

Maxwell, D., & McLennan, K. (2012). Case Study: Leveraging Government and Academic Partnerships in MOSES. In *Proceedings of World Conference on Educational Multimedia, Hypermedia and Telecommunications*, (pp. 1604-1616). Academic Press.

Mislove, A., Marcon, M., Gummadi, K. P., Drushel, P., & Bhattacharjee, B. (2007). Measurement and Analysis of Online Social Networks. In *Proceedings of the 7th ACM SIGCOMM Conference on Internet Measurement*, (pp. 29-42). ACM.

Mulliner, C., & Miller, C. (2009). Injecting SMS messages into smartphones for security analysis. In *Proceedings of the 3rd USENIX Workshop on Offensive Technologies*. Retrieved March 22, 2013 from https://www.usenix.org/legacy/events/woot09/tech/full papers/mulliner.pdf

Mustafa, M. (2012). *How to Customize the 'Via' Status on Facebook Posts, Hongkait.com Inspiring Technology*. Retrieved on April 18, 2013, from http://www.hongkiat.com/blog/customize-facebookstatus/

Myers, S. (2012). Operative BackTrack. *Journal of On Demand Hacking, 1*(3), 60-66.

Naismith, L., Lonsdale, P., Vavoula, G. & Sharples, M. (2006). *Literature review in mobile technologies and learning*. Futurelab Series. Retrieved March 22, 2013, from http://www2.futurelab.org.uk/resources/documents/1itreviews/MobileReview.pdf

Omar, M., & Dawson, M. (2013, April). Research in Progress- Defending Android Smartphones from Malware Attacks. In *Proceedings of 2013 Third International Conference on Advanced Computing and Communication Technologies* (pp. 288-292). Rohtak, India: IEEE.

Park, S. R., Nah, F. F., Dewester, D., & Eschenbrenner, B. (2008). Virtual World Affordances: Enhancing Brand Value. *Journal of Virtual Worlds Research, 1*(2), 1–18.

Parti, K. (2011). Actual Poling in Virtual Reality - A Cause of Moral Panic or a Justitied Need?. InTech. Retrieved March 22, 2013, from http://www.intechopen.com/books/virtua1-real ity/actua1poIicing-in-virtua1-real ity-a-cause-of-moralpanic-or-a-justified-need-

Perens, B. (1999). The open source definition. In *Open sources: Voices.from the open source revolution,* (pp. 171-85). Academic Press.

Popper, S., Bankes, S., Callaway, R., & DeLaurentis, D. (2004). *System-of-Systems Symposium: Report on a Summer Conversation.* Arlington, VA: Potomac Institute for Policy Studies.

Qualman, E. (2013). *Socialnomics: How Social Media Transforms the Way We Live and Do Business* (2nd ed.). Hoboken, NJ: John Wiley & Sons.

Raento, M., Oulasvirta, A., & Eagle, N. (2009). Smartphones: An Emerging Tool for Social Scientists. *Journal of Social Methods & Research, 37*(3), 426–454. doi:10.1177/0049124108330005

Rajabhushanam, C. C., & Kathirvel, A. A. (2011). System of One to Three Umpire Security System for Wireless Mobile Ad hoc Network. *Journal Of Computer Science, 7*(12), 1854-1858.

Rash, W. (2004). *Latest skulls Trojan foretells risky smartphone future.* Retrieved from www. eweek.com

Reed, D. (2003). *Applying the OSI seven layer network model to information security.* Retrieved March 22, 2013, from http://www.isd.mel.nist.gov/projects/processcontrol/members/minutes/7-Sep-2004/0SI.pdf

Roesch, M. (1999). SNORT-Lightweight Intrusion Detection for Networks. In *Proceedings of LISA '99: 13th USENlX conference on System administration.* Retrieved March 18, 2013, from https://www.usenix.org/legacy/events/!isa99/full papers/roesch/roesch.pdf

Sadasivam, K., Samudrala, B., & Yang, A. (2005). Design of Network Security Projects Using Honeypots. *Journal of Computing Sciences in Colleges, 20*(4), 282–293.

Salah, K., & Kahtani, A. (2009). Improving snort performance under linux. *Communications, JET, 3*(12), 1883–1895.

Sexton, S. (2011). *What is the Percieved Impact of Social Media on Personal Relationships in Adolescence?* (Doctoral Dissertation). Available from ProQuest Dissertations and Thesis Full Texts Database: http://gradworks.umi.com/15/03/1503092.html

Siegel, A., Denny, W., Poff, K. W., Larose, C., Hale, R., & Hintze, M. (2009). Survey on Privacy Law Developments in 2009: United States Canada, and the European Union, The American Bar Association Press. *The Business Lawyer, 65*(1), 285–307.

Snort. (2012). *What is Snort?.* Retrieved March 20, 2013, from www.snort.org

Socialcast. (2012). *Managing and Control Your Private Network.* Retrieved on April 22, 2013, from http://www.soc ialcast.com/adm in istration

Surman, G. (2002). *Understanding Security using the OSI Model.* Retrieved March 25, 2013, from http://www.sans.org/reading room/whitepapers/protocols/understanding-security-osi-model 377

TDC. (2012). *IDC Predicts 2013 Will Be Dominated by Mobile and Cloud Developments as the IT Industry Shifts Tnto Full-Blown Competition on the 3rd Platform.* Retrieved March 22, 2013, from https://www.idc.com/getdoc.jsp?containerId=prUS23814112

Turoff, M. (2000). An End to Student Segregation: No more separation between distance learning and regular courses. *Horizon, 8*(1), 1–7. doi:10.1108/10748120010803294

Tuteja, A. & Shanker, R. (2012). Optimization of Snort for Extrusion and Intrusion Detection and Prevention. *International Journal ofEngineering Research and Applications, 2*(3), 1768-1774.

Uitzil, L. (2012). Wireless security system implemented in a mobile robot. *International Journal of Computer Science Issues, 9*(4), 16.

Walker, J. J. (2012). Cyber Security Concerns for Emergency Management, Emergency Management. InTech. Retrieved April 2013, from http://www.i ntec hopen.com/books/emergency-management/cy ber-secu rity-concerns-for-emer gene ymanagement

Wang, P. A. (2010). *The Effect of Knowledge of Online Security Risks on Consumer Decision Making in B2C e-Commerce* (Dissertation Thesis). ProQuest LLC.

Weiser, M. (1991). The computer for the 21st century. *Scientific American, 265*(3), 94-104.

Wong, L. (2005). *Potential Bluetooth vulnerabilities in smartphones*. Retrieved March 18, 2013, from http://citeseerx. ist.psu.edu

Xie, L., Zhang, X., Chaugule, A., Jaeger, T., & Zhu, S. (2009). *Designing system-level defenses against cellphone malware*. Retrieved March 21, 2013, from www.cse.psu.edu

KEY TERMS AND DEFINITIONS

Authentication: Security measure designed to establish the validity of a transmission, message, or originator, or a means of verifying an individual's authorization to receive specific categories of information.

Availability: Timely, reliable access to data and information services for authorized users.

Cloud Computing: Comprised of both the application delivered as services over the internet and the hardware and systems software housed in the datacenters that provide those services (Armbrust, et al, 2010).

Confidentiality: Assurance that information is not disclosed to unauthorized individuals, processes, or devices.

Hyperconnectivity: Use of multiple means of communications such as instant messaging, phones, Web 2.0, Web 3.0, and other communication methods.

Integrity: Quality of an IS reflecting the logical correctness and reliability of the operating system; the logical completeness of the hardware and software implementing the protection mechanisms; and the consistency of the data structures and occurrence of the stored data. Note that, in a formal security mode, integrity is interpreted more narrowly to mean protection against unauthorized modification or destruction of information.

Non Repudiation: Assurance the sender of data is provided with proof of delivery and the recipient is provided with proof of the sender's identity, so neither can later deny having processed the data.

Open Source Software: Software that allows the original source code to be fi·ee available which may be freely redistributed or modified (Perens, 2009).

Section 3
Forensics, Malware Detection, and Analysis

Chapter 10
Similarity Measure for Obfuscated Malware Analysis

P. Vinod
SCMS School of Engineering and Technology, India

P. R. Rakesh
SCMS School of Engineering and Technology, India

G. Alphy
SCMS School of Engineering and Technology, India

ABSTRACT

The threats imposed by metamorphic malware (capable of generating new variants) can easily bypass a detector that uses pattern-matching techniques. Hence, the necessity is to develop a sophisticated signature or non-signature-based scanners that not only detect zero day malware but also actively train themselves to adapt to new malware threats. The authors propose a statistical malware scanner that is effective in discriminating metamorphic malware samples from a large collection of benign executables. Previous research articles pertaining to metamorphic malware demonstrated that Next Generation Virus Kit (NGVCK) exhibited enough code distortion in every new generation to defeat signature-based scanners. It is reported that the NGVCK-generated samples are 10% similar in code structure. In the authors' proposed methodology, frequencies of opcodes of files are analyzed. The opcodes features are transformed to new feature spaces represented by similarity measures (37 similarity measure). Thus, the aim is also to develop a non-signature-based scanner trained with small feature length to classify unseen malware and benign executables.

INTRODUCTION

Malware is generic term that refers to software which does undesired malicious activity in computer systems. As the amount of available data multiply, the problem of managing the information turn out to be more difficult. The increased use of internet file sharing has led to wide spread of malware. The consequence of this prevalence is that many computer systems are vulnerable and are infected with malicious programs. Zero day attacks cause great destruction to the computer world. Apart from the new attacks, existing malware threats are tansformed into new ones. Malware detectors have not evolved to mitigate sophisticated attacks.

DOI: 10.4018/978-1-4666-6158-5.ch010

Therefore, there is a need urgent need to develop robust detector which can identify not only the existing malwares but also unseen and obfuscated malwares. Static signature based detection technique has been a dominant within Antiviruses. Many writers make use of virus constructors for developing new malware. These malware kits allow hackers to generate new malware specimens with minimal knowledge. Some of the tools are Next Generation Virus Kits (NGVCK), G2, Mass Code Generation (MPCGEN), Virus Creation Lab (VCL 32) etc. We consider variants of a malware from various tools like NGVCK, G2 etc. Earlier studies have already shown that NGVCK tool provides enough obfuscation in subsequent malware generations. Thus, traditional signatures can prove to be ineffective when dealing with unknown variants. In this work, we propose static analyzing technique to extract relevant features from malware. Based on these relevant features we determine similarity amongst pair of files using 37 similarity measurement indices. In an effort to classify the samples, the objectives are as stated below:

1. To find whether various distance/similarity measures are effective in classification of malware and benign executables.
2. To evaluate the effectiveness of virus generation tool kits like NGVCK, G2 etc in the generation of strong metamorphic variants.
3. To evaluate the effects of feature reduction in classification accuracy.
4. To find which classifier produces better result for the test/train model.
5. To find actegory of features that contribute to the detection scheme.
6. To evaluate response of the proposed detector on imbalanced dataset.

In the remaining part of this chapter we briefly introduce different types of malware. Obfuscation methods adopted by metamorphic engine to generate strong metamorphic malware is also discussed. Subsequently, we discuss malware detection techniques proposed by researchers to identify metamorphic malware. Also, we introduce machine learning methods for the detection of malicious code. Later part of this chapter we discuss our proposed methodology based on similarity measurement indices. Finally experiments, results, inferences are covered. We close the chapter with pointers to future research in the challenging domain of desktop and mobile malware detection.

MALWARE AND DETECTION TECHNIQUES

Malicious programs have a long history and ever since the invention of malicious programs their detection have attracted the anti-malware community. Malicious programs aimed at detecting useful information confined to system and users, they remain dormant and undetected. Anti-detection mechanisms have evolved into complexity. However, sophisticated malicious program also known as *polymorphic* and *metamorphic* viruses have evolved in unprecedented rate. Detection of malcode that can obfuscate or morph future instances is a big challenge and needs to be addressed critically. In the following subsection, we discuss different types of malware with their detection techniques.

Malware

Malware or unwanted software's are the program created to compromise normal functionality of computer, gather sensitive information by gaining super user privilege and bypass access control. Malicious programs prevails itself in numerous forms such as codes, scripts, active contents and other software. Often, malware is confused as defective codes (also known as bug), whereas malware is skillfully implanted to disrupt the functioning of the host program.

Types

The most common types of malware are:

1. **Virus:** Virus is a piece of code that propagates from one system to other, infecting each system on its way. When an infected code is launched in a vulnerable machine it utlizes this machine to create a denial of service on the system.
2. **Worms:** Are *self-replicating* and independent codes that affects computer by exploiting operating systems vulnerability. In order to propagate in the network they take advantage of the information and file transport making it a network aware.
3. **Trojan Horses:** These malware are usually disguised as a legitimate applications. They appear in some eye catching program unknowingly downloaded by the users. The consequences range from deleting, stealing sensitive data or generating unwanted pop ups.
4. **Spyware:** Spy on user activity to collect keystrokes, harvest data, modify security settings of software or browser to interfere with unethical network connections.
5. **Adware:** Is a type of malware that is capable of delivering advertisements. These are often bundled with spyware that is capable of tracking user activity for stealing information.
6. **Encrypted Malware:** Encrypts the malware payload. The malicious code is encrypted using *block* or *stream ciphers* methods that thwart scanners employing pattern matching techniques. In this type of malicious code the decryption routine are constant and can be finally detected using signature based detectors.
7. **Polymorphic Malware:** Use a *polymorphic engine* to mutate syntactic structure of new variant while keeping the original algorithm intact. That is, the code changes itself each time it executes, but the function of the code (its semantics) does not change. More importantly, polymorphic malware have variable decryption routine. Thus, emulation based scanner can sometime be effective in their detection. However, limitation is to create a ideal emulator.
8. **Metamorphic Malware:** Metamorphic viruses can obfuscate their body by various techniques. The most applicable techniques are (refer Figure 1):
    a. **Register or Variable Exchange:** Use of different registers/variables in newly produced instance.
    b. **Instruction Substitution:** Replacement of instructions with their possible equivalents instructions blocks or subroutines.
    c. **Code Transposition:** Code and subroutines reorder or change of the flow control by using conditional or unconditional jumps.
    d. **Instruction Permutation:** Reorder independent instructions.

Figure 1. Metamorphic engine

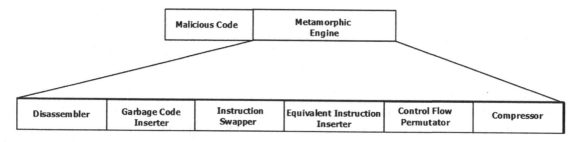

e. **Garbage Code Insertion:** NOP instruction and other instruction that has no effects on the operation of the code are inserted in the original program instructions.

Malware Detector

Malware detectors protect the system against the malicious code infection. Malware scanners may be configured to reside on the same computer it is trying to protect or could exist in an external computer. These detectors contain the knowledge of the malware (in form of signature or behavior) stored in the repository to flag any monitored samples as suspicious. According to Kindsight Security Labs Malware survey Report 2012, in fixed broadband deployment, 13% of home networks were found to be infected of which 6% are infected by high threat level malware such as botnets, rootkits or banking trojans, 7% of households are infected with a moderate threat level malware such as spyware, browser hijackers or adware. The Plankton-Apperhand-Tonclank family, which was reported as malware in 2011, have now been downgraded by the mobile security industry to "*aggressive adware*". Android infection rate has increased to an alarming rate in the order of 1 in 1000 devices which include the top android malware like Trojan.GGTracker, Trojan. Pjapps3.A, Adware.SndApp.B.

Sophos Security Threat Report 2012 anticipates growing sophistication in web-borne attacks, even broader use of mobile and smart devices, and rapid adoption of cloud computing bringing new security challenges. It reported United States (11.43%), India (8.02%), Russian Federation (7.52%), Brazil (5.62%), Italy (3.37%), Vietnam (3.07%), Indonesia (2.88%), Taiwan (2.85%), Ukraine (2.82%), Romania 2.64%), France (2.25%) as the top 12 spam producing countries in the world. Consequently, malware detectors with very high detection and robust techniques rates need to be devised.

Malware Detection Techniques

- **Anomaly Based:** In this approach the valid behavior of the system is studied and approximated to build the repository that has to be compared with the potentially unwanted infectors.
- **Signature Based:** Characteristics of the viruses are investigated and they are stored in the form of MD5 hashes for detection. Mostly, useful to identify known malware attacks.
- **Heuristic Bases:** Identifies the maliciousness by monitoring the behavior of software. Such detectors have high false alarms if heuristics are not well defined.
- **Behavior Based:** This approach inspect at how software would behave to determine hostile performance.
- **Integrity Check:** Detects the changes in files by comparing them to their original check-sum stored in a list of check sum table prepared in non-infection mode.

Malware Detection Methods

As malwares evolved in complexity, detection techniques have emerged in its sophistication. Several detection methods/models is proposed to effectively identify and classify zero day malware. Following subsection introduce various detection methods.

Statical Analysis

Static analysis is a process of analyzing the code before the execution in a system to classify samples as benign or malware. This method use the syntax or structural properties of the program to determine maliciousness.

Approach use varied features of malware files such as opcode, portable executable metadata, strings, function code length and/or Hex patterns. Tools of the trade are decompilers, disassemblers, source code analyzers, and even basic utilities such as *diff* or *grep* command. Detectors based on static analysis aim to develop a system by reverse engineering unknown binary executable code without the need for manual inspection of assembly code.

On successfully reversing malware, the analyst can understand malware infection life cycle. Static analysis has an advantage that it reveals how a program could behave under unusual conditions, as one can examine segment of the program that normally are not executed. Also, it is fast, as the detector fully predict the behavior of all but the smallest programs. However, it has the disadvantage of using disassemblers for analysis.

Dynamic Analysis

Dynamic analysis require the samples to be exeuted in an controlled environment to learn the behaviour of specimens. However, with dynamic analysis complete execution flow of a program is approximated to understand its nature. Certain malware that exhibit multiupersonality behaviour leads to increased levels of false alarms. As, the runtime behaviour of samples are used in dynamic analysis to determine maliciousness it incur high processing overhead. Therefore sometimes, static analysis is preferred, to understand in the initial phase of detection whether the sample is suspicious.

METAMORPHIC MALWARE DETECTION METHODS

Earlier research work in the area of metamorphic malware detection is introduced in (Vinod et. al, 2011a). They also discuss *longest common subsequence* techniques for detecting synthetic metamorphic malware where the extracted opcode sequence are used to create control flow graphs (CFG). In (Wong W, 2006) the author investigate the degree of metamorphism in different malware constructor like Generation 2 (G2), Virus Creation Lab (VCL32), MPCGEN (Mass Code

Generator), Next Generation Virus Creation Kit (NGVCK) obtained from (http://vx.netlux.org). They demonstrated that NGVCK generated variants depicted average similarity of 10%. However, non-malware files exhibited similarity close to NGVCK. Thus, to detect metamorphic malware variants created with NGVCK tool, Hidden Markov Model (HMM) based scanner was developed. Samples which could not have been detected with commercial antiviruses where however identified by their proposed HMM detector.

Authors in (Vinod et al, 2010a), proposed a method for detecting unseen malware samples by executing programs using STraceNTx in an emulated environment. Samples were generated with different malware kits (VCL32, IL_SMG, PS-MPC, MPCGEN and NGVCK). Common base signature from each malware constructor was developed. It was observed that unseen samples were detected using the base signature. Later, they investigated the degree of metamorphism amongst different constructors. Similarity amongst malware constructors were determined by computing proximity index. *Inter constructor* and *intra constructor* proximity was also determined. The research exhibited that all constructor demonstrated high *intra constructor* proximity except NGVCK. Unlike, NGCVK constructor, code distortion with other malware kits were not significant, indicating minimal degree of metamorphism. Also, *inter constructor* similarity was determined. Most of the samples were found to have higher proximity with other malware constructor. However, NGVCK generated variants depicted less *intra constructor* proximity. This indicated that metamorphic engine of NGVCK virus kit was robust in comparison to other malware constructor.

Authors (Attaluri, S, 2009) used opcode alignment sequences obtained from morphed malware, to create stronger detector based on Profile Hidden Markov Models (PHMMs), for the classification of unseen synthetic malware specimens. PHMMs are robust in comparison to standard HMM as the former capture positional information. The generated PHMM was tested on metamorphic malware samples generated from three malware constructors (VCL-32, PS-MPC and NGVCK). Detection rate of 100% was achieved for VCL-32 and PS-MPC samples, whereas, considering proper multiple aligned sequences of NGVCK malware, a better detection rate was obtained. The study also highlighted that PHMMs were not effective if code blocks were permuted. Under such scenario the standard HMM resulted in better accuracy. However, the primary disadvantage with PHMM is that they are computationally expensive for modeling malware.

Vinod et al, 2009, developed three malware samples and seven variants from the base malware by applying different code morphing technique (*equivalent instruction substitution, garbage insertion, code permutation using branch instruction*). Structure of variants were normalized with a custom built assembly code normalizer. Subsequently, normalized control flow graph (CFG) was constructed. Later, from this normalized CFG, sequence of opcode were extracted and compared with the opcode sequence of other variants using *Longest Common Subsequence (LCS)*. It was examined that variants of same base malware depicted higher similarity. Moreover, morphed malware could be differentiated from benign files. The only drawback of using LCS approach is that it has computational complexity of $O(m.n)$ where, *m and n* are the length of two opcode sequences extracted from malware/benign .asm files.

Authors in (Lin D., 2011) developed a metamorphic engine that could evade HMM based detector. The idea of the study was to investigate as to what extent the base malware could be morphed so as to fail HMM based scanners. The metamorphic engine morphed the NGVCK generated malware code using elementary code obfuscation techniques. More importantly, the basic idea was to generate morphed malware copies that are structurally similar to benign files. In order to carry the experiment Cygwin executables were considered as the benign samples (as they employ low level system functionality as malware specimens)

and code fragment of variable proportion from benign subroutines were extracted, which were subsequently inserted in malware samples keeping in view that maliciousness is not disturbed. The experiment was conducted for different fraction of injected code (extracted from benign files) in range of 5% to 35%. It was observed that even 5% of block of benign fragment inserted as dead code in malware sample could thwart HMM detector. This research article opened a new direction for malware analyst to understand that the metamorphic engine employing basic obfuscation method as *insertion of dead code* (from subroutine of benign files) could defeat both pattern based as well as spectrum based scanners.

In (Runwal N, 2012), authors devised a method for determining similarity between the files using opcode graphs (directed graph). An opcode graph is constructed from opcode extracted from malware assembly files. Nodes are denoted as opcode and the directed edge between the nodes are represented as the probability of a successor opcode in a file with respect to a given opcode under consideration. The study showed that the opcode graph similarity method outperformed HMM based detector and yielded no false positives or negatives. As there existed good separation between the similarity scores of malware v/s malware and benign v/s benign. Hence, a threshold could be easily established. Using this threshold, unseen samples can be classified as malware/benign. The authors also tested the effectiveness of the opcode graph model based on two attacks (a) removal of rare opcode and (b) transforming base malware into complex form (where junk code from benign samples are injected into malware samples so that malware and benign samples appear structurally similar). The investigation demonstrated that metamorphic malware could be discriminated from benign executable even after the elimination of uncommon opcode. Also, the detection rate of HMM scanners and opcode graph based detector are comparable if benign code is injected in malicious files as dead code.

Studies in (Lin D., 2011) depicted that HMM based detector failed to detect strong metamorphic malware invariants injected with benign opcode as dead code. Annie H, 2012, devised a method to improve the detection rate of HMM scanner by combining it with statistical methods such as *chi-squared test*. It was observed from the experiments that HMM detectors performed better if short sequence of benign opcode were added as junk code. Moreover, for a block of benign code added to malware file the detection rate of HMM based scanner degraded. Thus, *chi-square* based classifier was developed. This hybrid model devised by integrating HMM and *Chi-square* classifier resulted in improvement of classification accuracy.

Authors in (Donabelle B, 2013) proposed a method for identification of metamorphic malware based on byte features, using structural entropy and wavelet transform techniques. Image transformation methods were applied on malicious files to segment them using different scaling parameter. Subsequently, it was noticed that the scaling parameter with values 3 and 4 segmented malware files appropriately. The segmented files were then compared based on edit distance. The entropy score depends on the length of malware files. Hence, in some cases the detector did not perform well as the NGVCK generated malware differed largely with respect to its length.

Vinod et al, 2012b, created a probabilistic signature for the identification of metamorphic malware inspired by bio informatics multiple sequence alignment method (MSA). For each malware family, single, group and MSA signature was developed. Threshold were determined for 37 malware families. The results depicted promising outcome when compared to the detection rate achieved with 14 commercial antivirus scanners. Their study showed that the signatures generated using sequence alignment method were far superior in comparison to those generated by commercial AV. The proposed detector was found to have better detection rate (73.2% approximately) and was ranked third best compared to other commercial malware scanners.

DATA MINING TECHNIQUES FOR MALWARE DETECTION

The authors in (Md.Enamul, K, 2005) proposed a *"phylogeny"* model, particularly used in areas of bioinformatics, for extracting information in genes, proteins or nucleotide sequences. The *n-gram* feature extraction technique was proposed and fixed permutation was applied on the code to generate new sequence, called *n-perm*. Since new variants of malware evolve by incorporating permutations, the proposed *n-perm* model was developed to capture instruction and block permutations. The experiment was conducted on a limited data set consisting of 9 benign samples and 141 worms collected from VX Heavens (http://vx.netlux.org). The proposed method showed that similar variants appeared closer in the phylogenetic tree where node represented a malware variant. The method did not depict how the *n-perm* model would behave if the instructions in a block of code are replaced by equivalent instructions which could either expand or shrink the size of blocks (with respect to number of instructions in a block).

The authors (Schultz et al, 2001) introduced malware detection using data mining method. Three types of features were extracted: *PE Header*, *strings*, and *byte sequence*. To detect unknown computer viruses, classifiers like *decision tree*, *Naive Bayesian network* and *RIPPER* were used. The results demonstrated that the machine learning method outperformed signature based techniques. The *boosted decision trees* performed better with respect to classification and an area of 0.996 under the ROC curve was obtained.

Jeremy et al, 2004, extracted *n-grams* of byte from a collection of 1971 benign and 1651 malware samples. Top 500 *n-grams* were selected, and evaluated on various inductive methods like Naive Bayes, decision trees, support vector machines and boosted versions of these classifiers. The authors indicated that the results obtained by them was better compared to the results presented by Schultz et al, 2001. Better classification accuracy was obtained with boosted decision trees with area an under ROC curve of 0.996. In an extension to their study, the authors evaluated the effectiveness of earlier trained malware and benign models with new test data. It was noticed that the trained model were not good enough to identify unknown samples collected from the point after the training model was prepared. This study suggested that the training models also require updation for identification of unknown malware samples.

Dima S. et al 2009, proposed a method for malware detection using the opcode sequence obtained by disassembling executables. Opcode *n-grams* were extracted for *n = 1, 2,...., 6* from a large collection of malware and benign samples. Top *n-gram* was considered using three feature selection methods: *Document Frequency, Fischer Score* and *Gain ratio,* which finds prominence in text categorization. The frequency of terms in documents were computed and vector space model was represented for each sample. The experiment was evaluated on different *Malicious File Percentage (MFP)* levels to relate to real scenario. It was shown that *2-gram* features outperformed all *n-grams* models. The feature selection method like *Fischer score* and *Document Frequency* were found to be better as compared to Gain Ratio. Top 300 opcodes *n-gram* was found to be effective in classification of the executables with an accuracy of 94.43%. The Boosted decision tree, Artificial Neural Network (ANN) and decision tree produced low false positives compared to Naive and Boosted Naive Bayes. Also, the test set with MFP level of 30% was found to be better compared to other MFP levels with accuracy of 99%.

(Menahem et al, 2009a) proposed a method for improving malware detection using the ensemble method. Each classifier use specific algorithm for classification and each classifier is suited for a particular domain. In order to achieve higher detection rate using machine learning technique, the authors combined the results of individual classifier employing methods like weighted voting, distribution summation, Naive-Bayes combination, Bayesian combination, stacking and Troika

(Menahem et al, 2009b). The goal of this research was to evaluate whether ensemble based method would produce better classification accuracies as compared to individual classifier. Since ensemble methods require high processing time, the experiment was performed on a part of initially collected data set (33%). From their experiments, it was observed that the Troika and Distribution function were found to be the best methods with accuracy of 95% and 93% respectively but suffered with high execution time overheads. All ensemble methods that outperformed in accuracies suffered in execution time. PE file header information, byte *n-grams* and function based features were extracted and binary, multiclass classification was performed. Troika was found to perform better for multiclass classification followed by Bayesian-combination. The authors suggest that since execution time is of prime concern, Bayesian combination would be better choice for ensemble based classification of malware and benign instances.

Non-signature based method using Self-organizing maps (SOMs) was proposed in (Seon, Y., 2006). SOM is a feed-forward neural network for topological representation of the original data. This technique is used to identify files infected by malware. Using SOM, it was observed that the infected files projected a high density area. The experiment was conducted on 790 files infected with different malware. The proposed method was capable of detecting 84% of malware with false positive rate of 30%.

The authors in (Santos I, 2009) extracted *n-grams* from benign and malicious executables and used *k-nearest* neighbour algorithm to identify the unseen instances. In this method *n-grams* from malware and benign samples were extracted for *n = 2, 3, 4,...., 8* to form the training and test set. The number of coincidences of *n-grams* in the training set and test instance was determined. An unknown sample was considered as malware only if the difference of *k* most similar malware and benign instances was greater than a threshold *d.* The experiment was conducted on a data set collected from a software agency and the results depict that the detection rate for 2-gram was poor, 91% detection rate was obtained for 4-gram model.

Authors in (Henchiri, O., 2006) presented a method based on byte *n-gram* feature on different families of viruses collected from VX Heavens. For each family of virus an inter-family support threshold was computed, and a maximum of 500 features that have higher frequency than the threshold was retained. Likewise, features which have higher value than the inter-family support were retained and others were eliminated. The results were evaluated on the proposed classifier and compared with traditional classifiers like decision trees, Naive Bayes, and Support Vector Machine. From their experiments, it was observed that shorter byte sequences produced better detection rates between 93% to 96%. The performance degraded with feature length less than 200 features.

A non-signature based method using byte level file content was proposed in (Tabish, S.M, 2009). This method compute diverse features in block-wise manner over the byte level content of the file. Since blocks of bytes of a file was used for analysis, prior information regarding the type of file was not required. Initially, each sample was divided into equal sized blocks and different information theoretic feature selection technique were applied. The feature extraction module extracted 13 different type of features for each *n-gram* (*n = 1, 2, 3, 4*). Thus, for each block 52 features were extracted. The experiments were conducted on malware data set collected from VX Heavens (http://vx.netlux.org) and benign samples consisting of different file types: DOC, JPG, EXE etc. Results depict that the proposed method was capable of achieving an accuracy above 90%.

The authors in (Igor, S., 2010) proposed a novel method for detecting variants of malware making use of opcode sequence. This approach was based on determining frequency of the opcode. The relevant opcodes were mined using mutual information and assigned with certain weights. The proposed method was tested on dataset downloaded from VX Heavens (http://vx.netlux.org) and was not tested for packed malware. The

opcode sequence of fixed length *n = 1 or 2* was extracted for each base malware and its variants. Proximity between the variants was computed using *cosine similarity*. The similarity within malware data set was high as compared to benign set. Additionally, the similarity between malware and benign samples was low. Thus, it can be inferred that malware and benign samples are not as diverse as benign files; a characteristics that can be used for discriminating it from benign instances.

Analysis and detection of malware using structural information of PE was proposed by authors in (Merkel, R., 2010). PE header fields were extracted from executables and top 23 features were extracted. The analysis was performed on two test sets: (a) obfuscated and (b) clean malware samples. A hypothesis based classification model was developed and the results were compared with classifiers implemented in WEKA. The detection rate of 92% was reported with obfuscated malware executables.

In their study (Vinod et al, 2011b), different features from both malware and benign files like instruction opcode (consisting of opcode and addressing mode), portable executable header fields and mnemonic *n-grams* was extracted. The primary objective was to understand the degree of obfuscation introduced by malware writers either by modifying the PE header, substituting equivalent opcode or modifying the addressing modes. Features were processed with *scatter criteria* and classified with classification algorithm implemented with WEKA. The experiments revealed that *Random Forest* outperformed all classifier in terms of classification accuracy. Also, accuracy of 98.1% was obtained if classification was performed considering PE Header information. It was noticed that obfuscation was predominantly performed by modifying instruction either by replacing a given opcode with equivalent opcode or modifying the addressing mode of instruction. Therefore, the classification accuracy did not fair well when these features were used for the identification of malicious executables.

Authors in (Vinod et al, 2012a) devised a method for the discrimination of malware samples from large collection of benign executables. *Bigram* features were extracted after unpacking packed malware samples, provided by different user agencies making use of signature and dynamic unpackers. Reduced feature were obtained with *Principal Component Analysis* and *minimum redundancy and maximum relevance* techniques. Prominent features were extracted independently from malware and benign population. The objective of study was (a) to determine best feature (b) efficient classifier (c) appropriate feature selection methods and (d) optimal feature vector length that resulted in higher classification accuracy. They also investigated if the classification model performs well for imbalanced data set. Their results were also compared with previous literature and was found to produce detection rate of 97% with overall accuracy of 94.1%.

In (Vinod et al, 2013) proposed a novel method to create multicomponent feature (MCF features) composed of (a) opcode bi-gram (b) PE meta data (c) principal instruction code (opcode and addressing mode) and (d) prominent *uni-grams*. Features were reduced with minimum redundancy and maximum relevance, principal component analysis and extracting eigen vectors. They investigated different features and optimal feature vector length that yielded higher classification accuracy. Experiments were performed on total 2217 malware and 3307 benign PE files. It was observed that mRMR feature selection method produced higher classification accuracy. Overall accuracy of 96.1% was obtained with this proposed technique.

PROPOSED METHOD

Statistical analysis of malwares may be preferred over other methods due to advantages such as reduced memory usage, execution speed etc. Hence, statistical approach on portable executables is adopted in this study. Prior studies have exhibited

that *bi-grams* resulted in better accuracy in comparison to other features (Vinod P, 2012a & Vinod P, 2013). Robust similarity measurement indices computed on histogram of opcodes also indicated better classification of unseen executables. Proposed methodology is summarized in Figure 2.

Malwares variants are generated using various tools like NGVCK, G2, VCL32 etc. Benign files are collected from various internet sources. Each benign executable is scanned using commercial anti-virus scanner before they are included in data set. Independent samples are preprocessed and *bi-grams* are extracted. The two target classes of processed assembly files are then divided into test and train set. The opcode table or feature vector table is constructed and average distances are computed with various distance measures. This FVT is fed into the classifier to create malware and benign models which are subsequently used for predicting unseen samples.

Data Preprocessing

IDA (http://datarescue.com) disassembler is used to generate assembly language code from executable files. IDA Pro is also used as a debugger for Windows PE, Mac OS X, Mach-O, and Linux ELF executable. Assembly codes that are generated with IDA pro disassembler are parsed to extract opcodes from them using a custom parser (refer Figure 3).

It has been argued by researchers that opcodes alone can become good representation of features for identifying malware. Even though, using the entire instruction may lead to precise result, it causes high overhead which can be reduced if opcodes alone are used. So mnemonics or operations are isolated from the operands using a customized parser. For example, MOV is extracted from MOV eax,edx .

Later, from processed assembly files *n-grams* are extracted. *n-gram* are combination opcodes extracted in a sliding window fashion. The *n-gram* having a size of sliding window 1 is called *unigram*, 2 is called *bi-gram* and a size of 3 is

Figure 2. Proposed methodology for malware detection

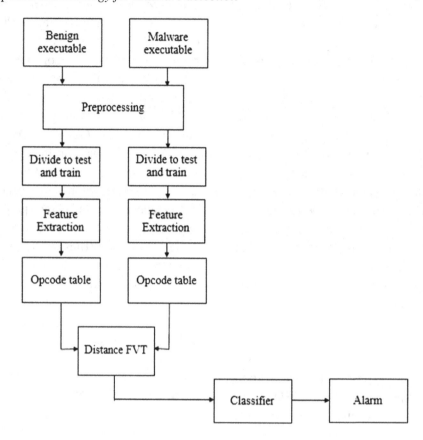

called as *tri-gram*. We use *n-grams* of size of 2 (*bi-grams*) in all our experiments. The following Table 1 depict *bi-grams* and *tri-gram* from generated from a *unigram*.

Experiment is performed in two phase. In the first phase included the extraction of prominent *bi-gram* features of malware files and subsequently determining the presence of these features in the benign samples. Second phase employed the extraction of features from the benign files and benign *bi-grams* in malware files was estimated.

Divide the Bigram Files into Test and Train

Entire data set is randomly divided into two set parts and train and test sets. Suppose that *x* % samples are considered in train set then *100-x* are used as test files (refer Figure 4).

Extraction of Prominent Features

Unique *bi-grams* appearing in malware/benign training files are determined. From the unique opcode list, a preprocessing operation is performed to extract the opcodes that appear predominantly in at least 40% of the files. This process is depicted in the Figure 5. We assume that this pruned unique list of opcodes acts as the footprint for malware/benign class. This also indicate that these opcodes may depict maliciousness in general. The pruned opcode list extracted from different proportion of training files (malware/benign), refer Table 2.

Opcode Table/Feature Vecttor Table

Entried of *Bigram* in the unique list are used to determine frequency of occurrence of the features in each file belonging to a specific target class.

Figure 3. Block diagram showing the preprocessing phase

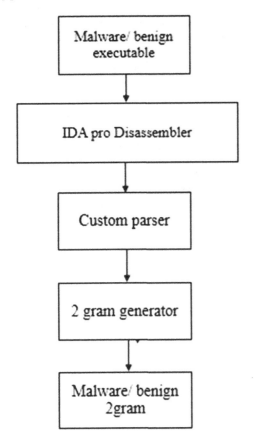

Table 1. Bi-gram tri-gram generation from unigram

Unigram	Bi-Gram	Tri-Gram
mov	movadd	movaddjmp
add	addjmp	addjmpmov
jmp	jmpmov	jmpmovinc
mov	movinc	movincsub
inc	incsub	incsubsub
sub	subsub	subsubjnc

Figure 4. Division of dataset into train and test set

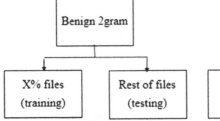

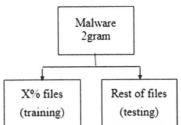

This frequency is recorded in a table also referred to us as opcode table (refer Figure 6).

Subsequently feature vector table is used to compute average distance between each file. We have used 37 distance measures. The average of each distance measure is copied to another table referred to us as distance table. The distance table is shown in Figure 7.

The steps mentioned in section 5.3 and 5.4 is repeated using malware/benign unique list (prominent *bi-grams*) to estimate the frequencies of features in training set of both the target classes and finally a distance table is developed.

Preparation of Distance Feature Vector Table

A FVT of training files is created by copying the distance tables of both training files with features of malware/benign (refer Figure 8). The structure of the distance FVT is as shown in the Figure 9.

Unknown samples (malware/benign) are identified using malware and being features (refer Figure 10). The classification accuracy and values of different evaluation parameters are measured.

Second round of experiment include extraction of features from the training set of target class (benign/malware) to generate two FVTs each for training feature of a specific class. This is done by repeating the processes from feature extraction of to FVT generation. The basic principle behind this is if discriminant feature lead to better accuracy. Also to prune semantically equivalent opcode patterns.

Figure 5. Block diagram showing the feature extraction

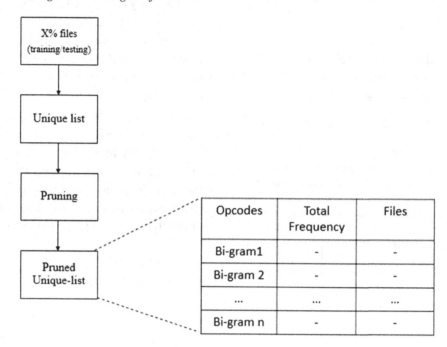

Figure 6. Block diagram showing the opcode table preparation

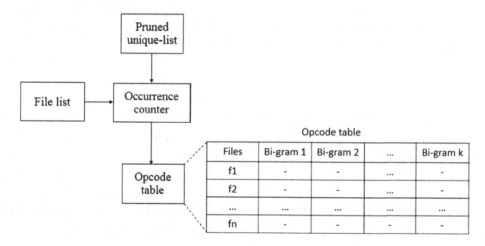

Classification

The train and test FVT is fed to the various classification algorithms implemented in WEKA to evaluate the performance of trained model. We assume that conventional distance measure cannot detect minor variations in each file, hence we consider 37 distance measures. These distance measures are effective in finding dissimilarities between files.

SIMILARITY MEASUREMENT INDICES

Distance or similarity measures are essential to solve many pattern recognition problems. There are a substantial number of distance/similarity measures encountered in many different fields.

From the scientific and mathematical points of view, distance is defined as a quantitative degree of how far apart two objects are. Synonyms for

Figure 7. Distance table

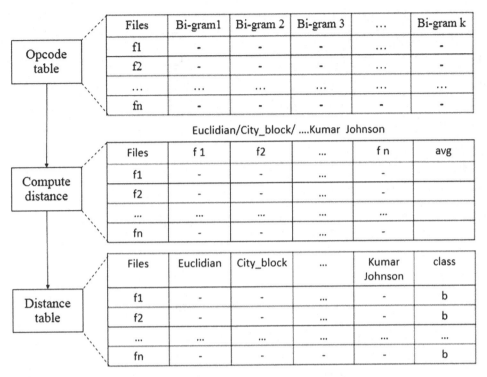

Table 2. Table shows pruned feature count

Percentage Division (train/test)	Class	Number of Entries in Uniquelist	Number of Entries in Pruned Uniquelist
80/20	Benign	10925	325
80/20	Malware	807	101
70/30	Benign	10789	309
70/30	Malware	782	98
60/40	Benign	9327	306
60/40	Malware	757	136
50/50	Benign	10525	349
50/50	Malware	734	139
40/60	Benign	7014	330
40/60	Malware	662	99

distance include dissimilarity and synonyms for similarity include proximity. The distance measures are classified into several families as shown in Figure 11. We have computed 37 distance measure which act as 37 features (S.-H. CHA (2007)) in our experiment (refer Table 3).

EXPERIMENTS AND RESULTS

The NGVCK (Next Generation Virus Creation Kit), G2 (Second Generation virus generator), MPCGEN (Mass Code Generator), VCL32 (Virus Creation Lab for Win32) (http://vx.netlux.org) tools were used to generate obfuscated malware executable from a single malware. These malware files are disassembled using the IDA disassembler to obtain the assembly code. This code is further parsed to obtain the opcode list. This constituted the malware data set for the experiment. The benign files are collected from various internet sources. Dataset constituted of 150 metamorphic malware variants and 800 benign files. The system on which the experiments were carried has 4GB RAM, i5 processor and 500GB hard disk installed on it.

The experiments are carried out using two different way (a) *cross validation* and (b) testing and training method. The cross validation is more efficient for smaller data set as each subset of data is iteratively included in train and test set.

Figure 8. Block diagram depicting FVT generation phase using benign features (training data)

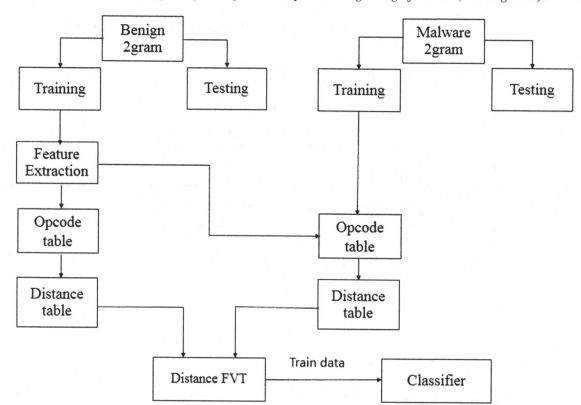

Figure 9. Block diagram showing the structure of distance FVT

Train /test data

Files	Euclidian	City_block	....	Kumar Johnson	class
f1	-	-	...	-	b
f2	-	-	...	-	b
...	...	...	...		...
fn	-	-	...	-	b
F1	-	-	...	-	m
F2	-	-	...	-	m
...	...	...	...	...	...
Fn	-	-	...	-	m

Distance FVT

The second is the *testing and training* method. In this method features are extracted from training set and unseen samples are classified into either of the target class.

Cross Validation

Cross-validation evaluates classification performance and compares algorithms. The process is executed by dividing data into two parts. One is

Figure 10. Block diagram depicting testing phase (features extracted using benign samples)

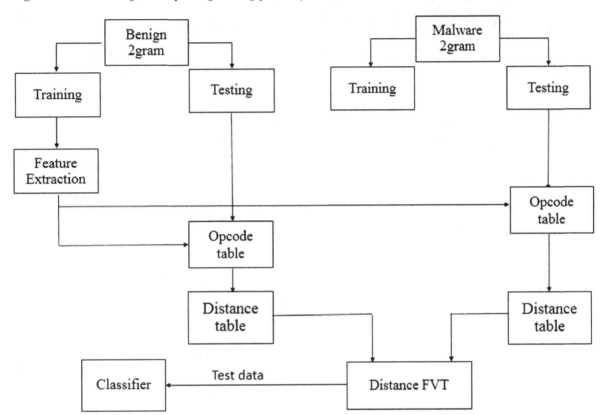

Figure 11. Taxonomy of similarity/distance measurements

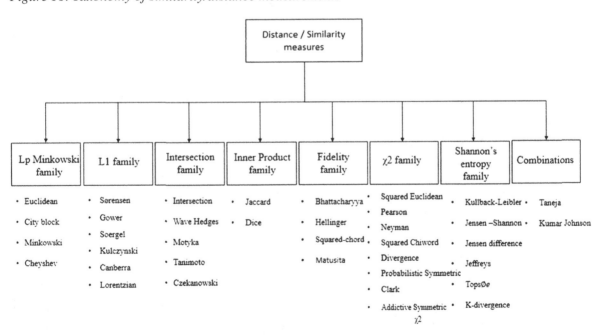

Table 3. Similarity measurement indices

S.No	Distance/Formula	S.No	Distance/Formula
1	Euclidean: $$d_{Euc} = \sqrt{\sum_{i=1}^{d}\left|P_i - Q_i\right|^2}$$	20	Matusita: $$d_{M} = \sqrt{\sum_{i=1}^{d}\left(\sqrt{P_i} - \sqrt{Q_i}\right)^2}$$
2	City block: $$d_{CB} = \sqrt{\sum_{i=1}^{d}\left|P_i - Q_i\right|}$$	21	Squared-chord: $$d_{sqc} = \sum_{i=1}^{d}\left(\sqrt{P_i} - Q_i\right)^2$$
3	Minkowski: $$d_{Mk} = \sqrt[P]{\sum_{i=1}^{d}\left|P_i - Q_i\right|^p}$$	22	Squared Euclidean: $$d_{sqe(P,Q)} = \sum_{i=1}^{d}\left(P_j - Q_j\right)^2$$
4	Cheyshev: $$d_{Cheb} = max\left|P_i - Q_i\right|$$	23	Pearson $\chi 2$: $$d_{p(P,Q)} = \sum_{j=1}^{n}\frac{\left(P_j - Q_j\right)^2}{Q_j}$$
5	Sørensen: $$d_{sor} = \frac{\sum_{i=1}^{d}\left|P_i - Q_i\right|}{\sum_{i=1}^{d}\left(P_i + Q_i\right)}$$	24	Neyman $\chi 2$: $$d_{n(P,Q)} = \sum_{i=1}^{d}\frac{\left(P_i - Q_i\right)^2}{P_i}$$
6	Gower: $$d_{gow} = \frac{1}{d}\sum_{i=1}^{d}\left|P_i - Q_i\right|$$	25	Squared $\chi 2$: $$d_{Schi}(P,Q) = \sum_{j=1}^{n}\left(\frac{P_j - Q_j^{2}}{P_j + Q_j}\right)$$ $$d_{Schi}(P,Q) = \sum_{j=1}^{n}\left(\frac{P_j - Q_j^{2}}{P_j + Q_j}\right)$$
7	Soergel: $$d_{sg} = \frac{\sum_{i=1}^{d}\left|P_i - Q_i\right|}{\sum_{i=1}^{d}\max\left(P_i, Q_i\right)}$$	26	Probabilistic Symmetric $\chi 2$: $$d_{pchi} = 2\sum_{i=1}^{d}\frac{(P_i - Q_i)^2}{P_i + Q_i}$$
8	Kulczynski: $$d_{kul} = \frac{\sum_{i=1}^{d}\left|P_i - Q_i\right|}{\sum_{i=1}^{d}\min\left(P_i, Q_i\right)}$$	27	Divergence: $$d_{clk} = \sqrt{\sum_{i=1}^{d}\left(\frac{\left|P_i - Q_i\right|}{P_i + Q_i}\right)^2}$$
9	Canberra: $$d_{can} = \sum_{i=1}^{d}\frac{\left|P_i - Q_i\right|}{P_i + Q_i}$$	28	Clark: $$d_{clk} = \sqrt{\sum_{i=1}^{d}\left(\frac{\left|P_i - Q_i\right|}{P_i + Q_i}\right)^2}$$

continued on the following page

Table 3. Continued

S.No	Distance/Formula	S.No	Distance/Formula
10	Lorentzian: $$d_{Lor} = \sum_{i=1}^{d} \ln\left(1 + |P_i - Q_i|\right)$$	29	Addictive Symmetric $\chi 2$: $$d_{Adchi} \sum_{j=1}^{b} \frac{(P_i - Q_i)^2 (P_i + Q_i)}{P_i Q_i}$$
11	Intersection: $$d_{Is} = \frac{1}{2} \sum_{i=1}^{d} |P_i - Q_i|$$	30	Kullback-Leibler: $$d_{KL} = \sum_{i=1}^{d} P_i ln \frac{P_i}{Q_i}$$
12	Wave Hedges: $$d_{WH} = \sum_{i=1}^{d} \frac{|P_i - Q_i|}{max(P_i, Q_i)}$$	31	Jeffreys: $$d_J = \sum_{i=1}^{d} (P_i - Q_i) ln \frac{P_i}{Q_i}$$
13	Czekanowski: $$d_{Cze} = \frac{\sum_{i=1}^{d} |P_i - Q_i|}{\sum_{i=1}^{d} |P_i + Q_i|}$$	32	K-divergence: $$d_{Kdiv} = \sum_{i=1}^{d} P_i ln \frac{2P_i}{P_i + Q_i} \quad d_{Kdiv} = \sum_{i=1}^{d} P_i ln \frac{2P_i}{P_i + Q_i}$$
14	Motyka: $$d_M = \frac{\sum_{i=1}^{d} max(P_i, Q_i)}{\sum_{i=1}^{d} (P_i + Q_i)}$$	33	Tops$\varnothing e$: $$d_T = \sum_{i=1}^{d} \left(P_i ln\left(\frac{2P_i}{P_i + Q_i}\right) + Q_i ln\left(\frac{2Q_i}{P_i + Q_i}\right) \right).$$
15	Tanimoto: $$d_T = \frac{(max(P_i, Q_i) - min(P_i, Q_i))}{\sum_{i=1}^{d} max(P_i, Q_i)}$$	34	Jensen –Shannon: $$d_{JS} = \frac{1}{2} \left[\sum_{i=1}^{d} P_i ln\left(\frac{2P_i}{P_i + Q_i}\right) + \sum_{i=1}^{d} Q_i ln\left(\frac{2Q_i}{P_i + Q_i}\right) \right]$$
16	Jaccard: $$d_J = \frac{\sum_{i=1}^{d} (P_i - Q_i)^2}{\sum_{i=1}^{d} P_i^2 + \sum_{i=1}^{d} Q_i^2 + \sum_{i=1}^{d} P_i Q_i}$$	35	Jensen difference: $$d_{JD} = \sum_{i=1}^{d} \left[\frac{P_i ln P_i + Q_i ln Q_i}{2} - \left[\frac{P_i + Q_i}{2}\right] ln\left[\frac{P_i + Q_i}{2}\right] \right]$$
17	Dice: $$d_D = \frac{\sum_{i=1}^{d} (P_i - Q_i)^2}{\sum_{i=1}^{d} P_i^2 + \sum_{i=1}^{d} Q_i^2}$$	36	Taneja: $$d_{Tj} = \sum_{i=1}^{d} \left(\frac{P_i + Q_i}{2}\right) ln\left(\frac{P_i + Q_i}{2\sqrt{P_i Q_i}}\right)$$ $$d_{Tj} = \sum_{i=1}^{d} \left(\frac{P_i + Q_i}{2}\right) ln\left(\frac{P_i + Q_i}{2\sqrt{P_i Q_i}}\right)$$

continued on the following page

used to train and whereas other part is used during the testing or validation phase. The train and test is carried out through successive rounds of computations. It focuses mainly on the idea that testing is used at least once. The available data population is divided into *k*-folds of which one part is used for testing and rest of the parts is used for training (refer Figure 12). The process is repeated *k*-times.

One fold and two fold cross validation are the two cross validation techniques mainly used. Two fold divides the data set into two equal parts and one fold builds a decision tree. Later the roles are swapped. The final accuracy is calculated as the average of the two model accuracies.

Table 3. Continued

S.No	Distance/Formula	S.No	Distance/Formula
18	$$d_{b=-\ln\sum_{i=1}^{d}\sqrt{P_i-Q_i}}$$ Bhattacharyya:	37	$$d_{KJ} = \sum_{i=1}^{d}\left(\frac{\left(\left(P_i^2-Q_i^2\right)^2\right)}{2\left(P_iQ_i\right)^{\frac{3}{2}}}\right)$$ Kumar Johnson: $$d_{KJ} = \sum_{i=1}^{d}\left(\frac{\left(\left(P_i^2-Q_i^2\right)^2\right)}{2\left(P_iQ_i\right)^{\frac{3}{2}}}\right)$$
19	$$d_{h=\sqrt{2\sum_{i=1}^{d}\left(\sqrt{P_i-Q_i}\right)^2}}$$ Hellinger:		$$d_{KJ} = \sum_{i=1}^{d}\left(\frac{\left(\left(P_i^2-Q_i^2\right)^2\right)}{2\left(P_iQ_i\right)^{\frac{3}{2}}}\right)$$ $$d_{KJ} = \sum_{i=1}^{d}\left(\frac{\left(\left(P_i^2-Q_i^2\right)^2\right)}{2\left(P_iQ_i\right)^{\frac{3}{2}}}\right)$$

Figure 12. Procedure of four-fold cross-validation

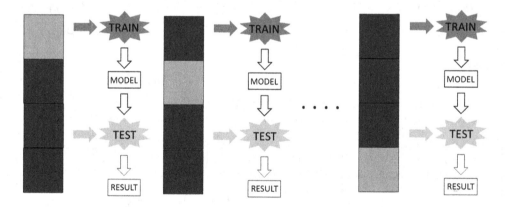

Experiment with Cross Validation

The entire dataset is used for this experiment; the distance FVT is fed to WEKA. The experiment is carried with different percentage split (40, 60 and 70) with 10 folds. The possible outcomes of the experiment are *true positive (TP), true negative (TN), false positive (FP) and false negative (FP)*. *True positive* denote the malware file is correctly classified as malware. *True negative* is benign file is correctly classified as benign.

The *false positive* indicate the total number of benign files classified as malware and *false negative* is the total number of malware files misclassified as benign (refer to Table 4). Perfect malware detector should have high *True Positive Rate (TPR)* with minimum *False Positive Rate (FPR)*.

A Receive Operating Characteristic (ROC) curve is used to evaluate the results of the experiments. An ROC is a graphical plot which illustrates the performance of a binary classifier system A

Table 4. Confusion matrix

Input\Output	Malware	Benign
Malware	TP	FN
Benign	FP	TN

ROC space is defined by FPR and TPR plotted on *x* and *y* axes respectively. The best possible prediction method would yield a point, and this point is called a perfect classification. Experiments is performed with different classification algorithm such as Naïve Bayes, J-48, AdaBoost M1 (with J-48 as base classifier), and Random Forest all algorithms implemented in WEKA. In all cases classification accuracy obtained with Random forest was found to be better. Primary reason is that Random forest is an ensemble based classifier and final decision is estimated by collecting voted decision from multiple classifiers. Due to lack of space we report the classification accuracy obtained with Random Forest and AdaBoost classifiers. ROC curve obtained is shown in Figure 13 and Figure 14.

Inference

The Figure 13 and Figure 14 depict that 100% accuracy is obtained in the cross validation. Standardizing the result using cross validation proves that the model developed precisely identified malware from files from large collection of benign samples. Experiment also suggest that *bi-gram* features are effective in identifying malware and benign executables. The study also indicate that *non-signature* based methods provide a better detection rate where signature based detector fail to recognize new instances.

Train and Test

In this experiment, the testing and training set is randomly split using customized random file splitter module generated by us. The training set

is identified, and supervised learning is performed where each instance is labelled in FVT. Feature vector table for test data is prepared where the class labels are not specified for any instances.

Initially, training model is developed using WEKA. Unseen samples are evaluated using performance metrics. We observe that an overall accuracy of 100% is obtained with classifier (refer Figure 15 and Figure 16) for different proportion of malware and benign programs.

Overall Inference

A Morphing or mutation engine is the heart of any metamorphic malware that incorporates structural change in new malware variant. The purpose of this metamorphic engine is to generate new patterns not found in signature repository to escape from the signature-based scanner. Although, the obfuscation techniques attempts to convert the binary sequence of the code. However, we feel that there is a limit to which an instruction could be modified, otherwise the maliciousness of the program will be lost, and sometime the resultant program would undesirable. The proposed system exhibited that the malware samples can be detected from an imbalanced data set consisting of large number of benign samples.

The NGVCK tool claims to produce highly obfuscated codes. Also, the metamorphic worm generated in earlier studies depict that obfuscation was in the form of dead code. These observations prove that the optimal feature vector can accurately identify the files. Therefore, the statistical method based on computed similarity/distance metrics is found to be effective in identifying obfuscated files.

CONCLUSION

A model was developed to identify the malware files from benign files. The opcodes from the train/ test files were extracted and the *bi-gram* opcode were generated. The robust features are developed

Figure 13. Cross validation using random forest

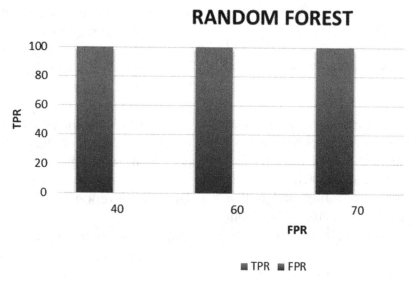

Figure 14. Cross validation using AdaBoost

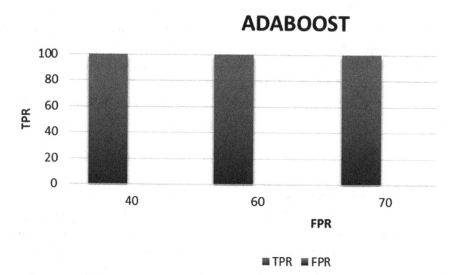

from the *bi-gram* using the similarity indices. It was observed that the proposed method could classify benign samples with better accuracy. The observations of the experiments carried out led to the following conclusions:

1. The results shows 100% accuracy in both experiments. This shows that the malware used in the study contained only minimal obfuscation.

2. The metamorphic engine develops the variants which concentrate on changing the opcodes with equivalent ones, whereas the prominent features remain more or less the same.

3. The changes brought about in the program may simply be produced by inserting junk benign codes which doesn't affect the analysis.

Figure 15. Test and train data using random forest

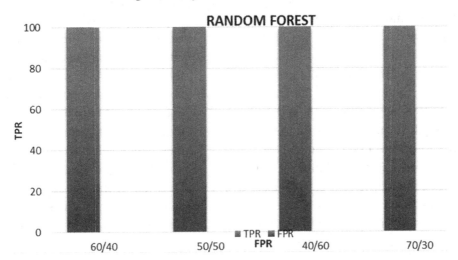

Figure 16. Test and train data using Adaboost

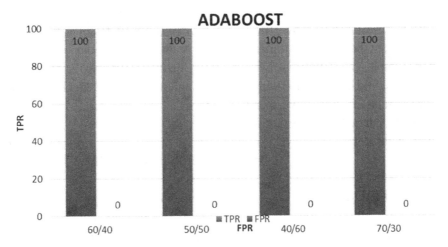

4. The data set used by the earlier researchers to claim that the metamorphic engines produce high degree of obfuscation, whereas our proposed method justifies that the obfuscation is weak. Also, dataset in prior study use large number of malware files in comparison to benign specimens. This setup of the dataset might bias identifying malware samples with high accuracy. Moreover, database used in our experiments is closer to real world since the number of malware is lesser than that of benign.

5. The experiments show that the feature set was reduced drastically from 10925 to 325 in benign class for 80/20. Whereas, in malware files the feature length was reduced from 807 to101. The reduced feature length delivered 100% accuracy, which shows that the proposed system is very efficient with respect to execution time during the detection phase.

FUTURE SCOPE

The proposed system has accurately identified and raised appropriate alarms. The efficiency when used in real malware samples needs to be tested.

The proposed system though have produced accurate results needs further advancement in the certain areas.

1. The efficiency of the system could be still evaluated by further reducing the feature length. Another advantage of the reduced feature length is that the overhead is decreased and the detection becomes faster.
2. In the proposed system, 37 similarity indices are used in order to find the similarity between two files. Investigation needs to done so as to further decrease the similarity measurement indices and still achieve higher accuracy.
3. The threshold can be determined (needs to be fixed) for identifying the malware and benign files. To find the threshold, a base file needs to be figured out that is highly similar to the rest of the samples in a family. Further distance of test file could be computed with the base file order to classify the files. Further experiments can be carried out in real and bigger malware dataset.

OPEN RESEARCH PROBLEMS

Like desktop malware detection, mobile malware especially Android malware research is attracting large number of researchers. The detection of mobile malware is in infancy stage. The domain is attracting huge number of researchers due to the increasing popularity and computational power of smart phones. Following are some research areas which can be useful to tackle the detection of injected malicious code.

1. Need to develop malicious program that are structurally similar to benign code but have malicious intents. This would help researchers understand the how the two classes of program differ at low level operations.

2. Identification and classification of prominent applications downloaded by users and inspect points of vulnerabilities.
3. Understand various sandboxes available for mobile/desktop malware detection and inspect different points in systems which are exposed to VM installation. This is mandatory as the future malware would exploit these vulnerable infection vectors to launch virtual machine attack.
4. Determine behavioral features for malware and benign applications. Study the default permissions and modifications during series of time interval. This could help us develop strong benign and malware models.
5. Investigate robust feature selection and reduction techniques to extract prominent/discriminant features for classification of samples (suspicious or benign).
6. Identification of malicious APIs and prepare white, grey and blacklist for the same.

ACKNOWLEDGMENT

We would like to especially thank Prof. Mark Stamp, Department of Computer Science, San Jose State University, USA, for sharing malware database for carrying out this study.

REFERENCES

Andrew, W., Michael, V., Matthew, H., Christopher, T., & Arun, L. (2007). *A: Exploiting Similarity between Variants to Defeat Malware: Vilo Method for Comparing and Searching Binary Programs.* Retrieved from https://blackhat.com/presentations/bh-dc-07/Walenstein/Paper/bh-dc-07-walenstein-W%P.pdf

Annie, H. T., & Mark, S. (2013). Chi-squared distance and metamorphic virus detection. Journal in Computer Virology, 9(1), 1-14

Asaf, S., Robert, M., Yuval, E., & Chanan, G. (2009). Detection of malicious code by applying machine learning classifiers on static features: A state-of-the-art survey. *Information Security Technical Report*, *14*(1), 16–29. doi:10.1016/j.istr.2009.03.003

Attaluri, S., McGhee, S., & Stamp, M. (2009). Profile hidden Markov models and metamorphic virus detection. *Journal in Computer Virology*, *5*, 151–169. doi:10.1007/s11416-008-0105-1

Aycock, J. (2006). Computer Viruses and Malware. Academic Press.

Baker, K. (2013). *Singular Value Decomposition Tutorial website*. Retrieved from http://www.ling.ohio-state.edu/~kbaker/pubs/Singular_Value_Decomposition_Tutorial.pdf

Baysa, D., Low, R. M., & Stamp, M. (2013). Structural entropy and metamorphic malware. Journal of Computer Virology and Hacking Techniques, 9(4), 1-14, doi: doi:10.1007/s11416-013-0185-4

Cha, S.-H. (2007). Comprehensive Survey on Distance/Similarity Measures between Probability Density Functions. *International Journal of Mathematical Models and Methods in Applied Sciences*, *1*, 300–307.

Chouchane, M. R., & Lakhotia, A. (2006). Using engine signature to detect metamorphic malware: In *Proceedings of the 4th ACM Workshop on Recurring malcode*, (pp. 73-78). ACM.

Dima, S., Robert, M., Zvi, B., Yuval, S., & Yuval, E. (2009). Using artificial neural networks to detect unknown computer worms. *Neural Computing & Applications*, *18*(7), 663–674. doi:10.1007/s00521-009-0238-2

Eitan, M., Asaf, S., Lior, R., & Yuval, E. (2009). Improving malware detection by applying multi-inducer ensemble. *Journal In Computational Statistics & Data Analysis*, *53*(4), 1483–1494. doi:10.1016/j.csda.2008.10.015

Henchiri, O., & Japkowicz, N. (2006). A Feature Selection and Evaluation Scheme for Computer Virus Detection. In Proceedings of ICDM (pp. 891-895). IEEE Computer Society.

Virus Collection Website. (n.d.). Retrieved from http://vx.netlux.org/lib

Igor, S., Felix, B., Javier, N., Yoseba, P., Borja, S., Carlos, L., & Pablo, B. (2010). Idea: Opcode-sequence-based malware detection: In Proceedings of Engineering Secure Software and Systems (LNCS) (vol. 5965, pp. 35-43). Springer.

Jeremy, Z. K., & Maloof, M.A. (2004). Learning to Detect Malicious Executables in the Wild. In *Proceedings of the Tenth ACM SIGKDD International Conference on Knowledge Discovery and Data Mining*, (pp. 470-478). New York, NY: ACM

Karim, M. E., Walenstein, A., Lakhotia, A., & Parida, L. (2005). Malware phylogeny generation using permutations of code. *Journal in Computer Virology*, *1*, 13–23. doi:10.1007/s11416-005-0002-9

Kephart, J. O., & Arnold, B. (1994). A Feature Selection and Evaluation of Computer Virus Signatures. In *Proceedings of the 4th Virus Bulletin International Conference*, (pp. 178-184). Academic Press.

Kolter, J. Z., & Maloof, M. A. (2006). Learning to Detect and Classify Malicious Executables in the Wild. *Journal of Machine Learning Research*, *6*, 2721–2744.

Lin, D., & Stamp, M. (2011). Hunting for undetectable metamorphic viruses. *Journal in Computer Virology*, *7*, 201–214. doi:10.1007/s11416-010-0148-y

Menahem, E., Rokach, L., & Elovici, Y. (2009a). Troika - An improved stacking schema for classification tasks. *Inf. Sci.*, *179*, 4097–4122. doi:10.1016/j.ins.2009.08.025

Menahem, E., Shabtai, A., Rokach, L., & Elovici, Y. (2009b). Improving malware detection by applying multi-inducer ensemble. *Computational Statistics & Data Analysis*, *53*, 1483–1494. doi:10.1016/j.csda.2008.10.015

Merkel, R., Hoppe, T., Kraetzer, C., & Dittmann, J. (2010). Statistical Detection of Malicious PE-Executables for Fast Offline Analysis. In B. De Decker & I. Schaumller-Bichl (Eds.), Communications and Multimedia Security, (Vol. 6109, pp. 93-105). Springer.

Moskovitch, R., Nissim, N., & Elovici, Y. (2009). Acquisition of Malicious Code Using Active Learning. In Proceedings of Privacy, Security, and Trust in KDD. Springer-Verlag.

Moskovitch, R., Stopel, D., Feher, C., Nissim, N., Japkowicz, N., & Elovici, Y. (2009). Unknown malcode detection and the imbalance problem. *Journal in Computer Virology*, *5*, 295–308. doi:10.1007/s11416-009-0122-8

Nissim, N., Moskovitch, R., Rokach, L., & Elovici, Y. (2012). Detecting unknown computer worm activity via support vector machines and active learning. *Pattern Analysis & Applications*, *15*, 459–475. doi:10.1007/s10044-012-0296-4

Open Source Machine Learning Software Weka website. (n.d.). Retrieved from http://www.cs.waikato.ac.nz/ml/weka/

Runwal, N., Low, R. M., & Stamp, M. (2012). Opcode graph similarity and metamorphic detection. *Journal in Computer Virology*, *8*, 37–52. doi:10.1007/s11416-012-0160-5

Santos, I., Penya, Y. K., Devesa, J., & Bringas, P. G. (2009). N-grams-based File Signatures for Malware Detection. In J. Cordeiro & J. Filipe (Eds.), ICEIS (vol. 2, pp. 317-320). Academic Press.

Schultz, M. G., Eskin, E., Zadok, E., & Stolfo, S. J. (2001). Data Mining Methods for Detection of New Malicious Executables. In *Proceedings of IEEE Symposium on Security and Privacy* (pp. 38-49). IEEE Computer Society.

Seon, Y., & Ulrich, U. N. (2006). Towards Establishing a Unknown Virus Detection Technique using SOM. Journal in Computer Virology, 2(3), 163-186.

Sridhara, S. M., & Stamp, M. (2013). Metamorphic worm that carries its own morphing engine. *Journal in Computer Virology*, *9*, 49–58.

Tabish, S. M., Shafiq, M. Z., & Farooq, M. (2009). Malware detection using statistical analysis of byte-level file content. In H. Chen, M. Dacier, M.-F. Moens, G. Paass & C. C. Yang (Eds.), *KDD Workshop on CyberSecurity and Intelligence Informatics* (pp. 23-31). ACM.

Vinod, P., Jain, Golecha, Gaur, & Laxmi. (2010a). MEDUSA: Metamorphic malware dynamic analysis using signature from API. In *Proceedings of the 3rd International Conference on Security of Information and Networks*. SIN.

Vinod, P., Laxmi, & Gaur. (2012a). REFORM: Relevant Features for Malware Analysis. In *Proceedings of 26th International Conference on Advanced Information Networking and Applications Workshops*. Academic Press.

Vinod, P., Laxmi, Gaur, Kumar, & Chundawat. (2009). Static CFG analyzer for metamorphic Malware code. In *Proceedings of the 2nd International Conference on Security of Information and Networks*. SIN.

Vinod, P., Laxmi, V., & Gaur, M. (2011a). Metamorphic Malware Analysis and Detection Methods. In Cyber Security, Cyber Crime and Cyber Forensics: Applications and Perspectives, (pp. 178-202). Hershey, PA: IGI Global. doi: doi:10.4018/978-1-60960-123-2.ch013

Vinod, P., Laxmi, V., & Gaur, M. S. (2011b). Scattered Feature Space for Malware Analysis. In Proceeding Advances in Computing and Communications. Springer.

Vinod, P., Laxmi, V., Gaur, M. S., & Chauhan, G. (2012b). MOMENTUM: MetamOrphic malware exploration techniques using MSA signatures. In Proceedings of International Conferenceon Innovations in Information Technology (IIT). IIT.

Vinod, P., Laxmi, V., Gaur, M. S., Naval, S., & Faruki, P. (2013). MCF: MultiComponent Features for Malware Analysis. In *Proceedings of the 27th International Conference*. doi: doi:10.1109/WAINA.2013.147

Wei, J. L., Wang, K., Stolfo, S.J., & Herzog, B. (2005). Fileprints: Identifying File types by n-gram analysis. In *Proceedings of the Sixth Annual IEEE SMC 4th Virus Bulletin Conference*. IEEE.

Wong, W., & Stamp, M. (2006). Hunting for metamorphic engines. *Journal in Computer Virology*, 2, 211–229. doi:10.1007/s11416-006-0028-7

Yan, W., Zhang, Z., & Ansari, N. (2008). Revealing Packed Malware. *IEEE Security & Privacy*, 6, 65–69. doi:10.1109/MSP.2008.126

KEY TERMS AND DEFINITIONS

Bi-Grams: Collection of two words or opcodes or term extracted in sliding window fashion.

Classifier: An algorithm that implements a classification task that assign a unique class to an instance.

Code Obfuscation: The process of code hiding important details of the program so as to conceal it form reverse-engineering.

Cross Validation: Model estimation technique based on rotation.

Evaluation Parameters: Various criteria for estimating the classification model.

Feature Reduction: The process which involves selection of prominent features (subset) from a large feature space.

Feature: Is representative of attribute.

Malware Constructors: Tool or kit that assist any user to develop synthetic malicious code without having the knowledge how the code is to be developed.

Malware: Is a generic term used to refer to all potential malicious software.

Metamorphic Engine: Is a heart of metamorphic malware which induces structural transformation in the code structure.

Metamorphic: The process by which a program undergoes transformation.

Opcodes: Is operation code, refer to a part of the complete instruction.

Similarity Measure: Is a function applied over any two objects in order to measure if the objects have high proximity.

Static Analysis: Structural analysis of malware samples without its execution.

Chapter 11
Mobile Worms and Viruses

Nidhi Goel
Delhi Technological University, India

Balasubramanian Raman
Indian Institute of Technology Roorkee, India

Indra Gupta
Indian Institute of Technology Roorkee, India

ABSTRACT

The ever-increasing use of mobile devices for communication and entertainment has made these devices an increasingly attractive target for malicious attacks. Thus, mobile device security has emerged as an important research area. Although malicious exploits for mobile phones have been steadily developing over the last decade, the emergence of smart-phone technology is proving to be a turning point in development of such malicious exploits. With the increase in sophistication of smartphones and their use for day-today activities, mobile threats (e.g., viruses, spyware, and malware) has also increased. This trend can be attributed to the fact that phone users want to communicate, and viruses want to be communicated. This chapter presents a state-of-the-art review of the developments in this important field of mobile malware.

INTRODUCTION

Mobile devices are much more connected to the outside world than PCs. The proliferation of mobile devices, with ever advancing technological features is mainly due to the platforms, like Android, iOS, Blackberry OS and Symbian that increasingly resemble traditional operating systems for PCs (Chen, 2008; Dagon, 2004). These mobile platforms can be extended by installing applications, which generally originate from third party providers. The various activities supported by these applications include sending or posting messages, organizing business or recreation,

making payments or reservations and many more (Leavitt,2005A; Leavitt,2005B).

Smartphones with these platforms started as expensive business models, but their popularity with consumers has recently taken off. Currently, smartphones make up most of the world's computers. And huge populations of users who have little or no experience with computers have started surfing the Web and sharing files with their phones. They would present mobile malware creators with an irresistibly large and unwary target. Bigger the target, bigger is the attraction for nefarious programmers (Ford,2004).

DOI: 10.4018/978-1-4666-6158-5.ch011

Viruses can let intruders access passwords or corporate data stored on a cell phone. Also, attackers can manipulate a victim's phone to make calls or send messages, a crime called theft of service. Apart from utilizing computing power provided by mobile devices, the attackers have also started targeting the data (Delac2011). This is due to the fact that the smart-phones are becoming storage units for personal information through use of various social networking applications, personal organizers and e-mail clients. Thus, the standard malicious attacks for PCs, like worms and trojans, as well as attack vectors, like the Internet access, are becoming applicable to the mobile platforms (Cisco,2010; Ahmad,2011).

Though PC and mobile phones are affected by similar malicious attacks, the threat is more severe in the case of mobile phones. The primary factor for this is the ever increasing user base and the emergence of smart-phone technology. Also, mobile phones are almost always switched on and stay connected to the network. Unlike a PC whose neighboring network nodes remain relatively fixed, the "neighbors" of a mobile device keep changing with every change of location of the user carrying the mobile device. Further, mobile phone users are less security conscious than the average Internet user.

Even though it took computer viruses twenty years to evolve, their mobile device counterparts have evolved in just few years. This increase may be attributed to the fact that phone users want to communicate, and viruses want to be communicated.

Recent reports show that there exist sufficient vulnerabilities in these devices that could be exploited to cause harm to the device, to reveal sensitive information or to use the mobile device in a malicious way (Gostev, 2006A;Gostev, 2006C). Earlier, the malicious exploits for mobile phones had limited range and impact due to the constraints in both hardware and operating systems. However, the emergence of smart-phone technology that provides more computing power and functionality, a turning point is expected in development of malicious exploits for mobile hand-held devices.

Statistics have revealed that there has been an exponential growth in mobile malware during the last few years. In 2006, there existed at least 31 families and 170 variants of known mobile malware. However, this has increased to a staggering 2500 different types of mobile malware in 2010 (Gostev, 2006A). The emergence of new malicious programs for the year 2012 has been indicated in Figure 1.

The present chapter gives an up-to-date treatise of the mobile malware and its development in the last one decade. The chapter also discusses about the various viruses, intention behind these malicious attacks, the modes of their spreading and the impact caused by them. Few viruses that has been launched on mobile devices has also been presented. Finally, the chapter concludes with the threat mitigation techniques.

DEVELOPMENTS OF MOBILE MALWARE

The most widely used processor platforms for cell phones include ARM, Motorola, and Texas Instruments. While the three dominant mobile-device OSs are android, Symbian, Palm, and two Windows CE versions: Pocket PC Phone Edition and Smartphone Edition. Analysis has revealed that if a generic language such as Java is used for creating the malicious code, it could affect devices that support Java. Thus, to reach a large number of victims, separate sets of malicious codes are required for each mobile operating system and each processor platform. This has discouraged some but not all the hackers from targeting wireless devices.

Analysis has revealed that currently, mobile world is dominated by android based phones and their various applications. Thus, Android based phones have become the focus of malware writers. A statistical representation for the distribution mobile malware on the basis of platform during the period 2004-2011 is indicated in Figure 2, while Figure 3 indicates the distribution for the year 2012.

Figure 1. Monthly fluctuations in the emergence of new malicious programs, 2012 (Ref. Kaspersky Security Bulletin 2012. The overall statistics for 2012).

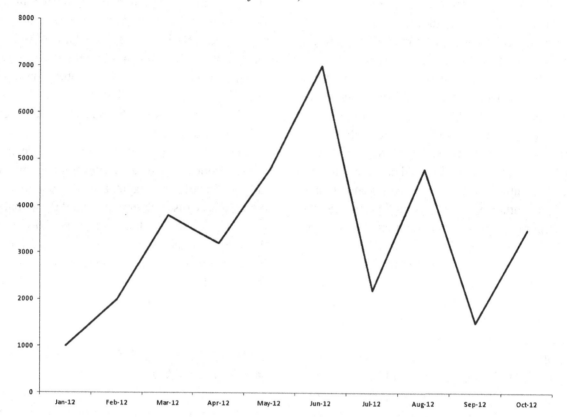

It can be easily observed that with time, popularity of Symbian has decreased; on the contrary, the popularity of Android has increased, and so is the malicious activities on Android based phones.

Since, mobile malware is relatively new, virus writers had released it primarily as proof-of-concept code. The first known mobile virus was identified in June 2000, when antivirus labs in Russia and Finland identified the "Timofonica" worm, which originated in Spain. The "Timofonica" sent SMS-messages to GSM mobile phones that read (in Spanish) "Information for you: Telefonica is fooling you"). These messages were sent through Internet SMS-gate of the MoviStart mobile operator (Ecomm, 2000). It is estimated hackers released about a dozen mobile viruses between 2001 and 2003. In 2004, security researchers discovered 21 variants of mobile viruses.

In June 2004, a company, Ojam had engineered an anti-piracy Trojan virus in older versions of their mobile phone game, Mosquito. This virus sent SMS text messages to the company without the users' knowledge. Though, it was removed from the game's more recent versions, but older, unlicensed versions are still affected. These older versions may still be distributed on file-sharing networks and free software download web sites.

In 2004, a proof-of-concept mobile virus Cabir was released by computer hobbyists that replicates itself on Bluetooth wireless networks Hypponen, 2006) http://en.wikipedia.org/wiki/Mobile_virus - cite_note-2. The other variants of the Cabir, Mabir.A.Mabir were one step ahead in the social engineering technique. It acted more smartly by sending itself and MMS reply to the SMS or MMS received so that people and hence the recipient were more inclined towards opening it.

Figure 2. Distribution of mobile malware by platform, 2004-2011 (FS_MTR2011)

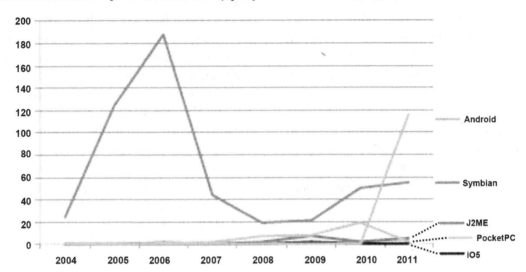

Figure 3. Distribution of mobile malware by platform, 2012 (KSB2012)

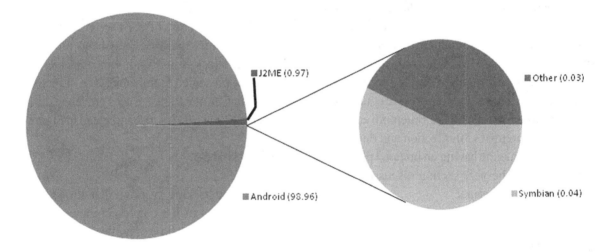

In March 2005, it was reported that a computer worm called Commwarrior-A had been infecting Symbian series 60 mobile phones (Infoplease,2005). This specific worm replicated itself through the phone's Multimedia Messaging System (MMS), sending copies of itself to other phone owners listed in the phone user's address book. Although the worm is not considered harmful, experts agree that it heralded a new age of electronic attacks on mobile phones. This is the social engineering technique used here just like in case of most of the viruses, worms and Trojans in the PC world.

Another Mobile phone Trojan that was first found in 2005 was the Fontal.A. It installs corrupted Font file into infected device, thus causing the device to fail at next reboot. However, there is only a small risk of infection and ones who are vulnerable to this are the people in the habit of installing warez mobile games files or some similar files onto their mobile phones. The first Trojan for J2ME (Java) was detected back in Feb 2006 and was called the Red Browser Trojan and it can run on a vast amount of mobile phones that supports Java.

In August 2010, Kaspersky Lab reported a trojan designated TrojanSMS.AndroidOS Fake Player.a. This was the first malicious program classified as a Trojan-SMS, which affects smartphones running on Google's Android operating system, and which had already infected a number of mobile devies, (Kaspersky,2010; MyPhoneFactor, 2013), sending SMS messages to premium rate numbers without the owner's knowledge or consent, and accumulating huge bills.

In the world of mobile phones smart phones have become a major target. Symantec's stats show that while 80 per cent of companies allow corporate data on handheld devices, only 25 per cent have so far addressed smartphone security.

There has not yet been a major outbreak of a mobile phone malware like that in the PC world except for the isolated outbreaks. However, experts are expecting it in near future. Research is ongoing on developing the products that prevent the spreading of these malwares not only through the browsers etc but also through a wireless technology like Bluetooth. These kinds of software could even help corporates to scan all the Bluetooth enabled phone in the premises for infection and thus alert them about someone having an infected phone in the premises. The next section discusses about the virus and its variants.

VIRUS AND ITS VARIANTS

A virus is a program that lives within another program. When the host program runs, the virus logic is activated first. The virus logic searches for another program to infect and copies itself into that program. This can best be modeled as an instance of an active network. The logic carried in a packet modifies the host node by inserting into the host node logic that infects packets as they pass through the host node.

Mobile viruses need to be detected as early as possible, because they have the ability to cause physical damage, denial of service, theft of data or even monetary loss by making unwanted phone calls and sending messages from an infected device. There have not yet been any significant and widespread outbreaks of a mobile virus, but a knowledge base in this area is required before it becomes a major problem.

With devices such as smart phones being used by businesses to give employees access to email and other work related material while on the move, it is important to ensure the integrity and security of sensitive information stored on these devices. A device that is on the move and has the ability to communicate using Bluetooth and MMS messaging is more vulnerable than a PC containing sensitive data behind a corporate firewall. Since the mobile platforms increasingly resemble traditional operating systems, the security threats characteristic for PCs are migrating to mobile devices.

In this subsection a brief overview of the most common mobile malwares has been presented. The actual attacks usually combine multiple variants of the presented mobile malware. A pictorial representation of various viruses prevalent during the period 2004-2011 is also indicated in Figure 4.

Trojan Horse

A Trojan is a hacking program that allows unauthorized access to the target's computer. It is a non-self-replicating type of malware which gains privileged access to the operating system while appearing to perform a desirable function.

Trojans can also be used to commit phishing activities. These may use drive-by downloads or install via online games or internet-driven applications in order to reach target computers. These backdoors tend to be invisible to average users, but may cause the computer to run slow. When activated, the malware can cause tremendous damage by infecting and deactivating other applications or the phone itself, rendering it unusable.

Trojans do not attempt to inject themselves into other files like a computer virus. Trojan horses may steal information, or harm their host computer systems. Usurpation data (spyware) syncs with

Figure 4. Distribution of the mobile malware during the years 2004 to 2011 (FS_MTR2011)

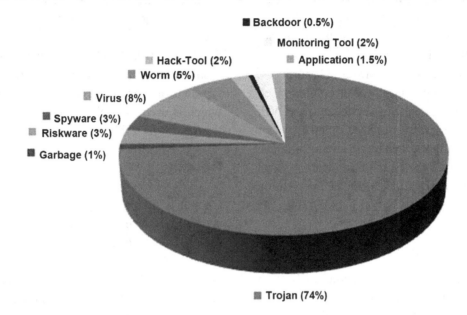

■ Backdoor (0.5%)

■ Monitoring Tool (2%)

■ Hack-Tool (2%) ▨ Application (1.5%)

▨ Worm (5%)

▨ Virus (8%)

■ Spyware (3%)

▨ Riskware (3%)

■ Garbage (1%)

▨ Trojan (74%)

calendars, email accounts, notes, and any other source of information before being sent to a remote server. Unlike worms, this type of mobile virus requires user interaction to be activated.

A computer system affected by Trojan may be used as part of a botnet. A trojan can crash the system, cause blue screen of death, electronic money theft, data theft (e.g. retrieving passwords or credit card information), installation of software, including third-party malware and ransomware, downloading or uploading of files on the user's computer, modification or deletion of files, keystroke logging, watching the user's screen, viewing the user's webcam and controlling the computer system remotely.

Botnet

A botnet is a collection of internet-connected programs communicating with other similar programs in order to perform tasks. Botnets sometimes compromise computers whose security defenses have been breached and control conceded to a third party. Each such compromised device, known as a "bot", is created when a computer is penetrated

by software from a malware (malicious software) distribution through drive-by download, exploiting web browser vulnerabilities, or by tricking the user into running a Trojan horse program, which may come from an email attachment.

This malware typically install modules that allow the computer to be commanded and controlled by the botnet's operator through communication channels formed by standards-based network protocols such as IRC (Internet Relay Chat) and HTTP (Hypertext Transfer Protocol). Though rare, more experienced botnet operators program command protocols from scratch. These protocols include a server program, a client program for operation, and the program that embeds the client on the victim's machine. These communicate over a network, using a unique encryption scheme for stealth and protection against detection or intrusion into the botnet.

Generally, the perpetrator has compromised multiple systems using various tools. Newer bots can automatically scan their environment and propagate themselves using vulnerabilities and weak passwords. An example of a botnet designed specifically for mobile devices is Waledac. Waledac uses SMS and MMS messages to exchange the data between nodes therefore enabling the botnet to remain active even if the nodes are not connected to the Internet.

Botnets are exploited for various purposes, utilizing the computing power of compromised devices, including denial-of-service attacks (CVE, 2006), creation or misuse of SMTP mail relays for spam (see Spambot), click fraud, mining bitcoins, spamdexing, and the theft of application serial numbers, login IDs, and financial information such as credit card numbers (Flo,2009).

Worm

Worm is a self-replicating malicious application designed to spread autonomously to uninfected systems (Orman,2003). These mobile worms are variants of internet worms, which spread by exploiting vulnerabilities in operating systems. Unlike viruses that always corrupt or modify files on a targeted device; worms tend to affect the network, even if only by consuming bandwidth.

There have been substantial efforts in modeling the propagation dynamics of Internet worms in the last few years. Staniford et al. used the classical logistic function to fit the propagation curve of the Code Red I worm (Staniford,2002) while Zou et al. proposed a two-factor worm model to characterize the epidemic spreading of Internet worms (Zou,2002). Many models have also been brought forward for special types of Internet worms, such as e-mail worms (Zou,2004), P2P worms (Thommes,2006), and so on.

Mobile worms are usually transmitted via text messages SMS or MMS, and do not require user interaction for execution. This type of malware's main objective is to reproduce and spread to other devices so that it can be copied endlessly to destroy the operating system of the mobile device. They may also contain harmful and misleading instructions.

This type of malware has been ported to mobile platforms since the introduction of Cabir (29A,2006). Cabir is a worm designed to attack Symbian S60 devices by spreading through Bluetooth links. A more recent example of a worm type malware for mobile devices is Ikee.B (IkeeB) which is used to steal financially sensitive data from jailbroken iPhones.

Rootkit

Rootkit is a type of malicious software that is activated each time a system boots up. Rootkits are difficult to detect because they are activated before system's Operating System has completely booted up. Further, rootkit may be able to subvert the software that is intended to find it. A rootkit often allows the installation of hidden files, processes, hidden user accounts, and more in the systems OS. Rootkits are able to intercept data from terminals, network connections, and the keyboard.

Rootkit detection methods include using an alternative and trusted operating system, behavioral-based methods, signature scanning, difference scanning, and memory dump analysis. Removal can be complicated or practically impossible, especially in cases where the rootkit resides in the kernel; reinstallation of the operating system may be the only available solution to the problem. When dealing with firmware rootkits, removal may require hardware replacement, or specialized equipment.

Although no current rootkit type threats for mobile devices exist, recent research efforts (Bickford,2010) indicate the potential of this attack strategy and classify it as an emerging threat to mobile security.

ATTACKER'S GOAL

With both the sophistication of smart phones and their increased technological capabilities, smart phones are being used as mini computers. Due to their widespread use and numerous vulnerabilities, these have become potential targets. Inherent weaknesses in the mobile IP protocol allow the launch of attacks that are relatively straightforward to mount but hard to detect and thwart.

Some mobile phone users store their credit card numbers and other financial information in electronic wallet software. Further, several users are just beginning to make purchases and conduct financial transactions over mobile devices, particularly in Europe and Japan. Viruses can let intruders access passwords or corporate data stored on a cell phone. Also, attackers can manipulate a victim's phone to make calls or send messages, a crime called theft of service.

In this subsection we present basic motives for breaching mobile device's security. These can be categorised as covert or harmful. Covert approach to executing an attack is to perform malicious operations while avoiding user's detection. The goal of such attacks is to disrupt the operation of the device as little as possible while performing activities useful to the attacker. On the other hand, harmful attacks are aimed at disrupting the normal operation of a mobile device.

Financial

Unlike, computers, mobile phones have a built-in billing system. This makes financial gain is one of the most important motives for virus writing. Every phone call placed and every text or multimedia message sent is a financial transaction. That opens up a flood of potential earning opportunities for profiteer hackers and virus authors.

A Trojan called RedBrowser sends a continuous stream of text messages from an infected phone to a Russian number until the user disables the phone. Each message is charged at a premium rate of about five dollars, resulting in huge bills for the unfortunate victims. Some cellular carriers hold their customers liable to collect the premium fees. Luckily, RedBrowser has so far only been spotted inside Russia.

Figure 5 indicates the principle of operation for premium SMS messages, while Figure 6 indicates the working of premium SMS message for an infected device. These two figures collectively indicate the financial theft performed in a mobile network.

Further, several service providers in North American markets are beginning to introduce "mobile wallets." Through this mobile wallet, customers will be able to use their phones to transfer funds from their accounts to others by sending specially formatted text messages. PayPal, a digital payments firm, offers a similar service that allows users to buy items using their phones. Such services could be of intense interest to malware authors.

Identity Theft

Hackers often attack mobile devices to obtain information. Two subcategories exist: attacks against transient information and against static information. Transient information includes the phone's location, its power usage, and other data which the device doesn't normally record. Using services such as Enhanced 911 (www.fcc.gov/911/enhanced), attackers can store a history of user movements through the city with some precision. Even without advanced location services, attacker can still locate phones with mobile regions, even if the phones aren't in active use.

Attacks on static information target information that cellular devices store or send over the network. Thus, instead of targeting meta-information about the device (where it is, what state it's in, and so on), these attacks try to get data such as contact information, phone numbers, and programs stored on smart phones. The BlueSnarfing attack is one example (see www.thebunker.net/release-bluestumbler.htm) (Herfurt, 2004). A snarf attack works against particular mobile devices, letting

Figure 5. How premium SMS works

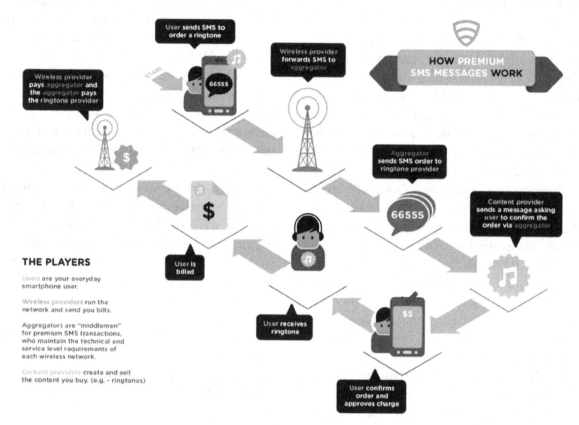

attackers connect without alerting the owner. Attackers can access most data on the device, including phonebook entries, calendars, cards, and even the phone's International Mobile Equipment Identity, which uniquely identifies it on the mobile network. At present, these attacks largely depend on misconfigured Bluetooth devices and other insecure default installations. These attacks will increase as attackers learn ways to break IEEE 802 protection schemes. For example, the 802.11 WEP protocol has demonstrated weaknesses that allow for both attacking message privacy and cipher key recovery. GSM-encrypted communications have also been vulnerable to ciphertext-only attacks.

Utilize Computing Resources

The increase in computing resources is setting the contemporary mobile devices into focus for malicious attacks with aim to covertly exploit the raw computing power in combination with broadband network access. Combined with high speed Internet links, mobile devices are becoming attractive for malicious exploits, such as deployment of botnets (Traynor,2009). For example, high end mobile devices have CPU operating frequencies in excess of 1GHz, and physical memory well over 512MB. In addition, multicore processors for mobile devices are under development.

Harmful Malicious Activities

Harmful malicious actions are aimed at generating device user's discomfort on performing useful operations for the attacker. Although such attacks are usually easily discoverable, they are aimed at causing the maximum possible damage. The attacks can range from data loss to draining the devices battery or exhausting other resources, like generating huge network traffic (Racic,2006).

Figure 6. How toll fraud malware works

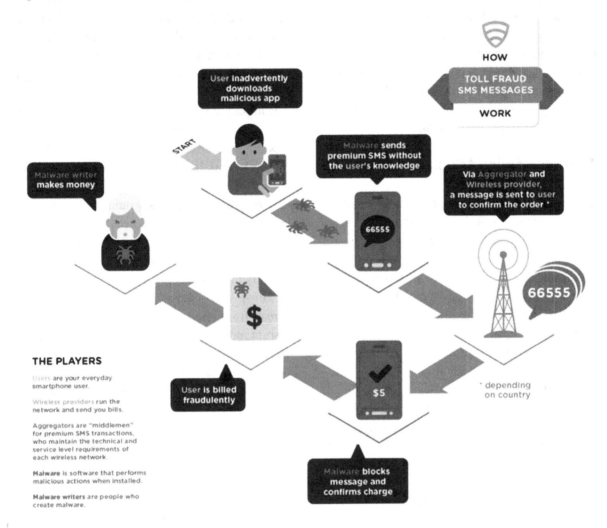

Ultimately, by gaining access to critical systems the attacker could disable the device permanently, i.e. brick the device.

Collect Private Data

Since the mobile devices are in effect becoming storage units for personal data, they are an attractive target for breaching user's privacy. The attackers target both the confidentiality and integrity of stored information. A successfully executed attack can empower the attacker with ability to read SMS and MMS messages, e-mail messages, call logs and contact details. Furthermore, the attacker can intercept or send fake SMS, forward e-mails to alternative inboxes, and access the information from personal organizers and calendars.

Additional information can be gathered by reading Instant Messaging client logs, data stored by applications used to access social networks or data stored by browsers. Any other data located in device's memory or on SD card, like documents, photos or videos, can also be compromised. In addition, tapping into phone's basic hardware features provides an opportunity to collect additional data from user's surroundings. By utilizing the voice recording hardware, the attacker can turn the infected mobile phone into a listening device.

Accessing the camera provides an opportunity to take photos or record video of the user's surroundings. Additional momentum to compromising user's privacy can be achieved by exploiting the location information. Mobile devices can provide location information by utilizing the GPS module, or by triangulating the position using the service provider's network infrastructure.

Theft-of-Service Attacks

Some malware might attempt to use the victim's phone resources, effectively hijacking services. Possibilities include placing long-distance or 900-number calls, sending expensive SMS messages, and so on. The recent Mosquitos virus is one example (see www.symbian.com/press-office/2004/pr040810.html). Pirated copies of a computer game were infected with a virus that sent (potentially) expensive SMS messages when users played the illicit copy of the game. The Brador WinCE virus poses a similar threat to services because it opens a backdoor on the infected device. Hijacking phone resources isn't unexpected— malware authors have been using victims' resources for quite a while (Chen, 2008).

Denial-of-Service Attacks

Two types of DoS attacks against mobile phones are possible—those that attempt to flood the device (for example, MAC Layer DoS attacks against 802.11 networks8) and attacks that attempt to drain power. At present, it's extremely easy to crash or overwhelm most Bluetooth applications on mobile devices just by sending repeated pieces of information, corrupted packets, and incorrect file formats. Experimentations at the Georgia Tech Information Security Center has revealed that many commercial and open source Bluetooth stacks are vulnerable to simple protocol attacks. The problems with these new, large, and complex protocol layer implementations are not unlike the

vulnerabilities that plagued IPv4 implementations years ago. Power demands always constrain mobile devices, so this latter category is more serious.

Another attack exhausts a device's battery by keeping the device active all the time, preventing it from going into lower-power idle and sleep states. The impact of this attack depends on the device's ratio of active to sleep power. On a mobile phone, this would mean the user's battery life would last only as long as the talk time, not the standby time, even if the phone is not in use. A carefully crafted battery exhaustion attack would lead the user to believe that the battery had become defective. As the ability to hold charge decreases with age of battery, users might believe that their batteries were dying naturally.

However, if battery exhaustion could rapidly spread from phone to phone, an attacker could disrupt mobile phone service on a wide scale or within a class of users. Another possibility would be to use battery exhaustion as a "secondary" attack to amplify the impact of another attack.

ATTACK VECTORS

The smartphones have the capability to download programs from the Internet and share software with one another through short-range Bluetooth connections, multimedia messaging service (MMS) communications and memory cards. These novel capabilities have created new vulnerabilities. The weaknesses were bound to be discovered and consequently exploited for mischief or criminal gain.

Though mobile devices are compared with the desktop computers, the viruses and the modes of spreading them are not exactly same. This is because of the more mobility of the mobile devices which leads to some relevant characteristics like moving velocity, moving scope etc. Due to this, the epidemic model of mobile phone virus is very different from the epidemic model of computer virus and worm. Conventional, stochastic mobile model (such as Random Waypoint model, Random Direction model) can be used to build spreading model of mobile phone virus. But due to their limitations, and for the simplification of problem, a model with uniform motion has been developed (Scorgie, 2009).

Mobile platforms provide multiple attack vectors for delivery of malicious content. This section discusses the various attack vectors, which are mainly classified into four categories: mobile network services, Internet access, Bluetooth, and access to USB and other peripheral devices.

SMS and MMS

SMS, a paging-like service for cell phones that use the Global System for Mobile and Code-Division Multiple-Access technologies, is used to send brief text messages (168 characters) to mobile phones. MMS, an advanced type of SMS for phones that are based on General Packet Radio Service technology, carries up to 50 Kbits of data, which is large enough for many viruses.

Cellular services like SMS, MMS and voice calls can be used as attack vectors for mobile devices. For example, SMS and MMS messages can be used to deliver malicious content and to maintain the communication with the attacker. This is especially applicable to MMS messages as they support rich content which allows the attacker to embed hidden XML messages. Furthermore, the cellular services provide opportunities for phishing attacks. Phishing is an attack strategy in which the attacker gains sensitive information from the user by presenting itself as a trustworthy entity.

Two basic phishing attacks over mobile networks exist: smishing and vishing. Smishing is a phishing attack executed using SMS messages. The attacker uses SMS to send URL links that when clicked automatically open a browser window rendering the device vulnerable to attack. On the other hand, vishing attack is carried out using voice calls. By masking the true voice call id, the attacker can trick the user into calling a certain number.

The attacker can then gain sensitive information from the user by pretending to be a trustworthy entity, like a bank or insurance company.

Internet Access

Mobile devices can access the Internet using Wi-Fi networks or 3G/4G services provided by mobile network operators. Although such high speed Internet connections ensure comfortable browsing, they also expose the mobile devices to the same threats as PCs. Since mobile devices are usually constantly switched on, they can maintain a continuous connection to the Internet. However, prolonged connection to the Internet also increases the chances of a successful malicious attack. The attack probability increases if the device is connected to a public network over a Wi-Fi hotspot.

In addition, the attackers can use multiple emerging Internet services to spread malicious content. For example, social networks, like Tweeter or Facebook, are commonly used to share URL links in order to indicate items of interest on the Web. Since links sometimes become long and unpractical to share, the URL shortening services are becoming a common way for reducing the link size. For example, the URL: http://www.mipro.hr/MIPRO2011.ISS/ELink.aspx could be shortened to: http://goo.gl/tL20e. Since the shortened link completely replaces the original, it is not possible to find out the destination without clicking on the link. By spreading the links over social networks, using previously compromised devices, the attackers can easily fool the users into clicking the harmful links. This way the attackers can trick users into downloading malicious content or navigating them to phishing sites.

Bluetooth

Bluetooth is a short-range radio technology aimed at connecting different wireless devices at low power consumption and at low cost (Bluetooth, 2008). A Bluetooth equipped smartphone can identify and exchange files with other blue-tooth devices from a distance of 10 meters or more. However, recent research has indicated that a Bluetooth connection can be establish from one mobile phone to another standard phone one mile away with a 19dbi panel antenna (BluetoothAt-tack, 2004).

Most of the people generally leave the Blue-tooth radios in their phones wide open, thus, of-fering a disturbingly effective vector for invisible parasites. As victims travel, their phones can leave a trail of infected bystanders in their wake. And any event that attracts a large crowd presents a perfect breeding ground for Bluetooth viruses (Gostev, 2006B). A particularly nasty form of Cabir, for example, spread so rapidly through the audience at the 2005 world track and field championships in Helsinki that stadium operators flashed warnings on the big screen (Gostev, 2006B). Most smart-phones can put Bluetooth into a "nondiscoverable" mode that protects them from invasion by worms. But few users avail themselves of this feature.

Bluetooth worms significantly differ from Internet worms in three ways. First, the limited transmission range of a Bluetooth device leads to a proximity-based infection mechanism: a Bluetooth-enabled device controlled by the worm can only infect neighbors within its radio range. This differs from Internet worms that often scan the entire IP address space for susceptible victims. Second, the bandwidth available to Bluetooth devices is usually much narrower than those of Internet links. For instance, the maximum trans-mission rate of a device operating on the class 2 Bluetooth radio is 1 Mbps. Finally, due to the mobility and limited transmission ranges of Blue-tooth devices, the underlying network topology on which Bluetooth worms propagate is much more dynamic than that of Internet worms.

Bluetooth attacks are a method used for device-to-device malware spreading (Haataja,2005). Once the two devices are in range, the compro-mised device pairs with its target by using default Bluetooth passwords. When the connection is established, the compromised device sends mali-cious content. However, the Bluetooth is a limited attack vector for injecting malicious content due to several security factors. First, the mobile devices usually are not set as discoverable by default and the period in which they can be discovered is limited. Second, the user has to confirm the file transfer and then manually install the file.

Research is being carried out to study the behaviour of mobile worms, and to model the propagation dynamics of Bluetooth worms (Bulygin, 2007). Bose and Shin (2006B) pre-sented a survey of existing Bluetooth viruses and worms. The simulations of the Bluetooth worm propagation have also been pursued from different perspectives (Bose, 2006B; Yan, 2006; Su, 2006). Several other work have also been carried out on Bluetooth worm, which mainly includes investigation of the impact of mobility patterns on Bluetooth worm propagation (Yan, 2007), detailed analysis of packet loss rates in Bluetooth networks (Yan, 2009), probabilistic queueing model for epidemic spreading in mobile environments (Mickens, 2005).

Bluebugging

One particularly pernicious attack is bluebugging, whereby a targeted phone becomes a bugging device. The attack requires the target device to im-properly offer a serial line service over Bluetooth. Most smart phones can record about an hour's worth of audio or more. The attacker can either record or broadcast the victim phone's audio, ef-fectively turning it into a mobile bugging device.

The basic idea of turning a mobile phone into a listening device has been done simply by using the hands-free interface on many phones. By setting the ringer to its lowest setting, turning off the vibrator, and turning on the "auto answer" mode, a phone will answer a call without any owner intervention. Although many phones will not let the phone be in "silent" mode while also in auto answer mode; the volume and ringtone can be set to unnoticeable in most environments. Even turning off a mobile phone might not be adequate protection. Most mobile phones use a "soft" power switch, which does not physically disconnect power to the phone but instead turns off the screen and puts the phone in a lower power state. A malicious program running on the phone could imitate this "power off" state when the user presses the power button. It would keep the phone operating to monitor the microphone, steal information from the user's phone, or even record audio for later recovery in the phone's memory.

Instant Messaging

The use of Instant messaging is increasing for personal and corporate communications. Individuals chat via IM; companies rely on its real-time capabilities, for collaborative design work; and e-businesses use IM to provide live, immediate customer service to shoppers. However, as IM becomes more popular, particularly for businesses, it has also increasingly become the target of attacks, such as those using malicious code and phishing.

These include the use of tricks to encourage victims to click on virusladen attachments or hyperlinks to Web pages that upload applets to either infect visitors with malware or drop unwanted software on their computers. The most dangerous part about the attacks is their speed of propagation, caused by IM's real-time capabilities. Simulations have shown that IM viruses can spread to 500,000 machines in less than 30 seconds (Symantec).

As mobile instant messaging's popularity grows, the same sorts of attacks seen on PCs are likely to appear, such as hijacking lists of IM names and sending links to recipients to direct them to malicious sites. Mobile viruses could also send out IM messages with the malicious code attached. In addition, IM supports the peer-to-peer transfer of files and messages with attachments, so they bypass most of email's server- and security-gateway based virus scanning. Password protection is limited in most IM systems, and the

communications are rarely encrypted. Without encryption, any off-the-shelf sniffer can reveal the content of IM communications

IM attacks can cause buffer overflows(Mulliner, 2006), which occur when a program or process tries to store more data in a buffer than it was designed to hold. The extra information overflows into adjacent buffers, corrupting or overwriting valid data. The overflowing data can contain instructions designed to cause problems such as client failure or the consumption of CPU or memory resources. Poor programming and memory management can enable buffer overflow attacks. Thus, major IM networks are revising their clients to ensure better memory management.

USB and Other Peripherals

Apart from the mentioned attack vectors, mobile devices can also be compromised by using other connections, like widely spread USB. The USB connection in commonly used to synchronize the mobile device with a personal computer. If the software used to synchronize the mobile device was compromised, the attacker can access private information and install malicious applications on the device. In addition, since some mobile platforms allow the device to connect as USB storage device, traditional USB malware can also be applied.

MOBILE MALWARE

Mobile malware is relatively new, thus, virus writers have released it primarily as proof-of-concept code. This section gives a brief overview of few of these mobile viruses and malwares.

Cabir

The well-known 29A Eastern European hacker group, specializes in creating proof-of-concept viruses, sent the first version of the Cabir worm, known as Cabir.A, to a number of antivirus firms. Cabir runs on smart phones from vendors such as Motorola, Nokia, Panasonic, and Sony Ericsson that support the Nokia-licensed Symbian Series 60 platform. Cabir spreads through a shared infected application or replicates via Bluetooth. The worm appears as an .SIS (Symbian installation system) application-installation file. Target devices display a message asking users if they want to receive a message via Bluetooth and then ask for further confirmation if the application is not digitally signed by an authorized Symbian authority. If the user chooses to receive the file, it installs and then sends itself to other Bluetooth-enabled devices within the 10- meter range.

After infecting a phone, Cabir.A displays the text "Caribe VZ/20a"and Cabir.B displays "Caribe" on the victim's screen. The worm also interferes with a host device's normal Bluetooth system by forcing it to constantly scan for other enabled devices. This reduces a device's battery life and either makes Bluetooth unavailable to legitimate applications or degrades Bluetooth performance.

Skulls

Skulls is a Trojan horse and thus masquerades as a useful application to convince users to install it. Its authors wrote Skulls to appear to be an application that lets users preview, select, and remove design themes for their phone screens. Hackers deliber-ately—and file sharers inadvertently—uploaded Skulls to several shareware sites, from which several users have downloaded the application. Skulls target the Nokia 7610 phone, although some other Symbian Series 60 phones can also install it. Skulls makes the original Symbian binaries for everyday functions, such as file management, Bluetooth control, messaging, Web browsing, and application installation and removal, useless by replacing them with non-functional binaries. The phones can then only make and receive calls.

As Skulls disables Symbian applications, only phones with third party file managers can remove the Trojan. Those using Symbian's file manager must perform a hard reset, thereby erasing all stored data. Skulls also replace each application icon with a skull and crossbones (Figure 7). Each of several Skulls variants and hybrids has a slightly different effect. For example, Skulls.D—posted to several Web discussion forums and warez sites—pretends to be a Macromedia Flash player for Symbian Series 60 devices. The variant replaces system binaries related to application uninstall and Bluetooth control with non-functional binaries, installs the Cabir.M worm, and disables antivirus programs and third-party file managers.

Mquito

Mquito is a version of the popular Mosquito game whose copy protection crackers have broken. Once the game is installed on a Symbian Series 60 device, it surreptitiously sends unauthorized SMS text messages to high-cost toll phone numbers in Germany, Holland, Switzerland, and the UK. Game-maker Ojom deliberately added Mosquito's hidden SMS functionality as a copy-protection technique. The Symbian OS provides the functionality required for any application to send and receive SMS messages with or without user intervention. Current versions of the game no longer have the hidden SMS functionality, but cracked versions with the capability are still available online for downloading.

Windows CE Virus

It is the first proof-of-concept virus for Microsoft's mobile operating system written by 29A hacker group. The WinCE.Duts.A virus sends recipients a message asking for permission to download. When the permission is granted, the virus tries to infect all executable files bigger than 4,096 bytes. During the infection process, the virus appends itself to a file. If a victim tries to run an infected

Figure 7. Representation of skulls infected mobile screen (Ref. F-Secure Corporation Report)

Image Copyright © F-Secure Corporation

file, the virus will function but the application won't. The virus then attempts to spread, looking for new files to infect. When files are exchanged between devices, the virus spreads along with them. Being a proof-of-concept virus, it has no payload. However, it could be easily adapted.

Metal Gear

Metal Gear is a Trojan camouflaged as a mobile version of the Metal Gear Solid video game. To get infected with the Trojan, users must open and install the fake Metal Gear game. Designers often port PC games to mobile platforms, so Metal Gear fans might believe the Trojan actually is a mobile version of the game. The Metal Gear Trojan disables antivirus programs and installs the Cabir.G worm, which tries to spread a second Trojan program, SEXXXY, to nearby phones via Bluetooth. Users will have difficulty repairing their phones because the Metal Gear Trojan effectively disables all tools on the phone necessary to undo the damage.

Lasco

Lasco.A, a proof-of-concept program, uses Bluetooth to infect mobile phones running on the Symbian Series 60 platform. Lasco can create its own .SIS installer file, which lets the application load itself onto other Bluetooth enabled devices within range. It can also insert itself into other .SIS files and thereby spread during file sharing. Lasco is the first mobile malware that can use both methods to infect devices, thereby increasing its ability to spread. Once installed, Lasco changes a phone's file directory to include the appended file. It also sets up the .SIS file to tell the target phone's application manager to run Lasco during installation. The file arrives in the phone's messaging inbox and asks, "Install Velasco?" If the user gives permission, the worm activates and looks for new devices to infect.

Gavno

Gavno, a Trojan reported to SimWorks but not yet found in the wild, contains an application file that hackers have deliberately rendered invalid by, for example, removing critical data. When the Symbian OS tries to use it as the type of file it is supposed to be, problems arise that cause a series of cascading errors in Nokia 6600 and 6630 phones. The errors cause the OS to become unstable, limiting infected phones to receiving calls. Gavno then makes the phone reboot, which produces similar errors.

One of two variants, Gavno.B, includes a Cabir version. This mobile malware will become more sophisticated as virus writers gain more experience and hackers publish the source code for various viruses, worms, and Trojans.

Commwarrior

It was found in 2005 and it is the first worm to use MMS messages, in order to spread to other devices. It can spread through Bluetooth as well. It infects devices running under OS Symbian Series 60. The executable worm file, once launched, hunts for accessible Bluetooth devices and sends the infected files under a random name to various devices.

Gingermaster

A Trojan developed for Android platform that propagates by installing applications that incorporate a hidden malware for installation in background. Exploit the frailty from the version Gingerbread (2.3) of operating system to use super-user permissions by privilege escalation. Then create a service that steals information from infected terminal (user ID, number SIM, phone number, IMEI,IMSI, screen resolution and local time) by sending the same to a remote server through petitions HTTP.

Droidkungfu

A Trojan content in Android applications, which when executed, obtains privileges root and install the file, com.google. ssearch.apk, which contains a backdoor that allows removing files, open home pages supplied, open web and download and install application packages. This virus collected and sent to a remote server all available data on the terminal.

Ikee

Ikee is the first worm known for platforms iOS. Only works on terminals that were previously made a process of jailbreak, and spreads trying to access other devices using protocol SSH, first through the subnet that is connected to the device. Then, repeat the process generating a random range and finally used some preset ranges corresponding to IP address of certain telephone companies. Once infected the computer, replace the wallpaper to a photograph of the singer Rick Astley.

VIRUS DETECTION AND PREVENTION

The idea of viruses that target mobile devices is relatively new, and it has not received the attention that the PC virus threat has seen. Most of the work that has been done regarding mobile viruses has looked at worm propagation models, or examined the differences and similarities between them and PC viruses (Yan,2007; Bose,2006A; Su,2006; Fleizach,2007). Research has been conducted on detecting and limiting mobile viruses with positive results (Venugopal,2006; Cheng,2007; Sarwar,2007).

The primary and most widely used method of virus detection for mobile devices is signature-based virus scanning. Signature scanning relies on a list of predefined virus signatures so that viruses can be identified in a mobile device. Each year, several virus signatures are added to the central database but still a virus can go undetected if the device is infected by a virus signature which is new for the scanner. Figure 8 graphically represents the number of antivirus signatures added in the last four years (Kaspesky Reports).

In the case of signature scanning technique, the device needs to have a regular connection to a central database of signatures so that updates can be received on the latest definitions. This is not as easy to achieve as it is on a PC with a constant Internet connection. Mobile devices have limited storage space and with every new virus definition download, the signature scanner uses more of the limited resource. This signature scanning method also means that the device needs to be infected by a virus.

Considering the limited battery life, processing power and memory, several other methods for virus detection are also being researched. One such method requires the device to keep a log of all communication activities, and send the log regularly to a central server. The server then checks the log for any unusual behaviour which

would indicate that a virus has infected the device. This method requires the virus to be active and spreading from a device in order to detect it. However, this would not be acceptable for a device that contains sensitive business data that could have been stolen in the meantime.

These schemes detect a virus on a mobile device after the device has been infected or some damage has been done. To avoid such damages, a technique has been proposed for virus detection at the time of infection (Scorgie,2009). This uses the concept of Auto-Start Extensibility Points (ASEP), which is described as any point in the OS or a commonly used application that can be "hooked" onto in order to enable auto-starting of programs without explicit user invocation. A system has been developed that would monitor ASEPs in Windows XP and alert the user of any hooking operations that were detected in an attempt to keep users informed of spyware that was being installed on a PC. The same technique could be adapted to the mobile environment to alert users of ASEP hooking operations that could indicate a virus infection. In addition to writing ASEP

Figure 8. Number of new antivirus signatures created each year to detect Mac OS X malware

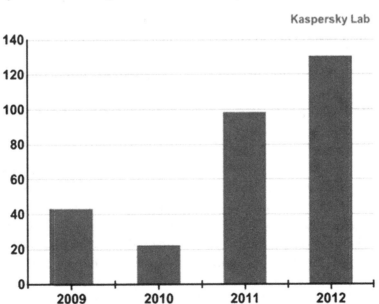

hooking event details to a log file, the application also displays an alert message on the screen for the user.

These various virus detection techniques will be used if the device is infected. To detect and prevent the viruses, several companies have launched antivirus solutions for mobile devices. The next section gives a brief overview of their principle of operation and the attacks that can be launched against them.

MOBILE ANTIVIRUS

Mobile applications are considered to be the most convenient method for performing malicious attacks. For virus detection and prevention, companies like Lookup (LookOut), COMODO (Comodo), F-Secure (F-Secure), TrustGo (Trust-Go), Trend Micro (TrendMicro2006), Symantec (Symantec) have started offering antivirus solution for the mobile devices. Mobile antivirus software is designed to shield smartphone from viruses, malicious threats, hackers and spam.

The antivirus research community has mainly focused on security model implemented over two widely spread platforms: the Android by Google and the iOS by Apple. The analyzed mobile platforms differ in their approaches to enforce application security. The Android isolates applications in order to prevent them from interfering with other applications or the operating system. On the contrary, the iOS applications are screened for malicious intentions by code reviewers, thus allowing implementation of simpler security mechanisms.

Because virus scanners rely on detecting certain key attributes of a virus's binary code, there has been an ongoing competition between virus writers and antivirus developers since the first virus scanner arrived. Two antivirus attack schemes stand out.

Polymorphism

The most important body blow to antivirus scanner developers was the concept of polymorphism, in which successive replications of the same virus type rearrange their code to appear differently when viewed in files. Thus, polymorphic viruses "look" different with each replication, making detection far more difficult than with static code. Scanner developers generally have been successful at detecting these viruses by applying multiple techniques. However, this detection approach usually hinges on easily identifying the virus code's entry point and applying various static analysis techniques. In fact, relying on entry-point identification is the Achilles heel of modern signature- based solutions.

Entry Point Obfuscation

When an entry-point obfuscation (EPO) virus successfully hides its location point; many signature-scanning tools fail. Coupled with polymorphism, EPOs might signal the beginning of the death knell for scanning systems—or at least their use as cure-alls.

To understand EPO virus impact, the advantage that virus writers have over scanner developers must be understood: virus writers don't have to achieve perfect infection. Infection attempts can sometimes fail. Even an imperfect virus can spread quite well in the real world. On the contrary, an antivirus product must be extremely reliable. Unreliable detection, either by identifying a benign file as infected or vice versa, is a fatal flaw. Thus, an EPO algorithm does not have to be perfect but an EPO-detection algorithm should be perfect. Virus writers can achieve EPO in many ways. Unlike a traditional virus that often subverts an infected application's initial entry point, an EPO virus can change any JMP or CALL in the body of an infected file, particularly for example, a call to an underlying C/C++ library call or an external dependency.

Potential start points for an EPO virus are unlimited, held in check only by the virus writer's skill and the size of the object which is to be infected. A virus scanner cannot check each possibility. Thus, EPO viruses do not make a virus-scanner's job impossible, but massively increase algorithmic complexity for signature-based work.

To circumvent the difficulty associated with virus infection, viz., virus detection, preventions using antivirus or withstanding the antivirus attacks, certain measures can be taken. Several such threat mitigation techniques have been presented in the next section.

THREAT MITIGATION

To combat the problem of mobile malware, a quick and concerted action at various levels is required from all the concerned entities (Gupta,2004). These different entities include the user, research community, mobile phone manufacturer, government, antivirus developers etc. Some of the required actions by these entities can be enlisted as follows:

1. **Antivirus Software:** Mobile antivirus programs are similar to those used for PCs; they scan files for code strings associated with viruses or watch for potentially harmful activities, that viruses frequently undertake. Such antivirus software, which are now available from many companies can immunize and disinfect smartphones. Due to the limitations of mobile devices, antivirus software must be simpler and economical. Mobile users should install such protection mechanisms.

2. **Firewall Protection:** Phones should also incorporate firewall software that warns the user when a program on the phone seizes the initiative to open an Internet connection. This is an especially important form of protection for smartphones that can connect to Wi-Fi networks and thus directly to the public Internet.

3. **Network Level Protection:** Open Wi-Fi networks are very insecure networks. This presents an opportunity for introduction of malicious exploits. Many cellular companies aggressively filter traffic on the GPRS or UMTS data networks that their mobile devices use. And while some carriers already filter their MMS streams to remove messages bearing malicious attachments, all should do so.

4. **Hardware Changes:** Some of the biggest phone manufacturers have joined the Trusted Computing Group, which has been hammering out industry standards for microcircuitry inside phones that will make it harder for malware to get at sensitive data in the device's memory or to hijack its payment mechanisms (Ravi,2006). Such an intiative has already started, other can also follow this trend.

5. **Digital Certification:** A new version of operating system has been launched by Symbian, that does an improved job of protecting key files and requires software authors to obtain digital certificates from the company. The new Symbian system refuses to install programs not accompanied by a digital certificate. This digital certification will prevent applications from being tampered with, such as by including malware.

6. **Governments Role:** Governments could also play a more constructive role than they have so far. Even though most countries have passed laws against hacking both ordinary computers and the computers inside cell phones, enforcement is lax or nonexistent in most of the world.

7. **Research Community:** Many of the nations are hit hardest by mobile malware outbreaks, such as Malaysia, Indonesia and the Philippines. Reliable and timely statis-

tics should be collected from them so that it helps to track software crimes. The security research community should proactively study the most widely used OS to look for vulnerabilities in the code and in the system designs that might afford entrée to malware. These holes should be identified so that they can be patched before the hackers exploit them.

8. **Mobile Companies:** While users now often protect their PCs with antivirus software, such measures are not so widespread in cellular phones. Most users aren't aware of potential mobile malicious code problems and thus aren't vigilant in preventing or avoiding attacks on their phones. Few mobile phones companies have started to install these antivirus software. For example, Japan's NTT DoCoMo now provides buyers of its new Symbian-based FOMA 901i phones with McAfee's VirusScan technology. Nokia has introduced two phones with Symantec Client Security software, which is preloaded on the memory card and can be updated wirelessly through Symantec LiveUpdate. Antivirus-software vendor Trend Micro recently rolled out Trend Micro Mobile Security, that provides antivirus and antispam protection for mobile devices' SMS applications.

9. **Customer Awareness:** Since mobile devices are connected through Bluetooth or other active network applications, mobile users should keep the network applications either turn-off or non-discoverable (Mulliner, 2006). Users should have knowledge of the types of attacks that can be mounted against mobile phones. Also, to circumvent mobile malware, mobile phones should provide visualizations and logs of their most critical statistics, such as battery level, rate of battery consumption, data transmission, and CPU activity. These visualizations can be inspected to determine potential problems, and find ways for their prevention.

CONCLUSION

Recent advancements in mobile technology have brought the mobile devices into focus of malicious attacks. In the present chapter, a detailed description of Mobile Worms and Viruses, and an up-to-date treatise of their mode of spreading, effects, and the risks involved have been presented. An analysis of contemporary mobile platform threats and an in-depth overview of threat mitigation mechanisms built into state of the art mobile operating systems have also been discussed.

The trends show a severe increase in mobile malware as many threats, designed for PC operating systems, migrate to mobile platforms. To counter the growing threat, antivirus companies have stepped up their research and development. In addition, vendors of phones and mobile operating systems are looking for ways to improve security. Antispyware and antivirus functionality will help mobile users become more resistant to such attacks, but like in the PC world, there will always be hackers who want to rise to the challenge. Mobile device users will have to learn to be more vigilant to ensure that their data and communications stay secure.

REFERENCES

Ahmad, M., Batz, D., Chasko, S., Dagon, D., Judge, P., & Lee, W. et al. (2011). *Emerging Cyber Threats Report for 2011*. Georgia Tech Information Security Center.

Android. (n.d.). Available at http://www.android.com/

Bickford, J., Hare, R., Baliga, A., & Ganapathy, V. (2010). Rootkits on Smart Phones: Attacks, Implications and Opportunities. In *Proceedings of the Eleventh Workshop on Mobile Computing Systems & Applications*, (pp. 49-54). Academic Press.

Bluetooth. (2008). *The Bluetooth Special Interest Group*. Available at http://www.bluetooth.com/

Bose, A., & Shin, K. G. (2006a). Proactive Security for Mobile Messaging Networks. In *Proceedings of ACM Workshop on Wireless Security* (pp. 95-104). ACM.

Bose, A., & Shin, K. G. (2006b). On Mobile Viruses Exploiting Messaging and Bluetooth Services. In *Proceedings of Second International Conference on Security and Privacy in Communication Networks*. Academic Press.

Bulygin, Y. (2007). Epidemics of Mobile Worms. In *Proceedings of IEEE International Conference on Performance, Computing and Communications*, (pp. 475-478). IEEE.

Cabir, 29A. (2006). *Source Code - Cabir*. Available at http://netsecurity

Chen, J. (2008). *An Introduction to Android*. Available at http://sites.google.com/site/io/an-introduction-to-android

Cheng, J., Wong, S. H. Y., Yang, H., & Lu, S. (2007). SmartSiren: Virus Detection and Alert for Smartphones. *MobiSys, 2007*, 258–271. doi:10.1145/1247660.1247690

Cisco Systems Inc. (2010). The Tipping Point: Cybercriminals Targeting Mobile Platforms. Cisco Annual Security Report 2010. Available at http://www.cisco.com

Common Vulnerabilities and Exposure. (n.d.). Available at http://www.cve.mitre.org

Comodo. (n.d.). Available at https://m.comodo.com/

Dagon, D., Martin, T., & Starner, T. (2004). Mobile Phones as Computing Devices: The Viruses are Coming! *IEEE Pervasive Computing*, 11–15. doi:10.1109/MPRV.2004.21

Delac, G., Silic, M., & Krolo, J. (2011). Emerging Security Threats for Mobile Platforms. In *Proceedings of 34th International Convention on Information and communication Technology, Electronics and Microelectronics* (MIPRO), (pp. 1468-1473). MIPRO.

Ecom200. (n.d.). *Mobile Phones Swamped by E-Mail Virus*. Available at ecommercetimes.com

F-Secure. (n.d.). Available at http://www.f-secure.com/en/web/home_global/mobile-security

Fleizach, C., Liljenstam, M., Johansson, P., Voelker, G. M., & Méhes, A. (2007). Can You Infect Me Now? Malware Propagation in Mobile Phone Networks. *Worm, 7*, 61–68.

Flo & Josang. (2009). Consequences of Botnets Spreading to Mobile Devices. In *Proceedings of the 14th Nordic Conference on Secure IT Systems*, (pp. 37-43). Academic Press.

Ford, R. (2004). The Wrong Stuff?. *IEEE Security & Privacy*, 86-89.

FS_MTR. (2011). *F-Secure, Mobile Threat Report, Q4, 2011*. Author.

Gostev, A. (2006a). *Mobile Malware Evolution: An Overview*, (Part 1). Available at https://www.securelist.com

Gostev, A. (2006b). *Mobile Malware Evolution: An Overview*, (Part 2). Available at https://www.securelist.com

Gostev, A. (2006c, January). Malicious programs for mobile devices. *Kaspersky Security Bulletin*. Available at http://www.viruslist.com/en/analysis?pubid=198981193

Gupta, A., & Daniel, C. D. V. (2004). Using Predators to Combat Worms and Viruses: A Simulation-Based Study. In *Proceedings of the 20th IEEE Annual Computer Security Applications Conference*. IEEE.

Haataja, K. M. J. (2005). Three practical attacks against Bluetooth security using new enhanced implementations of security analysis tools. In *Proceedings of the IASTED International Conference on Communication, Network and Information Security*, (pp. 101-108). IASTED.

Herfurt, M. (2004). *Bluesnarfing*. CeBIT 2004.

Hypponen, M. (2006). Malware goes mobile. *Scientific American*, 70–77. doi:10.1038/scientificamerican1106-70 PMID:17076086

IkeeB, F-Secure. (n.d.). *Worm:iPhoneOS/Ikee.B*. Available at http://www.f-secure.com

Infoplease. (n.d.). *Computer Virus Timeline*. Available at infoplease.com

Kaspersky. (2010). *First SMS Trojan detected for smartphones running Android*. Available at http://www.kaspersky.co.in

Kaspersky. (2012). *Kaspersky Security Bulletin 2012: The overall statistics for 2012*. Available at http://www.kaspersky.co.in

Leavitt, N. (2005a). Mobile Phones: The Next Frontier for Hackers?. *IEEE Computer*, 20-23.

Leavitt, N. (2005b). Instant Messaging: A New Target for Hackers?. *IEEE Computer*, 20-23.

LookOut. (n.d.). Available at https://www.lookout.com/mobile-antivirus-software

Mickens, J. W., & Noble, B. D. (2005). Modeling Epidemic Spreading in Mobile Environments. In *Proceedings of the Fourth ACM Workshop on Wireless Security* (pp. 77-86). ACM.

Micro, T. (2006). Trend Micro Mobile Security. Available at http://www.trendmicro.com

Mulliner, C. (2006). *Advanced Attacks Against Pocket PC Phones*. DEFCON 14.

Myphonefactor. (2013). *Information about Smartphone Virus and Prevention tips*. Available at myphonefactor.in

Orman, H. (2003). The Morris Worm: A Fifteen-Year Perspective. *IEEE Security & Privacy*, 35-43.

Racic, R., Ma, D., & Chen, H. (2006). Exploiting mms vulnerabilities to stealthily exhaust mobile phone's battery. In *Proceedings of SecureComm & Workshops*, (pp. 1-10). Academic Press.

Ravi, S. (2006). *Embedded System Security*. Princeton University.

Sarwar, U., Ramadass, S., & Budiarto, R. (2007). A Framework for Detection Bluetooth Mobile Worms. *In Proceedings of IEEE International Conference on Telecommunications*, (pp. 343-347). IEEE.

Scorgie, B., Prakash, V., & Ghosh, S. (2009). Early Virus Detection for Windows Mobile. In *Proceedings of the 9th IEEE Malaysia International Conference on Communications*, (pp. 295-300). IEEE.

Staniford, S., Paxson, V., & Weaver, N. (2002). How to Own the Internet in Your Spare Time. In *Proceedings of the 11th USENIX Security Symposium*. USENIX.

Su, J., Chan, K. K. W., Miklas, A. G., Po, K., Akhavan, A., Saroiu, S., et al. (2006). A Preliminary Investigation of Worm Infections in a Bluetooth Environment. In *Proceedings of the Fourth ACM Workshop on Recurring Malcode* (WORM). ACM.

Symantec. (n.d.). Available at http://www.symantec.com

Thommes, R., & Coates, M. (2006). Epidemiological Modelling of Peer-to-Peer Viruses and Pollution. In *Proceedings of the IEEE International Conference on Computer Communications*. IEEE.

Traynor, P., Lin, M., Ongtang, M., Rao, V., Jaeger, T., McDaniel, P., & Porta, T. L. (2009). On cellular botnets: Measuring the impact of malicious devices on a cellular network core. In *Proceedings of the 16th ACM Conference on Computer and Communications Security*, (pp. 223-234). ACM.

TrustGo. (n.d.). Available at http://www.trustgo.com

Venugopal, D. (2006). An Efficient Signature Representation and Matching Method for Mobile Devices. In *Proceedings of the 2nd Annual International Workshop on Wireless Internet*. Academic Press.

Yan, G., & Eidenbenz, S. (2006). Bluetooth Worms: Models, Dynamics, and Defense Implications. In *Proceedings of the 22nd IEEE Annual Conference on Computer Security Applications* (pp. 245-256). IEEE.

Yan, G., & Eidenbenz, S. (2009). Modeling Propagation Dynamics of Bluetooth Worms. *IEEE Transactions on Mobile Computing*, *8*(3), 353–367.

Yan, G., Flores, H. D., Cuellar, L., Hengartner, N., Eidenbenz, S., & Vu, V. (2007). Bluetooth Worm Propagation: Mobility Pattern Matters. In *Proceedings of the 2nd ACM Symposium on Information, Computer and Communications Security* (pp. 32-44). ACM.

Zou, C. C., Gong, W., & Towsley, D. (2002). Code Red Worm Propagation Modeling and Analysis. In *Proceedings of the Ninth ACM Conference on Computer and Communications Security*. ACM.

Zou, C. C., Towsley, D., & Gong, W. (2004). Email Worm Modeling and Defense. In *Proceedings of the 13th International Conference on Computer Communication and Networks*. Academic Press.

KEY TERMS AND DEFINITIONS

Botnet: A botnet is a collection of internet-connected programs communicating with other similar programs in order to perform tasks. Botnets sometimes compromise computers whose security defenses have been breached and control conceded to a third party.

Malware: Malware is any software that is used to disrupt computer operation, gather sensitive information, or gain access to private computer systems. It can appear in the form of code, scripts, active content, and other software. This includes viruses, worms, Trojan horses etc.

Rootkit: Rootkit is a type of malicious software that is activated each time a system boots up. Rootkits are difficult to detect because they are activated before system's Operating System has completely booted up.

Trojan: A Trojan is a hacking program that allows unauthorized access to the target's computer. It is a non-self-replicating type of malware which gains privileged access to the operating system while appearing to perform a desirable function.

Virus: A mobile virus is malicious software that targets mobile phones or wireless-enabled Personal digital assistants (PDA), by causing the collapse of the system and loss or leakage of confidential information.

Worm: Worm is a self-replicating malicious application designed to spread autonomously to uninfected systems. These mobile worms are variants of internet worms, which spread by exploiting vulnerabilities in operating systems.

Chapter 12
On Complex Crimes and Digital Forensics

Martin S. Olivier
University of Pretoria, South Africa

ABSTRACT

Science provides the basis for truth claims in forensics. Very little research has been done to explore the scientific basis of digital forensics. The work that has been done vary widely in what they propose; in most cases it is unclear how the philosophical remarks about such forensic science apply to digital forensics practice, or that the practical suggestions are a sufficient basis to claim that practice based on them is scientific. This chapter provides an initial exploration of the potential of decision problems from the field of algorithmics to form this scientific basis. There is no doubt that decision problems operate in the scientific domain and decision problems look similar to hypotheses to be of immediate practical use. The chapter suggests that, if decision problems are used in this manner, it is clear that current digital forensics have only scratched the surface of what is possible. Probabilistic complexity classes, for example, offer interesting possibilities for performing complex tests in relatively short times, with known error rates. Using decision problems as a demarcation criterion makes it possible to distinguish between digital forensic science (or simply digital forensics) and digital forensic craft, which should be called digital investigative technique or some other suitable term that does not imply that its use leads to scientific truths.

INTRODUCTION

Forensics entails the use of science to determine matters of fact where such facts are required to settle disputes (for example, in courts of law) or to determine the root cause of an event of interest. Forensics employs the notion that scientific knowledge is true and hence a good basis to settle such disputes and/or determine causes. Digital forensics is that branch of forensics that studies evidence that exists is digital form.

In order to make such truth claims forensics has to be 'scientific'. In some cases this is emphasised by using the term forensic science, which in this paper will be deemed to be synonymous with the term forensics. The notion of science (as well as the notion of truth) has been the subject of deep philosophical reflection over centuries; so much has been said that a paper that ultimately intends to deal with a small fraction of forensic science cannot hope to do justice to.

DOI: 10.4018/978-1-4666-6158-5.ch012

The obvious question then is what is the nature of digital forensic science or, with the same meaning, the science that underlies digital forensics? Cohen (2012) is the only author who has provided a coherent answer to this question by describing an information physics — 'natural laws' that apply to information and can be used as the basis for more complex truth claims. However, it is not yet clear that it is possible to always relate the behaviour of a complex system to truths about bits and related matters—see, for example, Hofstadter's argument (1979) that a complex system may be more than the mere sum of its parts and may exhibit characteristics that are not present in the parts.

A recent newspaper story (Koppl & Ferraro, 2012) provides some insight on what may go wrong if we rely on digital forensics that cannot be trusted—it may negatively affect innocent people. However, simply discarding digital forensics because of a lack of trust turns the cyberworld into a safe haven for criminals who can exploit others without fear of being caught. Clearly a digital forensics is required that maximises the chances that the guilt of the guilty can be proven, and that will ideally never implicate an innocent party. If these requirements are met the inhabitants of cyberspace can proceed with trust even in those cases where the proactive security mechanisms fail. Note that this problem is not only present in digital forensics; other branches of forensics have also failed because they used junk science or pseudoscience (Giannelli, 2007 ; Sasks & Faigman, 2008). Regarding digital forensics, Caloyannides (2006) boldly declares that "It is important for judges and juries to be highly sceptical of any claims by prosecution that digital 'evidence' proves anything at all."

This paper will examine the suitability of algorithmics or algorithmic complexity theory to form the basis of digital forensics. The justification of positing algorithmics as this basis is deferred to later in the paper when required underlying issues have been discussed. From the outset it is important to note that the paper distinguishes between expert testimony and forensics. In many jurisdictions forensic evidence can only be introduced in a court case by means of expert testimony. However, not all expert testimony is based on forensics. Consider, for example, the medical doctor who testifies as an expert about the current standard of care for some ailment. This testimony will be partly based on medical training (including continuing education), partly on professional observation of what colleagues do, partly by standards that may have been published by national and international bodies and partly by local conditions (such as affordability of various treatment options).

Clearly such testimony from an expert may be invaluable in a case where it is required. However, such evidence will not be classified as scientific evidence. In particular is this witness not basing evidence on forensic science. The remainder of the paper is structured as follows. The next section reviews some chacateristics of science, forensic science and expert testimony to provide context for the exploration of digital forensic science that follows. Section 3 initiates this exploration by discussing two simple (and common) scenarios at length. Section 4 uses these scenarios, the notion of decision problems and expectations about digital forensic science from the literature to begin to develop a theory of digital forensics that can claim to be scientific. Section 5 briefly mentions some competing theories. Section 6 concludes the paper.

ON SCIENCE, FORENSIC SCIENCE, AND EXPERT TESTIMONY

As noted earlier the intention of the current paper is not to explore the notion of science in depth. In the philosophy of science the following three landmarks are most important for the purposes of this paper. Firstly, in the period before the Second World War a group known as the Vienna Circle developed the notion of logical positivism. According to them the only meaningful judgements were the tautologies from mathematics and logic, and verifiable empirical claims from science. Everything else was nonsense. The second landmark is Popper's demarcation criterion for science: falsifiability. Only theories that can be falsified should be regarded as science. To be more specific, Popper foresees series of theories, where, when one theory is falsified, it is replaced by another theory that has greater explanatory power. Finally, Kuhn (1996) describes (rather than defines) science as an endeavour where during periods of normal science, scientists solve puzzles using the paradigm then prevalent. Once an existing theory becomes unsustainable, it is replaced by a new theory (again with greater explanatory power) during what he calls a scientific revolution.

Clearly much has to be added to this admittedly superficial descriptions of science to make them useful for forensic purposes. A theory that can be falsified but has not been tested at all may qualify as science, but not as grounds for the conviction of an alleged criminal. Similarly, the mere fact that a scientist has followed the appropriate paradigm may not ensure the reliability of the results. Rather than looking at the philosophy of science for deeper understanding, we turn our attention to the law.

Expert testimony in courts have a long history. In 1782 a civil engineer and scientist testified in the Wells Harbour case in the UK. Rather than just surmising from current observations what caused the silting up of the harbour he claimed that it was "necessary to shew the natural causes by which the port of Wells has been formed" (Smeaton, 1837, p.150). This was extraordinary since Mr Smeaton was testifying about something he did not observe, but derived from laws of nature (Golan, 2007). He also did not derive those laws or even tested them. Normally such testimony would have been classified as hearsay, or even irrelevant to the specific case being heard. The opposing side did indeed attempt to get his evidence excluded. However, Lord Mansfield who was presiding over the trial wrote "I cannot believe that when

the question is, whether a defect arises from a natural or an artificial cause, the opinions of men of science are not to be received [. . .] The cause of the decay of the harbour is also a matter of science, and still more so whether the removal of the bank can be beneficial. On this such men as Mr. Smeaton alone can judge. Therefore we are of the opinion that his judgement, formed on facts, was very proper evidence." This is often cited as the first use of science (or forensic science) in a court of law.

Of course the use of science enabled more informed judgments to be made, but over time much pseudoscience developed where claims were made based on some set of theories that was not scientific at all. A relatively modern example of a challenge that faces courts is the use of a polygraph to obtain evidence. The validity of such evidence is the topic of much debate; many reject polygraphy as pseudoscience, while others consider it to be very reliable. Many government agencies, for example, consider polygraphy as useful (Furedy, 1966). Even where such evidence is not accepted, a suspect who volunteers for such a test scores some credibility points.

It is therefore important that the court acts as a gatekeeper to only allow 'valid' or 'true' science to be accepted as scientific evidence. Of course it should not be necessary to qualify science using words such as valid or true because science itself implies those characteristics.

The best known 'modern' test for admissibility of expert testimony is the Daubert standard used in the USA. In this case the court decided, amongst others, that (U.S. Supreme Court, 1993). Faced with a proffer of expert scientific testimony under Rule 702, the trial judge, pursuant to Rule 104(a), must make a preliminary assessment of whether the testimony's underlying reasoning or methodology is scientifically valid and properly can be applied to the facts at issue. Many considerations will bear on the inquiry, including whether the theory or technique in question can be (and has been) tested, whether it has been subjected to peer review and publication, its known or potential error rate and the existence and maintenance of standards controlling its operation, and whether it has attracted widespread acceptance within a relevant scientific community. The inquiry is a flexible one, and its focus must be solely on principles and methodology, not on the conclusions that they generate.

While this standard has been slightly revised by other courts many of the phrases of this judgment reverberates in the minds of those who are trying to establish a scientific foundation for some forensic discipline. The key phrases include tested, peer review and publication, widespread acceptance and, perhaps the most challenging of all (and not present in some later formulations of the standard, but still frequently highlighted) the known or potential error rate of the theory. Note that it is easy to critique Daubert — the minority judgment that forms part of the decision cited above (U.S. Supreme Court, 1993) is a good starting point for such critique. However, some mechanism is required to keep pseudoscience out of courts, and Daubert is arguably the most prominent current standard used for this purpose.

Clearly then, for digital forensics to become (or remain) trusted, self reflection is necessary in the light of standards such as Daubert.

FORENSIC CRAFT AND SCIENCE

Let us consider just two typical scenarios encountered in 'digital cases' and distinguish between the craft and science involved.1 The first — and apparently most prevalent — example is one where it is necessary to show that some data is present on (or absent from) some medium. The nature of the content to find may vary. In the simplest case it may be some byte sequence, such as some credit card number (say 1234-5678-9012-3456) or a specific MP3 file. In a more complex case it may be an (any) email sent between two specific parties or a (any) JPEG image depicting certain

content. For ease of reference we will refer to the criteria used for searching as the search pattern even though the criteria may not be a typical pattern — such as when the criteria specify a certain file type. To find the search pattern a number of subtasks need to be completed. Firstly the disc (or other media) content needs to be acquired in a forensically sound manner. Secondly, the search pattern needs to be located. Thirdly, it has to be demonstrated that the search pattern does occur on the media (and it may be necessary to indicate what the full details are, for example the content of an email that has been found based on sender and recipient). Or it may be useful to indicate that the search pattern does not exist on the media (or, a weaker claim, indicate that the content was not found on the media).

The first of these three steps is typically not a scientific activity. On physical scenes crime scene investigators (CSIs) or first responders or some other group — rather than forensics scientists — collect (or bag and tag) the evidence. Contamination of evidence is one of the main concerns and therefore the collectors use specific collection (or acquisition) protocols to the letter. Legal issues (such as authority to collect evidence and questions about jurisdiction) may also play a role, but once again set protocols is followed or a legal expert (rather than a forensic scientist) is consulted.

Some scientific questions may arise. If, for example, it is (or becomes) clear that the container used to collect, say, some chemical or biological material reacts to its contents, it implies that such a container may contaminate such evidence. It then becomes a question of science to find (or develop) a container for which it can be scientifically shown that it will not contaminate the evidence. Similarly, if physical evidence may degrade over time it may be necessary to develop a container that restricts such degradation by, for example, maintaining the proper temperature or by preserving the evidence in some appropriate preservative compound. These are clearly questions for science.

However, in some cases the scientific knowledge, such as the temperature at which evidence will degrade, is already known and it becomes purely a question of engineering to construct a container that (for our example) maintains the appropriate temperature. There may be a question about the type of science involved in this step. The fact that some biological material does not degrade below a certain temperature may be a question of 'pure' biological science, rather than forensic science. However, we do not explore this possible distinction between 'pure' and forensic science further in the current paper.

We claim that, for the current scenario where some search pattern is to be located, acquisition is in principle very similar to physical acquisition. We have known for many years how to image disc drives. We know that we ought to use write blockers to prevent contamination or, if write blockers are not available, to use an operating system that allows the disc to be mounted as a read-only device. In the latter case we may know that it is best to boot that operating system from a read-only medium and to then bag and tag the medium as evidence in case any questions are later raised about the reliability of the operating system regarding not writing to media that are mounted in a read-only mode. We know that we have to calculate some hash (such as MD5 or SHA1) for the content of the original media as well as our evidentiary copies to demonstrate the integrity of our copy.

Note that very little of this process is based on science; most of it is a matter of common sense. Where science does play a role (for example in the integrity claims supported by message digests), that science is also widely used outside the realm of forensic science. Note again that this corresponds with physical forensics. The CSI who collects DNA from a suspect by brushing a swab inside the suspect's mouth to collect some saliva is typically not a scientist with a university degree in science.[2]

Similarly, the officers who collects fingerprints from a crime scene or even the officers who spray Luminol to detect spilled blood are not usually scientists. Note that this does not mean that they may be unqualified or inexperienced — their requirements and experience are just not as scientists and they are not expected to derive scientific truths.

A couple of remarks are in order about the digital forensic acquisition process described in the previous paragraph. Rather than imaging the device the CSI may simply seize the media and send it to the forensic laboratory to be imaged (and then analysed). However, the fact that imaging may occur in the laboratory does not make it a scientific process per se. The process of imaging described above has become known as "dead analysis", with many known shortcomings (such as its impact on business continuity for the entity being investigated). An alternative is so-called "live analysis" (Adelstein, 2006), which will not be explored further in the current paper. However, live analysis (also) desperately needs answers for the questions raised in this paper.

This concludes our discussion of the first step in the scenario described above. In summary, collection or acquisition in this scenario is primarily a technical activity (or craft), rather than a scientific activity.

Although we have distinguished between steps 2 (searching) and 3 (demonstrating presence or absence) above, the distinction does become blurred in many cases. We will, however, for the time being, use this distinction for the sake of exposition. What we do know at this point is that if digital forensics is a science, the science has to be part of step 2 or 3, since it was not present in step 1.

As noted, the second step of the given scenario entails searching for and finding (or not finding) the search pattern. Again we may use physical forensics as a point of departure. Consider an apparent murder case where the (possible) murder weapon needs to be found. It is possible that a knife is still stuck in the victim's body, in which case finding it is trivial and the process of finding it will not be considered forensic science. In a somewhat harder case the investigating officers may find a knife that they think may be the murder weapon in the suspect's home. Much now depends on the characteristics of the knife: Is it bloody? Is it similar to a set of knives from the victim's home and one such knife is missing from the victim's set? Does it have fragments of cloth stuck to it that correspond to the clothes the victim was wearing? Remember that we are assuming that there is some reason why the investigators think that this may be the weapon. If the knife is bloody, matches the set in the victim's house and contains 'obvious' fragments of cloth, the search may be over before the forensics have begun. Forensics will only come into play at step 3, where it needs to be proven that the found knife matches the victim's wound (and/or whatever other matches that may add scientific weight to the claim that the knife was indeed the murder weapon).

However, if there are not such a multitude of indicators that the identified knife is the correct one forensics may begin to play a role much earlier in the search. For example, it may be determined from the wound that a serrated or smooth knife was used; it may be possible to determine the length (and perhaps other measurements of the blade); paint or other traces from the knife may determine its colour, and so on. The investigators can now proceed with a (non-forensic) search based on what they have learnt from the forensic scientists about the weapon they are looking for. Finally, if the murder weapon was some poison, searching for (traces of) it may be a pure forensic exercise.

Our digital forensic scenario requires us to find some specified data on the disc image. Let us now make a sacrilegious claim: In general any tool may be used to search for the data. Of course the tool needs to be suitable for performing the search: if we are looking for a type of file (rather than exact text) we need a tool that is able to search for such files. To illustrate, suppose the investigator copies the image to a hard disc of a computer and then boots the computer from this disc.

Suppose the investigator opens the email application and uses its search fields to find the email messages between the two parties that are of interest. Or suppose we are indeed looking for some pattern; suppose the investigator uses grep or some other pattern matching program to find the required files. And, in any of these cases, suppose the investigators find what they were looking for. Is there any reason to object because 'non-forensic' or 'untrusted' tools have been used? I claim that there ought to be no objection. The claim is based on the assumption that we will during step 3 prove that the search pattern does indeed exist on the medium. Whatever methods we used to locate it are irrelevant.

Objections to these claims may come from multiple sources. Firstly, the notion of using untrusted tools in a regular forensic laboratory is unthinkable. Who knows what such tools may do to the evidence and in what way they may contaminate the evidence. But in the digital world we have the luxury of working with copies of evidence. Even if we destroy a copy we can just make a new copy from our master copy, check the message digests and no harm has been done (besides our time that may have been wasted).

Another objection may be that the non-forensic tool we are using may be 'biased' in some way; for some peculiar reason it may find incriminating evidence, but miss the exculpatory evidence. Say, for example, A emails a ransom note to B and five minutes later emails a note that it was an April fool joke. This behaviour may still be illegal, but these messages may be interpreted very differently depending on whether both or only the first message are discovered. This objection clearly has merit in some cases. However, the sad reality is that in many (possibly most) current digital forensic investigations this makes little difference: In so many current investigations investigators are looking for contraband; if the suspect is guilty hundreds (or more) of examples are typically found. Exculpatory evidence (if it can exist) will have a very different form from what is being searched for.

Say the disc contains many illegal (or unlicensed) MP3 files. Then it does not matter whether we find all of them; yet another MP3 will not serve as exculpatory evidence. Exculpatory evidence may exist in the form of a letter from a copyright holder granting permission to the suspect to copy their MP3 files without licences for, say, research purposes. This letter will typically be produced by the other party to explain the presence of the files. However, our claim that any tool may be used is dangerous when it is necessary to find all occurrences of the data of interest, or if the want to conclude that the data does not occur on the media at all. For such cases we need a tool we can trust; however, even for such cases there is no reason to use non-forensic tools if using them holds some benefit—such as the ability to find at least some occurrences faster than the trusted tool.

The final objection against the use of any tool to be considered may come from those who infer that our untested tool may go outside the boundaries of what we are legally allowed to access. This certainly is not the intention. The proper analogy to use when using these non-forensic tools is not the physical forensic laboratory, but the police officer who searches a room for evidence. This can only be done once an appropriate warrant has been issued and then the search has to be confined to the limits set out in the warrant. If this officer wants to use a flashlight to look into a dark corner of the room, it is ridiculous to require that it has to be a forensically sound flashlight. If the officer wants to read a label on a box that may be accessed and needs reading glasses, there is no need to ensure that they are forensically sound glasses. But when the officer looks into a cupboard that is beyond the limits of the warrant, evidence obtained will be inadmissable (in addition to punitive measures against the officer that should result). So, when using arbitrary tools to search data it is necessary to ensure that the limits of the warrant are respected. In many cases tools (such as grep) are simple enough to restrict to search within limits. Alternatively, the 'forbidden' areas of the disc may be redacted or the allowed areas may be copied to a clean disk. Either option, if executed correctly, will avoid any possible problems.

One practical consequence is this: If the investigator gives a copy of the (redacted) evidence to his or her sysadmin who is a Unix toolset, bash and scripting guru with the request to use his or her ingenuity to find the search pattern, whatever is found ought to be admissible. (This of course assumes that the sysadmin is authorised to access the evidence.) Note again that what the sysadmin does is not science — irrespective of how brilliant the search strategy may be.

We have spent an inordinate amount of space to the simple issue of searching for specific data in some data set. However, my sense is that most current forensic investigations occur in this space and that many who are looking for the science in digital forensic science are looking for it in this space. To illustrate the first point just consider the types of investigations that fit in this category. It includes searching for contraband, deleted logs, entries in the registry that indicate (former) presence of a specific program or device, credit card numbers, IP addresses, events in logs, events or modified files within some time period, fragments of known files and many more. Science may play a role in optimising the search strategies. However, the forensic investigation does not pose any specific requirements.

Therefore it seems inappropriate to consider 'forensic searching' as a relevant problem area for this scenario. Some search algorithms may hold certain benefits for forensics (and quite possibly other fields); for example strategies that yield initial results early in a specific search domain may be beneficial.

However, the requirements change when it is necessary to know that the search pattern does not occur on the disc at all or to find all instances of the search pattern. Similarly, issues arise when there is only sufficient time available to search a fraction of the available data. These cases are revisited after step 3 of the scenario has been considered. Step 3 entails proving that the search pattern exists or (equivalently) revealing the details of the found search pattern (by, for example, revealing the credit card number found if a pattern conforming to a credit card number was used as search pattern). In its first form the requirement is clearly that a decision problem has to be answered: Does the given search pattern occur on the disc? Decision problems are well known from the field of algorithmics (Harel, 1992) (or computational complexity). And, from that same field we know the second formulation above is computationally equivalent to the decision problem. And thus we find ourselves with a problem for which a solid theoretical framework exists and can be answered in a scientific manner. In the scenario under discussion the question about the presence of the search pattern may be answered positively in an incontrovertible manner by simply pointing to where the data occurs on the image. Formulated in its current form the problem is tractable and answerable in absolute terms. The error rate is 0%. The forensic scientist can answer this question with absolute scientific certainty in the witness box.

If scenario 1 deals with the possession of contraband, finding contraband on the disc allows the prosecution to introduce the disc image as evidence. If contraband has not been found it is possible to simply not introduce that disc as evidence. However, the defence is potentially faced with a bigger challenge: they want to prove that no contraband occurs on the disc (or any other disc either). Suppose that the message digests of files containing contraband are known. Then they simply have to compute the message digests of all the files on the disc and show that none of those digests corresponds with any of the contraband digests. This is again clearly a decision problem. However, this pushes the 'burden of proof' to step 2 of the scenario and there is no step 3 where one can simply point to the fact that nothing has been found. Ideally the defence needs to know that their search algorithm is correct and that the search problem itself is tractable. The issue of correctness may again be addressed from the perspective of algorithmics where the algorithm is formally proven correct (and where the accu-

racy of the algorithm is therefore 100%).3 A less desirable alternative is where trust develops in a certain search tool where opposing parties use it (and other tools) over many years and nobody finds any contraband missed by the other party. However, this only becomes scientific at the point where one can move from mere induction ('it has worked thus far and will therefore probably work in the next case as well') to where one may express one's confidence in the tool in scientific terms. Formal testing of the tool seems useful in this regard.

In addition to correctness the defence in our example ideally wants the search problem to be tractable (or even if it is tractable in general, they want the answer to be available before it is needed — for testimony in court, for example). As indicated by Cohen (2012) the field of computational complexity may provide us with the answer to the dilemma of whether it is even worth starting the computation. However, there may be another alternative available: a probabilistic algorithm may provide an answer that is correct with a given certainty. Executing the probabilistic algorithm repeatedly increases the certainty (or finds a counterexample). If the problem is intractable, probabilistic algorithms may provide us with a scientific answer with a quantifiable error rate. Even if the problem is tractable but requires more time than is available, it may be possible to use a much simpler probabilistic algorithm and run it repeatedly. This will again yield a scientifically valid answer with a quantified probability of being incorrect.

This, at long last, brings us to the end of scenario 1 that set out to locate or prove the absence of some data on a disc image in a scientific manner. We now turn our attention to just one other scenario that illustrates a different case where the craft may be turned into science.

Scenario 2 deals with file carving. File systems organise files in blocks, sectors, clusters or some other units (henceforth just referred to as blocks). Files typically consist of multiple blocks that are linked together using metadata. If these links are destroyed the file is effectively lost even though the file contents may physically still be present on the disc.

The links may be lost because of an attack or some accident. It is, for example, possible that a user deletes a file because it is no longer deemed necessary. Deleting the file typically deletes the links, but not the block contents. If it turns out that the information in such a deleted or lost file is important the question arises whether the blocks can be reassembled into the initial file. Such reassembly is known as file carving. Note that while the blocks are unlinked some of them may be reused for other files; therefore it is sometimes at best possible to carve a partial file.

Obviously file carving requires deep knowledge of the details of file systems. The carver needs to know how the metadata links blocks together in the specific file system as well as the other minutiae of the file system. In addition the carver needs to know the details of the file formats of the files being carved to recognise neighbouring blocks. In essence the carver is solving a jigsaw puzzle that has many extraneous pieces and where a few required pieces may be missing.

Now suppose that the carved file is used as evidence in a court case. Does the carver have scientific grounds to claim that the file has been reconstructed correctly? An intuitive answer may be that the mere fact that, say, a JPEG file that has been reconstructed from blocks scattered over a disc now successfully opens in an image viewer is sufficient evidence that reconstruction was done correctly. It seems just too improbable that a file with an incorrect block somewhere will still 'work'. But suppose the disc contained several versions of a given file with only minor differences between the versions. Is it not then possible that the reconstructed file may contain blocks from different versions forming a carved file that never existed in that exact form? And can it be guaranteed that there are no other situations where a combination of inappropriate blocks may seem like a valid file?

A somewhat different approach is to ask what can be said about the reconstructed file that is scientifically true (and hence truly forensic science). One example is the question whether the reconstructed file conforms to the expected format. File formats are often specified using some formal notation, such as a grammar. If not, it is in many cases possible to create a grammar-based specification from whatever specification exists—possibly even from reverse engineering an authoritative piece of software that creates such files. The notion of syntax checking is well understood from the field of compiler construction. The question whether the reconstructed file is syntactically correct is therefore one example of a question that may be phrased as a decision problem and answered in a scientific manner.

Many other properties may be checked in this manner. If certain values in a file are expected to have some relationship to one another this may be verified. The time stamps in a log file, for example, are supposed to be ordered according to time. In some (rare) cases it may be possible to show that no other blocks on the disc can possibly be part of a file of the given type. It may be possible to show that the blocks in the carved file are arranged on disc in a manner consistent with the block allocation strategy used by the operating system. It may be possible to allocate all blocks on the disc to files that are all syntactically, semantically and positionally correct. It may be possible to test all permutations of blocks (possibly after filtering those out that cannot possibly form part of the given file type) and show that the reconstructed file is the only permutation starting from some block that yields a syntactically valid file. Based on these scientific facts the expert may then offer a professional opinion about the correctness of the reconstructed file.

The opinion may take into account the complexity of the format, the consistency of the reconstructed file with other available information and other attributes of the file the professional may deem relevant. It is important to distinguish between science and opinion though. Different forensic scientists should arrive at the same scientific answers to questions that can be answered by forensic science. If their opinions differ, so be it. They are opinions after all, and should have less evidentiary weight than scientific facts. However, note that if it can be shown that an opinion is inconsistent with facts, that opinion is refuted.

Note that this second scenario conveniently ignored the fact that many real programs do not faithfully implement file format standards. It is therefore possible that an original file may not pass the syntax check — and if such a file is reconstructed correctly it should fail the syntax check. However, this may possibly be addressed by not only using de jure specifications, but also de facto specifications. We ignore this issue in the remainder of the paper.

To conclude note that this distinction between fact and opinion is also present in traditional (physical) forensic science. The DNA scientist cannot 'place' a person at a crime scene. The scientist can state as a scientific fact that, say, a hair and some saliva come from the same donor. The additional (non-scientific) information that the hair was found at the crime scene and the saliva sample was obtained from the suspect (as well as some convincing argument that there is no other logical explanation for the suspect's hair to be at the crime scene) is required to be certain that the suspect was indeed at the crime scene.

DIGITAL FORENSIC SCIENCE

The two scenarios discussed earlier in this paper show that decision problems may indeed provide the scientific basis for digital forensics for some cases; in such cases decision problems may be used to distinguish between forensic science and expert opinion. Those two scenarios are insufficient to claim that decision problems can be used as the underlying theoretical base of all of digital forensic science. However, it is a strategy that seems worth exploring. As Garfinkel (2010) points out, locating

incriminating information (such as contraband) in large datasets was the original challenge for digital forensics and the field needs to urgently cast its net wider to remain relevant. A digital forensic science based on decision problems (and the accompanying algorithmics or complexity theory) provides much scope for forensics to develop beyond its current state. Garfinkel's identification of the original challenge of digital forensics coincides with scenario 1 provided earlier in this paper. Much of digital forensics was originated by finding ways of solving crimes (or finding digital evidence) that may be useful to address such crimes. If we decide that decision problems underly digital forensics it also becomes possible to develop digital forensic science from the top down by determining what can and what cannot be proven by viewing the extensive body of knowledge about tractable and intractable problems from this new perspective.[4]

An initial argument that decision problems should form the basis of digital forensic science may read as follows. Many (or most) digital forensic investigators will be comfortable with characterising the examination process as a set of hypotheses that are tested and then rejected or not rejected.[5] The work by Carrier (2006) is a seminal text that frames digital forensics using hypothesis testing. The idea of using decision problems and determining the answers they yield (or concluding that they cannot be answered) appear rather similar to hypothesis testing. Hypothesis testing, however, typically assumes natural variation and testing a hypothesis is about determining whether minute differences between an observation and an ideal value may be ascribed to this natural variation. Digital data, on the other hand, being discrete, does not display such natural variation. The millions of statements produced by a bank on a monthly basis are not a little wrong each month because of natural variation. If the statement is not exactly correct it is because something is amiss. Natural variation may be introduced in a digital system because of external physical influences.

The time that data needs to traverse a network is one such example; this may result in a natural variation between times recorded in a log at the transmitter and times recorded for the same messages at the receiver. However, it is not clear that these differences are indeed natural. The digital realm is one that is inherently artificial. Users can influence congestion on the network and hence the differences in times. In fact, such times are often affected by multiple natural and artificial causes that make it impractical to measure a given characteristic and associate it with scientific accuracy with some specific cause or condition.

Decision problems may therefore fit digital data better than hypothesis testing would for forensic purposes. Note that decision problems, just like hypotheses, do not prescribe how an examination should be conducted, but clearly delineates what may be offered as evidence. An 'accepted' hypothesis makes a truth claim — as does a decision problem that has been decided.

The remainder of this section reviews the (well known) classes into which decision problems fall (Harel, 1992). The intention is twofold. Firstly, it shows how much of the field remains unexplored from a forensic perspective and therefore indicates a direction into which future forensic research may grow. It also shows how error rates naturally become an issue when decision problems become more complex. This potentially lends some credibility for a forensic investigator who claims 100% accuracy for a result based on a simple decision problem (relative to a whole field of varying complexity where error rates are no longer zero).

In general decision problems fall in one of four categories: they are decidable in polynomial time, probabilistically decidable in polynomial time, intractable or undecidable. The second category in this list gives us our first glimpse of what error rates may mean in the context of decidable digital forensics. We return to this topic below. When the question of interest is polynomially decidable there is no inherent need to quantify error rates. However, even polynomial time algorithms may

sometimes be too 'expensive': to search a petabyte of information in O(n) at 1 megabyte per second will take just over 30 years. A probabilistic algorithm that does not sample every byte of the petabyte and that yields a result that is reliable enough but terminates within some reasonable time will be preferable over the absolutely correct O(n) algorithm. In general, given the large data sets that digital forensics often has to deal with, it may be necessary to approximate the algorithm with an even faster one (one that, for example, only uses a fraction of the n inputs) if the results of the probabilistic algorithm are correct enough—that is, if the error rate can be quantified and it is deemed small enough to sufficiently substantiate the claim that it supports.

Probabilistic algorithms (also known as randomised algorithms) are algorithms that use a random number to determine their behaviour. The type of probabilistic algorithm alluded to above is a Monte Carlo algorithm — one that always terminates in polynomial time and produces an answer with a known error rate. Monte Carlo algorithms may be true biased, false-biased, or unbiased. When a true-biased algorithm returns true the answer to the problem is indeed true, which is often written as yes. When it returns false (or no), however, it may be wrong with some known (small) probability. The converse is true for false-biased algorithms. Unbiased algorithms may yield incorrect results (with some small probability) when they return either true or false. Monte Carlo algorithms are deigned such that the random number determines the execution of the algorithms, such that one execution of the algorithm is independent from the next and the probability of error from two executions of the algorithm are then the product of the probability of error during a single execution. To reach a particular level of certainty it is necessary to repeat the execution of the algorithm a sufficient number of times so that the combined error is small enough. Note that, if a true-biased algorithm returns yes during any execution, the final answer is true. It is only when it repeatedly returns no that the answer is no with a probability of error en, where e is the probability of error for a single execution and n is the number of executions. The same applies to false-biased algorithms, except that a no result is certain and a yes result is reached with a margin of error. We do not consider two-sided errors further in the current paper.

The class of problems that are solvable by probabilistic algorithms are known as the bounded-error probabilistic polynomial (BPP) class of problems. Let P (as usual) denote the class of problems that are solvable in polynomial time. Then we contend that probabilistic algorithms are indicated for any problems in BPP .. P. (Note that is is possible — and many indeed conjecture — that BPP = P.) As noted, Probabilistic algorithms may also be useful for problem in P, where available time simply does not allow execution of an exhaustive algorithm, even though it may be tractable.

ALTERNATIVE PERSPECTIVES ON ERROR RATES AND DIGITAL FORENSIC SCIENCE

As noted earlier, others have proposed strategies to deal with accuracy (or known error rates) of digital evidence. Cohen (2012), for example, notes that the error rates of CPUs are known and suggests that this may be used to quantify the accuracy of digital evidence.

However, such random CPU errors do not necessarily translate to specific error rates in digital evidence. In many cases data is, for example, subjected to error checks (such as integrity checks in databases, digitally signed messages, ordinary parity checks for memory, and so on). Some errors may cause a program to crash, rather than produce incorrect results.

Yet other errors may be inconsequential—such as when the colour of a single pixel on a screen is somewhat wrong. The fact is that such errors are extremely rare and of the few that occur, many will have no impact on evidence that is collected.

If it does affect the evidence it is possible that it may affect it in such a way that it is obvious that something is wrong. Once all of this is taken into account it is easy to see that errors may occur, but that this will occur so rarely that it is safe to ignore the possibility. However, with all these factor impacting on the error rates it becomes impossible to quantify the known error rates of our forensic techniques.

An earlier approach to describe (rather than quantify) error rates is Casey's certainty scale. It, for example, postulates that an event that has been logged in two independent logs may be accepted as fact with more certainty than an event only logged in one log (but this certainty will still be very low if the two logs are not properly secured). While this makes sense, it is not a scientific truth. An event logged in a number of highly secure, independent logs may lead to a high level of certainty that it really occurred. But it is possible that the administrators of all those systems colluded and entered a fake entry in all the logs. In contrast, an event logged in a single, unreliable log may indeed have occurred.

The higher degree of certainty is based—at least in part—on the assumption that a group of trusted individuals associated with independent systems will very rarely collude. While this is probably true, the average digital forensic scientist is not qualified to testify about human nature—and questions of human nature should arguably not be part of the domain of digital forensics. In any case, it seems unlikely that even a social scientist will be able to accurately estimate this probability. This does not mean that Casey's certainty scale is useless; it does mean that the certainty scale may be unsuitable to derive scientific facts. It may be very useful for an expert to express an opinion once the scientific facts have been determined.

Finally, Garfinkel et al (2009) emphasise the ability to independently verify test results as the hallmark of science and encourage the development of standardised corpora that may be used for independent testing (and provide some such corpora).

CONCLUSION

This paper identified a possible basis to ensure that digital forensics is indeed scientific, namely decision problems from the field of algorithmics. It illustrated that decision problems may indeed be useful for some investigative problems.

Decision problems also help to talk about facets of science such as truth and error rates. It provides a possible explanation for why it is currently hard to talk about such issues, because current research has only scratched the surface of this domain (once such research is rephrased in terms of decision problems).

Decision problems may be helpful to guide the construction of digital forensic tools that can be certified as reliable. Much remains to be done. Many other investigative scenarios need to be considered to determine whether decision problems form an appropriate solution, or whether there are better options to obtain scientifically valid evidence for such scenarios. Decision problems also potentially delimit the scope of digital forensics and delineation is often a source of contention. Do authorship attribution (Juola, 2006) and source camera identification (Olivier, 2008), for example, still form part of digital forensics or are they really about human and physical attributes that just happen to be represented in a digital format, but may just as well have been presented in a non-digital manner? If the proposal contained in this paper is accepted as a viable option by the digital forensics community only time will provide definitive answers to these latter questions.

ACKNOWLEDGMENT

The author would like to thank Stefan Gruner for providing some valuable insights after reading an earlier draft of this paper and Candice le Sueur for proofreading an almost final version of the paper. The author obviously remains responsible for any errors or inaccuracies that remain.

REFERENCES

Adelstein, F. (2006). Live forensics: Diagnosing your system without killing it first. *Communications of the ACM*, *49*(2), 63–66. doi:10.1145/1113034.1113070

Bunge, M. (1998). *Philosophy of Science: From Problem to Theory* (Vol. 1). Transaction Publishers.

Caloyannides, M. A. (2006). *Digital "Evidence" is Often Evidence of Nothing*. IGI Global.

Carrier, B. D. (2006). *A Hypothesis-based Approach to Digital Forensic Investigations*. (PhD thesis). Purdue University.

Cohen, F. (2012). *Digital Forensic Evidence Examination* (3rd ed.). Fred Cohen & Associates.

Furedy, J. J. (1966). The North American polygraph and psychophysiology: Disinterested, uninterested, and interested perspectives. *International Journal of Psychophysiology*, *21*, 97–105. doi:10.1016/0167-8760(96)00003-7 PMID:8792199

Garfinkel, S., Farrell, P., Roussev, V., & Dinolt, G. (2009). Bringing science to digital forensics with standardized forensic corpora. *Digital Investigation*, *6*, S2–S11. doi:10.1016/j.diin.2009.06.016

Garfinkel, S. L. (2010). Digital forensics research: The next 10 years. *Digital Investigation*, *7*(Supplement), S64–S73. doi:10.1016/j.diin.2010.05.009

Giannelli, P. C. (2007). *Wrongful convictions and forensic science: The need to regulate crime labs* (Working Paper 08-02). Case Western Reserve University.

Golan, T. (2007). *Laws of Men and Laws of Nature: The History of Scientific Expert Testimony in England and America*. Harvard University Press.

Gruner, S. (2010). Software engineering between technics and science — Recent discussions about the foundations and the scientificness of a rising discipline. *Journal for General Philosophy of Science*, *41*, 237–260. doi:10.1007/s10838-010-9116-y

Harel, D. (1992). *Algorithmics: The Spirit of Computing* (2nd ed.). Pearson Education.

Hofstadter, D. R. (1979). *Gödel, Escher, Bach: An Eternal Golden Braid*. Harvester Press.

Juola, P. (2006). Authorship attribution. In Foundations and Trends in Information Retrieval. Academic Press.

Koppl, R., & Ferraro, M. M. (2012). Digital devices and miscarriages of justice. *The Dayly Caller*. Retrieved from http://dailycaller.com/2012/06/15/digital-devices-and-miscarriages-of-justice/

Kuhn, T. S. (1996). *The Structure of Scientific Revolutions* (3rd ed.). University of Chicago Press. doi:10.7208/chicago/9780226458106.001.0001

Olivier, M. S. (2008). Using sensor dirt for toolmark analysis of digital photographs. In I. Ray, & S. Shenoi (Eds.), *Advances in Digital Forensics IV* (pp. 193–206). Springer. doi:10.1007/978-0-387-84927-0_16

Saks, M. J., & Faigman, D. L. (2008). Failed forensics: How forensic science lost its way and how it may yet find it. *Annual Review of Law and Social Science*, *4*, 149–171. doi:10.1146/annurev.lawsocsci.4.110707.172303

Smeaton, J. (1837). *Reports of the late John Smeaton, F.R.S., made on various occasions, in the course of his employment as a civil engineer* (2nd ed., Vol. 2). M. Taylor. doi:10.1680/rotljs-movoitcoheaace2ev1.51959

U.S. Supreme Court. (1993). Daubert v. Merrell Dow Pharmaceuticals, inc., 509 U.S. 579 (1993). Technical Report 92–102, Certiorari to the United Sstates Court of Appeals for the Ninth Ccircuit.

ADDITIONAL READING

Casey, E., Evidence, D., Crime, C., & Science, F. Computers, and the Internet, Third Edition, Academic Press, 2011. (This book is considered by many to be the standard reference work in digital forensics.)

Gratzer, W. (2000). *The Undergrowth of Science: Delusion, Self-Deception and Human Frailty*. Oxford University Press.

National Research Council. (2009). *Strengthening Forensic Science in the United States: A Path Forward*. Washington, DC: The National Academies Press.

NIST. Forensic Sciences, http://nist.gov/forensics/ - a portal that summarises the US response to the National Academies report

The Scientific Working Group on Digital Evidence (SWGDE). https://www.swgde.org/

The series of books on digital forensics published by Elsevier under the Syngress imprint, such as John Sammons, The Basics of Digital Forensics: The Primer for Getting Started in Digital Forensics, Syngress, 2012. (The books in this series are relatively short and allows one to obtain a thorough introductory overview of a specific area of interest.)

KEY TERMS AND DEFINITIONS

Digital Forensics: The applied science that studies the extraction of evidence that occur in digital form such that it may help to establish the root cause of an event.

Decision Problems: Problems that ask whether a particular claim is true or not - in particular problems of a computational nature where the veracity of the claim may, in principle, be determined algorithmically. (Note that some decision problems are too complex to solve in a reasonable time, while some others cannot be solved algorithmically, even though they may seem simple to solve.)

ENDNOTES

1   Note that many branches of computing combine craft and science and that a need to distinguish between craft and science — or even between art, craft, technics, engineering and science — becomes necessary. See the paper by Gruner [11] about the nature of this discourse in the software engineering discipline as an example.

2   As an example, to be formally recognised as a professional, candidate or certified natural scientist in South Africa a person has to meet the requirements specified by Act 27 of 2003 (Natural Scientific Professions Act, 2003); this act establishes the South African Council for Natural Scientific Professions which is responsible for registration of scientists who meet the prescribed requirements. In general a four year degree followed by three years of professional experience—or a higher degree followed by a shorter period of professional experience— is required to register as a professional natural scientist.

3   Note that correctness of the algorithm does not ensure correctness of the program; a simple option is to use multiple independent tools in parallel with the (probably valid) assumption that these independent programs will not contain coding errors that let them all fail in the same manner. However, this brings us back to an assumption, rather than a scientific fact. A deeper review of the field of software correctness is required than what can justifiably be provided here to be certain that the tool is correct.

4   Note that Garfinkel's plea for an extension of digital forensics refers primarily to the extension of technology used for digital forensics — that is, to digital forensic craft rather than digital forensic science.

5   Note that the mere use of hypotesis testing (outside a body of theory) would not be sufficient to make an activity scientific. For more details see [2, Chapter 5].

Chapter 13
Transform Domain Techniques for Image Steganography

Siddharth Singh
University of Allahabad, India

Tanveer J. Siddiqui
University of Allahabad, India

ABSTRACT

Recent advancement of multimedia technology has posed serious challenges to copyright protection, ownership, and integrity of digital data. This has made information security techniques a vital issue. Cryptography, Steganography, and Watermarking are three major techniques for securing information and ensuring copyright ownership. This chapter presents an overview of transform domain techniques for image steganography. The authors discuss the characteristics and applications of image steganography and briefly review Discrete Cosine and Wavelet transform-based image steganography techniques. They also discuss the various metrics that have been used to assess the performance of steganography techniques and shed light on the future of steganography.

INTRODUCTION

Steganography techniques were invented as a quest of human desire for communicating secret information. The term steganography refers to covered communication. Secret communication plays an important role in diplomacy and wars. Hence devising ways for secret communication has ever been fascinating. Codes and ciphers, invisible inks, wax coated wooden tablets, physical objects have been used thousands of years ago to communicate secret information. The oldest example of steganography is traced back to around 400 BC in the Greek history. The word steganography has been derived from the Greek words *steganos* (covered or secret) and *graphein* (writing) which

literally means "covered writing". In the "Histories of Herodotus" (1996), Herodotus reports an interesting story of Greek ruler Histiaeus. In order to inform his friends that it was time to begin a revolt against Mededs and Persians he tattooed a message on the shaved head of a slave. He waited till his hair grew back, and then sent him. The message reached to the intended recipients and the revolt was successful. Of course it took longer time, unlike emails, to grow hair back and to travel to the destination. Since then revolutionary changes have been occurred in the world of communication. We are now living in the digital era leading to enormous amount of digital content of various modalities. This has added new dimensions and brought new challenges to information security.

DOI: 10.4018/978-1-4666-6158-5.ch013

In particular, this poses serious challenges to copyright protection, ownership and integrity of digital data. This has made information security an emerging area of research. New applications have been emerged, new techniques have been invented and old techniques have undergone a sea change.

Cryptography, Steganography and Watermarking are the three main techniques used for securing information and ensuring copyright ownership. These techniques are closely related, have a great deal of overlap and share many technical approaches (Fridrich, 2010). However, there are fundamental differences. Cryptography secures data by scrambling it that it can not be understood by unintended recipient even if it is detected. The message is encrypted but its existence is not hidden.

Steganography is an art of hidden communication in which a secret message is communicated by hiding it in a cover file so that the very existence of the secret message is not detectable.

Watermarking is closely related to steganography, but in watermarking the hidden information is usually related to the cover object. Hence it is mainly used for copyright protection and owner authentication. Unlike steganography, watermarks do not always need to be hidden. Both visible and invisible watermarks are in use. In steganography the hidden data is important whereas in watermarking there is no problem even if an invisible watermark is detected. However, watermarking system requires resistance against removal. The fundamental difference between steganography and watermarking is that "the information hidden by a watermarking system is always associated to the digital object to be protected or to its owner while steganographic systems just hide any information (Katzenbeisser et al., 2000)". However, the use of invisible watermarking is blurring the distinction between steganography and watermarking at least at the level of technique. In invisible watermarking, watermark may be in the form of steganography where a party communicates secret message to another party. Like steganography, invisible watermarking requires that it should be nearly impossible for someone to guess that an image has been watermarked. Despite of obvious differences between watermarking and steganography techniques there are a lot of commonality and many of the watermarking techniques can be applied in steganography and vice versa. It is not possible to cover all these techniques in a single chapter. In this chapter, we limit our discussion to steganographic techniques. However, due to inherent commonalities between steganography and watermarking we will refer watermarking techniques as well.

As noted earlier steganography was in existence from ancient time. With newer development the slaves head and carved messages have been replaced by the digital content (cover media and embedded message). The cover media can be image, audio or video; the most commonly being the image files because of many reasons: (1) Digital images are being used quite frequently on the internet. (2) The size of image is large. (3) Digital images usually contain redundant bits. So, we can hide large amount of data in a digital image without being suspected by human visual system. The commonly used image file formats which are used for steganography are graphic interchange format (GIF), Joint Photographic Expert Group (JPEG) and bitmap format (BMP). We restrict the scope of this chapter to transform domain image steganography techniques only.

The message can be embedded directly in the cover image or in the transform domain. In this chapter, we will review transform domain techniques of digital image steganography. An extensive survey of digital image steganography can be found in (Cheddad et al., 2010).

The rest of the chapter is organized as follows:

In the next section, we introduce the basic concepts and major issues involved in steganography and discuss some of its applications. We then discuss various steganography techniques and classify them. We will focus on discrete cosine transform and wavelet transform based techniques. In the next section, we shed light on future of steganography. Finally, the chapter closes with conclusion.

PRELIMINARIES

Basic Framework

Figure 1 depicts a general framework for Image steganography. Any steganography system comprises of two main stages: embedding and recovery. During embedding, the sender first selects a cover image. It may be an image, a speech, or some text file. The most popular cover objects are image files. The secret message is embedded into the cover file using a secret key, called stego-key, to produce a stego file. The stego-file is transmitted through open channel to the receiver side. At the receiving end, the extraction process takes the stego file and using the stego-key applies the inverse algorithm to extract the hidden message (Johnson & Jajodia, 1998).

CHARACTERISTICS OF STEGANOGRAPHIC SYSTEM

The mere purpose of the steganography is to communicate secret information without inviting suspicions. In order to achieve this goal the first and foremost requirement is that hiding should not create any visible distortion, a property known as imperceptibility. Other key requirements include security and robustness. In the following lines we try to elaborate these concepts.

- **Imperceptibility:** The data hidden in host file has to be undetectable. This is only possible if the embedding does not cause any visible change in the stego image. If embedding creates visible distortion then any one can guess that the host image has been modified. This defeats the mere purpose of steganography. Hence, imperceptibility becomes an important criterion to measure the performance of any steganographic system.
- **Security:** Steganographic system requires high degree of security. The security of a steganographic system lies in the inability of an eavesdropper to distinguish cover image from stego image.
- **Robustness:** Robustness refers to the capability of hidden data to survive both intentional manipulation which aim to destroy the hidden information and unintentional manipulation, which do not aim to remove the hidden data.

STEGANOGRAPHY APPLICATIONS

Image steganography has been used for numerous applications like copyright protection, secure data hiding, ownership authentication, visible logo watermark for broadcasting, and medical imaging applications. We discuss few of the popular steganography applications here:

Figure 1. A general framework for image steganography

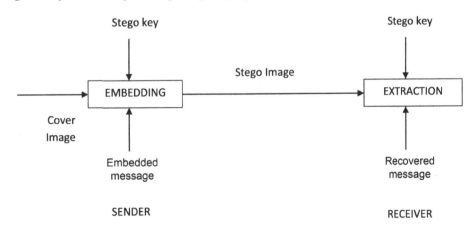

- **Copyright Protection:** Its main objective is to control access and stop illegal copying of data. This can be achieved by embedding a digital logo in the cover file extracted by comparing the stego file with the cover file. The printing and publishing industries use copyright protection for ownership identification as well.

- **Copy Control:** Copy control is required to prevent illegal reproduction of films, music, and other media. Steganography has found useful applications in copy control, particularly for audio data wherein serial number or author ID is secretly hidden in the media. If unlawful copies are found, then owner can trace the origin of the illegal copies.

- **Content Authentication:** Content authentication is required to certify that no tampering with data has been done. The conventional means of authentication was in the form of handwritten signature on document. Since signature is attached to document, it is difficult to change or modify to another document. A digital signature show robust authentication. There are several steganography applications related to authentication such as video surveillance (Bartolini et al., 2001), remote sensing applications, digital insurance claim evidence and digital right management.

- **TV Broadcasting:** Visible watermark logos are appropriate method for TV broadcast monitoring. Steganography can be easily used to insert visible watermark within the image. While, inserting the verification code is very complex as compared to the scrambling where the code is placed in the header file. Also, it degrades the perceptual quality of the image.

- **Medical Imaging Applications:** Protection of the integrity and confidentiality of the medical images and storage of electronic patient record (EPR) in the medical image is an important issue in medical applications such as tele-diagnosis. In recent years, researchers have used steganography techniques for secure transmission of medical records (Ulutas et al., 2011). In (Srinivasan et al., 2004) Bit-Plane Complexity Segmentation (BPCS) Steganography has been used to hide medical records in color cervical images. Lou et al. (2009) also used steganographic technique to hide EPR data into medical image.

PERFORMANCE METRICS

A number of performance metric have been used to assess the quality of the generated stego image with respect to original image and the extracted message. The most widely used metrics include: PSNR (Peak Signal to Noise Ratio), Universal Image Quality Index, SSIM (Structural Similarity Index Measure), CC (Correlation Coefficient), BER (Bit Error rate). In this section, we will discuss these metrics for image steganography.

Peak Signal-to-Noise Ratio

Peak Signal-to-Noise Ratio (PSNR) is one of the most commonly used performance metric to measure perceptual quality of images. PSNR is the ratio between the maximum value of a signal and the magnitude of background noise. It is calculated in decibel. The globally accepted PSNR value for good picture quality is > 40db (Cheddad et al., 2010, Atawneh et al., 2013). PSNR is defined as:

$$PSNR = 10 \log_{10} \left(\frac{L^2}{MSE} \right) \quad (1)$$

where, L is the peak signal value of the image i.e. L=255 for 8 bit gray scale image. Mean Square Error (*MSE*) between the original image I of size M × N and the stego image I_S is calculated as follows:

$$MSE = \frac{1}{MN}\left[\sum_{i=1}^{M}\sum_{j=1}^{N}\left(I(i,j) - I_s(i,j)\right)^2\right] \quad (2)$$

PSNR has been widely used in steganographic application to measure the perceptual quality of stego image with respect to the original image (Cheddad et al., 2010).

Universal Image Quality Index

The universal image quality index (Q) was investigated by Wang et al. (2002) for human visual system model. The dynamic range is [0, 1]. Higher value signifies better image quality. It is expressed as follows (Wang et al. 2002):

$$Q = \frac{4\sigma_{xy}\overline{xy}\left((\overline{x})^2 + (\overline{y})^2\right)^{-1}}{\left(\sigma_x^2 + \sigma_y^2\right)} \quad (3)$$

where $\overline{x}$, $\overline{y}$ are mean value of original image I and stego image $\left(I_s\right)$, σ_x, σ_y and σ_{xy} are variance of I and I_s and the cross variance of I and I_s respectively.

Structural Similarity Index Measure

The Structural Similarity Index Measure (SSIM) measures the similarity in the structure of two images. The visual quality of the stego image with respect to the original image can be measured in terms of SSIM. The structural similarity value lie between [-1, 1]. A value close to 1 indicates higher similarity. It is mathematically expressed as follows (Wang, 2004):

$$SSIM(I,I_s) = \frac{(2\mu_i\mu_{i_s} + C_1)(2\sigma_{ii_s} + C_2)}{(\mu_i^2 + \mu_{i_s}^2 + C_1)(\sigma_i^2 + \sigma_{i_s}^2 + C_2)} \quad (4)$$

where μ_i, μ_{i_s}, σ_i, σ_{i_s} and σ_{ii_s} are mean of i and i_s, variance of i and i_s and the covariance of i and i_S respectively. C_1, C_2 are constants.

Correlation Coefficient

The correlation coefficient (*CC*) is used to measure the similarity between embedded message (e.g., a logo image $\left(I_o\right)$) and the recovered message $\left(I_r\right)$ of size $M \times N$. The value lies in the range [0, 1]. It is defined as follows:

$$CC = \frac{\sum_{i=1}^{M}\sum_{j=1}^{N}(I_o(i,j) - \overline{I}_r)(I_r(i,j) - \overline{I}_r)}{\sqrt{\sum_{i=1}^{M}\sum_{j=1}^{N}(I_o(i,j) - \overline{I}_o)^2}\sqrt{\sum_{i=1}^{M}\sum_{j=1}^{N}(I_r(i,j) - \overline{I}_r)^2}} \quad (5)$$

where $\overline{I}_o$, $\overline{I}_r$ are mean of original and recovered logo image.

Bit Error Rate

The Bit error rate (BER) evaluates the difference between original and the recovered logo image. It is the ratio of the number of erroneous detected bits to the total number of original message bits (Hsieh et al.2011).

$$BER = \frac{\text{No. of erroneous recovered message bits}}{\text{total no. of original message bits}} \quad (6)$$

IMAGE STEGANOGRAPHY TECHNIQUES

A number of image steganographic methods have been proposed in literature. They differ on choice of cover media, recovery method and embedding domain. On the basis of cover object being used we can categorize them into text, image, audio and video steganography. Some authors have included protocol steganography and 3 D steganography as well in this categorization (Atawneh et al., 2013). On the basis of recovery method we can categorize a steganographic technique into three categories: blind, semi-blind and non-blind. In blind recovery, the cover image is not required for recovery. In semi-blind techniques some features of the cover object are required for recovery. The non-blind techniques require the original cover object to recover the hidden information.

Yet another classification is based on embedding domain wherein we can identify two broad categories: spatial domain techniques and transform domain techniques. Cheddad et al. (2010) considered adaptive techniques as a special case and classified existing techniques into spatial domain techniques, transform domain techniques and adaptive techniques. Adaptive techniques attempt to model the characteristics of the cover image and can be applied in both spatial and transform domain.

SPATIAL DOMAIN TECHNIQUES

In spatial domain approaches, the cover image is divided into bit planes and secret message bits are embedded directly by substituting the bits of the cover image. This method is computationally simple, straight forward and has large embedding capacity. Least significant bit (LSB) substitutions, Patchwork, Bit plane complexity segmentation and quantization index modulation are important spatial domain techniques. Among all these techniques, LSB substitution is most popular. It involves random selection of a pixel of the cover image and replacement of its LSB with a message bit. This process is repeated until all data bits are inserted. LSB retains the image quality, as the changes in the values of LSBs during embedding will have least effect on stego image quality.

Patchwork technique is also used for embedding a message in cover image as in Johnson & Jajodia (1998). They used a pseudo random generator to select two patches, A and B. Patch A pixels are lightened whereas patch B pixels are darkened. The changes of contrast in corresponding patches encodes one bit of embedding. The disadvantage of this method is that it has low embedding capacity. The advantage of this technique is that the secret image is spread over the whole cover image, even if one patch is damaged, the other will persist. This method is not dependent on cover image and is more robust against JPEG compression operation.

Bit plane complexity segmentation (BPCS) steganography is based on bit plane decomposition and the properties of human vision system introduced by Niimi et al. (1998). BPCS are used for larger bit plane for data hiding. In this method, every block is divided into bit plane. The decomposed bit plane is evaluated according to complexity and threshold value block is classified into informative and noisy region . It offers large embedding capacity and imperceptibility than conventional LSB substitution methods (Saha et al., 2012).

In general, spatial domain steganography techniques are less robust against common image processing attacks as compared to transform domain.

TRANSFORM DOMAIN TECHNIQUES

Transform domain steganography techniques embed secret message in significant areas of cover media. These techniques are generally more robust to common image processing operations than LSB substitution techniques. Moreover, the information hidden in cover media using transform domain techniques remains imperceptible to human eye. Most of the existing robust steganographic systems are based on transform domain (Provos & Honeyman, 2011; Westfeld, 2001). Various transforms that have been used include Discrete Fourier Transform (DFT), Discrete Cosine Transform (DCT) and Wavelet Transform (WT).

DISCRETE COSINE TRANSFORM DOMAIN TECHNIQUES

In early days, DCT was widely used by international data compression standards such as JPEG and MPEG file format. The use of DCT technique to hide information in digital media was introduced by Koch & Zhao (1995) and Cox et al. (1997).

DCT domain techniques provide better PSNR (Peak Signal-to-noise ratio), smaller BER (Bit Error Rate), good information integrity and low computational complexity. It is a real domain transform which represents an image as coefficient of different frequencies of cosine which is basis vector for this transform. It can separate image into high (f_h), middle(f_m) and low frequency (f_l) components as shown in Figure 2.

Two-dimensional discrete cosine transformation of input image I of size $N \times N$ is defined as (Amin et al., 2005):

$$C\left(u,v\right) = \alpha(u)\alpha(v) \sum_{x=0}^{N-1} \sum_{y=0}^{N-1} I\left(x,y\right) Cos\left[\frac{\Pi\left(2x+1\right)u}{2N}\right] Cos\left[\frac{\Pi\left(2y+1\right)v}{2N}\right]$$

(7)

where u, v = 0, 1, 2......... N-1 and $\alpha(u)$ is defined as follows:

$$\alpha(u) = \sqrt{\frac{1}{N}} \text{ u=0;}$$

$$\alpha(u) = \sqrt{\frac{2}{N}} \text{ u=1,2......N-1}$$

We find $\alpha(v)$ from $\alpha(u)$ by substituting u as v, where u, v ∈ {0, 1, 2 ....7}.

A number of openly available steganography tools embed data by modifying DCT coefficients including Jsteg (D. Upham), Outguess (Provos, 2001) and F5 (Westfield, 2001). Both Jsteg and F5 embed the data into the quantized DCT coefficients of JPEG image. F5 permutes the DCT coefficients before embedding and employs matrix embedding. An improvement of coding method used in F5 is proposed by Fan et al. (2011). Outguess also embeds data by flipping LSBs of DCT coefficient, but it spreads out changes by selecting coefficients with the user-selected password (Provos & Honeyman, 2011).

In (Johnson & Jadodia, 1998) a method of hiding information in images in transform domain. This method hides messages in significant areas of the cover-image. A number of watermarking algorithms have been proposed that use DCT co-

Figure 2. Middle frequency region of DCT for embedding

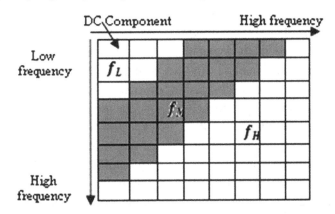

efficients for embedding secret data. Barni et al. (1998) proposed a digital watermarking based on DCT domain for copyright protection of multimedia data. The watermark was embedded in middle band DCT coefficient after Zig-Zag scanning to enhance perceptual invisibility. Their method is robust against image processing and geometrical attacks. Hernanddez et al. (2000) proposed a spread spectrum like DCT based watermarking technique for copyright protection of images. The DCT is applied on block of size 8×8 of cover image. The algorithm doesn't require original image for recovery process. Briassouli et al. (2005) presented a blind watermark detector based on statistical properties of DCT coefficient. This detector used the Cauchy statistical model i.e. class of heavy tailed alpha stable family which describes the behavior of the DCT coefficient. They implement the design of maximum likelihood watermark detector based on the alpha-stable modeling of DCT coefficients. Amin et al.(2005) proposed a statistically secure digital data hiding algorithm based on DCT domain. They improved statistical security and robustness against noise addition, filter processing, sharpening, blurring and JPEG compression attacks. Their method has better performance than the generic DCT method against all common image processing operations. Noda et al. (2006) proposed two methods, Histogram matching JPEG steganography in DCT domain and JPEG steganography using quantization index modulation (QIM) in DCT domain. They have shown performance comparison with F5 in which their method performed better in term of embedding rate and PSNR. Wong et al.(2007) proposed DCT based Mod 4 steganography method which uses blind recovery. The proposed method supports both uncompressed and compressed images for data hiding. They have reported performance comparison in terms of embedding capacity, PSNR, Universal Quality Index (Q) and steganalysis attacks. Chang et al. (2007) presented lossless and reversible data hiding scheme for DCT based compressed image. The proposed method hides

secret message bit in block of DCT middle band coefficients of compressed image. They exhibit acceptable image visual quality of stego image and provide good reversibility. Lin et al.(2010) proposed an improved DCT based image watermarking technique. They embed watermark into low frequency DCT coefficients of the cover image by using concept of mathematical remainder and improve the robustness against JPEG compression. Singh et al.(2011) introduced a DCT domain robust steganogrphy technique which embeds data in middle frequency DCT coefficients. From the analysis of log normal, Pareto, Weibull & Gaussian distribution, it is found that weibull distribution have better characteristics for embedding data in middle frequency DCT coefficients. Mali et al.(2012) presented robust and secure image adaptive energy threshold (AET) for selecting the embedding location in DCT domain. Their scheme exhibits more robustness against compression, tampering, resizing, filtering and addition of Gaussian noise.

Apart from DCT techniques, DFT (discrete fourier transforms) and DWT (discrete wavelet transform) are also used frequently.

WAVELET DOMAIN TECHNIQUES

The wavelet transform decomposes the image into three spatial directions i.e. horizontal, vertical and diagonal. Wavelet transform has been used extensively in data hiding techniques. The use of wavelet transform in steganography was proposed by Abdelwahab et al. (2008). The research on human perception reveals that the retina of the eye splits an image into frequency channels of approximately equal bandwidth which are processed independently. The multi-resolution property is expected to allow the independent processing of the resulting components without significant perceptible interaction between them. This will help in improving imperceptibility which is one of the most desirable properties of any steganography technique. Moreover, newer compression standards like JPEG2000 uses wavelet transform. This makes wavelet coefficients an obvious choice for data hiding.

A number of data hiding techniques (both watermarking and steganography) have been proposed for embedding data into the wavelet transform of the cover image. Barni et al.(2001) proposed wavelet based watermarking through pixel wise masking. They hide the watermark bit by modifying DWT coefficient of cover image and used HVS (Human visual system) characteristics for selecting the watermark strength. Their scheme outperforms other existing scheme in term of robustness against attacks. Kunder et al. (2004) introduced a new robust watermarking technique using discrete wavelet transform based image fusion principle for copyright protection. They use HVS model for determine salient image component for embedding the watermark bit. Kamstra et al.(2005) presented high capacity lossless reversible data embedding based on wavelet domain. They proposed two new techniques such as least significant bit prediction and Sweldens lifting scheme and an improvement of Tian method of difference expansion. These techniques outperform other existing data hiding techniques in terms of capacity distortion behaviour and capacity control.

Liu et al. (2006) suggested a robust watermarking scheme for copyright protection. They embed watermark in difference value between the original cover image and its reference. Ghouti et al. (2006) investigated a robust image watermarking using balanced multiwavelet transform. This transform is suitable for real time watermarking application like audio broadcasting monitoring. They used spread spectrum technique for watermark robustness. Lee et al.(2007) presented a reversible image watermarking scheme based on integer wavelet transform. First original image is divided into nonoverlapping blocks and hides watermark information into high frequency integer wavelet coefficient of each block by using LSB substitution. They have reported higher embedding capacity at low distortion than other existing

technique. Lin et al. (2008) suggested a blind image watermarking method based on the significant difference of wavelet coefficient quantization for copyright protection in which every seven consecutive wavelet coefficient of cover image have grouped into block. Chan et al.(2009) proposed a Haar Digital wavelet transform (HDWT) based reversible data hiding scheme. A new adaptive reversible data hiding scheme based on integer wavelet transform (IWT) was introduced by Peng et al.(2012). Bhatnagar et al. (2012) proposed robust logo watermarking scheme based on wavelet image fusion. They have reported higher visual quality of stego image and robustness against various intentional or unintentional attacks. Yeh et al. (2013) presented wavelet bit plane data hiding technique for compressed image. The compressed image is beneficial to reduced storage size and takes less time for transmission data. They use bit planes of DWT coefficient for hiding secret image based on multistage encoding.

Various hybrid domain watermarking techniques have been proposed (Rastegar et al., 2011; Rawat et al., 2012 ; Makbol et al.,2013). In Rastegar et al.(2011) a hybrid watermarking based on Finite Radon transform (FRAT), wavelet transform and singular value decomposition (SVD) for identification and authentication is proposed. They modified the singular value of all frequency band of cover image with singular values of watermark. Rawat et al. (2012) presented a dual watermarking scheme for copyright protection based on DWT, wavelet packet transform with best tree and SVD. They used two different grey scale images as watermark and embedded them by modifying singular values of two sub-images having largest sum of singular values. Makbol et al.(2013) proposed an image watermarking based on redundant discrete wavelet transform(RDWT) and SVD for copyright protection and ownership proof. The watermark image was directly inserted into singular value of RDWT subband of the cover image. Their scheme provides high capacity and high visual quality of stego image.

Contourlet transform (Sajedi et al.2009) was advancement over wavelet transform. Herein directionality and anisotropy properties are suitable for steganography. Sajedi et al. (2010) proposed a new adaptive contourlet transform based steganography scheme that embeds data in specific cover image, selected by best cover image measures such as Peak Signal-to-Noise Ratio (PSNR) and number of modifications of cover image. They hide the secrete data in contourlet coefficient through iterative embedding process to reduce the stego image distortion.

SPREAD SPECTRUM TECHNIQUES

Spread spectrum comes from wireless communication technology. It is also called as CDMA (code division multiple access). In spread spectrum, the signal (i.e. the watermark message), is transmitted on much larger frequency than required for the original message, in this case, the cover image.

One of the first work done in transform domain data hiding was by Cox et.al.(1997) which uses spread spectrum technology to insert a Gaussian random vector in perceptually most significant spectral components of the data to identify owner. Marvel et al. (1999) suggested an image steganography technique that combines spread spectrum technique, error control coding and image processing. They provide a technique for secure data hiding within cover image. Kutter et al.(2002) suggested visual mask model based spread spectrum image watermarking. It is based on the human visual system and taking its masking properties to reduce visual distortion and improve the robustness of watermark. Maity et al. (2011) introduced image watermarking technique based on hadamard transform and spread spectrum technique. The spread transform method is used for spreading transform coefficients of both cover and watermark image. Sadreazami et al. (2012) proposed a new blind spread spectrum watermarking based on ridgelet transform. The proposed method

improves imperceptibility of stego image by using spread spectrum technique and scrambling. They embed the watermark data in the best direction of ridgelet coefficient of cover image.

INTELLIGENT TECHNIQUES

Intelligent steganography techniques are based on the application of artificial intelligence techniques like Genetic Algorithm (GA) and Particle Swarm optimization (PSO). These techniques are generally used for optimizing various embedding parameters, e.g., embedding strength, embedding location, etc. Shieh et al. (2004) proposed a robust algorithm for DCT domain data hiding based on genetic algorithm to improve robustness against common image processing attacks. Li & Wang (2007) proposed a steganography technique that modified JPEG quantization table and embed secret message bits in middle frequency DCT coefficient by using Particle Swarm Optimization (PSO) for optimizing Least Significant Bit (LSB) substitution method of embedding which improves security level and imperceptibility. Ishtiaq et al.(2010) proposed a new method for adaptive watermark strength selection based on DCT and PSO. PSO is used for optimizing watermark strength in DCT domain. Their method provides better robustness against addition of noise, low pass filter, high pass filter and median filter, shifting and cropping operations. Wang et al.(2011) presented an intelligent watermarking technique using PSO in wavelet domain to improve fundamental issues like imperceptibility, robustness and security.

THE FUTURE OF IMAGE STEGANOGRAPHY

This provides an overview of image steganography techniques and discusses some of the existing transform domain techniques. Unlike images, audio and video steganography techniques are not well explored currently. Future steganography research may focus on these media. With the advancements in technology new platforms may emerge for hiding information. For example, Voice over IP may become important embedding platform because of the difficulty involved in detection. Presently, the most important application of image steganography seems in protecting intellectual property rights. In future, interesting industrial applications may catch sight. For example, digital camera manufacturers could incorporate steganography features in the firmware to tag pictures with copyright information. Other future applications may be tagging of video or multimedia content with hidden information. The use of steganography by criminals for communicating hidden messages is the darker side of the picture; It may lead to introduction of laws to limit the use of steganography in future.

CONCLUSION

This chapter presents the basic concepts involved in steganography, discusses its applications, and provide details of various transform domain techniques for image steganography. We review discrete cosine transform, wavelet transform, spread spectrum and intelligent based techniques for image steganography. We discussed various measures that have been used to assess the performance of steganography techniques and talk about the future scope of steganography.

REFERENCES

Abdelwahab, A. A., & Hassaan, L. A. (2008, March). A discrete wavelet transform based technique for image data hiding. In *Proceedings of Radio Science Conference*, (pp. 1-9). IEEE.

Amin, P. K., Liu, N., & Subbalakshmi, K.P. (2005). Statistically Secure Digital Image Data Hiding. In *Proceedings of the IEEE 7ᵗʰ Workshop on Multimedia Signal Processing*. IEEE.

Atawneh, S., Almomani, A., & Sumari, P. (2013). Steganography in Digital Images: Common Approaches and Tools, journal. *IETE Technical Review*, *30*(4), 344–358. doi:10.4103/0256-4602.116724

Barni, M., Bartolini, F., Cappellini, V., & Piva, A. (1998). A D.C.T. domain system for robust image watermarking. *Signal Processing*, *66*(3), 357–372. doi:10.1016/S0165-1684(98)00015-2

Barni, M., Bartolini, F., & Piva, A. (2001). Improved wavelet-based watermarking through pixel-wise masking. *IEEE Transactions on* Image Processing, *10*(5), 783–791.

Bartolini, F., Tefas, A., Barni, M., & Pitas, I. (2001). Image authentication techniques for surveillance applications. *Proceedings of the IEEE*, *89*(10), 1403–1418. doi:10.1109/5.959338

Bhatnagar, G., Jonathan Wu, Q. M., & Raman, B. (2012). Robust gray-scale logo watermarking in wavelet domain. *Computers & Electrical Engineering*, *38*(5), 1164–1176. doi:10.1016/j.compeleceng.2012.02.002

Briassouli, A., Tsakalides, P., & Stouraitis, A. (2005). Hidden messages in heavy-tails: DCT-domain watermark detection using alpha-stable models. *IEEE Transactions on* Multimedia, *7*(4), 700–715.

Chan, Y. K., Chen, W. T., Yu, S. S., Ho, Y. A., Tsai, C. S., & Chu, Y. P. (2009). A HDWT-based reversible data hiding method. *Journal of Systems and Software*, *82*(3), 411–421. doi:10.1016/j.jss.2008.07.008

Chang, C. C., Lin, C. C., Tseng, C. S., & Tai, W. L. (2007). Reversible hiding in DCT-based compressed images. *Information Sciences*, *177*(13), 2768–2786. doi:10.1016/j.ins.2007.02.019

Cheddad, A., Condell, J., Curran, K., & Kevitt, M. P. (2010). Digital image Steganography: Survey and analysis of current methods. *Signal Processing*, *90*(3), 727–752. doi:10.1016/j.sigpro.2009.08.010

Cox, I. J., Kilian, J., Leighton, F. T., & Shamoon, T. (1997, December). Secure spread spectrum watermarking for multimedia. *IEEE Transactions on Image Processing*, *6*(12), 1673–1687. doi:10.1109/83.650120 PMID:18285237

Fan, L., Gao, Yang, & Cao. (2011). An extended matrix encoding algorithm for steganography of high embedding efficiency. *Computers & Electrical Engineering*, *37*(6), 973–981. doi:10.1016/j.compeleceng.2011.08.006

Fridrich, J. (2010). *Steganography in Digital Media Principles, Algorithms and Application*. New York: Cambridge University Press.

Ghouti, L., Bouridane, A., Ibrahim, M. K., & Boussakta, S. (2006). Digital image watermarking using balanced multiwavelets. *IEEE Transactions on* Signal Processing, *54*(4), 1519–1536. doi:10.1109/TSP.2006.870624

Hernandez, J.R., Amado, M., & Perez Gonzalez, F.(2000). DCT-domain watermarking techniques for still images: Detector performance analysis and a new structure. *IEEE Tran on image proc*, *9*, 55-68.

Herodotus, . (1996). *The Histories*. London: Penguin Books.

Hsieh, S. L., Tsai, I. J., Yeh, C. P., & Chang, C. M. (2011). An image authentication scheme based on digital watermarking and image secret sharing. *Multimedia Tools and Applications*, *52*(2-3), 597–619. doi:10.1007/s11042-010-0520-4

Ishtiaq, M., Sikandar, B., Jaffar, M. A., & Khan, A. (2010). Adaptive watermark strength selection using Particle Swarm Optimization. *ICIC Express Letters: An International Journal of Research and Surveys, 4*(6).

Johnson, N. F., & Jajodia, S. (1998). Exploring Steganography: Seeing the unseen. *IEEE Computer, 31*(2), 26–34. doi:10.1109/MC.1998.4655281

Kamstra, L., & Heijmans, H. J. (2005). Reversible data embedding into images using wavelet techniques and sorting. *IEEE Transactions on* Image Processing, *14*(12), 2082–2090.

Katzenbeisser, S., & Petitcolas, F. A. P. (Eds.). (2000). *Information Hiding Techniques for Steganography and Digital Watermarking*. Norwood: Artech House, Inc.

Koch, E., & Zhao, J. (1995). Towards Robust and Hidden Image Copyright Labeling. In *Proceeding of IEEE Workshop on Nonlinear Signal and Image Processing*. Thessaloniki, Greece: IEEE.

Kundur, D., & Hatzinakos, D. (2004). Toward robust logo watermarking using multiresolution image fusion principles. *IEEE Transactions on* Multimedia, *6*(1), 185–198.

Kutter, M., & Winkler, S. (2002). A vision-based masking model for spread-spectrum image watermarking. *IEEE Transactions on* Image Processing, *11*(1), 16–25.

Lee, S., Yoo, C. D., & Kalker, T. (2007). Reversible image watermarking based on integer-to-integer wavelet transform. *IEEE Transactions on* Information Forensics and Security, *2*(3), 321–330.

Li, X., & Wang, J. (2007). A steganographic method based upon JPEG and particle swarm optimization algorithm. *Information Sciences*, *177*(15), 3099–3109. doi:10.1016/j.ins.2007.02.008

Lin, S. D., Shie, S. C., & Guo, J. Y. (2010). Improving the robustness of DCT-based image watermarking against JPEG compression. *Computer Standards & Interfaces*, *32*(1), 54–60. doi:10.1016/j.csi.2009.06.004

Lin, W. H., Horng, S. J., Kao, T. W., Fan, P., Lee, C. L., & Pan, Y. (2008). An efficient watermarking method based on significant difference of wavelet coefficient quantization. *IEEE Transactions on* Multimedia, *10*(5), 746–757.

Liu, J. L., Lou, D. C., Chang, M. C., & Tso, H. K. (2006). A robust watermarking scheme using self-reference image. *Computer Standards & Interfaces*, *28*(3), 356–367. doi:10.1016/j.csi.2005.07.001

Lou, D.-C., Hu, M.-C., & Liu, J.-L. (2009). Multiple layer data hiding scheme for medical images. *Computer Standards & Interfaces*, *31*, 329–335. doi:10.1016/j.csi.2008.05.009

Maity, S. P., & Kundu, M. K. (2011). Perceptually adaptive spread transform image watermarking scheme using Hadamard transform. *Information Sciences*, *181*(3), 450–465. doi:10.1016/j.ins.2010.09.029

Makbol, N. M., & Khoo, B. E. (2012). Robust blind image watermarking scheme based on Redundant Discrete Wavelet Transform and Singular Value Decomposition. *AEÜ International Journal of Electronics and Communications*.

Mali, S. N., Patil, P. M., & Jalnekar, R. M. (2012). Robust and secured image-adaptive data hiding. *Digital Signal Processing*, *22*(2), 314–323. doi:10.1016/j.dsp.2011.09.003

Malvar, H. S., & Florêncio, D. A. (2003). Improved spread spectrum: A new modulation technique for robust watermarking. *IEEE Transactions on* Signal Processing, *51*(4), 898–905. doi:10.1109/TSP.2003.809385

Marvel, L. M., Boncelet, C. G. Jr, & Retter, C. T. (1999). Spread spectrum image steganography. *IEEE Transactions on* Image Processing, *8*(8), 1075–1083.

Niimi, M., Noda, H., & Kawaguchi, E. (1998). A steganography based on region segmentation by using complexity measure. Trans. IEICE J81-D-II, 1132–1140.

Noda, H., Niimi, M., & Kawaguchi, E. (2006). High-performance JPEG steganography using quantization index modulation in DCT domain. *Pattern Recognition Letters*, *27*(5), 455–461. doi:10.1016/j.patrec.2005.09.008

Peng, F., Li, X., & Yang, B. (2012). Adaptive reversible data hiding scheme based on integer transform. *Signal Processing*, *92*(1), 54–62. doi:10.1016/j.sigpro.2011.06.006

Provos, N. (2001). Defending against statistical steganalysis. In *Proceedings of tenth USENIX Security Symposium '01*, (pp. 323–335). USENIX.

Provos, N., & Honeyman, P. (2011). Detecting Steganography Content on the Internet. CITI Technical Report.

Rastegar, S., Namazi, F., Yaghmaie, K., & Aliabadian, A. (2011). Hybrid watermarking algorithm based on Singular Value Decomposition and Radon transform. *AEÜ International Journal of Electronics and Communications*, *65*(7), 658–663. doi:10.1016/j.aeue.2010.09.008

Rawat, S., & Raman, B. (2012). Best tree wavelet packet transform based copyright protection scheme for digital images. *Optics Communications*, *285*(10), 2563–2574. doi:10.1016/j.optcom.2012.01.067

Sadreazami, H., & Amini, M. (2012). A robust spread spectrum based image watermarking in ridgelet domain. *AEÜ International Journal of Electronics and Communications*, *66*(5), 364–371. doi:10.1016/j.aeue.2011.09.001

Saha, B., & Sharma, S. (2012). Stenographic Techniques of Data hiding using Digital images. *Defence Science Journal, 62*(1), 11–18. doi:10.14429/dsj.62.1436

Sajedi, H., & Jamzad, M. (2009). ContSteg:Contourlet-based Steganography method. *Journal of Wireless Sensor Network, 1*(3), 163–170. doi:10.4236/wsn.2009.13022

Sajedi, H., & Jamzad, M. (2010). Using contourlet transform and cover selection for secure steganography. *International Journal of Information Security, 9*(5), 337–352. doi:10.1007/s10207-010-0112-3

Shieh, C. S., Huang, H. C., Wang, F. H., & Pan, J. S. (2004). Genetic watermarking based on transform-domain techniques. *Pattern Recognition, 37*(3), 555–565. doi:10.1016/j.patcog.2003.07.003

Singh, H. V., Rai, S., Mohan, A., & Singh, S. P. (2011). Robust copyright marking using weibull distribution. *Computers & Electrical Engineering, 37*(5), 714–728. doi:10.1016/j.compeleceng.2011.04.006

Srinivasan, Y., Nutter, B., Mitra, S., Phillips, B., & Ferris, D. (2004). Secure transmission of medical records using high capacity steganography. In *Proceedings of 17th IEEE Symposium on Computer Based Medical Systems*, (pp. 122–212). IEEE.

Ulutas, M., Ulutas, G., & Nabiyev, V. V. (2011). Medical image security and EPR hiding using Shamir's secret sharing scheme. *Journal of Systems and Software, 84*(3), 341–353. doi:10.1016/j.jss.2010.11.928

Upham, D. (n.d.). *JPEG–Jsteg*. Available from http://zooid.org/~paul/crypto/jsteg

Wang, Y. R., Lin, W. H., & Yang, L. (2011). An intelligent watermarking method based on particle swarm optimization. *Expert Systems with Applications, 38*(7), 8024–8029. doi:10.1016/j.eswa.2010.12.129

Wang, Z., & Bovik, A. C. (2002). A Universal Image Quality Index. *IEEE Signal Processing Letters, 9*(3), 81–84. doi:10.1109/97.995823

Wang, Z., Bovik, A. C., Sheikh, H. R., & Simoncelli, E. P. (2004). Image quality assessment: From error measurement to structural similarity. *IEEE Transactions on Image Processing, 13*(4), 600–612. doi:10.1109/TIP.2003.819861 PMID:15376593

Westfeld, A. (2001). *F5-a Steganographic algorithm: High capacity despite better Steganlysis.* Lecture Notes in Computer Science, 2137, 289–302. doi:10.1007/3-540-45496-9_21

Wong, K., Qi, X., & Tanaka, K. (2007). A DCT-based Mod4 steganographic method. *Signal Processing, 87*(6), 1251–1263. doi:10.1016/j.sigpro.2006.10.014

Yeh, H. L., Gue, S. T., Tsai, P., & Shih, W. K. (2013). Wavelet Bit-Plane Based Data Hiding for Compressed Images. *AEÜ International Journal of Electronics and Communications*. doi:10.1016/j.aeue.2013.04.003

ADDITIONAL READING

Cheddad, A. (2009). *Digital Image Steganography: Concepts, Algorithms, and Applications.* VDM Verlag Dr. Müller.

Cox, I. (2007). *Matthew Miller, Jeffrey Bloom, Jessica Fridrich and Ton Kalker, "Digital Watermarking and Steganography.* Morgan Kaufmann.

Information Hiding Techniques for Steganography and Digital Watermarking. (2000). *Stefan Katzenbeisser* (A. P. Petitcolas, Ed.). Artech House.

Neil, F. (2001). *Johnson, Zoran Duric, Sushil Jajodia, Information Hiding: Steganography and Watermarking-Attacks and Countermeasures: Steganography and Watermarking: Attacks and Countermeasures.* Springer.

KEY TERMS AND DEFINITIONS

Discrete Cosine Transform: The DCT is closely related to DFT, but offers a high energy compaction property in comparison with DFT for natural images. It is a real domain transform which represents an image as coefficient of different frequencies of cosine which is basis vector for this transform.

Image Steganography: It is process of hiding digital information into cover images so that it can conceal the information and prevent undetectability.

Spatial Domain Steganography: Spatial domain methods embed the secret data directly embedded into pixels of the cover image. Examples of spatial domain image steganography methods are least significant bit (LSB) and histogram based steganography method.

Transform Domain Steganography: Embed the secret information into the coefficients of transformed image in frequency domain. Such transformations are pyramid transforms, discrete cosine transform and wavelet transforms etc.

Wavelet Transform: A wavelet transform with real valued wavelet coefficient such as discrete wavelet transform (DWT).

Section 4
Cloud Security

Chapter 14
Experiences with Threat Modeling on a Prototype Social Network

Anne V. D. M. Kayem
University of Cape Town, South Africa

Molulaqhooa L. Maoyi
University of Cape Town, South Africa

Rotondwa Ratshidaho
University of Cape Town, South Africa

Sanele Macanda
University of Cape Town, South Africa

ABSTRACT

Supported by the Web 3.0 platform that enables dynamic content sharing, social networking applications are a ubiquitous information exchange platform. Content sharing raises the question of privacy with concerns typically centered on vulnerabilities resulting in identity theft. Identifying privacy vulnerabilities is a challenging problem because mitigations are implemented at the end of the software development life cycle, sometimes resulting in severe vulnerabilities. The authors present a prototype experimental social networking platform (HACKMI2) as a case study for a comparative analysis of three popular industry threat-modeling approaches. They focus on identified vulnerabilities, risk impact, and mitigation strategies. The results indicate that software and/or asset-centric approaches provide only a high-level analysis of a system's architecture and are not as effective as attacker-centric models in identifying high-risk security vulnerabilities in a system. Furthermore, attacker-centric models are effective in providing security administrators useful suggestions for addressing security vulnerabilities.

INTRODUCTION

Social networking applications have become a ubiquitous and popular Internet service enabling millions of users to share content dynamically (Westland, 2012), (Chen, 2013), (Story et al., 2012). This has been enabled in large part by the Web 3.0 technology that extends the Web 2.0 tech-

nology by enabling dynamic content distribution and/or sharing (Rowell, 2008), (Walters, 2009). As is the case with a lot of popular web applications storing or manipulating sensitive information, these applications are inherently vulnerable to privacy violations that can be exploited for identity theft and in certain cases compromises to professional integrity. Furthermore, scandals

DOI: 10.4018/978-1-4666-6158-5.ch014

such as the one that occurred in July of 2011, where security consultant (Ron Bowles) collected personal data off FaceBook and published it on the public site, Pirate Bay (Pirate Bay, 2010), have further compounded this problem (Boshmaf et al., 2013). Corporate organizations have responded to the potential threats that social networks pose by limiting and sometimes even completely prohibiting access to social networks using corporate infrastructure (Rooksby & Sommerville, 2012), (Wang et al., 2011).

The problem of security and privacy violations in web applications hinges mainly on the fact that security and/or mitigations are typically implemented at the end of the software development cycle (Hackmi2, 2012). As a consequence, there is often no clear strategy or plan to prevent security violations during the software development cycle. In general implemented mitigations are rushed jobs that can often result in more serious vulnerabilities. An added dimension to consider is that fixing vulnerabilities after an application has been deployed is more costly than if this were done during the design phase. The National Institute of Standards and Technology (NIST) in the United States of America estimates that code fixes performed after the release of a software product can result in 30 times the cost of performing these fixes during the design phase.

Threat modeling has received some attention with respect to integrating security and privacy modeling into the software design process. In general, threat modeling can broadly be described as an approach to security modeling whereby potential vulnerabilities or coding practices that are liable to result in security vulnerabilities are identified and categorized using security rating metrics. Threat modeling tools are typically packaged to addition- ally provide suggestions of implementable countermeasures. Approaches to threat modeling are categorized under two main themes namely, attack centric models and software/asset centric models. In attack centric models, as the name suggests, the focus is on the

attacker's goals and motivations for hacking into a system. The main motivation behind this model is that in order to design effective countermeasures for the identified security vulnerabilities, a security administrator needs to have a realistic perception of the potential weak points in the system that the attacker is most likely to exploit and why. The software/asset centric model by contrast aims at detecting the vulnerabilities that emerge in the design of the system. In this case, the idea is to have a sort of high-level parsing of the system's components with the goal being to identify potentially exploitable vulnerabilities. This is a proactive approach to discovering the vulnerabilities on a system from the system designer's perspective. The advantage is that vulnerabilities can then be addressed with situable countermeasures to protect against potential attacks and the other associated losses (cost-wise).

Having a blueprint of potential threats is useful from the system designer's viewpoint because potential attack scenarios as well as countermeasures can be simulated before the application is deployed. However, until recently, not much consideration has been given to comparing existing threat modeling approaches and that software tools that hinge on these models. Yet each one of the existing approaches has its pros and cons in the identification of security vulnerabilities in a system. In applying each one, it is important from an industry and academic perspective to be cognizant of the limitations of each with respect to the overall security modeling goal for the application and/or system.

In this chapter, we present a prototype experimental social networking platform (HACKMI2) as a case study basis for a comparative analysis of three popular industry threat modeling tools namely; the Microsoft Security Development Lifecycle (SDL), the SensePost Corporate Threat Modeling Tool (CTM), and the Microsoft Threat Analysis and Modeling (TAM) tool. The main reasons for selecting these tools are popularity of use in the industry and the fact that these tools are based on the basic threat modeling approaches of software and attack centrism. Using a social networking plat- form was motivated primarily by the fact that social networks are a popular communication tool, surpassing even email and social networks are an ideal platform for studying malicious behaviors and mitigation strategies.

Our comparison hinges on identified vulnerabilities, risk impact, and mitigation strategies. Our results indicate that software and/or asset centric threat models provide only a high level analysis of a system's architecture and are not as effective as attacker centric models in identifying high risk security vulnerabilities in a system. Furthermore, we noted that attacker centric models are more effective providing a security administrator effective suggestions for addressing security vulnerabilities without creating harmful side-effects.

The rest of the paper is structured as follows: in Section 2 we present background work on threat modeling in relation to social networking plat- forms. In Section 3, we discuss attacks, both identified and provoked, as well as mitigation strategies that we studied on the HACKMi2 social net- work platform (Dong et al., 2008).. We present the methodologies behind these attacks highlighting in each case the weakness in the threat modeling tools that made circumvention possible. Section 4, presents a comparative analysis of the threat modeling approaches that we studied, highlighting the pros and cons of each one in relation to vulnerability assessment in real systems. We offer concluding remarks and discuss open problems in Section 5.

BACKGROUND

Most systems contain valuable information assets that require protection from unauthorized access. In the case of social networks the sensitive information typically is user privacy related. For instance, if a user's account were compromised the stolen information could be used to deduce other more sensitive and less accessible information such as banking information. Threat modeling is useful therefore in detecting the kinds of vulnerabilities that can be exploited to access valuable information. In this section, we discuss threat modeling methodologies from the attacker and system centric perspectives. The attacker centric perspective is focused primarily on the process that an attacker uses to identify and attack valuable assets on the system, while the system centric approach is identify the assets on the system and evaluate the vulnerability of each component with respect to assets it is associated with.

Threat Modeling

Threat modeling is characterized by two key terms namely "threat" (potential to be attacked) and "risk" (value of information lost). In the threat modeling process, the goal is to identify in some formal way the entry points to a system, as well as the privilege boundaries. The entry points allow the modeler to identify all the possible access points to the system, both authorized and unauthorized (Dong et al., 2008).), (Boshmaf et al., 2013), 13]. The privilege boundary on the other hand evaluates conflicting access authorizations by mapping access right assignments to system objects. In order to conceptualize threat modeling, threat visualization serves as a follow up strategy to the entry points and privilege boundary process, involving formal representation techniques for constructing flow diagrams like attack trees (Mauw, & Oostdijk, 2006), (Bagnato et al., 2012), (Roy et al., 2010), fault trees (Cha, & Yoo, 2012), and attack nets (Zhou et al., 2003), (Wu, Li, & Huang, 2008), (Wang et al., 2013); and security pattern descriptions that are useful in correlating the effects of exploiting the vulnerabilities.

Since applications are dynamic in nature, threat modeling is iterative and is repeated to account for system changes. The threat modeling process can be broken down into six steps namely, asset identification, application overview, application decomposition, threat identification, threat documentation, and threat rating.

Asset identification can be viewed from both the attack and system centric perspective. In the attack centric perspective the aim is to simulate the most probable strategy that an attacker is likely to adopt in identifying assets that can be exploited for maximum gain. The system-centric approach adopts a more defensive strategy in identifying the assets that hold the most confidential data and therefore that are most likely to be attacked. Identify- ing assets of value in a system is key in making a difference between a useful threat modeling tool and a mediocre one. Setting clear objectives is vital in determining how to prioritize vulnerabilities.

The application overview is a follow-up procedure to asset identification, and in this case the goal is to evaluate in relation to the vulnerabilities identified, how the system's resources can be used and/or misused by documenting use cases. Use cases help to put the systems functionalities in context for easier understanding with respect to the impact the vulnerabilities can have. Examples of use cases in our HACKMi2 social network include updates to a user's profile, and administrator access to view a user's personal profile. In this case vulnerabilities involving unauthorized access might include misuse of business rules where an unauthorized user overrides administrator privileges for accessing a user's profile.

In decomposing the application, the threat modeling process aims to create an attack profile for the system based on the known (identified vulnerabilities). Data flow diagrams are particularly useful in this process because they provide a detailed representation of the system's components as well as boundaries and connections to other systems. Additionally, entry or exit points (data entry or exit) are highlighted. Data entry or exit points includes authentication forms, web applications for listening for HTTP(Hyper Text Transmission Protocol) requests, and related searches.

Identifying, documenting and rating threats are the next aspects that the threat modeler must consider. Typically, the Open Web Application

Security Project (OWASSP) serves as a guideline for classifying and categorizing web application risks. OWASP is an open source community dedicated to raising awareness about application security by classifying the top ten most critical web risks in terms impact (Kim et al., 2009). In order of priority, a list of the top ten OWASP vulnerabilities are: SQL injection attacks, Cross-Site Scripting, Broken Authentication and Session Management, Insecure Direct Object Reference, Cross-Site Request Forgery, Security Misconfiguration, In- secure Cryptographic Storage, Failure to restrict URL access, Insufficient Transport Layer Protection, and Unvalidated redirects and forwards.

This vulnerability list is used to scan for and identify, during the design phase, the vulnerabilities that are inherent to an application. In order to facilitate threat documentation, the STRIDE method (Xu et al., 2008) has been proposed for categorizing threats into six easy to remember categories namely, Spoofing, Tampering, Repudiation, Information Disclosure, Denial of Services and Elevation of privileges. These categories are used to classify the OWASP vulnerabilities that are identified in the application's design. For instance, broken authentication and session management could be classified under the Denial of Service attack category. However, not all threats are easy to categorize with the STRIDE model and in certain cases, the threats may fall into more than one category. For instance, the broken authentication and session management threats could also be classified under the spoofing and/or elevation if privileges category. A key advantage of STRIDE though, is that it shifts the focus of the threat modeling process from threat identification to threat mitigation. STRIDE is useful in capturing the intentions of an adversary but not very effective at identifying exactly what tools, knowledge, techniques, or combination thereof that an attacker might use to compromise the system. Spoofing attacks, for instance, generally affect authentication procedures and so

Table 1. Threat vs. property compromised

Threat	Property Compromised
Spoofing	Authentication
Tampering	Integrity
Repudiation	Non-Repudiation
Information Disclosure	Confidentiality
Denial of Service	Availability
Elevation of Priviledges	Authorization

tend to be ranked as embodying one of the more serious attack categories. The reason for this is that Spoofing can be used to provoke tampering attacks that affect the integrity of the system, while repudiation attacks result in refutations of non-repudiation, and information disclosure that can result in privacy violations such as identity theft, denial of service attacks that affect resource availability and/or elevation of service attacks that modify the access authorization policies.

Threat rating models support threat documentation and vulnerability assessment approaches by ranking threats according to the potential impact that exploitation of the threats can have on the system. The reason for this is that threats need to be prioritized to determine from a cost management perspective, which are the most important vulnerabilities and what the best order for addressing them might be (Futcher, & Von Solms, 2008), (Kainerstorfer, Sametinger, & Wiesauer, 2011), (Al-Ahmad, 2011). The DREAD (Damage, Reproducibility, Exploitability, Affected users, and Discoverability) rating or risk assessment model is rather subjective and is based primarily on a summation of the ratings of the identified vulnerabilities with respect to the rate of occurrence of exploits that take advantage of the vulnerabilities.

Attack Trees, Fault Trees, and Attack Nets

Threat modeling is facilitated by the use of threat visualization techniques such as attack trees, fault trees, and attack nets. Attack trees are used to describe directed graphs that provide a visual impression of security vulnerabilities (represented as nodes in the graph) and compromise methods (represented as edges in the graph) (Mauw, & Oostdijk, 2006).

Every node in the attack tree represents an adversary goal and the root node represents the overall goal. Intermediate nodes in the graph represent sub-goals that the adversary needs to achieve in order to reach an objective. Leaf nodes represent the aim of an attack that is the sub-goals or goals that cannot be refined any further. Attack trees have simple semantics to allow or enable cost propagation and facilitate specifying solutions to discourage attacks by making the cost of an attack very high. The semantics for specifying attacks trees however, do not contain enough information to facilitate logical reasoning about the threats represented and on what information can be deduced automatically from combining several threats (Mauw, & Oostdijk, 2006), (Kordy, Pouly, & Schweitzer, 2012). For example, when are two attack paths equal, what is the internal structure of an attack, and what impact is an event likely have on the overall system? An added consideration is that, attack trees suffer from the state space explosion problem and so need to be pruned for scalability (Mauw, & Oostdijk, 2006), (Kordy, Pouly, & Schweitzer, 2012). Pruning results in information loss and so a cost benefit tradeoff is required to decide when to prune an attack tree and by how much. In Figure 1 we present an attack graph depicting the possible execution paths that might arise in the case of a virus infecting a Windows NT operating system.

Fault trees build on the attack graph concept but represent only those vulnerabilities that result in system failures and show the correlations between the failures (Cha, & Yoo, 2012). The failures in this case are the system vulnerabilities that present threats to the system's integrity. A node in a fault tree represents an event and the edges represent a causal effect relationship between events.

Figure 1. An attack tree for a computer virus

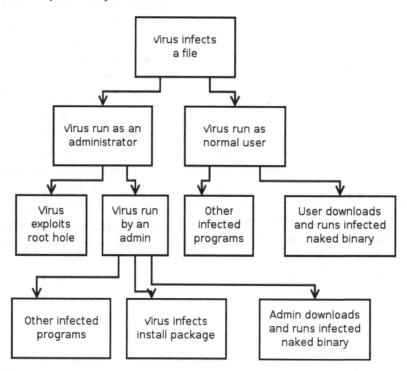

Finally attack nets are modeled on the concept of Petri Nets with a set $P = \{p_0, p_1, p_2, p_3, ..., p_n\}$ of nodes representing security vulnerability states to which is associated a set $T = \{t_0, t_1, ..., t_n\}$ of transitions that represent input events, commands, or data that cause one or more of the security vulnerability states to change or evolve (Br, Refsdal, & Stølen, 2010), (Zhou et al., 2003). Security states are interconnected by state transition edges that embody a casual effect relationship. An attack net has an attack vulnerability set that has a set of tokens that are held at each one of the security vulnerability node states, say p_i. Attack propagations can be simulated by monitoring the movement of the tokens. Attack nets are different from attack and fault trees in that attack events are clearly separated from attack goals, which is good because this enhances the descriptive power of the representation of attacks thereby allowing the security analyst to investigate the atomic components of attacks.

Security Pattern Description

While threat visualization techniques provide an abstract perception of existing threats in the application, security designers require more expresive languages for describing threats and the impact of these threats on vulnerability exploitation. This is particularly useful when composed threats need to be analyzed for potential impact to the system. Security pattern description provide a n are documents that describe the threat in a system in natural language (Cuevas et al., 2008), (Asnar, Paja, & Mylopoulos, 2011), (Edge, 2010). The advantage of security pattern descriptions is that they are more expressive than graphical representations because they are not bound by formalism constraints. Security pattern descriptions enable the capturing of atomic attributes of threats and background knowledge of the system. In this way, security pattern descriptions are a simple method of representing threat models in ways that are easy to interpret.

ONLINE SOCIAL NETWORKS AND THE ELGG FRAMEWORK

In the preceding section we discussed the threat modeling process highlighting in particular, the pros and cons of the different components in relation to the overall process. The HackMi2 prototype social network was built on the Elgg framework as a basis for our study of threat modeling approaches. We noted that the threat modeling process can be viewed as a stepwise procedure with the final goal being to build a clear picture of the security state of a system. We now describe our social network platform, HACKMi2 that is built on the Elgg framework (Sharma, 2008), (Elgg. 2013) and then proceed to explain in relation to the general threat modeling process, how assets and risks are identified.

Online Social Networks

As mentioned before, online social networks (OSN) have become quite popular with usage surpassing that of sites like Google, and Yahoo. There is no universally accepted definition for OSNs, but for simplicity we will use the one provided by INTECO and the Agencia Espahola de Protection de Datos (Krishnamurthy, & Wills, 2008), (INTECO, 2009).

"Online social networks are services that let their users create a public profile where they can introduce personal data and information. The users have different tools to interact with each other." Well known social networks include FaceBook, Twitter, LinkedIn, and MySpace (Lee et al., 2009). We opted to build the HACKMi2 social networking plat- form (Dong et al., 2008), in order to facilitate security experimentation hat would not have been possible on a closed commercial OSN like FaceBook for instance. HACKMi2 focuses primarily on the following three aspects and associated functionalities:

1. **Communication:** Enabling information sharing.
2. **Community:** Help finding and integrating communities (or groups).
3. **Cooperation:** Providing tools to develop activities collaboratively.

The Elgg Framework

For ease of implementation and conceptual simplicity, we used he Elgg framework to build the HackMi2 social network. Elgg (Elgg, 2013), (Sharma, 2008) is a social network framework that provides basic functionalities to run and/or create a social network. This framework has the advantage of being extensible, free to download and use as it is dual licensed under the General Public License (GNU) version 2. It runs on the Linux, Apache, MySQL, and PHP (LAMP) platform or Windows, Apache, MySQL, and PHP (WAMP) platform. Its creators Tosh and Wermuller describe it as being a "personal learning landscape" (Elgg, 2013), (Sharma, 2008) since it incorporates elements of social networking, collaborative document authoring, e-portfolios (user's online identity) and web-blogging. The Elgg platform supports an autonomous learner-centered approach through web publishing and promotes the formation of learning communities in which communication, information and knowledge sharing can take place.

Elgg offers two social networking features namely, keyword tags for content and friends or groups of users (Elgg, 2013), (Sharma, 2008), (Lee et al., 2009). The keywords enable users to find others who have published on similar topics and have the associated links appear as links at the bottom of a post that a user can click on in order to visit a webpage containing user posts with the keyword. Automatic tag suggestions are also offered and so this saves users from having to manually tag content as well as in avoiding errors that can be introduced when tagging is handled manually.

Like FaceBook, the Elgg framework allows users to invite other users and categorize them as "friends" by adding these users to a pre-defined friend catalogue. Friends can view each others' profiles, comment on each other's status updates and share resources such as photos, videos, and documents.

Elgg Architecture

Elgg is built on the Model-View-Controller (MVC) architecture which is basically a design pattern that defines a relationship between the model, view, and controller components of the Elgg social networking engine. The models are application components that implement the logic for the application data by retrieving and storing model states in a database (Curry, & Grace, 2008), (Lee et al., 2009). An example of this occurs when a blog object retrieves information from a database, performs some operations on the data, and then writes the updated information back to the blog's table in the database. Elgg stored models in the / actions directory which contains core actions of the system such as logging in, creating, updating or deleting content. Actions are executed when users post forms such as submitting a blog comment. The "action code" adjusts the submitted data and makes the relevant modifications to the database.

Views are useful in displaying graphical user interfaces and are useful in creating output from the layout of pages, footers down to form inputs. Controllers on the other hand handle user interactions with the system. For instance, the controller might handle query-string data and pass it to the model which will in turn use this data to query the database.

Finally, since Elgg is an extensible platform, plugins can be coded to ex- tend or replace core functionalities. For instance the email validation pluggin could be coded to override the existing Elgg core email validation functionality.

The Elgg Data Model

As with standard dynamic web applications, Elgg employs a database for the backend storage of data. In order to control duplication, Elgg has been designed to ensure that the author of a pluggin does not need to create a new database to support customized functionalities. This idea is facilitated by the fact that Elgg is underpinned by a flexible, generic data model which is advantageous because multiple servers and new data characterizations can be handled without requiring a complete overhaul of the database and/or system.

As shown in Figure 2, the Elgg data model consists of four main compo- nents namely, Objects, Users, Sites, and Groups, that are all controlled by an Elgg entity. Objects represent arbitrary objects with Elgg. Examples in- clude blog posts, uploaded files and bookmarks. User is an entity types that describes a user's profile and the sites represent the pages that compose the Elgg platform. Finally, groups are used to represent collaborations between users.

THREAT MODELLING APPROACHES: COMPARATIVE ANALYSIS

We implemented the HACKMi2 (Hackmi2, 2012) social networking platform as a basis for comparing the threat models that we studied and compared. As mentioned before, this is because we needed to experiment with a simple and open application without the risk of infringing on user privacy constraints in a real world application where the consequences of a violation could be a costly law suit. While the HackMi2 platform appear somewhat simplistic in comparison to sites like FaceBook, it contains all of the basic components required to run a social network successfully. The threat modeling tools that we focused on include:

Figure 2. Elgg data model [35]

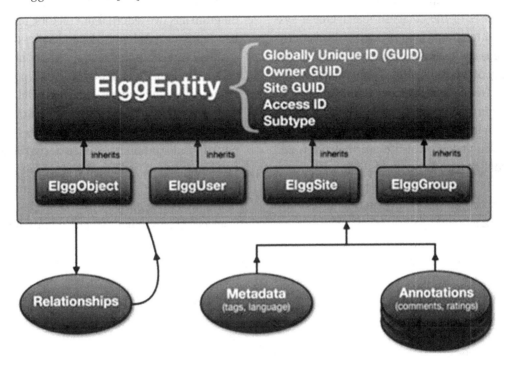

- Microsoft Threat Analysis and Modeling (TAM).
- Microsoft Software Development Lifecycle (SDL).
- Sensepost Corporate Threat Modeling (CTM).

The TAM and SDL models are mainly software centric whereas the CTM model is more attack centric then software centric. The HACKMi2 social network is built on the Elgg v1.8.8. framework and has the same data model as the one described in Section 3.4. This social network will serve as a testbed for studying the threat modeling approaches that we have cited with respect to analyzing the security vulnerabilities of social network platforms.

We implemented the HACKMi2 social network on a server with an Intel core i7-2600 CPU 3.40Ghz processor, 16GB of RAM and 3TB of hard disk space. The reason for selecting this hardware is that social networks tend to have huge databases of user profiles that include chat histories, photographs, videos, and blogs; and these operations tend to be processor and storage space intensive in addition to requiring concurrency handling. Open source technologies namely, Apache, PHP, MySQL Server and Ubuntu server edition, were used to enable the deployment of the HACKMi2 platform. The HACKMi2 social network uses a three-tiered architecture to segment the application into logical layers, namely the client, webserver, and data layer. The client layer is also known as the presentation layer and presents data to the user allowing for input and data manipulation. On the HACKMi2 social network, the presentation interface is the front-end that can be accessed using a browser. Users are able to post pictures and post blogs using the presentation layer and are able to interact with the social network.

The webserver is also referred to as the middle-tier and is where the business logic of the social network takes place. This is where the Elgg social networking engine is installed and in addition requires Apache 2 and PHP 5. The data layer consists of the database management system. The three tiered approach provides benefits such as reusability, flexibility, manageability, and scalability of the application. Components can be shared and reused and distributed across networks of computers as required.

In order to create a realistic social network that would mimic actual real-life user behavior, and in accordance with Boyd and Ellison's (Boyd, & Ellison, 2007) ideas of social networking sites, we incorporated the following features into HACKMi2 namely:

- Registration of new users.
- Retrieval of lost passwords, password changes, name display and email.
- Profile updates.
- Uploads of pictures and assorted files (video and audio).
- Status updates.
- Blogging:writing, commenting, and updates.
- Bookmarks to note interesting pages.
- Chatrooms and Horoscope views.
- Friendship group creation, friendship invitations, and "unfriending."
- Friendship profile views, searches, and messaging.
- Reporting of users.

In the following we compare the three threat modeling tools namely, the TAM, SDL, CTM tools, with respect to identifying the vulnerabilities on the HACKMi2 platform.

Threat Modeling Tools: A Comparison

All three threat modeling tools are similar in that they operate in general by creating a data flow diagram to begin with. the data flow diagram is primarily contextual and serves mainly to identify sources of input and out- put data. In the case of

the HACKMi2 platform we note that the data flow diagram has two external interactors, namely, the user and external pluggin dependencies that create security threats to the system. There are several actions or requests that a user can perform or request from the database and so the HACKMi2 engine needs to decide whether or not to allow cer-tain actions to be performed by users. Pluggins pose a similar problem in that external dependencies can result in malicious code being executed. For instance, the site http://www.eastrolog.com/free-daily-horoscopes/taurus-horscope-today.php is accessed to obtain updates for daily horoscope displays on HACKMi2. So, if a malicious user were to incorporate a virus in the horoscope display, HACKMi2 could become a vehicle to propagate the virus. Following on the specification of the data flow diagram, threat modeling tools incorporate methodologies for analyzing the data flow diagram. In this case, the threat is analyzed to decide on impact and to make a plan on how to mitigate the exploitation of the threat. Threat rating mechanisms are used at this stage to decide on the "seriousness" of the threat and also to prioritize mitigation work. Finally, once the data flow diagram and analysis is complete, a concise description of the environment is presented to demonstrate the dependencies, assumptions and external security notes that need to be taken into consideration during the design of the system.

In comparing the three threat modeling tools we discuss the advantages and disadvantages of each one. The Microsoft SDL threat modeling tool has the advantage of allowing users to create a hight level over of the application's architecture using data flow diagrams. By defining the data flow patterns between components of the application and pointing out trust boundaries in the application landscape the SDL tool highlights spots where security attention is required. With the Microsoft threat analysis and modeling tool on the other hand, one needs to first define the application's requirement and then define the application's architecture which is more cumbersome but provide more detail in terms of user roles, use cases and business objectives. The SensePost threat modeling tool allows the user rank threat according to the impact the threats might have on the system and the probability that the vulnerability is likely to be exploited. This has the advantage of facilitating threat categorization.

The Microsoft SDL and Microsoft TAM threat modeling tools are software centric whereas the SensePost threat modeling tool is more attacker-centric. Both the SDL and TAM tools are designed to enable non-technical experts to use them. For instance, the SDL tool embeds prescriptive, at-a-glance help throughout the modeling process and builds on activities that all software developers and architects are familiar with such as design diagrams of the software architecture. Reports generated by both SDL and TAM can easily be imported into Microsoft one note and further more documentation on the usage of both tools is easily accessible online. In the SensePost threat modeling tool by contrast, the security modeler needs to be an expert and so is expected to define threats and prioritize them. The advantage is that the process can be focused solely on te system being modeled. For instance, if two machines with 10TB and 50GB of hard disk space were identified to be vulnerable to a denial of service attack, SDL and TAM would rank the threat on the same level of seriousness for both machines whereas SensePost CTM would take the hard disk space into consideration during the analysis.

Since the SDL tools produces a rather high level analysis of the system, it is difficult to prioritize threats and describe concrete use case scenarios that security experts cam use for mitigation planning. Furthermore there is a tendency to over represent the system using data flow diagrams which can lead to unnecessary clutter making it difficult to discern the real problem areas especially for the non-expert security modeler. The downside of the TAM tool is that the images generated (threat tree, attack surface, and system call flaws) are not easily adaptable and when the complexity in the application increases, the images can get confusing to interpret accurately. Furthermore, while automatic threat generation highlights a good number of threat most highlighted threats are not useful or even applicable to the application's context.

Attack Methodologies and Mitigations: Case Studies

In this section we describe our experiences after the threat modeling process and the deployment of the HACKMi2 social network. We had roughly 200 users join the site mostly from a population of students and the site was used mainly for discussions of games or party planning. Users were provided with a privacy agreement document and discouraged strongly from posting any personal information as would have been the case on a real social network platform. The reason we opted for this strategy, was in order to avoid any negative consequences of privacy violations that might arise during experimentation. We tested four attacks namely, Session Hijacking, Account Lockout, Phishing, and Spamming; after the HACKMi2 platform had been deployed following the threat modeling process.

The session hijacking attack was successful because it was accomplished through a blog comment that none of the threat modeling tools had been able to identify. In this case the attacker opens up a blog and then injects a malicious code as a blog comment which is then reflected in the activity page. When a user views the activity page the code starts execution. Since Elgg stored its session tokens in a cookie on a client-side browser, the malicious code exploits this feature to obtain the session cookie that it sends to the attacker's server. This attack is actually quite difficult to detect because the user does not notice any changes after the session token has been stored on the attacker's end, as he/she will be quite naturally redirected to the HACKMi2 site after viewing the blog. A further attack step would be to provoke the same sort of session hijack attack using a chat application instead.

The impact of the session hijack attack is that the attack can gain complete control of a user's account and as a consequence read all of the user's private information including private messages. Session hijack attacks are a key method of obtaining information for identity theft. The impact is more severe if the hijacked user is the site's administrator.

Since this attack relies on the application's vulnerability to cross-site scripting attacks that were identified by both the TAM and CTM tools, circumventing the cross-site scripting attack solves the problem in this case.

We provoked a cross-site scripting attack on the HackMi2 social network platform to determine whether or not it is vulnerable to cross-site injections. The procedure we followed to do this was to use TamperIE which is a browser extension for HTTP analysis and tampering. This tool allows the attacker to tamper with the GET and POST requests. By default the attack parameters are set to tamper only with POST requests. When a POST request is launched during a browsing process, TamperIE intercepts that submission and presents the screen shown in Figure 3.

As shown in Figure 4, we then selected the "PrettyPOST" tab which shows all the fields that can be tampered with. In this case we tampered with the description field by inserting a simple Java script that just pops out an alert box in which is written "You got Hacked!!! by UCT Compsci."

```
Script: '"<script>alert("You got
Hacked!!! By UCT Compsci");</script>
```

Figure 5 shows the result of the cross-site script injection indicating that the attack was successful.

Figure 5. Cross-site script vulnerability

The solution we implemented as to sanitize user inputs before storing them in the database. Sanitization works by modifying the HTML entries into forms that are interpretable only by browsers.

The above example seems pretty harmless but consider the case in which the script were to be modified with just one extra Java script instruction such as: *Loaction.reload( )*thereby modifying the injected script to:

```
'"<script>alert ("You Got Hacked!!!
By UCT Compsci");</script>
Location.reload()
```

This will result in a continuous generation of the alert boxes each the the victim clicks on the ok button. This process will continue until the machine is rebooted. This type of attack is known as a temporary denial of service attack.

Cookie theft attacks allow a malicious user to steal cookie sessions form users. For instance, in order to steal a users seesion cookie and store it on an attacker's machine say "cheetah.cs.ucy.ac.za"

```
<a href="javascript:document.
location='http://cheetah.cs.uct.
ac.za/logger.php?cookie='+document.
cookie;">CLICK ME!</a>
```

In order to patch this vulnerability, we used a java script patch to sanitize input so as to block cross-site scripts that might lead to Denial-of-Service attacks. We did this with the following javascript

```
<script language = "javascript">
        var id = <%=Anti-
Xss.JavaScriptEncode(Request.
Querystring["userinput"])%>
</script>
```

The account lockout attack was tested to verify that the mitigations implemented on HACKMi2, after the threat analysis with the CTM tool, were

Figure 3. Running tamperIE

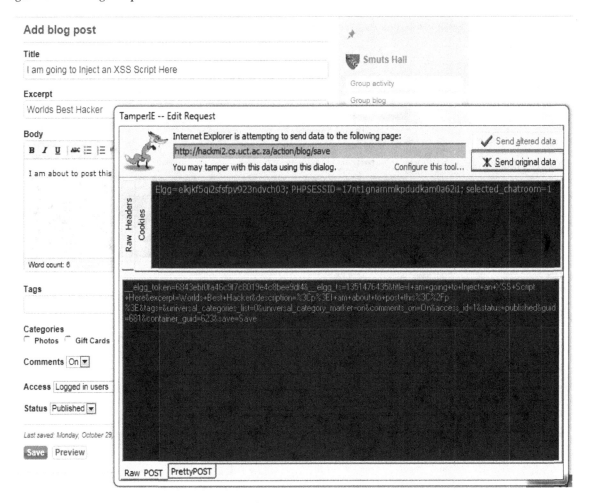

effective in preventing brute force attacks. We found that while brute force attacks are circumvented, an interesting problem arises, namely the account lockout attack. In the HACKMi2 initial implementation, we prevented users from testing passwords repeatedly (brute-force attack) by requiring that the user be locked out of the account for x seconds after a first try. Subsequent failed password entry requests were handled by growing the lockout time exponentially. However, the problem with this strategy is that it can be exploited to lockout a legitimate user from his/her account. We mitigated the account lockout attack by using a challenge-response system implemented as a CAPTCHA (Completely Automated Public

Turing Test to tell Computers and Humans Apart) where a user is forced to enter the characters in am image to provide authentication of being human. So instead of locking out the user on a failed attempt at logging in we check to verify whether or not the user is human or machine. Machines are typically used to provoke brute force attacks because of the large number of guesses required to obtain a "correct" password.

The phishing attack takes advantage of the cross-site scripting attack that we highlighted earlier in relation to the session hijack problem and has a similar impact in terms of identity theft. We mitigated this by patching the cross-site scripting vulnerability and also by sending out periodic

Figure 4. Injecting a cross-site attack script

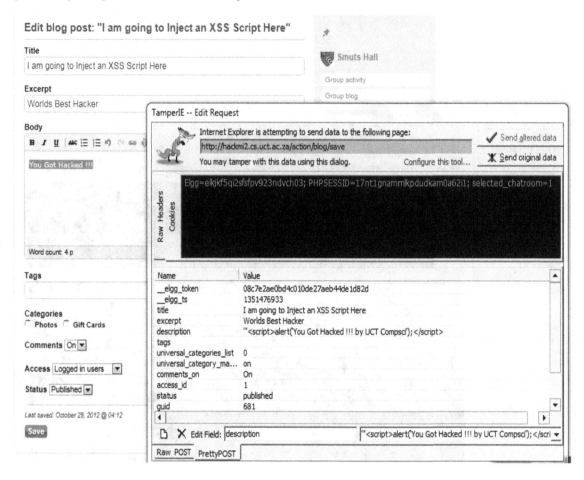

messages to the sites users about messages to be on the alert for. We also incorporated report buttons to allow users report suspicious messages or activity. We could have blocked urls to mitigate this attack but this would have impacted negatively on the usability of the social network.

Finally, spamming began almost a week into the deployment of the HACKMi2 social network. Spammers were able to register because the threat modeling tools had not picked up on the fact that registrations needed to be validated. The solution we employed here was to as a first step require some form of authentication to distinguish between human and machine. We did this by using a challenge-response system as we did in the case of handling account lockouts.

DISCUSSION

We note that only the CTM and TAM tools picked up the cross-site scripting attack vulnerability that impacts on session hijacking and phishing attacks. This is probably due to the fact that, as mentioned earlier, the SDL tool is very high level and so does not flag attacks that emerge from sources that are not directly related to the system's model. The CTM tool on the other hand identifies the more serious attacks like the brute force attack that can be used to gain unauthorized access into a user account but fails to identify the consequence of exponential lockout (Denial of Service Attack). The TAM model identifies a denial of service attack that is related to a cross-

Figure 6. Example of a letter CAPTCHA

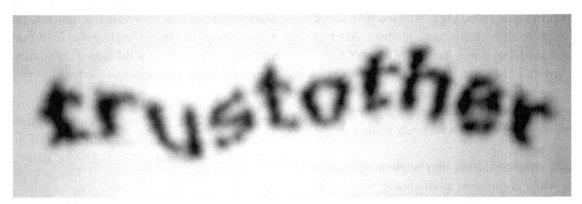

site scripting vulnerability but again not one that is related to the account lockout issue. We noted however, that in employing the TAM and SDL tools with an attacker-centric philosophy we were able to get a better analysis of the system in terms of what could go wrong. Also noteworthy was the fact that we used the CTM tool from a system administrator's perspective but considering that this is an attack centric tool we were able to better anticipate vulnerabilities in the HACKMi2 platform than would have been the case if TAM or SDL had been our primary method of analyzing the system. Finally, by comparing the three tools on the same platform we believe that we obtained a better threat analysis result than if only one of the three had been used.

A number of attacks that we tested were unsuccessful mainly because adequate precautions have been taken in the Elgg framework. For instance, SQL injection attacks are blocked because Elgg requires that all SQL queries be sanitized before they are used. Likewise, Broken Authentication and Session Management, as well as Insecure Direct Object Reference attacks are unsuccessful on HackMi2.

Elgg uses PHP's session handling with custom handlers. Session data is stored in the database. The session cookie contains the identifier that links the user to the browser and the user's meta data is stored in the session including the globally unique identifier, username, and email address. The session's lifetime is controlled through the server's PHP configuration. Sessions end automatically when the browser is closed.

Elgg further protects the system against session fixation by regenerating the session id when a user logs in. This way, even if the attacker were to steal the session identified he/she would be unable to exploit it usefully.

Session hijacking occurs if the identifier is compromised. Elgg counteracts this by storing the hash of the browser's user agent and a site secret such as a session fingerprints. However, it is still possible that an attacker get the user agent's identifier by using Jquery commands.

Finally insecure direct object references occur when a developer exposes a reference to an internal implementation object which as a file, directory or database key. Without access control checks or some other form of protection, attackers can manipulate these references to access unauthorized data.

Elgg restricts user for access certain oaths or directories. This was accomplished by having a method call gatekeep(), which whenever called, checks whether or not a user has the rights to have access to the directory or file.

CONCLUSION

In conclusion we present a summary of our findings as well as potential avenues for future work. HACKMi2 is the experimental social network platform that we built from an open source social network engine called Elgg. We used HACKMi2 to evaluate the effectiveness of three different threat modeling tools namely Microsoft SDL, Microsoft TAM and SensePost CTM in evaluating the security vulnerabilities in HACKMi2. Currently, HACKMi2 has nearly 200 registered members even though it was only made public 1 month ago.

We concluded from our comparative analysis that while al the tools studied have useful plus sides in relation to threat modeling and identifying security vulnerabilities, threat modeling tools that are attack as opposed to software centric are more effective in vulnerability analysis. In terms of at- tack methodologies and mitigations, we drew our list potential attacks from the OWASP document and focused on the first four because these are the more difficult ones to identify and mitigate. HACKMi2 was found to be vulnerable to cross site scripting attacks, and broken authentication and session management which are listed as numbers 1 and 3 on the OWASP list. We presented a methodology that we employed to patch both attacks and noted that patching the problem of cross site scripting also solves the problem of the session management attack.

As future work coming up with a hybrid threat modeling tool that integrates the best aspects of all of the threat modeling tools that we studied, would be helpful in better and more effective security modeling. More threats can be studied and a sort of security scaffolding system created to help novice designers with coding secure applications.

REFERENCES

Al-Ahmad, W. (2011). Building secure software using xp. *International Journal of Secure Software Engineering*, 2(3), 63–76. doi:10.4018/jsse.2011070104

Asnar, Y., Paja, E., & Mylopoulos, J. (2011). Modeling design patterns with description logics: a case study. In *Proceedings of the 23rd international conference on Advanced information systems engineering*. Springer-Verlag.

Bagnato, A., Kordy, B., Meland, P. H., & Schweitzer, P. (2012). Attribute decoration of attack-defense trees. *International Journal of Secure Software Engineering*, 3(2), 1–35. doi:10.4018/jsse.2012040101

Boshmaf, Y., Muslukhov, I., Beznosov, K., & Ripeanu, M. (2013). Design and analysis of a Social Botnet. *Computer Networks*, 57(2), 556–578. doi:10.1016/j.comnet.2012.06.006

Boyd, D. M., & Ellison, N. B. (2007). Social network sites: Definition, history, and scholarship. *Journal of Computer-Mediated Communication*, 13(1), 210–230. doi:10.1111/j.1083-6101.2007.00393.x

Br, G., Refsdal, A., & Stølen, K. (2010). Modular analysis and modelling of risk scenarios with dependencies. *Journal of Systems and Software*, 83(10), 1995–2013. doi:10.1016/j.jss.2010.05.069

Cha, S., & Yoo, J. (2012). A safety-focused verification using software fault trees. *Future Generation Computer Systems*, 28(8), 1272–1282. doi:10.1016/j.future.2011.02.004

Chen, R. (2013). Member use of social networking sites - An empirical examination. *Decision Support Systems*, 54(3), 1219–1227. doi:10.1016/j.dss.2012.10.028

Cuevas, A., Khoury, P. E., Gomez, L., & Laube, A. (2008). Security patterns for capturing encryption-based access control to sensor data. In *Proceedings of the 2008 Second International Conference on Emerging Security Information, Systems and Technologies*. IEEE Computer Society.

Curry, E., & Grace, P. (2008). Flexible self-management using the model-view-controller pattern. *IEEE Software, 25*(3), 84–90. doi:10.1109/MS.2008.60

Dong, X., Clark, J. A., & Jacob, J. L. (2008). Threat modelling in user performed authentication. In *Proceedings of the 10th International Conference on Information and Communications Security.* Springer-Verlag.

Edge, C. C. (2010). *Quantitative assessment of the modularization of security design patterns with aspects.* (Ph.D. thesis).

Elgg. (2013). *Elgg social network engine.* Retrieved from http://elgg.org/

Futcher, L., & Von Solms, R. (2008). Guidelines for secure software development. In *Proceedings of the 2008 annual research conference of the South African Institute of Computer Scientists and Information Technologists on IT research in developing countries: riding the wave of technology.* ACM.

Hackmi2. (2012). Retrieved from http://hackmi2

INTECO. (2009). *Study on the privacy of personal data and on the security of information in social networks.* Retrieved from https://www.inteco.es/file/vuiNP2GNuMjfCgs9ZBYoAQ?

Kainerstorfer, M., Sametinger, J., & Wiesauer, A. (2011). Software security for small development teams: A case study. In *Proceedings of the 13th International Conference on Information Integration and Web-based Applications and Services.* ACM.

Kendall, K. E., & Kendall, J. E. (2002). *Systems Analysis and Design.* Upper Saddle River, NJ: Prentice-Hall, Inc.

Kim, S., Han, H., Shin, D., Jeun, I., & Jeong, H. (2009). A study of international trend analysis on web service vulnerabilities in owasp and wasc. In *Proceedings of the 3rd International Conference and Workshops on Advances in Information Security and Assurance.* Springer-Verlag.

Kordy, B., Pouly, M., & Schweitzer, P. (2012). Computational aspects of attack—Defense trees. In *Proceedings of the 2011 international conference on Security and Intelligent Information Systems.* Springer-Verlag.

Krishnamurthy, B., & Wills, C. E. (2008). Characterizing privacy in online social networks. In *Proceedings of the first workshop on Online social networks.* ACM.

Lee, C.-J., Tsai, C.-C., Tang, S.-M., & Liang-Kai, W. (2009). Innovation: web 2.0, online-communities and mobile social networking. *Trans. on Comp., 8*(11), 1825–1834.

Mauw, S., & Oostdijk, M. (2006). Foundations of attack trees. In *Proceedings of the 8th international conference on Information Security and Cryptology.* Springer-Verlag.

Pirate Bay. (2010). Retrieved from http://www.pattayadailynews.com/en/2010/07/29/facebook-security-breach-private-details-published-on-pirate-bay/

Rooksby, J., & Sommerville, I. (2012). The management and use of social net- work sites in a government department. *Computer Supported Cooperative Work, 21*(4-5), 397–415. doi:10.1007/s10606-011-9150-2

Rowell, L. (2008). In search of web 3.0. *netWorker, 12*(3), 18–24. doi:10.1145/1435535.1435540

Roy, A., Kim, D. S., & Trivedi, K. S. (2010). Cyber security analysis using attack countermeasure trees. In *Proceedings of the Sixth Annual Workshop on Cyber Security and Information Intelligence Research.* ACM.

Sharma, M. (2008). Elgg Social Networking: Create and manage your own social network site using this free open-source tool. Packt Publishing.

Story, H., Blin, R., Subercaze, J., Gravier, C., & Maret, P. (2012). Turning a web 2.0 social network into a web 3.0, distributed, and secured social web application. In *Proceedings of the 21st international conference companion on World Wide Web*. ACM.

Walters, R. (2009). Joining the dots: Joining the dots. *Network Security*, *2009*(5), 16–19. doi:10.1016/S1353-4858(09)70054-6

Wang, Y., Li, J., Meng, K., Lin, C., & Cheng, X. (2013). Modeling and security analysis of enterprise network using attack-defense stochastic game petri nets. *Security and Communication Networks*, *6*(1), 89–99. doi:10.1002/sec.535

Wang, Y., Norcie, G., Komanduri, S., Acquisti, A., Leon, P. G., & Cranor, L. F. (2011). I regretted the minute I pressed share: A qualitative study of regrets on facebook. In *Proceedings of the Seventh Symposium on Usable Privacy and Security*. ACM.

Westland, J. C. (2012). The adoption of social networking technologies in cinema releases. *Information Technology Management*, *13*(3), 167–181. doi:10.1007/s10799-012-0114-0

Wu, R., Li, W., & Huang, H. (2008). An attack modeling based on hierarchical colored petri nets. In *Proceedings of the 2008 International Conference on Computer and Electrical Engineering*. IEEE Computer Society.

Xu, D., Goel, V., Nygard, K. E., & Wong, W. E. (2008). Aspect Oriented specification of threat driven security requirements. *Int. J. Comput. Appl. Technol.*, *31*(1/2), 131–140. doi:10.1504/IJCAT.2008.017725

Zhou, S., Qin, Z., Zhang, F., Zhang, X., Chen, W., & Liu, J. (2003). Colored petri net based attack modeling. In *Proceedings of the 9th international conference on Rough sets, fuzzy sets, data mining, and granular computing*. Springer-Verlag.

ADDITIONAL READING

Almorsy, M., Grundy, J., & Ibrahim, A. S. (2013). Automated software architecture security risk analysis using formalized signatures. In *Proceedings of the 2013 International Conference on Software Engineering* (ICSE '13). IEEE Press, Piscataway, NJ, USA, 662-671.

Almulhem, A. (2012, October). Threat Modeling for Electronic Health Record Systems. *Journal of Medical Systems*, *36*(5), 2921–2926. doi:10.1007/s10916-011-9770-6 PMID:21870030

Hu, Y., Zhang, X., Ngai, E. W. T., Cai, R., & Liu, M. (2013, December). Software project risk analysis using Bayesian networks with causality constraints. *Decision Support Systems*, *56*, 439–449. doi:10.1016/j.dss.2012.11.001

Keunwoo, R., Dongho, W., Sang-Woon, J., Sooyoung C., & Sangwoo, P. 2013. Threat modeling of a mobile device management system for secure smart work. 13, 3 (September 2013), 243-256.

Kusumo, D. S., Staples, M., Zhu, L., & Jeffery, R. (2012). Analyzing differences in risk perceptions between developers and acquirers in OTS-based custom software projects using stakeholder analysis. In *Proceedings of the ACM-IEEE international symposium on Empirical software engineering and measurement* (ESEM '12). ACM, New York, NY, USA, 69-78.

Rene Robin, C. R., & Uma, G. V. (2011). Development of educational ontology for software risk analysis. In *Proceedings of the 2011 International Conference on Communication, Computing & Security* (ICCCS '11). ACM, New York, NY, USA, 610-615.

Steven, J. (2010, May). Threat Modeling Perhaps It's Time. *IEEE Security and Privacy, 8*(3), 83–86. doi:10.1109/MSP.2010.110

Zalewski, J., Drager, S., McKeever, W., & Kornecki, A. J. (2013). Threat modeling for security assessment in Cyber Physical systems. In *Proceedings of the Eighth Annual Cyber Security and Information Intelligence Research Workshop* (CSIIRW '13), Frederick Sheldon, Annarita Giani, Axel Krings, and Robert Abercrombie (Eds.). ACM, New York, NY, USA, Article 10, 4 pages.

KEY TERMS AND DEFINITIONS

Attack Nets: A network of interconnected attacks that result from one or several attacks creating a ripple effect of interdependent security violations.

Attack Trees: These are conceptual flow state diagrams illustrating how an asset or target device might be attacked.

Authentication: Method that enables a computing system establish and verify the identity of a user in realtion to granting resource access.

Cross-Site Scripting Attacks: Also know as XSS attacks are a type of computer security vulnerability that typically arises in web-based applications. This attack enables the attacker to inject client-side code into webpages that are viewed/accessed by other users.

Fault Trees: This is a top-down deductive analysis approach to identifying the undesired states that a system can enter into. Typically, this is done by using boolean logic to combine a series of lower-level events.

SQL Injection Attacks: This is a code inject technique that is used to attack data-centric or data-driven applications.

Threat Modeling: This is a structured software design procedure for optimizing application security by identifying objectives and vulnerabilities, and then proceeding to specify countermeasures to prevent security violations.

Chapter 15

Solving Security and Availability Challenges in Public Clouds

Maxim Schnjakin
Potsdam University, Germany

Christoph Meinel
Potsdam University, Germany

ABSTRACT

Cloud Computing as a service-on-demand architecture has grown in importance over the previous few years. One driver of its growth is the ever-increasing amount of data that is supposed to outpace the growth of storage capacity. The usage of cloud technology enables organizations to manage their data with low operational expenses. However, the benefits of cloud computing come along with challenges and open issues such as security, reliability, and the risk to become dependent on a provider for its service. In general, a switch of a storage provider is associated with high costs of adapting new APIs and additional charges for inbound and outbound bandwidth and requests. In this chapter, the authors present a system that improves availability, confidentiality, and reliability of data stored in the cloud. To achieve this objective, the authors encrypt users' data and make use of the RAID-technology principle to manage data distribution across cloud storage providers. Further, they discuss the security functionality and present a proof-of-concept experiment for the application to evaluate the performance and cost effectiveness of the approach. The authors deploy the application using eight commercial cloud storage repositories in different countries. The approach allows users to avoid vendor lock-in and reduces significantly the cost of switching providers. They also observe that the implementation improved the perceived availability and, in most cases, the overall performance when compared with individual cloud providers. Moreover, the authors estimate the monetary costs to be competitive to the cost of using a single cloud provider.

INTRODUCTION

Cloud Computing is a concept of utilizing computing as an on-demand service. It fosters operating and economic efficiencies and promises to cause an unanticipated change in business. Using computing resources as pay-as-you-go model enables service users to convert fixed IT cost into a variable cost based on actual consumption. Therefore, numerous authors argue for the benefits of cloud computing focusing on the economic value (Carr, 2008), (Armbrust et al., 2010).

DOI: 10.4018/978-1-4666-6158-5.ch015

However, despite of the non-contentious financial advantages cloud computing raises questions about privacy, security and reliability. Among available cloud offerings, storage services reveal an increasing level of market competition. According to iSuppli (Burt, 2009) global cloud storage revenue is set to rise to $5 billion in 2013, up from $1.6 billion in 2009. One reason is the ever increasing amount of data which is supposed to outpace the growth of storage capacity. Currently, it is very difficult to estimate the actual future volume of data but there are different estimates being published. According to IDC review (Gantz, & Reinsel, 2009), the amount of digital information created and replicated is estimated to surpass 3 zettabytes by the end of this year. This amount is supposed to more than double in the next two years. In addition, the authors estimate that today there is 9 times more information available than was available five years ago.

However, for a customer (service) to depend solely on one cloud storage provider (in the following provider) has its limitations and risks. In general, vendors do not provide far reaching security guarantees regarding the data retention (Ponemon Institute, 2011). Users have to rely on effectiveness and experience of vendors in dealing with security and intrusion detection systems. For missing guarantees service users are merely advised to encrypt sensitive content before storing it on the cloud. Placement of data in the cloud removes the physical control that a data owner has over data. So there is a risk that service provider might share corporate data with a marketing company or use the data in a way the client never intended.

Further, customers of a particular provider might experience vendor lock-in. In the context of cloud computing, it is a risk for a customer to become dependent on a provider for its services. Common pricing schemes foresee charging for inbound and outbound transfer and requests in addition to hosting the actual data. Changes in features or pricing scheme might motivate a switch

from one storage service to another. However, because of the data inertia, customers may not be free to select the optimal vendor due to immense costs associated with a switch of one provider to another. The obvious solution is to make the switching and data placement decisions at a finer granularity then all or nothing. This could be achieved by distributing corporate data among multiple storage providers. Such an approach is pursued by content delivery networks (for example in (Broberg, Buyya, & Tari, 2009), (Buyya, Yeo, & Venugopal, 2008) and implies significant higher storage and bandwidth costs without taking into account the security concerns regarding the retention of data. A more economical approach, which is presented in this paper, is to separate data into unrecognizable slices, which are distributed to providers - whereby only a subset of the nodes needs to be available in order to reconstruct done for years at the level of file systems and disks. In our work we use RAID like techniques to overcome the mentioned limitations of cloud storage in the following way:

1. **Security:** The provider might be trustworthy, but malicious insiders represent a well known security problem. This is a serious threat for critical data such as medical records, as cloud provider staff has physical access to the hosted data. We tackle the problem by encrypting and encoding the original data and later by distributing the fragments transparently across multiple providers. This way, none of the storage vendors is in an absolute possession of the client's data. Moreover, the usage of enhanced erasure algorithms enables us to improve the storage efficiency and thus also to reduce the total costs of the solution.

2. **Service Availability:** Management of computing resources as a service by a single company implies the risk of a single point of failure. This failure depends on many factors such as financial difficulties (bank-

ruptcy), software or network failure, etc. In July 2008, for instance, Amazon storage service S3 was down for 8 hours because of a single bit error (The Amazon S3 Team., 2008). Our solution addresses this issue by storing the data on several clouds - whereby no single entire copy of the data resides in one location, and only a subset of providers needs to be available in order to reconstruct the data.

3. **Reliability:** Any technology can fail. According to a study conducted by Kroll Ontrack[1] 65 percent of businesses and other organizations have frequently lost data from a virtual environment. A number that is up by 140 percent from just last year. Admittedly, in recent times, no spectacular outages were observed. Nevertheless failures do occur. For example, in October 2009 a subsidiary of Microsoft, Danger Inc., lost the contracts, notes, photos, etc. of a large number of users of the Sidekick service (Sarno, 2009). We deal with the problem by using erasure algorithms to separate data into packages, thus enabling the application to retrieve data correctly even if some of the providers corrupt or lose the entrusted data.

4. **Data Lock-In:** By today there are no standards for APIs for data import and export in cloud computing. This limits the portability of data and applications between providers. For the customer this means that he cannot seamlessly move the service to another provider if he becomes dissatisfied with the current provider. This could be the case if a vendor increases his fees, goes out of business, or degrades the quality of his provided services. As stated above, our solution does not depend on a single service provider. The data is balanced among several providers taking into account user expectations regarding the price and availability of the hosted content. Moreover, with erasure codes we store only a fraction of the total amount of data on each cloud provider. In

this way, switching one provider for another costs merely a fraction of what it would be otherwise. In recent months we conducted an extensive experiment for our application to evaluate the overall performance and cost effectiveness of the approach. In the current work we present the design of our application and the results of the experimental study. We show, that with an appropriate coding configuration Cloud-RAID is able to improve significantly the performance of the data transmission process, whereby the monetary costs are competitive to the cost of using a single cloud.

ARCHITECTURE

The ground of our approach is to find a balance between benefiting from the cloud's nature of pay-per-use and ensuring the security of the company's data. The goal is to achieve such a balance by distributing corporate data among multiple storage providers, supporting the selection process of a cloud provider, and removing the auditing and administrating responsibility from the customer's side. As mentioned above, the basic idea is not to depend on solely one storage provider but to spread the data across multiple providers using redundancy to tolerate possible failures. The approach is similar to a service-oriented version of RAID (Redundant Arrays of Inexpensive Disks). While RAID manages sector redundancy dynamically across hard drives, our approach manages file distribution across cloud storage providers. RAID 5, for example, stripes data across an array of disks and maintains parity data that can be used to restore the data in the event of disk failure. We carry the principle of the RAID-technology to cloud infrastructure. In order to achieve our goal we foster the usage of erasure coding technics (see chapter IV). This enables us to tolerate the loss of one or more storage providers without suffering any loss of content (Weatherspoon & Kubiatowicz 2002), (Dingledine, Freedman, & Molnar, 2000).

The system has a number of core components that contain the logic and management layers required to encapsulate the functionality of different storage providers. Our architecture includes the following main components:

- **User Interface Module:** The interface presents the user a cohesive view on his data and available features. Here users can manage their data and specify requirements regarding the data retention (quality of service parameters). User can upload, view, modify or delete existing content. Further, the user is presented with options to specify parameters regarding security or storage and transfer budget.
- **Resource Management Module:** This system component is responsible for intelligent deployment of data based on users' requirements. The component is supported by:
  - A registry and matching service: assigns storage repositories based on users requirements (for example physical location of the service, costs and performance expectations). Monitors the performance of participating providers and ensures that they are meeting the agreed SLAs.
  - A resource management service: takes operational decisions regarding the content storage.
  - A task scheduler service: has the ability to schedule the launch of operations at peak-off hours or after specified time intervals.
- **Data Management Module:** This component handles data management on behalf of the resource management module and is mainly supported by:
  - A data encoding service: this component is responsible for striping and encoding of user content.
  - A data distribution service: spreads the encoded data packages across multiple providers. Since each storage service is only accessible through a unique API, the service utilizes storage "service connectors", which provide an abstraction layer for the communication to storage repositories.
  - A security service: manages the security functionality based on a user's requirements (encryption, secret key management).

Further details can be found in our previous work (Schnjakin, & Meinel, 2011), (Schnjakin, Alnemr, & Meinel, 2010), and (Schnjakin, Alnemr, & Meinel, 2011).

DESIGN

Any application needs a model of storage, a model of computation and a model of communication. In this section we describe how we achieve the goal of the consistent, unified view on the data management system to the end-user. The web portal is developed using Grails, JNI and C technologies, with a MySQL back-end to store user accounts, current deployments, meta data, and the capabilities and pricing of cloud storage providers. Keeping the meta data locally ensures that no individual provider will have access to stored data. In this way, only users that have authorization to access the data will be granted access to the shares of (at least) k different clouds and will be able to reconstruct the data. Further, our implementation makes use of AES for symmetric encryption, SHA-1 and MD5 for cryptographic hashes and an improved version of Jerasure library (Plank, Simmerman, & Schuman. 2008) for using the Cauchy-Reed-Solomon and Liberation erasure codes. Our system communicates with providers via "storage connectors", which are discussed further in this section.

Service Interface

The graphical user interface provides two major functionalities to an end-user: data administration and specification of requirements regarding the data storage. Interested readers are directed to our previous work (Schnjakin, Alnemr, & Meinel, 2010) which gives a more detailed background on the identification of suitable cloud providers in our approach. In short, the user interface enables users to specify their requirements (regarding the placement and storage of user's data) manually in form of options, for example:

- Budget-oriented content deployment (based on the price model of available providers).
- Data placement based on quality of service parameters (for example availability, throughput or average response time).
- Storage of data based on geographical regions of the user's choice. The restriction of data storage to specific geographic areas can be reasonable in the case of legal restrictions.

Storage Repositories

Cloud Storage Providers

Cloud storage providers are modeled as a storage entity that supports six basic operations, shown in Table 1. We need storage services to support not more than the aforementioned operations.

Further, the individual providers are not trusted. This means that the entrusted data can be corrupted, deleted or leaked to unauthorized parties. This fault model encompasses both malicious attacks on a provider and arbitrary data corruption like the Sidekick case (section 1). The protocols require $n = k + m$ storage clouds, at most m of which can be faulty. Present-day, our prototypical implementation supports the following storage repositories: Amazons S3 (in all available regions: US west and east coast, Ireland, Singapore and Tokyo), Box, Rackspace Cloud Files, Azure, Google Cloud Storage and Nirvanix SND. Further providers can be easily added.

Service Repository

At the present time, the capabilities of storage providers are created semi-automatically based on an analysis of corresponding SLAs which are usually written in a plain natural language. Until

Table 1. Storage connector functions

Function	Description
create(ContainerName)	creates a container for a new user
write(ContainerName, ObjectName)	writes a data object to a user container
read(ContainerName, ObjectName)	reads the specified data object
list(ContainerName)	list all data objects of the container
delete(ContainerName, ObjectName)	removes the data object from the container
getDigest(ContainerName, ObjectName)	returns the hash value of the specified data object

now the claims stated in SLAs need to be translated into WSLA statements and updated manually (interested readers will find more background information in our previous work (Schnjakin, Alnemr, & Meinel, 2010). Subsequently the formalized information is imported into a database of the system component named service repository. The database tracks logistical details regarding the capabilities of storage services such as their actual pricing, SLA offered, and physical locations. With this, the service repository represents a pool with available storage services.

Matching

The selection of storage services for the data distribution occurs based on user preferences set in the user interface. After matching user requirements and provider capabilities, we use the reputation of the providers to produce the final list of potential providers to host parts of the user's data. A provider's reputation holds the details of his historical performance plus his ratings in the service registries and is saved in a Reputation Object (introduced in our previous work). By reading this object, we know a provider's reputation concerning each performance parameter (e.g. has high response time, low price). With this information the system creates a prioritized list of repositories for each user. In general, the number of storage repositories needed to ensure data striping depends on a user's cost expectations, availability and performance requirements. The total number of repositories is limited by the number of implemented storage connectors.

Data Management

Data Model

In compliance with (Abu-Libdeh, Princehouse, & Weatherspoon, 2010), we mimic the data model of Amazon's S3 by the implementation of our encoding and distribution service. All data objects

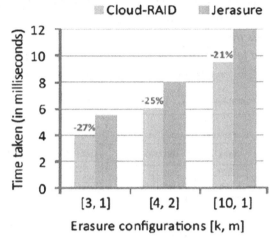

Figure 1. Total time taken when Jerasure and Cloud-RAID libraries are used to encode data objects of varying sizes

(a) Encoding of a 100kB data object

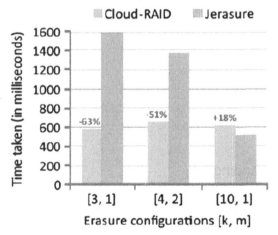

(b) Encoding of a 100MB data object

are stored in containers. A container can contain further containers.

Each container represents a flat namespace containing keys associated with objects. An object can be of an arbitrary size, up to 5 gigabytes (limited by the supported file size of cloud providers). Objects must be uploaded entirely, as partial writes are not allowed as opposed to partial reads. Our system establishes a set of n repositories for each data object of the user. These represent different cloud storage repositories (see Figure 2).

Figure 2. Data unit model at different abstraction levels. At a physical layer (local directory) each data unit has a name (original file name) and the encoded k+m data packages. In the second level, Cloud-RAID perceives data objects as generic data units in abstract clouds. Data objects are represented as data units with the according meta information (original file name, cryptographic hash value, size, used coding configuration parameters m and k, word size etc.). The database table "Repository Assignment" holds the information about particular data packages and their (physical) location in the cloud. In the third level, data objects are represented as containers in the cloud. Cloud-RAID supports various cloud specific constructions (buckets, tree nodes, containers etc.).

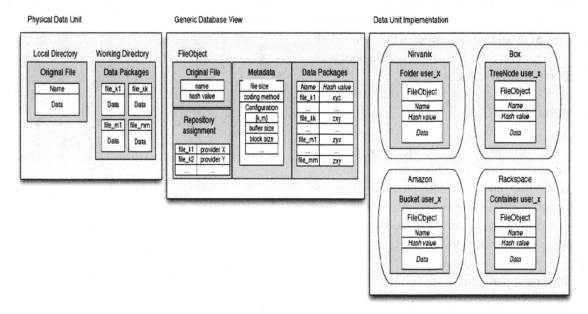

Encoding

Upon receiving a write request the system splits the incoming object into k data fragments of an equal size - called chunks. These *k* data packages hold the original data. In the next step the system adds *m* additional packages whose contents are calculated from the *k* chunks, whereby *k* and *m* are variable parameters (Plank, Simmerman, & Schuman. 2008). This means, that the act of encoding takes the contents of *k* data packages and encodes them on m coding packages. In turn, the act of decoding takes some subset of the collection of $n = k + m$ total packages and from them recalculates the original data. Any subset of *k* chunks is sufficient to reconstruct the original object of size s (Rhea et al., 2001). The total size of all data packets (after encoding) can be expressed with the following equation: $(s/k * k)+(s/k * m) = s$

$+ (s/k * m) = s * (1 + m/k)$. With this, the usage of erasure codes increases the total storage by a factor of *m/k*. Summarized, the overall overhead depends on the file size and the defined m and k parameters for the erasure configuration. Figure 3 visualizes the performance of our application using different erasure configurations. In our work we make use of the Cauchy-Reed-Solomon algorithm for two reasons. First, according to (Plank, Simmerman, & Schuman. 2008) the algorithm has a good performance characteristics in comparison to existing codes. In their work, the authors performed a head-to-head comparison of numerous open-source implementations of various coding techniques which are available to the general public. Second, the algorithm allows free selection of coding parameters k and m. Whereas other algorithms restrict the choice of parameters. Liberation Code (Plank, 2008) for example is a

Figure 3. The average performance of the erasure algorithm with data objects of varying sizes (100kB, 500kB, 1MB, 10MB and 100MB)

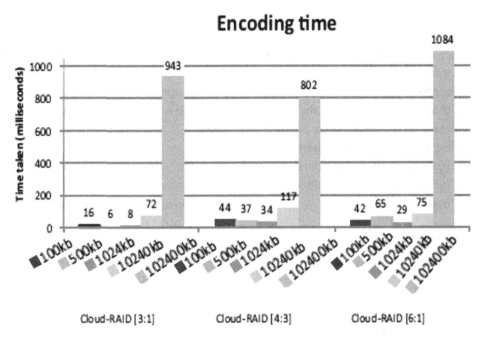

specification for storage systems with $n = k + 2$ nodes to tolerate the failure of any two nodes (the parameter m is fix and is equal to two). However, the functionality of the encoding component is based on the Jerasure library (Plank, Simmerman, & Schuman. 2008) which is an open C/C++ framework that supports erasure coding in storage applications. In our implementation we were able to improve the overall performance of the library by more than 20%. Figure 1 summarizes the results of 20 runs executed on test machine 1.

Competitive storage providers claim to have SLAs ranging from 99% to 100% uptime percentages for their services. Therefore choosing $m = 1$ to tolerate one provider outage or failure at time will be sufficient in the majority of cases. Thus, it makes sense to increase k and spread the packages across more providers to lower the overhead costs.

In the next step, the distribution service makes sure that each encoded data package is sent to a different storage repository. In general, our system follows a model of one thread per provider per data package in such a way that the encryption, decryption, and provider accesses can be executed in parallel.

However, most erasure codes have further parameters as for example w, which is word size 2. In addition, further parameters are required for reassembling the data (original file size, hash value, coding parameters, and the erasure algorithm used). This metadata is stored in a MySQL backend database after performing a successful write request.

Data Distribution

Each storage service is integrated by the system by means of a storage-service-connector (in the following service-connector). These provide an intermediate layer for the communication between the resource management service and storage repositories hosted by storage vendors. This enables us to hide the complexity in dealing with proprietary APIs of each service provider.

The basic connector functionality covers operations like creation, deletion or renaming of files and folders that are usually supported by every storage provider.

Such a service-connector must be implemented for each storage service, as each provider offers a unique interface to its repository. As discussed earlier in this chapter all accesses to the cloud storage providers can be executed in parallel. Therefore, following the encoding, the system performs an initial encryption of the data packages based on one of the predefined algorithms (this feature is optional).

Reassembling the Data

When the service receives a read request, the service component fetches k from n data packages (according to the list with prioritized service providers which can be different from the prioritized write list, as providers differ in upload and download throughput as well as in cost structure) and reassembles the data.

This is due to the fact, that in the pay-per-use cloud models it is not economical to read all data packages from all clouds. Therefore, the service is supported by a load balancer component, which is responsible for retrieving the data units from the most appropriate repositories. Different policies for load balancing and data retrieving are conceivable as parts of user's data are distributed between multiple providers. A read request can be directed to a random data share or the physically closest service (latency optimal approach).

Another possible approach is to fetch data from service providers that meet certain performance criteria (e.g response time or throughput). Finally, there is a minimal-cost aware policy, which guides user requests to the cheapest sources (cost optimal approach). The latter strategy is implemented as a default configuration in our system. Other more sophisticated features as a mix of several complex criteria (e.g. faults and overall performance his-

tory) are under development at present. However, the read optimization has been implemented to save time and costs.

Resource Management Service

This component tracks each user's actual deployment and is responsible for various housekeeping tasks:

1. The service is equipped with a MySQL back-end database to store crucial information needed for deploying and reassembling of users data.
2. Further, it audits and tracks the performance of the participated providers and ensures, that all current deployments meet the corresponding requirements specified by the user.
3. The management component is also responsible for scheduling of not time-critical tasks. Further details can be found in our previous work (Schnjakin, Alnemr, & Meinel, 2011).

PERFORMANCE EVALUATION

In this section we present an evaluation of our system that aims to clarify the main questions concerning the cost, performance and availability aspects when erasure codes are used to store data on public clouds.

Methodology

The experiment was run on Hasso Plattner Institute (HPI), which is located close to Berlin, Germany, over a period of over 377 (24x7) hours, in the middle of July 2012. As it spans seven days, localized peak times (time-of-day) is experienced in each geographical region. HPI has a high speed connectivity to an Internet backbone (1 Gb), which ensures that our test system is not a bottleneck during the testing. The global testbed spans eight cloud providers in five countries on three continents. The experiment time comprises three rounds, with each round consisting of a set of predefined test configurations (in the following sequences). Table 2 provides a summary of the conducted experiment.

We used test files of different sizes from 100 kB up to 100MB, deployed by the dedicated test clients. Prior to each test round the client requires a persistent connection to the APIs of the relevant cloud storage providers, so that requests for an upload or download of test data can be send. In general, providers will refuse a call for the establishment of a new connection after several back-to-back requests. Therefore we implemented an API connection holder. After two hours of an active connection the old connection is overwritten by a new one. Further, we determine a timeout of one second between two unsuccessful requests, each client waits for a think time before the next request is generated.

Machines for Experimentation

We employed three machines for experimentation. Neither is exceptionally high-end, but each represents middle-range commodity processor, which should be able to encode, encrypt, decrypt

and decode comfortably within the I/O speed limits of the fastest disks. These are: Windows 7 Enterprise (64bit) system with an Intel Core 2 Duo E8400 @3GHz, 4 GB installed RAM and a 160 GB SATA Seagate Barracuda hard drive with 7200 U/min.

Experiment Setup

Figure 4 presents the workflow of the experiment. In general we use two machines to transfer test data to cloud storage providers. The first machine (the upper part of the graph) uses erasure codes. This means, upon receiving a write request the test system splits the incoming object into k data fragments of an equal size - chunks . These k data packages hold the original data. In the next step the system adds m further packages whose contents are calculated from the k chunks, whereby k and m are variable parameters (Plank, Simmerman, & Schuman. 2008). With this, the act of encoding takes the contents of k data packages and encodes them on m coding packages. In turn, the act of decoding takes some subset of the collection of $n = k + m$ total packages and from them recalculates the original data. Any subset of k shares is sufficient to reconstruct the original data object (Rhea et al., 2001).

Table 2. Experiment details

Category	Description
Cloud storage provider	8
Locations	Europe, USA, Asia
Total experiment time	about 15d 9h (377h)
Total number of test rounds	about 3 rounds
Total number of requests (read/write) / round	281,900
Service time out for each request	1 sec
Test file size	100 kB - 100 MB
Coding Method	cauchy_good
Coding configuration [k,m]	k=[2..4,6,10], m=[1..2], k>=m

Figure 4. Workflow of the experiment

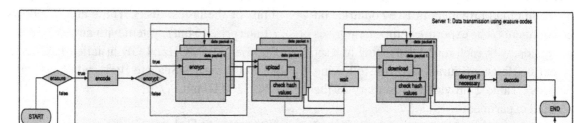

In the next step, the application makes sure that each data package is sent to a different storage repository. In general, our system follows a model of one thread per provider per data package in such a way that the encoding, encryption, decryption, and provider accesses can be executed in parallel. The second machine (the lower part of the graph in the Figure 4) uploads the entire data object to a single provider without any modifications. As we are interested in the direct comparison between these two approaches, we want each data transmission to start simultaneously.

Therefore we used the third machine as a "sync-instance" running a Tomcat 7 server with a self-written sync-servlet which controls the workflow of the experiment.

Erasure Configuration

In our experiment we make use of the Cauchy-Reed-Solomon algorithm for two reasons. First, according to Plank et al. (Plank et al., 2009a) the algorithm has a good performance characteristics in comparison to existing codes. In their work, the authors performed a head-to-head comparison of numerous open-source implementations of various coding techniques which are available to the public. Second, the algorithm allows free selection of coding parameters k and m, whereas other algorithms restrict the choice of parameters. Liberation Code (Plank, 2008) for example is a specification for storage systems with $n = k + 2$ nodes to tolerate the

failure of any two nodes (whereby the parameter *m* is fix and is equal to two).

In our test scenario we tested more than 2520 combinations of k and m. We will denote them by $[k,m]$ in the course of the chapter, whereby the present evaluation focuses on an encoding configuration [4,1]. Which means, that the setting provides data availability toward one cloud failure at the time of read or write request. Most of the providers have SLAs with 99% and 99.9% monthly up-time percentages. Thus, we believe that adding enough redundancy to tolerate provider outage or failure at a time will be sufficient in most cases.

Schemes and Metrics

The goal of our test is to evaluate the performance of our approach. Mainly we are interested in availability of APIs, overhead caused by erasure codes and transmission rates. Therefore, we implemented a simple logger application to record the results of our measurements. In total we log 34 different events. For example, each state of the workflow depicted in Figure 4 is captured with two log entries (START and END).

Erasure Overhead

Due to the nature of erasure codes, each file upload and download is associated with a certain overhead. As discussed in before the total size of all chunks (after encoding) can be expressed with the following equation: $s+(s/k * m) = s * (1 + m/k)$, whereby variable s is defined as the original file size. Again, the usage of erasure codes increases the total storage by a factor of m/k. Further, we need to encode data prior to its upload and accordingly decode the downloaded packets into the original file. Both operations cause an additional computational expense.

Transmission Performance and Throughput

We measure the throughput obtained from each read and write request. In general the throughput is defined as the average rate of successful message delivery over a communication channel. In our work we link the success of the message delivery to the success of the delivery of the entire data object. In our approach, a data object is completely transferred, when the last data package is being successfully transferred to the transfer destination. This means that in case of data upload, the transfer is only completed, when (upon a write request) our client receives a confirmation message in the form of individual digest values that correspond

with the results of the local computation (this applies for all transferred data packages). In the event of a mismatch the system will delete the corrupted data and initiate a re-upload procedure. With this, the value of throughput does not only represent the pure upload or download rate of the particular providers, as the measured time span includes also possible failures, latency and the bilateral processing of get-hash calls.

Empirical Results

This section presents the results in terms of read and write performance, as well as throughput, response time and availability based on over 281.000 requests. Due to space constraints, we present only some selected results from the conducted experiment.

Erasure Overhead

As described in IV-B1 the erasure coding leads to a storage overhead of factor m/k. For instance, an *[k=4, m=1]* encoding results in a storage overhead of 14 100% = 25% . In order to reduce the storage

Figure 5. The computational overhead caused by erasure with different configurations and file sizes. In general, the overall overhead increases with growing file size regardless of the defined m and k parameters for the erasure configuration.

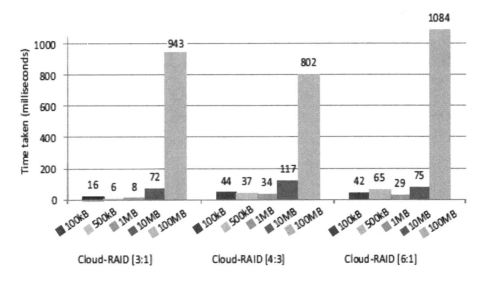

overhead, it would be advisable to define high k and preferably low m values. For example, an encoding configuration *[k = 10, m = 1]* produces a storage overhead of ¼ * 100% = 25%. In order to reduce the storage overhead, it would be advisable to define high *k* and preferably low *m* values. For example, an encoding configuration *[k=10, m=1]* produces 1/10 * 100% = 10%. Erasure causes also a computational overhead. During the experiment we scrutinized 12 different configurations. A selection of the results is presented in Figure 5. The figure illustrates, that the computational expense increases with the file size regardless of the erasure configuration. As the encoding of a 100 MB data object takes approximately one second, the encoding overhead can be neglected in view of the significantly higher transmission times. In (Schnjakin et al., 2013) we showed, that the average performance overhead caused by data encoding is less than 2% of the entire data transfer process to a cloud provider.

Using encryption, we can say that the total performance decreases as individual data packages have to be encrypted locally before moving them to the cloud. In our experiments the costs for encryption were less than 3% of total time which is also negligible in view of the overall transmission performance. This point has been addressed in our previous work (Schnjakin et al., 2013) and (Schnjakin et al., 2013).

Transmission Performance and Throughput

Due to space constraints the current evaluation focuses on the Cloud-RAID configuration with k = 4 and m = 1. For performance comparison we experimented with different combinations among eight clouds, which are: Amazon US, Amazon EU, Azure, Box, Google EU, Google US, Nirvanix and Rackspace. The particular combinations are represented in Table 3.

Figure 6. Average throughput performance in milliseconds and seconds observed on all reads and writes executed for the [4,1] Cloud-RAID configuration (4 of 5 data packages are necessary to reconstruct the original data, m = 1). The Cloud-RAID bars (CR) correspond to the complete data processing cycle: the encoding of a data object into data packages and the subsequent transmission of individual chunks in parallel threads.

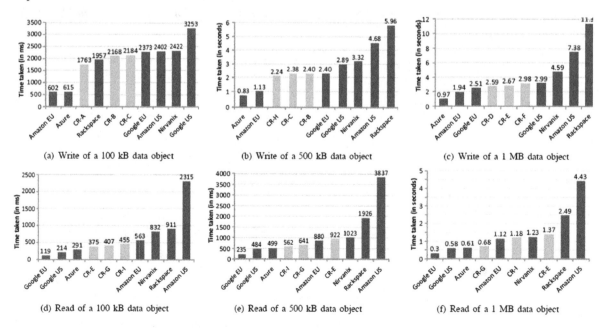

(a) Write of a 100 kB data object

(b) Write of a 500 kB data object

(c) Write of a 1 MB data object

(d) Read of a 100 kB data object

(e) Read of a 500 kB data object

(f) Read of a 1 MB data object

In general, we observed that utilizing Cloud-RAID for data transfer improves the throughput significantly when compared with cloud storages individually. This can be explained with the fact, that Cloud-RAID reads and writes a fraction of the original data (more specific 14 th with [4,1] setting, see IV-B1) from and to clouds simultaneously.

However, the total time of data transfer depends on the throughput performance of each provider involved into the communication process. The throughput performance of Cloud-RAID increases with higher performance values of cloud providers involved into the data distribution setting.

During the performance evaluation we observed, that storage providers differ extremely in their upload and download capabilities. Moreover, some vendors seem to have optimized their infrastructure for large files, while others focused more on smaller data objects. In the following we will clarify this point.

As we mentioned above there is a striking difference in the up- and download capabilities of cloud services. Except Microsoft Azure all the tested providers are much faster in download than in upload. This applies to smaller and larger data objects. At one extreme, with Google EU or Google US services a write request of a 100 kB file takes up to 19 times longer than a read request (see Figures 6a and 6d). This behavior can also be observed with larger data objects (although less pronounced). Here the difference in the throughput rate may range from 4 to 5 times, with the exception of the provider Rackspace, where an execution of a write request is up to 49 times slower than of a read request (e.g. an upload of a 100 MB file takes on average 17,3 minutes, whereas the download of the same file is performed in less than 21 seconds, see Figures 7b and 7d). Then again, Google US service improves its performance clearly with the growing size of data objects (see Figures 6a and 7a).

The explanation for this could be that with larger files the relatively long reaction time of the service (due to the long distance between our test system and the service node) has less impact on the measuring results. Similar to the US service Google EU performs rather mediocre in comparison to other providers when it comes

Table 3. Cloud-RAID setting with k = 4 AND m = 1

Cloud-RAID	Provider Setting
CR-A	Amazon EU, Amazon US, Azure, Nirvanix, Rackspace
CR-B	Amazon EU, Amazon US, Azure, Google EU, Rackspace
CR-C	Amazon US, Azure, Google EU, Nirvanix, Rackspace
CR-D	Amazon EU, Amazon US, Azure, Google EU, Nirvanix
CR-E	Amazon EU, Azure, Google EU, Google US, Nirvanix
CR-F	Amazon EU, Google EU, Google US, Nirvanix, Rackspace
CR-G	Amazon EU, Amazon US, Azure, Google EU, Google US
CR-H	Amazon EU, Amazon US, Google EU, Google US, Nirvanix
CR-I	Amazon EU, Azure, Google EU, Google US, Rackspace
CR-K	Amazon EU, BoxNet, Google EU, Google US, Nirvanix
CR-L	Amazon EU, Amazon US, BoxNet, Google EU, Google US
CR-M	Amazon EU, Amazon US, Azure, BoxNet, Google EU

Figure 7. Throughput observed in seconds on reads and writes executed for the [4,1] Cloud-RAID con-figuration. Here again, CR bars correspond to the complete data processing cycle.

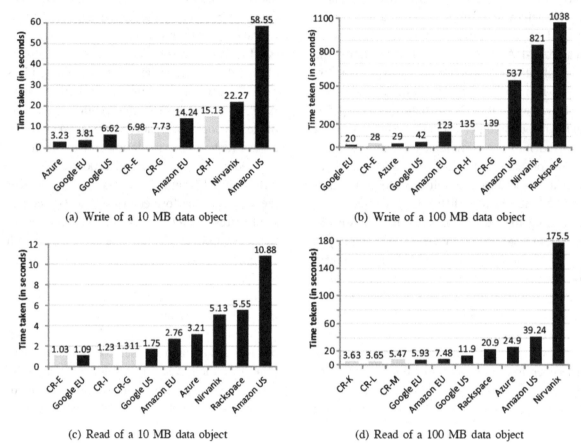

(a) Write of a 10 MB data object

(b) Write of a 100 MB data object

(c) Read of a 10 MB data object

(d) Read of a 100 MB data object

to read speeds for data objects up to 1 MB, (see Figures 6a and 6b). In terms of performance for writing larger files,

Google EU becomes the clear leader and even outperforms the fastest Cloud-RAID setting, which consists of the five fastest providers: Amazon EU, Azure, Google EU, Google US and Nirvanix (see Figure 7b). Similar phenomena have been observed by read requests. Microsoft Azure belongs to the leading providers for reading 100 kB data objects (see Figure 6d) and falls back by reading 100 MB files (see Figure 7d).

Hence, the performance of Cloud-RAID differs depending on the provider setting and file size. It is observed that our systems achieves better throughput values for read requests. The reason is that the test client fetches less data from the

cloud (only k of n data packages) than in case of a write request, where all n packages have to be moved to the cloud.

As expected, we observe that the fastest read and write settings consist of the fastest clouds. Concerning writing 100 kB data objects, the fastest Cloud-RAID setting CR A improves the overall throughput by an average factor of 3 (compared to the average throughput performance of the providers in the current Cloud-RAID setting). For reading 100 kB, CR-E achieves an improvement factor of 5. In terms of performance for writing 1 MB and 10 MB objects, Cloud-RAID setting CR-D and CR-E achieve already an average improvement factor of 7. Then again, for reading 10 MB, Cloud-RAID improves the average performance by a factor of 13 and even outperforms the fastest cloud providers (see figure 7c). By smaller data objects, execution of both read and write requests is highly affected by erasure overhead, DNS lookup and API connection establishment time. This can lead to an unusual behavior. For example, the transmission of a 100 kB data object to Google US can take our system more time than the transmission of a 500 kB or even 1 MB file (see Figure 6a, 6b and 6c). Hence, increasing the size of data objects improves the overall throughput of Cloud-RAID. Concerning read and write speeds for 100 MB data objects, Cloud-RAID increases the average performance by a factor of 36 for writes (despite of the erasure overhead of 25 percent) and achieves an improvement factor of 55 for reads (see Figures 7c and 7d).

There is also an observed connection between the throughput rate and the size of data objects. Charts 6a to 6f show results from performance tests on smaller files (up to 1 MB). Microsoft Azure and Amazon EU achieve the best results in terms of write requests. When writing 10 MB or 100MB data objects Amazon EU falls back on the fourth place (see Figures 7b and 7d). Form these observations, we come to the following conclusions. The overall performance of Cloud-RAID is not only dependent on the selection of k and m values, but also on the throughput performance of the particular storage providers. Cloud-RAID increases the overall transmission performance compared to the slower providers. Beyond that we are able to estimate, that the more providers are involved into the data distribution process, the less weight slower providers carry in terms of overall throughput performance. The underlying reason is again the size of individual data packages, which decrease with the growing number of *k* data packages (see chapter IV-B1).

Observations and Economic Consequences

Finally, based on the measured observations, we determine users benefits from using our system. In order to assert the feasibility of our application we have to examine the cost structure of cloud storage services. Vendors differ in pricing scheme and performance characteristics. Some providers charge a flat monthly fee, others negotiate contracts with individual clients. However, in general pricing depends on the amount of data stored and bandwidth consumed in transfers. Higher consumption results in increased costs.

As illustrated in Tables 4 and 5 providers also charge per API request (such as read, write, get-hash, list etc.) in addition to bandwidth and storage. The usage of erasure codes increases the total number of such requests, as we divide each data object into chunks and stripe them over multiple cloud vendors. The upload and download of data takes on average two requests. Considering this, our system needs $(4+1)2 = 10$ requests for a single data upload with a [4, 1] coding configuration. The download requires only $4\,2 = 8$ requests, as merely 4 packets have to be received to rebuild the original data. Thus, erasure [k,m] increases the number of requests by a factor of $k + m$ for upload and k for download.

Consequently, the usage of erasure codes increases the total cost compared to a direct upload or download of data due to the caused storage and API request overhead. Tables 4 and 5 summarize the cost in US Dollars of executing 10,000 reads and 10,000 writes with our system considering 5 data unit sizes: 100 kB, 500 kB, 1 MB, 10 MB and 100 MB. We observe, that the usage of erasure is not significantly more expensive than using a single provider. In some cases the costs can be even reduced.

SECURITY

Although erasure algorithms perform a series of coding operations on data, they do not provide far reaching security functionality. There may be enough data in the encoded fragments that useful content (a username and a password or a social security number for example) could be reassembled. The only protection measure

Table 4. Costs in dollars for 10,000 reads

Provider	Filesize in kB				
	100	500	1024	10240	102400
CR-B	0.15	0.55	1.07	10.21	101.61
CR-G	0.16	0.52	0.99	9.28	92.25
CR-I	0.15	0.55	1.07	10.21	101.61
CR [6,1][1]	3.61	4.12	4.78	16.50	133.69
Azure	0.11	0.53	1.08	10.74	107.42
Amazon/Google	0.13	0.59	1.19	11.74	117.21
Rackspace	0.17	0.86	1.76	17.58	175.78
Nirvanix	4.14	4.72	5.46	18.65	150.48

[1] The setting CR [6,1] consist of nearly all providers involved in the test setting: Amazon EU, Amazon US, Azure, Boxnet, Google EU, Nirvanix, Rackspace.

Table 5. Costs in dollars for 10,000 writes

Provider	Filesize in kB				
	100	500	1024	10240	102400
CR-B	0.12	0.12	0.12	0.12	0.12
CR-G	0.16	0.16	0.16	0.16	0.16
CR-I	0.12	0.12	0.12	0.12	0.12
CR [6,1]	8.14	8.20	8.29	9.75	24.40
Azure	0.00	0.00	0.00	0.00	0.00
Amazon/Google	0.02	0.02	0.02	0.02	0.02
Rackspace	0.00	0.00	0.00	0.00	0.00
Nirvanix	4.10	4.48	4.98	13.77	101.66

provided through erasure coding is the logical and physical segregation of the data packages, as these are distributed between different providers. Thus, we implemented a security service which enables users of our application to encrypt individual data packages prior to their transmission to cloud providers.

The encryption algorithm depends on the user's security requirements specified in the user interface. In general, our implementation makes use of the AES-128 and AES-256 algorithms for data encryption. On top of this, we use SHA-1 and MD5 cryptographic hash functions to test the integrity of cloud-stored data.

Encryption

Concerning the security strategy, it is important to determine the point when the encryption occurs and who holds the keys to decrypt the data. In general, we performed two sets of experiments with different erasure configurations - one for initial encryption prior to the encoding step and another vise versa.

Figures 9 shows the results of 100 runs (per machine) executed in a random order. The test encompasses the complete data processing cycle: the encoding of a data object, its subsequent encryption, its decryption and finally the decoding step. We observe, that the processing order (encode encrypt vs. encrypt encode) does not really matter with the dual-core processor. This applies despite the fact that the usage of erasure algorithms causes an additional storage overhead. With regard to erasure configuration there is another factor of importance: whether the sum of the configuration attributes k and m is odd or even (see erasure configurations [4,1] and [4,2] as well as [10,1] and [10,2] in Figure 9). This has an impact on the parallel processing (encryption of the data) in the following step. However, the test with a quad-core processor provides the expected results: first, the encoding of smaller data objects causes a significant higher I/O overhead and second, the encryption of larger files (executed in parallel threads) after an initial encoding step is more efficient than the opposite. With this, we made a decision to encrypt data after its being encoded into n coding packages.

Key Possession

Another important part when developing an encryption strategy is key the possession. The only encryption option for most of the available cloud solutions is that the keys are managed by the cloud storage providers, which is convenient to the user (the provider can assist with data restoration for example) but it entails a certain amount of risk. On one hand there are laws and policies that allow government agencies easier access to data on a cloud than on a private server. For example, in the USA the Stored Communication Act enables the FBI to access data without getting a warrant or the owner's consent. Furthermore, closed subpoenas may prohibit providers to inform their customers that data has been given to the government. On another hand there is always the chance of a disgruntled employee circumventing security and using the data in a way the user never indented.

In order to provide the user 100% control over the encryption process, we store the keys locally so that no third party is able to access and read the secured data. This, however also creates a single source of failure and means that the backup of the keys and metadata required for reassembling the data is in the responsibility of the user. However, the mitigation of this issue is part of our future work and analysis.

Observations

To assess the impact of encryption and encoding on the overall performance of the data transmission process we performed a further experiment on our dual-core test machine. We utilized the system to transfer some data to a set of randomly selected providers. The results represented in Figure 8 capture the end-to-end transmission performance of our application with files of varying sizes (1MB and 10MB). Compared with the results presented in the Figure 9 we conclude that in the case of significantly higher transmission rates, encryption can be added with no noticeable performance impact.

RELATED WORK

The main idea underlying our approach is to provide RAID technique at the cloud storage level. In (Bowers et al., 2009) the authors introduce the HAIL (High-Availability Integrity Layer) system, which utilizes RAID-like methods to manage remote file integrity and availability across a collection of servers or independent storage services. The system makes use of challenge-response protocols for retrievability (POR) (Ateniese et al., 2007) and proofs of data possession (PDP) (Ateniese et al., 2007) and unifies these two approaches. In comparison to our work, HAIL requires storage providers to run some code whereas our system

Figure 8. Time taken for the encoding and upload of data objects with Cloud-RAID. The encoding step requires not more than 0,5% of the entire data upload process. The data packages were sent to the following providers: Google US, Amazon EU, Amazon (US-west-1), Nirvanix, Azure and Google EU.

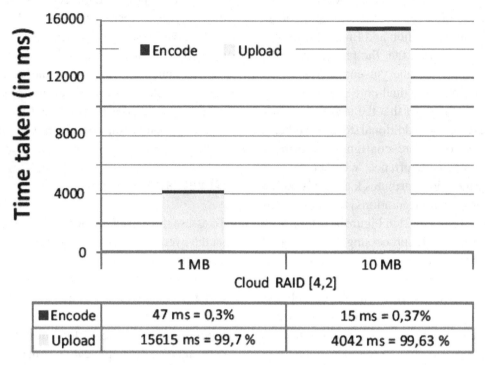

	1 MB	10 MB
■ Encode	47 ms = 0,3%	15 ms = 0,37%
Upload	15615 ms = 99,7 %	4042 ms = 99,63 %

deals with cloud storage repositories as they are. Further, HAIL does not provide confidentiality guarantees for stored data.

In (Dabek et al., 2001) Dabek et al. use RAID-like techniques to ensure the availability and durability of data in distributed systems. In contrast to the mentioned approaches our system focuses on the economic problems of cloud computing described in chapter I. Further, in (Abu-Libdeh, Princehouse, & Weatherspoon, 2010) authors introduce RACS, a proxy that spreads the storage load over several providers. This approach is similar to our work as it also employs erasure code techniques to reduce overhead while still benefiting from higher availability and durability of RAID-like systems. Our concept goes beyond a simple distribution of users' content.

RACS lacks sophisticated capabilities such as intelligent file placement based on users' requirements or automatic replication. In addition to it,

the RACS system does not try to solve security issues of cloud storage, but focuses more on vendor lock-in. Therefore, the system is not able to detect any data corruption or confidentiality violations.

The future of distributed computing has been a subject of interest for various researchers in recent years. The authors in (Buyya, Yeo, & Venugopal, 2008) propose an architecture for market-oriented allocation of resources within clouds. They discuss some existing cloud platforms from the market-oriented perspective and present a vision for creating a global cloud exchange for trading services. The authors consider cloud storage as a low-cost alternative to dedicated Content Delivery Networks (CNDs).

There are more similar approaches dealing with high availability of data trough its distribution among several cloud providers. DepSky-A (Bessani et al., 2011) protocol improves availability and integrity of cloud-stored data by replicating

Figure 9. Total time taken when encryption occurs either before or after the encoding step. Tests were executed on a dual-core/quad-core CPU. The bars correspond to the complete data processing cycle: the encoding of a data object into data packages, the subsequent encryption of individual chunks in parallel threads, the decryption of data packages and finally the reassembling of the data in the decoding step. The opposite order encompasses the following operations: encryption, encoding, decoding and decryption.

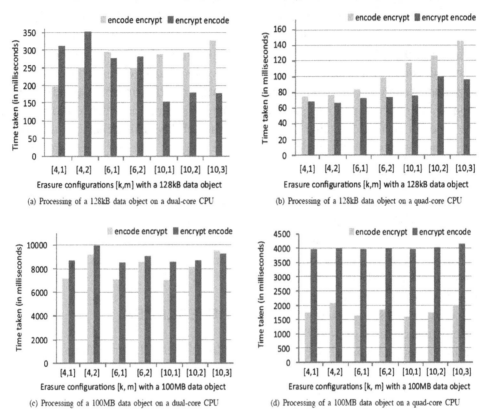

it on cloud providers using quorum techniques. This work has two main limitations. First, a data unit of size S consumes *n x S* storage capacity of the system and costs on average n times more than if was stored on a single cloud. Second, the protocol does not provide any confidentiality guaranties, as it stores the data in clear text. In their later work the authors present DepSky-CA, which solves the mentioned problems by the encryption of the data and optimization of the write and read process. However, the monetary costs of using the system is still twice the cost of using a single cloud. On top of this, DepSky does not provide any means or metrics for user centric data placement. In fact, our approach enables cloud storage users to place

their data on the cloud based on their security policies as well as quality of service expectations and budget preferences.

CONCLUSION

In this chapter we outlined some general problems of cloud computing such as security, service availability and a general risk for a customer to become dependent on a service provider. In the course of the paper we demonstrated how our system deals with the mentioned concerns. In a nutshell, we stripe users' data across multiple providers while integrating with each storage provider via appropriate service-connectors. These connectors provide an abstraction layer to hide the complexity and differences in the usage of storage services.

The main focus of the paper is an extensive evaluation of our application. From the results obtained, we conclude that our approach improves availability at costs similar to using a single commercial cloud storage provider (instead of 100% and more when full content replication is used). We use erasure code techniques for striping data across multiple providers. The experiment proved, that given the speed of current disks and CPUs, the libraries used are fast enough to provide good performance - whereby the overall performance depends on the throughput performance of the particular storage providers. The throughput performance of Cloud-RAID increases with the selection of providers with higher throughput performance values. Hence, with an appropriate coding configuration Cloud-RAID is able to improve significantly the data transmission process when compared with cloud storages individually.

Further, performance tests showed that our system is best utilized for deployment of large files. Utilization of our system for storing of smaller data objects is subject to further test and analysis. In the long term, our approach might foster the provision of new and even more favorable cloud storage services. Today, storage providers surely use RAID like methods to increase the reliability of the entrusted data to their customers. The procedure causes costs which are covered by providers price structure. With our approach, the on-site backups might become redundant, as users data is distributed among dozens of storage services. Furthermore, we enable users of cloud storage services to control the availability and physical segregation of the data by themselves. However, additional storage offerings are expected to become available in the next few years. Due to the flexible and adaptable nature of our approach, we are able to support any changes in existing storage services as well as incorporating support for new providers as they appear.

FUTURE WORK

Our performance testing revealed that some vendors have optimized their systems for large data objects and high upload performance, while others have focused on smaller files and better download throughput. We will use these observations to optimize read and write performance of our application. During our experiment we also observed that the reaction time of read and get-hash requests may vary from provider to provider at different times of day. This behavior might be related to the usage of different consistency models and is subject of further analysis.

In addition, we are also planing to implement more service connectors and thus to integrate additional storage services. Any extra storage resource improves the performance and responsiveness of our system for end-users.

REFERENCES

Abu-Libdeh, H., Princehouse, L., & Weatherspoon, H. (2010). *Racs: A case for cloud storage diversity*. Paper presented at SoCC'10. New York, NY.

Armbrust, M., Fox, A., Griffith, R., Joseph, A. D., Katz, R., & Konwinski, A. et al. (2010, April). A view of cloud computing. *Communications of the ACM, 53*(4), 50–58. doi:10.1145/1721654.1721672

Ateniese, G., Burns, R., Curtmola, R., Herring, J., Kissner, L., Peterson, Z., & Song, D. (2007). *Provable data possession at untrusted stores*. Paper presented at the 14th ACM CCS. New York, NY.

Bessani, A., Correia, M., Quaresma, B., Andre, F., & Sousa, P. (2011). Depsky: Dependable and secure storage in a cloud-of-clouds. In *Proceedings of the Sixth Conference on Computer Systems*, (pp. 31–46). New York, NY: ACM.

Bowers, K. D., Juels, A., & Oprea, A. (2009). *Hail: A high availability and integrity layer for cloud storage.* Paper presented at CCS'09. New York, NY.

Broberg, J., Buyya, R., & Tari, Z. (2009). *Creating a 'cloud storage' mashup for high performance, low cost content delivery.* Paper presented at Service-Oriented Computing. New York, NY.

Burt, J. (2009). *Future for cloud computing looks good, report says.* Academic Press.

Buyya, R., Yeo, C.-S., & Venugopal, S. (2008). Market-oriented cloud computing: Vision, hype, and reality for delivering it services as computing utilities. In *Proceedings of the 10th IEEE International Conference on High Performance Computing and Communications.* IEEE.

Carr, N. (2008). The Big Switch. Norton.

Dabek, F., Kaashoek, M. F., Karger, D., Morris, R., & Stoica, I. (2001). *Wide-area cooperative storage with cfs.* Paper presented at ACM SOSP. New York, NY.

Dingledine, R., Freedman, M., & Molnar, D. (2000). *The freehaven project: Distributed anonymous storage service.* Paper presented at the Workshop on Design Issues in Anonymity and Unobservability. New York, NY.

Gantz, J., & Reinsel, D. (2009). *Extracting value from chaos.* Academic Press.

Plank, J. S. (2008). The raid-6 liberation codes. In *Proceedings of the 6th USENIX Conference on File and Storage Technologies.* Berkeley, CA: USENIX Association.

Plank, J. S., Luo, J., Schuman, C. D., Xu, L., & Wilcox-O'Hearn, Z. (2009a). A performance evaluation and examination of open-source erasure coding libraries for storage. In *Proceedings of the 7th conference on File and storage technologies,* (pp. 253–265). Berkeley, CA: USENIX Association.

Plank, J. S., Simmerman, S., & Schuman, C. D. (2008). *Jerasure: A library in C/C++ facilitating erasure coding for storageapplications - Version 1.2* (Technical Report CS-08-627). University of Tennessee.

Ponemon Institute. (2011). *Security of cloud computing providers study.* Author.

Rhea, S., Wells, C., Eaton, P., Geels, D., Zhao, B., Weatherspoon, H., & Kubiatowicz, J. (2001, September). Maintenance free global storage in ocean store. *IEEE Internet Computing.*

Sarno, D. (2009, October). Microsoft says lost sidekick data will be restored to users. *Los Angeles Times.*

Schnjakin, M., Alnemr, R., & Meinel, C. (2010). Contract-based cloud architecture. In *Proceedings of the second international workshop on Cloud data management,* (pp. 33–40). New York, NY: ACM.

Schnjakin, M., Alnemr, R., & Meinel, C. (2011). A security and high-availability layer for cloud storage. In Proceedings of WebInformation Systems Engineering (LNCS) (vol. 6724, pp. 449–462). Springer.

Schnjakin, M., Goderbauer, M., Krueger, M., & Meinel, C. (2013). Cloud storage and it-security. In *Proceedings of the 13th Deutscher IT-Sicherheitskongress* (Sicherheit 2013). Academic Press.

Schnjakin, M., Korsch, D., Schoenberg, M., & Meinel, C. (2013). Implementation of a secure and reliable storage above the untrusted clouds. In *Proceedings of Computer Science & Education (ICCSE),* (pp. 347-353). ICCSE.

Schnjakin, M. & Meinel, C. (2011). Platform for a secure storage-infrastructure in the cloud. In *Proceedings ofthe 12th Deutscher IT-Sicherheitskongress* (Sicherheit 2011). Academic Press.

The Amazon S3 Team. (2008). *Amazon s3 availability event: July 20, 2008.* Author.

Weatherspoon, H. & Kubiatowicz, J. (2002). *Erasure coding vs. replication: A quantitative comparison*. IPTPS.

ADDITIONAL READING

Dimitrios Zissis and Dimitrios Lekkas. (2012). Addressing cloud computing security issues. *Future Gener. Comput. Syst.* 28, 3 (March 2012), 583-592. DOI=10.1016/j.future.2010.12.006

Krutz, R. L., & Vines, R. D. (2010). *Cloud Security: A Comprehensive Guide to Secure Cloud Computing*. Wiley Publishing.

Madhan Kumar Srinivasan, K. Sarukesi, Paul Rodrigues, M. Sai Manoj, and P. Revathy. (2012). State-of-the-art cloud computing security taxonomies: a classification of security challenges in the present cloud computing environment. In *Proceedings of the International Conference on Advances in Computing, Communications and Informatics* (ICACCI '12). ACM, New York, NY, USA, 470-476. DOI= doi:10.1145/2345396.2345474 http://doi.acm.org/10.1145/2345396.2345474

Perez-Botero, D., Szefer, J., & Lee, R. B. (2013). Characterizing hypervisor vulnerabilities in cloud computing servers. In *Proceedings of the 2013 international workshop on Security in cloud computing* (Cloud Computing '13). ACM, New York, NY, USA, 3-10.

S. Subashini and V. Kavitha. (2011). Review: A survey on security issues in service delivery models of cloud computing. *J. Netw. Comput. Appl.* 34, 1 (January 2011), 1-11. DOI=10.1016/j.jnca.2010.07.006 http://dx.doi.org/10.1016/j.jnca.2010.07.006

KEY TERMS AND DEFINITIONS

Availability of Cloud Services: Model of cloud computing where resource availability is considered to be a strong constraint.

Cloud Computing Security: Model of cloud computing where security policies are designed and implemented to enforce protection of cloud resources both in soft and hardware form.

Cloud Computing: Describes a variety of computing concepts that involve a large number of computers connected through a real-time communication network such as the Internet. (Abu-Libdeh, Princehouse, & Weatherspoon, 2010). It is very similar to the concept of utility computing. In science, cloud computing is a synonym for distributed computing over a network, and means the ability to run a program or application on many connected computers at the same time.

Cloud Storage: Is a model of networked enterprise storage where data is stored in virtualized pools of storage which are generally hosted by third parties. Hosting companies operate large data centers, and people who require their data to be hosted buy or lease storage capacity from them.

Infrastructure as a Service: Offers cloud computing resources as an infrastructural service to external services requiring infrasture to run.

Reliability of Cloud Services: Fault tolerant model of cloud computing where resource reliability in terms of service delivery is considered to be a strong constraint.

Storage as a Service: Model of cloud computing where the storage resource availability is considered to be a strong constraint.

ENDNOTES

[1] http://www.krollontrack.com/resource-library/case-studies/

Chapter 16

Information Security Innovation:
Personalisation of Security Services in a Mobile Cloud Infrastructure

Jan H. P. Eloff
SAP Innovation Center Pretoria, South Africa & Department Computer Science, University of Pretoria, South Africa

Mariki M. Eloff
University of South Africa, South Africa

Madeleine A. Bihina Bella
SAP Innovation Center Pretoria, South Africa

Donovan Isherwood
University of Johannesburg, South Africa

Moses T. Dlamini
University of Pretoria, South Africa

Ernest Ketcha Ngassam
University of South Africa, South Africa

ABSTRACT

The increasing demand for online and real-time interaction with IT infrastructures by end users is facilitated by the proliferation of user-centric devices such as laptops, iPods, iPads, and smartphones. This trend is furthermore propounded by the plethora of apps downloadable to end user devices mostly within mobile-cum-cloud environments. It is clear that there are many evidences of innovation with regard to end user devices and apps. Unfortunately, little, if any, information security innovation took place over the past number of years with regard to the consumption of security services by end users. This creates the need for innovative security solutions that are human-centric and flexible. This chapter presents a framework for consuming loosely coupled (but interoperable) cloud-based security services by a variety of end users in an efficient and flexible manner using their mobile devices.

INTRODUCTION

The increasing demand for cost-effective always on connectivity on all types of end-user computing devices (e.g. desktop computer, laptop, MP3 player, tablet, smartphone) results in the need for new business models (mobile, cloud, services, platforms) that increase the level of

exposure to a company's assets. This creates new security challenges for networked businesses as a number of 3rd-party services and infrastructures within complex ecosystems are integrated. For instance, many actors are involved in the service provisioning ranging from the customer, the service provider, the content provider, the network provider, the cloud provider and the electronic or

DOI: 10.4018/978-1-4666-6158-5.ch016

mobile payment provider. Each of these actors has an entry point to the service and therefore is a potential security risk.

Investigating a security breach thus requires the collection of data from all these different sources. In addition, the existence of various mechanisms to access the network (e.g. wired, wireless, 3G, modem, VPN) creates many access points that can be exploited for unauthorized access to and misuse of the company's information.

Detecting such events requires the continuous exchange of information between all service elements and network devices (Bihina Bella, Eloff, & Olivier, 2009). Furthermore, entities involved in the service provisioning can have conflicting security policies that need to be aligned to the company's policy.

In this collaborative environment, security risks shifts from the IT system as a whole to the services it offers to a multitude of independent users and to the data that travel across systems (e.g. in cloud computing applications hosted on public infrastructures). For example applications hosted on public cloud infrastructures are not only open to the general public but are also open to malicious individuals. Such applications become a public good and are susceptible to excessive and malicious use. Malicious or disgruntled individuals may decide to flood such applications with targeted distributed denial of service (DDoS) attacks so that the general public could not have access to them.

Maintaining a secure configuration in such heterogeneous IT landscapes is complex a security requirements are multi-lateral and diverse. This creates the need for innovative security solutions that are human-centric, flexible and also robust. Potential avenues for innovation within the information security domain include, amongst others, the following:

1. The definition of data-centric policies that travel with the services as well as the data.

2. The usage of privacy-preserving computing (Wang, Zhao, Jiang, & Le, 2009) to ensure the privacy of all parties involved.

3. Access control policies and mechanisms that take care of conflict management (Cuppens, Cuppens-Boulahia, & Ghorbel, 2007) between the members of an ecosystem.

4. The possible aggregation of different access control approaches such as usage and optimistic based access control (Padayachee, 2010).

5. Simple and basic authentication services on mobile devices.

6. Forensic tools for mobile-cum-cloud environments (Ruan, Carthy, Kechadi, & Crosbie, 2011) services utilization, using mobile devices.

This is an opportunity to capitalize on the advantages offered by cloud computing for accessing value-added business services, by end-users. In general, end-users are not concerned by the complexity of the technical infrastructure required to set up cloud-based services for large consumption but rather the intended business outcome offered by exposed services.

This paper presents an innovative framework for accessing loosely coupled (but interoperable) cloud-based security services by a variety of end-users, in a secure, elective and flexible manner, anywhere and anytime, using their mobile devices. The remaining part of this paper is structured as follows: the next section provides some background information discussing the concept of innovation within the domain of information security.

Furthermore, background information is provided on the current state-of-the-art in information security services and existing approaches to services oriented architectures. In the next section, a generic SiYP (Security-In-Your-Pocket) platform is presented from a Service Oriented Architecture (SOA) point of view. The following section presents a conclusion and future work.

BACKGROUND AND RELATED WORK

From the previous section it is clear that various technologies, tools and devices will form part of this proposed framework in order to provide the required flexibility, efficiency and security. In this section the different terms and technologies will be discussed as well as how they relate to each other. IDC (Christiansen, 2008) identified the importance of leveraging the strengths of both innovation and security in order to gain a competitive advantage over companies who do not do it. However, no extensive research was found that addresses how information security can strengthen innovation and vice versa. In this section these terms will be defined as well as their interrelationship. Some well-known terminologies are associated with information security such as information security services, privacy and trust. However, it is important to understand how, for example, trust, relates to service oriented architecture and innovation.

Innovation

For any organization to gain and maintain a competitive advantage and be an economic leader, being innovative is of utmost importance. Innovation should not be confused with invention, which is only the idea or model for a new or improved product, process, device or system, whereas innovation is bringing this idea to market as a real product, process, system or device that is part of the economic system (Roth, 2009). Innovation is only accomplished with the first commercial transaction involving this new invention. Schumpeter said, in as far back as 1943, that Economic change revolves around innovation, entrepreneurship and market power (Schumpeter, 1943).

Information Security Services

According to the ISO 7498-2 standard, produced by The International Standards Organization (ISO) information security can be defined in terms of the five security services, namely identification & authentication, authorization, confidentiality, integrity and nonrepudiation (ISO, 1989). These services are required to ensure that information are protected and secured at all times, whether in storage of any nature, during transmission or usage. A definition for each of these services follows:

The identification and authentication of any subject who wants to access any computer system is the first step towards enforcing information security. A subject requesting access needs to present a user-id that uniquely identifies it. On presentation of such a user-id, the user-id should be verified to ensure that it does, in fact, belong to the subject who presented it.

The next step is to determine if the authenticated subject has the right to access the computer facilities in question. In terms of the authorization process, control is, therefore, exerted over the access rights of all authenticated subjects. All information must be strictly accessible to authorized parties only. Protecting the confidentiality of information, therefore, gives the assurance that only authorized parties will have access to the information in question.

Information should not only be kept confidential, but its integrity should also be guaranteed. Only authorized parties should be able to change the content of protected information. In other words, unauthorized changes to information must be prevented, ensuring that the information can be deemed accurate and complete. The last step is to ensure that no action is performed to affect information security, for example, changing some of the content of information that could be denied at a later stage. This process is referred to as non-repudiation. It may be argued that the security services are not applicable in current computing applications; however, various authors have proven through research that these services are essential, especially in mobile and cloud computing (Chetty & Coetzee, 2011; Huang, Ma, & Li, 2010).

Privacy

Privacy, which is closely related to information security, is defined as the right of an individual or a group to isolate information about themselves from others. This ability allows individuals to reveal themselves selectively. The Oxford English Dictionary refers to privacy as the condition of free from public attention, undisturbed, or the freedom from interference or intrusion (Proffitt, 2012).

Trust

Trust is in principle a human action. A person may trust another to behave in a certain manner, where trust is based on past experience, recommendation or the reputation of the other person. The Oxford English Dictionary (Proffitt, 2012) defines trust as the confidence in or reliance on some quality or attribute of a person or thing, or the truth of a statement. This definition of trust does not take all aspects of trust into consideration nor does it satisfy the requirements of trust as required in the Web 2.0 environment (OReilly, 2007). . Trust is bi-directional with mainly two parties involved, namely the truster and the trustee. The truster is the party who trusts, confides, or relies on the other party; he/she is the one who believes or credits; the one that gives credit, a creditor. The trustee is, on the other hand, the party who is trusted, or to whom something is entrusted; a person in whom confidence is put (Proffitt, 2012). Josang, Ismail, and Boyd (2007) go further and distinguish between reliability trust and decision trust. Reliability trust implies that trustee will act as expected, while decision trust refers to the situation where the truster depends on the trustee, even though some risks may be involved.

Service Oriented Architecture and Cloud Computing

Service oriented architecture (SOA) developed from older concepts such as distributed computing and modular programming into cloud computing. Cloud computing can be seen as a service-oriented architecture (SOA) exploring almost every computing component including, but not limited to distributed computing, grid computing, utility computing, on-demand, open source, Peer-to-Peer and Web 2.0 (Weinhardt, Anandasivam, Blau, & Stosser, 2009). It is a natural next step from the grid model to a supply and demand utility model. In minimizing potential security and trust issues as well as adhering to governance issues facing Cloud computing, prerequisite control measures are required to ensure that a concrete Cloud computing Service Level Agreement (SLA) is put in place and maintained when dealing with mobile applications.

Mobile Computing

Mobile computing refers to any computing device that possesses processing and storage capabilities and that can connect to other computing devices, preferably through wireless connections. Devices include, but are not limited to cellular phones, tablets, PDAs, laptops, notebooks etc.

Security in Mobile and Cloud Computing

Trust is a key element of security in cloud computing. If one party is not trustworthy, it is clear that this party's security, even if claimed to be strong, is not security at all (Masnick, 2011). One of the most important protocols in ensuring transparency and security within Cloud computing is the SLA. The SLA is the only legal agreement between the service provider and client and its importance should not be under estimated (Balachandra, Ramakrishna, & Rakshit, 2009). The only means that the cloud provider can gain the trust of clients is through the SLA; therefore the SLA has to be standardized. The following are the main aspects as a guideline for SLA:

1. Services to be delivered and performance.
2. Tracking and Reporting.
3. Problem Management.
4. Legal Compliance.
5. Resolution of Disputes Customer Duties.
6. Security Responsibility.
7. Confidential Information Termination.

However, ensuring mobile and cloud security is still a serious challenge as identified and addressed by various research studies (Leavitt, 2011; Lin, 2011; Oberheide, & Jahanian, 2010). From the above discussions it is clear that for the proposed framework it will be important that the existing security services should be embedded in the SOA as well as in the mobile-cloud infrastructure. The user will play an important part in these security services. The mobile applications, being loosely coupled, propose unique security challenges.

A GENERIC SERVICE MODEL FOR THE SECURITY IYP PLATFORM

As alluded to in previous sections, the intended purpose of a user centric security platform is to supply the user with the ability to bind available apps to be consumed as service. This requires a range of security services for ensuring that all transactions performed during the consumption of cloud-based services are secured and guaranteed, not only for good quality of services, but also to adhere to prescribed service level agreements amongst interoperable services.

In general, the SiYP platform is regarded as a container of apps grouped together and supported by a range of loosely coupled, security-based, services deployed in the cloud. Security-based services will be implemented and deployed in the cloud for consumption based on the various constraints required for ensuring that any app consumed by end-users adhered to the prescribed security standard. However, the approach adopted in this new paradigm provides the flexibility for the end-user to wrap the business app with the minimum necessary security app (and therefore service) required for an effective consumption without any security breach. For illustration purpose, an end user who would like his device to be secured based on its location while using a given business app would configure the business app such that the location service provided in the platform is activated. This approach provides interested users, to only rely on the consumption of security services that are necessary while consuming a given business app through the cloud. Equally, the end-user would have the ability to enforce the traceability of all its operations while consuming the service, provided that he has activated the secured security app in the platform, dedicated to such a role. Of course, one may argue that security enforcement would require that all security-based services are activated (ISO, 1989). However with the limited computational resources available on mobile devices as well as the complexity that could arise if all those services are invoked, it makes perfect sense to adopt the approach of delivering those services on-demand, to be consumed by end-users on an as-needed basis.

It follows that the overall structure of the platform would reflect the manner in which apps are usually grouped together based on the kind of services being rendered by any given app. In the app world, each app as presented to end-users contains the necessary functionality that reflects the service to be provided to the consumer. As such, there is a range of services at the lower level of the hierarchy that are invoked and aggregated in order to meet end-user's expectation. Therefore two different apps may share many services although their end-result appears different to the end-users. This is a true reflection of the principles of loosely coupling and interoperability that make up a service model following modern

Service Engineering (and therefore SOA) paradigm (Bullingera, Fhnrichb, & Meirena, 2003). As such the conceptualization of our proposed SiYP platform would equally be based on current trends, as reflected in the state-of-the-art of Services Engineering (Bullingera et al., 2003).

We perceive the SiYP service model, therefore, as a four-tier architecture, see Figure 1. As a naming convention, all the apps are called "My" followed by "App name" and the term security is implied. For instance My Device indicates that

this is the app for the user device security. The description of each layer of the architecture as well as components thereof follows.

The Presentation Layer

This layer represents the entry-point to the security innovation platform by end-users using the necessary computational medium for the consumption of any given business app. For instance, the Business in Your Pocket (BiYP) interface available on

Figure 1. An extract SiYP security service model

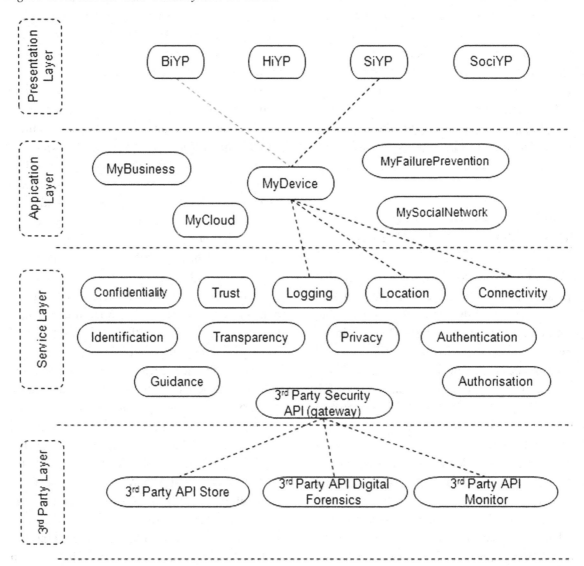

the end-user's device would enable him/her to consume business services in the cloud anywhere and anytime. In order to do so, the edit-ability of the platform would allow the user to personalize a range of security apps required for the secure consumption of all business services attached to the app. Discussion on those business services are beyond the scope of this work. Since the end user might require that security, with respect to the device being used for service consumption, be enforced, he/she then has to "wrap-on" the business app, the appropriate security app available from the lower layer in the hierarchy. This security app also invokes a range of security services from lower layers as well as required security services for interaction with third party API's that are not part of the SiYP platform. The presentation layer is therefore the environment used by consumers to personalize their required security services in order to ensure that security is enforced during the consumption of a given business app.

The Application Layer

This layer provides a pool of security apps that can be added to and removed from a business service based on the user requirements. Examples of some possible security apps are described below. They are My Device, My Failure Prevention, My Cloud and My Social Network.

My Device App

This application enables users to select the level of security for the specific device they are using to connect to the corporate network. Security levels will differ from one computing device to another based on the device features and usage profile of the user. To this effect, MyDevice will use services such as Location, Connectivity and Logging. For instance, one user may use his laptop and smartphone mainly in the office but his iPad and iPod mainly out of the office.

The laptop is mostly used for processing power intensive usage such as creating and editing documents, running and installing applications while the iPad is used primarily to read documents as well as to read and write emails. The iPad may be used for Wi- Fi access to his corporate emails. This information could be recorded in his corporate user profile along with identifiers of all the devices he/she uses. This can allow single sign-on with his corporate user credentials on all devices. The security level for a device will be defined in terms of various services such as Location, Connectivity, and Logging.

The Location service recognizes whether the user is in a trusted familiar environment (e.g. home, office, regular coffee shop) and adjusts the security features accordingly. In an unknown location, security will be tighter (e.g. 2- step authentication) and geo-location data will only be sent to authorized recipients.

The Logging service keeps a record of the user's activity and the data stored on the device that is not linked to any application (e.g. multimedia le, software and hardware identifiers). This is used to specify the level of security for the user data according to the selected device (e.g. encryption of transmitted data). This is also applicable to the SIM card data. If one SIM card is transferred from one device to another, security policies applicable to this device can be enforced on the SIM card as well.

The Connectivity service specifies the security level required based on the connection channel used (e.g. 3G, Wi-Fi or VPN). For instance, accessing the corporate network from a public non-encrypted Wi-Fi access point will require tighter controls than access through a more secure VPN.

My Failure Prevention App

This application will monitor the service consumed to detect unsafe events and situations that can lead to a failure. The application will use the Logging service to log such events and any associated data for a possible future root cause analysis and to prevent the recurrence of such events. An example of such an event, referred to as a near miss, is the near exhaustion of critical resources (e.g. memory or battery power). The user will have the choice to specify a near miss threshold that indicates how close the near miss is to cause a failure to generate an alert (Bihina Bella, Olivier & Eloff, 2012).

This app can also be used to prevent misuse of the business service by creating a service profile. The service profile specifies how the business service is normally used by the average user. It can thus help detect suspicious activity that deviates significantly from the normal usage pattern and which can indicate that the service is being misused. The profile will provide information such as the average spending and the usual time and duration of the service usage.

My Cloud App

My Cloud app uses the cloud infrastructure to deliver security services to customers and other cloud service providers. This is referred to as Security as a Service (SECaaS) (Cloud Security Alliance, 2011). SECaaS is defined as the on-demand provisioning of cloud-based security services either to hosted cloud infrastructure and software or to clients on premise private systems (Cloud Security Alliance, 2011). My Cloud leverages a cloud-based model to deliver security service-based offerings which include end point protection, on-demand transparency-enhancing technology, identity as a service, risk-based authentication etc.

Cloud-based end point protection leverages the SECaaS model to provide cost effective anti-virus and anti-spyware services to all types of end point devices (desktop, laptops, tablets and smartphones) that each user employs when connecting to corporate resources. This service also maintains and manages all updates to each of these end points.

On-demand transparency-enhancing technology leverages the auditing and logging capability of cloud based systems. It provides customers with a clear indication of all the data centers where their data is hosted and/or replicated and who is accessing it and for what purposes. The customers can query their cloud service providers for the exact location of where their data sits at any particular time. And they could also query the cloud service provider for all access to their resources within a given time period, for example over the past 12 months. Providing the customer with such transparency can help ensure that customer data can only be stored in data centers in approved geographical locations. The cloud security app will help solve most of the jurisdictional compliance challenges.

Nowadays, organizations are faced with a workforce that is highly mobile. This type of a workforce constantly require access to corporate resources from wherever they are (on-premise or hosted), at all times, from any location, using a plethora of devices (Dlamini, Venter, Eloff, & Mitha, 2012). This raises concerns on how to keep corporate resources available to only those who must have access. How to ensure that the right people, systems, and end point devices have the necessary access privileges to both on-premise and hosted cloud services. Cloud computing through Identity as a Service (IDaaS) presents a platform that does exactly that. It decouples the provisioning, de-provisioning, maintaining and managing users from the apps. This app provides digital identity as a service. IDaaS provides an API that authenticates users from different directories (e.g. Active Directory, LDAP or Web Service) on cloud-based apps and supports cross-domain authentication.

My Social Network App

My Social Network app monitors and manages all social media accounts of a user from one place. This app offers social network Single Sign-On portal. You sign-in on one Social Network and gain access to everything you need. For a first time user, he/she will register once and then choose from a wide pool of all the social networks that he/she wishes to gain access to. The app will then use the provided registration information to register the user on all the other social network sites. For those users who are already registered with different Social Networks and have different credentials, this app integrates all their accounts and put them under one umbrella called My Social Network app. The user can use this app to log on supplying it with his/her credentials for one Social Network where he/she is registered e.g. Facebook and then gain access to all his/her social media accounts.

This app use federated identity to authenticate the user only once and then share the credentials in assertions across all registered Social Networks. It provides the user in real-time with all the RSS feed updates happening in all of the social networks where he/she is registered, all in one place. This app ensures that the users are no longer required to manage multiple user accounts for multiple Social Networks. When the user logs out of the My Social Network app it automatically logs him/her out in all of the social networks.

Furthermore, this app uses a mobile devices built-in GPS to determine a user's location at any given time. After picking the user's location, it then scans the friend lists on each of his/her registered social media accounts to see if any one of them is in the same area. It then notifies the user of all friends who are within his/her vicinity giving their distance, time it will take to reach them, a detailed route plan and a good restaurant where they could meet and have coffee after a day's long work.

The Services Layer

In this layer, loosely coupled (but interoperable) security services required for consumption by apps in the application layer are available. These services should be designed in such a way that they can be consumed, depending on the needs of the user within the context of selecting an appropriate business app. For example it will not make sense for a security service such as authentication to be used by the MyDevice app in that it is supporting an application as opposed to a device. Therefore, although services in this layer are loosely coupled, interoperability will only be applicable amongst those services that are deemed to be interoperable according to security standards at both hardware and software levels. We briefly describe a selected number of services in this layer along the following lines.

3rd Party Security API (Gateway)

This service is a specialized service required for interaction with a 3rd party application. In order to facilitate integration with other third party applications foreign to the platform, a range of API would be necessary for facilitating such interactions. This justifies the presence of this specialized service that is made available for ensuring that there is no breach in the security of the application being invoked outside the platform. Equally, third party applications would also want to prevent any security breach in their system, hence the importance of this specialized service in the platform.

Furthermore, the monitoring of operation in the platform might be necessary if such a service has not yet been implemented in the platform. This is equally true when some forensic tools are required for enforcing the security in the platform should a breach arise. Hence the importance of the 3rd party gateway that is used for interaction with other security services not yet available in the platform.

Trust

The Trust service is an important security service that has the function of providing a truster with information that will assist in determining whether the trustee can be trusted. Such information would be derived from past experiences as well as the trustees reputation according the general public or community, based on the trust model used. This service would make use of existing data, feedback from users, 3rd party data, and social position to determine the trustworthiness of stakeholders in the iYP ecosystem. This Trust service would be consumed by apps such as My-Business and MySocialNetwork, where personal relationships and business collaborations are established. For example, a user of the BiYP application, wrapped with the MyBusiness security app, would like to collaborate with another user, for business purposes. The collaboration could be in the form of bulk-buying, selling products on credit, or customer recommendations.

The MyBusiness app would be able to provide trust ratings and recommendations to the parties involved through the use of the Trust service, therefore facilitating trustworthy collaborations. Similarly, the MySocial-Network security app could consume the Trust services functionality to facilitate trusting personal relationships.

The 3rd Party Layer

This layer is the extension of the API services gateways mentioned above. But the layer is physically situated in the service providers' environment (e.g. suppliers, banks, etc.) and has the purpose of uploading and/or receiving information from the specialized API services in the third layer, for further processing. In summary, the service model forms the basis for the decision of an appropriate generic cloud-based technical infrastructure required for implementing and deploying the SiYP platform. However, discussions on the architectural model are beyond the scope of this paper.

CONCLUSION AND FUTURE WORK

The Security-in-Your-Pocket (SiYP) platform is innovative in the sense that it provides a user-centric approach towards the personalization of security services with specific reference to mobility within cloud infrastructures. SiYP, as discussed in this paper, also highlights the acute need for new security services that will support apps such as MyBusiness, MyDevice, and the like. Interesting examples of such services, amongst others, include a Transparency service and a Trust service. Future work will focus on the construction and usability aspects of the proposed SiYP platform.

ACKNOWLEDGMENT

The support of SAP Research Pretoria and Meraka CSIR towards this research is hereby acknowledged. Opinions expressed and conclusions arrived at are those of the authors and not necessarily to be attributed to the companies mentioned in this acknowledgement.

REFERENCES

Balachandra, R. K., Ramakrishna, P. V., & Rakshit, A. (2009). Cloud Security Issues. In *Proceedings of the Services Computing* (pp. 517-520). Bangalore, India: IEEE.

Bihina Bella, M. A., Eloff, J. H. P., & Olivier, M. S. (2009). A fraud management system architecture for next-generation networks. *Forensic Science International*, *185*(1-3), 51–58. doi:10.1016/j.forsciint.2008.12.013 PMID:19168299

Bihina Bella, M. A., Olivier, M. S., & Eloff, J. H. P. (2012). Near miss Detection for Software Failure Prevention. In *Proceedings of the Southern African Telecommunication Networks and Applications Conference* (SATNAC 2012) (pp. 165-170). George, South Africa: Telkom.

Bullingera, H., Fhnrichb, K., & Meirena, T. (2003). Service engineering methodical development of new service products. *International Journal of Production Economics*, *85*(3), 275–287. doi:10.1016/S0925-5273(03)00116-6

Chetty, J., & Coetzee, M. (2011). Information Security for Service Oriented Computing: Ally or Antagonist. In *Proceedings of the Availability, Reliability and Security conference (ARES)* (pp. 460-465). Vienna: IEEE.

Christiansen, C. A. (2008). *Innovation and Security: Collaborative or Combative*. International Data Corporation (IDC) White Paper. Retrieved from http://www.techrepublic.com

Cloud Security Alliance. (2011). SecaaS: Defined categories of Service. Retrieved from https://cloudsecurityalliance.org

Cuppens, F., Cuppens-Boulahia, N., & Ghorbel, M. B. (2007). High level conflict management strategies in advanced access control models. *Electronic Notes in Theoretical Computer Science, 186*, 3-26.

Dlamini, M. T., Venter, H. S., Eloff, J. H. P., & Mitha, Y. (2012). Authentication in the Cloud: A Risk-based Approach. In *Proceedings of the Southern African Telecommunication Networks and Applications Conference* (SATNAC 2012) (pp. 469-478). George, South Africa: Telkom.

Huang, Y., Ma, X., & Li, D. (2010). Research and Application of Enterprise Search Based on Database Security Services. In *Proceedings of the Second International Symposium on Networking and Network Security* (ISNNS '10) (pp. 238-241). China: Academy Publisher.

ISO 7498-2. (1989). *Information processing systems Open systems Interconnection Basic Reference Model Part 2: Security architecture.*

Josang, A., Ismail, R., & Boyd, C. (2007). A Survey of Trust and Reputation Systems for Online Service Provision. *Decision Support Systems, 34*, 618–644. doi:10.1016/j.dss.2005.05.019

Leavitt, N. (2011). Mobile Security: Finally a Serious Problem? *Computer, 44*(6), 11–14. doi:10.1109/MC.2011.184

Lin, X. (2011). Survey on cloud based mobile security and a new framework for improvement. In *Proceedings of the International Conference on Information and Automation* (ICIA) (pp. 710-715). Shenzen: IEEE.

Masnick, M. (2011). Innovation. In Security: It's All About Trust. Retrieved from http://www.techdirt.com

Oberheide, J., & Jahanian, F. (2010). When mobile is harder than fixed (and vice versa): Demystifying security challenges in mobile environments. In *Proceedings of the Eleventh Workshop on Mobile Computing Systems & Applications* (pp. 43-48). Annapolis, MD: ACM.

OReilly, T. (2007). What Is Web 2.0: Design Patterns and Business Models for the Next Generation of Software. *Communications & Strategies, 1*, 1738.

Padayachee, K. (2010). *An aspect-oriented approach towards enhancing Optimistic Access control with Usage Control.* (PhD thesis). University of Pretoria, Pretoria, South Africa.

Proffitt, M. (2012). *The Oxford English Dictionary.* Oxford University Press.

Roth, S. (2009). New for whom? Initial images from the social dimension of innovation. *International Journal of Innovation and Sustainable Development, 4*, 231–252. doi:10.1504/IJISD.2009.033080

Ruan, K., Carthy, J., Kechadi, T., & Crosbie, M. (2011). Cloud Forensics. In Advances in Digital Forensics VII, (pp. 35-46). Orlando, FL: Springer.

Schumpeter, J. A. (1943). *Capitalism, Socialism, and Democracy.* Routledge.

Wang, J., Zhao, Y., Jiang, S., & Le, J. (2009). Providing Privacy Preserving in cloud computing. In *Proceedings of the International Conference on Test and Measurement* (pp.213-216). Hong Kong: IEEE.

Weinhardt, C., Anandasivam, A., Blau, B., & Stosser, J. (2009). Business Models in the Service World. *IT Professional, 11*(2), 28–33. doi:10.1109/MITP.2009.21

ADDITIONAL READING

Dinh, H. T., Lee, C., Niyato, D., & Wang, P. (2013). A survey of mobile cloud computing: architecture, applications, and approaches. *Wirel. Commun. Mob. Comput, 13*, 1587–1611. doi:10.1002/wcm.1203

Fernando, N., Loke, S. W., & Rahayu, W. (2013). Mobile cloud computing: A survey. *Future Generation Computer Systems, 29*(1), 84–106. doi:10.1016/j.future.2012.05.023

Garg, S. K., Versteeg, S., & Buyya, R. (2013). A framework for ranking of cloud computing services. *Future Generation Computer Systems, 29*(4), 1012–1023. doi:10.1016/j.future.2012.06.006

Grobauer, B., Walloschek, T., & Stöcker, E. (2011). Understanding Cloud Computing Vulnerabilities. *IEEE Security & Privacy, 9*(2), 50–57. doi:10.1109/MSP.2010.115

Huang, D. (2011). Mobile cloud computing. *IEEE COMSOC Multimedia Communications Technical Committee (MMTC). E-Letter, 6*(10), 27–31.

Khan, A. N., Kiah, M. L., Khan, S. U., & Madani, S. A. (2013). Towards secure mobile cloud computing: A survey. *Future Generation Computer Systems, 29*(5), 1278–1299. doi:10.1016/j.future.2012.08.003

Kshetri, N. (2013). Privacy and security issues in cloud computing: The role of institutions and institutional evolution. *Telecommunications Policy*, 373–386.

Li, L., Huang, D., Shen, Z., & Bouzefrane, S. (2013). A cloud based dual-root trust model for secure mobile online transactions. In *Proceedings of IEEE Wireless Communications and Networking Conference (WCNC): SERVICES & APPLICATIONS* (pp. 4404-4409). Shanghai, China: IEEE.

Subashini, S., & Kavitha, V. (2011). A survey on security issues in service delivery models of cloud computing, *Journal of Network and Computer Applications archive, 34*(1), 1-11.

Xiao, H., Ford, B., & Feigenbaum, J. (2013). Structural cloud audits that protect private information. In *Proceedings of ACM Cloud Computing Security Workshop* (pp. 101-112). Berlin, Germany: ACM.

Zhou, Z., & Huang, D. (2012). Efficient and secure data storage operations for mobile cloud computing. In *Proceedings of Network and Service Management conference* (pp. 37-45). Las Vegas, U.S.: IEEE.

Zissis, D., & Lekkas, D. (2012). Addressing cloud computing security issues. *Future Generation Computer Systems, 28*(3), 583–592. doi:10.1016/j.future.2010.12.006

KEY TERMS AND DEFINITIONS

Cloud Computing Architecture: Refers to the components and subcomponents required for cloud computing. These components typically consist of a front end platform (fat client, thin client, mobile device), back end platforms (servers, storage), a cloud based delivery, and a network (Internet, Intranet, Intercloud). Combined, these components make up cloud computing architecture.

Cloud Computing: Is a model for enabling on-demand network access to a shared pool of configurable IT capabilities and resources (e.g., networks, servers, storage, applications, and services) that can be rapidly provisioned and released with minimal management effort or service provider interaction.

Cloud Service Provisioning: Is through three service delivery models (Cloud Software as a Service (SaaS), Cloud Platform as a Service (PaaS), and Cloud Infrastructure as a Service (IaaS)) (CNSSI, 4009)

Information Security: The protection of information and information systems from unauthorized access, use, disclosure, disruption, modification, or destruction in order to provide confidentiality, integrity, and availability. (CNSSI No. 4009)

Innovation: This is the process of bringing an idea to market as a real product, process, system or device that is commercially marketable involving new inventions. The process of translating an idea or invention into a good or service that creates value or for which customers will pay.

Mobile Cloud: Is Internet-based data, applications and related services accessed through smartphones, laptop computers, tablets and other portable devices.

Mobile Computing: Is a generic term used to refer to the use of a variety of mobile devices such as laptops, cell phones and tablets that allow people to access data and information from where ever they are.

Security Services: Are the capabilities that support one, or more, of the security requirements (Confidentiality, Integrity, Availability). Examples of security services are key management, access control, and authentication.

Concluding Thoughts on Information Security in Diverse Computing Environments

This final chapter presents an overview of the topics discussed in chapters 1 through 15, noting that security solution design in resource-constrained environments requires a new look at implementation strategies and algorithms. While in certain cases tweaking or re-adapting current solutions is sufficient, there is an increasing need for more radical approaches to security problem resolution in resource-constrained environments.

The idea of producing an edited book on the topic of information security in diverse computing emerged on the back of observations we have made in terms of designing security solutions for the developing world. We have noted that oftentimes, the scenarios that emerge in the context of the developing world hinge on limited resource availability. For instance, power outages impede access to data on backend servers thereby nullifying the need for standard access control schemes that aim to satisfy strong quality of service requirements. Likewise mobile device popularity imposes a need for dependable backend cloud servers on to which data can be stored when device storage limitations make this necessary. Cloud computing also raises issues of security and privacy in relation to the storage of the data and the notion of trust management in the case of the involvement of third-party service providers.

Generally, computer security and information security in particular, are topics that rely primarily on the conception of preventing adversarial access to computer systems and to the data stored on these computing systems. Consequently, the security solutions that we propose hinge on notions of easing access for authentic user but on the opposite end deterring malicious use. However, resource constrained environments present new scenarios that require rethinking security solutions. For instance, having the best access control scheme that is reliant on high speed Internet access, is completely useless in situations where reliable access to bandwidth is problematic. Likewise, using a biometric scheme in a context of intermittent power connections could annul the effectiveness of the scheme if one of the key presumptions for security was a stable connection. Effective solutions to enforcing security in these resource constrained environments can be designed by rather unconventional approaches to security solution design.

In certain cases, we might note as is the case for the work we have presented in this book, that workable solutions simply require slight changes to the constraints on which the model or prototype hinges. In other cases we might find that we need other sources of inspiration. For instance, to specify adversarial models we might draw inspiration from biological defense processes such as the human body's ability to fight disease by generating suitable antibodies. Likewise a chameleon's behavior could serve as inspiration for modeling anonymity schemes or slime mould, instead of threat modeling tools, to make decisions about network attack progression models.

Each model offers pros and cons. For instance, while security and privacy have become important issues when dealing with Internet Protocol version 6 (IPv6) networks. We still have to deal with issues such as anonymity enforcement where, on the one hand anonymity, by its privacy enforcing character makes distinguishing between legitimate users and illegitimate users a difficult problem. On the plus end a user has a guarantee of keeping his/her identity secret in cases where remaining anonymous is advantageous. On the downside when a user needs to be authenticated by systems whose services he/she requires we have the problem of deciding how to authenticate the user without requiring information that might compromise his/her true identity. Other considerations to evaluate include the fact that, a lack of privacy exposes legitimate users to abuse, which can result from the information gained from privacy related attacks.

In adversarial modeling we note that while the security and integrity of exterior gateway protocols such as the Border Gateway Protocol (BGP) and interior gateway protocols have been investigated in relation to adversarial modeling, neither has much attention has been paid to the problem of availability and timeliness that is crucial for ensuring quality of service in critical infrastructure areas such as financial services and electric power (smart grid) networks. Al-Mutairi and Wolthusen, in Chapter 8, present a method for modeling adversaries for the analysis of attacks on quality of service characteristics underpinning such real-time networks. By using an abstraction of the problem we are able in this case, to analyze and make predictions about behavioral patterns that can be used to distinguish between security violations and regular system failures.

Furthermore, the growing number of security vulnerabilities make an efficient detector of known and unknown malware necessary. The threats imposed by metamorphic malware often bypass a detectors that are based on pattern matching techniques. Therefore, signature or non-signature based scanners that not only detect zero day malware but also are self-adapting to new malware threats are needed. In Chapter 10, Vinod et al. propose a statistical malware scanner that is effective in discriminating metamorphic malware samples from large collection of benign executables. Two types of experiments (a) cross validation and (b) test and train are used and the results indicate that the proposed statistical generator is effective in the identifying synthetic metamorphic malware and benign instances.

Viewed, as we have analyzed in the preceding paragraphs, security is an area in which we as specialists in the field are often guilty of misunderstanding the very people we are trying to protect. As Marsh et al. present in Chapter 2, oftentimes people (users) are the weak link in the security chain. However, as the authors of chapter 2 go on to point out, this may be true, but there are nuances that make this allegation difficult to defend. The key it seems lies in designing the models in ways that help users understand their information and device security and make informed, guided, and responsible decisions.

Finally we look at cloud computing as a service-on-demand architecture that has grown in importance in recent years. A key reason behind this is the ever increasing amount of data which is supposed to outpace the growth of storage capacity. Cloud storage is a cost-effective option for organizations and individuals, but these benefits of cloud computing come tagged with challenges and open issues such as security, reliability and the risk of dependency on the provider for service provision. Schnjakin and Meinel, in Chapter 16, present a system that improves availability, confidentiality and reliability of data stored in the cloud. To achieve this objective, they propose that a user's data be encrypted and the RAID-technology principle used to manage data distribution across cloud storage providers. They proceed to discuss the security functionality and present a proof-of-concept experiment for our application to evaluate the performance and cost effectiveness of their approach. Experimental results of deploying the application using eight commercial cloud storage repositories in different countries improves the perceived availability and, in most cases, the overall performance when compared with individual cloud providers.

Exciting avenues for future work in the area of enforcing security in resource-constrained environments would include:

1. Re-evaluating existing solutions for suitability and potential extensions to suit the new scenario.
2. Coming up with new paradigms and/or models to support the design process.
3. Discovering cost-effective solutions that are generic and not confided to specific narrow scenarios.

Anne V. D. M. Kayem
University of Cape Town, South Africa

Compilation of References

Abdelwahab, A. A., & Hassaan, L. A. (2008, March). A discrete wavelet transform based technique for image data hiding. In *Proceedings of Radio Science Conference,* (pp. 1-9). IEEE.

Abu-Libdeh, H., Princehouse, L., & Weatherspoon, H. (2010). *Racs: A case for cloud storage diversity.* Paper presented at SoCC'10. New York, NY.

Adams, A., & Sasse, A. (1999). Users are not the enemy. *Communications of the ACM, 42*(12), 40–46. doi:10.1145/322796.322806

Adelstein, F. (2006). Live forensics: Diagnosing your system without killing it first. *Communications of the ACM, 49*(2), 63–66. doi:10.1145/1113034.1113070

Aggarwal, C., Han, J., Wang, J., & Yu, P. (2003). A framework for clustering evolving data streams. In *Proceedings of the 29th international conference on Very large data bases* (vol. 29, pp. 81-92). VLDB Endowment.

Aggarwal, C., & Philip, S. (2008). *A general survey of privacy-preserving data mining models and algorithms.* Springer. doi:10.1007/978-0-387-70992-5_2

Agrawal, Cruz, Okino, & Rajan. (1999). Performance bonds for flow control protocols. *IEEE/ACM Transactions on Networking, 7*(3), 310–323.

Agrawal, R., Kiernan, J., Srikant, R., & Xu, Y. (2002). Hippocratic databases. In *Proceedings of 28th International Conference on Very Large Data Bases*, (pp. 143-154). Morgan Kaufmann.

Ahmad, M., Batz, D., Chasko, S., Dagon, D., Judge, P., & Lee, W. et al. (2011). *Emerging Cyber Threats Report for 2011.* Georgia Tech Information Security Center.

Al-Ahmad, W. (2011). Building secure software using xp. *International Journal of Secure Software Engineering, 2*(3), 63–76. doi:10.4018/jsse.2011070104

Alexander, D. (2011). *U.S. reserves right to meet cyber attack with force.* Academic Press.

Al-Harbi, A. L., & Osborn, S. L. (2011). *Mixing privacy with role-based access control.* Paper presented at the Fourth International C* Conference on Computer Science & Software Engineering. Montreal, Canada.

Alkahtani, M. S., Woodward, M. E., & Al-Begain, K. (2003). An overview of quality of service (qos) and qos routing in communication networks. In *Proceedings of 4th PGNET2003 Symposium*, (pp. 236-242). Liverpool, UK: PGNET.

Amin, P. K., Liu, N., & Subbalakshmi, K.P. (2005). Statistically Secure Digital Image Data Hiding. In *Proceedings of the IEEE 7th Workshop on Multimedia Signal Processing.* IEEE.

Andersson, Doolan, Feldman, Fredette, & Thomas. (2007). *LDP specification.* IETF, RFC 5036.

Andrew, W., Michael, V., Matthew, H., Christopher, T., & Arun, L. (2007). *A: Exploiting Similarity between Variants to Defeat Malware: Vilo Method for Comparing and Searching Binary Programs.* Retrieved from https://blackhat.com/presentations/bh-dc-07/Walenstein/Paper/bh-dc-07-walenstein-W%P.pdf

Android. (n.d.). Available at http://www.android.com/

Annie, H. T., & Mark, S. (2013). Chi-squared distance and metamorphic virus detection. Journal in Computer Virology, 9(1), 1-14

Arends, R., Austein, R., Larson, M., Massey, D., & Rose, S. (2005, March). DNS Security Introduction and Requirements. *RFC*. Retrieved March 2005, from http://www.ietf.org/rfc/rfc4033.txt

Arkko, J., Kempf, J., Zill, B., & Nikander, P. (2005, March). *SEcure Neighbor Discovery (SEND)*. Retrieved from http://tools.ietf.org/html/rfc3971

Armbrust, M., Fox, A., Griftlth, R., Joseph, A. D., Katz, R., Konwinski, A., & Zaharia, M. (2010). A view of cloud computing. *Communications oft he ACM, 53*(4), 50-58.

Armbrust, M., Fox, A., Griffith, R., Joseph, A. D., Katz, R., & Konwinski, A. et al. (2010, April). A view of cloud computing. *Communications of the ACM, 53*(4), 50–58. doi:10.1145/1721654.1721672

Asaf, S., Robert, M., Yuval, E., & Chanan, G. (2009). Detection of malicious code by applying machine learning classifiers on static features: A state-of-the-art survey. *Information Security Technical Report, 14*(1), 16–29. doi:10.1016/j.istr.2009.03.003

Asnar, Y., Paja, E., & Mylopoulos, J. (2011). Modeling design patterns with description logics: a case study. In *Proceedings of the 23rd international conference on Advanced information systems engineering*. Springer-Verlag.

Atawneh, S., Almomani, A., & Sumari, P. (2013). Steganography in Digital Images: Common Approaches and Tools, journal. *IETE Technical Review, 30*(4), 344–358. doi:10.4103/0256-4602.116724

Ateniese, G., Burns, R., Curtmola, R., Herring, J., Kissner, L., Peterson, Z., & Song, D. (2007). *Provable data possession at untrusted stores*. Paper presented at the 14th ACM CCS. New York, NY.

Atkins, D., & Austein, R. (2004, August). Threat Analysis of the Domain Name System (DNS). *RFC*. Retrieved August 2004, from http://www.ietf.org/rfc/rfc3833.txt

Attaluri, S., McGhee, S., & Stamp, M. (2009). Profile hidden Markov models and metamorphic virus detection. *Journal in Computer Virology, 5*, 151–169. doi:10.1007/s11416-008-0105-1

Audsley, N. C., Burns, A., Davis, R. I., Tindell, K. W., & Wellings, A. J. (1995). Fixed priority pre-emptive scheduling: An historical perspective. *Real-Time Systems, 8*(2-3), 173–198. doi:10.1007/BF01094342

Aura, T. (2005, March). *Cryptographically Generated Addresses (CGA)*. Retrieved from http://www.ietf.org/rfc/rfc3972.txt

Awduche & Agogbua. (1999). *Requirements for traffic engineering over mpls*. IETF, RFC 2702.

Awduche, Berger, Gan, Li, Srinivasan, & Swallow. (2001). *Rsvp-te: Extensions to rsvp for lsp tunnels*. IETF, RFC 3209.

Aycock, J. (2006). Computer Viruses and Malware. Academic Press.

Azad, M., Ahmed, A., & Alam, A. (2010). Digital Rights Management. *International Journal of Computer Science and Network Security, 10*, 11.

BackTrack Linux. (2011). *BackTrack Linux*. Retrieved March 22, 2013, from www.backtracklinux.org

Bagnato, A., Kordy, B., Meland, P. H., & Schweitzer, P. (2012). Attribute decoration of attack-defense trees. *International Journal of Secure Software Engineering, 3*(2), 1–35. doi:10.4018/jsse.2012040101

Baker, K. (2013). *Singular Value Decomposition Tutorial website*. Retrieved from http://www.ling.ohio-state.edu/~kbaker/pubs/Singular_Value_Decomposition_Tutorial.pdf

Balachandra, R. K., Ramakrishna, P. V., & Rakshit, A. (2009). Cloud Security Issues. In *Proceedings of the Services Computing* (pp. 517-520). Bangalore, India: IEEE.

Barker, K., Askari, M., Banerjee, M., Ghazinour, K., Mackas, B., & Majedi, M. et al. (2009). A data privacy taxonomy. *Lecture Notes in Computer Science, 5588*, 42–54.

Barni, M., Bartolini, F., Cappellini, V., & Piva, A. (1998). A D.C.T. domain system for robust image watermarking. *Signal Processing, 66*(3), 357–372. doi:10.1016/S0165-1684(98)00015-2

Barni, M., Bartolini, F., & Piva, A. (2001). Improved wavelet-based watermarking through pixel-wise masking. *IEEE Transactions on Image Processing, 10*(5), 783–791.

Bartolini, F., Tefas, A., Barni, M., & Pitas, I. (2001). Image authentication techniques for surveillance applications. *Proceedings of the IEEE, 89*(10), 1403–1418. doi:10.1109/5.959338

Basu, A., Corena, J., Kiyomoto, K., Marsh, S., Vaidya, J., & Guo, G. (2014b). Privacy preserving trusted social feedback. In *Proceedings of the ACM Symposium on Applied Computing (SAC) TRECK track*. New York: ACM Press.

Basu, A., Corena, J., Kiyomoto, S., Vaidya, J., Marsh, S., & Miyake, Y. (2014a). PrefRank: Fair aggregation of subjective user preferences. In *Proceedings of the ACM Symposium on Applied Computing (SAC) RS track*. New York: ACM Press.

Bayardo, R., & Agrawal, R. (2005). Data privacy through optimal k-anonymization. In *Proceedings. 21st International Conference on* (pp. 217-228). IEEE.

Baysa, D., Low, R. M., & Stamp, M. (2013). Structural entropy and metamorphic malware. Journal of Computer Virology and Hacking Techniques, 9(4), 1-14, doi: doi:10.1007/s11416-013-0185-4

Becher, M., Freiling, F., & Leider, B. (2007). On the effort to create smartphone worms in Windows Mobile. In *Proceedings of the 2007 IEEE Workshop on Information Assurance*. United States Military Academy. Retrieved March 22, 2013, from http://pil.informatik.uni-mannheim.de/filepool/publications/on-the-effort-to-create-smartphone-worms-in-windows-mobile.pdf

Beidleman, S. W. (2009). Defining and Deterring Cyber War. Barracks, PA Army War College. Retrieved March I0, 2013, from http://www.hsdl.org/?abstract&doc=ll86 53&coll=limited

Bessani, A., Correia, M., Quaresma, B., Andre, F., & Sousa, P. (2011). Depsky: Dependable and secure storage in a cloud-of-clouds. In *Proceedings of the Sixth Conference on Computer Systems*, (pp. 31–46). New York, NY: ACM.

Bhatnagar, G., Jonathan Wu, Q. M., & Raman, B. (2012). Robust gray-scale logo watermarking in wavelet domain. *Computers & Electrical Engineering*, 38(5), 1164–1176. doi:10.1016/j.compeleceng.2012.02.002

Bhattacharya, D. (2008) *Leardership styles and information security in small businesses: An empirical investigation*. (Doctoral dissertation, University of Phoenix). Retrieved March 9, 2013, from www.phoenix.edu/apololibrary

Bicakci, V. (2013). *Anomaly Detection for Mobile Device Comfort*. (Masters of Applied Science Thesis). Carleton University.

Bickford, J., Hare, R., Baliga, A., & Ganapathy, V. (2010). Rootkits on Smart Phones: Attacks, Implications and Opportunities. In *Proceedings of the Eleventh Workshop on Mobile Computing Systems & Applications*, (pp. 49-54). Academic Press.

Bihina Bella, M. A., Olivier, M. S., & Eloff, J. H. P. (2012). Near miss Detection for Software Failure Prevention. In *Proceedings of the Southern African Telecommunication Networks and Applications Conference* (SATNAC 2012) (pp. 165-170). George, South Africa: Telkom.

Bihina Bella, M. A., Eloff, J. H. P., & Olivier, M. S. (2009). A fraud management system architecture for next-generation networks. *Forensic Science International*, 185(1-3), 51–58. doi:10.1016/j.forsciint.2008.12.013 PMID:19168299

Bilski, T. (2009). Fluctuations and lasting trends of qos on intercontinental links. *Quality of Service in Heterogeneous Networks*, 22, 251–264. doi:10.1007/978-3-642-10625-5_16

Bishop, M., & Taylor, C. (2009). A Critical Analysis of the Centers of Academic Excellence Program. In *Proceedings of the 13th Colloquium for Information Systems Security Education* (pp. 1-3). Retrieved March 9, 2013, from http://nob.cs.ucdavis.edu/bishop/papers/2009-cisse/

Blake, Black, Carlson, Davies, Wang, & Weiss. (1998). *An architecture for differentiated services*. IETF, RFC 2475.

Bluetooth. (2008). *The Bluetooth Special Interest Group*. Available at http://www.bluetooth.com/

Bodden, E., Hermann, B., Lerch, J., & Mezini, M. (2013). *Reducing human factors in software security architectures. In Proceedings Fraunhofer Future Security Conference 2013*. Germany: Fraunhofer Verlag.

Bohnet, I., & Zeckhauser, R. (2004). Trust, risk and betrayal. *Journal of Economic Behavior & Organization*, 55(40), 467–484. doi:10.1016/j.jebo.2003.11.004

Bose, A. (2008). *Propagation, detection and containment of mobile mal ware*. (Doctoral dissertation, University of Michigan). Retrieved March 11, 2013, from www.phoenix.edu/apololibrary

Bose, A., & Shin, K. G. (2006a). Proactive Security for Mobile Messaging Networks. In *Proceedings of ACM Workshop on Wireless Security* (pp. 95-104). ACM.

Bose, A., & Shin, K. G. (2006b). On Mobile Viruses Exploiting Messaging and Bluetooth Services. In *Proceedings of Second International Conference on Security and Privacy in Communication Networks*. Academic Press.

Boshmaf, Y., Muslukhov, I., Beznosov, K., & Ripeanu, M. (2013). Design and analysis of a Social Botnet. *Computer Networks*, *57*(2), 556–578. doi:10.1016/j.comnet.2012.06.006

Bowers, K. D., Juels, A., & Oprea, A. (2009). *Hail: A high availability and integrity layer for cloud storage.* Paper presented at CCS'09. New York, NY.

Boyd, D. M., & Ellison, N. B. (2007). Social network sites: Definition, history, and scholarship. *Journal of Computer-Mediated Communication, 13*(1), 210–230. doi:10.1111/j.1083-6101.2007.00393.x

Brenner, S. W., & Clarke, L. L. (2010, October). Civilians in cyberwarfare: Conscripts. *Vanderbilt Journal of Transnational Law, 43*(4), 10111076.

Br, G., Refsdal, A., & Stølen, K. (2010). Modular analysis and modelling of risk scenarios with dependencies. *Journal of Systems and Software, 83*(10), 1995–2013. doi:10.1016/j.jss.2010.05.069

Briassouli, A., Tsakalides, P., & Stouraitis, A. (2005). Hidden messages in heavy-tails: DCT-domain watermark detection using alpha-stable models. *IEEE Transactions on Multimedia, 7*(4), 700–715.

Briggs, P., & Olivier, P. (2008). Biometric daemons: Authentication via electronic pets. In *Proceedings CHI 2008* (pp. 2423–2432). New York: ACM Press.

Briscoe, B. (1999). MARKS: Zero side eect multicast key management using arbitrarily revealed key sequences. In *Proc. First International Workshop On Networked Group Communication* (NGC'99). NGC.

Broberg, J., Buyya, R., & Tari, Z. (2009). *Creating a 'cloud storage' mashup for high performance, low cost content delivery.* Paper presented at Service-Oriented Computing. New York, NY.

Brown, B. (2009). *Beyond Downadup: Security expert worries about smart phone, TinyURL threats: Malware writers just waiting for financial incentive to strike, F-Secure exec warns.* Retrieved March 20, 2013, from http://business.highbeam.com/409220/article-1G1-214585913/beyond-downadup-securityexpert-worries-smart-phone

Bullingera, H., Fhnrichb, K., & Meirena, T. (2003). Service engineering methodical development of new service products. *International Journal of Production Economics, 85*(3), 275–287. doi:10.1016/S0925-5273(03)00116-6

Bullock, J., Haddow, G., Coppola, D., & Yeletaysi, S. (2009). *Introduction to homeland security: Principles of all-hazards response* (3rd ed.). Burlington, MA: Elsevier Inc.

Bulygin, Y. (2007). Epidemics of Mobile Worms. In *Proceedings of IEEE International Conference on Performance, Computing and Communications,* (pp. 475-478). IEEE.

Bunge, M. (1998). *Philosophy of Science: From Problem to Theory* (Vol. 1).Transaction Publishers.

Burke, M. J., & Kayem, A. V. D. M. (2014). K-Anonymity for Privacy Preserving Crime Data Publishing in Resource Constrained Environments. In *Proceedings for the 8th International Symposium on Security and Multinodality in Pervasive Environments*. Academic Press.

Burt, J. (2009). *Future for cloud computing looks good, report says.* Academic Press.

Buyya, R., Yeo, C.-S., & Venugopal, S. (2008). Market-oriented cloud computing: Vision, hype, and reality for delivering it services as computing utilities. In *Proceedings of the 10th IEEE International Conference on High Performance Computing and Communications*. IEEE.

Byun, J.-W., & Li, N. (2008). Purpose based access control for privacy protection in relational database systems. *The VLDB Journal, 17*(4), 603–619. doi:10.1007/s00778-006-0023-0

Cabir, 29A. (2006). *Source Code - Cabir.* Available at http://netsecurity

Caloyannides, M. A. (2006). *Digital "Evidence" is Often Evidence of Nothing.* IGI Global.

Cao, J., Carminati, B., Ferrari, E., Member, S., & Tan, K. (2011). Castle: Continuously anonymizing data streams. *IEEE Transactions on Dependable and Secure Computing, 8*(3), 337–352.

Carr, N. (2008). The Big Switch. Norton.

Carrier, B. D. (2006). *A Hypothesis-based Approach to Digital Forensic Investigations*. (PhD thesis). Purdue University.

Celeda, P. (20II). *Network security monitoring and behavior analysis*. Retrieved March 22nd, 2013 from http://www.terena.org/activities/campus-bp/pdf/gn3-na3-t4-cbpd133.pdf

Chang, H., & Schroeter, K. (2010). Creating safe and trusted social networks with biometric user authentication, ethics and policy of biometrics. In *Proceedings 3rd International Conference on Ethics and Policy of Biometrics and International Data Sharing*. Retrieved on March 29, 2013 from http://www.comp.polyu.edu.hk/conference/iceb/

Chang, C. C., Lin, C. C., Tseng, C. S., & Tai, W. L. (2007). Reversible hiding in DCT-based compressed images. *Information Sciences, 177*(13), 2768–2786. doi:10.1016/j.ins.2007.02.019

Chan, Y. K., Chen, W. T., Yu, S. S., Ho, Y. A., Tsai, C. S., & Chu, Y. P. (2009). A HDWT-based reversible data hiding method. *Journal of Systems and Software, 82*(3), 411–421. doi:10.1016/j.jss.2008.07.008

Cha, S.-H. (2007). Comprehensive Survey on Distance/Similarity Measures between Probability Density Functions. *International Journal of Mathematical Models and Methods in Applied Sciences, 1*, 300–307.

Cha, S., & Yoo, J. (2012). A safety-focused verification using software fault trees. *Future Generation Computer Systems, 28*(8), 1272–1282. doi:10.1016/j.future.2011.02.004

Chatfield, C., Carmichael, D., Hexel, R., Kay, J., & Kummerfeld, B. (2005). Personalisation in intelligent environments: Managing the information flow. In *Proceedings OZCHI '05: 17th Australian conference on Computer-Human Interaction*. Canberra: Computer-Human Interaction Special Interest Group (CHISIG) of Australia.

Cheddad, A., Condell, J., Curran, K., & Kevitt, M. P. (2010). Digital image Steganography: Survey and analysis of current methods. *Signal Processing, 90*(3), 727–752. doi:10.1016/j.sigpro.2009.08.010

Chen, J. (2008). *An Introduction to Android*. Available at http://sites.google.com/site/io/an-introduction-to-android

Chen, T., & Zhong, S. (2012). Emergency Access Authorization for Personally Controlled Online Health Care Data. *J. Med. Syst., 36*(1), 291-300. DOI=10.1007/s10916-010-9475-2

Cheng, J., Wong, S. H. Y., Yang, H., & Lu, S. (2007). SmartSiren: Virus Detection and Alert for Smartphones. *MobiSys, 2007*, 258–271. doi:10.1145/1247660.1247690

Chen, J. L., Chen, M. C., & Chian, Y. R. (2007). QoS management in heterogeneous home networks. *Computer Networks, 51*(12), 3368–3379. doi:10.1016/j.comnet.2007.01.032

Chen, R. (2013). Member use of social networking sites - An empirical examination. *Decision Support Systems, 54*(3), 1219–1227. doi:10.1016/j.dss.2012.10.028

Chen, T. M., Walrand, J., & Messerschmitt, D. G. (1989). Dynamic priority protocols for packet voice. *IEEE Journal on Selected Areas in Communications, 7*, 632–643. doi:10.1109/49.32327

Chen, T.-S., Liu, C.-H., Chen, T.-L., Chen, C. S., Bau, J.-B., & Lin, T. C. (2012, December). Secure Dynamic Access Control Scheme of PHR in Cloud Computing. *Journal of Medical Systems, 36*(6), 4005–4020. doi:10.1007/s10916-012-9873-8 PMID:22926919

Cheok, A. (2009). Mixed Reality Entertainment and Art. *International Journal Of Virtual Reality, 8*(2), 83–90.

Cheok, A., Fernando, 0., & Liu, W. (2008). The magical world of mixed reality. Innovation: The Magazine of Research and Technology. *National University of Singapore and World Scientific Publishing, 8*(1), 70–73.

Cheok, A., Man Fung, H., Yustina, E., & Shang Ping, L. (2005). Mobile Computing With Personal Area Network and Human Power Generation. *International Journal of Software Engineering and Knowledge Engineering, 15*(2), 169–175. doi:10.1142/S0218194005002348

Cheshire, S., & Krochmal, M. (2013, February). *Multicast DNS*. Retrieved from http://tools.ietf.org/html/rfc6762

Cheswick, B. (1990). The design of a secure internet gateway. In *Proc. Summer USENIX Conference*. USENIX.

Chetty, J., & Coetzee, M. (2011). Information Security for Service Oriented Computing: Ally or Antagonist. In *Proceedings of the Availability, Reliability and Security conference (ARES)* (pp. 460-465). Vienna: IEEE.

Chiu, C., Huang, H., & Yen, C. (2010). Antecedents of trust in online auctions. *Electronic Commerce Research and Applications*, 9(2), 148–159. doi:10.1016/j.elerap.2009.04.003

Chouchane, M. R., & Lakhotia, A. (2006). Using engine signature to detect metamorphic malware: In *Proceedings of the 4th ACM Workshop on Recurring malcode*, (pp. 73-78). ACM.

Christiansen, C. A. (2008). *Innovation and Security: Collaborative or Combative*. International Data Corporation (IDC) White Paper. Retrieved from http://www.techrepublic.com

Ciriani, V., Foresti, S., & Samarati, P. (2007). Microdata Protection. In Secure Data Management in Decentralized Systems (pp. 291-321). Springer.

Cisco Systems Inc. (2010). The Tipping Point: Cybercriminals Targeting Mobile Platforms. Cisco Annual Security Report 2010. Available at http://www.cisco.com

Clark, D. D., & Landau, S. (2010). The problem isn't attribution: It's multi-stage attacks. In *Proceedings of the Re-Architecting the Internet Workshop*. ACM.

Clark, D., Braden, B., & Shenker, S. (1994). *Integrated service in the internet architecture: an overview*. Program on Internet and Telecoms Convergence.

Clarke, R. & Knake, R. (2010). *Cyber war: The next threat to national security and what to do about it*. New York, NY: Ecco.

Cloud Security Alliance. (2011). SecaaS: Defined categories of Service. Retrieved from https://cloudsecurityalliance.org

Cofta, P. (2006), Distrust. In *Proceedings of Eight International Conference onElectronic Commerce* (pp. 250-258). New York: ACM Press.

Cohen, F. (2012). *Digital Forensic Evidence Examination* (3rd ed.). Fred Cohen & Associates.

Common Vulnerabilities and Exposure. (n.d.). Available at http://www.cve.mitre.org

Comodo. (n.d.). Available at https://m.comodo.com/

Conti, M., Hasani, A., & Crispo, B. (2011). Virtual Private Social Networks. In *Proceedings of the First ACM Conference on Data and Application Security and Privacy*. New York, NY: ACM.

Cooper, A., Tschofenig, H., Aboba, B., Peterson, J., Morris, J., Hansen, M., & Smith, R. (2013, July). *Privacy Considerations for Internet Protocols*. Retrieved from http://tools.ietf.org/html/rfc6973

Cox, I. J., Kilian, J., Leighton, F. T., & Shamoon, T. (1997, December). Secure spread spectrum watermarking for multimedia. *IEEE Transactions on Image Processing*, 6(12), 1673–1687. doi:10.1109/83.650120 PMID:18285237

Cox, J. (2004). How to identify trust and reciprocity. *Games and Economic Behavior*, 46(2), 260–281. doi:10.1016/S0899-8256(03)00119-2

Crawford, H. (2013). *A Framework For Continuous, Transparent Authentication On Mobile Devices*. (PhD Thesis). University of Glasgow, Glasgow, UK.

Crocker, D. (1997). *Mailbox Names for Common Services, Roles and Functions*. RFC 2142 (Proposed Standard), May 1997.

Cruickshank, H., Howarth, M., & Iyengar, S. A. (2005). *Comparison between satellite DVB conditional access and secure IP multicast*. Paper presented at the 14th IST Mobile and Wireless Communications Summit. New York, NY.

Cruz, R. L. (1991). A calculus for network delay. Part I. network elements in isolation. *IEEE Transactions on Information Theory*, 37(1), 114–131.

Cuevas, A., Khoury, P. E., Gomez, L., & Laube, A. (2008). Security patterns for capturing encryption-based access control to sensor data. In *Proceedings of the 2008 Second International Conference on Emerging Security Information, Systems and Technologies*. IEEE Computer Society.

Cuppens, F., Cuppens-Boulahia, N., & Ghorbel, M. B. (2007). High level conflict management strategies in advanced access control models. *Electronic Notes in Theoretical Computer Science, 186*, 3-26.

Curry, E., & Grace, P. (2008). Flexible self-management using the model-view- controller pattern. *IEEE Software, 25*(3), 84–90. doi:10.1109/MS.2008.60

Dabek, F., Kaashoek, M. F., Karger, D., Morris, R., & Stoica, I. (2001). *Wide-area cooperative storage with cfs.* Paper presented at ACM SOSP. New York, NY.

Daglish, D., & Archer, N. (2009). Electronic Personal Health Record Systems: A Brief Review of Privacy, Security, and Architectural Issues. In *Proceedings of the IEE 2009 World Congress on Privacy, Security, and Trust and the Management of e-Business*, (pp. 110-120). IEE.

Dagon, D., Martin, T., & Starner, T. (2004). Mobile Phones as Computing Devices: The Viruses are Coming! *IEEE Pervasive Computing*, 11–15. doi:10.1109/MPRV.2004.21

Dalenius, T., & Reiss, S. (1982). Data-swapping: A technique for disclosure control. *Journal of Statistical Planning and Inference*. doi:10.1016/0378-3758(82)90058-1

Dawson, M. (2011). Applicability of Web 2.0: Training for Tactical Military Applications. Global TIME, 1, 395-398.

Dawson, M. E. Jr, Crespo, M., & Brewster, S. (2013). DoD cyber technology policies to secure automated information systems. *International Journal of Business Continuity and Risk Management, 4*(1), 1–22. doi:10.1504/IJBCRM.2013.053089

Dawson, M. E., & Saeed, AI, T. (2012). Use of Open Source Software and Virtualization in Academia to Enhance Higher Education Everywhere. *Culling-edge Technologies in Higher Education, 6*, 283–313. doi:10.1108/S2044-9968(2012)000006C013

Debatin, B., Lovejoy, J. P., Horn, A. K., & Hughes, B. N. (2009). Facebook and Online Privacy: Attitudes, Behaviors, and Unintended Consequences. *Journal of Computer-Mediated Communication, 15*(1), 83–108. doi:10.1111/j.1083-6101.2009.01494.x

Deering, S., & Hinden, R. (1998, December). Internet Protocol, Version 6 (IPv6) Specification. *RFC*. Retrieved from http://www.ietf.org/rfc/rfc2460.txt

Delac, G., Silic, M., & Krolo, J. (2011). Emerging Security Threats for Mobile Platforms. In *Proceedings of 34th International Convention on Information and communication Technology, Electronics and Microelectronics (MIPRO)*, (pp. 1468-1473). MIPRO.

Denning, D. E. (2012). Stuxnet: What Has Changed? *Future Internet, 4*(3), 672–687. doi:10.3390/fi4030672

Dima, S., Robert, M., Zvi, B., Yuval, S., & Yuval, E. (2009). Using artificial neural networks to detect unknown computer worms. *Neural Computing & Applications, 18*(7), 663–674. doi:10.1007/s00521-009-0238-2

Dingledine, R., Freedman, M., & Molnar, D. (2000). *The freehaven project: Distributed anonymous storage service.* Paper presented at the Workshop on Design Issues in Anonymity and Unobservability. New York, NY.

Dlamini, M. T., Venter, H. S., Eloff, J. H. P., & Mitha, Y. (2012). Authentication in the Cloud: A Risk-based Approach. In *Proceedings of the Southern African Telecommunication Networks and Applications Conference (SATNAC 2012)* (pp. 469-478). George, South Africa: Telkom.

Dolev, D., & Yao, A. C. (1983). On the security of public key protocols. *IEEE Transactions on Information Theory, 29*(2), 198–208.

Dong, X., Clark, J. A., & Jacob, J. L. (2008). Threat modelling in user performed authentication. In *Proceedings of the 10th International Conference on Information and Communications Security*. Springer-Verlag.

Dossia. (2014). *Dossia.* Retrieved from http://www.dossia.org

Droms, R., Bound, J., Volz, B., Lemon, T., Perkins, C., & Carney, M. (2003, July). Dynamic Host Configuration Protocol for IPv6 (DHCPv6). *RFC*. Retrieved July 2003, from http://www.ietf.org/rfc/rfc3315.txt

Dudenhoffer, C. (2012). Pin It! Pinterest as a Library Marketing Information Literacy Tool. *College & Research Libraries News*, *73*(6), 328–332.

Dwyer, N. (2011). *Traces of digital trust: an interactive design perspective.* (PhD thesis). Victoria University, Victoria, Australia.

Dyck, J., Pinelle, D., Brown, B., & Gutwin, C. (2003). Learning from Games: HCI Design Innovations in Entertainment Software. In Proceedings of Graphics Interface, (pp. 237-246). Retrieved March 18, 2013, from http:/lhci. usask.ca/publica tions/view.php?id=88

Ecom200. (n.d.). *Mobile Phones Swamped by E-Mail Virus.* Available at ecommercetimes.com

Edge, C. C. (2010). *Quantitative assessment of the modularization of security design patterns with aspects.* (Ph.D. thesis).

Eitan, M., Asaf, S., Lior, R., & Yuval, E. (2009). Improving malware detection by applying multi-inducer ensemble. *Journal In Computational Statistics & Data Analysis*, *53*(4), 1483–1494. doi:10.1016/j.csda.2008.10.015

Elgg. (2013). *Elgg social network engine.* Retrieved from http://elgg.org/

EPOC Features. (2012). Retrieved fromhttp://www.emotiv.com/epoc/features.php

EU DPD. (1995). *European Union Data Protection Directive: Processing of Personal Data and on the free movement of such data.* Retrieved from http://eur-lex.europa.eu/LexUriServ/LexUriServ. do?uri=CELEX:31995L0046:en:HTML

EU DPD. (2012). *European Union Data Protection Directive.* Retrieved from http://europa.eu/rapid/press-release_IP-12-46_en.htm?locale=en

European Telecommunications Standards Institute. (1997). *Digital Video Broadcasting: Framing structure, channel coding and modulation for 11/12 GHz satellite services.* European Standard EN 300-421. Author.

European Telecommunications Standards Institute. (2009). *Digital Video Broadcasting: Transport of MPEG-2 TS Based DVB Services over IP Based Networks.* ETSI TS 102 034, August 2009. Author.

European Telecommunications Standards Institute. (2011, September). Digital Video Broadcasting: Support for use of the DVB Scrambling Algorithm version 3 within digital broadcasting systems. *ETSI TS*, *100*, 289.

FaceBook. (2014). *FaceBook.* Retrieved from https://www.facebook.com

Fan, L., Gao, Yang, & Cao. (2011). An extended matrix encoding algorithm for steganography of high embedding efficiency. *Computers & Electrical Engineering*, *37*(6), 973–981. doi:10.1016/j.compeleceng.2011.08.006

Federal Bureau of Investigation. (2011). *International cyber ring that infected millions of computers dismantled.* Author.

Fineberg. (2003). *Qos support in mpls networks.* White Paper.

Finn, J. (2004). A Survey of Online Harassment at University Campus. *Journal of Interpersonal Violence*, *19*(4), 468–483.

Fitzgerald, D. C. (2008). *Intersections of the Self: Identity in the Boom of Social Media* (Doctoral Dissertation). Available from ProQuest Dissertations and Thesis Full Texts Database: http:!/search.proguest.com/docview/304607151

Fleizach, C., Liljenstam, M., Johansson, P., Voelker, G. M., & Méhes, A. (2007). Can You Infect Me Now? Malware Propagation in Mobile Phone Networks. *Worm*, *7*, 61–68.

Flink, C. W. (2002). Weakest Link in Information System Security. In *Proceedings of Workshop for Application of Engineering Principles to System Security Design.* Retrieved on October 3rd, 2013 from http://www.acsac.org/waepssd/papers/01-flink.pdf

Flo & Josang. (2009). Consequences of Botnets Spreading to Mobile Devices. In *Proceedings of the 14th Nordic Conference on Secure IT Systems*, (pp. 37-43). Academic Press.

Floyd, S., Jacobson, V., Liu, C., McCanne, S., & Zhang, L. (1997, December). A reliable multicast framework for light-weight sessions and application level framing. *IEEE/ACM Transactions on Networking*, *5*(6), 784–803. doi:10.1109/90.650139

Ford, R. (2004). The Wrong Stuff?. *IEEE Security & Privacy*, 86-89.

Frangopoulos, E. D., Eloff, M. M., & Venter, L. M. (2013). Psychosocial risks: Can their effects on the security of information systems really be ignored? *Information Management & Computer Security*, *21*(1), 53–65. doi:10.1108/09685221311314428

Frankel, S., Graveman, R., Pearce, J., & Rooks, M. (2010, December). *Guidelines for the Secure Deployment of IPv6*. Retrieved from http://csrc.nist.gov/publications/nistpubs/800-119/sp800-119.pdf

Fraser, M., Hindmarsh, J., Best, K., Heath, C., Biegel, G., Greenhalgh, C., & Reeves, S. (2006). Remote Collaboration Over Video Data: Towards Real-Time e-Social Science. *Computer Supported Cooperative Work*, *15*(4), 257–279. doi:10.1007/s10606-006-9027-y

Fridrich, J. (2010). *Steganography in Digital Media Principles, Algorithms and Application*. New York: Cambridge University Press.

FS_MTR. (2011). *F-Secure, Mobile Threat Report, Q4, 2011*. Author.

F-Secure. (n.d.). Available at http://www.f-secure.com/en/web/home_global/mobile-security

Furedy, J. J. (1966). The North American polygraph and psychophysiology: Disinterested, uninterested, and interested perspectives. *International Journal of Psychophysiology*, *21*, 97–105. doi:10.1016/0167-8760(96)00003-7 PMID:8792199

Futcher, L., & Von Solms, R. (2008). Guidelines for secure software development. In *Proceedings of the 2008 annual research conference of the South African Institute of Computer Scientists and Information Technologists on IT research in developing countries: riding the wave of technology*. ACM.

Gantz, J., & Reinsel, D. (2009). *Extracting value from chaos*. Academic Press.

Garfinkel, S. L. (2010). Digital forensics research: The next 10 years. *Digital Investigation*, *7*(Supplement), S64–S73. doi:10.1016/j.diin.2010.05.009

Garfinkel, S., Farrell, P., Roussev, V., & Dinolt, G. (2009). Bringing science to digital forensics with standardized forensic corpora. *Digital Investigation*, *6*, S2–S11. doi:10.1016/j.diin.2009.06.016

Ghouti, L., Bouridane, A., Ibrahim, M. K., & Boussakta, S. (2006). Digital image watermarking using balanced multiwavelets. *IEEE Transactions on Signal Processing*, *54*(4), 1519–1536. doi:10.1109/TSP.2006.870624

Giannelli, P. C. (2007). *Wrongful convictions and forensic science: The need to regulate crime labs* (Working Paper 08-02). Case Western Reserve University.

Golab, L., & Özsu, M. (2003). Issues in data stream management. *SIGMOD Record*, *32*(2), 5–14. doi:10.1145/776985.776986

Golan, T. (2007). *Laws of Men and Laws of Nature: The History of Scientific Expert Testimony in England and America*. Harvard University Press.

Gont, F. (2013). *A method for Generating Stable Privacy-Enhanced Addresses with IPv6 Stateless Address Auto-configuration (SLAAC)*. Retrieved from http://tools.ietf.org/html/draft-ietf-6man-stable-privacy-addresses (Work In Progress)

Goodman, S., & Harris, A. (2010, December). The Coming African Tsunami of Information Insecurity. *Communications of the ACM*, *53*(12), 24–27. doi:10.1145/1859204.1859215

Google Project Hosting. (2012). *Emu-as- EmuOS Is an Open-source Hacking Game and Simulator*. Retrieved March 11, 2013, from http://code.google.com/p/emu-os/

Gostev, A. (2006a). *Mobile Malware Evolution: An Overview*, (Part 1). Available at https://www.securelist.com

Gostev, A. (2006b). *Mobile Malware Evolution: An Overview*, (Part 2). Available at https://www.securelist.com

Gostev, A. (2006c, January). Malicious programs for mobile devices. *Kaspersky Security Bulletin*. Available at http://www.viruslist.com/en/analysis?pubid=198981193

Grainger, J. (2010). *Social Media and the Fortune 500: How the Fortune 500 Uses, Perceives and Measures Social Media as a Marketing Tool* (Doctoral Dissertation). Available from ProQuest Dissertations and Thesis Full Texts Database: https://cdr.lib.unc.edu/indexablecontent?id=uuid:ae530f99-9b8d-43a4-9fa4-9f12c5b00a21&ds=DATA FILE

Grayson, D., Guernsey, D., Butts, J., Spainhower, M., & Shenoi, S. (2009). Analysis of security threats to mpls virtual private networks. *International Journal of Critical Infrastructure Protection*, 2(4), 146–153. doi:10.1016/j.ijcip.2009.08.002

Gruner, S. (2010). Software engineering between technics and science — Recent discussions about the foundations and the scientificness of a rising discipline. *Journal for General Philosophy of Science*, 41, 237–260. doi:10.1007/s10838-010-9116-y

Guernsey, D., Engel, A., Butts, J., & Sheno, S. (2010). Security analysis of the mpls label distribution protocol. In *Proceedings of the Fourth Annual IFIP Working Group 11.10 International Conference on Critical Infrastructure Protection*, (vol. 342, pp. 127–139). IFIP.

Guo, K., & Zhang, Q. (2013). Fast clustering-based anonymization approaches with time constraints for data streams. *Knowledge-Based Systems*. doi:10.1016/j.knosys.2013.03.007

Gupta, A., & Daniel, C. D. V. (2004). Using Predators to Combat Worms and Viruses: A Simulation-Based Study. In *Proceedings of the 20th IEEE Annual Computer Security Applications Conference*. IEEE.

Gurijala & Molina. (2004). Defining and monitoring qos metrics in the next generation wireless networks. In *Telecommunications Quality of Services: The Business of Success, 2004. QoS 2004* (pp. 7–42). IEE.

Haataja, K. M. J. (2005). Three practical attacks against Bluetooth security using new enhanced implementations of security analysis tools. In *Proceedings of the IASTED International Conference on Communication, Network and Information Security*, (pp. 101-108). IASTED.

Hackmi2. (2012). Retrieved from http://hackmi2

Harel, D. (1992). *Algorithmics: The Spirit of Computing* (2nd ed.). Pearson Education.

Haroon, J. (2004). *Decentralized key management for large dynamic multicast groups using distributed balanced trees*. (Master's thesis). National University of Computer and Emerging Sciences, Lahore, Pakistan.

He, L., & Botham, P. (2008). Pure mpls technology. In *Proceedings of Availability, Reliability and Security*, (pp. 253–259). ARES.

Henchiri, O., & Japkowicz, N. (2006). A Feature Selection and Evaluation Scheme for Computer Virus Detection. In Proceedings of ICDM (pp. 891-895). IEEE Computer Society.

Herfurt, M. (2004). *Bluesnarfing*. CeBIT 2004.

Hernandez, J.R., Amado, M., & Perez Gonzalez, F. (2000). DCT-domain watermarking techniques for still images: Detector performance analysis and a new structure. *IEEE Tran on image proc, 9*, 55-68.

Herodotus, . (1996). *The Histories*. London: Penguin Books.

Hiltz, S. R., Benbunan-Fich, R., Coppola, N., Rotter, N., & Turoff, M. (2000). Measuring the Importance of Collaborative Learning for the Effectiveness of ALN: A Multi-Measure, Multi-Method Approach. *The Journal of Asynchronous Learning*, 4(2), 103–125.

Hochman, N., & Schwartz, R. (2012). Visualizing Instagram: Tracing Cultural Visual Rhythms, Association for the Advancement of Artificial Intelligence. In *Proceedings of Sixth International AAAI Conference on Weblogs and Social Media*. Retrieved March 18, 2013 from, http://www.aaai.org/ocs/index.php/lCWSM/lCWSM12/paper/viewFile/4782/5091

Hofstadter, D. R. (1979). *Gödel, Escher, Bach: An Eternal Golden Braid*. Harvester Press.

Hogg, S., & Vyncke, E. (2009). *IPv6 Security*. Cisco Press.

Hoisington, M. (2009). Cyberwarfare and the use of force giving rise to the right of self-defense. *Boston College International and Comparative Law Review*, 32(1), 439.

Hollis, D. (2011, January). Cyberwar case study: Georgia 2008. *Small Wars Journal*.

Hsieh, S. L., Tsai, I. J., Yeh, C. P., & Chang, C. M. (2011). An image authentication scheme based on digital watermarking and image secret sharing. *Multimedia Tools and Applications*, *52*(2-3), 597–619. doi:10.1007/s11042-010-0520-4

Hsu, J. (n.d.). U.*S considers open-source software for Cyber security*. Retrieved March 22, 2013, from http://www.teclmewsdaily.com/2644-cybersecurity-open-source.html

Huang, Y., Ma, X., & Li, D. (2010). Research and Application of Enterprise Search Based on Database Security Services. In *Proceedings of the Second International Symposium on Networking and Network Security* (ISNNS '10) (pp. 238-241). China: Academy Publisher.

Hummel, K. A., & Hlavacs, H. (2003). *Anytime, Anywhere Learning Behaviour Using a Web Based Platform for a University Lecture. In Proceedings of SSGRR 2003*. Aquila.

Hypponen, M. (2006). Malware goes mobile. *Scientific American*, 70–77. doi:10.1038/scientificamerican1106-70 PMID:17076086

Igor, S., Felix, B., Javier, N., Yoseba, P., Borja, S., Carlos, L., & Pablo, B. (2010). Idea: Opcode-sequence-based malware detection: In Proceedings of Engineering Secure Software and Systems (LNCS) (vol. 5965, pp. 35-43). Springer.

IkeeB, F-Secure. (n.d.). *Worm:iPhoneOS/Ikee.B*. Available at http://www.f-secure.com

Infoplease. (n.d.). *Computer Virus Timeline*. Available at infoplease.com

Instagram. (2014). *Instagram*. Retrieved from http://instagram.com

INTECO. (2009). *Study on the privacy of personal data and on the security of information in social networks*. Retrieved from https://www.inteco.es/file/vuiNP2GNuMjfCgs9ZBYoAQ?

Internet Assigned Numbers Authority (IANA). (2008). *ICMP type numbers*. Author.

Irdeto, B. V. (2011). *Irdeto*. Retrieved from http://www.irdeto.com/

Ishtiaq, M., Sikandar, B., Jaffar, M. A., & Khan, A. (2010). Adaptive watermark strength selection using Particle Swarm Optimization. *ICIC Express Letters: An International Journal of Research and Surveys, 4*(6).

ISO 7498-2. (1989). *Information processing systems Open systems Interconnection Basic Reference Model Part 2: Security architecture*.

Issa, R. (2009). *Satisfying K-anonymity: New Algorithm and Emirical Evaluation*. (Masters Thesis). Carleton University.

Iyengar, V. (2002). Transforming data to satisfy privacy constraints. In *Proceedings of the eighth ACM SIGKDD international conference on Knowledge discovery and data mining*, (pp. 279–288). ACM.

Jacobson, Frederick, Casner, & Schulzrinne. (2003). *Rtp: A transport protocol for real-time applications*. IETF, RFC 3550.

Jain (1998). *Myths about congestion management in high speed networks*. Arxiv preprint cs/9809088.

Jamoussi, L., Andersson, R., Callon, R., Dantu, L., Wu, P., Doolan, T., … Girish, M. (2002). *Constraint-based lsp setup using ldp*. IETF, RFC 3212.

Jensen, C. (2010). The role of trust in computer security. In *Proceedings of the 4th IFIP WG 11.11 International Conference on Trust Management*. Morioka, Japan: Springer.

Jeremy, Z. K., & Maloof, M.A. (2004). Learning to Detect Malicious Executables in the Wild. In *Proceedings of the Tenth ACM SIGKDD International Conference on Knowledge Discovery and Data Mining*, (pp. 470-478). New York, NY: ACM

Jiang, W., & Clifton, C. (2006). A secure distributed framework for achieving k-anonymity. *The VLDB Journal*, *15*(4), 316–333. doi:10.1007/s00778-006-0008-z

Johnson, N. F., & Jajodia, S. (1998). Exploring Steganography: Seeing the unseen. *IEEE Computer*, *31*(2), 26–34. doi:10.1109/MC.1998.4655281

Josang, A., Ismail, R., & Boyd, C. (2007). A Survey of Trust and Reputation Systems for Online Service Provision. *Decision Support Systems*, *34*, 618–644. doi:10.1016/j.dss.2005.05.019

Juola, P. (2006). Authorship attribution. In Foundations and Trends in Information Retrieval. Academic Press.

Kabir, M., Wang, H., & Bertino, E. (2011). Efficient systematic clustering method for k-anonymization. *Acta Informatica*, 51–66. doi:10.1007/s00236-010-0131-6

Kainerstorfer, M., Sametinger, J., & Wiesauer, A. (2011). Software security for small development teams: A case study. In *Proceedings of the 13th International Conference on Information Integration and Web-based Applications and Services*. ACM.

Kaminski, P., Agrawal, P., Kienle, H., & Müller, H. (2005). <username>, I need you! initiative and interaction in autonomic systems. In *Proceedings of the 2005 workshop on Design and evolution of autonomic application software*. Retrieved on 25th April, 2013 from http://www.deas2005.cs.uvic.ca/

Kamstra, L., & Heijmans, H. J. (2005). Reversible data embedding into images using wavelet techniques and sorting. *IEEE Transactions on Image Processing*, *14*(12), 2082–2090.

Karim, M. E., Walenstein, A., Lakhotia, A., & Parida, L. (2005). Malware phylogeny generation using permutations of code. *Journal in Computer Virology*, *1*, 13–23. doi:10.1007/s11416-005-0002-9

Kaspersky. (2010). *First SMS Trojan detected for smartphones running Android*. Available at http://www.kaspersky.co.in

Kaspersky. (2012). *Kaspersky Security Bulletin 2012: The overall statistics for 2012*. Available at http://www.kaspersky.co.in

Katzenbeisser, S., & Petitcolas, F. A. P. (Eds.). (2000). *Information Hiding Techniques for Steganography and Digital Watermarking*. Norwood: Artech House, Inc.

Kayem, A. V. D. M., Akl, S. G., & Martin, P. (2010). Adaptive Cryptographic Access Control. Springer.

Kendall, K. E., & Kendall, J. E. (2002). *Systems Analysis and Design*. Upper Saddle River, NJ: Prentice- Hall, Inc.

Kent, S., & Seo, K. (2005, December). Security Architecture for the Internet Protocol. *RFC*. Retrieved December 2005, from http://www.ietf.org/rfc/rfc4301.txt

Kephart, J. O., & Arnold, B. (1994). A Feature Selection and Evaluation of Computer Virus Signatures. In *Proceedings of the 4th Virus Bulletin International Conference*, (pp. 178-184). Academic Press.

Kim, S., Han, H., Shin, D., Jeun, I., & Jeong, H. (2009). A study of international trend analysis on web service vulnerabilities in owasp and wasc. In *Proceedings of the 3rd International Conference and Workshops on Advances in Information Security and Assurance*. Springer-Verlag.

Koch, E., & Zhao, J. (1995). Towards Robust and Hidden Image Copyright Labeling. In *Proceeding of IEEE Workshop on Nonlinear Signal and Image Processing*. Thessaloniki, Greece: IEEE.

Kolter, J. Z., & Maloof, M. A. (2006). Learning to Detect and Classify Malicious Executables in the Wild. *Journal of Machine Learning Research*, *6*, 2721–2744.

Koppl, R., & Ferraro, M. M. (2012). Digital devices and miscarriages of justice. *The Dayly Caller*. Retrieved from http://dailycaller.com/2012/06/15/digital-devices-and-miscarriages-of-justice/

Kordy, B., Pouly, M., & Schweitzer, P. (2012). Computational aspects of attack— Defense trees. In *Proceedings of the 2011 international conference on Security and Intelligent Information Systems*. Springer-Verlag.

Kraak, V. I., Story, M., & Wartella, E. A. (2012). Government and school progress to promote a healthful diet to American children and adolescents: A comprehensive review of the available evidence. *American Journal of Preventive Medicine*, *42*(3), 250–262. doi:10.1016/j.amepre.2011.10.025 PMID:22341162

Krishnamurthy, B., & Wills, C. E. (2008). Characterizing privacy in online social networks. In *Proceedings of the first workshop on Online social networks*. ACM.

Kuhn, T. S. (1996). *The Structure of Scientific Revolutions* (3rd ed.). University of Chicago Press. doi:10.7208/chicago/9780226458106.001.0001

Kundur, D., & Hatzinakos, D. (2004). Toward robust logo watermarking using multiresolution image fusion principles. *IEEE Transactions on Multimedia*, *6*(1), 185–198.

Kutter, M., & Winkler, S. (2002). A vision-based masking model for spread-spectrum image watermarking. *IEEE Transactions on Image Processing*, *11*(1), 16–25.

Kwak, H., Lee, C., Park., H., & Moon, S. (2010). What is Twitter, a Social Network of News Media?. In *Proceedings of the 19111 International Conference on World Wide Web*. Academic Press.

Langheinrich, M. (2003). When trust does not compute: The role of trust in ubiquitous computing. In *Proceedings of Privacy Workshops of Ubicomp'03*. Retrieved on 16 May 2006 from http://www.ubicomp.org/ubicomp2003/program.html?show=workshops

Laurie, D., Sisson, G., Arends, R., & Blacka, D. (2008, March). *DNS Security (DNSSEC) Hashed Authenticated Denial of Existence*. Retrieved from http://tools.ietf.org/html/rfc5155

Leavitt, N. (2005a). Mobile Phones: The Next Frontier for Hackers?. *IEEE Computer*, 20-23.

Leavitt, N. (2005b). Instant Messaging: A New Target for Hackers?. *IEEE Computer*, 20-23.

Leavitt, N. (2011). Mobile Security: Finally a Serious Problem? *Computer*, *44*(6), 11–14. doi:10.1109/MC.2011.184

Lecigne, C., & Neville-Neil, G. V. (2006, August). *Walking through FreeBSD IPv6 stack*. Retrieved from http://clem1.be/gimme/ipv6sec.pdf

Lecture Series, Krete. (n.d.). Retrieved 17 Jan 2011 from http://www.forth.gr/onassis/lectures/2010-06-28/presentations_10/Identity_management_and_privacy.pdf

Lee, C.-J., Tsai, C.-C., Tang, S.-M., & Liang-Kai, W. (2009). Innovation: web 2.0, online-communities and mobile social networking. *Trans. on Comp.*, *8*(11), 1825–1834.

Lee, S., & Knight, D. (2005). Realization of the next-generation network. *IEEE Communications Magazine*, *43*(10), 34–41. doi:10.1109/MCOM.2005.1522122

Lee, S., Yoo, C. D., & Kalker, T. (2007). Reversible image watermarking based on integer-to-integer wavelet transform. *IEEE Transactions on Information Forensics and Security*, *2*(3), 321–330.

Lehoczky, J. P. (1990). Fixed priority scheduling of periodic task sets with arbitrary deadlines. In *Proceedings of Real- Time Systems Symposium*, (pp. 201–209). Academic Press.

Lenhart, A., Purcell, K., Smith, A., & Zickuhr, K. (2010). *Social Media & Mobiler Internet Use Among Teens and Young Adults*. Pew Research Center. Retrieved March 20, 2013, from http://web.pewinternet.org//media/Files/Reports/2010/PlPSocialMediaandYoungAdultsReportFina!withtoplines.pdf

Lewis, B. K. (2012). *Social Media and Strategic Communications: Attitudes and perceptions Among College Students* (Doctoral Dissertation). Available from ProQuest Dissertations and Thesis Full Texts Database: http://www.prsa.org/Intelligence/PRJ ournal/Documents/2012LewisN ichols.pdf

Li, A. B., & Liebeherr, J. (2007). A network calculus with effective bandwidth. *IEEE/ACM Transactions on Networking*, *15*(6), 1442–1453.

Li, F., Sun, J., Papadimitriou, S., Mihaila, G. a., & Stanoi, I. (2007). Hiding in the Crowd: Privacy Preservation on Evolving Streams through Correlation Tracking. In *Proceedings of 2007 IEEE 23rd International Conference on Data Engineering*, (pp. 686–695). IEEE. doi: doi:10.1109/ICDE.2007.367914

Li, J., Ooi, B., & Wang, W. (2008). Anonymizing streaming data for privacy protection. In *Proceedings of Data Engineering*, (pp. 1367-1369). IEEE.

Li, N., Li, T., & Venkatasubramanian, S. (2007). t-Closeness: Privacy beyond k-anonymity and l-diversity. *International Conference on Data Engineering (ICDE)*, (3), 106–115.

Lialina, O. (2012). *The Turing Complete User*. Retrieved on 30th November, 2013 from http://contemporary-home-computing.org/turing-complete-user/

Lin, X. (2011). Survey on cloud based mobile security and a new framework for improvement. In *Proceedings of the International Conference on Information and Automation (ICIA)* (pp. 710-715). Shenzen: IEEE.

Lin, D., & Stamp, M. (2011). Hunting for undetectable metamorphic viruses. *Journal in Computer Virology*, *7*, 201–214. doi:10.1007/s11416-010-0148-y

Lin, S. D., Shie, S. C., & Guo, J. Y. (2010). Improving the robustness of DCT-based image watermarking against JPEG compression. *Computer Standards & Interfaces*, *32*(1), 54–60. doi:10.1016/j.csi.2009.06.004

Lin, W. H., Horng, S. J., Kao, T. W., Fan, P., Lee, C. L., & Pan, Y. (2008). An efficient watermarking method based on significant difference of wavelet coefficient quantization. *IEEE Transactions on Multimedia, 10*(5), 746–757.

Liu, J. L., Lou, D. C., Chang, M. C., & Tso, H. K. (2006). A robust watermarking scheme using self-reference image. *Computer Standards & Interfaces, 28*(3), 356–367. doi:10.1016/j.csi.2005.07.001

Li, X., & Wang, J. (2007). A steganographic method based upon JPEG and particle swarm optimization algorithm. *Information Sciences, 177*(15), 3099–3109. doi:10.1016/j.ins.2007.02.008

LookOut. (n.d.). Available at https://www.lookout.com/mobile-antivirus-software

Lopez, C. (2009). Immersive technology melds Hollywood, warrior training. *Soldiers, 64*(5), 27.

Lotring, A. (2005). Training the millennlal sailor. *U.S. Naval Institute Proceedings, 131*(12), 36–37.

Lou, D.-C., Hu, M.-C., & Liu, J.-L. (2009). Multiple layer data hiding scheme for medical images. *Computer Standards & Interfaces, 31,* 329–335. doi:10.1016/j.csi.2008.05.009

Lyon, J. F. (2009). *Nmap Network Scanning: The Official Nmap Project Guide to Network Discovery and Security Scanning.* Academic Press.

Mac, R. (2013). *No One Is More Excited For Google Glass Than Facebook CEO Mark Zuckerberg.* Retrieved March 28, 2013 from http://www.forbes.com/sites/ryanmac/2013/02/21/no-one-is-moreexcited-for-google-glass-than-facebook-ceo-mark-zuckerberg/

Machanavajjhala, A., Kifer, D., & Johannes, G. (2007). l-diversity: Privacy beyond k-anonymity. *ACM Transactions on Knowledge Discovery from Data, 1*(1), 3.

Maity, S. P., & Kundu, M. K. (2011). Perceptually adaptive spread transform image watermarking scheme using Hadamard transform. *Information Sciences, 181*(3), 450–465. doi:10.1016/j.ins.2010.09.029

Makbol, N. M., & Khoo, B. E. (2012). Robust blind image watermarking scheme based on Redundant Discrete Wavelet Transform and Singular Value Decomposition. *AEÜ International Journal of Electronics and Communications.*

Mali, S. N., Patil, P. M., & Jalnekar, R. M. (2012). Robust and secured image-adaptive data hiding. *Digital Signal Processing, 22*(2), 314–323. doi:10.1016/j.dsp.2011.09.003

Malvar, H. S., & Florêncio, D. A. (2003). Improved spread spectrum: A new modulation technique for robust watermarking. *IEEE Transactions on Signal Processing, 51*(4), 898–905. doi:10.1109/TSP.2003.809385

Manson, G. P. (2011). Cyberwar: The united states and china prepare for the next generation of conict. *Comparative Strategy, 30*(2), 121–133. doi:10.1080/01495933.2011.561730

Marsh, S. (1994). *Formalising Trust as a Computational Concept.* (PhD Thesis). University of Stirling, Stirling, UK.

Marsh, S. (2010). Comfort Zones: Location Dependent Trust and Regret Management for Mobile Devices. In Proceedings LocationTrust 2010: workshop on location as context for trust at IFIPTM 2010. Springer.

Marsh, S., & Briggs, P. (2010). Defining and Investigating Device Comfort. In *Proceedings of the 4th IFIP WG 11.11 International Conference on Trust Management.* Morioka, Japan: Springer.

Marsh, S., & Dibben, M. (2005). Trust, Untrust, Distrust and Mistrust – An Exploration of the Dark(er) Side. In P. Herrmanm, V. Issarny, & S. Shiu (Eds.), Trust Management (LNCS) (vol. 3477, pp. 17–33). Berlin: Springer. doi:doi:10.1007/11429760_2 doi:10.1007/11429760_2

Marsh, S., Basu, A., & Dwyer, N. (2012). Rendering unto Cæsar the things that are Cæsar's: Complex trust models and human understanding. In *Trust Management VI, Proceedings of IFIPTM 2012* (AICT) (vol. 374, pp. 191-200). New York: Springer.

Marsh, S., Basu, A., & Dwyer, N. (2012a). Security Enhancement With Foreground Trust, Comfort, And Ten Commandments For Real People. In Proceedings INTRICATE-SEC 2012. Academic Press.

Marsh, S., Wang, Y., Noël, S., Robart, L., & Stewart, J. (2013). Device Comfort for mobile health information accessibility. In *Proceedings Privacy, Security and Trust (PST), eleventh annual conference.* IEEE.

Marsh, S., Briggs, P., El-Khatib, K., Esfandiari, B., & Stewart, J. (2011). Defining and Investigating Device Comfort. *Information and Media Technologies*, *6*(3), 914–935.

Marvel, L. M., Boncelet, C. G. Jr, & Retter, C. T. (1999). Spread spectrum image steganography. *IEEE Transactions on Image Processing*, *8*(8), 1075–1083.

Masnick, M. (2011). Innovation. In Security: It's All About Trust. Retrieved from http://www.techdirt.com

Mauw, S., & Oostdijk, M. (2006). Foundations of attack trees. In *Proceedings of the 8th international conference on Information Security and Cryptology*. Springer-Verlag.

Maxwell, D., & McLennan, K. (2012). Case Study: Leveraging Government and Academic Partnerships in MOSES. In *Proceedings of World Conference on Educational Multimedia, Hypermedia and Telecommunications*, (pp. 1604-1616). Academic Press.

McGrew, D. A., & Sherman, A. T. (1998). Key establishment in large dynamic groups using one-way function trees. *IEEE Transactions on Software Engineering*.

McMahan, J. (1994, January). Self-defense and the problem of the innocent attacker. *Ethics*, *104*(2), 252290. doi:10.1086/293600

McSherry, F. (2010). Privacy integrated queries: an extensible platform for privacy- Preserving data analysis. *Communications of the ACM*, *53*(9), 89–97. doi:10.1145/1810891.1810916

Menahem, E., Rokach, L., & Elovici, Y. (2009a). Troika - An improved stacking schema for classification tasks. *Inf. Sci.*, *179*, 4097–4122. doi:10.1016/j.ins.2009.08.025

Merkel, R., Hoppe, T., Kraetzer, C., & Dittmann, J. (2010). Statistical Detection of Malicious PE-Executables for Fast Offline Analysis. In B. De Decker & I. Schaumller-Bichl (Eds.), Communications and Multimedia Security, (Vol. 6109, pp. 93-105). Springer.

Mickens, J. W., & Noble, B. D. (2005). Modeling Epidemic Spreading in Mobile Environments. In *Proceedings of the Fourth ACM Workshop on Wireless Security* (pp. 77-86). ACM.

Micro, T. (2006). Trend Micro Mobile Security. Available at http://www.trendmicro.com

Mislove, A., Marcon, M., Gummadi, K. P., Drushel, P., & Bhattacharjee, B. (2007). Measurement and Analysis of Online Social Networks. In *Proceedings of the 7th ACM SIGCOMM Conference on Internet Measurement*, (pp. 29-42). ACM.

Mockapetris, P. (1987, November). *Domain Names - Implementation and specification*. Retrieved from http://tools.ietf.org/html/rfc1035

Möllering, G. (2005b). *Understanding trust from the perspective of sociological neoinstitutionalism: The interplay of institutions and agency*. MPIfG Discussion Paper 05/13, Max Planck Institute for the Study of Societies, Cologne. Retrieved 11 February 2009 from http://edoc.mpg.de/270955

Möllering, G. (2001). The nature of trust: from Georg Simmel to a theory of expectation, interpretation and suspension. *Sociology*, *35*(2), 403–420. doi:10.1177/S0038038501000190

Möllering, G. (2006a). Trust, institutions, agency: Towards a neoinstitutional theory of trust. In R. Bachmann, & A. Zaheer (Eds.), *Handbook of trust research*. Cheltenham, UK: Edward Elgar. doi:10.4337/9781847202819.00029

Montpetit, M., Mirlacher, T., & Ketcham, M. (2010). IPTV: An end to end perspective. *The Journal of Communication*, *5*, 5.

Moskovitch, R., Nissim, N., & Elovici, Y. (2009). Acquisition of Malicious Code Using Active Learning. In Proceedings of Privacy, Security, and Trust in KDD. Springer-Verlag.

Moskovitch, R., Stopel, D., Feher, C., Nissim, N., Japkowicz, N., & Elovici, Y. (2009). Unknown malcode detection and the imbalance problem. *Journal in Computer Virology*, *5*, 295–308. doi:10.1007/s11416-009-0122-8

Mulliner, C. (2006). *Advanced Attacks Against Pocket PC Phones*. DEFCON 14.

Mulliner, C., & Miller, C. (2009). Injecting SMS messages into smartphones for security analysis. In *Proceedings of the 3rd USENIX Workshop on Offensive Technologies*. Retrieved March 22,2013 from https://www.usenix.org/legacy/events/woot09/tech/full papers/mulliner.pdf

Murayama, Y. F., Saito, Y., & Nishioka, D. (2012). Usability issues in security. In *Proceedings Security Protocols XX - 20th International Workshop, Revised Selected Papers* (LNCS) (vol. 7622, pp. 161–171). Cambridge, UK: Springer Verlag.

Mustafa, M. (2012). *How to Customize the 'Via' Status on Facebook Posts, Hongkait.com Inspiring Technology.* Retrieved on April 18, 2013, from http://www.hongkiat.com/blog/customize-facebookstatus/

Myers, S. (2012). Operative BackTrack. *Journal of On Demand Hacking, 1*(3), 60-66.

MyHealtheVet. (2014). *MyHealtheVet.* Retrieved from https://www.myhealth.va.gov/index.html

Myphonefactor. (2013). *Information about Smartphone Virus and Prevention tips.* Available at myphonefactor.in

Nagravision, S. A. (2011). *Nagravision.* Retrieved from http://www.nagravision.com/

Naismith, L., Lonsdale, P., Vavoula, G. & Sharples, M. (2006). *Literature review in mobile technologies and learning.* Futurelab Series. Retrieved March 22, 2013, from http://www2.futurelab.org.uk/resources/documents/1itreviews/MobileReview.pdf

Naor, D., Naor, M., & Lotspiech, J. (2001). Revocation and tracing schemes for stateless receivers. In *Advances in Cryptology* (pp. 41–62). Springer-Verlag. doi:10.1007/3-540-44647-8_3

Narten, T., Draves, R., & Krishnan, S. (2007, September). *Privacy Extensions for Stateless Address Autoconfiguration in IPv6.* Retrieved from http://tools.ietf.org/html/rfc4941

Narten, T., Nordmark, E., Simpson, W., & Soliman, H. (2007, September). Neighbor Discovery for IP version 6 (IPv6). *RFC.* Retrieved September 2007, from http://www.ietf.org/rfc/rfc4861.txt

National Security Agency, Common Criteria Evaluation and Validation Scheme (CCEVS). (2008). *Common criteria evaluation and validation scheme -- Organization, management, and concept of operations* (Version 2.0). Retrieved from National Information Assurance Partnership website: http://www.niap-ccevs.org/policy/ccevs/scheme-pub-l.pdf

NDS. (2011). *NDS VideoGuard.* Retrieved from http://www.nds.com/

Niimi, M., Noda, H., & Kawaguchi, E. (1998). A steganography based on region segmentation by using complexity measure. Trans. IEICE J81-D-II, 1132–1140.

Nikander, R., Kempf, J., & Nordmark, E. (2004, May). *IPv6 Neighbor Discovery (ND) Trust Models and Threats.* Retrieved from http://tools.ietf.org/html/rfc3756

Nissim, N., Moskovitch, R., Rokach, L., & Elovici, Y. (2012). Detecting unknown computer worm activity via support vector machines and active learning. *Pattern Analysis & Applications, 15*, 459–475. doi:10.1007/s10044-012-0296-4

Noda, H., Niimi, M., & Kawaguchi, E. (2006). High-performance JPEG steganography using quantization index modulation in DCT domain. *Pattern Recognition Letters, 27*(5), 455–461. doi:10.1016/j.patrec.2005.09.008

Nooteboom, B. (2002). *Trust: forms, foundations, functions, failures and figures.* Cheltenham, UK: Edward Elgar. doi:10.4337/9781781950883

Norman, D. (2010). When security gets in the way. *Interactions (New York, N.Y.), 16*(6).

Notoatmodjo, G., & Thomborson, C. (2009). Passwords and Perceptions. In *Proceedings of the 7th Australasian Conference on Information Security.* Academic Press.

Nt'l Telecommuncation Union (2011). *ITU-T Recommendation Y.1540, Internet protocol aspects Quality of service and network performance-Internet protocol data communication service IP packet transfer and availability performance parameters.* Author.

OASIS. (2005). *eXtensible Access Control Markup Language (XACML) version 2.0.* Retrieved from http://docs.oasis-open.org/xacml/2.0/access_control-xacml-2.0-core-spec-os.pdf

Oberheide, J., & Jahanian, F. (2010). When mobile is harder than fixed (and vice versa): Demystifying security challenges in mobile environments. In *Proceedings of the Eleventh Workshop on Mobile Computing Systems & Applications* (pp. 43-48). Annapolis, MD: ACM.

OECD. (1980). *Guidelines on the protection of privacy and transborder ows of personal data.* Retrieved from http://www.oecd.org/http://www.oecd.org/document/1 8/0,3746,en_2649_34223_1815186_1_1_1_1,00.html

Oikawa, Y. F. H., & Murayama, Y. (2008). Towards an interface causing discomfort for security: A user survey on the factors of discomfort. In *Proceedings Second International Conference on Secure System Integration and Reliability Improvement* (pp. 173–174). Yokohama, Japan: IEEE Press.

Oliver, P., & Green, G. (2009). Adopting new technologies: Self-sufficiency and the DIY artist. In *Proceedings UK Academy for Information Systems Conference 2009.* Retrieved 17 July 2010 from http://aisel.aisnet.org/ukais2009/38

Olivier, M. S. (2008). Using sensor dirt for toolmark analysis of digital photographs. In I. Ray, & S. Shenoi (Eds.), *Advances in Digital Forensics IV* (pp. 193–206). Springer. doi:10.1007/978-0-387-84927-0_16

Olsen, O. (2005). *Adversary modeling.* (Master's thesis). Gjovik University College.

Omar, M., & Dawson, M. (2013, April). Research in Progress- Defending Android Smartphones from Malware Attacks. In *Proceedings of 2013 Third International Conference on Advanced Computing and Communication Technologies* (pp. 288-292). Rohtak, India: IEEE.

Open Source Machine Learning Software Weka website. (n.d.). Retrieved from http://www.cs.waikato.ac.nz/ml/weka/

OReilly, T. (2007). What Is Web 2.0: Design Patterns and Business Models for the Next Generation of Software. *Communications & Strategies, 1,* 1738.

Orman, H. (2003). The Morris Worm: A Fifteen-Year Perspective. *IEEE Security & Privacy,* 35-43.

Osborn, S., Sandhu, R., & Munawer, Q. (2000). Conguring role-based access control to enforce mandatory and discretionary access control policies. *ACM Transactions on Information and System Security, 3*(2), 1–23. doi:10.1145/354876.354878

Ostrom, E. (1998). Behavioral approach to the rational choice theory of collective action. *The American Political Science Review, 92*(1), 1–22. doi:10.2307/2585925

Ottow, C., Vliet, F. V., Boer, P. D., & Pras, A. (2012). The Impact of Ipv6 on Penetration Testing. Springer.

Padayachee, K. (2010). *An aspect-oriented approach towards enhancing Optimistic Access control with Usage Control.* (PhD thesis). University of Pretoria, Pretoria, South Africa.

Park, S. R., Nah, F. F., Dewester, D., & Eschenbrenner, B. (2008). Virtual World Affordances: Enhancing Brand Value. *Journal of Virtual Worlds Research, 1*(2), 1–18.

Parti, K. (2011). Actual Poling in Virtual Reality - A Cause of Moral Panic or a Justitied Need?. InTech. Retrieved March 22, 2013, from http://www.intechopen.com/books/virtua1-rea1ity/actua1po1icing-in-virtua1-rea1ity-a-cause-of-moralpanic-or-a-justified-need-

Payne, C. A. (2007). Cryptographic Access Control Architecture Secure Against Privileged Attackers. In *Proceedings of the 2007 ACM workshop on Computer security architecture.* ACM.

Peng, F., Li, X., & Yang, B. (2012). Adaptive reversible data hiding scheme based on integer transform. *Signal Processing, 92*(1), 54–62. doi:10.1016/j.sigpro.2011.06.006

Perens, B. (1999). The open source definition. In *Open sources: Voices.from the open source revolution,* (pp. 171-85). Academic Press.

Perkins, C., Johnson, D., & Arkko, J. (2011, July). *Mobility Support in IPv6.* Retrieved from http://tools.ietf.org/html/rfc6275

Perlman, R. (1997). *"LKH+": Simplication of LKH, an observation from the conference floor.* Academic Press.

Pirate Bay. (2010). Retrieved from http://www.pattaya-dailynews.com/en/2010/07/29/facebook-security-breach-private-details-published-on-pirate-bay/

Plank, J. S. (2008). The raid-6 liberation codes. In *Proceedings of the 6th USENIX Conference on File and Storage Technologies.* Berkeley, CA: USENIX Association.

Plank, J. S., Luo, J., Schuman, C. D., Xu, L., & Wilcox-O'Hearn, Z. (2009a). A performance evaluation and examination of open-source erasure coding libraries for storage. In *Proceedings of the 7th conference on File and storage technologies,* (pp. 253–265). Berkeley, CA: USENIX Association.

Plank, J. S., Simmerman, S., & Schuman, C. D. (2008). *Jerasure: A library in C/C++ facilitating erasure coding for storageapplications - Version 1.2* (Technical Report CS-08-627). University of Tennessee.

Ponemon Institute. (2011). *Security of cloud computing providers study.* Author.

Poppe, R., Rienks, R., & van Dijk, B. (2007). Evaluating the future of HCI: Challenges for the evaluation of emerging applications. In Artifical Intelligence for Human Computing, (pp. 234-250). Berline: Springer.

Popper, S., Bankes, S., Callaway, R., & DeLaurentis, D. (2004). *System-of-Systems Symposium: Report on a Summer Conversation.* Arlington, VA: Potomac Institute for Policy Studies.

Preneel, B. (2010). *Identity management and privacy.* Onassis Foundation Science.

Proffitt, M. (2012). *The Oxford English Dictionary.* Oxford University Press.

Provos, N. (2001). Defending against statistical steganalysis. In *Proceedings of tenth USENIX Security Symposium '01,* (pp. 323–335). USENIX.

Provos, N., & Honeyman, P. (2011). Detecting Steganography Content on the Internet. CITI Technical Report.

Qiu, L., Li, Y., & Wu, X. (2007). Protecting business intelligence and customer privacy while outsourcing data mining tasks. *Knowledge and Information Systems, 17*(1), 99–120. doi:10.1007/s10115-007-0113-3

Qualman, E. (2013). *Socialnomics: How Social Media Transforms the Way We Live and Do Business* (2nd ed.). Hoboken, NJ: John Wiley & Sons.

Racic, R., Ma, D., & Chen, H. (2006). Exploiting mms vulnerabilities to stealthily exhaust mobile phone's battery. In *Proceedings of SecureComm & Workshops,* (pp. 1-10). Academic Press.

Raento, M., Oulasvirta, A., & Eagle, N. (2009). Smartphones: An Emerging Tool for Social Scientists. *Journal of Social Methods & Research, 37*(3), 426–454. doi:10.1177/0049124108330005

Rafiee, H., & Meinel, C. (2013). *Router Advertisement based privacy extension in IPv6 autoconfiguration.* Retrieved from http://tools.ietf.org/html/draft-rafiee-6man-ra-privacy

Rafiee, H., & Meinel, C. (2013). SSAS: A Simple Secure Addressing Scheme for IPv6 AutoConfiguration. In *Proceedings of the 11th IEEE International Conference on Privacy, Security and Trust (PST).* IEEE.

Rafiee, H., Loewis, M. V., & Meinel, C. (2013). Challenges and Solutions for DNS Security in IPv6. In Architectures and Protocols for Secure Information Technology Infrastructures. Hershey, PA: IGI Global. DOI: doi:10.4018/978-1-4666-4514-1.ch006

Rafiee, H., Mueller, C., Niemeier, L., Streek, J., Sterz, C., & Meinel, C. (2013). *A Flexible Framework For Detecting IPv6 Vulnerabilities.* Submitted to ACM Conference.

Rajabhushanam, C. C., & Kathirvel, A. A. (2011). System of One to Three Umpire Security System for Wireless Mobile Ad hoc Network. *Journal Of Computer Science, 7*(12), 1854-1858.

Rash, W. (2004). *Latest skulls Trojan foretells risky smartphone future.* Retrieved from www.eweek.com

Rastegar, S., Namazi, F., Yaghmaie, K., & Aliabadian, A. (2011). Hybrid watermarking algorithm based on Singular Value Decomposition and Radon transform. *AEÜ International Journal of Electronics and Communications, 65*(7), 658–663. doi:10.1016/j.aeue.2010.09.008

Ravi, S. (2006). *Embedded System Security.* Princeton University.

Rawat, S., & Raman, B. (2012). Best tree wavelet packet transform based copyright protection scheme for digital images. *Optics Communications, 285*(10), 2563–2574. doi:10.1016/j.optcom.2012.01.067

Reed, D. (2003). *Applying the OSI seven layer network model to information security.* Retrieved March 22, 2013, from http://www.isd.mel.nist.gov/projects/processcontrol/members/minutes/7-Sep-2004/OSI.pdf

Renaud, K., & Galvez-Cruz, D. (2010). Privacy: Aspects, dentitions and a multi-faceted privacy preservation approach. In *Proceedings of Information Security South Africa Conference 2010.* ISSA.

Republic of South Africa. (2002) *Electronic communications and transactions act.* Author.

Rhea, S., Wells, C., Eaton, P., Geels, D., Zhao, B., Weatherspoon, H., & Kubiatowicz, J. (2001, September). Maintenance free global storage in ocean store. *IEEE Internet Computing.*

Rivest, R. L., Shamir, A., & Adleman, L. (1978, February). A method for obtaining digital signatures and public-key cryptosystems. *Communications of the ACM, 21*(2), 120–126. doi:10.1145/359340.359342

Roesch, M. (1999). SNORT-Lightweight Intrusion Detection for Networks. In *Proceedings of LISA '99: 13th USENIX conference on System administration.* Retrieved March 18, 2013, from https://www.usenix.org/legacy/events/!isa99/fuII papers/roesch/roesch.pdf

Rogers, Y. (2006). Moving on from Weiser's vision of calm computing: Engaging UbiComp experiences. In *Proceedings of International Conference of Ubiquitous Computing.* Retrieved 9 July 2009 from http://dx.doi.org/doi:10.1007/11853565_24

Rooksby, J., & Sommerville, I. (2012). The management and use of social net- work sites in a government department. *Computer Supported Cooperative Work, 21*(4-5), 397–415. doi:10.1007/s10606-011-9150-2

Roschke, S., Cheng, F., & Meinel, C. (2010). Using Vulnerability Information and Attack Graphs for Intrusion Detection. In *Proceedings of the 6th International Conference on Information Assurance and Security (IEEE),* (pp. 68 - 73). IEEE. doi: doi:10.1109/ISIAS.2010.5604041

Rosen, A. V., & Callon, R. (2001). *Multiprotocol label switching architecture.* IETF, RFC 3031.

Rosen, Y. R., Tappan, Farinacci, Fedorkow, Li, & Conta. (2001). *MPLS label stack encoding.* IETF, RFC 3032

Roth, S. (2009). New for whom? Initial images from the social dimension of innovation. *International Journal of Innovation and Sustainable Development, 4,* 231–252. doi:10.1504/IJISD.2009.033080

Rowell, L. (2008). In search of web 3.0. *netWorker, 12*(3), 18–24. doi:10.1145/1435535.1435540

Roy, A., Kim, D. S., & Trivedi, K. S. (2010). Cyber security analysis using attack countermeasure trees. In *Proceedings of the Sixth Annual Workshop on Cyber Security and Information Intelligence Research.* ACM.

Ruan, K., Carthy, J., Kechadi, T., & Crosbie, M. (2011). Cloud Forensics. In Advances in Digital Forensics VII, (pp. 35-46). Orlando, FL: Springer.

Runwal, N., Low, R. M., & Stamp, M. (2012). Opcode graph similarity and metamorphic detection. *Journal in Computer Virology, 8,* 37–52. doi:10.1007/s11416-012-0160-5

Sadasivam, K., Samudrala, B., & Yang, A. (2005). Design of Network Security Projects Using Honeypots. *Journal of Computing Sciences in Colleges, 20*(4), 282–293.

Sadreazami, H., & Amini, M. (2012). A robust spread spectrum based image watermarking in ridgelet domain. *AEÜ International Journal of Electronics and Communications, 66*(5), 364–371. doi:10.1016/j.aeue.2011.09.001

Saha, B., & Sharma, S. (2012). Stenographic Techniques of Data hiding using Digital images. *Defence Science Journal, 62*(1), 11–18. doi:10.14429/dsj.62.1436

Sajedi, H., & Jamzad, M. (2009). ContSteg:Contourlet-based Steganography method. *Journal of Wireless Sensor Network, 1*(3), 163–170. doi:10.4236/wsn.2009.13022

Sajedi, H., & Jamzad, M. (2010). Using contourlet transform and cover selection for secure steganography. *International Journal of Information Security, 9*(5), 337–352. doi:10.1007/s10207-010-0112-3

Saks, M. J., & Faigman, D. L. (2008). Failed forensics: How forensic science lost its way and how it may yet find it. *Annual Review of Law and Social Science, 4,* 149–171. doi:10.1146/annurev.lawsocsci.4.110707.172303

Salah, K., & Kahtani, A. (2009). Improving snort performance under linux. *Communications, JET, 3*(12), 1883–1895.

Samarati, P. (2001). Protecting respondents identities in microdata release. *IEEE Transactions on Knowledge and Data Engineering,* 1–29.

Sandhu, R. S. (2000). Engineering authority and trust in cyberspace: The om-am and rbac way. In *Proceedings of ACM Workshop on Role-Based Access Control*, (pp. 111-119). ACM.

Santos, I., Penya, Y. K., Devesa, J., & Bringas, P. G. (2009). N-grams-based File Signatures for Malware Detection. In J. Cordeiro & J. Filipe (Eds.), ICEIS (vol. 2, pp. 317-320). Academic Press.

Sarno, D. (2009, October). Microsoft says lost sidekick data will be restored to users. *Los Angeles Times*.

Sarwar, U., Ramadass, S., & Budiarto, R. (2007). A Framework for Detection Bluetooth Mobile Worms. *In Proceedings of IEEE International Conference on Telecommunications*, (pp. 343-347). IEEE.

Sasse, M. A., Brostoff, S., & Weirich, D. (2001). Transforming the 'Weakest Link' — A Human/Computer Interaction Approach to Usable and Effective Security. *BT Technology Journal*, *3*(19), 122–131. doi:10.1023/A:1011902718709

Schnjakin, M. & Meinel, C. (2011). Platform for a secure storage-infrastructure in the cloud. In *Proceedings of the 12th Deutscher IT-Sicherheitskongress* (Sicherheit 2011). Academic Press.

Schnjakin, M., Alnemr, R., & Meinel, C. (2010). Contract-based cloud architecture. In *Proceedings of the second international workshop on Cloud data management*, (pp. 33–40). New York, NY: ACM.

Schnjakin, M., Alnemr, R., & Meinel, C. (2011). A security and high-availability layer for cloud storage. In Proceedings of WebInformation Systems Engineering (LNCS) (vol. 6724, pp. 449–462). Springer.

Schnjakin, M., Goderbauer, M., Krueger, M., & Meinel, C. (2013). Cloud storage and it-security. In *Proceedings of the 13th Deutscher IT-Sicherheitskongress* (Sicherheit 2013). Academic Press.

Schnjakin, M., Korsch, D., Schoenberg, M., & Meinel, C. (2013). Implementation of a secure and reliable storage above the untrusted clouds. In *Proceedings of Computer Science & Education (ICCSE)*, (pp. 347-353). ICCSE.

Schultz, M. G., Eskin, E., Zadok, E., & Stolfo, S. J. (2001). Data Mining Methods for Detection of New Malicious Executables. In *Proceedings of IEEE Symposium on Security and Privacy* (pp. 38-49). IEEE Computer Society.

Schumpeter, J. A. (1943). *Capitalism, Socialism, and Democracy*. Routledge.

Scorgie, B., Prakash, V., & Ghosh, S. (2009). Early Virus Detection for Windows Mobile. In *Proceedings of the 9th IEEE Malaysia International Conference on Communications*, (pp. 295-300). IEEE.

Seon, Y., & Ulrich, U. N. (2006). Towards Establishing a Unknown Virus Detection Technique using SOM. Journal in Computer Virology, 2(3), 163-186.

Setia, S., Koussih, S., Jajodia, S., & Harder, E. (2000). *Kronos: A scalable group rekeying approach for secure multicast*. Paper presented at the IEEE Symposium on Security and Privacy. Oakland, CA.

Setia, S., Zhu, S., & Jajodia, S. (2002). A comparative performance analysis of reliable group rekey transport protocols for secure multicast. Performance Evaluation, 21-41.

Sexton, S. (2011). *What is the Percieved Impact of Social Media on Personal Relationships in Adolescence?* (Doctoral Dissertation). Available from ProQuest Dissertations and Thesis Full Texts Database: http://gradworks.umi.com/15/03/1503092.html

Sharma, M. (2008). Elgg Social Networking: Create and manage your own social network site using this free open-source tool. Packt Publishing.

Shieh, C. S., Huang, H. C., Wang, F. H., & Pan, J. S. (2004). Genetic watermarking based on transform-domain techniques. *Pattern Recognition*, *37*(3), 555–565. doi:10.1016/j.patcog.2003.07.003

Shute, T. (2009). Towards a newer urbanism: Talking cities, networks, and publics with Adam Greenfield. *Ugotrade*. Retrieved 3 March, 2012 from http://www.ugotrade.com/2009/02/27/towards-a-newer-urbanism-talking-citiesnetworks-and-publics-with-adam-greenfield/

Siegel, A., Denny, W., Poff, K. W., Larose, C., Hale, R., & Hintze, M. (2009). Survey on Privacy Law Developments in 2009: United States Canada, and the European Union, The American Bar Association Press. *The Business Lawyer*, *65*(1), 285–307.

Silberschatz, A., Korth, H. F., & Sudarshan, S. (1997). Database Concepts. McGraw-Hill.

Silva, P. M., Dias, J., & Ricardo, M. (n.d.). *Survey on Privacy Solutions at the Network Layer: Terminology, Fundamentals and Classification*. Retrieved from http://paginas.fe.up.pt/~prodei/dsie11/images/pdfs/s6-4.pdf

Singh, H. V., Rai, S., Mohan, A., & Singh, S. P. (2011). Robust copyright marking using weibull distribution. *Computers & Electrical Engineering*, *37*(5), 714–728. doi:10.1016/j.compeleceng.2011.04.006

Smeaton, J. (1837). *Reports of the late John Smeaton, F.R.S., made on various occasions, in the course of his employment as a civil engineer* (2nd ed., Vol. 2). M. Taylor. doi:10.1680/rotljsmovoitcoheaace2ev1.51959

Snort. (2012). *What is Snort?*. Retrieved March 20, 2013, from www.snort.org

Socialcast. (2012). *Managing and Control Your Private Network*. Retrieved on April 22, 2013, from http://www.soc ialcast.com/adm in istration

Sokoler, T., & Svensson, M. (2007). Embracing ambiguity in the design of nonstigmatising digital technology for social interaction among senior citizens. *Behaviour & Information Technology*, *26*(4), 343–352. doi:10.1080/01449290601173549

Spainhower, M., Butts, J., Guernsey, D., & Shenoi, S. (2008). Security analysis of rsvp-te signaling in mpls networks. *International Journal of Critical Infrastructure Protection*, *1*(1), 68–74. doi:10.1016/j.ijcip.2008.08.005

Speakman, T., Crowcroft, J., Gemmell, J., Farinacci, D., Lin, S., & Leshchiner, D. et al. (2001). *PGM Reliable Transport Protocol Specication. Request for comments 3208*. Internet Engineering Task Force.

Sridhara, S. M., & Stamp, M. (2013). Metamorphic worm that carries its own morphing engine. *Journal in Computer Virology*, *9*, 49–58.

Srinivasan, Y., Nutter, B., Mitra, S., Phillips, B., & Ferris, D. (2004). Secure transmission of medical records using high capacity steganography. In *Proceedings of 17ᵗʰ IEEE Symposium on Computer Based Medical Systems*, (pp. 122–212). IEEE.

Ssembatya, R., Kayem, A., & Marsden, G. (2013). On the challenge of adopting standard EHR systems in developing countries. In *Proceedings of the 3rd ACM Symposium on Computing for Development* (ACM DEV '13). ACM. DOI=10.1145/2442882.2442911

Staniford, S., Paxson, V., & Weaver, N. (2002). How to Own the Internet in Your Spare Time. In *Proceedings of the 11ᵗʰ USENIX Security Symposium*. USENIX.

Stoimenov, N., Chakraborty, S., & Thiele, L. (2010). An interface algebra for estimating worstcase traversal times in component networks. Leveraging Applications of Formal Methods, Verification, and Validation, 6415, 198–213.

Storer, T., Marsh, S., Noël, S., Esfandiari, B., & El-Khatib, K. (2013). Encouraging second thoughts: Obstructive user interfaces for raising security awareness. In *Proceedings PST 2013: Privacy Security and Trust, Eleventh Annual Conference*. IEEE.

Story, H., Blin, R., Subercaze, J., Gravier, C., & Maret, P. (2012). Turning a web 2.0 social network into a web 3.0, distributed, and secured social web application. In *Proceedings of the 21st international conference companion on World Wide Web*. ACM.

Su, J., Chan, K. K. W., Miklas, A. G., Po, K., Akhavan, A., Saroiu, S., et al. (2006). A Preliminary Investigation of Worm Infections in a Bluetooth Environment. In *Proceedings of the Fourth ACM Workshop on Recurring Malcode* (WORM). ACM.

Subramanian, L., Caesar, M., Ee, C. T., Handley, M., Mao, M., Shenker, S., & Stoica, I. (2005). HLP: a next generation inter-domain routing protocol. *ACM*, *35*(4), 13–24.

Suchman, L. (1987). *Plans and situated actions: The problem of human-machine communication*. New York: Cambridge University Press.

Sun, H., Chen, C., & Shieh, C. (2008, October). Flexible-Pay-Per-Channel: A New Model for Content Access Control in Pay-TV Broadcasting Systems. *IEEE Transactions on Multimedia*, *10*(6), 1109–1120. doi:10.1109/TMM.2008.2001381

Surman, G. (2002). *Understanding Security using the OSI Model*. Retrieved March 25, 2013, from http://www.sans.org/reading room/whitepapers/protocols/understanding-security-osi-model 377

Sveen, F. O., Hernantes, J., Gonzalez, J. J., & Rich, E. (2010). Towards understanding recurring large scale power outages: An endogenous view of inter-organizational effects. In *Proceedings of the 5th international conference on Critical Information Infrastructures Security* (CRITIS'10). Springer-Verlag.

Sweeney, L. (2001). *Computational disclosure control: A Primer on Data Privacy Protection.* (Doctoral Dissertation). MIT, Cambridge, MA.

Sweeney, L. (2002a). Achieving k-anonymity privacy protection using generalization and suppression. *International Journal of Uncertainty, Fuzziness and Knowledge-Based Systems, 10*(5), 1–18. doi:10.1142/S021848850200165X

Sweeney, L. (2002b). k-anonymity: A model for protecting privacy. *International Journal of Uncertainty, Fuzziness and Knowledge-Based Systems, 10*(5), 1–14. doi:10.1142/S0218488502001648

Symantec. (n.d.). Available at http://www.symantec.com

Syverson, Tsudik, Reed, & Landwehr. (2001). *Towards an analysis of onion routing security.* Academic Press.

Tabish, S. M., Shafiq, M. Z., & Farooq, M. (2009). Malware detection using statistical analysis of byte-level file content. In H. Chen, M. Dacier, M.-F. Moens, G. Paass & C. C. Yang (Eds.), *KDD Workshop on CyberSecurity and Intelligence Informatics* (pp. 23-31). ACM.

Tassa, T., & Gudes, E. (2012). Secure Distributed Computation of Anonymized Views. *ACM Transactions on Database Systems, 37*(2). doi:10.1145/2188349.2188353

Taylor, P., Reiter, J. P., Duncan, G., Lambert, D., & Singer, E. (2003). Estimating Risks of Identification Disclosure in Microdata. *Journal of the American Statistical Association, 37*–41. doi:10.1198/016214505000000619

TDC. (2012). *IDC Predicts 2013 Will Be Dominated by Mobile and Cloud Developments as the IT Industry Shifts Tnto Full-Blown Competition on the 3rd Platform.* Retrieved March 22, 2013, from https://www.idc.com/getdoc.jsp?containerId=prUS23814112

Techhive. (2012). *Users are still the weakest link. David Jeffers, editorial.* Retrieved June 30, 2002 from http://www.techhive.com/article/260453/users_are_still_the_weakest_link.html

Thaler, R., & Sunstein, C. (2008). *Nudge: Improving decisions about health, wealth, and happiness.* New Haven, CT: Yale University Press.

The Amazon S3 Team. (2008). *Amazon s3 availability event: July 20, 2008.* Author.

Thiele, Chakraborty, & Naedele. (2000). Real-time calculus for scheduling hard real-time systems. In *Proceedings of Circuits and Systems,* (vol. 4, pp. 101–104). IEEE.

Thommes, R., & Coates, M. (2006). Epidemiological Modelling of Peer-to-Peer Viruses and Pollution. In *Proceedings of the IEEE International Conference on Computer Communications.* IEEE.

Thompson, M. (2010). *Mariposa botnet analysis* (Technical report). Defence Intelligence.

Tikk, E., Kaska, K., Rnnimeri, K., Kert, M., TalihŠrm, A-M., & Liis Vihul. (2008). *Cyber attacks against georgia: Legal lessons identied.* Academic Press.

Toffler, A. (1980). *The third wave.* Bantam Books.

Traynor, P., Lin, M., Ongtang, M., Rao, V., Jaeger, T., McDaniel, P., & Porta, T. L. (2009). On cellular botnets: Measuring the impact of malicious devices on a cellular network core. In *Proceedings of the 16th ACM Conference on Computer and Communications Security,* (pp. 223-234). ACM.

TrustGo. (n.d.). Available at http://www.trustgo.com

Truta, T. M., & Vinay, B. (2006). Privacy Protection: p-Sensitive k-Anonymity Property. In *Proceedings of the 22nd International Conference on Data Engineering workshops.* IEEE.

Turoff, M. (2000). An End to Student Segregation: No more separation between distance learning and regular courses. *Horizon, 8*(1), 1–7. doi:10.1108/10748120010803294

Tuteja, A. & Shanker, R. (2012). Optimization of Snort for Extrusion and Intrusion Detection and Prevention. *International Journal ofEngineering Research and Applications, 2*(3), 1768-1774.

Twitter. (2014). *Twitter.* Retrieved from https://twitter.com

U.S. Supreme Court. (1993). Daubert v. Merrell Dow Pharmaceuticals, inc., 509 U.S. 579 (1993). Technical Report 92–102, Certiorari to the United Sstates Court of Appeals for the Ninth Ccircuit.

Uitzil, L. (2012). Wireless security system implemented in a mobile robot. *International Journal of Computer Science Issues, 9*(4), 16.

Ulutas, M., Ulutas, G., & Nabiyev, V. V. (2011). Medical image security and EPR hiding using Shamir's secret sharing scheme. *Journal of Systems and Software, 84*(3), 341–353. doi:10.1016/j.jss.2010.11.928

Upham, D. (n.d.). *JPEG–Jsteg*. Available from http://zooid.org/~paul/crypto/jsteg

Usui, T., Kitatsuji, Y., & Yokota, H. (2011). A study on traffic management cooperating with ims in mpls networks. *Telecommunication Systems*, 1–10.

Venugopal, D. (2006). An Efficient Signature Representation and Matching Method for Mobile Devices. In *Proceedings of the 2nd Annual International Workshop on Wireless Internet*. Academic Press.

Vermeulen, J. (2012). *Subscriber selected DStv channels demanded, My Broadband Tech News*. Retrieved from http://mybroadband.co.za/news/broadcasting/56271-subscriber-selected-dstv-channels-demanded.html

Vinod, P., Jain, Golecha, Gaur, & Laxmi. (2010a). MEDUSA: Metamorphic malware dynamic analysis using signature from API. In *Proceedings of the 3rd International Conference on Security of Information and Networks*. SIN.

Vinod, P., Laxmi, & Gaur. (2012a). REFORM: Relevant Features for Malware Analysis. In *Proceedings of 26th International Conference on Advanced Information Networking and Applications Workshops*. Academic Press.

Vinod, P., Laxmi, Gaur, Kumar, & Chundawat. (2009). Static CFG analyzer for metamorphic Malware code. In *Proceedings of the 2nd International Conference on Security of Information and Networks*. SIN.

Vinod, P., Laxmi, V., & Gaur, M. (2011a). Metamorphic Malware Analysis and Detection Methods. In Cyber Security, Cyber Crime and Cyber Forensics: Applications and Perspectives, (pp. 178-202). Hershey, PA: IGI Global. doi: doi:10.4018/978-1-60960-123-2.ch013

Vinod, P., Laxmi, V., & Gaur, M. S. (2011b). Scattered Feature Space for Malware Analysis. In Proceeding Advances in Computing and Communications. Springer.

Vinod, P., Laxmi, V., Gaur, M. S., & Chauhan, G. (2012b). MOMENTUM: MetamOrphic malware exploration techniques using MSA signatures. In Proceedings of International Conferenceon Innovations in Information Technology (IIT). IIT.

Vinod, P., Laxmi, V., Gaur, M. S., Naval, S., & Faruki, P. (2013). MCF: MultiComponent Features for Malware Analysis. In *Proceedings of the 27th International Conference*. doi: doi:10.1109/WAINA.2013.147

Virus Collection Website. (n.d.). Retrieved from http://vx.netlux.org/lib

Vuorimaa, P., Harmo, P., Hämäläinen, M., Itälä, T., & Miettinen, R. (2012). Active life home: a portal-based home care platform. In *Proceedings of the 5th International Conference on PErvasive Technologies Related to Assistive Environments* (PETRA '12). ACM. DOI=10.1145/2413097.2413133

Walker, J. J. (2012). Cyber Security Concerns for Emergency Management, Emergency Management. InTech. Retrieved April 2013, from http://www.intechopen.com/books/emergency-management/cyber-security-concerns-for-emergene ymanagement

Wallner, D. M., Harder, E. J., & Agee, R. C. (1999). *Key management for multicast: Issues and architectures*. Request for comments 2627, Internet Engineering Task Force (June 1999).

Walters, R. (2009). Joining the dots: Joining the dots. *Network Security, 2009*(5), 16–19. doi:10.1016/S1353-4858(09)70054-6

Wang, J., Zhao, Y., Jiang, S., & Le, J. (2009). Providing Privacy Preserving in cloud computing. In *Proceedings of the International Conference on Test and Measurement* (pp.213-216). Hong Kong: IEEE.

Wang, K., Xu, Y., Wong, R. W., & Fu, A. C. (2010). Anonymizing temporal data. In *Proceedings of Data Mining (ICDM)*, (pp. 1109–1114). ICDM. doi: doi:10.1109/ICDM.2010.96

Wang, P. A. (2010). *The Effect of Knowledge of Online Security Risks on Consumer Decision Making in B2C e-Commerce* (Dissertation Thesis). ProQuest LLC.

Wang, P., Lu, J., Zhao, L., & Yang, J. (2010). B-CASTLE: An Efficient Publishing Algorithm for K-Anonymizing Data Streams. In *Proceedings of Intelligent Systems (GCIS), 2010 Second WRI Global Congress on* (Vol. 2, pp. 132-136). IEEE. doi: doi:10.1109/GCIS.2010.196

Wang, W., Li, J., Ai, C., & Li, Y. (2007). Privacy protection on sliding window of data streams. In *Proceedings of Collaborative Computing: Networking, Applications and Worksharing,* (pp. 213-221). IEEE.

Wang, Y., Norcie, G., Komanduri, S., Acquisti, A., Leon, P. G., & Cranor, L. F. (2011). I regretted the minute I pressed share: A qualitative study of regrets on facebook. In *Proceedings of the Seventh Symposium on Usable Privacy and Security.* ACM.

Wang, Y. R., Lin, W. H., & Yang, L. (2011). An intelligent watermarking method based on particle swarm optimization. *Expert Systems with Applications, 38*(7), 8024–8029. doi:10.1016/j.eswa.2010.12.129

Wang, Y., Li, J., Meng, K., Lin, C., & Cheng, X. (2013). Modeling and security analysis of enterprise network using attack-defense stochastic game petri nets. *Security and Communication Networks, 6*(1), 89–99. doi:10.1002/sec.535

Wang, Z., & Bovik, A. C. (2002). A Universal Image Quality Index. *IEEE Signal Processing Letters, 9*(3), 81–84. doi:10.1109/97.995823

Wang, Z., Bovik, A. C., Sheikh, H. R., & Simoncelli, E. P. (2004). Image quality assessment: From error measurement to structural similarity. *IEEE Transactions on Image Processing, 13*(4), 600–612. doi:10.1109/TIP.2003.819861 PMID:15376593

Wang, Z., & Crowcroft, J. (1996). Quality-of-service routing for supporting multimedia applications. *IEEE Journal on Selected Areas in Communications, 14*(7), 1228–1234.

Waxman, M.C. (2010). Cyber-Attacks and the Use of Force: Back to the Future of Article 2(4). *Yale Journal of international Law, 36*(2).

Weatherspoon, H. & Kubiatowicz, J. (2002). *Erasure coding vs. replication: A quantitative comparison.* IPTPS.

Web. (2014). *Merriam Webster On-line dictionary.* Retrieved from www.merriam-webster.com

Weber-Jahnke, J.H., & Obry, C. (2012). Protecting privacy during peer-to-peer exchange of medical documents. *Information Systems Frontiers, 14*(1), 87-104. DOI=10.1007/s10796-011-9304-2

Wei, J. L., Wang, K., Stolfo, S.J., & Herzog, B. (2005). Fileprints: Identifying File types by n-gram analysis. In *Proceedings of the Sixth Annual IEEE SMC 4th Virus Bulletin Conference.* IEEE.

Weinhardt, C., Anandasivam, A., Blau, B., & Stosser, J. (2009). Business Models in the Service World. *IT Professional, 11*(2), 28–33. doi:10.1109/MITP.2009.21

Weiser, M. (1991). The computer for the 21st century. *Scientific American, 265*(3), 94-104.

Westfeld, A. (2001). *F5-a Steganographic algorithm: High capacity despite better Steganlysis.* Lecture Notes in Computer Science, 2137, 289–302. doi:10.1007/3-540-45496-9_21

Westland, J. C. (2012). The adoption of social networking technologies in cinema releases. *Information Technology Management, 13*(3), 167–181. doi:10.1007/s10799-012-0114-0

WhatsApp. 2014. *WhatsApp.* Retrieved from https://www.whatsapp.com

Wong, L. (2005). *Potential Bluetooth vulnerabilities in smartphones.* Retrieved March 18, 2013, from http://citeseerx. ist.psu.edu

Wong, C. K. (2000). Secure group communications using key graphs. *IEEE/ACM Transactions on Networking, 8*(1), 16–30. doi:10.1109/90.836475

Wong, K., Qi, X., & Tanaka, K. (2007). A DCT-based Mod4 steganographic method. *Signal Processing, 87*(6), 1251–1263. doi:10.1016/j.sigpro.2006.10.014

Wong, W., & Stamp, M. (2006). Hunting for metamorphic engines. *Journal in Computer Virology, 2*, 211–229. doi:10.1007/s11416-006-0028-7

Wu, R., Li, W., & Huang, H. (2008). An attack modeling based on hierarchical colored petri nets. In *Proceedings of the 2008 International Conference on Computer and Electrical Engineering.* IEEE Computer Society.

Xiao, X., & Ni, L. M. (1999). Internet qos: A big picture. *IEEE Network, 13*(2), 8–18. doi:10.1109/65.768484

Xie, L., Zhang, X., Chaugule, A., Jaeger, T., & Zhu, S. (2009). *Designing system-level defenses against cellphone malware.* Retrieved March 21, 2013, from www.cse.psu.edu

Xu, D., Goel, V., Nygard, K. E., & Wong, W. E. (2008). Aspect Oriented specification of threat driven security requirements. *Int. J. Comput. Appl. Technol., 31*(1/2), 131–140. doi:10.1504/IJCAT.2008.017725

Yamada, T., & Matsumura, T. (2012). Battery-Aware IT Control Method for Effective Battery Use During Power Outage. In *Proceedings of the 2012 IEEE International Conference on Green Computing and Communications (GREENCOM '12).* IEEE Computer Society.

Yan, G., & Eidenbenz, S. (2006). Bluetooth Worms: Models, Dynamics, and Defense Implications. In *Proceedings of the 22nd IEEE Annual Conference on Computer Security Applications* (pp. 245-256). IEEE.

Yan, G., Flores, H. D., Cuellar, L., Hengartner, N., Eidenbenz, S., & Vu, V. (2007). Bluetooth Worm Propagation: Mobility Pattern Matters. In *Proceedings of the 2nd ACM Symposium on Information, Computer and Communications Security* (pp. 32-44). ACM.

Yan, J., Blackwell, A., Anderson, R., & Grant, A. (2004). Password Memorability and Security: Empirical Results. *IEEE Security & Privacy,* 25–31.

Yang, Y., Li, X., Zhang, X., & Lam, S. (2001). Reliable group rekeying: design and performance analysis. In Proceedings of ACM SIGCOMM 2001 (pp. 27-38). ACM.

Yan, G., & Eidenbenz, S. (2009). Modeling Propagation Dynamics of Bluetooth Worms. *IEEE Transactions on Mobile Computing, 8*(3), 353–367.

Yan, W., Zhang, Z., & Ansari, N. (2008). Revealing Packed Malware. *IEEE Security & Privacy, 6,* 65–69. doi:10.1109/MSP.2008.126

Yeh, H. L., Gue, S. T., Tsai, P., & Shih, W. K. (2013). Wavelet Bit-Plane Based Data Hiding for Compressed Images. *AEÜ International Journal of Electronics and Communications.* doi:10.1016/j.aeue.2013.04.003

Yerraballi, R., & Mukkamalla, R. (1996). Scalability in real-time systems with end-to-end requirements. *Journal of Systems Architecture, 42,* 409–429. doi:10.1016/S1383-7621(96)00031-8

Zakerzadeh, H., & Osborn, S. (2011). FAANST: fast anonymizing algorithm for numerical streaming data. In *Data Privacy Management and Autonomous Spontaneous Security* (pp. 36–50). Springer. doi:10.1007/978-3-642-19348-4_4

Zakerzadeh, H., & Osborn, S. (2013). Delay-sensitive approaches for anonymizing numerical streaming data. *International Journal of Information Security.* doi:10.1007/s10207-013-0196-7

Zhang, J., & Yang, J. (2010). KIDS: K-anonymization data stream base on sliding window. In *Proceedings of Future Computer and Communication (ICFCC),* (pp. 311–316). IEEE.

Zhou, B., Han, Y., Pei, J., Jiang, B., Tao, Y., & Jia, Y. (2009). Continuous privacy preserving publishing of data streams. In *Proceedings of the 12th International Conference on Extending Database Technology: Advances in Database Technology* (pp. 648-659). ACM.

Zhou, S., Qin, Z., Zhang, F., Zhang, X., Chen, W., & Liu, J. (2003). Colored petri net based attack modeling. In *Proceedings of the 9th international conference on Rough sets, fuzzy sets, data mining, and granular computing.* Springer-Verlag.

Zhu, S., Setia, S., & Jajodia, S. (2003). Adding reliable and self-healing key distribution to the subset dierence group rekeying method. In *Proceedings of the 5th COST 264 International Workshop on Networked Group Communications.* Springer-Verlag.

Zhu, S., & Jajodia, S. (2010). Scalable group key management for secure multicast: A taxonomy and new directions. In S. C. H. Huang, D. MacCallum, & D. Du (Eds.), *Network Security* (pp. 57–75). Springer. doi:10.1007/978-0-387-73821-5_3

Zou, C. C., Gong, W., & Towsley, D. (2002). Code Red Worm Propagation Modeling and Analysis. In *Proceedings of the Ninth ACM Conference on Computer and Communications Security.* ACM.

Zou, C. C., Towsley, D., & Gong, W. (2004). Email Worm Modeling and Defense. In *Proceedings of the 13th International Conference on Computer Communication and Networks.* Academic Press.

About the Contributors

Anne V. D. M. Kayem is currently a Senior Lecturer at the University of Cape Town's Department of Computer Science and head of the Information Security Laboratory. Since January 2013, she is coordinator of the Hasso-Plattner-Institute's PhD Research School in Information and Communication Technologies for Development at the University of Cape Town, South Africa. She holds a PhD degree in Computer Science obtained from Queen's University, Kingston, Ontario, Canada. Her PhD thesis was on Adaptive Cryptographic Access Control in Dynamic Data Sharing Environments and her current research interests lie in the areas of Cryptographic Key Management, Data Anonymization, Autonomic Computing, Access Control, and Unconventional Security Methodologies for resource constrained environments. She is a member of ACM and IEEE, and a member of the editorial board of Parallel Processing Letters. In addition, she is on the reviewing board of a couple of local (South African) and International Conferences and Journals. She co-chairs the INTRICATE-SEC (Theories and Intricacies of Information Security Problems) workshop.

Christoph Meinel is a professor and CEO of the Hasso-Plattner-Institut affiliated with the University of Potsdam, where he leads the Internet Technologies and Systems research group. His research interests include security and trust engineering, Web 3.0, and eLearning. Meinel has a PhD in computer science from the Humboldt-University in Berlin.

* * *

Jonathan Abramson is a faculty lead for information systems at Stratford University and faculty member for Everest University. He holds a Doctorate of Computer Science (DCS) from Colorado Technical University. His research focus is mobile learning and E-learning. Prior to entering academia Abramson served in the United States Army. He has taught at Northwestern Connecticut Community College, Post University, Capital Community College, and Education Connection. He is most recognized for his skills in adult education, distance learning, E-learning, and instructional design. His recent scholarly work was with the Academic Business World International Conference as a coauthor on the topics of cyber security.

Abdulrahman Al-Mutairi holds a BSc in Information Technology and Computing and a MSc in Information Security (with Distinction) from Royal Holloway College-University of London. Abdulrahman also is a GIAC Certified Digital Forensic Analyst. He is a third year doctoral student in information security group at Royal Holloway College-University of London. His research interest includes network security, digital forensics, cloud computing security, cyber crime, distributed systems, critical infrastructure and electronic commerce security. Currently, his research is about the security of real-time networks and the associated mechanisms including differentiated services, traffic engineering and policy routing, under the supervision of Dr. Stephen Wolthusen.

George Alphy received his Bachelor in Technology from SCMS School of Engineering and Technology, Ernakulam, Kerala, India in 2013. His area of Interest is information and system security, information forensics, and open source architecture.

R. Balasubramanian is associated as an Associate Professor in the Department of Computer Science and Engineering at the Indian Institute of Technology Roorkee. He has obtained his BSc and MSc degree in Mathematics from the University of Madras in 1994 and 1996, respectively. He obtained his PhD Degree from the Indian Institute of Technology Madras in 2001. He was a Post Doctoral Fellow at the University of Missouri Columbia, USA in 2001-02 and a Post Doctoral Associate at Rutgers, the State University of New Jersey, USA in 2002-03. He has been associated with the Indian Institute of Technology Roorkee since 2004. He was a Visiting Professor and a member of Computer Vision and Sensing Systems Laboratory in the Department of Electrical and Computer Engineering at the University of Windsor, CANADA during May - August 2009. Balasubramanian has guided 6 Doctoral and 64 Master's theses, has published three book chapters in Springer Verlag, and has more than 135 research publications in reputed journals and conference proceedings. He has also successfully completed a number of research projects of national importance. His area of Research includes Vision Geometry, Digital Watermarking using Mathematical Transformations, Image Fusion, Biometrics, Secure Image Transmission over Wireless Channel, Content Based Image Retrieval and Hyperspectral Imaging.

Anirban Basu is a Senior Researcher at KDDI R&D Laboratories in Japan. Prior to that, he worked as a Post-doctoral Researcher at Tokai University. He is also a Visiting Research Fellow at the University of Sussex. He holds a PhD in Computer Science and a Bachelor of Engineering (Hons.) in Computer Systems Engineering from the University of Sussex. His research interests are in computational trust, privacy and security and peer-to-peer networks. He is particularly active within the IFIPTM computational trust management community.

Dustin Bessette is a doctoral candidate at The National Graduate School of Quality Management. He is completing a Doctor of Business Administration with a concentration in quality systems management. He completed his undergraduate degree in real estate studies from Marylhurst University. Additional graduate coursework was completed in green development and renewable energy. Currently, he is employed with the Oregon Parks and Recreation Department (OPRD) as a park ranger. Previously he was employed with the New York State Parks and Recreation Historic Preservation (NYSOPRHP) as a regional water safety coordinator. He served as the associate editor for *The International Journal of Environmental Sustainability*.

Mehmet Vefa Bicakci graduated from Carleton University with a bachelor's degree in computer systems engineering and a master of applied science degree in electrical and computer engineering in 2011 and 2013, respectively. His masters thesis title was "Anomaly Detection for Mobile Device Comfort." Vefa's research interests are broad, and they include security, operating systems, and machine learning and data mining.

Madeleine A. Bihina Bella is currently pursuing a PhD in Computer Science, specialising in digital forensics, at the University of Pretoria in South Africa. She has received several local and international awards for her doctorate research. Notable ones include the 2011 L'Oréal-UNESCO Regional Fellowship for Women in Science in Sub-Saharan Africa, the 2013 Google Anita Borg Memorial Scholarship Europe, Middle East and Africa and the 2013 Tata Africa PhD scholarship for women in science, engineering and technology as part of the national South African Women in Science Awards. She is currently appointed as a Research Associate at SAP Innovation Center Pretoria and worked previously as a business analyst and an IT auditor in the private sector, where she obtained a CISA (Certified Information Systems Auditor) certification. Her research interests include digital forensics, computer fraud detection and intrusion detection systems.

Mark John Burke holds two bachelor's degrees from Potchefstroom University, South Africa, in both Computer Science and Language Technology. He graduated from the University of Cape Town with an MSc in Computer Science and he is currently studying at Cambridge University. His master's thesis title was "Enabling anonymous crime reporting on mobile phones in the developing world." His research experience and interests are varied, and include cryptography, security, privacy, artificial intelligence, machine learning and the policies surrounding these aspects

Maurice Dawson serves as an Assistant Professor of Information Systems at University of Missouri-St. Louis, Visiting Assistant Professor (Honorary) of Industrial and Systems Engineering at The University of Tennessee Space Institute, Visiting Professor at University of Gambia, and Fulbright at South Ural State University, Russia. Dawson is recognized as an Information Assurance System Architect and Engineer Level 1 and 2 by the U.S. Department of Defense. His research focus area is cyber security, systems security engineering, open source software (OSS), mobile security, and engineering management.

Moses T. Dlamini has a BSc in Computer Science and Mathematics from the University of Swaziland. He received his BSc-Honours and MSc in CS from the University of Pretoria. He has written and presented a number of research papers. His research interest lies in cloud security.

Natasha Dwyer is a Senior Lecturer in Digital Media at Victoria University in Australia. She is a design researcher exploring the dynamics of trust in digital environments, an area she worked in as a Research Fellow at British Telecom. For ten years, she worked as a public servant in the capacity of 'Interactive Designer' for the Australian Centre for the Moving Image (ACMI), a cultural institution at Federation Square, Melbourne. Her role was to facilitate public access to ACMI's collections. Projects she designed included the Memory Grid (2003), a touch-screen interface that provided a video-on-demand service to ACMI's visitors. The work was available across multiple access points on ACMI's ground floor for five years. The MAP (memory and place) project (2007) invited visitors to submit films about locations in Victoria to an interactive map.Natasha has also been involved in the not-for-profit arts organization bigHart (www.bighart.org.au). In this capacity, she created interactive documentaries to support television programmes broadcast on Australian national television.

Jan H. P. Eloff is currently appointed as a Research Expert at SAP P&I Mobile Empowerment in Pretoria. His main expertise is in the area of Software Innovation and Information Security. Under his leadership, a number of innovative software prototypes were developed for industry related use cases. He is the co-inventor of a number of patent registrations and filings in the U.S.A. From 2009 – 2012 he was appointed as Research Director of SAP Meraka UTD, a private public partnership between the South African government and SAP. He is currently appointed as an Extraordinary Professor in Computer Science at the University of Pretoria. He worked on and managed many industry related projects and served as an expert advisor on ICT to industry.

Mariki M. Eloff received a PhD Computer Science degree in 2000, from the then Rand Afrikaans University, South Africa, now known as the University of Johannesburg. In October 2002, she was appointed as an associate professor in the School of Computing at UNISA. In July 2009, she was promoted to full professor. She joined the Institute of Corporate Citizenship at Unisa as chief researcher in August 2012. In 2010, she received the Unisa Women in Research award for Research Leadership. She participated in many information security management research projects. She has presented research papers at international and national conferences mostly focusing on information security. She has assisted in the organisation and management of international conferences in information security. She served as the South African representative on ISO (the International Standards Organisation) from 2005 to 2007 and contributed to the development of computer and information security standards on an international level.

Babak Esfandiari is an Associate Professor in the Department of Systems and Computer Engineering at Carleton University. He obtained his PhD in Computer Science in 1998 (University of Montpellier, France), then worked for two years at Mitel Corporation as a software engineer before joining Carleton in 2000. His research interests include agent technology, network computing and object-oriented design.

Nidhi Goel is working as an Assistant Professor in Department of Electronics and Communication Engineering Department at Delhi Technical University, New Delhi. She received her BE degree in Electronics and Communication and M.Tech. Degree in Digital Communication in 2001 and 2006, respectively. She pursued her research interest and completed her PhD from Department of Electrical Engineering at the Indian Institute of Technology Roorkee, India. She has several research papers in reputed journals and International Conferences. She has guided several Masters theses and published a book chapter in Springer Verlag. Her area of interest includes wireless communication, multimedia transmission over packet networks, image encryption and visual cryptography.

Indra Gupta received her B.Tech. degree in electrical engineering from HBTI, Kanpur, in 1984. She completed her ME and PhD degrees from the University of Roorkee, India. She is currently an associate professor in the Department of Electrical Engineering, Indian Institute of Technology Roorkee, India. Her areas of interest includes advanced microprocessor applications, information security, multimedia processing, process control applications, biomedical imaging, content based image retrieval and online computer applications.

Gregory L. Harding graduated from the University of Cape Town with a Bachelors and Masters degrees in Computer Science in 2007 and 2013 respectively. His Masters thesis title was "A Practical Key Management and Distribution system for IPTV Conditional Access." Greg's interests include distributed systems, networking, and security. He has previously worked as a software engineer developing digital receivers in the pay-television industry, and currently works in the field of cloud computing.

Barry Irwin has a PhD in Computer Science, and holds the CISSP certification. He is an Associate Professor in the Department of Computer Science at Rhodes University, South Africa. He leads the Security and Networks Research Group (SNRG), having founded it in 2003. This group serves as a home for postgraduate students conducting research in the fields of information security and IP networking. His primary research interests are network traffic analysis, information security data analysis and visualisation, cyber conflict and botnets identification and mitigation. He has presented at a number of academic and industry conferences, including BruCon and CyCon.

Donovan Isherwood born in South Africa, is an IT-consultant, software developer, and masters graduate. He graduated with a MSc IT degree from the University of Johannesburg, South Africa in 2014. The research for his masters dissertation considered the role of trust and reputation in different cultures. He consequently proposed a new trust model, known as Trust$_{CV}$, to support reputation-based trust for collectivist cultures in digital business ecosystems. Apart from his academic involvement, Donovan was also a researcher at SAP Research in Pretoria, South Africa from 2011 until 2013. He participated in several research and development projects aimed at addressing economic and social challenges in emerging regions, particularly in Africa. Currently, Donovan lives and works in Berlin, Germany at the company SD&C (Solutions Development & Consulting). There, he provides his IT-knowledge and development skills for innovative business software solutions.

Sanele Macanda graduated from the University of The Western Cape with a BSc majoring in Computer Science and an Information System and BSc (Hons) in Computer Science from the University of Cape Town in 2011 and 2012 respectively. His Honours thesis title was "Threat Modeling in Social Networks using The Sense Post threat modeling tool." His research interests are Information security and trading on the financial market. He is currently working as a Front Arena Developer/Analyst at Absa Capital (Barclays Africa Group) and planning to continue studying towards becoming a Chartered Financial Analyst (CFA)

Molulaqhooa Linda Maoyi graduated from the University of Cape with a BSc majoring in Computer Science, Ocean and Atmospheric science and a BSc (Hons) in Computer Science in 2011 and 2012 respectively. His Honours thesis title was "Threat Modeling in Social Networks using attack centric Model." His research interests are Information security, High Performance Computing, Weather and Climate Modeling. He is currently working as a Weather Anchor at an International TV station (eNews Channel Africa) and pursuing an MSc in Atmospheric Science (Climate Modeling) with the University of Cape Town.

Steve Marsh is a Trust Scientist and a thought leader in the phenomenon of trust for computational systems. He is an Assistant Professor of Information Systems in the Faculty of Business and Information Technology, University of Ontario Institute of Technology. His PhD (University of Stirling, 1994) was a seminal work that introduced the first formalisation of the phenomenon of trust (the concept of 'Computational Trust'), and applied it to Multi Agent Systems. As a milestone in trust research, it brought together disparate disciplines and attempted to make sense of a vital phenomenon in human and artificial societies and is still widely referenced today, being in the top tenth of one percent of Citeseerx's most cited articles in computer science. Steve's current work builds extensively on this model, applying it to network security, Critical Infrastructure Protection, and mobile device security. His research interests include computational trust, trust management, regret and regret management, and socially adept technologies. He is the Canadian delegate to IFIP Technical Committee 11: Security and Privacy Protection in Information Processing Systems. He is an adjunct professor at UNB (Computer Science) and Carleton University (Systems and Computer Engineering and Cognitive Science). Steve's Google Scholar page is at http://scholar.google.co.uk/citations?user=Qz73wh4AAAAJ. Steve lives in rural Ontario, Canada with dogs, cats, horses and people, all of which creatures that have their own things to teach us about trust.

Ernest Ketcha Ngassam is a Research Expert at SAP P&I BIT Mobile Empowerment, South Africa, Pretoria. He has lead a number of projects within SAP such as, Rustica, GaRO and CoSMoS. Ernest is currently appointed as a Professor Extraordinaire at the Tshwane University of Technology (Faculty of ICT) and the University of South Africa (School of Computing).

Sylvie Noël has a Ph.D. in cognitive psychology and an M.Sc. in cognitive ergonomics. After studying the impact of expertise on knowledge for her doctoral thesis, she moved to Perth, Australia where she worked for five years on a project to build a computer-supported learning system. After returning to Canada, she joined the federal government where she worked on a variety of human-computer interaction projects. These included working on the interface for a group videoconferencing tool, helping to develop a computer-supported collaborative editing tool, improving human-to-human interactions in a collaborative virtual world, exploring the impact of emotional avatars in virtual worlds, and improving trust and security in a mobile environment.

Martin Olivier is a professor in the Department of Computer Science in the School of Information Technology at the University of Pretoria. His current primary research interest is digital forensics. He is author or co-author of more than 200 academic publications. Thirty-two students obtained their doctorates or masters degrees under his (co-) supervision. He is a member of the editorial board of Data and Knowledge Engineering. He is a member of IFIP working group 11.9 on digital forensics, the ACM, the Suid-Afrikaanse Akademie vir Wetenskap en Kuns (South African Academy for Science and Art) and an associate member of the American Academy of Forensic Sciences. Prof Olivier holds a BSc degree in Mathematical Sciences, BSc (Honours), MSc and PhD degrees in Computer Science, a BA degree in Humanities, a BA (Honours) degree in Philosophy and an MPhil degree in Workplace Ethics. He is also a Certified Cyber Forensic Professional (CCFP).

Marwan Omar is a computer science faculty at Nawroz University. He holds a Doctor of Computer Science (DCS) from Colorado Technical University. Omar's research focus is mobile security, human factors security engineering for mobile security, and smartphone exploits. Prior to entering academia, he was a contractor to the United States military in Iraq and worked for a large communications company in Houston, Texas. He has published in the 2013 IEEE Third International Conference on Advanced Computing and Communication Technologies, and the *Journal of Information Systems Technology and Planning*. He is an active member of IEEE, ACM, and the Intellectbase International Consortium.

Sylvia Osborn is currently a professor in the Department of Computer Science at the University of Western Ontario, London, ON, Canada. She holds a PhD degree in Computer Science obtained from the University of Waterloo, Canada. Her research interests lie in the field of Database Management Systems and Database Security in particular

P. R. Rakesh received his Bachelor in Technology from SCMS School of Engineering and Technology, Ernakulam, Kerala, India in 2013. His area of Interest is computer security information forensics and software testing.

Rotondwa Ratshidaho graduated from the University Of Cape Town with a Bachelors degree in computer science specializing in computer engineering and an honours degree in computer science in the year 2011 and 2012 respectively. His Honours project was entitled "Threat models in social networks." In particular, his focus was on the Microsoft Security Development Lifecycle (SDL) threat modeling tool that he studied and compared to the SensePost Corporate Threat Modeling tool and the Microsoft Threat Analysis and Modeling tool. Rotondwa's interests include security, machine learning, performance management, and mobile development. He is also interested in learning about new technologies that can be used to enhance software development.

Hosnieh Rafiee is a researcher at Hasso-Plattner-Institut at the University of Potsdam. Her research interests are in network security including integration of privacy and security in IPv6 networks and the authentication problems that occur in the application layer services such as DNS and email and the deployment of SEcure Neighbor Discovery (SEND). Rafiee recently finished her PhD at the university of Potsdam and has a MSc in IT-Computer networks engineering from Amirkabir University of Technology in Tehran.

Karen Renaud is a Scottish Computer Scientist and Senior Lecturer at the University of Glasgow. She was educated at the Universities of Pretoria, South Africa and Glasgow. She has made contributions in the fields of usable security, technology adoption, email usage, electronic voting and design patterns and works with research collaborators in Germany, the US, South Africa and the UK.

Aderonke B. Sakpere is a second year PhD student at the University of Cape Town's Department of Computer Science. She holds a scholarship from the Hasso-Plattner-Institute and works in the field of information security. Her thesis is centred around data stream anonymization with an application to crime report datasets in the context of the developing world.

Maxim Schnjakin studied computer science at the University of Trier and moved to Hasso-Plattner-Institute after graduation. Since 2008, he works as a scientific assistant at the chair of Professor Christoph Meinel. The main focus of his research is enforcement of high availability and security requirements in public clouds.

Tanveer J Siddiqui received her PhD degree from University of Allahabad, Allahabad (India) in 2006. She is currently an assistant professor with the Department of Electronics and Communication at University of Allahabad, Allahabad. Her current research interests cover Natural language Processing and Information Processing. She has co-authored / edited five books and published a number of publications in the scientific journals and leading International conferences.

Siddharth Singh obtained his B.Tech degree in Electronics Engineering from Purvanchal University, Jaunpur (India) and M.Tech in Electronics and Communication Engineering from Integral University, Lucknow in 2009. Currently, he is pursuing his PhD from University of Allahabad, Allahabad. His areas of interest are information security, steganography and digital image processing.

Richard Ssembatya graduated from Mbarara University of Science and Technology (MUST) with a bachelors degree in computer science and a Masters of Science degree in computer science in 2002 and 2006, respectively. His master's thesis title was "Towards a Decision Support system for Universal Primary Education in Uganda." He recently completed and submitted for examination, a PhD thesis on the topic of Securing Mobile Health Records in Rural Areas. Richard's research interests are broad, and they include usable security, Human Computer Interaction (HCI), Mobile design and applications and E-Health.

Tim Storer is a Lecturer in Software Engineering at the University of Glasgow. His research interests are in the dependability of software, and in particular of large scale complex software based systems. He is interested in both the design and management of the systems themselves, but also the engineering methods that need to be developed to support these activities in the future. This interest has taken him into a variety of problem domains in which a variety of heterogeneous software systems have become essential to the operation of wider socio-technical processes. These domains include critical infrastructure management, electronic voting, scientific programming and digital forensics.

P. Vinod completed his PhD in Computer Engineering from Malaviya National Institute of Technology, Jaipur, Rajasthan, India. He received his Masters of Technology in Information Technology as well as Bachelors of Engineering in Computer Science and Engineering from Rajiv Gandhi Proudyogiki Vishwavidyalaya, Bhopal, Madhaya Pradesh. He has more than 30 publications to his credit in international conferences and journals to his credit. Also, he has executed a project entitled "PROSIM: Probabilistic Signature for Metamorphic Malware Detection," funded by the Department of Information Technology, MCIT, New Delhi. Presently, he is working as an Associate Professor in the Department of Computer Science and Engineering, SCMS School of Engineering and Technology, Ernakulam, Kerala, India. His research interest are desktop and mobile malware analysis, intrusion detection, cryptography, natural language processing and image analysis.

Stephen Wolthusen received his Dipl.-Inform. degree in computer science in 1999 and completed his PhD in theoretical computer science in 2003, both at TU Darmstadt. He was with the Security Technology Department at Fraunhofer-IGD from 1999-2005 serving as deputy division chief from 2003 onwards and as senior visiting scientist from 2005 onwards. He is currently a Reader in Mathematics with the ISG, having joined Royal Holloway in 2006. He also is Full Professor of Information Security (part-time) at Gjovik University College, Norway, where he has held a position since 2005. His research focuses on models of adversaries and resilient networks, with applications in defense networks and particularly in critical infrastructure networks and control systems security. He has led a number of national and European projects, including the Internet of Energy project, is author and editor of several books as well as over 100 peer-reviewed publications. He has served as editor-in-chief of Computers and Security and as vice-chair of the IEEE Task Force on Information Assurance and is currently vice-chair of the IEEE Task Force on Network Science.

Index